Rebecca Harding Davis

REBECCA HARDING DAVIS

A LIFE AMONG WRITERS

Sharon M. Harris

WEST VIRGINIA UNIVERSITY PRESS
MORGANTOWN

Copyright © 2018 by West Virginia University Press
All rights reserved
First edition published 2018. Paperback edition 2019.
Printed in the United States of America

ISBN:
Cloth 978-1-946684-30-1
Paper 978-1-949199-18-5
EPUB 978-1-946684-32-5
PDF 978-1-946684-33-2

The Library of Congress has cataloged the hardcover edition as follows:
Names: Harris, Sharon M., author.
Title: Rebecca Harding Davis : a life among writers / Sharon M. Harris.
Description: Morgantown : West Virginia University Press, 2018. | Includes bibliographical references and index.
Identifiers: LCCN 2018000765| ISBN 9781946684301 (hardback) | ISBN 9781946684332 (pdf)
Subjects: LCSH: Davis, Rebecca Harding, 1831-1910. | Women authors, American--Biography. | Davis, Rebecca Harding, 1831-1910--Family. | Davis, Rebecca Harding, 1831-1910--Friends and associates. | Authors, American--19th century--History. | Women and literature--United States--History--19th century. | Literature and society--History--19th century. | BISAC: BIOGRAPHY & AUTOBIOGRAPHY / Literary. | BIOGRAPHY & AUTOBIOGRAPHY / Women.
Classification: LCC PS1517 .Z67 2018 | DDC 813/.4--dc23
LC record available at https://lccn.loc.gov/2018000765

Cover design by Than Saffel / WVU Press
Cover photograph courtesy of the Rachel Loden Collection, Palo Alto, California

Contents

Preface 1
Acknowledgments 5

1. Southern Roots (Ancestry to Mid-1861) 9
2. Treason and Fame (April 1861–March 1863) 31
3. A New Life (May 1863–May 1865) 73
4. New Ventures (June 1865–December 1867) 94
5. A National Author (1868–1870) 124
6. A Conservative Progressive (1871–1875) 147
7. Centennial Celebrations and the Failure
   of Reconstruction (1876–1879) 177
8. Exposing Government Corruption (1880–1884) 204
9. An Era of Nonfiction (1885–1889) 228
10. "A Message to Be Given" (1890–1893) 255
11. A Return to Novel-Writing (1894–1896) 294
12. War Years (1897–1899) 313
13. Transitions (1900–1904) 339
14. The Widowed Writer (1905–1910) 375
15. Final Pages: Richard, Charles, and Nora 399

Notes 411
Bibliography 469
Index 471

Preface

The Real Rebecca Harding Davis

Rebecca Harding Davis is an internationally recognized author most often defined as a pioneering realist. Readers have long garnered a sense of Davis through her classic story, "Life in the Iron-Mills," assuming that her life among the iron foundries of Wheeling, West Virginia, was not only the source of her realist turn, which it was, but the final definition of her life, which it was not. It is an understandable error. Having studied Davis's writings for the last three decades, I assumed when I began this biography that I had a keen sense of her life and would simply need to tweak and slightly expand our understanding of her. What a surprise I had in store! The woman who wrote most often about working-class conditions and the cost of poverty to human endeavors knew that life well from her thirty years of living in Wheeling. But the remaining nearly fifty years of her life were lived among the most elite circles of Philadelphia society where she developed friendships with US presidents and international figures.

It is not only our knowledge of the circles she moved in and the ways in which they shaped her life that need redefining. Her life as an author was coupled with her status as one of America's early and notable women journalists. Perhaps no aspect of her life has been as overlooked as that of her forty-plus years as a newspaper editorial writer for prestigious national and regional papers from the *New-York Tribune* to the *Philadelphia Press* to the *New York World*. In 1894, Moses Purnell Handy, a reporter for the *Tribune* and publisher of the *Press*, asserted she "may be said to be the pioneer in the editorial discussion of social topics in daily newspapers.... After Harriet Martineau...I know of no other woman who is entitled to more honor as a journalist than Rebecca Harding Davis."[1] And Ida Tarbell, a pioneer in investigative journalism, identified Davis as one of the "representative women" in nineteenth-century journalism.[2] As a biographer, I therefore had the wonderful and daunting task of both correcting errors in our knowledge about Davis and expanding that knowledge to the many unrecognized avenues she took in her life and writing.

Correcting misconceptions about this author turned from the usual dutiful work of the biographer to a fascinating recognition that we had misread or failed to recognize some of the most important aspects of her life and reputation. The first biography of Davis was a master's thesis by Helen Woodward Shaeffer. It is an important contribution to Davis studies because Shaeffer had access to primary materials that no longer exist due to loss and to a fire that destroyed a significant portion of Davis's private papers, including a major diary. Only snippets of her other known diary remain, since an unidentified scholar—I use the term loosely—of her eldest son had the audacity to cut the diary into tiny strips and retained only those that mentioned the son, apparently destroying the rest. Thus her private comments on the last years of the Civil War, on her early years of marriage, on the birth of her children, and numerous other events in her life are largely lost to us. Letters reveal some of these perspectives, but letters are always shaped by the writer's relationship to the recipient and are typically less forthcoming than a private diary.

Shaeffer's biography is also rife with errors and with assertions that are undocumented. Perhaps none is as important to correct as the assertion that the Harding family was absolutely in agreement about the Civil War and thoroughly supported the Union. In fact, the Harding family was torn apart by the war as were most families. One of her brothers ardently supported the Confederacy and was charged with treason for his actions; it was years before he and Rebecca tenuously reconciled. Though many late twentieth-century scholars at first used Shaeffer's biography as a reliable source, myself included, my own research has exposed the problems with Shaeffer's study, and I now use it as a source for quoting primary texts only. Both I and Jean Pfaelzer included some biographical information on Davis in studies of her work in the 1990s, and Jane Atteridge Rose published a Twayne Series biography in 1993. All of these works are valuable but limited, and my own thinking about and knowledge of Davis's life has changed radically since I published *Rebecca Harding Davis and American Realism* in 1991, which was a revision of my doctoral dissertation. An academic lifetime of research now informs this biography.

As one of the major reform writers of the nineteenth century, Davis sought sweeping changes to the nation's social and socioeconomic structures. Her life story is indelibly linked to her role as author and journalist, of course, but it is a highly unusual life because she was one of only a handful of nineteenth-century authors to live in a family of writers. Her husband, L. Clarke Davis, was one of the premier newspaper editors of the century, first with the *Philadelphia Inquirer* and later with the prestigious and influential *Public*

Ledger; he also published a few short stories and several essays in literary periodicals. Their sons, Richard Harding Davis and Charles Belmont Davis, were nurtured in both literature and journalism by their parents; they became established authors, had careers in the newspaper industry, and became editors of literary magazines (Richard for *Harper's Weekly* and Charles for *Collier's Weekly*). The Davises' daughter Nora was the only family member who did not become an author, preferring the life of a socialite; she was supported in this choice by her mother and, with her marriage, Nora moved into the highest circles of British royalty.

Unlike the competitive James family of authors (William, Henry, Alice), the Davises were extraordinarily supportive. They critiqued each other's work in manuscript and promoted one another throughout their lifetimes. Rebecca was particularly skilled at the latter avenue of familial support. To study her and her family's careers is to understand how she created a pattern that would be embraced by all of the writers in the family: first establishing herself with a literary magazine and then opening the door for one or more of her family members to publish there as well. The same pattern was used with newspapers. The process was well recognized among nineteenth-century literati, as the Davises soon became known nationally as "The Davis Family" of writers.

Equally important, *Rebecca Harding Davis: A Life among Writers* moves beyond a single author or even a single family to analyze the changing literary landscape of the nineteenth century. Davis and her family capture the extraordinary changes that occurred between her lifetime and that of her children. While Rebecca and Clarke embraced the idea that their work should stand on its own, shunning the cult of celebrity that emerged in the post–Civil War years, their sons embraced the self-promotion of celebrity. Richard and Charles also demonstrated the keen difference between their parents' nineteenth-century world and the early twentieth century's turn to melding literature, the stage, and film.

Rebecca Harding Davis embraced a world very different from and yet rooted in her life in Wheeling. She loved the theater and attended frequently, both in Philadelphia and New York; dined at Delmonico's when in New York; associated with the famous and the infamous; and crafted a life as an artist that was as inclusive as it was incisive in its critique of the culture of the nineteenth and early twentieth centuries. To read Davis's life and work is to have an eye-view on the changing world of literature and culture in these eras.

Acknowledgments

Numerous scholars have offered support over the many years during which I have studied Davis's life and works. I hope I have sufficiently acknowledged my appreciation along the way. A few individuals, however, deserve special recognition for their encouragement to see this project to its fruition and for their own scholarship, which has added so much to my knowledge of Davis: Alicia Mischa Renfroe, Robin Cadwallader, Arielle Zibrak, and Donna Campbell.

Integral to this project as well has been the generosity of many large and small archives in allowing me access to their manuscripts and rare books. My sincere appreciation to the American Antiquarian Society, Worcester, Massachusetts; Barnard College Library, Columbia University; Rare Book and Manuscript Library, Columbia University; Rare Book Room, Buffalo and Erie County Public Library; Boston Public Library; Connecticut Historical Society; David M. Rubenstein Rare Book and Manuscript Library, Duke University; Huntington Library, San Marino, California; Special Collections, Lehigh University, Linderman Library, Bethlehem, Pennsylvania; Massachusetts Historical Society; Manuscripts and Archives Division, The New York Public Library, Astor, Lenox and Tilden Foundations; Princeton University Library; West Virginia Collection, Manuscripts Division, West Virginia University Library; University of Iowa; Albert and Shirley Small Special Collections Library, University of Virginia; and the Beinecke Rare Book and Manuscript Library, Yale University.

Many librarians, archivists, and city historians have given generously of their time in aid of my research. Again, a few deserve special recognition: Rebekah Karelis, Wheeling National Heritage Area; Anna Mae Moore, Washington and Jefferson College Library; Janet Wareham, the LeMoyne House; and Clayton Gilmore, The Bradford House.

Perhaps the most valuable and under-recognized keepers of important historical documents and knowledge are individuals in a community or family who serve as private archivists and historians. Several such people have been immensely generous and helpful with this project: Margaret Brennan, former President of the Wheeling Area Historical Society, who gave me a guided walking tour of the city's historical sites relating to Davis, provided introductions to various archival sources in the city, and shared her knowledge of the city and Harding family history; Wendy Bidstrup of Marion, Massachusetts, who generously shared privately held diaries, photographs, and local history, and amazingly donated several items to me; and Rachel Loden of Palo Alto, California, whose Loden Collection is a treasure trove of family history relating to the Hardings, Leets, and other relatives. Without these many helping hands, this biography would not have been possible.

Nor would *Rebecca Harding Davis: A Life among Writers* have been published without the exceptional support of my editor at West Virginia University Press, Derek Krissoff. Every author should be so fortunate in an editor.

I have identified archives that have provided permissions to publish in the notes as follows:

    AAS—American Antiquarian Society
    BCL—Overbury Collection, Barnard College Library, Columbia University
    BEPL-JFG—James Fraser Gluck Collection, Rare Book Room, Buffalo and Erie County Public Library
    BEPL-CWM—Charles Wells Moulton Collection, Rare Book Room, Buffalo and Erie County Public Library
    BPL—Boston Public Library/Rare Books
    CHS—Rose Terry Cooke Correspondence, Connecticut Historical Society
    CUL—Rare Book and Manuscript Library, Columbia University
    DUL—David M. Rubenstein Rare Book and Manuscript Library, Duke University
    HL—Huntington Library, San Marino, California
    HLH—Houghton Library, Harvard University
    LUL—Richard Harding Davis Correspondence and Other Documents, SC MS 0001, Special Collections, Lehigh University, Linderman Library, Bethlehem, Pennsylvania
    MHS—Massachusetts Historical Society
    NYPL-AC—Alfred Williams Anthony Collection, Manuscripts and Archives Division, The New York Public Library, Astor, Lenox and Tilden Foundations
    NYPL-CC—Century Company Records, Manuscripts and Archives Division, The New York Public Library, Astor, Lenox and Tilden Foundations

NYPL-JGH—J. G. Holland Papers, Manuscripts and Archives Division, The New York Public Library, Astor, Lenox and Tilden Foundations
NYPL-WCC—William Conant Church Papers, Manuscripts and Archives Division, The New York Public Library, Astor, Lenox and Tilden Foundations
PUL-DRD—D. and R. Dodge Collection, Princeton University Library
PUL-CSS—Charles Scribner's Sons Archives, Princeton University Library
PUL-MMD—Mary Mapes Dodge Collection, Princeton University Library
RLC—Rachel Loden Collection, Palo Alto California
UI—University of Iowa Library
UVA—Richard Harding Davis Papers, Albert and Shirley Small Special Collections Library, University of Virginia
WVUL—Archibald Campbell Papers, West Virginia Collection, Manuscripts Division, West Virginia University Library
YUL—Yale Collection of American Literature, Beinecke Rare Book and Manuscript Library, Yale University

Chapter 1

Southern Roots
(Ancestry to Mid-1861)

The *St. Paul* eased out of New York City's harbor on the cloudy morning of March 17, 1896. On board were a number of renowned Americans—noted business leaders and one of the nation's most admired authors and journalists, Rebecca Harding Davis. Heading for Europe, Davis was accompanied by her daughter Nora, a young woman who had not followed the literary path of her family of writers, preferring instead the role of Philadelphia socialite. At home in Philadelphia, Rebecca's husband Clarke, whose reputation for integrity as managing editor of the *Public Ledger* offered him access to the nation's leaders and a voice in the major political issues of the day, was preparing to join his wife and daughter in June. Rebecca and Clarke had a loving and egalitarian marriage; they shared careers and raised a family that they considered their greatest achievement. Although their elder son Richard frequently joined his parents when they were in Europe, this year he remained in New York where he was a noted author-celebrity and war correspondent. Rebecca and Nora were traveling to see the Davises' middle child, Charles, the American consul in Florence, Italy, and an emerging author.

Few families in the nation had achieved such distinction for all of their members, and Davis could look on her family's and her own accomplishments with warmth and pride. But it had not always been an easy climb to national recognition for the woman raised in a family that struggled to enter the middle class in a town of mill works and much poverty. Talent had afforded Rebecca the means to escape this difficult early life, but it was a strong will and a vibrant imagination for the possibilities of a different path that sustained her through early years of war and uncertainty about her future.

* * *

The dreams and determination that guided Rebecca Blaine Harding were rooted in generations of dreamers and risk-takers. She drew on this heritage to immerse herself in the grit and grime of a milltown in West Virginia as well as to become an internationally recognized writer who moved among the renowned authors and artists of her day and whose insightful cultural critiques affected the nation.

Her mother, Rachel Leet, was born in 1808, among the extended Wilson, Leet, and Blaine families of Washington County, Pennsylvania.[1] Rachel's grandparents, Margaret (?–?) and James Wilson, Sr. (?–1791), were farmers from Ireland who immigrated to eastern Pennsylvania around 1740. The area gained the name of Burnt Cabins after it was destroyed during the volatile years of conflicts between Native Americans and new settlers. James and Margaret survived the destruction of the settlement and remained in the area until 1781, when they moved to the southwestern part of the state. Their new home was in what became the town of Washington, a community that would play a large part in the childhood of their great-granddaughter, Rebecca Harding. The Wilsons established friendly relations with an elderly tribal chief, Tinguanquali, and they thrived, eventually buying large tracts of land in addition to their homestead claim.

In 1786, James gave his eldest son Hugh Wilson (1763–1832) the deed to a block on Main Street in Washington. Hugh was even more successful at property accumulation than his father. As Rebecca later recalled, Hugh's holdings were so large "that when he made his yearly journey on horseback to Philadelphia over the mountains he used to boast that he slept every night on his own land."[2] Hugh's home on Main Street was the largest house in town and served as the center of town activities from meetings to public entertainments.

Hugh Wilson married Rachel Leet (?–1811), daughter of Rebecca Vahan (sometimes given as "Vaughan" or "Vaughn"[3]) and Isaac Leet (1726–1802), two years after he was deeded the Main Street property. The Leet family liked to claim that Rachel Leet's brothers had fought with George Washington in the Revolutionary War,[4] but their granddaughter later acknowledged that these men were hard drinkers who loved to fight but "were not fond of work." They did, however, bequeath their descendants "certain artistic tastes . . . and with a good tough quality of endurance."[5] The Leet family was also among the early property owners of Washington County. Isaac and Rebecca Leet arrived in the area in 1779, two years before the town of Washington was established; by 1807 the family owned 351 acres known as Leet's Fancy.[6]

Rebecca Harding's grandparents continued the family tradition of property accumulation, largely due to James Wilson, Sr.'s generosity. Hugh was involved in politics and helped raise funds to build the First Baptist Church. He and

Rachel had four children—Rebecca, Margaret, Rachel, and Hugh W. Wilson. In 1786 James gave Hugh and Rachel another lot, and Hugh began his business as a merchant in a building he constructed on the property. In spite of his success at property accumulation and as a merchant, Hugh made one significant mistake late in his life: he ignored much-overdue taxes and had to sell a large portion of his property to pay off his debt.[7] But in the years when they were raising their family, life was good for Hugh and Rachel. She managed their estate with great skill. The family, which entertained often, had several household servants—"bound men and women, black slaves and white Redemptionists," as their granddaughter recalled.[8] Hugh was a zealous Baptist, and they often had itinerant ministers and other poor travelers in the household as well.

Hugh and Rachel's daughter, Rachel Leet Wilson (1808–1884) would become Rebecca Harding Davis's mother. Rachel was very close to her older sister, Rebecca Leet Wilson (1789–1866), who married James Blaine (1787–1848), a lawyer, in 1809. In that year Blaine also opened a dry goods store next to Hugh Wilson's home, probably with Hugh's assistance. Rebecca Harding would be born in the Blaine's home, and she and her siblings loved their aunt and uncle dearly. Indeed, her Uncle James was the adult male whom she most admired. Her father was a kind man and a wonderful storyteller but was incapable of turning his imagination to building a successful career. The Harding family often hovered on the edge of financial ruin. In contrast, Uncle James, or "The Old Squire" as he was known in the Washington community, may have dressed in "shabby brown clothes and wig," but he was the lawyer who successfully settled local disputes for many years. "He brought into our lives," Rebecca fondly recalled, "most of the joy and happiness that ever came" to her mother, herself, and her siblings.[9]

James G. Blaine (1830–1893), a cousin[10] and the future US Senator and Secretary of State under Presidents Garfield and Harrison, was a lifelong friend of Rebecca's, and they met often as young people in Aunt Rebecca and Uncle James's Old Stone House on South Main Street in Washington.[11]

The quiet and happy girlhood of Rachel Leet Wilson underwent a sea change when her mother died in 1816. Her two eldest siblings, Rebecca and Margaret, had already married and established homes of their own. Rachel and her younger brother Hugh W. Wilson were alone with their struggles to confront the loss of their mother and to adjust to life with their new stepmother, Margaret Fleming Wilson, who married their father on February 14, 1818.[12] Within a few years, however, the family seemed to be settling into the new routines of their altered relations.

In the midst of this familial turmoil, Rachel met a young Anglo-Irish immigrant from Munster, Ireland, who had recently arrived in Pennsylvania. This was the man who would become Rebecca Harding Davis's father. Richard William Harding (1792–1864[13]), according to family legend, was a descendant of one of the English families that had settled Ireland as part of Queen Elizabeth I's granting of large tracts of land to young English officers.[14] However, these families, Rebecca Harding Davis would later record in a history for her own children, brought their prejudices with them to Ireland; they "despised Puritans and Catholics alike . . . and it is three centuries since . . . and they never have become assimilated with the natives and never will."[15]

Within these Harding families, every generation had at least one male relative who would abandon work and become a wanderer. There was also the Harding family tradition of elopement. Richard's father, Thomas Harding, had been forbidden to marry the sixteen-year-old Isabel Harris, but they defied their parents and eloped. Richard adored his father, often telling his children about this adventurous man who was noted in his community as a raconteur. Isabel and Thomas worked hard and judiciously saved their money; eventually they were able to build a large stone house, Cherry Hill, in Munster, where they raised their eight children. Richard was the seventh child, and he had numerous advantages growing up in this unique family.

Cherry Hill was distant enough from town that the Hardings had to be self-supporting of all necessary staples. Twice a year a tailor, a dressmaker, and a shoesmith came to the house, spending several weeks preparing clothes for the family. Living full time in the household, in addition to several Irish servants, were tutors, governesses, and music teachers—and poor relations, who seemed to come in a steady stream and stay for various periods of time. Thomas and Isabel Harding valued education and also proudly housed young scholars who needed rooms for a term or more.[16]

Richard Harding was a tall, handsome man with a keen intellect and a playful sense of humor. In spite of the significant difference in their ages, Richard knew he had met the young woman he wanted to marry, and Rachel returned his feelings. Her father, however, wanted no suitor for his fifteen-year-old daughter, and especially not a newly arrived immigrant. Richard's parents were as well-to-do as the Wilsons, but he had assigned his inheritance to his sister Emily when he left Ireland,[17] and he had yet to make his mark in the US. Although her father forbade Rachel to see her suitor, Richard promised he would return when she was old enough to marry. For the next seven years, neither forgot that promise.

Wanting to make himself a more appealing suitor in the eyes of Rachel's father, Richard left Pennsylvania in pursuit of better-paying employment and relocated to Florence, Alabama, locally known as "Big Spring." The town was becoming known for its textile manufacturing, and a cotton factory had been built there five years before Richard arrived. It seemed a city in which a young immigrant could live cheaply and save his money.

While Richard was making his way in Alabama, Rachel was growing into a highly intelligent young woman who was afforded an unusual education for females of her era. Her older sisters had only been given one year's "finishing" in Philadelphia, but Rachel was offered an extraordinary opportunity. Her father was a close friend of Bishop Alexander Campbell who, with his brother Thomas, founded the Christian Church (Disciples of Christ). In the late 1840s, with Barton Stone, in what became known as the Stone-Campbell Movement, Campbell would become a pioneer in higher education for women.[18]

Rachel lived with the Campbell family as a paying pupil who was educated by Campbell with his own daughters in what was largely a classical education. Rachel was recognized for her keen intellect, and she excelled at history. As her daughter would later acknowledge, she "had enough knowledge to fit out half dozen modern college-bred women."[19] Through Campbell, Rachel garnered a thorough education and deepened her strong faith, traits she would pass on to her eldest daughter. Through Campbell's teachings of anti-sectarianism, Rachel was exposed to a conservative but inclusive religion that accepted everyone who followed the teachings of the Bible.[20]

In 1830, seven years after first proposing, Richard Harding returned to Pennsylvania and asked Rachel to marry him. Again Rachel's father objected.[21] This time, however, the couple would not be thwarted, and they eloped. They were married in nearby Uniontown on August 12, 1830, by the Reverend Mr. Fielding.[22] The couple left immediately for Florence, Alabama.

Situated in a northeastern district of cotton plantations, Florence was a village that housed a general store, a forge, a shoemaker, and a tavern. A portion of the community was Protestant Irish, another portion was French Catholics whose ancestors had settled in the region after escaping the French Revolution. Even more important in this region than the cotton was its fame for having some of the best running horses in the country, including a few that competed in Louisville. The town was situated in a wide basin surrounded by hills, and Native Americans who lived just beyond the hills brought their pelts into town to sell at the general store.[23]

What Rachel discovered in Florence was a mixture of "magnificence and squalor" on the cotton plantations that surrounded the village. The planters were welcoming to the young couple, but Rachel was discomfited by the mud pits below the houses that were built on pilings and by the strange combination in the locals' homes of abundant flowers but bare, unkempt floors.

Years later Richard told his family about his first experiences in Florence. The first thing he had seen was a man shot to death on the street, and more than thirty such deaths occurred during his first six months in Florence—"the outcome of the creed which rated honor higher than life," in his daughter's view.[24] It was not as lawless when Rachel arrived, but it was unlike any community she had known. Women's lives in these small villages were not that of picturesque Southern belles. They typically experienced hard labor, poverty, and rare access to books other than the Bible. Rachel missed her family and friends, and she had a hard time adjusting to the cultural differences she encountered in Alabama.

Soon the Hardings were overjoyed with the news that Rachel was pregnant. They worked hard to flourish in their new home and prepare for the baby, but, for all his efforts, Richard made little headway in establishing himself on the economic basis he desired. When the birth date neared, Rachel was determined to return to Washington to give birth where she could have the support of her beloved sister, Rebecca Blaine. In a large, back bedroom on the second floor of the Blaines' Old Stone House, Rachel gave birth to Rebecca Blaine Harding on June 24, 1831. Like all parents, the Hardings had great hopes for their first child, but little could they foresee that she would become one of nineteenth-century America's premier fiction writers and female journalists.

Within weeks, the young family returned to Florence, where they stayed for nearly six years. During these years, Rachel gave birth to two boys, William, who died in infancy, and Hugh Wilson ("Wilse") Harding, born in 1835. Like his older sister, Wilse had been born in Washington, Pennsylvania, and he was named after his maternal grandfather and uncle. The growing family did not thrive in Alabama, however. With the Hardings, two young children, and a boarder living in a small house,[25] the future did not appear prosperous. So around 1837 they decided to return north where they hoped they would find better opportunities and have the support of family. They did not return to Washington, however.

In 1831 Wheeling, Virginia, had become a port of entry under an Act of Congress, a change that meant the area was already developing into a manufacturing center for the region, and the Hardings chose this promising town on the Ohio River for their new home. It was about thirty-five miles from Rachel's family in Washington. In 1832 when Rachel's father died, he had bequeathed the Old Stone House to her as the eldest child,[26] but since the Blaines had been living in the house for several years and its upkeep would have been a burden to the young Harding family, they determined to establish their new home in Wheeling. It had the advantage, too, of being close enough that the families could visit regularly, but far enough apart that the Hardings could create an independent life for themselves.

The Hardings first lived in a relatively poor area of Wheeling near the east channel of the Ohio River. Rebecca recalled the town at that time as consisting of "two sleepy streets lined with Lombardy poplars, creeping between a slow-moving river and silent, brooding hills. Important news from the outside world was brought to us when necessary by a man on a galloping horse."[27] But this sleepy-town atmosphere was a child's perspective. Wheeling had already become the region's commercial hub by the time the Hardings arrived. Situated on the National Road that connected the North and South and on the Ohio River that allowed for an ease of transporting goods, the village was a bustling manufacturing town.

Unfortunately, the Hardings' arrival coincided with the economic Panic of 1837, which led to a recession that would last for nearly seven years. If Rebecca's early days in Wheeling were filled with the romance of seeing two stage coaches arrive each day with passengers from the East who then boarded steamboats bound for St. Louis or New Orleans and great Conestoga wagons that occasionally passed through with families headed for the West,[28] that romance would soon be overwhelmed by two realities: the faster-paced and soot-filled life of an industrial town, and the ravages of a civil war that played out on their doorstep. Although these events made Rebecca feel that Wheelingites "had rocked the cradle of the new-born nation,"[29] they were tumultuous years for the family and the nation.

Richard had formed a business partnership with a local businessman, Reddick McKee. When the Hardings arrived in Wheeling, McKee was an agent for the Wheeling Cotton Manufacturing Company,[30] and Richard's work as a merchant in the cotton-manufacturing region of Florence may have served as the initial connection for the two men.[31] They soon became partners in McKee, Harding, and Company, initially formed through the buyout of a rope manufacturing business. In the early years of the partnership they were primarily commission merchants, but by 1839 they had become officers of the Fire and Marine Insurance Company of Wheeling, with Richard serving as director.[32]

Richard and Rachel's family grew quickly. Rebecca and "Wilse" (as she always called her eldest brother) were joined in 1838 by a brother, Richard Harris Harding, named after his father and his paternal grandmother Isabel Harris Harding's family. Their brother Henry Grattan Harding was born in 1840, and their only surviving sister, Emilie Mary Harding,[33] named after her father's beloved sister, was born in 1842.[34] Richard Harding's brother William immigrated to the US in 1836 and lived with the Harding family for a while before becoming a professor in Burlington, Indiana.[35]

In 1839 the Hardings moved into a multistoried row house in a nicer part of town on Webster Street. It was close to Richard's downtown office in the McLure House at 67 Monroe Street.[36] To make the move feasible, however, Richard had to go into debt to his in-laws in the amount of $400 to buy beds, living room chairs, carpets, plates and silverware, washtubs, two wire cages and five canaries, and other household items.[37]

The Hardings had a household servant, but unlike some of their neighbors, they never owned slaves.[38] Each room in the Webster Street house had a large fireplace that burned bituminous coal, and Rebecca long remembered its dusting of the household day in and out: "The black soot hung and swayed in the chimneys like a mass of sable mosses, and, beneath, yellow and red and purple flames leaped up from an inky base of coal to reach them, while on this base, black and shining as jet, was a gray lettering that incessantly formed itself almost into words then crumbled away."[39]

But there was also a field nearby in which a number of old trees offered shade in the summer, and in the back of the house was a large garden with hillocks. In winter the children played on the icy hills, pretending they were the great Swiss Alps. Their mother encouraged outdoor adventures, equipping the explorers with alpenstocks, bottles of spruce beer, and small cakes.[40] She also taught them to care for neighbors who were poorer than themselves; it was a lesson Rebecca would carry with her always.[41]

Rachel and Richard invested their children with a sense of the importance of local history as well, and the family loved to tell visitors that the large wooden chairs in their living room had once been occupied by Native American chiefs who stopped to see Richard as they traveled to the nation's capital. While the guests' painted faces were recalled by the children as "live horrors . . . to shiver over when you were in bed and the candles were out and you pulled the clothes over your head," Rachel corrected these attitudes, insisting the children treat their guests cordially.[42]

Mysteries, adventures, and storytelling were a beloved part of the Hardings' lives. Both parents nourished the children's imagination, and Richard created a mysterious character, a French nobleman, Monsieur Jean Crapeaud, who had been driven out of his country and had come to live on the high shelf of a closet in their dining room. Richard created fanciful adventures for the nobleman that entertained his youngsters for years. The children's nurse, Barbara, once tried to add to the legend of Monsieur Crapeaud, but when she described him as smoking a corn-cob pipe, Rebecca was having none of it. If details were to be added to the myth, they must be accurate, and to think of a nobleman smoking a cob pipe such as she had seen the poor negroes smoke lacked common sense to her child's mind.[43]

The Harding children benefited from their contact with Barbara, however. She was as creative in her own way as the other members of the family. Recognizing Rebecca's love of reading and the need for a quiet space in a household of seven, Barbara, "having an architectural turn of mind," built a treehouse for young Rebecca. Years later, after viewing the great architectural wonders of St. James's and the Vatican, Rebecca could assert, "I can't imagine any house as satisfactory as Barbara's."[44] It was there young Rebecca first discovered Hawthorne's short stories and there she became a budding literary critic, a role she would play as an adult as well. When stories were "thin and cheap as the paper" on which they were printed, she rejected them. She had honed her critical skills over the years by reading the periodicals found in her home, including the *United States Gazette* and the *Gentleman's Monthly Magazine*. Her parents allowed her to read broadly, though they pinned pages together if they thought something within the periodicals was inappropriate for her age.

The family that thrived on storytelling also often gathered together in the evenings for the reading of novels such as *Ivanhoe*.[45] It was an environment that nourished Rebecca's already active young imagination. Yet the idea that she could become a writer was only beginning to form in her mind. She attended a local school for a period of time, and one day the pupils were shocked when "an authoress" visited their classroom. "None of the children had ever before seen a woman who had written a book," she recalled with amusement. "She was to us a something apart from the actual world, like a comet or a two-headed dog. . . . We watched her with bated breath. Was she an abolitionist? Or an atheist? Something monstrous she must be. Only a genius could write a book; and to our simple souls 'A genius' was outside of nature—disguised, perhaps, with a body like other men and women, but inside of it, an angel or a ravening beast. We only breathed freely when the door closed behind her."[46]

The Hardings were a deeply religious family, and they regularly attended St. Matthew's Episcopal Church. The magnificent structure of Grecian Doric design had been built in 1837. Located on a hill up the road from the Harding home, the church had a dozen rows of wide steps leading to an entrance that was reached through six mammoth pillars.[47] Its congregation, primarily well-to-do families whose ancestors had ties to the Anglican Church, was led by Rev. William Armstrong.[48] It suited the intellectually engaged Harding family, as the church rejected the emotionalism that marked Methodists in these years and was tolerant of alcohol, dancing, and a variety of theological opinions.[49] There were sixty families in the congregation at the time, and the church supported an active Sunday School.[50] Additionally, space was created on the second floor for slave benches. These were hard, narrow benches, tucked back against the wall so the people sitting there could not see the preacher or most of the congregation on the main floor; the minister's disembodied voice could only float up to them. Although members of the Episcopalian church, the Hardings believed in religious tolerance, and the local Catholic priest, Father Vaughan, was a frequent visitor in their home along with their own minister.[51]

At age fourteen, Rebecca began one of the most important phases of her youth: she was sent to the Female Seminary in Washington, Pennsylvania. When young, she and her siblings had attended a local school as well as being schooled at home by their mother and several tutors, but sending Rebecca to the Washington Female Seminary (WFS) was a major commitment for the family. It is likely her Uncle Hugh helped fund her education. Board and lodging was fifty dollars per term, plus five dollars in winter term to cover additional fuel costs, and tuition fees were nine dollars per term for the first year, eleven dollars for the second, and fourteen dollars for the third. Although there were local female academies, the Hardings chose the WFS because of its growing reputation as a distinguished and progressive Presbyterian school of higher learning for young women.[52]

The school had been organized by a distinguished group of citizens, including Dr. F. Julius LeMoyne, Alexander Reed, and Rebecca's uncle Hugh W. Wilson. In 1840 the WFS had attracted as its principal Sarah Foster, a prized graduate of Emma Willard's Troy Female Seminary who had taught for nine years in New York. Foster appointed highly educated assistant teachers, and within a short period, the WFS became known as a preeminent institution for young women, drawing students from thirteen states, the District of Columbia, and Canada. Most of its graduates became teachers in the West and South, although a few, like Rebecca's classmate Sarah Sweeney, became businesswomen. As the WFS's promotion materials liked to assert, the reputation of the school went with its graduates.[53]

When Rebecca entered her first year, there were nine teachers in addition to Miss Foster as principal and teacher. Seven of the teachers lived at the institution, and Mrs. Clarine Freeland served as the girls' governess. The school offered a three-year course of study. Miss Foster taught Bible, intellectual philosophy, and composition. In the first year, Rebecca took grammar, advanced arithmetic, ancient and modern geography, ancient and modern history, geology, and natural philosophy (first lessons). For her second year, courses included algebra, advanced geometry, geography of the heavens, chemistry, botany, rhetoric, and analysis of the English language. As a senior, she advanced to natural philosophy at large, elements of criticism, analogy of natural and revealed religion, logic, and mental and moral science.[54]

Through all of these years she had continuing courses in orthography, reading, calisthenics, composition, and scripture history. For additional fees ranging from four to sixteen dollars per course, students could take more typical "finishing" courses such as French, German, Latin, drawing, painting, piano, vocal music, needle work, and lectures in chemistry. Miss Foster also believed her students should have an extensive extracurricular agenda that included daily walks in the woods (which undoubtedly appealed to Rebecca who was an avid walker all her life[55]), morning and evening religious services, deportment classes on Saturday mornings, and exposure to major cultural events.[56]

Semesters at the WFS ran from November through March and May through September, with vacations in April and October after the completion of rigorous end-of-term examinations. Students' days began at 7:30 a.m. with breakfast followed by a brisk walk, then they took part in opening exercises and classes, which were prelude to recitations and followed by study time until 1:00 p.m. Lunch was followed by another walk, classes, evening chapel, and more study time. All students were required to retire at 9:20 p.m., except seniors, who were allowed to stay up until 10:00 p.m. Wednesdays and Saturdays were half days, giving the students time twice a week to socialize or visit their families, if they lived nearby.[57]

At the end of the three-year period, graduation examinations consisted of two-day public ordeals in which students were tested by trustees and teachers. But it was not all academic rigor. As Charlotte LeMoyne Wills recalled for the institution's fiftieth anniversary, lunch recess was all about "romps and games" that enlivened their sense of playfulness, and on Friday nights schoolmates could gather in the dining room for games and sometimes amateur theatricals.[58] The religious influence of the seminary's teachings had a profound effect on Rebecca in these formative years as well; it was here that she took communion for the first time on Easter Sunday in 1847.[59]

While in Washington, Rebecca had an opportunity to visit almost daily with Harriet Preble Barlow, a relative by marriage of Hugh W. Wilson. Rebecca and her cousins Edward Preble Wilson, James Blaine Wilson, and Clara Wilson often gathered at Aunt Harriet's house. Harriet had lived in France for a number of years, and she helped Rebecca hone her French. Clara, who was only four when Rebecca first entered the WFS, became deeply fond of her older cousin, whom she and the family called "Cuddie."[60] The cousins remained close for many years, with Clara an ardent supporter of Rebecca's literary career. The family attended Rebecca's graduation ceremonies, and Clara thought her cousin delivered the valedictory address to great effect.[61]

Washington in these years was a manufacturing center, producing everything from coal and oil to tinplate, iron, and glass, and it was a central crossroads for travelers, especially between the North and South. Among the major cultural figures Rebecca had an opportunity to see while studying at the WFS was Henry Clay. As a five-year-old living in Alabama, she had heard him discussed with near reverence by her father and his friends, and in Wheeling she had immersed herself in his speeches, which were often printed in the *United States Gazette*. He frequently visited the city of Washington on his travels during the years she was attending the seminary. He was, she proclaimed many years later, the "only hero" of her childhood because he treated all people as old friends and never forgot a person's name, no matter how slight their acquaintance.[62]

The same talent for memory and names was vested in another national figure she knew when she was at school, her cousin James G. Blaine. He was a law student at Washington College,[63] which was situated next to the WFS. Rebecca's familial connection to James gave her personal insights into his character, and they remained close throughout their lives. His "warm heart and ardent instincts came to him from his Irish forefathers," and his impact on the nation was in large part due to his personal magnetism, she felt.[64]

As important as Sarah Foster, Henry Clay, and James G. Blaine were in shaping Rebecca's thinking in these years, perhaps even more so was Dr. F. Julius LeMoyne. A founder of the WFS and a member of the Board of

Trustees, LeMoyne knew many of Rebecca's relatives, and he recognized her exceptional talents. His daughter Romaine was one of Rebecca's classmates, and he attended the school's events and the end-of-term examinations. He had been a major voice in the abolition movement in the region since the 1830s, arguing that slavery violated the most basic human rights and was abhorrent to the principles of Christianity. Thus he insisted on the immediate and unconditional emancipation of all slaves. He was the first president of the Washington County Anti-Slavery Society, founded in 1835, and he faced sometimes violent opposition within the community. Dr. LeMoyne ran unsuccessfully three times for governor of Pennsylvania on the abolitionists' Liberty Party ticket. African Americans from the region were an active and vital force in the local party, unlike in many other regions of the country. In 1840 LeMoyne ran for Vice President of the United States, again on an abolitionist ticket.[65]

During the years Rebecca was in Washington, LeMoyne and other abolitionists established an active underground railroad throughout the southwestern part of the state. The Washington County abolitionists were so successful that Democrat Sherrard Clemens, a Wheeling lawyer and cousin of Samuel Clemens, complained to the governor of Virginia about their successful tactics of "luring" enslaved African Americans from Wheeling into the free state of Pennsylvania.[66] Not only was the LeMoyne house in Washington, which Rebecca often visited, a central station on the underground railroad, but LeMoyne also invited abolitionists to offer public lectures in the area during Rebecca's time in Washington. The Harding family's yearly visits to see relatives and friends in Washington typically included seeing LeMoyne, and Rebecca knew him as a man who "made his own creeds and customs.... Doctor LeMoyne was probably the truest representative of the radical Abolitionist in this country. He never gave his adherence to any temporizing or experiment of expediency," and she acknowledged his true commitment to racial equality through his work after emancipation in which he used his money and influence to improve educational opportunities for the formerly enslaved, including $20,000 to endow the LeMoyne Normal Institute for African American students in Memphis, Tennessee.[67]

It was not only LeMoyne's work as an abolitionist that made its mark on Rebecca, however. As a physician, his reputation was equally strong, and he welcomed her curiosity about his pharmacy, located on the first floor of the home, and all of its fascinating bottles and jars of pharmaceuticals. That so many of her later stories included physicians and a notable knowledge of medical practice and theories certainly must have been influenced by these years of access to the man and his practice.[68]

The Hardings did not escape the ravages of a slave culture in the northwestern panhandle of Virginia, in spite of its small slave population. The area offered easy transportation to the lower South, making it a central point on the slave-trading routes, and weekly slave auctions were held in the city well into the 1850s.[69] There were a few free African Americans living in Wheeling, many of whom worked as household servants rather than in the mills, but the majority were enslaved. In her old age, Rebecca claimed that slavery was not a significant issue in Wheeling, because they were so close to the Ohio River that anyone could cross it at Wheeling and be in Ohio within half an hour.[70]

At the time, however, she more honestly acknowledged the tensions over slavery that emerged every time the family crossed the border from Virginia into Pennsylvania: in Pennsylvania, they felt it necessary to defend their slaveholding friends at home because the abolitionists wanted to see all such people as Simon Legrees, and in Wheeling, they had to defend their Pennsylvania abolitionist friends from charges of being "emissaries of hell."[71] By the Civil War, it had become an explosive issue in the prosperous city, dividing the Wheeling community, and the Harding family would feel firsthand the devastating clash of differing political loyalties.

Rebecca graduated valedictorian from the Washington Female Seminary in 1848, the first in a class of seventeen. The only sadness to mark the occasion was that her uncle James Blaine had died in February, and she felt his loss immensely. The erudition that marked Rebecca from her youth had been greatly expanded during her years at the WFS and became a hallmark of her literary and political writings throughout her life. But still she returned home to Wheeling without a clear sense of what her future would be. She had little interest in teaching, and there seemed to be no viable marriage prospects on the horizon. She had developed a passion for writing and she wanted to test her talents in that direction, but how did a seventeen-year-old female in Wheeling, Virginia, find an outlet for such talents? She was expected to help with the household chores and the care of her siblings, although the hardest household work was done by their live-in Irish American servant, the forty-seven-year-old Jane Hadden, and Rebecca had time for writing and wandering through the town on her frequent walks.[72]

At this time, her father was established as a civic leader and continued his partnership in the insurance business. Though Richard's positions meant the family moved among the town's well-to-do and civic leaders, financially they were anything but well off. In contrast to their extended family of achievers and risk-takers, Richard's poor management of his money left the family always teetering on the brink of poverty. "He was a man of stern integrity," Rebecca acknowledged, but he had "strong prejudices and no energy or business ability whatever. He would persevere steadily for years at any work set for him, but he never would add to it, nor move an inch to look for any better."[73] Whereas her Uncle James Blaine, a successful lawyer and active civic leader, offered her great joy in her youth, her father never earned a similar admiration; his great storytelling could not erase the tensions of his sternness and his lack of ambition that left the family often having to borrow from relatives or do without. Although Rebecca knew her parents loved her, she understood that as the eldest, unmarried daughter, she would quickly become a burden to the family, especially since marriage did not seem to be in her future.

Fortunately, she became acquainted with several people new to Wheeling on her return from Washington. These new friends helped direct her energies into personally satisfying avenues that at times also aided the Harding family. One of these new friends was the Reverend Cyrus Dickson, who had arrived in Wheeling in April to serve as pastor of the Second Presbyterian Church. His church was on the corner of the block where the Hardings lived. Dickson effected a strong revival in the Wheeling church. When he arrived, there were only fourteen members of the congregation, but his charismatic personality drew many new members. Dickson, like Rebecca's own minister, offered her religious guidance, but even more, he and his wife quickly became her friends. Dickson was known for his keen intellect as well as compassionate pastoral endeavors.[74] Even after the Dicksons left Wheeling in late 1856 to head a church in Baltimore,[75] Rebecca remained in touch with them.

In 1850 Richard Harding was elected Treasurer of the city of Wheeling, a post to which he would be re-elected until his death in 1864, and he continued to serve as Secretary of the Fire and Marine Insurance Company.[76] His election confirmed his reputation as a trustworthy man, but it did little to change the family's economic status. At the same time, Rebecca's brother Wilse left home to attend Washington College and to live with his Aunt Rebecca Blaine. Wilse was always Rebecca's closest sibling, in age and in her heart, and his departure was a notable loss of companionship. When he returned home in the summers, they would continue their studies together, including his emphasis in German.[77]

The increasing prosperousness of Wheeling also began to afford its residents a number of new cultural opportunities. The economic change for the city was largely the result of the Baltimore and Ohio Railroad's decision in 1852 to build tracks into Wheeling. If the Ohio River had given the city important market connections in the early decades, the railroad link made the river even more popular for manufacturing transportation, and the city's economy boomed. The LaBelle Nail Works was founded almost immediately and several smaller iron foundries were established as well.[78] Although these changes would result in prosperity for the city, the environmental costs were something that long-time residents noted quickly. A decade later Rebecca would describe such effects in one of her most famous stories, "Life in the Iron-Mills": "The idiosyncrasy of this town is smoke. It rolls sullenly in folds from the great chimneys of the iron-foundries, and settles down in black slimy pools on the muddy streets."[79]

Many positive changes also occurred, however. A new newspaper, the *Wheeling Intelligencer*, was established the same year that the railroad and LaBelle Nail Works opened, becoming the first daily newspaper in the region and, in spite of the fact that Virginia was a slaveholding state, the *Intelligencer* ran an advertisement for *Uncle Tom's Cabin* with the full table of contents in its September 1852 issue.

Within two years, when Wilse graduated from Washington College and returned to Wheeling, the business owners and manufacturers were seeking more advanced educations for their sons, and he was able to find a position as a teacher at Wheeling's Classical Academy, where he would remain for the next twelve years. Student testimonials praised Wilse's teaching abilities—"He was a very good disciplinarian, an aspiring teacher, and he was popular with both the little boys and the young men who studied under him. He was a man of rare courtesy, and met his students with a friendly esteem that stimulated the best in each of them."[80] For at least one semester, Henry Harding joined Wilse at the Academy as a teacher, but he did not remain.[81] He found work as a clerk, and in the mid-1860s he became Assistant Secretary of the Aetna Fire and Marine Insurance Company.[82]

A former student at the Academy who became a business owner in Wheeling asserted that Rebecca had assisted Wilse at the Academy for a period of time,[83] but her name never appeared in the newspaper accounts of the school's activities. Having been trained at WSF, a teaching career would have been an easy and expected path for her to follow, but it did not become the preferred field for anyone in the family except the exceptional teacher, Wilse. In 1859 he would become principal of the Academy.

Equally exciting for the city and its residents was the opening in 1855 of the Athenaeum where families could see traveling theatricals. The subject matter of the dramas, comedies, and farces ranged from "Norah Creina; or, The White Boys of the Mountains" in January 1855 to a production of "Romeo and Juliet" the following year with the American Shakespearean actress Annette Ince in the role of Juliet. Performances at the Athenaeum engaged racial issues that were as wide ranging as their dramatic counterparts. July 4th and 5th of 1859 saw back-to-back performances of *Uncle Tom's Cabin* and *Omaha Indians*. With the nearing of war, the Athenaeum also became a meeting place for local guards and the site of the debates over secession.[84] For young families like the Hardings, the Athenaeum offered both entertainment and intellectual stimulation. Such entertainments, as well as family visits to Washington, became a key part of Rebecca's life in the years between when she left the WFS and began her writing career in earnest.

All of Rebecca's siblings remained at home, though Wilse had his teaching career and Richard was now old enough to work as a clerk. Richard had followed in his brother's footsteps and attended Washington College while living with Aunt Blaine, but their younger brother Henry did not have an interest in education and was the only Harding child not to receive some form of higher education. Henry lived his entire short life in Wheeling, unlike all of the other children who would venture near and far to try their hand at a different life. Emilie followed in Rebecca's footsteps in the late 1850s and attended the WFS before returning to Wheeling,[85] though she, too, would eventually leave the city and later travel to the Pacific Northwest.

Friendships in this period were of special importance to Rebecca, formed both with relatives and with figures such as Cyrus Dickson. Most important among these relationships, however, was Archibald Campbell. Campbell probably knew the Hardings before he arrived in Wheeling in the spring of 1856 since his uncle, Alexander Campbell, had been Rachel Harding's teacher when she was a girl. Archibald became one of Rebecca's best friends for nearly a decade. A graduate of Bethany College and Hamilton College Law School in New York, Campbell was an erudite man and a brilliant conversationalist; he was equally well known as a thoughtful listener who treated the opinions of the poor and the wealthy with the same respect. Beginning as an attaché for the *Wheeling Intelligencer*, within several months Campbell formed a partnership with John F. McDermot and purchased the paper, becoming its editor.[86] Before long he recognized Rebecca Harding's talents as a writer and encouraged her to write for the *Intelligencer*.

This initial stage of Harding's career in journalism was one of the most important influences on her future as a writer and journalist. As did other notable author-journalists of the nineteenth century, Harding learned that her fiction, like her journalism, had to be invested with "something to say," a simple-sounding adage but one that marked the insightful analyses of cultural issues and contexts for a generation of authors, from Harding to Stephen Crane, who began their careers as journalists and continued both avenues of writing throughout their lives. Harding's first known publication in the *Intelligencer* was in February 1859, but she may have started as early as 1856 when her name began to be listed separately in the city directory, although she was still living at home and it was highly unusual for a single woman's name to be listed. Even more suggestive of her early involvement with the newspaper was the increased attention to the Harding family in its pages beginning in 1857. For example, an account of the Classical Academy's public examinations noted Rebecca's brother Henry had answered "quite extensively and interestingly" his question, "Did the movement of the Crusades exercise a purifying influence on society in Europe?" while another item praised Wilse's "academic regime" at the Academy.[87]

Unlike many women writers of her generation, Harding had strong support from her family for her journalistic and literary endeavors. Her first identifiable publication for the *Intelligencer* was an editorial on "Women and Politics." The balance between the domestic and the professional lives she was living, as well as her sense of humor, were evident in a note she sent Campbell with the submitted editorial: "In the intervals of that all important cooking today I have written this 'to order.'" She emphasized to Campbell how much she relished her opportunities to write editorials: "You see like all new editors I am going to define my position, with my say's. If it had not been for a due regard for your prospects with your lady readers, I should have been unmerciful. Please correct it, & trust me to do better when you are safely gone & I am not afraid of your criticism. . . . If you put this in at all it must go in as an editorial. I have a most insane ambition in that way."[88] Harding was referencing the fact that Campbell was soon to travel out of town for several days, during which he offered her the opportunity not only to write editorials but to serve as editor in his absence. Rebecca would fulfill her dream of becoming an editorial correspondent beyond anything she could have conceived in these early years.

"Women and Politics" criticized the tendency in the US "to ignore the existence of women in the body politic, bar them from the bench, the rostrum, the ballot box." The commentary asked *why* that should be so. She advised women not just to embrace their fathers' and brothers' political positions but to analyze the issues and come to their own conclusions. She concluded the editorial pessimistically, however:

> "The heart of a woman," says the old German, "is older than her head," and it never fails sooner or later to assert its birth-right—to put a stop to her ambition. . . . So we may safely allow our Lucy Stones and George Sands to lecture and write—they carry with them the elements of their own defeat. . . . just when they think they have overcome, it will assert its divine power, and with a touch—cripple and bless them.[89]

The conundrum of women's right to careers but ultimate roles as mothers was an attitude Rebecca would struggle with throughout her life.

That Harding focused on political issues would not have surprised readers of the newspaper even if they had known the unsigned article was written by a woman. Almost immediately after purchasing the *Intelligencer,* Campbell aligned it politically with liberal politics and soon thereafter with the Republican Party. This was an audacious and at times dangerous decision on his part. By 1850 Wheeling's population was 18,008, with 164 slaves,[90] but the issue of slavery and the Republican Party's antislavery position was not popular in the region.

That Rebecca chose to align herself with this newspaper, rather than the other papers in town that supported the extraordinary control of the region by the eastern part of the state and were known to echo Richmond's opinions, was a political act in itself. As many citizens of Wheeling felt, to be a Republican was little better than admitting to being an abolitionist. Racial politics in Wheeling were volatile at the time Campbell took over the *Intelligencer.* In that year the circuit judge of the Wheeling district asserted in his charges to a grand jury that Republicans were suspicious persons and opposed to the laws and traditions of Virginia; a speech by Horace Greeley, editor of the *New-York Tribune,* was blocked even though it was rather conservative in its subject matter, with only a passing reference to slavery. Additionally, a Baptist minister of impeccable reputation felt forced to leave the city after his decision to teach African American children in his Sunday school created a public fervor. Proslavery postmasters were known to refuse to deliver the antislavery New York *Christian Advocate*; political meetings of Republicans were sometimes disrupted by mobs and their processions were stoned by angry opposition members.[91] It was doubtful initially if the *Intelligencer* under Campbell's editorship could survive in this atmosphere, but he and his partner persevered in spite of the ongoing dissension, and by 1860 the newspaper had enough subscribers and advertisers to be financially stable.

Harding wrote a number of unsigned editorials over her years with the *Intelligencer* as well as reviews of newly published books.[92] An editorial likely by Harding was on a topic that haunted her for many years—that of a young woman, Ellen Carroll, who was jailed in Wheeling in the summer of 1861 because she manifested "symptoms of insanity." As the *Intelligencer* editorial reported, shortly after Ellen's brother had enlisted in the 24th Ohio Regiment, her mother died and she was left alone. Determined to join her brother, Ellen set out for western Pennsylvania but, unable to locate him, became "despondent and finally deranged" and was brought to Wheeling for her own safety. Recovering, she sought to return to Ohio. The article concluded, "It would be an act of humanity to have her sent as she desires, and we hope some of our citizens will see to it."[93] Harding would return to the subject of Ellen Carroll in the 1860s and in her 1904 autobiography.

While Rebecca was immersed in her work for the *Intelligencer*, her brothers Richard and Henry became privates in Captain Alonzo Loring's militia company known as the Virginia State Fencibles. Their company had been called to Harper's Ferry in 1859 in the aftermath of John Brown's raid, and they served as security at Charles Town during Brown's trial. By 1860 they had returned to their work in Wheeling, Richard as a druggist and Henry continuing his work as a clerk. Rebecca said the family was "on the fence, so to speak" on the subject of abolition; they "could see the great question from both sides" and were subject to defending each side depending on the political position of those with whom they debated the topic.[94] When Rebecca wrote to her pro-Union uncle Hugh Wilson in November 1860, she reflected the split nature of local politics:

> What do you do to amuse yourself? Read the WORLD and abuse the South? You must want somebody to tease you terribly. Don't you wish I was back? The election here came off on Monday. Clem and Hubbard, Union men were elected. There was more excitement than at any election I ever saw here. However, I breathe freely now, our liberties are safe. Sherrard said in his speech at the Athenaeum, '*My* spear has struck the leviathan of disunion. Virginia and *I* will save the Union.' That's a fact.[95]

No one had been more strategic in forcing issues to a head in the city than her editor, Archibald Campbell. He had become popular enough in the region to be elected a Republican delegate from Virginia to the national convention and cast his vote for Abraham Lincoln. Thereafter, the *Intelligencer* ardently supported Lincoln in its pages, the only daily in Virginia to openly do so and to argue in favor of the preservation of the Union.[96]

Violence continued to break out in the city over political differences, especially when it became evident that most of the Republican votes in the city came from men working in the iron mills, especially the LaBelle mill.[97] Figures like Campbell and working men in the iron industry were the core of Union supporters who would eventually build enough strength to effect the establishment of a separate state when the eastern part of Virginia moved to secede from the Union.

Rebecca's cousin, James G. Blaine, was also an ardent supporter of Lincoln; after college he had moved to Maine, where he became a newspaper editor. Known as the "Magnetic Man" because of his charismatic speaking style, Blaine worked tirelessly on behalf of the Lincoln candidacy.[98] Rebecca's own attitudes seemed to shift back and forth. She could be offended when her abolitionist friends clumped all southerners into a stereotypic sameness, and yet she worked for Campbell, admired LeMoyne's ardent passion for abolition, identified herself as an abolitionist, and was an admirer of William Douglas O'Connor's abolition novel, *Harrington*, which was published in 1860 and which O'Connor hoped "would rout and vanquish the South utterly."[99] With the election of Lincoln in November 1860, Wheeling and the western section of Virginia had to confront their conflicted alliances and decide where their allegiances would ultimately lie.

While the world around her seemed about to shatter, Rebecca had determined to move beyond the reporting she was doing for the *Intelligencer* and to test her skills in the broader literary world. She set herself an almost unimaginable task: to be published in the premier literary periodical of her day, the *Atlantic Monthly*. It was where she had read Hawthorne, Whittier, Holmes, and so many other favorites, and she wanted to be judged by the highest standards endemic to the *Atlantic*. With her ever-observant eye and a habit of walking throughout the community, she had studied the rapidly changing environment of a now-industrialized city, and she incorporated those impressions into her first submission to the *Atlantic*, "A Story of To-Day," sent to the periodical in late 1860. The magazine's assistant editor, James T. Fields, was about to take over as editor and was looking for ways to revitalize the scope of the magazine, which was seen as a vehicle primarily for New England writers.

Fields responded quickly to Harding's submission, but when she received the letter, its import seemed more than she could bear to have revealed. If he liked her story, it was the beginning of a whole world of opportunities for a young Virginian writer; if he did not, the narrowness of life in Wheeling would close around her. For half a day, she carried the letter with her, afraid to open it and convinced it would be a rejection. At last she could wait no longer. Inside was not only an acceptance letter but a check for $50.[100] Considering her father's entire personal estate upon his death was $150,[101] it was an enormous amount of money for a woman in her late twenties to earn, and an even greater accomplishment for a writer who wanted to be among the best of the high-literary writers of her day. Harding could not yet know that she would never again have to worry if a publisher would accept her work. For the next forty-eight years her writings would be sought by the major literary periodicals and by nationally renowned newspapers.

Fields wanted a different title for the story, and he and Harding ran through several possibilities. Although she preferred "A Story of To-Day," she also offered "Beyond?" or "The Korl-Woman," and they finally settled on "Life in the Iron-Mills." As "Life" was being prepared for press, Fields encouraged her to submit additional manuscripts, and he offered to advance her $100 toward future publications. She was thrilled and more than a little nervous about living up to his high expectations after "Life" had so impressed him. She carefully cautioned him that he might be disappointed in whatever she sent next and declined the advance payment: "Money is enough a 'needful commodity' with me to make me accept with a complacent smile whatever you think the articles are worth. But if I were writing with a hundred dollar bill before me in order to write in it 'I have paid him' I am afraid the article would be broad and deep just $100-and no more;—dollarish all over."[102] Integrity as a writer and insisting on the freedom to express herself as she wished would remain hallmarks of Rebecca Harding Davis's career.

Chapter 2

Treason and Fame (April 1861–March 1863)

As the nation entered into war, "Life in the Iron-Mills" was published in the April 1861 issue of the *Atlantic Monthly*. The themes that Harding engaged in "Life" were subjects she would return to repeatedly in her nearly fifty years as a writer. Foremost was a critique of capitalism and its inherent class inequities. Written in the aftermath of several major labor strikes in New York and Pennsylvania, the story assessed the very meaning of work and its relation to workers, manufacturers, and the nation, as would many of her subsequent writings.[1] In this context, Harding emphasized the ethnic diversity of workers in the mills and refuted a simple "white" distinction to her characters. Here, too, was an early example of Harding's interrogation of gender as she depicted millworkers referring to Hugh Wolfe as "Molly Wolfe" because of his artistic tendencies and because he would not stop at a tavern after work every night. In later works her characterizations often integrated ideas of "womanish" men and "mannish" women. As in "Women and Politics," Harding asserted in "Life" that conventional expectations for men and women might seem to offer security but in fact could cripple the most talented, intellectually aspiring people, to the nation's detriment.

This crippling was both metaphorically and literally embodied in "Life," literally through Deb's malformed body. After the war and its consequent amputations and gunshot wounds, the disabled body would become a key facet of both realism and naturalism, and it positioned authors to turn to societal reactions and causes as well as to challenge the antebellum emphasis on beauty and perfection, especially of women. It was a subject Harding would explore repeatedly over the course of her career, examining ways in which disability (psychological and physical) symbolized the consequences of unregulated industrialization and the inability of society to confront such consequences.

Further, the mechanization of Deb's and Hugh's bodies placed these workers at the heart of one of the most pervasive themes in Harding's body of fiction and journalism: the law. Lawyers were in the process of using the body's capacities and limitations to argue for shorter work days. Typographers, nailmakers, and ironworkers—constituting nearly half of Wheeling's population—had unionized in 1859–60 over just this issue.[2] Within months of the publication of "Life," Harding would create a series of stories confronting legal issues about class, inheritance, and slavery that melded her interests in labor with the ongoing war.

Equally important in "Life" was Harding's interest in exploring religious diversity, the complexities of which she would address throughout her life.[3] In "Life" she emphasized the difference between the reform minister, whose preaching was cast in a language inaccessible to Hugh, and the Quaker woman who exemplified Christian charity by aiding those in need on a one-to-one basis. In an era in which religious sects were often in conflict and families typically followed the same sect for generations, Harding had experienced a surprising variety of religious teachings within her own family: her mother's education in a Baptist household; her father's preference for Anglican traditions; her friendship with the Presbyterian minister Cyrus Dickson; family friends who were Unitarian, Catholic, and numerous other faiths; and the family's attendance for many years at an Episcopal church.

While embracing religious diversity, she was unafraid to expose what she felt were the failings of certain sects or individuals. In her critique of the reform minister in the original manuscript of "Life," for instance, she had written a more thorough analysis of religious figures who failed to touch the lives of the town's poorer citizens because the preacher failed to truly understand Christ's example. Much of this assessment was cut from the publication of "Life" for its publication in the *Atlantic*. Its importance to Harding, however, was evident a few years later when Ticknor and Fields sought to reprint "Life" in a collection of their best publications from the 1860s. Harding agreed to the reprinting, but insisted on reinserting a version of the excised paragraph.[4]

The response to "Life" was immediate and powerful. People from around the country wrote to her, at least two of whom became of lasting importance in her life: Nathaniel Hawthorne, the famous romantic author, and L. Clarke Davis, a lawyer from Philadelphia. In an effort both to acknowledge her indebtedness to Hawthorne and to promote her own work, Rebecca sent him a copy of "Life" after its publication. "I do not think for a moment," she wrote in a letter sent with the story, "you will care what partial glimpse of this To-day has come to a woman's eyes in her corner but I want to send you *something*—because, when the woman's eyes were child's eyes, your words used to bring the tears to them, often—bring them still, and I wish to thank you for the words, if you will allow me, in even this uncouth fashion."[5] Clarke Davis, on the other hand, initiated contact. He wrote to Harding, complementing her on a powerfully effective story. They began a correspondence that would last for nearly two years and culminate in marriage.

What should have been a time of unabated joy was clouded by the looming war. On April 12, hostilities between the North and South erupted in the first battle at Fort Sumter in South Carolina, and on April 17, Virginia seceded from the Union. The local secessionist newspaper, the *Wheeling Union*, had supported Richmond; but in the months leading to secession by the Richmond government, Archibald Campbell of the *Wheeling Intelligencer* played a central role in activating Republicans' resistance to secession. For the next six months, until the western section of the state determined to remain in the Union and form the state of New Virginia (later West Virginia), the city was awash in turmoil. There had long been distinct differences between the eastern and western parts of the state; the east's economy was built on slave labor and agriculturally fed by large plantations, while the west's economic base was small farms, ties to the nearby free states, and few slaves. The small farmers of the west begrudged the dominance of the state legislature by the eastern mercantile elites.[6] Tucked into the panhandle between the free states of Ohio and Pennsylvania, Wheeling was in a precarious position.

Several nationally powerful Republicans, including William H. Seward, who would become Secretary of State in the Lincoln administration the following month, became financial backers of the *Wheeling Intelligencer* to help promote resistance to secession. Prior to the convention calling for the state's separation from the Union, Campbell published numerous articles about that resistance, and thirty-two of the forty-seven delegates from the western region voted against it. Pro-Unionists determined to meet in Wheeling on May 13, ten days before the statewide ratification vote was to be held, and the announcement appeared in the *Intelligencer*. On that same day, however, Rebecca's uncle Hugh Wilson died, and she and her mother traveled to Washington for the funeral.[7] Hugh's death seemed a foreshadowing of the sorrows to come.

At the same time Harding's emerging sense of herself as a national writer was jarred when she received a negative response from James Fields about her second submission, a story she had sent him in mid-April with the working title "The Deaf and The Dumb." It was not a rejection, but Fields felt the story was too gloomy for the political atmosphere of the moment. After her glorious beginning with the success of "Life," this was a blow. She felt his kindness covered a "veil of disappointment": "Whatever holier meaning literature or music has for me, has reached me through the 'pathetic minor'—I fear that I only have power to echo the pathos without the meaning." She had intended the character of Lois to be the "sunshine" that Fields sought, she explained, representing that "even the meanest things in life, were 'voices in the world,' and none of them without signification.'" It was crafting the character Stephen Holmes that had thwarted her effort toward a positive resolution because she wanted to show the effects "in common vulgar life of a Fichtean philosophy and its effect upon a selfmade man, as I view it."[8] Although she accepted Fields's criticism and asked if she should try again or if he wanted her to continue to be a contributor to the *Atlantic*, the letter posited her own writing theories in a manner that subtly suggested he may have misread some of the characterizations. That pattern would prevail in their years of working together.

The other pattern that began at this time was Fields's determination to have his wife, Annie Adams Fields, respond on his behalf and encourage Harding to revise and resubmit her manuscript—and to assure Harding that he wanted her as a contributor. It was a strange moment for deflection, when she most needed to hear that *he* was not abandoning her as an author, but the warmth and graciousness with which Annie stepped in as the substitute editor established a bond between the three individuals that would develop into a friendship as well as a business enterprise.[9]

With Annie, Rebecca frequently discussed the impact of the war for people like herself living in a border state. Even in her response to Annie's first letter, the cordiality and a freer range of topics was evident in comparison to her exchanges with James, as she assumed Annie had more time for these discussions. Rebecca thanked Annie for affirming James wanted her to continue to write for the *Atlantic* and promised, "I will try and meet his wishes by being more cheerful," but she emphasized that her "story of to-day" made it difficult: "humor had need to be high and warm as God's sunshine to glow cheerily on Virginia soil just now."[10] Yet she determined to revise the story, extending it into a novel so she could develop her ideas more fully.

While Rebecca and her mother were at her uncle's funeral, the First Wheeling Convention met over a three-day period, and the most powerful Unionist, Carlisle Jackson, called for the drafting of a constitution for New Virginia, a term for the region that the *Intelligencer* immediately began to use.[11] They intended Wheeling as the new state's capital. Tensions developed over such a radical move, however, and the idea was tabled. At the convention's conclusion, there was a call to vote against secession with no reference to developing an independent state. If the statewide May 23 vote favored secession, they would reconvene in June.

Although the anti-secession vote in the western region was nearly twice as large as the pro-separation vote, the state moved to secede. Determined to pursue their goal of remaining in the Union, the western Virginians petitioned the federal government for protection of the area. The Confederates had destroyed the railroad between Grafton and Wheeling just days before the first convention, and Republicans knew if they were to succeed in holding the region, federal assistance was needed. General George B. McClellan's troops, part of the federal Department of the Ohio, arrived just before the first convention. Union troops could be seen practicing drills in the city and the first infantry had responded to Lincoln's May 3 call for volunteers. Wheeling was under siege, battling for survival on its own terms. For some in the region this simply meant remaining in the Union; for others, it meant entering the Union as a free state.[12]

In the midst of these regional conflicts, Rebecca Harding was building her reputation as an author. Although she could not imagine it at this moment of war and sorrow, she would remain in Wheeling for less than two years before moving to the East Coast, beginning a new life with a family of her own, and becoming part of the nationally recognized literati. At present, the destruction of the railroad into Wheeling had a notable impact on her personally. To Rebecca's wondrous surprise, Nathaniel Hawthorne responded to her letter, indicating he intended to go to Harper's Ferry where John Brown had led a raid on the armory and then on to visit Rebecca. The thrill she felt at this news remained vivid decades later when she recalled receiving his letter; he was coming to see "*Me*. Well, I suppose Esther felt a little in that way when the king's scepter touched her."[13]

With the seizure by Confederates of the Baltimore and Ohio Railroad, however, it became impossible for Hawthorne to reach the town. Against her disappointment, she worked arduously to produce work that was both meaningful to her and that met the editor's expectations. Although these criteria typically coincided, she at times struggled to find the balance. Writing "of to-day" was her most unflinching desire. With Fields's encouragement to submit more stories to the *Atlantic*, Harding developed a complicated but ultimately successful authorial relationship with him.

By June Rebecca had sketched a revision of "The Deaf and The Dumb." She took advantage of Fields's comment that he was indifferent to length and crafted a longer work that allowed her both to explore more fully the laboring class issues she had begun in "Life" and to integrate labor themes with the ravages of war. Though she initially anticipated the story would run in three numbers, "A Story of To-Day," as it was retitled, would actually run from November 1861 to March 1862 with multiple negotiations along the way between Harding and the Fieldses.

She submitted the full manuscript in July, asking James to "read it in a real July humour," but she was frustrated with the final product—in part from the multiple revisions but mostly because she felt she had to curtail what she could say either about industrialization or the war for an American audience in these early months of national disruption. Harding longed to write for an English audience, where she felt she would have more freedom of expression. As she lamented to James, "If I could have dared write a true history of today! but even in its poorest phrases, I was afraid to touch forbidden subjects so just the husk of the thing was left," adding later, "It was so much like giving people broken bits of apple-rind to chew."[14]

In spite of her concerns, Fields replied ten days later with a positive review of the manuscript and an acceptance. What she preferred was that he return all but the first section, which she wanted to begin publishing as soon as possible because of its timeliness; she could revise all but that first chapter before publication. "Besides," she added, "if I could send you each division as you need it, I could make it more truly a story of the day." Fields agreed, returning the first section as well and allowing her to revise it before he began its serialization in November. This process allowed her to incorporate specific battles and war issues into the novel, sometimes within days of when they occurred.

In an unusual editorial decision for the time, Fields had instigated a policy of paying on acceptance rather than publication and at times even paying in advance if he thought the author's financial situation required it. For their core group of authors, Ticknor and Fields maintained royalty accounts as well, allowing authors to draw against these funds when needed.[15] At this time, Harding became more specific as to how she wanted to be paid, agreeing to a forty-dollar payment on acceptance of "A Story of To-Day" and the remainder in monthly installments.[16] It would offer the Harding family an additional income for several months.

At the time Rebecca finished the initial version of the novel, the political tensions in the city were building. The Second Wheeling Convention was even more volatile than the first as creating a new state came to the forefront. The convention ran from June 11–25 and began with a repudiation of the Richmond government. By June 19 they had determined to reorganize as a separate state, although details would continue to develop late into the summer. The response from Richmond was immediate, and Archibald Campbell sought to expose the control the eastern legislature demanded over its western resisters. On August 31, he published an editorial announcing Confederate President Jefferson Davis's notice that "Union men in the Seceded States, had only forty hours to leave the state or be arrested for treason." Campbell ardently condemned this action, arguing it treated pro-Union citizens in the west "as alien enemies."[17] Eventually, nearly 35,000 West Virginia troops would support the Union, of which 212 were "Colored Troops," while slightly more than 10,000 Confederate troops came from the region, and the area's volatile differences raged throughout the fall.[18]

On December 4, General William S. Rosecrans established his winter headquarters in Wheeling and lodged at the McClure House.[19] The Cheat Mountain area southeast of Wheeling, which would figure in much of Harding's early writings about the war,[20] was a focal point of conflict, since a significant portion of people in that area still supported the Confederacy. The entire western region was overwhelmed with violence, largely instigated by guerillas and bushwhackers. This was not an area that saw only the organized battles depicted in the pages of *Harper's Weekly*, with troops standing shoulder to shoulder in battle. It was a place of military command but equally an area of lawless sniping and brutal attempts to resist Union control by some citizens. When Harding famously declared that "war may be an armed angel with a mission but she has the personal habits of the slums," she had precisely this style of warfare in mind.[21]

The impact of the war on the Harding family and on Rebecca's perspectives about war was immense. Their own church was split apart by the secession debates, and Episcopalians, who were viewed as aligned with Richmond because of the church's connections in that area, became suspect within the community, though the pro-Union members of the Wheeling church ultimately prevailed. The tensions became so fraught that Rev. E. T. Perkins and his family slipped out of town one night and traveled to Richmond, leaving all of their household goods behind. He later offered to return if he could forego including President Lincoln in his public prayers; the congregation declined. A new minister, Thomas G. Addison, was appointed; he was willing to pray for the Union cause and the President.[22] Many business leaders, some of whom were friends of the Hardings, left Wheeling. In September secessionist women were brought before the US Court on perjury charges, having falsely testified when friends or relatives were brought up on charges for their pro-South allegiance.

Nowhere was the evidence more clear that war divided families and former friends, indeed entire communities. For the Harding family, the loss of so many friends was painful, especially for Rebecca's father. He identified as a southerner, as did most of his friends. The family seriously considered moving to the free state of Pennsylvania, but in the end they remained in Wheeling as New Virginia joined the United States as a free state.[23]

It was not merely the loss of friends that devastated the Harding family, however. Rebellion was in their very midst. When Rachel and Rebecca returned from Hugh Wilson's funeral in May 1861, the First Wheeling Convention had already been held, federal troops were coming into the region, and dissension was widespread in the town. Rebecca's father had struggled with his alliances but sided with the Union; her brother Richard, however, was adamant about his alliances from the beginning—and they were with the Confederacy.

Shortly after her return from Washington, Rebecca wrote her cousin Jim Wilson, Hugh's son, to offer continuing condolences. After sympathizing with him, she admitted "how dreary" it was in Wheeling and that her mother had been ill since their return. She noted about 160 Union volunteers from Wheeling had headed for Harper's Ferry that week, and a significant number of families were also leaving for the South. Then she turned to a topic that had apparently been discussed while they were in Washington: "One pain was spared [mother]. Dick consented to stay. He was all ready to start on Monday, but the Mayor sent him and the other boys word that if they went it would ruin their families—spoke of Pa particularly, so Dick gave it up."[24] Richard had clearly made public his intentions, and for a while it seemed that the mayor's efforts had worked.

In spite of the fact that the paper reported the success officials had in capturing those who were viewed as disloyal to the Union, Richard was undeterred and soon thereafter slipped out of Wheeling under cover of night. He intended to travel through Cincinnati, purportedly on business, and then head south to join the Confederacy. But Richard's actions had not gone unobserved, and the Custom House officer in Wheeling sent a telegram to his counterpart in Cincinnati, warning him that Richard was in route to their city "under suspicious circumstances." Richard was arrested on a mail boat about to leave for Louisville and charged with treason. He was found to be carrying letters of introduction from Wheeling merchants that he had used as a cover for traveling on business; he was also carrying a packet of money, and he refused to profess loyalty to the Union. The Cincinnati papers claimed he was a captain in the Confederate army who "had evaded the vigilance of the Virginia officials," though it is unlikely he had actually joined the Confederacy yet.[25]

On September 3, 1861, the *Wheeling Intelligencer* published the news of Richard's arrest under the headline "The Case of Richard Harding." The article detailed the arrest of Rebecca's brother, the hearing in Cincinnati during which the district attorney demanded he take the new loyalty oath, and the fact that Richard had refused to swear allegiance to the federal government. The judge thereafter prepared a bench warrant for his removal to the prison at Camp Carlile, a Union Army training facility in Wheeling. The article concluded, "Harding is now at Camp Carlile, where it is understood, he will remain, until tried by the Federal Court, which meets on Friday next."[26]

The humiliation this cast on the Harding family was extraordinary, particularly on the senior Richard Harding who had spent two and a half decades building his reputation in the city. Whether the younger Richard finally agreed to take a loyalty oath is unknown. He simply disappeared from all public records until 1863. No Federal Court hearing was recorded, and although Richard and his siblings would eventually reconcile, only the briefest of whispers about him appeared in family commentaries for the next twenty years.

Through all the trauma of Richard's arrest, Rebecca was corresponding with Annie and James Fields, yet not a word of the family dilemma appeared in her letters. There was clearly a friendship growing between the three of them, but Rebecca knew they were fervent Unionists and, more importantly, she felt that, living in Boston and removed from the war zone, they could not understand the realities of war faced by people in the border states. So she discussed revisions to her novel, the health of her family, the war in general—but never a word about the real focus of their lives at that moment.

A professional battle was brewing as well as Rebecca learned the complexities of negotiating with an editor. She was both demanding and accommodating as an author, picking her battles. "Can the division between the 2nd and 3rd parts as *I* made it, be a division in your arrangement?" she asked Fields, adding, "The sense demands a break there, imperatively."[27] Their correspondence suggested again that Fields had misread her characterization, most notably when he wanted to title the novel *Margret Howth*. Harding insisted Margaret was "the completest failure in the story, besides *not* being the nucleus of it."[28] But then she shifted tone, "However if you do not see this, and really think it a more apt title, alter it, certainly. You know best about what is attractive, and I do not care, myself. I put that *all* into your hands. 'What is *today* fifty years hence?'"[29] To suggest she did not care, after adamantly asserting her dislike of the title, was hardly credible, but it captured her conflicting desires for wide audience appeal and the right to express her views as uncensored as possible. For the serial, Fields accommodated Harding's rejection of his title preference; the story appeared in the magazine as "A Story of To-Day," but its book publication early the next year used the title of *Margret Howth*.

The war presented constant challenges to sending manuscripts back and forth to Boston. As Rebecca noted in mid-August, "the mails between here and Pittsburgh have run 'clean daft' like everything else. . . . If Gen Lee can pass Rosecrans' force, it is probable he will scatter our Wheeling government, and our mails will be deranged. I do not think it likely, but it is as well to be safe" and thus she requested Fields not send the manuscript back to her. With "'New Virginia' and its capitol . . . in a state of panic and preparation not to be described," she requested correspondence be sent to her cousin James Wilson in Washington.[30] Although they had initially expected the serial to begin in September, the necessity of making revisions via correspondence rather than directly to the manuscript delayed its publication.

At the end of August, General John C. Frémont issued a proclamation declaring emancipation and martial law in Missouri. Rebecca had followed Frémont's career for some time and admired his views. Within a few months, he and his wife would become close friends, and she liked to tell the heroic story of his refusal to allow what he viewed as "apologetic Whereases" to be inserted into the introduction of the proclamation. After his review, all such remarks had been eliminated. "'The proclamation of emancipation,' he said quietly 'needs no apology. I will do this thing simply because it is right.'"[31] Although Lincoln would rescind Frémont's proclamation, Rebecca felt the General's document reflected "the total lack of posing, of self-consciousness" that was the trait of men who achieved distinction because they could abandon themselves to the importance of the moment.[32]

Her growing support of Lincoln, Frémont, and other Unionists was evident, though she would continue to admonish friends on both sides for homogenizing northerners and southerners into stereotypic figures. In fact, Rebecca became adamant in her resistance to sitting on the fence, including the "sham of neutrality" taken by Kentucky.[33] Her correspondence with L. Clarke Davis may have been influential as well. An ardent abolitionist, he countenanced no compromise in the move toward the eradication of slavery. Yet Rebecca would never be as fully one-sided about the war as Clarke and the Fieldses. Her abiding love of the South would always shape her thinking.

Even as the turmoil of the war situated Wheeling in the midst of panic and military maneuvering and her family struggled through the fear and worry of Richard's imprisonment, Rebecca was able to push away such horrors by concentrating on her writing. She had successfully tested the possibilities of contributing to America's premier literary magazine, and she longed now to try those of England as well. She approached James Fields on the subject by suggesting she wanted his advice and asking, "Would it not be good for me to next year if I could contribute occasionally to some English magazine? Even if you still wish me to write for you I have much time unemployed." This should not have been an unexpected question, since some of the *Atlantic*'s writers appeared in *Macmillan's* as well, but Fields apparently viewed this as a possible loss of one of his newest and most provocative writers. Instead he asked her to devote herself to the *Atlantic*; she agreed, appreciating the offer, but saying she hoped he would aid her with English publication in the future. He also invited her to visit him and Annie in Boston, but that seemed impossible at present. Fields probably believed that the war was the sole cause of her hesitation, but she had friends who had just traveled to Boston and thus her assertion, that "I cannot tell when I can leave home now. Not until the war is over. So I fear I must remain for a long time here," was as likely about the family drama playing out as the complications of travel.[34]

She signed the letter to Fields about English publication "invisibly R. B. H.,"[35] and she was "invisible" to the Fields for nearly a month. Fields finally contacted her, requesting a short story that could appear immediately after the completion of "A Story of To-Day." Her reply that she had been ill was accompanied by an embarrassing but necessary request to change their arrangement of payments for the novel and have the remaining $160 sent immediately rather than in installments. Undoubtedly, the loss of Richard's income as a druggist, added to the legal costs of his treason case, was desperately felt in a family that always lived hand-to-mouth. Fields complied immediately and the check arrived in less than a week. In spite of the payment, she had not yet started the new story, "being worried about other things," but she promised to begin the next day. In the interim between letters, news had arrived of the fighting at Edwards Ferry in Maryland and of the Union defeat at the Battle of Ball's Bluff, and she closed her letter with wishes that the disaster had not touched James and Annie personally: "God grant the war may never be to you in Boston what it is to us here."[36]

After much debate within her family, it had been decided Rebecca should use her name for the publication of "Life," yet after discussions with Fields, she determined not to identify herself in print. Still, her reputation became known among publishers, and with the first installment of "A Story of To-Day" appearing in October, their interest was piqued. Charles Godfrey Leland, editor of the

Continental Monthly, wrote to her. His magazine published literary works but was also devoted to national policy, and it was vocal in its pro-Union stance. The explicit rendering of labor problems and the war in "A Story of To-Day" was in line with the kind of items Leland sought for the *Continental*. He invited her to become one of his corps of writers. This was a tantalizing offer and recognition of the talents she brought to the literature of her day. But loyalty was an integral part of Rebecca's nature, so she contacted James Fields immediately and asked if Leland's magazine was a rival or would it be acceptable for her to write for it as well.[37]

Fields did not hesitate to reign in his prized new author. He did not mind that she was going to contribute anonymously to a popular publication, *Peterson's Magazine*, but the *Continental Monthly* was too much of a high-literature competitor for Fields, and he asked her again to write only for the *Atlantic*. Although many *Atlantic* writers wrote for other periodicals, this diversity meant the possibility of demands for higher payments for their stories, and all publishers sought to keep their best writers solely aligned with their magazines. Leland would continue to pursue Harding, writing in February 1862 again to invite her to become a regular contributor; Fields would likewise repeat his request that she remain exclusively with his magazine, and she again agreed.[38] Yet it was an issue that would continue to recur during her years with the *Atlantic*.

The summer after Leland contacted her, Charles Eliot Norton wrote to Harding as well. At the time Norton was a well-known writer and in two years would become editor of the *North American Review*. An admirer of Harding's fiction, Norton recommended to her the British author Arthur Clough who was in the States and wanted to come to Wheeling to meet her. Norton continued to stay in contact with Harding, often sending her information about people he thought she would like to meet or to learn about. These early months of her literary career introduced her to many important figures in the arts who would be part of the wide circle of writer-friends she developed over the years, including the poet, Transcendentalist, minister, and abolitionist David Atwood Wasson, who corresponded with Harding.[39] Wasson, the Reverend Cyrus Bartol, and James Freeman Clarke were all part of the *Atlantic*'s cadre of liberal theological writers known for their anti-dogmatism.[40]

Harding's connection with *Peterson's Magazine* had come through her acquaintance with the Philadelphia lawyer L. Clarke Davis, who had written to her after the publication of "Life in the Iron-Mills." Clarke was an editor of *Law Reports* and the *Legal Intelligencer*, but he also served as a literary editor for

Peterson's Magazine. Its editor, Charles J. Peterson, was a member of Philadelphia's T. B. Peterson Publishing family; he valued Clarke's assessment of literary works and had allowed the young lawyer to cultivate writers of particular interest. Clarke's initial appreciation of "Life" was followed by other letters and at least one visit to Wheeling to meet Rebecca and her family.[41]

Clarke encouraged Harding to write for *Peterson's*, which was one of the most popular women's magazines of the day, with a circulation exceeding that of *Godey's* in the 1860s. Although many such periodicals declined during the war, *Peterson's* actually grew in subscriptions, and it became an important and propitious affiliation for Harding, one that would last for thirty-two years. Equally important was that Rebecca and Clarke's relationship was established first through correspondence and then in person. Writing would be a core part of their relationship for the rest of their lives as they supported one another's careers, edited each other's texts, worked in tandem to write about political issues of the day, and nurtured two sons into nationally recognized literary careers.

Writing for *Peterson's* fulfilled Harding's desire to write more prolifically than the *Atlantic* could accept, but it also meant she now had to juggle commitments and relationships with two editors. Such training at an early stage of her career proved to be immensely beneficial. The experience of negotiating payment, fulfilling a particular magazine's needs while maintaining her own literary voice and political perspectives, and juggling due dates were important lessons in authorship. In her post-1860s career, she would often be writing for half a dozen periodicals at one time, some of them high literary magazines, some popular women's magazines, others religious or special-topic periodicals, and all demanding more contributions from her because her name drew an audience to the magazine.

When she began her alliance with *Peterson's* in November 1861, she was thus entering a new phase of her writing career. She would at times berate her writings for this popular magazine, most often because they had been rushed rather than nurtured into existence, yet it served two important purposes in her development as a writer: she found in Peterson an editor who allowed her to express herself with far less control than James Fields wielded, though she largely appreciated Fields's advice and learned from their negotiations; and she had the opportunity to explore new kinds of writings in *Peterson's*, such as mysteries, gothic literature, and politically charged stories about the South, the law, and women's cultural status. By working across such diverse periodicals as the *Atlantic* and *Peterson's*, Harding developed into a writer who could express herself in multiple genres and for multiple audiences. It was the key to her long career as a writer. Just as the *Wheeling Intelligencer* offered her apprenticeship as a journalist, the *Atlantic* and *Peterson's* both nurtured her early years as a fiction writer and aided the explosion of her talents within their pages.

This was also a transitional moment for James Fields. He had been editing the *Atlantic* since January 1861, and he wanted to build its circulation by creating an identifiable group of "*Atlantic* authors" who would be proclaimed the best writers in the nation. For New England authors, the salon that he and Annie hosted in their home was an effective means of building such a group,[42] but for a distant author such as Rebecca Harding, he needed to use other tactics. He worked on several fronts to keep Harding solely within his stable of high literary authors. He sent small gifts and portraits of famous authors and soon engaged her as a book reviewer for the magazine.

Equally important, he sent her recent publications from Ticknor and Fields such as Dr. John Brown's *Rab and His Friends* and a copy of a forthcoming book, *Cecil Dreeme* by Theodore Winthrop. She thought the 1859 book by the Scot physician Brown was "of a homely nature that ought to bring tears to anybody's eyes,"[43] but it was *Cecil Dreeme* that most interested her. Winthrop was a lawyer and a rising young author who had enlisted in the Union Army at the beginning of the war, only to be killed on June 10. *Cecil Dreeme* was a gothic novel he had finished before his death; it explored social customs among young, educated Americans that included cross-dressing and sexual ambiguity. Harding thanked Fields for the advance copy of the novel, "I wish the friends of the author could hear the quick recognition his bravery drew from the Confederates. Some friends of mine were in the Virginia howitzers who were nearest when he fell, and their praise is worthy of the man."[44]

James and Annie also sent Rebecca beautifully framed portraits of Longfellow, Hawthorne, and Holmes that she treasured as seeing them brought back many childhood memories. James asked to have a picture of Rebecca as well, a compliment as large as she could ever hope for, since it placed her in the context of these remarkable and remarkably famous authors who were long-time *Atlantic* writers. She admitted she had only one copy of a photograph of herself but promised to have another taken soon. This was the beginning of a long history of Rebecca's refusal to have her image preserved. The one extant copy, which she did send to the Fieldses,[45] had been taken the previous summer; she was dressed in what she called an "airy costume" for summer, her hair was in long curls surrounding her oval face, and, most notably, her compelling eyes were staring boldly and directly at the viewer. Why this photograph was not used for *Atlantic Monthly* promotions is unclear, although she may well have indicated it was for their private viewing only. It would be more than thirty years before another image of her would appear, and then it would be taken in a public setting in which she could not escape the camera's lens. The refusal to have her picture taken was part vanity and partly because she wanted her work to stand on its own. In later years, as celebrity became a key facet of literary fame, her ongoing decision to refuse to have her portrait published impacted the status of her career, but she would not acquiesce.

The most important effort on Fields' part to retain Harding as an *Atlantic* author, however, was the publication of "A Story of To-Day" in book form. The negotiations began again, in earnest. Fields wanted to rename the novel *Margret Howth*, and in spite of her earlier protestations, Harding agreed, as she waffled between liking and disliking the title. In these months she established a pattern with Fields of stating forthrightly what she preferred in terms of revisions in her work, then saying if he thought something else was better that was fine, and concluding, "I don't care."[46] She used this pattern with issues such as titles and mottos for her writings, but she fought for styles of phrasing she used that were indigenous to western Virginia and to use the English spelling she preferred ("my spelling calls out most rebelliously to your proof-reader to be let alone"[47]).

In these early months of her relationship with Fields, Harding also often shifted her ideas about whether to use her name for the book publication as well as how and when to be paid. On the issues of style, spelling, and payment methods, Fields typically agreed to her requests. Although she had asked to have monthly installments paid for "A Story of To-Day," by December she had recanted that decision: "Do not send me any money for Margret Howth until she has earned it. So far from belonging to the clan Croesus I belong to a race from whom money runs away like water, so please keep it safe for me till I need it."[48] She would learn over the next few years to be a keen negotiator for payment, and once she left her father's home, she was so adept at managing money that she and her family would become as financially successful as they were famous.

What Harding was adamant about was the need to revise *Margret Howth* before it went to press. Letters flew back and forth for a few weeks, since Fields did not want to grant this request, but Harding won the day by agreeing to write only for the *Atlantic* for the next year in exchange for the right to make the desired revisions.[49] She significantly altered the entire book, especially in terms of honing her phrasing, paragraph by paragraph.[50] Revisions to the ending of the novel were especially important. The last four to five pages of the serialization were separated into a final chapter for the book that detailed the fate of several of the characters. This was an important revision since the novel traced a range of poverty levels among workers, manufacturers, professionals, and townspeople in a manufacturing town. Stephen Holmes was a Fichtean-bred zealot whose quest for self-reliance made him blind to the needs of others, while Dr. Knowles was the ardent cause-driven philanthropist who dreamed of abandoning manufacturing to build a commune for people who had been ravaged by the conditions of capitalism at mid-century. Margret was the young Euro-American woman whose literal and figurative hunger led her to work in the mills, and Lois was a disabled, impoverished, free-born mulatta who was the most loving and kind character in the novel. These characterizations were not at all typical of the literary scene of 1860 when Harding wrote the novel, especially the move to have Lois be, in some ways, the most heroic figure of the novel. But none of the characters were purely heroic nor were their lives resolved in conventional or romanticized ways. That was the major point of the revisions Harding made in the conclusion of "A Story of To-Day" before it appeared as *Margret Howth*.

Perhaps the most important line Harding added before preserving the novel's final depiction of Lois was to ask the reader, "It does not satisfy you?" Using a final question was a technique Harding turned to frequently throughout her career, in her journalistic writings as well as her fiction. Like all reform writers, Harding wanted her readers to be engaged with the subject matter, to be frustrated and outraged to the point of taking action. But in the midst of the war, the novel—even with its purported "sunnier" tone—embraced the feelings of loss and lack of ability to change the course of the nation, in terms of capitalism or war.

At the same time Harding was making final revisions to *Margret Howth*, she sent her next contribution to the *Atlantic* and published her first short story for *Peterson's Magazine*, "The Murder of the Glen Ross," under the authorship of "New Contributor." Working on all three projects throughout December, it hardly seemed that she had published in a national magazine for the first time only eight months earlier. The war intruded into every aspect of her writing efforts, however. The story sent to Fields, "John Lamar," was not received, and since she did not keep copies of her submissions, most likely because of the cost and scarcity of paper and because of the time it would take to make copies of all her writings, she feared the manuscript was lost.

This was a very stressful moment for Harding, as she confessed to Fields, "John Lamar" "is my pet you see, my 'shay dorver'—as Mr. Poliphon says"; it was one of the most provocative war stories she wrote in these years, and its loss would have been immense. The reference to "Mr. Poliphon" was a pun on the musical term *polyphone*, a piece consisting of many voices or sounds. This description was exemplary of Harding's writing style, one she would more explicitly define in her *Peterson's* stories; and "John Lamar" captured numerous voices—of the slave owner, the abolitionist, the enslaved, the radicals of the border-state region, and many others. Finally, it was discovered that the person who had agreed to send the manuscript for her had simply addressed it to Fields at "Atlantic Monthly, Boston." "Possibly it is still in the Boston P.O.," she wrote in late December. Eventually, the manuscript was found, and the story appeared in the April 1862 issue.[51]

Harding's relationship with Charles Peterson was quite different from that with James Fields. With Fields and the *Atlantic*, she often felt she was writing, as she told Fields, "'with one hand tied behind my back' as Artemus Ward says."[52] As close as her relationship with the Fieldses was becoming, she always felt they did not understand the South or at least southerners like herself. Peterson, on the other hand, surprised her in a different way. Even as a southerner transplanted to Philadelphia, he did not object to her depictions, in a series of stories published during and after the war, of the South as a region that had brought about its own destruction by holding on to philosophies of "honor" and "chivalry" that were mere covers for the massively abusive system of slavery.

In her first story for *Peterson's*, "The Murder of the Glen Ross" in November 1861, Harding introduced the character of John Page, an unmarried Virginia lawyer who narrated this and a series of subsequent stories.[53] The John Page stories became the vehicle by which Harding could articulate her opinion as a West Virginian that the plantation elite of the Richmond area were deluded by their own traditions of slavery and chivalry.[54] Page at first seems like an aging lawyer who over time has become passive about his practice but is a benevolent man in most ways, and he offers insights into the real lives of people who are involved in his legal cases. But as the stories unfold, aspects of his character are revealed that offer a more unsettling picture of a lawyer whose passivity can cause great harm to others, and it becomes evident that Page is not a reliable narrator; he is often part of the problem rather than the solution to the South's immersion in traditions that enslave and oppress. As revealed in the fourth story in the series, he owned a large plantation and was himself a slave owner. On one level, the John Page stories were simply good mysteries, but on more careful examination of the nuances embedded in the stories, a critique of southern slavery and the plantation traditions and of Page himself emerge.

In this world of the Virginia plantation system, Harding created her own version of a Yoknapatawpha County a century before William Faulkner. Although John Page was the recurring narrator, numerous other characters appeared throughout the stories that ran into the late 1860s, with Page or members of his clan appearing randomly in a few stories and novels in the 1870s. Recurring characters included Thomas Flint, a law student in Page's practice; Brady, a prosecutor against whom Page appears in several cases but who is later an active partner in Page's firm when John has moved into semi-retirement; Sholter, a barely competent lawyer who is usually hired only by people so poor they can afford no one else; Dr. Tom Berkley, a plantation owner and friend of Page; the Champernoun plantation family; numerous physicians who serve the plantation owners; and, most importantly, Pine, a slave owned by Page who is his "office boy" and manservant. Numerous other friends and relatives in the plantation community near Richmond populate the stories as well, and after a story or two, the reader comes to a rich understanding of the cultural values and habits of this community.

Set in the 1820s to the 1860s, the stories in no chronological order traced Page's experiences from middle age to semi-retirement. The stories always placed Page at the center of a mysterious case, one he inevitably won and that demonstrated his concern for people more than mere legal issues. But what was also revealed was his admiration of the "careless ease of gesture of the Virginia 'colonels' and 'generals'" like Berkley, with their "prodigality, careless idleness, unbounded hospitality."[55] He remarked on Berkley's warm and genial heart—just before he drove past the Negro quarters on Berkley's plantation. Page perpetuated the theory of "happy" slaves and repeatedly described slaves as drunken and especially as lazy. Moreover, he mentions in passing and without recrimination that slaves could not give evidence at the trials in which he participated.

Most importantly, it was through the characterization of Pine that the true nature of the lawyer and slave owner was revealed over the course of the series of stories. Pine's dialect was always that of the uneducated slave (numerous dialects were used throughout the stories, for store clerks, plantation owners, etc., offering a rich flavor of various southern dialects), but from the first of Harding's John Page stories, it became evident that Pine was highly intelligent, perceptive of people's actions and motives, and had educated himself to the law. When a case seemed hopeless, Page did not turn to his co-counsel but to a very different counselor. Pine. Never in white or black have I ever found a more subtle, acute genius for discovery, combination. Do you laugh? Then you do not know the instinct of the negro. It had often happened that some curious hint, some lucky hit, had gained me a victory, which was due to the intuitive knack of Pine for odd bits of knowledge. How or in what way he obtained his acquaintance of the leading points of civil cases was a perpetual mystery.[56]

Although this was notable praise, Page never acknowledged Pine's astute intellectual abilities; it was a "lucky hit," of "intuitive knack." Nor could he accept what was evident: Pine had learned the law because he was always with Page in the law office and often in the courtroom. The harshness of Page's slaveholding values was revealed in "The Murder of the Glen Ross" and continued to emerge in later stories.

The themes that ran throughout the John Page stories were diverse. In addition to the indictment of slavery, there were several stories that examined the importance of inheritance through wills and lost letters; although these stories seemed to focus on the white plantation culture, they often included mixed-race characters whose very presence questioned the privilege of heritage that the white race claimed as their own. The legal rights of white women and all slaves within this culture were examined, as were slave owners' unscrupulousness when it came to the law and their purported benevolence toward their slaves.

Another major theme that ran throughout the stories was that of "blood." While Harding used the common idea of the white characters' insistence on their purity of blood when interacting with mixed-race slaves, she also attended to "blood" traditions within the white community, such as the belief that family blood was the true marker of a person's character. A man might live all his life as an upright citizen, but should he once make a tragic mistake, the community would insist it was family "blood" that had finally been revealed. Numerous plantation owners and their kin were defined by their "pride of blood";[57] as affirmed by Page, "In Virginia, you know, as in all unchanging societies of landed proprietors, the test of rank is blood, not bank-notes."[58]

Other timely issues appeared in the John Page stories as well. "My First Case," published in August 1862, nearly a year after Harding's brother Richard had been charged with treason, examined that issue. Setting the story in the 1820s with reflections back to the Revolution seemed to remove it from the Civil War era, but published in the midst of war, the displaced timeframe was unlikely to diminish the impact of the theme on contemporary readers.

While Harding was establishing herself as a prolific and sought-after writer, she also had the opportunity to cement several friendships that would be vitally important in the coming years. Certainly James and Annie Fields's friendship was one of the most important as it was intimately entwined with her writing career. That was both its strength and its challenge. In the year prior to her first visit with the Fieldses, a friendship was clearly emerging, but their correspondence retained as much of the flavor of business associates as true friends. They recognized affinities—such as a love of Sir Thomas Browne—and Rebecca became comfortable enough to reveal her sense of humor and to offer "the warmest kiss" to Annie for the New Year.[59] But the necessity of attending to business matters in their letters, from revisions to money matters to copyright issues, maintained a more formal nature in their early letters. Rebecca also had to accept certain rejections on James's part. She wanted, for instance, to have a friend of hers, probably Archibald Campbell, write an article for the *Atlantic*. As she explained to Fields in a letter in January 1862,

> I am a patriotic West Virginian you know and I think an article describing the private history of the struggle in our new state during the past year with especial reference to the question whether she shall be admitted as free or slave would interest your readers, both as a political query and a drama—Don't you? If you do, I have a friend that I will persuade to write it— . . . It is a hobby of mine—West Virginia, and I want to see her "fitly sung."[60]

Fields apparently declined, as no such article appeared. He did like Harding's war stories, however, and when she needed an advance of $100 in February, she offered to write them "ad-infinitum until I am clear of debt." Fields generously sent her $200.[61]

Rebecca's letter describing herself as a "patriotic West Virginian" captured her commitment to separation of the western part of the state from the secessionist east, but these issues were not comfortably reconciled for her during the Civil War. She maintained a border-state sense of rights and wrongs on both sides. What she hated was war itself, and yet it seemed almost impossible to openly express this idea when the war was being fought on such important principles. Being a patriotic West Virginian allowed her to align herself politically with the North but to maintain close ties her southern roots. In later years, she would articulate a more open anti-war stance, but throughout the

Civil War, she insisted she was able to see the realities of both sides; she condemned slavery without overtly condemning the South.

Rebecca's friendship with Annie was tenuous in these months, etched in a few letters to encourage Harding whenever she and James were in discussions that seemed to be stagnating. As their friendship developed through correspondence, Rebecca invited the Fieldses to visit her and her family in Wheeling and to experience a West Virginian winter: "I can promise you nothing but a welcome from all the family, half Irish and half Virginia"; they reciprocated with the request she come to Boston.[62] To reinforce their enticement, the Fieldses apparently encouraged Nathaniel Hawthorne to invite her as well, for within days Rebecca received a letter from him.[63] As much as Rebecca longed to go to Boston and meet her friends, she could not arrange at this time to do so. It was a desire that would not be squelched, however, and when they did finally meet four months later, their friendship was cemented.

Margret Howth was published in April. Before reviews appeared, Fields wrote to Harding to convey the positive comments Oliver Wendell Holmes had made about the serial version at one of their dinner parties. "Indeed I *was* glad about that dinner praise," she responded. "It has put me in a good humour. Perhaps though your Clicquot was good and gave my story a rosy light."[64] Holmes had one question that particularly amused Harding, "Why did Dr. Holmes think me a foreigner? *Please* tell me. . . . Do I write 'wid a bit o' the brogue?"[65] She was delighted with the appearance of the novel, but she was most interested in receiving reviews, "especially any finding fault[.] I would rather see those though of course you don't believe me when I say so."[66]

The reviews were strongly favorable. An early response in *Godey's* proclaimed the novel was "likely to prove one of the best if not the most attractive, books of the season. . . . it fairly sparkles with originality." The *Christian Examiner*'s reviewer was also impressed with its "marked and original power . . . a welcome exception to the common run of sensational or sentimental novels. Here is an author who has something to say that demands utterance, and says it in words not skimmed from magazines and dictionaries, but stamped with the writer's own personality." The reviewer for the *North American Review* found some of her "mannerisms of style" not to his liking but, in spite of his gendered assumption that one would scarcely expect a young woman author to know about the darker experiences of life, was impressed with her explorations of each character's "inner life" in which "she has achieved a high degree of success." He concluded, "no one can read the book without feeling its power, and wishing to know more of so vigorous and subtle a writer."[67]

Two editors who had been pursuing Harding, one hoping to retain her and the other to attract her as a regular contributor, also published glowing reviews of *Margret Howth*. After predicting the author would soon "be acknowledged by our best critics, to be foremost among female novelists America has yet had," the review in *Peterson's* declared she was "a new genius, who has, so suddenly risen in our midst." Charles Godfrey Leland's published assessment was presented under his name and, surprisingly, it revealed the author's identity. Referring to "that noble book 'Margret Howth,'" he added, "by the great-hearted REBECCA HARDING."[68] Although she chose to continue for a few more years to publish anonymously, her identity was now known and subsequent publications that identified her as "The Author of *Margret Howth*" did little to cloak her identity. *Margret Howth* went into three editions, with the first selling fifteen hundred copies; she was disappointed that the last two editions sold only three hundred books each and that no fourth edition was anticipated.[69] But the repeated recognition of her originality had to have eliminated any concerns she might have harbored about how the novel would be received.

At the time of Rebecca's request for reviews from Fields, she was leaving for a stay in the country near Washington, Pennsylvania. She initially claimed she would be "out of sight of the 'civilized' world of books and papers," but a few weeks later, while still in the country, she had already drafted the beginnings of a new story for Fields. When she became dissatisfied with that version, however, she "burnt it and began again this morning," insisting to Fields, "I am sure you would rather I would take time and write when I *can* write and so do you and myself and The Atlantic justice, wouldn't you?"[70] She had destroyed the original version of "David Gaunt." Rebecca stayed in the country residence near Washington for about six weeks, returning to Wheeling in early April. She had nursed both her parents during the winter months, and she may have used this time in the country to recover her own health and to have the countryside as her "room of one's own."

Shortly after her return, "John Lamar" was published in the *Atlantic*. She was paid seventy-five dollars for the story. Fields had begun a policy of publishing authors' names in a biannual index of the *Atlantic* as a means of advancing his corps of writers, identifying them as "the leading American authors."[71] That Harding was now determined to publish anonymously kept her from being promoted in the same way as Fields's other major authors, including Emerson, Longfellow, and Whittier. She had submitted the second version of

"David Gaunt" to Fields just before her return, and he asked for a rewrite. She agreed with this suggestion, she explained, "or I shouldn't have yielded so easily," adding, "You may expect a very abolitionist story in David Gaunt. How can I help it? Here Sen. Fremont has confiscated one of my friends' house for headquarters just across the street and Zagonyi is charging continually past the windows.... My secession proclivities (if I had any) are oozing out of my ribbons, like Bob Acres' courage—."[72] The shock of returning from the country to find the city in even greater turmoil over the increased military presence and Stonewall Jackson's attempts to take over much of the northwestern region for the Confederacy left everyone in Wheeling on edge.

Harding's other important new friendship of these early years of the war was with General John C. Frémont and his wife, Jessie Benton Frémont. The Union Army's Mountain Department was established in Wheeling on March 11, 1862, first under General Rosecrans and then, on March 28, under General Frémont's command.[73] Rebecca soon became a valued friend of the Frémonts; she admired his military skill and their supportive marriage: "Frémont was the ideal soldier,—simple, high-bred, courteous, always at a white heat of purpose. His wife was constantly beside him, urging the cause with all the wonderful magnetism which then made her the most famous of American women." John Frémont's abolitionist views also drew her to him, as he "made of Freedom a religion."[74]

But she was not wholly without an awareness of his shortcomings, observing that he may not have "had any especial liking for the negro—very few Abolitionists ... had that. But the slavery of the black man—of any man—was abhorrent to him."[75] Although Rebecca appreciated Jessie's public role in support of her husband and her country, she came to know her personally as an extraordinary woman: "There was doubtless something in her of the French *grande dame*. De Staël had not a more piercing wit, nor Récamier a finer quality of beauty, but below and apart from either was her personal magnetism. Whatever might be the room into which she came ... she was the fire burning in it, ...the instrument of music that struck a note to which your secret self replied."[76] Jessie's return to New York left a notable gap in Rebecca's life.

In the summer of 1862, after numerous invitations and stalled plans, Rebecca's desired journey east was about to become a reality. She had postscripted a note to James in May revealing her greatest wish, "I *must* say it—I do hope you will all like me."[77] She need not have worried; she was a success with her new acquaintances in New England, just as much as with her dear friends whom she also visited in New York, Newport, Philadelphia, and Baltimore.

There was another "friend" about which she was concerned. In mid-May she sent the revised "David Gaunt" to Fields: "Won't you let me know if you give him cordial welcome as soon as possible for if not I must stay at home and write something else. But I hope you will make a friend of David." As encouragement to view the story favorably, she added, "I had a letter from a publisher the other day saying if I would write a novel on 'the rebellion' & have it ready by fall he would make 'liberal offers' etc. What do you think? Had I better still abide by 'the old flag?' meaning T&F?"[78] Clearly, Harding was developing into a more astute negotiator to have her work published as she wished. "David" received a warm welcome.

She learned with James to be more assertive and to remind him, when needed, that she could easily publish elsewhere; with Annie Fields she wisely maintained a genteel discourse that appealed to Annie's sensibilities. Rebecca could rant about proofreaders and negotiate money with James, but Annie resented such haggling. As Annie wrote about one author who tried to use her to negotiate with James, "as if it were not enough to pester my husband they prick him again through me."[79] At the end of the month, Rebecca reiterated her desire to have "David Gaunt" published as written, "I have one request like Queen Esther. Don't leave anything out of it in publishing. A deformity is better than a scar you know."[80] Fields apparently agreed, as very few revisions were required.

Family problems seemed about to thwart her trip, however. Her father's health was again precarious, and the plans of her necessary escort, brother Wilse, changed repeatedly. On the east coast, negotiations were also being undertaken. Both the Fieldses and the Frémonts wanted Rebecca to visit them first. As Jessie Frémont explained to James, "She has never seen the sea & I want to shew it to her—& she is proud & shy & I want to help her to a coat of armor against she gets into your formidable sharpshooters' circle."[81] Annie tried to change Jessie's mind by inviting her and her daughter Lily to come to Boston as well, but Jessie declined. With her husband at war, she explained, "I am not quiet enough at heart just now to live out of myself—it is so hard to have one's body in one place when all one's heart & soul & strength are in another."[82] There was no arguing against such a heartfelt assertion, and Rebecca went first to the Frémont home, though she would divide her time there with an interim visit to Boston and Concord.

Rebecca, escorted by Wilse as far as New York City, arrived in early June. She spent a week with Jessie and Lily Frémont before she left for Boston, where she spent nearly two weeks. Even then, it was a whirlwind visit, and the relaxation of the Frémont home afterward was a welcome rest. But the two weeks in Boston and Concord made an indelible impression on Rebecca. From their first face-to-face meeting, Rebecca developed a true friendship with Annie and James Fields. More than a year of correspondence had laid the groundwork, but nothing could have prepared Rebecca for how quickly these two people became dear to her and how much she came to love their Boston home and its renowned visitors. From the isolation of Wheeling, she had come into the midst of the greatest literary coterie in America at the time, and she was heralded by all. To everyone, she was "the author of *Margret Howth*" and, to her surprise, enjoyment, and not a little amusement, a celebrity.[83]

Sophia Hawthorne was staying with the Fieldses for a few days as well, so Rebecca had an opportunity to get to know her before she was introduced to Nathaniel. Sophia had eagerly read *Margret Howth* as it was serialized, commenting on it periodically in her diary.[84] Rebecca liked Sophia, finding her to be "a soft, affectionate, feminine little woman, with intuitions subtle enough to follow her husband into his darkest moods, but with, too, a cheerful practical Yankee 'capacity' which fitted her to meet baker and butcher."[85] That first evening, Oliver Wendell Holmes and his wife Amelia dined with them, and the next morning Rebecca joined Annie, Sophia, and the Hawthornes' daughter Rose for services at the West Church where Dr. Cyrus Bartol, a Transcendentalist and abolitionist, preached a sermon on the congregants' duties to the dead.[86] Annie, Sophia, and Rebecca had tea with Reverend Bartol and his wife Elizabeth in the afternoon. Rebecca liked the Bartols and their daughter Lizzie, who would become a well-regarded painter and sculptor; Rebecca thought Lizzie was "healthful in every way."[87] But it was Dr. Holmes who most impressed Rebecca and who retained her admiration in ways that some of the other New England greats would not. "Physically, he was a very small man, holding himself stiffly erect," but his eyes were "full of a wonderful fire and sympathy."[88] The next morning dawned full of sunshine and everyone went to Swamscot and Nahant for the day, "dining on the rocks" as Sophia noted.[89]

That evening the Fieldses hosted a party to introduce Rebecca to a number of their friends and Boston notables. Among the dinner guests were Governor John Albion Andrew and his wife Eliza. They had both been active in antislavery societies, and he had been instrumental in establishing the first African American troops in the Union Army. Other guests included the essayist, critic, and abolitionist Edwin P. Whipple and his wife, and Louisa May Alcott, who had just begun her writing career with the *Atlantic*. Louisa admired Rebecca's work and liked her immediately. When they first met, Alcott explained to

Rebecca, "These people may say pleasant things to you, . . .but not one of them would have gone to Concord and back to see you, as I did to-day. I went for this gown. It's the only decent one I have. I'm very poor."[90] As Alcott wrote in her diary, "Saw Miss Rebecca Harding, author of 'Margret Howth,' which has made a stir and is very good. A handsome, fresh, quiet woman, who says she never had any troubles, though she writes about woes. I told her I had had lots of woes, so I write jolly tales, and we wondered why we each did so."[91] For a long time thereafter, Louisa compared women writers she met to Rebecca, noting a year later when she met Gail Hamilton, for instance, "didn't like her as well as Miss Harding."[92]

The days with the Fieldses passed quickly, but Rebecca had an opportunity to spend more time with Holmes. When she mentioned she liked old graveyards, he insisted she accompany him to Mount Auburn. She felt privileged to have this man whom everyone in the country adored completely to herself for an entire morning. She appreciated that he did not take her to the famous graves but to those of the lesser-known, telling her of their lives, honorable or tragic. "I search out the histories of these forgotten folk . . . ," he explained to her, "[and] when I have found out all about them they seem like my own friends, lying there forgotten. But I know them! And every spring, as soon as the grass begins to come up, I go my rounds to visit them and see how my dead men do!'"[93] She was introduced to several other people, including women writers who published in the *Atlantic*. Among them were Kate Field, Celia Thaxter, and Harriet Prescott. She also met a group of abolitionists who had admired "John Lamar," including Mrs. and Rev. R. C. Waterston and the author and lawyer Richard Henry Dana.

Then on June 17, Rebecca went to Concord to stay with the Hawthornes for a few days and meet the literary giants who were their friends and neighbors. Rebecca was not as naïve as Jessie Benton Frémont had suggested, but she came to Concord with a writer's awe for these renowned literati. She was never one to be swept away by someone's fame, however, and she carefully made her own judgments about each of them. On the second day of her visit, Sophia and Nathaniel took Rebecca to Sleepy Hollow, the Monument, and the Old Manse. It was as if she had wandered into a collection of Hawthorne stories, for here were all of the places she had read about while secluded in her tree house. Along the way they met Sophia Ripley; she and her husband, the Unitarian minister George Ripley, had developed Brook Farm and were leading Transcendentalists. On their return, Rebecca and the Hawthornes stopped at the Emersons' home, and Lydia Emerson showed Rebecca their lush gardens and the summerhouse. That evening Elizabeth Palmer Peabody and Abby Alcott, Louisa's mother, dined with them. Elizabeth Peabody was quite taken with Rebecca and would correspond with her after she returned to Wheeling. Joining the group later that evening also was Ralph Waldo Emerson and his daughter Edith, Bronson and Louisa May Alcott, and several other guests.[94] Rebecca was nervous when she was about to meet the renowned Emerson, "When I heard him coming into the parlor at the Wayside my body literally grew stiff and my tongue dry with awe."[95]

Although this was an extraordinary experience for a newly acclaimed writer, Rebecca was not completely enamored of everyone she met. "They did not," she reflected, "appear precisely as they do in the portraits drawn of them for posterity by their companions"; in part, she felt, it was because the "'Atlantic' coterie" stood "always apart from humanity." It was their power but also their shortcoming, because they guided the world but "never would see it as it was." Unlike Holmes, they were, to her mind, impractical dreamers, and Harding was the writer who wanted to capture the world of "to-day." This gap between their romantic ideals and reality as she knew it was most evident when they discussed the war. During the evening at Wayside hosted in her honor, Bronson Alcott "chanted paeans to the war, the 'armed angel which was wakening the nation to a lofty life unknown before.'" His recitation seemed stale, as if often repeated, as indeed Hawthorne's mocking eyes suggested. Her vision of war was of uncalibrated corruption and hatred in which honorable men became adept at political machinations and the "filthy spewings" of war that included "burning homes and outraged women." In response to Alcott's glorification of war, she reflected, "War may be an armed angel with a mission, but she has the personal habits of the slums" and Bronson Alcott was merely a "would-be seer."[96]

She was surprised by the tempering of her admiration for Emerson on this occasion as well. It was based on Emerson's adoration of Bronson Alcott, and his own momentarily intense interest in people that waned like a bee who has taken "from each man his drop of stored honey, and after that the man counted for no more to him than any other robbed bee." The two men's discussions of the "eternal verities" was fascinating but ultimately unsatisfying, Rebecca felt, since "their theories were like beautiful bubbles blown from a child's pipe, floating overhead, with queer reflections on them of sky and earth and human beings, all in a glow of fairy color and all a little distorted."[97]

Hawthorne, however, seemed to be what she had imagined. His love of his friends was tinged with an ironic sense of their pontifications, which was appreciated by Rebecca, an author who used irony as powerfully as anyone in the nineteenth century. In spite of her criticisms, she quickly developed a fondness for this group of influential writers; Bronson Alcott may have held what she felt was an unwarranted sense of his own importance, but he was "a kindly old man," and Rebecca would see Emerson, Louisa May Alcott, and several other of the Boston-Concord literary aristocracy over the coming years when they visited Philadelphia where she would soon be living. It was Hawthorne who left the best impression, perhaps because he stood outside the Boston fraternity, friends with all but not really a part of the club that embraced the grandness of either Emerson or Bronson Alcott. Yet she also realized that he maintained this aloofness even in his own home. She had time with Sophia and Nathaniel alone, however, when his personality blossomed before her in ways she would never forget. When Rebecca left their home, Nathaniel took her hand and remarked, "I am sorry you are going away. It seems as if we had known you always."[98] It meant everything to Rebecca, especially since she would never see Nathaniel again. He died two years later.

Perhaps most of all, Rebecca relished the time she had with the Fieldses, getting to know them far more intimately than she had even hoped. For the next several years the three of them would be as close friends as they were professional associates. James was "a keen man of business, but he had a kindly, hospitable soul," and she credited him as the force behind the success of the *Atlantic* coterie. Although Dr. Holmes, Henry Wadsworth Longfellow, Emerson, and George Ticknor all headed different New England literary "clans" at the time, she credited Fields with the greatest talent: "He was the wire that conducted the lightning so that it never struck amiss."[99] Annie's genteel nature and her genuine regard for Rebecca were evident from moment she arrived at their Charles Street home: "You never knew did you Annie how downrightly scared and lonesome I felt that night and how your cordial greeting took it all away. You met me *at the door* you know, it was *good* in you to do that."[100]

It had been an extraordinary visit, Rebecca reflected as she left to spend more time with the Frémonts. Coming into the New York City train station, however, she felt "my old scare of being left alone coming on fast, the great inhospitable world being represented just then by hack-drivers and scuffling newsboys."[101] Her fears abated when she saw Jessie and Lily waiting for her. With the Frémont women in their Staten Island residence, Rebecca felt at home in a way she had not with the hustle and constant entertainments of Boston. While she was visiting, however, John Frémont faced the last crisis of his military career. On June 26 the federal Army of Virginia was created, and to Frémont's dismay, John Pope was put in command. Rather than serve under a junior officer, he ended his military career and returned home. Rebecca was still at the Frémonts' the night he arrived. She was surprised when he took time the next day to attend to her as his guest, sketching a map of places she should visit in the city. As she later recalled, "he was the great man of my youth."[102]

While at the Frémonts, she also met Sarah Blake Sturgis Shaw. Sarah and her husband Francis George Shaw were Unitarians known for their intellectualism and for the ardency of their abolitionist views. Their son, Robert Gould Shaw, was leading the first all-African American regiment, the 54th Massachusetts Infantry. Standing on the front porch of the Shaw home, Sarah showed Rebecca a watch Robert had sent her that had been damaged by a bullet. It had saved her son's life. Within weeks, however, Robert and most of the men in the 54th would be killed at Charleston, South Carolina.[103]

From New York, she wrote to Annie, struggling to tell her how much the two weeks in Boston had meant: "when I sincerely feel anything, I can say least. But *you know*—don't you? Not long ago a friend of mine said to me, her eyes full of tears, 'You, every woman has a right to summer days in her life.' I only want to say that you—both of you—have commanded such days into mine, and that I won't forget."[104] She also mentioned that the Fieldses should be on the lookout for her brother Wilse who was on his way to Montreal but hoped to stop by Boston on his return to meet them. "Now you must like him, if he does," she commanded. "He is—well, just the best brother now alive."[105] Once Wilse had visited the Fieldses, he became as true a convert as Rebecca.

At the beginning of July, Rebecca left New York on her way to Baltimore to visit Rev. Cyrus Dickson and his wife who had left Wheeling in 1856. She made two stops along the way. First in Newport, Rhode Island, where she visited friends,[106] and then in Philadelphia to see Clarke Davis, the lawyer who had initiated contact with her after reading "Life in the Iron-Mills." Since his visit to Wheeling, their attraction to one another had grown, and this time together confirmed their feelings. She and Clarke explored Philadelphia, romantically rowed up the Wissahickon by early dawn,[107] and forged a friendship into love. Yet not a word of this visit or any mention of Clarke appeared in her correspondence with Annie or James while she was visiting him. After she returned home, she mentioned to the Fields in passing only that she had had a "happy week" in Philadelphia.[108] As she had told Annie, when she cared most, she could say the least. And she cared deeply for Clarke.

In Baltimore, Rebecca resumed her correspondence with Annie, claiming the seat near the Fieldses' fireplace as her own, hoping it was "miserably vacant" for Annie. It was strange to be in a border state again, Rebecca admitted, "I am in the midst of Southern sultriness & secessionism—now I have fallen into the old habits of sleeping all afternoon—and making my dinners in water-ice and bananas and I wish from the innermost soul of me for a Boston east wind—" She was already beginning a process that would continue for several years in her correspondence with Annie: reminiscing about all of the fascinating people she had met in Boston. The journalist Kate Field often came to mind: "When I think of Boston her face with its true beauty comes up surely among the first—I have a fancy she and I are to be fellow pilgrims on the good road somewhere again." Rebecca also reflected on how happy she was to have had the opportunity to know Sophia Hawthorne well, and she wanted to be kept informed of everything relating to Dr. Holmes, Elizabeth Peabody, and Celia Thaxter and "all the news—new ideas—spirits—books—people—scandal—who and what will be in the next Atlantic," and she asked that "if anybody speaks of me—water their memory—dip under it, keep it alive. I want to be remembered by somebody in Boston. For *I love* Boston. I don't often say that of anything—you know." She signed her letter, "*Yours* in or out of the Union."[109]

While she was in Baltimore, the Dicksons escorted her around the city. She was particularly impressed with Druid Hill, a park she found to be "old and solitary and wild enough for you to not be surprised if some Druid priestess should come out and begin her invocation."[110] It was not all ease in Baltimore, however. One day as they were traveling near Mount Vernon Place, their carriage was halted by a mob protesting some facet of the war.[111] Otherwise, she liked the city, which she found beautiful, and after the "barred windows of New York," the "lighted drawing rooms and fresh faces grouped on the balconies" harbored an openness she admired.[112] In the evenings, she and the Dicksons were reading Elizabeth Sara Sheppard's memorial *Charles Auchester*, and Rebecca was pursuing the writings of another British author, Edward Dicey, whom she had met while in Boston. She was amused after her return home to learn that Dicey had found them all quite curious. "How very English that is!" she laughingly declared to Annie.[113]

Rebecca had promised Annie she would send a photograph of herself, so she had three taken while in Baltimore, but since her friends said they presented her as completely expressionless, she destroyed the pictures. In spite of numerous promises to Annie, she would never again have a photograph taken.[114] Yet this was not a casual request from Annie. Rebecca's refusal to supply a photograph stymied her inclusion in James's plans to promote her as part of the *Atlantic* coterie. Although she would be given the coveted position of the lead story in the January issue of 1863—the lead in the January issues was given only to Fields's premier authors—he was also using their portraits to market the journal. New subscribers would soon be offered a picture of their favorite *Atlantic* writer, and these images would populate hundreds of New England and Midwestern homes.[115] But none would be available of the author of "Life in the Iron-Mills" and *Margret Howth*. Fields was at the forefront of recognizing the importance of the emerging cult of personality, but Rebecca wanted no part of this kind of promotion, preferring that her work stand on its own. It was a mark of her artistic integrity, but one that hindered her reputation as one of the century's leading authors.

From Baltimore, Harding continued to push James about publishing *Margret Howth* in England with Macmillan. She was also collecting materials for an article she wanted to publish in the *Atlantic* on "Blind Tom," as Thomas Wiggins was known. He was an African American autistic savant whose remarkable abilities on the piano were fascinating the country. A musician in Boston gave her the gift of a full-length likeness of Wiggins, and she was trying to locate a phrenological chart of his head. If she could not do so, she intended to send a photograph to one of the Fowler brothers, the leading phrenologists of the time, so he could give her his opinion.[116] Harding was both concerned about the truth of Wiggins' abilities and felt he represented so many individuals with extraordinary talents who were oppressed within the slavery system.

By the middle of August Rebecca was back in Wheeling, "in the midst of dust and smoke."[117] Over the next few years, her correspondence with the Fieldses, especially Annie, would keep alive her wondrous memories of Boston and all the people she met there. She also again encouraged them to visit her in Wheeling, though one of her brothers worried that all they would have to show the Bostonians was grime from the mills.[118] As soon as she was home, Rebecca sent her article on Thomas Wiggins to James. While she finalized her next serial for the *Atlantic*, "David Gaunt," she used Annie as an intermediary for some people she wished to keep in contact with, such as Kate Field, sending notes to Field via Annie. Others, such as Elizabeth Peabody, whose forthrightness sometimes startled Rebecca, needed no intermediaries to maintain contact.[119] Rebecca had been struck by Peabody's refusal to accommodate her brother-in-law Nathaniel Hawthorne's moodiness and inclination toward reclusiveness. She admired Peabody as "a woman of wide research and a really fine intelligence," but the woman, she felt, had "the discretion of a six-year-old child," and one evening when Rebecca was staying with Sophia and Nathaniel, she had been abashed to learn that Elizabeth had invited a group of people to Wayside to meet her without first informing the Hawthornes.[120] Rebecca was extremely discomfited when Elizabeth sent her a collection of private letters exchanged between Mrs. and Dr. William Ellery Channing without the family's knowledge. Elizabeth had mentioned them to Rebecca when she was in Concord, and she sent them hoping the author would use their story in one of her future writings. Rebecca quickly wrote to Annie, revealed the situation, and asked that Annie explain to Elizabeth "that such a thing *could not be* if I had any regard for decency. . . . You see I felt she did it all for the best and from kind motives to me—so my lips were sealed—She *is* a good woman."[121]

In long letters to Annie and James, Rebecca delighted in discussing recent publications in the *Atlantic*, such as Mary Abigail Dodge's "A Complaint of Friends," which Rebecca thought was done "excellently well,"[122] and especially in reminiscing about her time in Boston. It kept the experience alive for her and, equally important to Rebecca, instantiated her in their midst so as not to be forgotten. She missed the intellectual stimulation she had experienced in both Boston and Concord and repeatedly asked to be remembered to those who had impressed her and to be kept abreast of the activities of others, such as Louisa May Alcott. Rebecca also kept in touch with the Frémonts and reported on their activities to the Fieldses.[123] The intimacy that had developed between Rebecca and the Fieldses also allowed her to speak more openly with them about the war, especially with Annie. The more Rebecca experienced of war, the more fully her anti-war philosophy was developed. As she reported in late August of 1862,

> These are sad lonesome days for us here. The war is surging up close about us. O Annie if I could put into your and every true woman's heart the inexpressible loathing I have for it! If you could only see the other side enough to see the wrong the tyranny on both! God rules. Yes I know. But God in His inscrutable wisdom suffered great wrongs to work out His ends—and *this* is one of them.

She reminded Annie of how fortunate she was to be far from the warfront and reminded her Bostonian friends that she could tell them "things *I know* that would make your heart sick. Yet it is not because of these apparent horrors that I think the war unjust—You will say, I know, that my judgment is warped by sympathy. From the first I upheld the right of revolution, granted to the south what Garibaldi[,] Emmet[,] Washington claimed, though *I* never would—never *could* have lived in a slave confederacy—." As if she felt she had gone too far, Rebecca pulled back, "Forgive me. I don't know what wrung that out. Let us go back to pleasanter thoughts." Yet she could not withhold her attitudes for long, and as she concluded an account of her time in Baltimore at the end of the letter, she added,

> I do wish you knew some of my Baltimore friends, though—could see a glimpse or two of Maryland plantation life. One acquaintance of mine—I tell you this as a set-off to poor Tom's story—was having a boy—her slave—instructed in drawing with her own children, fancying he was a genius and meant to send him to Italy—My dear, hush, I know that is nothing. I think slavery wrong, as you do.[124]

She was trying to convince Annie, who had never been to Baltimore, that southerners were not all alike, just as she was trying to convince herself.

The provocative "David Gaunt" proved to be a success, and with that assurance, Harding bolstered herself to tell James Fields in October that she truly wanted to write only for the *Atlantic* because she liked the sophistication of their readers,

> But I'm going to be perfectly honest now. If I wrote stories suitable for other magazines, I could make more. The Peterson's in Phila. sent me in September $300 for a story very little longer than David Gaunt and very inferior. I wrote it in two weeks. It was anonymous, of course. They offered more if I would allow them to say by the author of Margret Howth. Now I would *rather* write for you—alone—I don't like to write that sort of articles even anonymously. It does me no good and for others is neither harmful not helpful. Yet as times are, I am not justified in refusing "the higher price." So I thought I would say to you as a friend to whom I *can* be candid that I hope Mr. Ticknor and you will give as much for future articles as you can legitimately afford so that I can write solely for the A.M. You would understand me "all right" don't you?[125]

Two goals were accomplished with this letter: she emphasized her concerns over the relatively low pay of the *Atlantic*, which as Gail Hamilton would reveal in a few years was better for male than female writers, and that she was continuing to write for *Peterson's* and would do so in the future. To her satisfaction, Fields raised her rate of payment to eight dollars per page rather than a flat fee.[126] She would remain with the well-paying *Peterson's* for decades after leaving the pages of the *Atlantic* and writing for other high literary magazines. In these months as well, Rebecca was feeling a great personal frustration. She wrote longingly to Annie about her time in Boston—"sometimes I reproach myself so much for my visit to Boston. I think, why did I not show more how happy I was? Make them love me more?" and she added, "At times, looking back over all the wasted years I feel as if I could say, I have lost not a day—but a life."[127]

Perhaps because of this lamentation, Annie sent news that they were planning to visit her in the spring. This promise, after so many invitations from the Harding family, delighted Rebecca. She had just spent weeks of caring for her mother and sister through illnesses, and she felt "tired out, most of the time in body and mind,"[128] but the news cheered her immensely. More importantly, by the end of October she hinted to Annie, obliquely, the truly significant way in which her life was about to change. She had agreed to marry Clarke Davis. For now she would not discuss it or even say more than that she would tell Annie something important soon. She was also in close contact with Jessie Benton Frémont in these months, to whom she gave one of her highest accolades—that of being a *"genuine woman."*[129]

Rebecca had encouraged Jessie's interest in writing and was delighted to learn that she had finished a book she had been working on for some time. Rebecca made every effort to ensure the success of her friend's work, writing to editors she knew to encourage them to publish the book. Jessie also asked Rebecca to review it when it was published, which Rebecca not only agreed to do but let the Fieldses know that she wished to do so. James had already approached her about reviewing books for the *Atlantic*, and he embraced this opportunity. Her review of Frémont's book, which Ticknor and Fields agreed to publish, would soon appear in its pages.

Rebecca was able at this time to achieve one of her longstanding dreams. "Blind Tom" was published in the *Atlantic Monthly* in November, and Harding's desire for English publication had not abated. Although Macmillan had written to Fields that he would like to publish some of her work, he wanted to do so without indicating it was by an American author.[130] Her work was so specifically about US industrial life and about the war from the perspective of a resident of the border-state region that she could not meet Macmillan's criterion. With Macmillan's failure to commit to publication, Harding had suggested to Fields that "Blind Tom" might find a home in Charles Dickens' periodical, *All the Year Round*. This time she was successful. When Fields sent the article to Dickens, it immediately captured the interest of the British author and editor. "I have read that affecting paper you had the kindness to send me, with strong interest and emotion," Dickens wrote Fields after reading "Blind Tom" in manuscript. "You may readily suppose that I have been most glad and ready to avail myself of your permission to print it."[131] By arrangement between the two editors, it appeared in England as "Blind Black Tom" the month before its US publication. Harding at last had broken into the English publishing market.

At home, the responses to "Blind Tom" were expansive. On a personal level, friends greatly admired it. Jessie Benton Frémont wrote to a friend, "Didn't you like 'Blind Tom' thoroughly? Miss Harding (who wrote it) is to be married on Thursday of next week & to live in Philadelphia. So we shall save her out of Virginia. She remains the one agreeable result of my stay in Wheeling & she is an acquisition."[132] On a public level, the response was even more extensive. Because Thomas Wiggins' owners were marketing him as a musical prodigy, *Dwight's Journal of Music* reprinted "Blind Tom" and received numerous letters, some highly critical, others fascinated with Harding's commentary, reflecting the ongoing cultural debate over Tom's abilities and the exhibition of his talents by his owners. The response to the reprinting of her article in *Dwight's* was so overwhelming that finally in January 1863 they announced they would publish no further discussions of the article and Thomas Wiggins because it had received "too much space." As Rebecca discerned from the many letters she received about the article, "those who have heard Tom believe the story—those who never did disbelieve it at which I am not surprised."[133]

Rebecca's abolitionist writings over the last year led a Boston abolitionist, probably David Wasson with whom she had been in correspondence, to ask her to help the French scientist and professor Joseph-Charles d'Almeida enter the South in order to study the war in that region as well as in the North. She found d'Almeida naïve about what it might mean to travel surreptitiously in the South at this time, but she liked him immensely even while thinking his goal of helping slaves escape north was ill-conceived under the current war conditions. She was asked to intervene with some southern leaders to assure his safety or, that failing, to help him slip through lines in disguise. d'Almeida brought with him letters of introduction from Horace Greeley, Charles Sumner, and Rev. Elijah Lovejoy of St. Louis; he assumed that, as a foreigner, he would be afforded the courtesy of traveling in the South and promoting his abolitionist ideals. As Rebecca reflected, this was a moment in which young girls in Wheeling, under martial law, had been arrested for playing "Dixie" on the piano. Because West Virginia had remained with the North, the antagonism from southern leaders, Rebecca feared, would never be set aside for concerns over d'Almeida's nationality. It was another instance, she felt, of the extraordinary naiveté of Boston abolitionists about the true conditions of war.

Before she arranged for d'Almeida's transport to St. Louis she had directed him north in the hope of deterring his southern adventures. In December she sent a letter of introduction for d'Almeida to James Fields.

> He has been travelling through our country for the purpose of observing... the motive causes of our present struggle. I know no one who can bring him more immediately in contact with representative men of New England than you—men who will convey to him most clearly the northern ideas. He is quite worthy that you should do this thing.... Whatever courtesy you extend to him I will accept so done to me until you know him. Then you will do it for other reasons.[134]

In March 1863 he visited Fields, who embraced Rebecca's request by introducing his guest to Longfellow, Emerson, and the Swiss-American scientist Louis Agassiz. But he returned to Wheeling and reported to friends that because of Miss Harding's kindness, he had been introduced to *"la société rebelle."*[135] Eventually, a Harding family friend, a southern "rebel and slave-owner," would take d'Almeida with him to St. Louis, but the Frenchman was arrested the same day he crossed into the South. He spent nearly a year in Confederate prisons, finally returning to Washington in a prisoner exchange. Revealed in Rebecca's account of this experience was the acknowledgement that she retained connections to southern sympathizers even as she aligned herself with the northern cause. She wrote abolitionist stories; though she detested war, she deemed the war to preserve the union and abolish slavery a "great and holy" cause; and yet she loved the South and, at times, rationalized southerners' behavior. She personified the realities of a civil war that was as psychologically challenging as it was physically and culturally brutal.

Amidst her negotiations for d'Almeida, Rebecca had visited Clarke and his sister in Philadelphia in late November in order to make arrangements for their married life.[136] In spite of Rebecca and Clarke's preparations for a Christmas wedding, they had to postpone their plans, probably due to her father's precarious health. It was a solemn Christmas in Wheeling but by January 1863 her plans had been solidified. She would marry Clarke in March and then move to Philadelphia. Only then did she reveal her plans to Annie, explaining there was "a certain cozery . . . all ready for *me* you know Annie—in Philadelphia—and I'm going there in a few weeks now. . . . it is'nt easy for me to tell you this I don't know why. I would rather tell other women's stories than my own. But you, who are so happy in your married life, will know how to ask for a blessing in mine." Yet Rebecca revealed to Annie almost nothing about Clarke in this first confession, simply saying that her name would be Davis and that Annie could form her own opinion about him when she and James visited them in the spring. She asked Annie not to tell anyone yet, but she expressed her joy, "*My summer days are coming now.*"[137]

When Annie responded with numerous questions, Rebecca finally revealed more about her fiancé. In addition to his full name, she related,

> Except the stories Miss Peabody told me of Mr. Hawthorne, I never heard of a more reserved sedentary life than his has been—He is a lawyer, about my age—holding an office under government just now—for the past few months. He is *not* the editor of whom I spoke. He was—is I mean, a friend—just as I said—you know Annie, if he had been more I would not have spoken of him at all.

As to Rebecca and Clarke's acquaintance, "*Not* a very old thing nor very new— years enough to satisfy the most rigourous rules of proprieties—."[138]

The editor about whom Rebecca had spoken frequently during her time in Boston was Archibald Campbell. Although Rebecca denied any interest in Campbell, the few extant letters between her and the *Intelligencer* editor suggest an intimacy that went beyond casual friendship, as seen in a letter Rebecca sent to Archibald after an apparent disagreement:

> You did not come last night, so I am going to take this way of expressing my seeming rudeness. For I wish to explain it—in justice to myself—& in courtesy to you. Besides, I can write more plainly than I can speak. I left you so abruptly, not from any unkind feelings towards yourself— they were never farther from my heart than on that day—but because I had been made painfully conscious before you entered that every one present regarded you in a false position which I *knew* to be distasteful to yourself—You did not take the seat voluntarily—was given you. Of course you could not leave it—& if we remained there, I felt that the impression would be confirmed which you would dislike. So I went away— too suddenly perhaps—but that was unintentional—You know—
>
> "My manners have not that repose
> That marks the caste of Vere de Vere."

> I am tired of being misunderstood—so I am going to be so plain as you were the other evening—You were unjust in saying that I "was ashamed to be seen at the front door with you." You know I never had refused any attention from you voluntarily offered.
>
> I had intended telling you of a remark of Mr. Binghams—which had made me act so unreasonably at Mrs. Acheson's—but it is no difference. I was wrong to allow my wounded pride that *he* should care to dismiss me to make me [] you by any hasty words—Is that enough? You have not asked for an apology—but I have made it—for I cannot bear that you should have thought me selfish and ill-tempered.
>
> You spoke truthfully to me the other evening—Since then I have had the most perfect confidence in you—*more than you have in yourself*—May I ask you to do the same? Will you believe *I* too can "act honorably" And if I ever do it again—will you believe that it is prompted *only* by a simple sense of justice and delicacy due to your position and mine? I think you will understand me.
>
> If you do not—at least, never accuse me of "whims or caprice"— even if you think it, do not say it with as angry a look as you did the other night—never—*never* again. I have enough to bear without that—Perhaps I ought not to have written this note, but it does not seem wrong to me. I do not think it will to you. Only answer it by saying that you understand me—and I will know I am forgiven for now & all future times—*Always* your friend R.[139]

Whatever she may have felt for Archibald Campbell previously, once Rebecca met Clarke Davis, she knew he was the man whose life would best meld with her own.

At the same time, Rebecca was publishing prolifically. "The Second Life" began serialization in *Peterson's* and "The Promise of Dawn" was published in the *Atlantic*. "The Second Life" serial constituted her second novel and was set in western Virginia; it exposed the brutalities a woman endured in a forced marriage. The serial's success led Peterson again to request Harding as a publicly identified regular contributor to his magazine, but she continued to insist on anonymity. For a long time thereafter, she was identified in *Peterson's* only as "The Author of 'The Second Life.'"

"The Promise of Dawn" received the coveted position in the *Atlantic* of lead story in a January issue. This was a particularly important story personally for Rebecca. She knew she was treading on taboo subject matter by writing about a prostitute for the *Atlantic*, but she had paved the way by encouraging Annie to understand the importance of the subject. When James Fields had first asked her to write a Christmas story, she contemplated submitting a children's story, "but another thought so took possession of me" that she had to write it.[140] When she submitted the manuscript, she informed James, "I am sure my heart never wrote one as much before."[141] Because the subject matter was provocative—the main character Lot was a prostitute whom Harding depicted as capable of redemption—James initially felt uncomfortable with the story. It was Annie who interceded, and as Rebecca acknowledged, "You were right not to let Mr. Fields think the Christmas story overdrawn. 'Lot' is from life. You know, here, in a town like this it is easy to come into direct contact with every class and the longer I live—the more *practical* my observation is—the more I am concerned that the two natures remain in the most degraded soul until the last and struggle until the end for victory."[142]

Living in Wheeling, Rebecca could hardly have remained ignorant of the realities of prostitution. The city had seen a significant rise in brothels due to the establishment of military posts and training centers there. A police sting organized on August 5 had resulted in the arrest of several brothel owners and prostitutes and was reported in the *Intelligencer*, for which Harding was still writing. The sting did little to solve the issue, however. Many unattached young women came to Wheeling at this time, via the National Road or on the railways, and many ended up in prostitution, often heading for Mrs. Hugen's brothel in the Fifth Ward. With the troops and prostitutes came corruption and violence unknown to those outside the war zone.[143]

The subject matter of "The Promise of Dawn" disturbed many readers, including her friend Jessie Benton Frémont, who complained to James Fields and Rebecca about its Fantinish proclamation."[144] Harding was undaunted by her friend's criticism, as she explained to Annie, "I *know* I was right. I was sorry Mrs. Frémont did not think the effort one of [] utility—but I have Christ on my side."[145] Her response revealed several changing aspects of Rebecca's sense of herself as a writer. She may, indeed, have been uncomfortable with the subject matter, but her assertions were also part of the performative nature of her epistolary exchanges with Annie, more than any of her other correspondents. Rebecca wanted to be beloved by Annie, as she made clear in several letters, and emphasized her integrity as a writer in the face of censure, whether it came from friends, editors, or the public. It was meant to impress Annie, but it was also an important transition in her own parameters for artistic integrity. Her frustration with some of her writings was often due to the sense that she had not been able to write as unguardedly as she would have liked, and whenever she compromised, she regretted it. But it was also typical of talented authors who pushed themselves artistically. Harding never claimed to be satisfied with a finished work, always wanting more from herself as a writer.

Before her marriage she also completed a three-part serial initially titled "The Gurneys" (it would be published as "Paul Blecker"; this time the change in title was made solely at Harding's request[146]). She felt the pages read "fagged" and admitted to being tired when she wrote the story, working through significant revisions before its serialization began in May. In spite of having been paid $120 for "The Promise of Dawn" in early December, she asked for a $225 advance against the serial's publication, undoubtedly to assuage the cost of her wedding and the concerns over the Harding family finances.[147] At the same time, she published the first of many unsigned reviews she would write for the *Atlantic*—the review of Jessie Benton Frémont's *The Story of the Guard*.[148]

At last, the day of her wedding arrived. On March 5, 1863, Rebecca married L. Clarke Davis in the Harding home in Wheeling, with Rev. Thomas G. Addison presiding.[149] It was a day later than they had initially planned, since a snow storm had blasted through the region, making it impossible for Clarke to arrive on time. The ceremony had been so modestly planned, however, it was not difficult to hold it on the fifth of March rather than the fourth. Rebecca, just shy of her thirty-second birthday, and Clarke, four years her junior, were old enough to adapt easily to such contingencies, and they left later that day for Philadelphia. Only her immediate family attended the wedding, but far across the states, Annie Adams Fields was keeping the day in honor of her friend by writing a wedding poem, "Espoused," for her.[150]

In Clarke, Rebecca had found a truly kindred spirit. Politically, they were aligned, though Clarke was the more radical of the two. His dedication to a life of integrity and a determination to reform social policies in order to aid the downtrodden closely matched her own. Although not without its early challenges, it would be an extraordinarily successful marriage that blended their careers into a lifestyle that sustained both of them through more than forty years of marriage.

Lemuel Clarke Davis was born on a farm near Sandusky, Ohio. His ancestors were of Welsh and Scotch-Irish heritage. Clarke's parents had followed the life of pioneers, traveling in one of the Conestoga wagons that had captured Rebecca's fancy as a child; the Davises initially settled in an area still largely populated by Native Americans. By the time of Clarke's birth in 1835, however, the family had determined to return to the East Coast, buying a farm in

Harford County in northeastern Maryland. The move may have been precipitated by his mother's ill health, as she died soon thereafter. Several moves followed, but eventually the family—his father, David Davis (1797–1852), Clarke, his two brothers, and his sister Carrie—settled in Philadelphia.[151]

When he was sixteen, Clarke was sent to the Treemount Seminary outside of Norristown, Pennsylvania, directed by Rev. Samuel Aaron, a Baptist. Students were taught the basics of spelling, reading, writing, phonography, composition, grammar, arithmetic, elocution, rhetoric, geography, and logic; their advanced courses included Latin, Greek, French, and German, and courses designed to give them a foothold into the business world, such as bookkeeping, practical accounting, algebra, and geometry. They were also taught courses in natural philosophy and chemistry. The cost was seventeen dollars per month for students such as Clarke who boarded. It was at Treemount that Clarke's dedication to learning and his education in abolitionism took place. As a highly regarded teacher, scholar, and abolitionist, Aaron invested his students with a superb education and a political consciousness. His teaching was not merely the recitation of lessons but a development of student's writing in a literary style that would serve Clarke in both his career as a writer and a newspaper editor.

This initial training was supplemented by Clarke's advanced education at the esteemed Episcopal Academy in Philadelphia. His father died while he was at the Academy, but Clarke finished his courses, graduating in 1855. He knew by then that he wanted to pursue the law and enrolled at the University of Pennsylvania's law school, after which he apprenticed with Thomas Balch, an important figure in Clarke's life. Balch would later be recognized for the development of international arbitration as a peaceful means to resolve international disputes, a policy that Clarke Davis embraced throughout his life.

While working in Balch's firm, Clarke began to develop his other professional love by engaging in editorial work for the *Law Reports* and the *Legal Intelligencer*. Even after he had passed the bar, he continued his association with the *Intelligencer* for several years, both in editorial work and as a lead writer. Although Clarke initially received little pay for this work, it was through these experiences that he began to make the political and literary associations that became an integral part of his life. On the staff at the time were John Russell Young, later a managing editor of the *New-York Tribune* and a minister to China in the Arthur administration; and Frank R. Stockton, the journalist and author. Clarke found editorial work far more gratifying than his legal work, which primarily involved small real-estate transactions.[152] He soon became the editor of both the *Law Reports* and the *Legal Intelligencer*. But his engagement to Rebecca forced him into more stable and remunerative work as a postal clerk, a position he retained until 1864, while continuing his editorial positions. He was at this transitional stage of his career when he met and then married Rebecca, just as she was advancing in her writing career and about to turn those early years of editorial writing for the *Wheeling Intelligencer* into the touchstone for new directions. Perhaps most important, Rebecca and Clarke were about to enter into a period of development in their marriage that would result in one of the most powerful and unique marriage/career collaborations of the nineteenth century.

Chapter 3

A New Life (March 1863–May 1865)

Rebecca and Clarke traveled directly from Wheeling to Philadelphia. The Davises had accepted the offer of Clarke's widowed sister, Carrie Davis Cooper, to live with her and her children at 1429 Girard Avenue. Clarke wanted to transition his work; he would retain his position in the legal office but hoped to leave his postal position before long so he could devote more time to editing legal periodicals. Annie Fields had invited them to come to Boston en route, but Rebecca declined, "I have new relations to meet whom I scarcely know, and I wish to know them *soon* and feel at home with them. You understand?"[1] Living with Carrie allowed the Davises to plan for their future. What Rebecca called her "cozery" in Carrie's three-story home constituted a bedroom and two rooms. She personalized their "parlours" by placing portraits of the Fieldses and *Atlantic* writers on the walls and filling the rooms with gifts from loved ones and a few items brought from home so she could blend her old life with her new one.[2]

Although Rebecca had anticipated spending only a couple of months in Carrie's home, it would be nearly a year and a half before she and Clarke were able to move into a residence of their own, so the newlyweds' process of learning to meld their lives had to be developed in the midst of another family, their burgeoning careers, and a steady stream of visitors who expected to be escorted around the city. Quickly, however, the Davises settled into a few patterns that would become fixtures of their marriage. Their love for one another was deep, abiding, and affectionate. Clarke called her "Cuddy," and "Pet" was an endearment each used. One of the patterns they developed in these early months of marriage would last a lifetime—reading together in the evenings and discussing contemporary and classic literature as well as current events. They read everything from "The Brier-Wood Pipe" by the Irish poet Charles Dawson Shanly to political assessments of Gettysburg that appeared a few months after the devastating battle.[3] They were also struggling at this point with what would eventually become a much more comfortable pattern in their careers: when they should read one another's work—in manuscript, so they could offer critiques for revision, or after it was in print? Initially, Clarke resisted reading

Rebecca's work until it was published; gradually, however, he became comfortable offering comments while her stories were still in manuscript. Their comfort with one another's criticism and recognition of how it could strengthen her fiction and journalism and his editorials would grow into a mutually supportive practice.

Unlike many women of her time, Rebecca felt no need to align her political opinions in accordance with her husband's. Although they agreed on most issues, when they did not, they openly expressed their differences to each other and to others. Within a month of their marriage they were debating the merits of the controversial General Benjamin Butler. Rebecca had written a critical line about Butler in "Paul Blecker," and when the proofs for that section of the story were sent to her, the line had been excised. She was livid and wrote to Annie immediately:

> Mr. Davis says to tell you that if you were the one who took a sentence out of Paul Blecker alluding to (your demigod) Gen Butler—he thanks you—and applauds it highly. *I* want to know who did it—Mr Nichols [the proofreader] or Mrs Fields? Because—
>
> _____
>
> What abysms of wrath lie in that blank you may imagine—.[4]

Other political differences would occasionally arise between Rebecca and Clarke (and between her and Annie), and she freely voiced her own opinions; it was the perfect testing ground before she expanded her career in journalism. Such rifts in opinions did not impact her marriage or her friendships. At the end of the letter to Annie, for example, she added, "Do write a long good letter," and later that month she joked with Annie: "Only look at this patriotic paper! It is all I have—you'll say it is the only sign of patriotism you ever saw in me, I don't doubt, you satirical soul—who—believes—in—*Butler*—."[5]

Where Rebecca and Clarke heartily agreed was in relation to religious practices. Coming from a family that had experienced several religious sects, Rebecca was open to many faiths, and both she and Clarke were members of Episcopal churches, but she did not like the exclusivity of many of the Philadelphia churches: "'Christians and *patriots* were invited' only," so the Davises kept holy days by going to "our church—the trees in Laurel Hill" along the Schuylkill River. Rebecca loved her native South, supported abolition, and yet felt war was wrong; she often wrote about the brutalities of war as damaging people on both sides. Rather than embrace the politicization of church services that was rampant in these years, Rebecca and Clarke turned to nature for spiritual sustenance. On one such occasion, a "grand thunderstorm" came up suddenly while they were walking, and they rushed into a secluded area "and watched the gray misty walls closing up the river." It was very romantic, Rebecca confessed. Clarke shared her love of walking, and they walked every day, in town or preferably in the countryside just outside the city. "Nobody ever drew their breath from Nature as directly as he," Rebecca remarked about her husband.[6] The same was true of her.

Moving to Philadelphia gave Rebecca an opportunity to know her *Peterson's* editor better as well, and she quickly became friends with Charles and Elizabeth Peterson. Rebecca's love of the outdoors was embraced by these new friends as well. The Davises often visited Ridgewood, the Petersons' estate in Lebanon Hills east of Reading, where the two couples roamed the hills, "rooting and trowelling for moss, and trailing arbutus," which Rebecca took home and arranged about their rooms in Carrie's house. The Petersons, part of the Peterson family publishing dynasty, were members of the upper echelon of Philadelphia society and they introduced the Davises to this social world. As Rebecca and Clarke advanced in their professions, they would move among the Philadelphia elite due to their own accomplishments, and the young woman from West Virginia would become a fixture in Philadelphia's high society world.

In the early months of her marriage, Rebecca was so busy she could hardly keep up with letters to friends, and what letters she did write were almost breathless in their brevity. She often added funny notes of apology, such as "Half a loaf *is* better—but this is only a biscuit—isn't it?"[7] Part of her time was spent with new friends she was making in Philadelphia, including several well-known Quakers families. Among this group were Lucretia Mott and her children. Rebecca became closest to Thomas and Marianna Pelham Mott, Lucretia's son and daughter-in-law. When Annie asked Rebecca if Marianna was a relative, she replied, "No . . . no relation of ours, only as a woman and a sister."[8] Rebecca and Elizabeth Peterson visited Marianna in April, shortly after Rebecca settled in Philadelphia. Marianna was only six years her senior, and Rebecca quickly came to love her for her wit and intelligence. They remained close friends until Marianna's death in 1872.

Rebecca was disappointed not to meet Lucretia Mott on this first visit, but they finally met in mid-June. After visiting Marianna and her sister and brother-in-law, Maria and Edward Davis, with whom the Davises also became friends, they went to Lucretia Mott's home. "What a grand carving her life has done in her face!" Rebecca declared after meeting her. Frances Gage was visiting

Mott at the time, but Rebecca found her off-putting: "Ugh! if I should be sick and she should have to nurse me! That is a mean thing to say. She's had a hard life, they say, and it may have been vice-like enough to wring all the sap and freshness out but leave tough strong helpful fibre." In spite of her reaction to Gage, the visit was a grand success, as Rebecca found all of the Motts to be so natural that she instantly felt at home. She managed to engage in one of her favorite activities as well, "I brought in flowers and branches and a small tree and a hanging basket and divers ants and spiders who are careening over my cozery."[9]

Rebecca came to know many Quakers in Philadelphia, drawn to their abolitionist and anti-war stances. Living in Philadelphia also gave her an opportunity to attend lectures by many of the famous abolitionists who spoke there during the war years, including Wendell Phillips (his charm sometimes made her "so interested in the man that [she] forgot the cause"), William Still ("a grave, shrewd negro" who was an agent of the Philadelphia underground railroad "by which thousands of flying slaves escaped"), John Greenleaf Whittier ("he did not consciously pose, but he never forgot his mission"), James Russell Lowell (whose "politics and poetry were, as a rule, kept inside of his books"), Frances Watkins Harper ("an able, ambitious woman, who lectured with a strange, bitter eloquence"), and Henry Ward Beecher ("so oddly unconscious of himself. . . . He was an Abolitionist not so much from love of Freedom as love of the poor black man himself").[10]

Most of all, however, she loved the Quaker women activists in Philadelphia whom she came to know well. She viewed them as the heart of the abolition movement, especially Eliza Randolph Turner and Mary Grew and her partner Margaret Burleigh. Rebecca was often in the home where the three women lived and worked together. She especially admired their sense of purpose: "It never occurred to them that they had come into the world for any other purpose than to reform it."[11] As she came to know Lucretia Mott better, Rebecca admired her most of all. Mott was, she proclaimed, "one of the most remarkable women that this country has ever produced. Fugitive slaves, lecturers, reformers, everybody who wanted to give help, found their way to her quiet little farmhouse on the Old York Road." Rebecca found herself often at the farmhouse as well, and she felt no one in the abolitionist movement had a better brain or was more eloquent than Lucretia Mott.[12]

In these early months, Rebecca was inundated with visitors while she was writing, caring for sick family members, and trying to find time to send out the requisite post-wedding cards with her new address. Soon she felt she "scarcely . . . had time to breathe." By the beginning of May, everyone was healthy again, or comparatively so, but "*I* still breathe 'Bay-rum' and sick room nausea—it hangs about my lungs, somehow." Within a week she became ill after working in the garden when it was damp. The chest cold kept her from writing for more than a week. More frustrating was that the abolitionist and women's suffrage advocate Anna Dickinson was lecturing in Philadelphia at the time, and Rebecca was unable to attend. It was unusual for her to be ill, but taking time from her writing to nurse family members would be a reality she had to face for decades to come.

She was barely recovered when Clarke developed a bad cold as well, and Rebecca began what would be an unsuccessful if lifelong campaign to have him stop smoking cigars. She had managed to reduce his smoking to three cigars a day and then planned to cut him off completely, but in this Clarke would never acquiesce. Carrie's health remained precarious, and she seemed so worn out and nervous that Rebecca made plans for her sister-in-law to stay with the Hardings in Wheeling over the summer in order to recover fully. Before she could fulfill these plans, Carrie became quite ill again in mid-May, recovered briefly, and then was even more seriously ill in July with bilious fever, which kept her bedridden.[13]

None of these events alleviated Rebecca's other commitments, and she continued to feel constantly rushed. Their numerous visitors expected to be escorted around Philadelphia, which fell to Rebecca since Clarke worked in an office downtown and guests assumed her writing could be set aside in order to entertain them. Even when one or another of the family members was ill, Rebecca felt she had to serve as local host. When a friend from Wheeling visited while Carrie was ill, for instance, Rebecca had to "'do' Girard College, the Academies etc." as tour guide. On Carrie's first day out of bed, Rebecca's beloved brother Wilse arrived. She was delighted to see him, but Carrie was frail and it was a tense time in the community, as General Robert E. Lee was threatening to invade the city. Yet Rebecca wanted Wilse to feel that Philadelphia was his second home, and so she tried to entertain him thoroughly with the city's attractions while serving as her sister-in-law's nurse and attempting to meet publishing deadlines. It was a pattern she would come to know well. She would learn to balance multiple publications, family obligations, travel, and work in the community, but it was a steep learning curve in these early months of marriage.[14]

In spite of their hectic schedules, the Davises were delighted when Annie and James Fields visited them in April 1863. They took the Fieldses on one of Rebecca's favorite ventures: going up into the hills to gather moss and flowers.[15]

It was a successful visit, as Rebecca confirmed in a letter sent immediately after Annie and James left: "I never thought you cared for me *half* so much until you came and we never really knew each other before, I think. We—Mr. Davis and I—speak of you both every day since and when we shall see you again."[16] The visit, like Rebecca's visit to Boston the previous year, strengthened the Davises' friendship with Annie and James and melded Davis's personal and professional relationships with the Fieldses. That synthesis worked well for a period of time, but as both James Fields's and Rebecca Harding Davis's career paths took divergent routes, it would demand effort to again separate the business and personal sides in order to maintain their friendship.

The more forthright nature of the correspondence with the Fieldses about her work was evident immediately after their visit to Philadelphia. Rebecca's new and more powerful business voice was due in part to her assurance of their friendship but also to the fact that she was being pursued by other publishers and had been successful in having her rate of pay increased by the *Atlantic*. Davis more openly expressed her desires for how her work should be published, such as when she submitted "The Great Air-Engine." The manuscript was longer than the magazine's usual single-issue story, but she insisted it could not be condensed.[17] Agreeing, Fields published the story in one issue even though it ran to twenty-six pages.

Clarke was also attentive to Rebecca's need for both time and space in which to write. Indeed, he came quickly to value people based on how well they appreciated his wife and her talents. Knowing she often spent considerable time in research before writing about an issue, Clarke contacted the head librarian at the Philadelphia Library and asked that Rebecca have a table set aside for her own exclusive use in a quiet corner of the library. As Clarke informed the head librarian, he ought to know who the author of *Margret Howth* was and that she was a "greatly admired" author deserving of such attention. His request was granted,[18] and Davis would use her research area in the library for decades to come.

Another pattern the Davises established early in their marriage was frequent travel. Clarke was required to travel on business at times, most often to New York City, and they liked to see friends and family often. It was necessary to limit their travel to short trips in these years for economic reasons, but also because Clarke could only take a few days from work. In early June they were able to visit Jessie and John Frémont in New York,[19] and within a week of returning, the Davises were on their way to visit the Petersons for a few days at their country home and were already planning a summer trip to Wheeling, in spite of the difficulties of travel during war.[20] Wilse came to Philadelphia and escorted Rebecca and Carrie to Wheeling in August, where they spent a month. Rebecca traveled to Wheeling and later to Washington, Pennsylvania, numerous times in the early years of their marriage, frequently with Clarke coming later for a few days and traveling home with her, as he did this first year, and they typically went at least twice a year to the Petersons' country home as well.

As a newlywed and as a rising author, Rebecca saw Annie Fields as an important touchstone. Annie modeled a loving marriage, and her business acumen was unmatched among the women of the Boston literati. Writing to Annie allowed Rebecca to hone her assessments of other authors as well. When, for instance, the Fieldses sent the Davises a portrait of Emerson and a collection of his work as a wedding gift, Rebecca combined a thank you note with her sense of Emerson: "outside of my feeling for him as the truth-seeker, the most earnest if not the most successful among us—I have the *man* so identified with my visit last summer." Perhaps most of all, writing Annie allowed Rebecca both to convey the news of her new life in Philadelphia and to recall "that odd stay at Concord. . . . I told you, I think, how weird and uncanny that time seemed to me? Even absolute Mr. Dicey felt it—I remember—I wonder Thoreau did not find the lotus on Walden pond. And Emerson in that unhomelike library of his with the pines shivering outside and that blanched wife and her ghostly eyes—are the most vivid recollections—."[21]

Rebecca also maintained correspondence with Kate Field and David Wasson. After receiving a long letter from Field, Rebecca remarked to Annie, "How much earnest power there is cased up there!" Wasson, on the other hand, was a conundrum. Rebecca felt he was yet searching for his calling, though he had already established himself as a vibrant preacher. When she read some of his poetry, she wrote Annie, "What do you think of Mr Wasson as a poet? He sends me the Commonwealth now. It gives him pleasure to do those things I suppose—but I cannot help but think it is a pity."[22]

She was also comfortable enough with the Fieldses at this point to ask a favor. A local Presbyterian minister and editor of the *Presbyterian Quarterly*, Rev. Benjamin J. Wallace, had died leaving a widow and children with no support. His wife Sarah was energetic with good common sense and hoped to move to western Pennsylvania where she could live more cheaply and support her family by opening a circulating library. Rebecca asked the Fieldses if they could aid Mrs. Wallace by appointing her as an agent for Ticknor and Fields to sell their publications on commission, or if that was not possible, to think of some way to help. She was delighted when they responded more generously than she had even hoped by sending Wallace a wide selection of their books as a gift to help furnish her circulating library.[23] This type of aid through her literary connections was something Rebecca offered to those in need throughout her lifetime, and it was representative of a theme that would become integral to her writings: charity should be a one-on-one system of aid.

Having been assured of her friendship with Annie after the Boston and Philadelphia visits, Rebecca was much more willing to reveal her sense of humor to her friend as well, often in a self-deprecating way. Lamenting that she had to go out to return bridal calls, which she had put off for as long as possible, Rebecca joked,

> There is conventionalism for you—isn't it? But you see, I have such a cloak—"Literary women always affect eccentricity" with a slight curling of the lip and you are forgiven. Only write for a magazine Annie— and come live in the west and you can wear feathers in July or pin your shawl behind with impunity if you like—And you needn't grow thin or eat only one spoonful of chowder to do it.

Her humor was again revealed later in the letter when she recounted her attempt to pose as an art connoisseur. While showing a gentleman guest some of the local artworks, she "explained a fresco satisfactorily to myself as the eternal bridge over Hades when an unfortunate note turned up and the label 'Jonah and the whale'"![24]

Rebecca continued to reveal to Annie both her concerns about the war and about Clarke's constant attention to battles and the war's progress. She would be happy, she explained, "if I could persuade Mr Davis that God has the war in His hand—and not he."[25] Rebecca was deeply worried about the national conflict as well, however. News out of Virginia had been horrific with the battles of Fredericksburg and Chancellorsville in April and May. Reading literature of the day sometimes brought the war too close to home. Louisa May Alcott's "Hospital Sketches" had been serialized in *Commonwealth* in May and June 1863, and the second part, especially the story of John that would appear in the book chapter titled "A Night," haunted Rebecca. "How much I like Louisa Alcott's second sketch!" she wrote Annie Fields.

> *Like* is not the word—it cost me a nervous miserable night last night— as every glimpse of the war does lately. Such a weak puppet-like feeling comes over me—How long—oh Lord how long? is the prayer such real sights of horror gives—I don't know if they are healthful or not. That story of John is terrible in its truth and simplicity—I was so weak

Annie that I shut my ears part of the time while [Clarke and Carrie] were reading it. Not for this man—but the thousands.[26]

Rebecca had reason to be frightened of the horrors of war. Shortly after she sent this commentary to Annie, the rumors about Robert E. Lee's intent to invade Pennsylvania proved true. Major-General Napoleon J. T. Dana became commander of the Philadelphia military district on June 26, and he tried to prepare the city's residents for the possibilities of war on their doorsteps. This turn of events brought new worries for Rebecca, as she feared Clarke would feel compelled to enlist. "It's not easy for any man, much less one of his temperament to feel that his home is invaded and be quiet," she reflected. She was surprised, then, when the draft was instated and Clarke chose not to enlist, instead opting to pay $300 to a substitute. "Clarke was drafted," she explained to Annie, "and says very heroically $300 is very little service for him to offer his country, which is all very well for patriots of his and your persuasion to say. I notice however that he is nursing the rheumatism into one foot very assiduously ever since Saturday. Of course I don't guess for what."[27]

This was one of the rare instances in which Rebecca criticized Clarke to someone else; it was equally a snipe at Annie's sense of patriotism that Davis felt was easy for New Englanders who were distanced from the ravages of war. This ongoing theme appeared in her letters and in her fiction. Her argument that New Englanders refused to see anything other than stereotypes of southerners was reinforced in the pages of the *Atlantic* where the intellectual New Englander was always contrasted with the southerner, depicted as a sensualist who was devoid of true faith and lacking in intellect.[28] Although this may not have been surprising in the midst of war, to Rebecca's mind it was intellectually dishonest.

Discussing publications in the *Atlantic Monthly* with Annie allowed Rebecca to hone her skills as a literary critic as well as to recall her time in Boston and Concord. The July 1863 issue brought a cascade of assessments. Hawthorne's "Outside Glimpses of English Poverty" was one of the best in the volume Rebecca thought: "Do you notice what an attraction his meaning has for firm and delicate expression? I read this article over again curiously for that reason. The words *se rangent* about his thought in as just forms as steel filings about a magnet." The issue also reminded her of when she had met Louisa May Alcott, although she thought "Debby's Debut falls far below her Hospital Sketches—she knows hospital perhaps is the reason—and fashionable society she evidently don't know. It is so long since it was thought necessary for a girl of untainted nature to make hay and eat bread & milk out of a bowl." Gail Hamilton (Mary Abigail Dodge), on the other hand, was "herself again in this number. What a thoroughly Western woman she is! I don't know how she made the mistake to be born in New England. Rough, democratic, hardy, common sense is the strength of Western people and if she had belonged out there we'd have crowned her the genius of it—surely." Rebecca liked "womanly women" like Annie Fields, but her greatest complement was to assert someone was a "Western woman," a term she always used for herself. That winter she would also be deeply moved by Edward Everett Hale's "The Man Without a Country," and she and Clarke had debated whether or not the story could be true.[29]

The first six months of married life in Philadelphia had brought extraordinary changes for Rebecca: deepening her relationship with Clarke, replenishing old friendships and forging new ones, navigating a new city and its demarcated social structures, and confronting the ravages of war close at hand. Time in Wheeling over the late summer gave her an opportunity to catch her breath and visit with family in a world she knew indelibly. Yet this was one of the most transitional moments for the proud West Virginian who would soon become an internationally recognized "Philadelphia writer." When she returned to the city in September, she began to make a number of changes that would unfold over the next few years, personally and professionally.

Family continued to demand a great deal of Rebecca's time, often to her joy but not without recognition of the time taken from her writing. When she returned to Philadelphia from Wheeling, her sister Emilie came with her. Rebecca showed Emmy as much of the city as she could, "at a most thorough pace." One afternoon alone entailed lunch, a visit to the museum, and then a tour of Turners Lane Hospital where soldiers with neurological damage were being brought for treatment.[30] This was the hospital in which Dr. S. Weir Mitchell, who was the Davises' family physician in these years, developed his neurological expertise and was the military hospital established by Dr. William A. Hammond, whom Rebecca probably first met when he was stationed in Wheeling. Within a few years, the Davises would know most of the famous, elite Philadelphia physicians, including the world-renowned Dr. William Osler. Davis undoubtedly drew on these friendships for the numerous depictions of physicians in her fiction.

Before leaving for Wheeling, Rebecca had felt unhealthy and had not been sleeping well. She had tried allopathic and homeopathic remedies, but nothing helped until, back in Philadelphia, she returned to her routine of long, fatiguing daily walks. They resulted in the return of her "old healthy cheerful days and dreamless nights. I'm so glad of it, for I didn't know how to be sick & thought like Mrs. Gummidge 'nobody ever had berlinks like mine.'"[31]

Though Rebecca felt better, Emmy's visit left her scrambling to finish a Christmas story, "Stephen Yarrow," that James Fields had asked her to write. Davis would pen a Christmas story almost every year as a gift to Clarke, who loved the tradition. Christmas was the holiest day to him, which was why they had originally planned to be married on the holiday, and these Christmas stories were both a gift to him and a remembrance of their love.[32] By late October Rebecca was asking Fields when was the latest it could be sent, explaining she had "suffered a thousand interruptions,"[33] though she had managed to publish another John Page story, "Success," in *Peterson's*. She was shocked and embarrassed to discover in November that she was actually in arrears on her account with Ticknor and Fields. It was quickly rectified,[34] but the incident exacerbated her financial concerns.

Davis had become increasingly unhappy about certain aspects of her business relationship with the *Atlantic*. Part of her frustration continued to be its low rate of pay. She was frequently approached by editors of other literary magazines, all of whom promised higher pay for her work. Charles Eliot Norton was persistent, repeatedly inviting her to write for a magazine, the *North American Review*, that would begin publication the next year, and he often sent papers that praised her work. In response, she invited him to visit whenever he came to Philadelphia so they could become friends in reality and not just in correspondence.[35]

Perhaps the most frustrating part of her relationship with the *Atlantic*, however, was the editorial attempt to curtail her opinions. Though not frequent intercessions, these incidents went to the heart of her political and literary values. She had been furious over the exclusion of her comment about General Butler in "Paul Blecker," but the issue of free expression came to a head over a review she was asked to write of a new edition of Robert Browning's *Sordello*, a discussion between James Fields and Davis that began in April and lasted through early 1864. Davis had been penning unsigned book reviews for the *Atlantic* for some time, but Browning was a friend of the Fieldses.

"I do not agree with you about the book," she told Annie in April. "You will see but I expressed my honest opinion—and after all a notice is only to suggest inquiry—so I hope J.T.F. don't require his critiques to be in accordance with his own judgment. Does he?" But indeed he did. When Annie cautiously approached a revision, Davis agreed. "You must *not* be afraid I will hate you for playing refracting midm[an?]. I often know and care too little for criticism or style etc. but unless the motive with which I write is impugned it don't touch me much."[36] The revised review still did not please James, however. "I was sorry Mr. Fields did not like the review," she told Annie, "but hardly thought he would—being a personal friend of Mr. Browning's. I had to say what I honestly think though." She simply asked that the review be returned to her, and another author's assessment of Browning's book, one that praised it, finally appeared in May 1864. Book reviewing for the *Atlantic* had changed under Fields's editorship. As part of his promotion of *Atlantic* writers and writers popular with the public such as Browning, he increasingly used reviews as advertisements and as a promotional venue.[37] The whole situation left a distasteful aftermath that both sides tried to bridge. They were only partially successful.

That winter Rebecca's cousin Clara Wilson spent a week with the Davises. The cousins had been close since Rebecca's days at the Washington Female Seminary when they spent many hours together. No one was a greater champion of Rebecca's talents than Clara. Clara had encouraged her cousin's early attempts at writing, reported on the quality of her writings to family and friends, and remained a lifelong supporter. The week in Philadelphia with her beloved cousin meant everything to Clara. As she told her fiancé, Andrew Todd Baird, "That week has been truly one of the brightest pages of my life, it is so homelike there—we can talk of the same things with interest, of the joys and sorrows, that are past. Mr. Davis is so very pleasant, they really have a delightful home."[38] There was more important news, however, in the Davis household: Rebecca was pregnant.

She was feeling well enough in December to return to Wheeling before Christmas as a gift to her father, whose health was in decline. Clarke followed her a few days later so everyone could be together for the holiday. It was the first Christmas "since the family was broken up" by Rebecca's marriage and her brother Richard's departure. For the first time since Richard's charges of treason, Rebecca mentioned him to Annie, though she simply said that one of her brothers had moved to Kentucky during the last year.[39]

Her father was weaker than she expected, but she did not believe he was dangerously ill. He was extremely nervous, however, and she felt he was "even morbid in his desire to have me with him." Changes in Wheeling were blatant as well. The Athenaeum where Wilse had established his Classical Academy had been turned into a military prison, barracks, and hospital. Some people in the city called it the "Lincoln Bastille" because it held not only Confederate prisoners of war, spies, and captured bushwhackers, but also people who had refused to take the oath of allegiance. Rebecca had to admit, "It was not a very merry Christmas, though a quiet and deeply happy one for us," since she had been able to share with her family the news of her pregnancy.[40]

With the New Year, Rebecca was not only writing and entertaining visitors but sewing clothes for the expected baby. February 1864 brought a brief visit from the Fieldses. Annie thought the Davises were "both rare characters; brave in self-denial and self-discipline," living as they did with Carrie and working to be able to afford a home of their own. Like so many other people who knew the Davises over the years, it was the strength of their marriage that was most remarkable to Annie, however: "What a satisfaction such a marriage is!"[41] While visiting, James had suggested Rebecca write a series of short sketches, an idea that appealed to her, but she first submitted "The Wife's Story." Although it detailed a woman who was torn between family and work obligations, Rebecca herself was feeling joyful. As she wrote to Annie, "all good things lie in the future—I'm so sure of that these days—God is keeping them for us, like a mother holding back the baby's toys till he is old enough to use them."[42]

By the end of February, James Fields had indicated his pleasure with "The Wife's Story" and accepted it for publication.[43] But Davis's hope about the future began to wane as the month leading to the birth of her first child became more and more difficult. In March Clarke was seriously ill, causing Rebecca considerable anxiety, since she was not feeling well herself and Carrie was out of town. Atypically nervous, Rebecca described herself as feeling "as if every faculty had been rasped and handled unbearabley and *must* rest."[44] The fact that she hated feeling as she did only exacerbated her condition, but there was no time for rest. She tried taking Hoffman's anodyne, a popular cure-all remedy, but found it ineffective. Their doctor, Weir Mitchell, was called in.

The Davises had been friends of Lucretia Mitchell and George Leib Harrison since shortly after Rebecca's arrival in Philadelphia. Lucretia was Weir's sister, and it was probably she who introduced the Davises to Dr. Mitchell. By early April, "The doctor," Rebecca wrote to Annie, "forbids the least reading or writing for fear of bringing back the trouble in my head."[45] Mitchell would not fully develop his rest cure theories until much later in the century, but already he was prescribing a version of such treatments.

It was not a prescription Rebecca followed, however. She was in the midst of serializing a six-part mystery for *Peterson's*, "The Lost Estate," and she continued to write home to Wheeling weekly as well as correspond occasionally with Annie Fields and other friends. A significant part of Rebecca's ill health during March and April was her fear of dying in childbirth, as she revealed in an April letter to Annie.[46] Rachel Harding came to Philadelphia to be with her daughter during this difficult time, and Rebecca was comforted by the decisions she and Clarke had made that he would conclude his work as a postal clerk and they would find a home of their own.

Rachel Harding brought tragic news, however. On March 21, Rebecca's father had died. No one told her immediately because of her poor health, waiting until Rachel could be with her before she learned of her father's death from "congestion of the brain."[47] Richard Harding's death had brought forth extensive honors from his business associates, city leaders, and family in Wheeling. His obituary in the *Wheeling Intelligencer* described him as "universally respected for the exemplary course of life which he pursued." The mayor asked the newspaper to announce that he, members of the City Council, Aldermen, all officers of the city, and the directors of the Fire and Marine Insurance Company would attend the funeral and walk in the procession.[48] Yet all of this occurred without Rebecca being aware he had died.

A week before Rebecca gave birth, William Ticknor also died. He and Nathaniel Hawthorne were visiting Philadelphia when he became ill. Clarke went immediately to offer his assistance, but physicians were already in attendance when he arrived. Ticknor died the next day.[49] There was little time for the Davises to react; Rebecca gave birth to Richard Harding Davis on April 18, 1864. What should have been a joyous occasion was tempered by the loss of her father, her child's namesake, and the ill health of both baby and mother.

The baby was not strong in its early months, and Rebecca's health was even worse. She was confined to her bed for a month, during which time the whole household was overtaken with sickness. Rebecca's mother became ill first, not yet recovered from her husband's death, then so did Carrie. The family hired nurses to care for Rebecca and the baby, and even when she could finally leave her room, it was some time before she could resume many of her usual activities. She was suffering still from dysentery and remained morbidly anxious about whether or not everyone loved her and, like many new mothers, feared it could all be taken from her.[50]

By late June, however, the baby was at last healthy again and Rebecca was able to walk in the nearby hills, in spite of the intense heat. Annie Fields was deeply concerned about her and offered to come to Philadelphia, but Rebecca declined as graciously as possible, emphasizing how much the offer meant: "How dear you are to me I never have told you, nor how tenderly I feel every new word and sign of your love to me and mine." The Davises were planning to leave shortly for the seashore, and Rebecca did not want Annie to see her baby when he was so frail.[51]

Two priorities now became central to Rebecca and Clarke's plans for the future: finding a place to summer where they could replenish their health, "by the sea-shore quiet & cheap,"[52] as Rebecca put it, and finding a new home. They settled on Point Pleasant, New Jersey, for a mid-summer retreat, leaving Philadelphia on July 5.[53] Before going to the shore, they spent several days at the Petersons' country home,[54] but they were anxious to settle for the summer months, and Point Pleasant was the answer to their dreams: not a resort with social obligations, but rather a remote seaside area.

They and two other families boarded at the Curtis House, owned by Phoebe and Captain Eben Curtis whose sons, Lloyd and Tom, helped run the establishment.[55] The inn had long wooden porches where Rebecca and Clarke could sit in the evening, and the thick woods on one side were perfect for the walks they loved to take, while the shelter of trees on the other side could be traversed to find a beautiful river. They bathed in the strong surf and caught up on their reading, which had been set aside during Rebecca's illness. The baby, nicknamed Hardy, was rapidly gaining his health, and Clarke, an avid fisherman, spent his days crabbing and fishing in the hot sunshine. He had resigned his position as a postal clerk before they left Philadelphia, intending to devote himself to the law and editing.

Rebecca relished being a mother. When Hardy became frightened by a stranger's attention and nestled into her arms, it seemed as if no one else had ever had such loving experiences. This summer retreat offered another advantage. Rebecca was already describing the area in letters that served as prelude to the many stories about the New Jersey shore that she soon began writing. The area fascinated her; as she looked out over the vast scene before her, she reflected one evening on "the rising sea mists moving slowly over these marshes—on a dark gray day it is a new feature in scenery to me—, and has an indescribably weird and dreary effect—they look like gigantic ghosts, passing on their way to some council in Hades—." She was fascinated by the customs of the people, especially their superstitions about the sea, and the history of the region with its tales of "wrackers" and "Barnegat pirates."[56]

Point Pleasant was a place for relaxation, but Rebecca always continued writing on her summer retreats. Two of her stories were published while they were at the shore—"The Story of a Song" in *Peterson's* and "A Wife's Story" in the *Atlantic*. Whether writing for the *Atlantic* or *Peterson's*, Davis's central theme was human nature. Living in Philadelphia, she studied the conglomeration of transplanted Americans from the west, south, and Europe who re-created their traditions in Philadelphia. The theme of "The Story of a

Song" would become prevalent in her fiction: once people actually meet, they can cross social ranks and national backgrounds to form lasting friendships. A number of themes that would fascinate Davis throughout her career began to emerge in her work at this time: critiques of the elite classes, the shift to female as well as male narrators in her stories, and the contrast of selfish and self-righteous New England women with the caring, hardscrabble Western woman.

When the family left Point Pleasant, Clarke returned to Philadelphia while Rebecca traveled west to visit her mother who was in the midst of moving to Pennsylvania to live with her widowed sister. Rebecca's visits to Wheeling would become rarer after her mother left, but this visit in their old home was memorable as it was her mother's last weeks in the house where her children had been raised. Clarke joined Rebecca in time for them to travel home together, and her sister Emmy again returned with them. This time, returning to Philadelphia meant settling into her new home. Rebecca loved Carrie and she felt sentimental about their rooms in the Cooper household since it was her first home as a married woman and where her baby was born, but the idea of being able to establish her own home was exciting.[57] The Davises still could not afford to buy a home of their own, but they rented a three-story row house at 1817 North Twelfth Street. Carrie and her children had made every effort to prepare the rooms in ways they knew would cheer Rebecca when she first saw it, with trimmings of wood-leaves and ferns.

After several hectic weeks of arranging the house, Davis was ready to write again, with the goal of having a Christmas story for the *Atlantic* as a gift for Clarke.[58] On the first Sunday in which the Davises could actually relax, write letters, and read, Rebecca picked up her correspondence with Annie, reporting that Clarke was sitting next to her, "Thinking of Lincoln 'while he smokes tobacco' I suppose, for he growls out something now & then about 'That is a disgraceful peace'—'How stands Lincoln here'? I think—outside of office-holders—his party have swallowed him as a bitter pill at which the gorge rises—a choice between bad & worst—But enough of politics." With the baby now healthful and always laughing "as if all the world was a puppet show gotten up for his especial fun," they were planning to leave shortly for a week with the Petersons at Ridgewood.[59]

Davis managed to write one story for *Peterson's* in between her trips. The story was rooted in the 1791 slave revolt at Santo Domingo. Davis had asserted in letters that she did not believe African Americans would rise up against their masters if they were freed, but she wrote several stories in this period in which characters did precisely that, including "John Lamar" and this story of

Santo Domingo, "The Alsatian Hound." In each the act of revenge was cast as horrific, but it was paired with an assertion that the system of slavery had created such a response.

In November Rebecca and the baby again went to see her mother, this time in the Old Stone House in Washington, Pennsylvania. Clarke had to remain in Philadelphia as demanded by his legal work and editing responsibilities, but they wrote to one another almost daily while she was away. The Petersons sympathized with Clarke's temporary bachelorhood and invited him to dine with them every other night until Rebecca's return. He liked that Charles Peterson, when he was not entertaining his socially elite friends, could be very "easy and natural" and offered Clarke a "dinner with no state affair." In spite of the Petersons' care, Clarke was again recovering from an illness, and he soon felt bogged down by work. Writing to Rebecca for assistance, he prefaced his request with a detailed list of items he had to do—draw up a "very long and tedious" charter for the Shafton Coal Company, prepare a number of conveyances and two deeds, batches of mortgages, bonds, articles of agreement and a Sheriff's deed—in order to explain why he was in need of her help: "And now dearest Pet will you help your old Boy a little in his work," he asked.[60]

He had promised James Fields a notice for the *Atlantic* to appear in the *Legal Intelligencer*, and he did not have time to write it as promised. He carefully described what he wanted the notice to say about the importance of the *Atlantic* to "the learned professions," to include mention of its eminent contributors, and so on. He also asked her to write a review of *Emily Chester*, a novel anonymously published by Anne M. Seemuller.[61] The lamentations of overwork mixed with love for "Pet" worked, and Davis wrote the notice and the book review which appeared in the December 23 issue of the *Legal Intelligencer*.[62] It was becoming more common for Rebecca and Clarke to intertwine their careers, at first in these minor ways but soon as an integral part of their writing lives.

In December, the Davises happily planned for their first Christmas in their own home. They decorated a little tree for the baby, and Clarke returned to his love of carpentry work. Rebecca felt that he was becoming a true artist in the craft, though it meant shavings tracked throughout the house. Rebecca again spent Christmas week, and Clarke part of the week, in Wheeling where her brother Henry still lived in the family home and where everyone had gathered for the holiday. There was sorrow because of their father's absence, but the new baby enlivened everyone. The Davises returned to Philadelphia before the New Year. Although traveling over the mountains at night as they did on their return was exhausting, they held a belated family celebration in their own home. Rebecca felt "as if our little home held more love and summer than all the world beside to me that night."[63]

The year 1865 arrived in Philadelphia with a blast of cold weather, and it would bring radical changes to Rebecca's life and to the nation. As the Davises settled into their comfortable new home, Rebecca would return to writing with her usual productivity, in spite of her constant struggles to manage the household and care for a baby. Their son would grow rapidly in size and in their hearts, and Rebecca would begin, slowly yet definitely, to reduce her contributions to the *Atlantic*, which would mean redoubled and sometimes strained efforts for the Davises and Fieldses to remain close friends. Most importantly, after four bloody and brutal years, the Civil War would end with the defeat of the South.

Life now demanded even more of a balance between family and household obligations and Rebecca's writing career. They had a nurse for the baby, but Clarke was making business trips to New York still, and Rebecca filled page after page of correspondence in early 1865 with pithy details about caring for an infant, often revealing typical concerns of a first-time mother: "Think what a woman is worth by night when all day she has been in momentary expectation of seeing that infant hope of the world brought in choked by a pin or strangled on a coal or whatever else its fingers can lay hands on."[64] Although she constantly felt the pressure for enough time to write, Rebecca insisted on some time for "feeding what lies with the body by a little writing & reading." As busy as they both were, Rebecca and Clarke were happy, and in January they were already planning to return to Point Pleasant for the summer, though the battles of war hovered all about them. The joy they felt in their home was necessary, to Rebecca's mind, "to temper the outside influence in these times."[65]

Writing to Annie was another means of tempering the tensions of war. Their letters always combined their business and personal lives. In early March, Annie sent a note reminding Davis she had not yet submitted two sketches that were due. Rebecca responded with a long letter, promising to submit the sketches soon. She emphasized that these short pieces were "*true*—in all essential points though I told them for convenience sake under an assumed name [as narrator]—The heroine of the second is still living—a century old, if not more." Reflecting on her upcoming wedding anniversary, Rebecca added: "Two years ago and it seems but a day or two. This good life flies so fast."[66]

It was with a tempered joy that Union supporters marked Lee's surrender at Appomattox on April 9, 1865. Joy was scarce when nearly 620,000 men had lost their lives as had 50,000 civilians, and the wounded numbered more than

380,000.[67] There was no time to reflect on what the end of the war might mean when five days later the news of President Lincoln's assassination was received. It was a week before Rebecca felt she could express her despair to Annie:

> You as well as I doubtless felt that the few days just past were no time for talking either by voice or pen—All subjects but one were impertinencies and upon that I felt no words were fitting.
>
> For the last month I have thought—God was dealing with us as with His chosen people of old—by such great visible judgments that we almost heard His voice and saw His arm, a present God even to the dullest.
>
> For selfish reasons I shall be glad when this present pain is in a measure past. The continuous excitement & nervous tension is more than one can bear—
>
> Mr Davis has been ill—you know how deeper—than his life, I almost said—is his love of his country & honor—Our little boy's face is the only bright-cheerful spot I can turn my eyes to—God grant his life may be given some day to as great and holy a cause as that for which Abraham Lincoln died—
>
> Think of us *all*—both dear friends—and let us hear from you soon.
>
> Yours always, R H Davis[68]

If the extent of the tragedies over the previous four years seemed almost impossible to comprehend, the demands of everyday life did not evaporate. In spite of giving birth, the loss of her father, dealing with several family illnesses, and moving into a new home, Rebecca continued to write, indeed needed to write, as she often remarked. Her stories for *Peterson's* in early 1865 maintained her usual productivity. Between January and May, she published four short stories and a two-part serial. Some of these works offered new stylistic and content explorations for Davis. As was the case with "A Wife's Story," "A New Year's Story" and "The Clergyman's Wife" were part of Davis's move to include in her repertoire stories narrated by female characters.

"The Clergyman's Wife," in spite of a rather contrived ending, was a fascinating study of a marriage in peril, a theme Davis would return to several times over her career. The core of the story was in a new format for her as well: the woman's fears are revealed through her writings in a journal. The story's critique of New England's self-aggrandizing intellectualism was continued in "The Missing Diamond," one of Davis's best mysteries. It included a female character who believed herself to be a great intellectual of the Concord stripe: "Born in the healthy atmosphere of Ohio or Pennsylvania, she would have made an unpretending, narrow-brained house wife and mother; but she had been one of those mediocre people in the outer circles of New England society, who are drunk for life with the fumes they have smelled afar off of Boston transcendentalism; so she went about, as her class do to-day, giving out dilutions of Margret Fuller and Emerson."[69] *Peterson's* may have been less prestigious than the *Atlantic Monthly*, but Davis explored many important themes in its pages and, equally important, her contributions to the periodical served as the backbone of her family's income for the next decade.

At the same time, Davis's relationship with the *Atlantic Monthly* was changing noticeably. In 1862 she had published "John Lamar," the serial "David Gaunt," the novel "A Story of To-day" (*Margret Howth*), and the article "Blind Tom." By 1864 she had reduced her contributions to the *Atlantic* to two stories a year, a pattern she would largely follow until she ended her regular-contributor association with the magazine in 1867. This was not from a lack of interest on the part of James Fields, who often asked her to contribute a story. The sense that other high-literature magazines were paying better rates continued to nag at Davis, as did Fields's failure to secure a British publisher for her works other than "Blind Tom" and she had been the one to initiate the idea of Dickens' magazine for that piece. So she turned to her new pattern of producing two stories a year for the *Atlantic* while continuing a significant literary output for *Peterson's*, and soon she would no longer be able to resist the repeated offers from other periodicals to become a contributor to their magazines.

It was May before Davis published her first story of 1865 in the *Atlantic*. "Out of the Sea" was a vivid portrayal of the lives of sailors and their families on the New Jersey shore, with the atmosphere drawn from her experiences the previous summer as she studied the unique landscape and the tenacious people who made a living from the sea. Davis's Jersey shore stories allowed her to explore both the realities of maritime life and the almost mystical aspect of the environment. The fact that "Out of the Sea" did not appear until May marked the notable shift in her work for the *Atlantic*, since previously she had published in the January issue and throughout the year. One of the dangers of the intimate friendship she had built with the Fieldses was that business and personal lives intermingled, and this alteration could not help but impact their friendship. Nothing was overt. Rebecca and Annie continued to exchange warm and supportive letters, and in them they talked about the literature of the day and the personalities of authors and activists they knew, but the letters were sometimes shorter, and the hopes of visiting one another became almost pro forma rather than a real expectation. The war had ended, and they all felt their lives could truly begin again in its aftermath, but for the Davises that new life would gradually move away from the close association with James and Annie Fields. Both Rebecca and Clarke were about to enter into new career ventures, and they were building their lives among the famous authors and artists of Philadelphia.

Chapter 4

New Ventures (June 1865–December 1867)

In the summer of 1865 Rebecca was still struggling to confront the meaning of the war in its aftermath. As returning troops marched through the streets of Philadelphia, she reflected, "I could scarcely keep the tears back awhile ago, thinking that the cannon spoke of peace and freedom at last—If we only do not hold peace & freedom as *surely* won in our hands, when only the hand-work of victory is done—But God will guard it."[1] Rebecca, and especially Clarke, became involved in efforts to aid veterans. She would soon find a way to respond to the needs beyond "the hand-work of victory" through one of her most important novels, but first she had to confront a battle closer to home.

In July, as she was packing for the summer at the seashore after having been inundated with visitors for the past few weeks, Rebecca was looking forward to the usual blend of relaxation with Clarke and Hardy and a quiet space for writing at Point Pleasant. She had prepared "Ellen," the first of the series of sketches of real life that she had promised James Fields for the *Atlantic* that would also eventually include other works such as "The Luck of Abel Steadman" and "The Harmonists." "Ellen" was a return to her interest in Ellen Carroll, the young woman who had wandered into Wheeling during the war in search of her soldier-brother. Before its publication, Annie had written Davis to remark on how much she liked the sketch, and Davis explained, "The story is quite true—and one of the simplest clearest proofs of a *living* Christ leading us, I think, that I ever heard."[2]

When "Ellen" appeared in the *Atlantic*, however, a reader wrote to James Fields complaining that the "story" had already been published in *Peterson's*. Fields contacted Davis asking for an explanation. She had, indeed, used Ellen's experiences as "groundwork" for a *story* in *Peterson's*, she acknowledged, but reminded Fields he had wanted sketches rooted in real life. Writing about Carroll again for the *Atlantic*, she stated "the bald facts of her history . . . thinking them interesting and hoping in that way to obtain some clue to her fate. My doing so did not appear to me then irregular, nor does it now. The case is the same as if Mr Hale should found a story on the tragic career of L.E.L. and afterward tell what he knew about her in your pages."[3]

This was no longer the acquiescent "Miss Harding" who had said "I don't care" to Fields's inquiries. There was no apology, as she did not feel one was needed, but she did offer an understanding of his concerns, "I am quite willing to make an explanation public if you think it necessary." She offered to forego payment for the story if he felt they were wronged in a "pecuniary sense," implying it could be in no other way.[4] Fields initially said it would be "made right" but then remained silent—"J.T.F. the Silent" as she referred to him a month later after no response,[5] and no public explanation was published. The incident simply passed into the oblivion of silence. Rebecca continued to correspond with James and Annie over the summer as usual, and James sent the Davises copies of *Atlantic* publications and the British periodical *The Reader*, which he knew they liked.

It was not only through narratives such as "Ellen" that Rebecca reflected on the aftermath of war. Many soldiers returned to a world of "hopeless confusion" that forever altered their lives. "When Johnny came marching home again," she later remarked, "he was a very disorganized member of society, and hard to deal with. You cannot take a man away from his work in life, whether that be selling sugar, practicing law, or making shoes, and set him to march and fight for five years, without turning his ideas and himself topsy-turvy." The age of the man made a significant difference as well, she observed:

> The older men fell back into the grooves more readily than the lads, who had been fighting, when, in ordinary times, they would have been plodding through Cicero or algebra. Some of them harked back to college to gather up the knowledge they had missed; some of them took up awkwardly the tools of their trades, and some of them took to drink and made an end of it. The social complications of the readjustments were endless and droll.[6]

It was little wonder she soon turned to writing about the tragic impact of both war and alcoholism for the individual, families, and the culture. Rebecca never joined a temperance society, but she became a strong voice in asserting alcoholism was a national issue in need of serious attention.

The summer at Point Pleasant was enjoyable and refreshing for the whole family. Wilse and three of his friends joined them this year, and they engaged in crabbing, cricket, and "gunning." In spite of these activities, Rebecca loved that it was such a "quiet, lonely place" with "the rustle of pine woods and the eternal throb of the surf in my ears. . . . Nature looks at you with so sad abstracted a face through all the changes of bright skies and cool driving winds that you fancy you have come upon her in one of her melancholy un-reticent moods and that presently you will learn her secrets as never before."[7] Rebecca and Clarke had moved to a two-story cottage next to the inn for their summer sojourns, which they would buy in a few years. Yet Rebecca could already see that change was coming, since people in the Manasquan area that encompassed Point Pleasant were becoming immersed in postwar resort fever, talking about the benefits of converting the quiet area into a resort with a railroad and large hotels.[8]

Hardy had been very ill with teething in July, but he quickly recovered at the shore. He was no longer a baby, Rebecca observed, but rather "a rough little ruffian"; she wanted Hardy to love the sea, swimming, and the outdoors as heartily as she and Clarke did.[9] The summer months also restored Clarke's health, even though he typically went back into Philadelphia for several days each week. Summer was Rebecca's time to write long letters, which she could rarely manage during the rest of the year, and she was able to catch up with Annie about news of their mutual friends, among them David Wasson. Rebecca continued to follow Wasson's career and was glad to learn "he has found his place at last" in Boston.[10]

In September "The Luck of Abel Stedman" was published in the *Atlantic*. It was especially interesting for its preludes to lifelong issues in Davis's writing, not the least of which was her refusal to adhere to conventional genre definitions. What was fiction and what was nonfiction? Her explanation in relation to "Ellen" did little to resolve the issue, and she had determined to use an assumed name for the narrators of these sketches—some male and some female. "Abel Steadman" continued the blurring of genres as a "sketch" drawing on the real-life figure of Mrs. Cruger, a Wheeling resident, but encased in what seemed to be a fictional narrative told by the character Zack Humphreys. The story about inheritance claims was problematic, however, in its representation of the ways in which Euro-Americans casually depleted Native burial grounds and viewed "Indian antiquities" as of insignificant value. Although Davis could be advanced in much of her work and thinking about racial issues, she was not free from some of the biases typical of her time and, in fact, she often both advanced racial matters and undermined them with terms such as "picaninnies" and "savages." Just as her writings frequently argued for national recognition and support of African Americans, "Steadman" was the first in what would be a long series of stories and essays in which Davis explored Native

American issues. She would eventually mature into a far different view about Native American rights than this story represented.

When at home in Philadelphia, the Davises kept Sundays as letter-writing days, and in the fall, Rebecca penned a long letter to Annie Fields that recaptured their correspondence when it was at its height: longing for a time when they could summer together, discussing her writing and critiquing that of other authors, and relating family issues.[11] Rebecca also noted that Thomas Wiggins, about whom she had written in "Blind Tom," was in Philadelphia before he and his master left for Europe. She did not like the way in which he was paraded before the public, however, and did not go to his performance. As to other writers, she was particularly interested in Harriet Beecher Stowe's "Chimney Corner" writings. Encouraging James to continue Stowe's series, she declared, "Her sound vigorous sense comes to me once a month—a real time of refreshing for which if I knew her I would send her the strongest word of thanks I know."[12] This was notable praise for Stowe, since Davis had often criticized *Uncle Tom's Cabin*. But she had since given a copy of Stowe's newly published *House and Home Papers* to her cousin Clara Wilson as a pre-wedding gift. Although Rebecca concluded her letter with a wish to have the Fieldses visit again, it would be a few years before they saw one another in person.

Davis continued to write for *Peterson's*, publishing several stories in the last months of 1865. Of particular note was "The Little Street-Sweeper." The poor child as a street-sweeper was a common image in the 1850s and 1860s and representative of the scores of impoverished Americans who needed assistance.[13] However, Davis's depiction of the underground world where the desperately poor lived was unusually graphic:

> There are cellars, inlets to hell, in New York, to give them their plain name, running deep underground, ventilated only by the door of entrance. Boards swung in these from the ceiling, bunks in the wall, and benches over the floor, are dignified by the name of beds, and hired to white and black of both sexes for a couple of pence. The police know them as dens, from which a criminal can rarely be drawn, as deep are they sunk, and so extensive are their channels of egress under the streets.[14]

Peterson's was advertising at this time that it paid more for original stories than any of the other women's magazines, including two stories in the next year for which it would pay $1,000.[15] One of these was Davis's five-part novella, "The

Stolen Bond." This was far more than the *Atlantic* was paying and set a high bar for the various publishers who were pursuing her.

In addition to their careers and family life, the Davises were also beginning to develop public roles in Philadelphia through their work for various artistic and charitable institutions. Although Rebecca occasionally participated in civic events, it was Clarke who most fully embraced this role. One of his first endeavors was with the Academy of Music in Philadelphia, heading their Book Department and serving as one of the managers for the 1865 Sanitary Fair that opened at the Academy. Philadelphia had held several Sanitary Fairs during the War, organized by volunteer civilians in pro-Union patriotic gestures to help support the Sanitary Commission and other charitable entities. Philadelphia was known for having one of the most active branches, and a subsidiary, the Women's Pennsylvania Branch of the US Sanitary Commission, had been formed to solicit donations from hundreds of local aid societies.[16] Clarke, as head of the Academy's Book Department, sought contributions of reading materials from publishers, booksellers, and stationers for the Soldiers' and Sailors' Home in the city.[17]

Rebecca did not like the committee work that was considered an important part of a rising couple's social obligations in the nineteenth century. Though Clarke was one of the most active managers, Rebecca assisted little with the Fair, "I suspect for many reasons of which lack of interest was certainly not one—I was only down there one evening—though I believe my name was on a committee—The fact is when our sex get into corporate bodies I have an instinct that warns me off.... 'I am never less a woman than when I have been among women,' as Seneca *didn't* say."[18] It was an attitude she would retain throughout her life.

The last months of the year were more hectic than usual, with Clarke's work for the Fair and Rebecca's writing for the *Atlantic* and *Peterson's*, including the novella that would begin publication in January. When a horrific fire broke out in a nearby impoverished neighborhood leaving forty families homeless in the frigid December weather, however, Rebecca immediately put into action a process to help those in need. Newspaper accounts of the fire and special notices seeking aid for its victims noted that "Contributions in clothing of all kinds, but especially for women and children, will be received and distributed by Mrs. L. Clarke Davis, No. 1817 North Twelfth street," with funds going to a local lawyer and business owner Robert Pennick King.[19] Rebecca did not reveal her own role when she wrote Annie about the aftermath of the fire, but focused on the many "instances of unselfish heroism among those poorest poor which not having seen you would scarcely believe."[20]

The early months of 1866 brought several major changes in the Davises' lives. Clarke had always been an avid connoisseur of the theater, a role he would expand in coming years and which Rebecca would fully embrace, and he had already made friends among the famous actors who lived or performed in Philadelphia. But it was an unusually political stance taken by the Davises when they strongly supported Edwin Booth's return to the stage in January 1866. Booth had bought the Walnut Street Theater in Philadelphia in 1863, and he continued to manage the Winter Garden Theater in New York City until 1867. For all of his success as an actor and theater manager, the infamy cast on the family name when his estranged brother, John Wilkes Booth, assassinated President Lincoln forced him to leave the stage for many months. Theirs was the classic story of how the war tore apart families, since Edwin had sided with the Union and John embraced the Confederacy. Although Edwin had disowned his brother and publicly condemned his actions, the newspapers vilified him.[21]

Rebecca and Clarke stood by Edwin in the aftermath of the assassination. As she wrote to Annie Fields, "The Press of this country—has made itself infamous by its cowardly attacks on him, adding a thousand fold to his great sorrow, to gratify the lowest taste of the lowest class of readers."[22] The theater and its actors would be a focus of many of Rebecca's and Clarke's literary and civic endeavors in coming years as well as a source of many books of shared reading. At the time she wrote Annie, they were reading Dr. John Doran's *"Their Majesties' Servants": Annals of the English Stage.*

An even greater change for the family occurred in the new year. Their second son, Charles Belmont Davis, was born on January 24, 1866. He was named after Clarke's brother Charles who had been killed at the battle of Belmont, Missouri, in the early months of the war. Four days after his birth, Rebecca recorded in her diary her first thoughts about Charley, "He gets a tighter hold about one's heart each new day."[23] She was saddened, however, by the lack of attention he was receiving. As she told Annie Fields, "Nobody was enthusiastic about Charley. His brother had carried off all the plaudits—as first child and first grandchild, and this boy was a sequel to the story—an afterpiece—an every-day matter."[24]

Although he was already developing distinctive traits, this assessment of Charley would last his entire lifetime; his flamboyant brother always stole the attention, though Charley would actually become the more talented writer. Yet the boys would build a bond based on Charley's adoration of his older brother that would also last throughout their lives, and he never seemed to feel the "afterpiece" status from Hardy that everyone else appended to him.

Just as Charley arrived, Rebecca's works were appearing in the *Atlantic* ("The High Tide of December") and in *Peterson's* (the first part of "The Stolen Bond" serial). At this time, too, Clarke's legal work began to require him to be in New York City more frequently than in the past. Although they were pleased with Clarke's steady progress in establishing himself in Philadelphia's legal and civil communities and that his trips allowed him to see the Frémonts regularly, his travel meant Rebecca often had the sole oversight of a nearly-two-year-old and a newborn as well as the entire household and a demanding career. They were fortunate to have a wonderful nurse, Annie, a German woman who Rebecca praised highly for her skill and generosity in caring for the children, but Rebecca's continuing productivity in this period was a testament to how well she had learned to balance work and family. She was even learning to write while in the nursery with Charley.[25]

The publication of "The Stolen Bond" revealed Davis's ongoing concentration on the effects of war:

> The tide of war in that time had surged up from the depths of our national life, done its work, and ebbed more rapidly than it came, leaving a land ghastly with the wrecks of old systems, and pregnant with the promise of those to come. The sun, that set on the last of our battle-fields, had marked no day with a meaning so clear or decisive, in the long history of the march of humanity to its promised land . . . and with every stroke gave a death-blow to the soul-serfism which had lasted for many centuries.[26]

The serial was also the beginning of a series of works, culminating in *John Andross* (1874), that exposed corruption in politics and business as integral to capitalism.

Although Rebecca rarely wrote publicly about legislative affairs in these years, she occasionally did so in the privacy of her diary, as she did on January 31, recording her support of the Civil Rights Act. After noting that Clarke, "my darling," and the boys were all recovering from colds, she added, "The new Constitutional Amendment regulating the appointment of members passed by over a two-thirds vote after a grand speech by that grand old man Stephens. The world moves—."[27] Thaddeus Stevens was a member of the House of Representatives from Pennsylvania and a leader among the Radical Republicans. He was a powerful voice for racial equality, and this speech was explicitly designed to thwart the rise of power among representatives from the former slave states that were now seeking to increase their seats in the House, because each African American in their states could now be counted as one citizen rather than as three-fifths. Stevens argued that unless suffrage was granted to all male residents of the former Confederacy, the states' representation in Congress should be diminished. The speech became a key element in the passage of the Fourteenth Amendment, granting equal civil and legal rights to African Americans.[28]

The year 1866 again brought several major changes for Rebecca's family. On February 28, her beloved aunt Rebecca Blaine died. In spite of the sadness this death brought, there was good news in relation to Rebecca's two brothers who still lived in Wheeling. Henry, like their father, had become involved in civic events, worked in the insurance field, and still lived in the Harding home in Wheeling; like all of the Harding children, he was better at handling his finances than his father. However, it was Rebecca's brother Wilse who was excelling in his career at this point. After years of running the Classical Academy, he was appointed to a professorship at Bethany College in the chair of mathematics and astronomy. A beloved teacher who was respected by colleagues as a man of the "highest mental and moral type,"[29] Wilse would continue to advance in academics and would be a frequent visitor at the Davis home in Philadelphia and at Point Pleasant in the summers.

By spring Davis was again frustrated by Fields's delay in publishing a submitted manuscript, "The Harmonists." When they had first discussed the idea that she would contribute a series of sketches based in real life, she had requested they be published one after the other in a timely manner. She had sent the manuscript for her study of the Rappite community nearly a year earlier with the understanding it would be published shortly after "The Luck of Abel Steadman." Davis sensed James might still harbor concerns about the publication of "Ellen" and added in the midst of her discussion of "The Harmonists," "By the way, I heard lately of 'Ellen' through the Colonel of her brother's regiment—You remember the girl whose story I sent you? (a true story, unfortunately despite your correspondent's letter). The brother was still in the army, but had procured a furlough to search for her—his only clue being that which we gave—I do not know if he was at all successful." If Fields had delayed publication because he did not like the story of George Rapp's utopian religious community but was hesitant to say so, she asked that he simply let her know and she would publish it elsewhere. This assertion gave Fields an out if he did not wish to publish "The Harmonists," but it also reminded him that she had other options than the *Atlantic* among the high-literary magazines. The material was important, she felt, and if he did not want the sketch, she would use it as background for a story, or if he preferred to have a *story*, she was willing to prepare that as well. "The Harmonists" was finally published in the *Atlantic* in May.[30]

Davis had closed her letter to Fields with another important issue: "I would so like the benefit of your advice about a book which is now a little more than a project."[31] This "project" would become one of the most important novels of Davis's career, *Waiting for the Verdict*. Although Fields published "The Harmonists," he was silent on the issue of a book project. This was surprising, since he had just started a new scheme to increase subscriptions: publishing novels over the span of two years, so readers who had begun a novel in 1865, for instance, would need to subscribe for 1866 in order to read the conclusion of the novel. He had commissioned both Charles Reade's *Griffith Gaunt* and Donald G. Mitchell's *Doctor Johns* in this manner, but each was scheduled to conclude in 1866—June for *Doctor Johns* and December for *Griffith Gaunt*— which would have seemed the perfect timing for Davis to begin her novel in mid-1866.

But to Fields' surprise, *Griffith Gaunt* had received wide criticism as a sensationalistic novel, a response to its move toward naturalism.[32] Since Davis wanted to write about racial conditions and national responsibilities toward the newly freed, Fields may have worried it was too volatile a subject to publish in the aftermath of responses to Reade's novel. For whatever reason, he passed on what would become one of Davis's most notable, highly praised, and profitable novels. And his silence offered her the path to publishing elsewhere.

In the midst of these discussions, Rebecca received two letters from Annie Fields, in an apparent attempt to smooth the conversation between Davis and James Fields. Rebecca responded slowly to the first missive, because she was again nursing family members. Just like Hardy, Charley was ill for much of his early months, and Clarke was suffering from a severe case of pneumonia. Charley, with his "gravest of baby faces," had hardly been out of Rebecca's arms for several days when she sent the quick note to Annie. Charley and Clarke were well again within a few weeks, though Clarke went to Marianna and Thomas Mott's country home for a period of time to restore his health.[33]

In spite of the stress of these responsibilities, Rebecca was soon able to respond to Annie with news of family and friends. She had received a card from Harriet Prescott Spofford about her recent marriage, liked Kate Field's lead story in the April issue, and thought the issue particularly effective with the serials of Reade's and Mitchell's stories. But she also revealed her continuing frustration with living in Philadelphia. "We have a dear little home warm with love and beautiful in its quiet way," she admitted, "but with all one grows homesick for the country." With scarlet fever in the house next door, the city seemed a particularly dangerous place, and the public was always hungry for fashion or the gruesome details about the latest murder.[34] For all of her dissatisfaction with living conditions in Philadelphia, it would be her home for the rest of her life.

Once the discussion of "The Harmonists" publication and the silence about her projected novel had passed, Annie did not write again, so in late May, Rebecca finally sent her a note, "What *has* become of you? It is so long since one of your tiny reminders of a letter came wandering in here that we are beginning to regard you as a thing of the past."[35] It was not unusual for Annie to create a strong emotional bond with a woman writer and then largely drop her as a friend when differences of opinion arose, maintaining a surface relationship without a true closeness.[36] It would take a period of several years for Annie and Rebecca's friendship to fade out completely, but the foreshadowing of this eventuality was already evident.

Rebecca was involved in other important changes in her personal and professional life, however. Clarke's sister Carrie remarried in May and settled in New York City with her new husband. The joy of this event was in stark contrast to the Davises' ongoing concerns about President Andrew Johnson's policies, as he returned confiscated lands to plantation owners and supported Black Codes that deprived African Americans of their civil rights. It was becoming apparent that, rather than a Reconstruction of American life the Radical Republicans supported, Johnson was making efforts to restore the slave-owning society to its former status. It made the publication of Davis's new novel of even greater importance.

With impeccable timing, Frank Church wrote to her in June, seeking Davis as a regular contributor to the new magazine, *The Galaxy*, that he and his brother William had just founded. Davis quickly responded, "Both Mr Davis and I have been interested in 'The Galaxy' from the first issue, hoping to find in it that which would fill a vacuum in our literature more apparent every year—a national magazine—in which the current of thought in every section could find expression so thoroughly as that of New England does in *The Atlantic*." Although she initially declined to serialize her novel and indicated she could not become a regular contributor during the present year because of other commitments, she promised to send the novel to them when it was completed and agreed to write one or two short stories for them in the current year.[37]

The *Galaxy* was conceived as direct competition to the *Atlantic* and *Harper's New Monthly Magazine*, and it quickly drew authors from these periodicals to its pages, beginning the rivalry between Boston and New York as the center of American publishing.[38] "Waiting for the Verdict" would be considered one of the best serials published by the *Galaxy* and its first by an American author,[39] but the road to publication was not as pleasant as the initial exchange of letters between Davis and the Church brothers had seemed to foretell.

As the Davises were preparing to leave for Point Pleasant at the beginning of July, a note from Annie finally arrived. Writing letters had received little of Rebecca's attention in recent weeks, due to her negotiating with James Fields and the Church brothers, writing for *Peterson's*, caring for a rambunctious little boy and a new baby, being concerned about her widowed mother, hosting five guests who were just preparing to leave, and solo parenting with Clarke once again out of town.

Rebecca did take a moment, however, to remark to Annie on "The Case of George Dedlow" by S. Weir Mitchell that had just appeared in the *Atlantic*. "He is a friend of ours—our physician by the way—I was a little surprised at finding him write so well a merely popular article" because, as she explained, "He ranks near to [Dr. Joseph] Pancoast here as a practitioner and has written only on scientific subjects so far as I know—heretofore—for the use of government during the war—One little treatise on the effect of gunshot wounds on the nerves and brain is interesting to any one—." Rebecca had heard Mitchell speak "of mental phenomena much more curious than those he instances" in "George Dedlow." She also revealed her understanding of his position in Philadelphia's highly structured social system, "He not only belongs to the narrow royal line of Philadelphia but has nature's blue blood in his views—an aristocracy of which I know but half a dozen," and yet she was an admirer of Mitchell. "I am a little enthusiastic, maybe," she explained, "but I owe much to him—life—and what is better than life—I hope he will write more for the A. There is more life in what men of vigor & high culture throw off from the mere fullness of spirit than in the forced work of literary hacks."[40] Though the Davises were only beginning to circulate in Philadelphia's society circles, it was a world in which they would soon be common travelers and a world in which they would immerse their children.

The summer at Point Pleasant was much needed. The Davises brought with them to the shore this year a Philadelphia friend who was invalided,[41] and Rebecca's cousin Clara and her new husband Andrew Todd Baird joined them. The group played croquet, swam, and fished, and thoroughly enjoyed their time together. The Davises had developed such keen friendships at Point Pleasant that it had become their second home. New friends included John S.

Powell, a Philadelphia attorney, and Henry Steel Olcott, who was residing in Philadelphia for the year on special commission with the US Navy. Both men would become frequent dinner guests at the Davises' Philadelphia home when they all returned to the city in the fall.[42] The boys thrived at the shore, and at last Charley was gaining health. He was still small but now "fat . . . with a good humored little face, and *blue* eyes. Where *they* came from," Rebecca remarked, "I can't imagine."[43]

The family returned to Philadelphia in early September just as a letter from Annie Fields arrived commenting on the sparsity of Rebecca's letters. It was a fair criticism, as the summer was usually when Rebecca wrote long letters to Annie. But Rebecca merely replied, "But my dear, some time ago I mounted a certain family horse which goes on, trot, trot, day after day—giving me precious little time for greetings by the way or meditations on the prospect."[44] The cooling of the friendship was coming from both sides.

Davis's writings for *Peterson's* at this time had turned away from the lives of patriarchal plantation-owning Virginians in the John Page series to studies of the tragic lives of impoverished women, such as "The Story of Christine." Being at the shore had also meant that the Davises were absent when Philadelphia hosted the controversial pre-election National Unionist Convention (also known as the Southern Loyalist Convention) in August, though Davis did report that the ferment had not totally died down even by September.[45] The convention was intended as support of President Johnson's policies against the challenges of the Radical Republicans. Although Rebecca rarely revealed her alliances with any political party, she was developing a plan for the novel she would publish in the *Galaxy*; it explicitly embraced the actions and policies of the Radical Republicans.

As had become her custom, Rebecca spent a month in Wheeling from late September to late October. Just before leaving, she received a letter from Annie criticizing one of Rebecca's stories of graphic poverty. Like Clarke, Annie preferred sentimental stories. "But I don't see it as you and he do," Rebecca replied. "By which I mean neither to be slangy nor obstinate. Only—let the 'youth comb his hair' 'Paint me with all my wrinkles.'" This was also the first time Rebecca mentioned a new young writer who was of interest to her, Elizabeth Stuart Phelps. Although she had not yet met Phelps, she and Clarke knew her father, the professor and minister Austin Phelps, from his educational activities in the city. Over the coming years Davis and Elizabeth Stuart Phelps would become good friends. Clarke added a note to Annie with an amusing detail about S. Weir Mitchell, "By the way, what have you people been doing to Dr Mitchell?

He came up to call the other day and confidentially informed me he meant to vote the Republican Ticket this Fall. He was always a warm personal friend & admirer of 'Lordy George' and a bit Copperish—."[46]

While in Wheeling, the smoke and grime weighed increasingly heavily on Rebecca, and she found it hard to write while she was there: "all I said or did there bore the mark of the beast or it came out saddened and cloudy—as if smoke & soot had got into the brain as well as skin, in spite of its being my old home," and with her brothers Wilse and Richard now absent, the old home hardly seemed the same.[47] When Rebecca returned to Philadelphia, finding her own residence became more of an adventure than she had expected. Clarke had planned to meet her and the babies in Pittsburgh and travel home with them, where he would surprise her with the new residence, but they missed each other. When she arrived home, or thought she had, she rang and rang the bell, but no one answered. Finally,

> a stranger's face appeared at the next door—"Nobody lives there." I looked up—Philadelphia houses are all twins, but this was certainly ours—I then civilly inquired if I did not live there & was told I had moved to the next street. Going round—to 1816 [North Camac] a square off—I rang again and this time the open sesame opened home. . . . We had to move sometime this fall & Clarke had had it done to surprise me.[48]

The house was a twin of their former rental, "only clean in paper and paint." In preparing the house for Rebecca's return, Clarke purchased a new English Brussels carpet in a mossy green shade to bring even more warmth into their parlor.[49]

Hardy was now old enough to go out with his father on walks about the city, while Charley, "*My* boy," stayed at home with Rebecca. They all settled happily home in the North Camac rowhouse. As Rebecca said, "It is enough to be alone in days like this—when the earth sets quiet—thinking before she lies down for the winter's sleep." In spite of her lamentations about conditions in Wheeling, a week later she was thinking fondly of the visit when she wrote Annie, "It was so good and *resting* to go West. Nature there is prodigal of life. There is such absence of struggle, or straining, such excess of beauty—of vigor,—such quiet strength in absolute repose. . . . New England may be the brain—of the country—but I think its heart, the centre of its warm strong, life-giving blood out yonder—I'm *glad* it is my home." She added amusedly, "I wonder what called out that effort of patriotism."[50]

After returning from her visits to Wheeling and western Pennsylvania, Davis often wrote stories with that setting, as she did this year with "In the Dark," published in November. These stories combined a sense of the tragedy of so many rural lives, not unlike the shipwrecked lives of her Jersey shore stories, and of people who had a talent for one kind of work but by necessity or error were led into another. During the past several months she had continued writing the novel she intended to place with the *Galaxy*. On a trip to New York at the end of October, Clarke had served as emissary with the Church brothers for Rebecca to discuss publishing the novel, but she decided almost immediately thereafter that she was unhappy with the work and destroyed the entire copy of the first version of *Waiting for the Verdict*.[51]

As she explained to the Church brothers, she was "determined to entirely remodel and extend it. The subject is one of which has interested me more than any other, and I wish to put whatever strength I have into that book, and make it, if possible, different from any thing which I have yet been able to do." She wanted to move ahead, however, with arrangements to accept the talented William John Hennessey's offer to illustrate the novel. The Churches wished the novel to be published in January, but such a date was impossible to Davis's mind, as she could not "do justice to myself or it" in so short a timeframe. She agreed to send them "the full outline of the story and a sufficient number of chapters for you to judge whether it would suit your pages,—and to base your offer on."[52]

In the interim, she met her earlier promise and sent them the manuscript for "The Captain's Story," a study of Spiritualism that foreshadowed the work of William James in thought transference. Philadelphia had been a hotbed for Spiritualism's growth in the postwar years, and the *Religio-Philosophical Journal* and the *Banner of Light* had published an account in 1866 about the progress of the movement in the city. Davis rejected Spiritualism in general, mesmerism, and other such phenomena, but she was open to the discussions that were just beginning about thought transference. She was paid one hundred dollars for the story, which appeared in the December issue of the *Galaxy* under the byline "The Author of *Margret Howth*." Although *Margret Howth* had been serialized in the *Atlantic* and published in book form by Ticknor and Fields, her subsequent short fiction and sketches in the *Atlantic* had used "Author of 'Life in the Iron-Mills'" as her byline. When *Peterson's* had attempted to identify her as "Author of *Margret Howth*," Davis cautioned them to use only "Author of 'The Second Life.'" No objection was made, however, to the usage in the *Galaxy* of her authorship of *Margret Howth* from either Davis or Fields. The fee paid for the story, as for most of their short stories, was actually somewhat less than what she would have received from the *Atlantic*, which suggests just how important it was to Davis to move away from the New England literary cult and have a wider audience, especially one in New York. The same held true for other young and coming authors such as Henry James and John DeForest.[53]

Davis was corresponding with James Fields at this time as well. With the rising competition of the *Galaxy*, he sought to reinforce their relationship, sending her "an unusually beautiful book," *The Atlantic Tales*, that included the best of their 1860s publications. "Life in the Iron-Mills" was among the selections. He could hardly complain that she was writing for the *Galaxy* when James, DeForest, and other *Atlantic* writers were doing the same.[54]

What appealed to Davis and the other writers who joined the *Galaxy* pantheon, even if it meant discomfort in their relationships with the editors of the *Atlantic* and *Harper's*, was its commitment to being a national magazine. This was an important new venue for Davis, but it would be a very rugged path to see "Waiting for the Verdict" through publication to its conclusion. Some of Davis's harshest comments to an editor were directed at Frank Church and yet, as with her relationship with Fields, she would find a means to move past any differences with Frank Church and remain friends with his brother William.

William came to Philadelphia in late November to finalize contract details for serialization of the novel. Davis was to be paid ten dollars per printed page. As she told her cousin Clara, she had not intended to allow publication to begin until the novel was completed, "but the publishers of the new New York magazine, *The Galaxy*, were so very winning in their arguments that I will write it as a serial beginning in February."[55] The contract was quite brief and did not address some of the promises made verbally to her prior to its signing—an error Davis would never again make.

Almost immediately, the Church brothers pushed to begin publication before the agreed-upon start date by announcing in the magazine that the novel would begin serialization in January. Davis wrote to them immediately, insisting they adhere to the mid-February publication date, "or I am afraid there will be a break down.... I always write slowly and I must have a number or two done in advance—If I knew there was no reserve for me to depend on—I would be sure to grow imbecile out of sheer nervousness. Besides I must have a start in case sickness of ourselves or the children should interrupt me."[56]

She had good reason for the latter concern. At the end of November Clarke had again been ill with a severe cold from which he was slowly recovering.

Though Annie, the children's nurse, was wonderfully helpful, taking "the care of the boys off me as much as I will let her," Rebecca still needed time to care for Clarke, begin preparations for Christmas, stop in the midst of her writing to hug Charley when he fell and cut his face, and a myriad of other interruptions typical of tending to family and home.[57] She sent the first two sections of the serial by December 14, and the novel began publication in the February issue.

Other complications began as the *Galaxy* was preparing to publish "The Captain's Story." They changed the size of the periodical's pages, which meant a change in the per-page rate and differences for chapter breaks, and the magazine would soon alter the length she was allowed for the novel, though she had been verbally promised it could be as long as she wished. The *Galaxy* editors, especially Frank Church, quickly became known in the industry for heavy-handed alterations of manuscripts. Experienced writers balanced an acceptance of some changes and demands for their work to appear as written in other instances. Women writers were especially subject to changes in their manuscripts at the *Galaxy*, often without consultation before publication,[58] to the extent that Harriet Prescott Spofford felt they had enacted a "ruinous mutilation" of her story "The Black Bess."[59] Still, Davis moved forward with the novel. Clarke aided the prospects of both Davis's novel and the *Galaxy* by sending notices of the upcoming publication of "Waiting for the Verdict" to all of the Philadelphia newspapers.[60]

Throughout December and into the new year, Davis had to negotiate item after item with the Church brothers, though each side attempted to do so with as pleasant exchanges as possible. On Davis's part, the change in page size created unending difficulties. When she submitted the two chapters she wanted to constitute the second part of the serial, so it would end in a crisis as the editors had requested, she was told they needed more material for that issue, and she sent a short third chapter.[61] When they approached her about owning or selling the copyright, she was explicit,

> I wish to dispose of it as profitably as possible. Two other publishers—a New York and a Boston firm, have wished me to write a novel for them but you have the refusal of this and if you are willing to give as much as they will do, I should be pleased to leave it in your hands and continue the relations so pleasantly begun between us. As you wish some arrangement made now, please let me know what per-centage you would pay if I retain the copyright or what sum if you bought

it at once. I would stipulate that the book be printed on good paper & durably bound in cloth.[62]

She finally determined to retain the copyright,[63] a decision that would prove highly beneficial when negotiations turned sour.

The extent to which Davis was publishing more widely was evident at the beginning of 1867. In January she began a six-part Jersey shore serial in *Peterson's*, "The Longest Journey," that combined the realities of maritime life with a romance that crossed class differences. In February, the first section of "Waiting for the Verdict" appeared in the *Galaxy* while the beginning of a two-part story, "George Bedillion's Knight," set in western Pennsylvania, was published in the *Atlantic*. Although not intended at the time, this story would be the last of Davis's publications in the *Atlantic* until long after James Fields had ended his editorship.

The *Galaxy* editors did not raise an issue about her continuing to publish in the *Atlantic*, since many of their authors were now writing for both periodicals; it was the *Peterson's* serial that raised concerns for them. "The Longest Journey" was a previous commitment, and Davis was used to James Fields lack of concern about competition from *Peterson's*. But the Church brothers questioned the time writing for *Peterson's* would take away from Davis's productivity for their periodical. She chose to respond only in terms of the difference in styles she used for each magazine, "The story in Peterson . . . is entirely different in aim and treatment from 'Waiting for the Verdict' and I might suggest written for an altogether different audience from the readers of the Galaxy."[64] That crisis, at least, had been averted.

In spite of the seemingly unending need for clarifications with the *Galaxy*, 1867 brought time for Rebecca and Clarke to enjoy family outings together. On January 5, they took Hardy to the theater for the first time—to a pantomime. It was "the best I ever saw," Rebecca recorded in her diary that night. "It was as great a treat to me as to our boy. It was the first place to which we three had gone together. Hardy was a little frightened I think at first & a *good* deal awed." At home that evening he tried running through a wall "like Harlequin & showed Charley how Columbine danced, which as he is a clumsy little fellow was very funny. I am so glad he can see it while he is so [young]."[65] As an avid fan of the theater, Clarke often stopped after work to view some new performance in one of the numerous theaters in Philadelphia.[66] The boys were not only taken to the theater from a young age but also raised in a household that counted numerous actors as frequent guests. With the new year, Rebecca reflected on how happy she was with her writing life and her family of four: "I felt as if the old Year had taught me no word to write but one of thanksgiving. It does not matter, after all, if 'The May of Life blooms once—and not again' when June and July are filled with warmer sunshine and light."[67]

In late January, the Davises and Fieldses were at last united again in person. Annie and James visited the Davises while spending a few days in Philadelphia. Rebecca and Annie were still corresponding, if somewhat sporadically. The Fieldses had sent the Davises a copy of Longfellow's *Flower-de-Luce* as a Christmas present. Rebecca liked the appearance of the book better than the poetry, and they debated the merits of Longfellow's work during the Fieldses' stay.[68] Shortly after their visit, "Waiting for the Verdict" began serialization in the *Galaxy* as Davis worked on proofs for subsequent issues and wrote later chapters. The novel examined the life of an African American physician who passed as white in order to practice his profession; ultimately, however, the physician embraces his African American heritage. There had been no novel in US literature prior to "Waiting" with a mixed-race physician as its protagonist,[69] and the rarity of licensed black physicians in these years was evidenced in Philadelphia where there was at the time only one degreed African American physician, Dr. David Rossell, and he, like Davis's Dr. Broderip, had received his degree in Europe.[70]

The novel posited the question of what the US was going to do to ensure the successful transition of the formerly enslaved into lives of freedom and accomplishment. As an African American freed woman asserts at the novel's end, they were waiting for the verdict of the nation on this important question. Davis had written about medicine from the beginning of her career, but in "Waiting" she turned directly to the issue. Medicine long fascinated her—in her seventies she would still recall where the medicine jars had been kept in her childhood home and the "terrible skeleton" that was housed in Doctor Tanner's office in Wheeling;[71] as a teenager, she had been drawn to Julius LeMoyne's medical office and its curiosities; and for the rest of her career, the medical debates of each era would be incorporated into her literary works as she argued for a wide variety of medical reforms and the abandonment of nonsensical treatments such as mesmerism and hypnosis.

Davis received $3,600 for the *Galaxy* serial, more than six times what Fields would have paid her at the *Atlantic*[72] for a novel; it was an especially notable figure considering the economic crisis of 1867–69. The *Atlantic* raised its rates somewhat after the war, but it did not keep pace with most of the other high-literary magazines of the day.[73] The initial reviews of the serial were strong. The Philadelphia *Evening Bulletin*'s assessment appeared on the front-page: "A *real* new novel is a literary epoch. We earnestly hope 'Waiting for the Verdict' will be such a one. The first few chapters . . . shows [sic] plainly that the writer is devoting to this book the best of her thought, her knowledge of life, and her beliefs about humanity. It is, moreover, the first novel by an author of real power, in which the war or its principles become constituent forces." If the novel continued with the power of its opening chapters, the reviewer asserted, it would "typify the new relations and conditions of the races of men in the United States during and since the rebellion with as much force, breadth, intensity and truth, as 'Uncle Tom's Cabin' gave to the picture of things as they were before the war."[74]

The *Boston Advertiser* praised her as a "vigorous writer" who already had "a considerable reputation" that was continuing with this novel.[75] However, as the novel progressed and its emphasis on race relations before and during the war became more explicit, some negative reviews began to appear in conservative periodicals. The reviewer for the *Sunday School Teacher*, for instance, wrote: "Mrs. Davis is one of the most powerful writers in the English language; and this announcement will doubtless attract many readers to the *Galaxy*. For ourselves, we confess to a stern determination to read no more of her writings. The stories we have read of hers presented life as an inexorable fate. Her universe is an atheistic one. The soul answers to such writers, as Joubert remarks, by saying, 'You harrow me.'"[76] But positive reviews far outweighed the occasional disparaging ones. The depiction of a black physician even attracted the attention of the *Medical and Surgical Reporter*, which praised the novel and noted the "considerable attention" it was receiving.[77]

Davis always wanted to write stories of "to-day," but the urgency with which she felt this was necessary for this serial was evident in a letter she wrote to one of the Chase sisters (probably Lucy), Quaker activists from Philadelphia who were working with the Freedman's Bureau in the South:

My dear Miss Chase,

I write to you by the advice of Mrs Lucretia Mott, who named you to me as a person who would be able to give me some needed information, and willing she was sure, judging from the deep interest you have always shown in freedmen.

I will tell you as briefly as I can what I wish. I have been writing short articles for The Atlantic for some time (Life in the Iron Mills &c &c) and am now engaged in a long work intended to show as forcibly as I can the present *needs* of the colored race in both North and South.

I use the word in its broadest sense. I would not have attempted such an undertaking without going myself to the South, but two baby children make me perforce a "keeper at home" and I must rely on others for information.

Will you help me? I understand that you have been in the Carolinas and Georgia for two or three years and observing, no doubt with a quick and anxious eye, must have a clear insight into the chances of success in elevating these people. If you have time and will be so good as to assist me I would like to know what are the *present* obstacles legally interposed to their education or the proper remuneration of their labour, and also what is the usual temper and relation existing between the freedmen and their old masters—so far as they have fallen under your observation. I limit my questions to these knowing how much your time is filled. But whatever information you can give me on these two points, will be of the very greatest aid to me—Of course the more you can tell me—the better. But I feel as if I was [ink blot covers word] a stranger heavily in asking even so much. I would not do it were it a personal matter.

But you will understand how I, here at home wish anxiously to add my mite to the good which you and your co-laborers have so nobly begun. As the book is already begun in serial, I would be glad if you would write as soon as would suit your convenience.

R. H. Davis
Author Life in the Iron Mills[78]

In spite of her efforts to make this the best work she had yet written, Davis was faced with ongoing problems coming from new policies at the *Galaxy*. Initially, the author and editors worked cooperatively to promote the novel and the journal. While the Churches placed notices in literary magazines, they asked Clarke to use his connections to place notices in the leading newspapers outside of Philadelphia as well. Still, conflicts arose. Davis had tried to accommodate the changed page size and font type, but when William Church informed her that they were changing their payment policies as well, she responded quickly. While assuring him she had "a gratified sense that our business relations will be pleasant ones," she clearly presented her dissent:

> In reference, however to your proposition to pay for the balance of the story on the first of each month, it does not agree with either Mr. Davis's or my own understanding of our agreement. Our recollection of it is that upon my asking you if you would pay for the story as each installment was published you replied that it was your habit to write a cheque for each contributor on the day the magazine is dated—on the 1st and 15th of each month.

She explained she had made commitments based on their understanding; "I would prefer then, if it is convenient to you, that we would adhere to the first plan."[79]

She was learning the dangers of relying on oral agreements. In a deft maneuver, she followed her request to adhere to the original payment plan with an emphasis on the importance of one's word, "As to the copyright, please draw up the agreement at your leisure. I have come to regard your word as your bond." She also reiterated that the three chapters she had just sent should remain with the breaks she had indicated. Although Frank Church felt free to edit at will, William Church agreed to use a hands-off approach to her novel. She thanked him for his willingness "to let the story stand or fall on its own merit. I will do all I can to do justice to myself and you, and if I fail it will be for want of ability, and not for honest effort and feeling."[80] Although Davis was always invested in her writing, her insistence on having her say about how the nation should respond to the thousands of formerly enslaved men and women was at its most powerful in this novel.

Dealing with Frank Church, however, was a completely different experience. More abrupt in manner and decidedly less concerned with an artist's wishes, he caused untold conflicts that repeatedly had to be smoothed over by his brother. Rebecca had a far more heated temper than Clarke, and it was often he who had to smooth over disputes from their side. The Davises developed in these months a process they would continue for the rest of their lives whereby Clarke would "hold the pen for her" when Rebecca either was too angry to respond with her usual politeness to an editor or had responded in anger and a calming influence was needed.[81] Thus Clarke wrote Frank Church on February 15 after an accounting dispute to remind him of the "spirit" of their agreement as well as its literal intent.[82]

In spite of their disputes with Frank Church, the Davises' friendship with William grew; he visited them in Philadelphia and invited them to join him and his wife on a trip to the South. Clarke was just recovering from another illness, so Rebecca declined, also citing her young children as a reason they could not join the Churches.[83] By mid-April, however, discussions with the Church brothers had reached a peak of frustration for Davis when they informed her of additional changes to paper and font size. She was livid but, as much as possible, circumspect when she responded to the editors:

> My dear Messrs Church,
>
> I was very sorry to learn from your letters of your intended change, as your difficulty must follow unavoidably. With your sized page you cannot finish two serials before next year without giving up most of the magazine to them. I understand the trouble, and will most willingly do all I can to help you. Still, I would like you to perceive that the embarrassment to which I am so abruptly subjected is equally annoying, as it is by no will of mine and will prove in every way a loss.
>
> You recollect that it was not my intention to publish this story except in book-form, after giving it care and time, and that it was only at your urgent request that I gave to the Galaxy to publish serially. When the agreement was made with you, however, I adhered to it—That was, you remember, for a story of the length of [British author Annie Edwards'] 'Archie Lovell' and in the plot and conduct of the novel, I have kept that in view. Mr. F. P. Church's arrangement—to comprise the remainder unpublished, into seven numbers of 30 pages each would take off over 60 pages at the last, when every page is of importance. It would be equivalent to asking Mr. Hennessy to cut off the heads of his figures because you wanted to alter the size of your page! You must allow me the feeling which the humblest workman has for his work. The loss in money would be about $500 besides delaying the time of issue as a book. You must not think me cross about it—I have no doubt that it was a prudent thing to start another serial after mine and to twice alter the arrangement of the magazine but it is hardly fair that *I* should pay the penalty.
>
> I went over the outline of the unfinished part carefully yesterday, anxious to do all I could to help you and which I will do—without injury to the story. But I cannot consent to omit a word which would affect its meaning or what I conceive to be its artistic development for any injury to it is a permanent one to my reputation.
>
> What I *can* do is to finish the story this year, provided you give me not less than 35 pages in each number after May 1st, including December. That would shorten it by about 35 pages. I cannot spare more. The book can be issued in November, as before arranged. It would be in

time then for the fall trade sale, and the appearance of one number in the Galaxy afterwards would hurt neither magazine nor book—it is usual—I believe in the publication of all serials.

If you cannot do this, the story must run into next year & the book be delayed in which case my loss would be equivalent to your own.

I regret very much that the difficulty has arisen. If I had heard earlier of your wish to shorten the story it could have been done—but at this advanced state—it is impossible to do more than I propose—With Mr Davis regards to both

Very truly R. H. Davis[84]

She had expected "Waiting" to run sixteen issues, a point that was acknowledged throughout their correspondence in late February and March, but after the Churches demanded more cuts, it would end up at only eleven issues, the majority of cuts made from the ending. William Church wrote expressing his regret that their correspondence seemed so harsh. As Clarke replied, once again "holding her pen," Davis "too would have been glad to have *talked* with you about your mutual troubles in preference to waiting, for words on paper *seem* harsh though they may come from a mind full of gentleness."[85]

Complicating matters, Clarke had agreed to handle a volatile legal matter for William Church—a case that would eventually be decided by the US Supreme Court in 1874 (*Garsed v. Beall*) and which the Court itself would define as a "peculiar case."[86] Exactly how Church was involved remains unclear, as Clarke managed to keep his name out of the legal proceedings; it is likely he was an investor with Thomas Metcalf, who was a part owner with Jeremiah and William Beall in a lot of cotton valued at $2 million. The Bealls and Metcalf would claim when the case went to the Supreme Court that John Garsed and George Schley had pretended they had military orders to seize the cotton but intended to sell it for their own profit.

In 1867, Clarke served as Church's representative when a man named Stephen Knopf presented himself as working on behalf of Metcalf and a Mr. Roth, whose involvement was even shadier than the unseen Metcalf's. Knopf attempted to blackmail Church for $10,000. Clarke arranged for Knopf and Roth to meet at the Davis home rather than his office. Before the meeting, Rebecca helped Clarke compare the handwriting of a letter from Knopf and one purportedly from Roth, determining they had been written by the same man. Clarke repeatedly recommended having the men arrested, but Church refused, probably to avoid a public airing of the situation. When the case reached the courts, Clarke had been successful in extricating Church from the suit. The negotiations with the blackmailers had lasted through much of April, however, and several letters from Clarke to Church included messages about Rebecca's manuscript and references to his negotiations with the blackmailers in a blending of legal and literary machinations that blurred the lines between Clarke's legal career, Rebecca's literary career, and their professional and personal relationships with the Church brothers.[87]

The stress of all of these literary and legal negotiations was certainly part of the cause of an illness that overcame Rebecca in late April, and it was early May before she was again "beginning to creep about." As she told Annie Fields, "I am *so* unaccustomed to be weak and useless that I proved a most impatient patient, I am afraid. *Most* impatient for the spring. The cold dreary rains of the last weeks were thoroughly depressing seen through a chamber window. We are going early to the country this summer. I am making fresh attacks on 'Papa' to move out of town altogether—seconded by Hardy."[88]

In reality, she and Clarke had too much business to attend to at present to think seriously of moving. Her mid-April letter did not alter the financial need the Churches had for asking her to shorten the length of her novel, but they did try to accommodate her requests as much as possible because they wanted the right to publish the serial in book form. Davis was more reticent after her illness, and when William Church indicated how much he liked the story, she was pleased, "I did not want you to think you had been wrong in taking it."[89] Frank Church also sought to mend relations, although he sent praise for an article Clarke had written, not Rebecca!

"Among the Comedians" for the *Atlantic* was Clarke Davis's first publication outside of the Philadelphia newspapers and legal publications, and it offered a particularly astute analysis of Joseph Jefferson's acting as he was becoming famous for his role as Rip Van Winkle. This was a new phase in Clarke's career as a critic. His reputation grew rapidly and within a few years he would wield national influence as a theater critic. Equally important, this publication began a new pattern in the indelible link between Rebecca and Clarke's writing careers. They had always helped one another in minor ways, discussing their work or with Rebecca writing the review for the *Legal Intelligencer* when Clarke needed help, and Clarke meeting with the Church brothers in New York to smooth tensions between the publishers and author. But this was a different stage of that mutual commitment to one another's careers, and one that would be followed throughout their lifetimes. The process was the same each time: Rebecca would establish her reputation and a cordial relationship with the editors of a major literary periodical, and then Clarke would publish one or two articles or short stories in the periodical as well. Clarke was a brilliant newspaper editor and a good writer; he may eventually have found his way into high-literary publications, but her connections escalated his opportunities.

To her astonishment, Davis's frustrations with the editors of the *Galaxy* were far from over. In early June she received separate letters from Frank and William Church about the need to cut the length of her story by thirty-four pages. Whether it mutilated the story was obviously a secondary consideration to them, Davis argued in a letter addressed to both men. There was little tempering of her anger this time: "I would have cut out a hundred pages rather than bear the chagrin and annoyance of the last two or three days." She intended, she continued, to present the "business side" of the situation, an emphasis that sought to separate the growing friendship between William Church and the Davises, in order to correct errors both men had made in their assertions about the need for her to cut more pages:

> And first, as to your impression that I intended forcing you to expense, and loss, by sending a longer story than you engaged from me? *No* such agreement as that on which you based your very peremptory demand the other day ever was made between us, oral or written. I never bind myself—no writer other than the merest penny-liner could bind himself—to write a story of exactly 279—or any given number of pages. "Archie Lovell" was instanced by Mr. W. C. Church as about the desired length and an imperfect copy which he had brought containing 300 pages—cited. During our first interview he repeatedly assured me that I was not to be limited as to length.... As late as March 29 Mr. F. P. Church wishes cannot you keep the (semi-monthly) parts down to 24 printed pages? which would have brought the story to 384 pages—new type.... Then—nine full parts being in your hands and the story so far advanced that it was impossible to change it without mutilation you demanded its curtailment to give space to Mrs Edwards,[90] and to accommodate the change of publication. If you find it necessary (unless I comply) *for these reasons* to add extra pages to the magazine, am *I* fairly chargeable with the blame or loss? I too might have had complaints if I had wished to be captious—that you delayed the issue of the book from October until December by your altering[?]

from a fortnightly to a monthly issue, making it too late for the fall leads—Another misapprehension under which you labor and which gives to your letters a peculiarly distasteful tone, is that the story is a joint venture in which you are suffering pecuniary loss and consequently conferring a favor on me by publishing it. You will remember that the novel was published in The Galaxy by no solicitation of mine: you took it at a time when I had offers from two large publishing houses for a novel, in which I would have been circumscribed by neither time nor quantity. Having engaged it to you I wrote it as I have done many other stories for other publishers. I gave you conscientiously my best and most earnest effort, and then, my part was done. When the last word is written all obligation ceases on my side. As to whether the Atlantic or the Galaxy increases or not in circulation while I wrote for them, beyond personal good wishes—is a matter with which I surely have nothing to do and have never heretofore been held responsible, pecuniarily or otherwise.

You are the first publishers who have ever complained that in what I had written they had not received a due equivalent for their money. You are also the first in the six years I have been writing for the press who have asked me to alter or abridge a line. I have been perhaps unusually favored by the old etiquette of the editorial sanctum.

I am very sorry to say all this. Our personal intercourse has been exceedingly pleasant. But I will be as frank as you have been with regard to our business relations, and I feel that while I have made every effort to fulfil my part of the contract, I have most unjustly been held chargeable—pecuniarily and morally, with difficulties brought on by your frequent changes of type, mode of publication, etc—and with the success or non-success of The Galaxy. No money could pay me for the annoyance to which I have been subjected.

I think your own good sense cannot blame me if I desire to free myself from it as soon as possible and desire that our business relations may cease upon the conclusion of the story in The Galaxy.

Mr. W. C. Church spoke of some contemplated arrangements with Sheldon & Co. I desire that no farther steps may be taken in the matter—

Very respectfully
R. H. Davis[91]

The final words of Davis's letter hit the mark. The possibility of not being able to publish the novel in book form would mean a major financial loss for the editors. Their correspondence again became cordial, yet Davis still had to write each month to remind them to send payment. The Churches worked arduously to soothe Davis back into an agreement to publish "Waiting" as a book through them via the arrangements they had been in the midst of negotiating with Sheldon and Company. It took time, not the least because she again became ill in the midst of these frustrations, and the illness lasted for nearly two weeks.

By mid-June she was again able to write, though she especially found solace in gardening. With a rowhouse, the Davises had only an eight-by-ten-foot lawn, but they had created a flower hedge around the yard. It was the creation of the rows of flowers that helped restore her spirits. The garden consisted "not of costly flowers—but rare ones as I had a fancy to collect all the old fashioned growths of a garden, which used to be fairy land to me long ago. So I sent every where for the queer half-forgotten blossoms."[92] The extent to which the Davises and the William Churches were attempting to separate their business differences was nowhere so evident as in the invitation the Davises extended to William and his wife to join them at the shore, which they accepted.[93] The willingness of each side to budge a little bridged the latest break, and by mid-July Davis agreed they could continue to negotiate with Sheldon and Company for book publication.[94]

The summer of 1867 was a particularly restful one at Point Pleasant. "I think we never have enjoyed our little solitary corner of the world so much as this summer," Rebecca confessed to Annie Fields. Clarke had a sailboat which he took out almost daily to explore neighboring islands, and Hardy was learning to swim. The Davises and their friends played cricket and croquet, but Rebecca also continued to study the region and its people as subject matter for her stories. She found many of the local people to be "curious studies as Nature, seeing that the great passions of human nature go on unceasingly with ebb and flow, making new and terrible shipwrecks—as we have felt since we came here." Rebecca claimed at this time that she would never again agree to a serial that needed to be written while publication was in progress.[95]

Rebecca's lingering distaste over her experiences with the *Galaxy* did not deter Clarke from writing an article on croquet for the magazine that appeared in August, replicating their pattern with the *Atlantic*: Rebecca concluded publication with that journal for several years but not before Clarke began publishing in it. Clarke faced the same editorial challenges as Rebecca when writing his article for the *Galaxy*, however, and he had to write directly to Frank Church to ensure large sections were not excised.[96]

His article appeared just as Rebecca signed the contract with the Church brothers to have Sheldon and Company publish the book version of *Waiting for the Verdict*. This time, she negotiated a much more detailed contract, including the percentages she was to receive as copyright holder, that illustrations from the *Galaxy* would be replicated in the book, and that the book would be published on good paper with a cloth binding.[97]

When the Davis family returned to Philadelphia in September, exchanges continued between Rebecca and the Churches with her insistence that proofs be retained as she had indicated, instead of the substitutions made by the printer. During these negotiations, she was writing a new story, "At Bay," for *Peterson's*. In May 1867, Elizabeth Stuart Phelps had published a story of the same title in *Harper's* in which she had paid tribute to Davis for writings such as "Life in the Iron-Mills" and "Paul Blecker." As one of Phelps's characters remarked about Davis's stories: "It made you feel as if she knew all about you, and were sorry for you; and as if she thought nobody was too poor, or too uneducated, or too worn-out with washing-days, and all the things that do not sound a bit grand in books, to be written about. . . . It makes me love her."[98] It is likely Davis meant a return complement by using the same title for her own story when it was published in October.

"At Bay" was an unusual story in Davis's canon to date. Set in the era of Andrew Jackson's presidency, the story began in France and ended in South Carolina. Like "Life" and *Margret Howth*, it suggested a person's character was revealed by how he or she responded to a person with disabilities. Characters with disabilities were becoming common in Davis's work and would be as varied as any other of her characterizations. Sometimes their disabilities symbolized a corrupt nature, while at other times their ability to construct meaningful lives cast them as moral exemplars.

As "At Bay" appeared in print, William Church invited Davis to write a Christmas story for the *Galaxy*. She declined. In spite of their friendship, she intended to hold to her refusal to publish with them at present, and it was two years before she could be convinced to return to the *Galaxy*. What the Churches did not yet know was that Davis was turning to the opportunities offered her by a new literary magazine to be published in Philadelphia, *Lippincott's New Monthly Magazine*, and her next novel-length work would appear in its pages. Just as the penultimate issue of "Waiting for the Verdict" was published, Henry James published in the *Nation* a review of the novel in which he insisted Davis employed "lachrymose sentimentalism" in her writing.[99] It was an odd moment in which to make this charge, since the latest episode included the taut scenes in which Dr. Broderip was revealed to be of mixed-race heritage, a man born in slavery who had risen to the top of his profession but was now rejected by almost everyone when his racial identity was revealed. James was only beginning his own career at this point and attacked many women writers, though with little detriment to their careers. His primary criticism was Davis's focus on the impoverished as he believed class did not impact the frailties of human nature, a point with which Davis disagreed.

Considering the importance of war stories for nineteenth-century literature, the most unusual implication of James's review was that Reconstruction and miscegenation were inappropriate subject matters for fiction.[100] Davis's choice of a character such as Dr. Broderip was in part a reflection of the knowledge of the black community she had gained since moving to Philadelphia. African Americans numbered more than 22,000 in the city at the time, and there were several prominent black men who had made a mark in Philadelphia.[101] Additionally, the nation was aflame with debates about miscegenation in the early years of Reconstruction. In a radical characterization for the time, Davis cast the white woman character who rejects her beloved once she knows he is of mixed race as a failure who could not move beyond insipid prejudices.

Several women writers were outraged at James's review and none more so than Harriet Beecher Stowe. Although they had never met, she wrote Davis indicating her disdain for the review. To Stowe's mind, the *Nation* "has no sympathy with any deep and high moral movement—no pity for infirmity. It is a sneering respectable middle aged sceptic who says I take my two glasses & my cigar daily," and she encouraged Davis to ignore them.[102] It was well-meaning advice, but Davis never fretted over reviews. She was moving on to new ventures.

Davis had submitted a Christmas story to the *Atlantic* that argued for recognizing God's presence in this life rather than always looking to the next, but James Fields replied with a surprisingly negative response—not to its quality but to its length. She had intended, with Clarke's encouragement, to use "Mrs. R. H. Davis" with this story, for the first time identifying herself in the *Atlantic*. Whether from mutual agreement or her decision to withdraw the story rather than cut its length, "The Story of Christmas Eve" was published in *Peterson's* rather than the *Atlantic*, and it was the end of her publishing relationship with the *Atlantic Monthly* for many years.

Davis had a larger issue to address with Fields as well and one that may have impacted the decision about whether to publish the Christmas story: her name had been eliminated from their major notice of "Eminent Writers" who were regular contributors to the *Atlantic*. "I must tell you frankly, that I did not understand the manner in which I was dismissed from your list of contributors for the coming year," she chided Fields.

> It would have been more business-like—(not to say friendly) in T. and F. if they wished our relation to end to let me know before my engagements were made for next year. I made them with reference to writing for you—declining to write for other Boston magazines which I supposed were unfriendly to the A.—I was the more surprised at it as I have been writing for the Atlantic for a year and a half at half the price per page paid and offered me by all the other magazines—I did not intend to speak of this to you, as I preferred to write for the Atlantic at even a pecuniary loss because it was my oldest friend and because too there were so many among its readers whom I liked and whom I think liked me.[103]

This was clearly a painful rejection, one that Rebecca never fully understood, but she turned to other subjects, asking Fields to thank Annie for her two notes and to say that she would write soon. What was equally surprising in the notice for the coming year's list of authors for the *Atlantic* was that, in addition to having her name moved from regular contributor to a nonalphabetized list of contributors the publishers "are still able to promise contributions from," Clarke's name was listed several spaces above hers, even though he had published only one article in the periodical.

It was an exhausting and in some ways disappointing end to the year. Rebecca maintained courteous relations with the Fieldses, but this was the beginning of the end of their friendship. It would take one more affront from Annie in a few years to finally close this chapter of her life. Her frustration with James Field may have altered her memories of the *Galaxy* negotiations, since in December she surprisingly ended a note to William Church, "You must allow me, too, Mr Church to acknowledge the uniform courtesy of yourself and your brother—a thing which has no value on paper" but which she valued dearly and perhaps felt she had not received from Fields in this most recent event.[104] In spite of the frustrations and setbacks of these months, Davis was turning a new page—with publishers and in her life. She could write in her diary on Christmas evening 1867: "The happiest Christmas I have had for a long long time. God has been so loving and so tender in His love—our lives seem like a beautiful hymn of joy."[105]

Chapter 5

A National Author (1868–1870)

The beginning of 1868 saw the publication of two important novels by Davis: the book publication of *Waiting for the Verdict* and the serialization of "Dallas Galbraith." In marketing the former, Sheldon and Company created a designation that would resonate throughout literary studies in perpetuity: *Waiting for the Verdict* was "The Great American Novel."[1] The reviews of *Waiting* continued to be strong, but they again at times ascribed the novel to a "masculine pen," as the reviewer for *Godey's* asserted, adding that it was a "novel of more than ordinary interest." Even more enthusiastic, if equally gendered, was the reviewer for *The Round Table*, a New York periodical that had begun publication in 1863 with the goal of attracting nationally established reporters and authors. Anyone who had read "Life in the Iron-Mills" or *Margret Howth*, the reviewer noted, did "not need to be told that Mrs. Davis is one of our most vigorous and thoughtful writers, not only among the best of living American novelists, which is not saying much, but (which is saying a great deal) worthy to rank with that Brilliant English sisterhood of talent . . . both in the quality of her genius and her intellectual bent." The two-page review cast *Waiting for the Verdict* as Davis's "best work" to date and of "original character." Its one criticism, however, was indicative of the radical nature of her novel. Referring to the white woman, Miss Conrad, who had loved Dr. Broderip but ended their engagement because she could not overcome her racial prejudices, the reviewer insisted Broderip could not have been mistaken for a white man, "A woman of Miss Conrad's keen instincts and strong antipathies would surely have taken alarm at the obvious physical signs of race." Yet the reviewer's conclusion was that the novel's greatest merit was "the skill displayed in the use of those two elements of war and slavery which so often suffice to swamp less practiced or more pretentious artists" and the thesis on slavery served

> to bring out its crushing wrong and shame more forcibly than a thousand harangues of the professional freedom-shriekers whose art so made the better cause appear the worse. Mrs. Davis writes like one who has taken an inside view of the peculiar institution; a surmise

which the accuracy of her negro dialect would go to strengthen.... It is a pleasure to read, a pleasure to criticize, such a book as this.

Private evaluations were equally positive if more succinct. In the inside cover of her copy of *Waiting for the Verdict*, the reformer Caroline Dall wrote, "A brave good book."[2]

Davis's decision to move to *Lippincott's* to publish "Dallas Galbraith" began a fifteen-year association, and it was in *Lippincott's* that many of her best short stories and novellas of the 1870s would be published. Lloyd P. Smith was the magazine's first editor; he moved into the role from his position as Head Librarian at the Philadelphia Library and was probably the person who had heeded Clarke's suggestion of granting Rebecca her own writing space in the library. Years earlier, before taking the position at the Philadelphia Library, Smith had edited the literary magazine *Smith's Weekly Volume*, and his commitment to what he termed "the best popular literature" helped to make *Lippincott's* a very successful magazine with a wide circulation.[3] "Dallas Galbraith" began its serialization in the first issue of the magazine. The novel combined her Jersey shore and West Virginia locales, but its primary focus was an issue to which she would return over the coming years: that American society inexcusably shunned the convicted man, and Davis emphasized that many men were imprisoned not because of evidence of guilt but because they were poor. By constructing a figure who, through long years of endeavor, builds a life of integrity for himself in spite of having been falsely imprisoned, Davis demonstrated a belief in the ability of individuals to overcome tragic events in their lives—and that society needed to recognize character was not written on the surface or in the pocket.

Initial reviews were enthusiastic. The *Round Table* reviewer again commented on the strength of Davis's writing, and the *Lancaster Intelligencer* remarked in a front-page article: "A lady like Mrs. Rebecca Harding Davis would be a lion in the most fashionable circles of Boston. In New York she would not be unknown in those circles if she chose to move in them, and, if she chose to avoid them, she might still move in a circle where letters are the symbol of aristocracy."[4] More tempered but still positive was William Gilmore Simms' review. Simms was known for his efforts to present both fault-finding and praise in every review, and he assessed Davis's novel in that manner. Her book was a "strange compound of a good story well told, with characters that do violence to the popular conception of nature.... in the conception of the plot she has displayed considerable tact and skill, and in her portrayings of the characters she has met in one or two instances with success."[5] Again, the only negative review

Davis's novel received was from Henry James who oddly termed Galbraith a "woman's boy"; he also found the powerful and dominating Mrs. Galbraith to be a "monster" and against female nature, though he grudgingly acknowledged that Davis "may probably be congratulated on a success."[6] Indeed, the novel garnered wide success, insuring Davis's long association with *Lippincott's*.

To have two novels published at this time and with such acclaim was remarkable. Just over 2,200 books were published in the US in 1868, and a large portion was imported editions or reprints of English works. As *Appleton's* noted in their annual analysis of national publishing and literary progress, "Of the six novels which achieved the largest sales during the year, three, Mrs. Rebecca Harding Davis's 'Dallas Galbraith,' Mr. [Henry Ward] Beecher's 'Norwood,' and Miss Anna Dickinson's 'What Answer,' were by American authors."[7] The recognition of her talent and successful sales placed Davis among the nationally recognized authors of the period.

Rather than creating a sense of pressure on Davis to reproduce the same types of works, the success of "Dallas Galbraith" freed her creatively. One of the major fields into which she moved at this time was narratives that realistically examined women's lives, including "'In the Market'" for *Peterson's*. Although Davis had previously touched on women's needs for greater economic and social opportunities, this story analyzed society's treatment of women as property to be bartered in the capitalist marketplace. It was the beginning of numerous stories and articles in which Davis suggested how opportunities could be made for women to become economically independent in urban centers or rural communities. She never wrote explicitly in favor of women's rights or joined women's suffrage organizations, but in many stories and articles she created arguments for women's economic and social rights. These stories were varied and did not always present women as virtuous emblems of American society, however. She followed "'In the Market,'" for instance, with "The Daughter-in-Law," another John Page legal story; in this instance, the title character was a female con artist. Con artists fascinated Davis, and they would populate her writings for decades to come.

Although Davis turned to *Lippincott's* as a new publisher, she and Clarke maintained cordial relations with Charles Peterson, William Church, and, though they were in less contact than in the past, James Fields. These connections were important for the personal relationships they afforded the Davises with each editor and his family, but on a professional level, they were particularly important to Clarke who would continue to publish in both the *Atlantic* and the *Galaxy*. He also continued to be Davis's go-between, as evidenced in a

February 1868 letter he wrote to Church, "Thank you for your proffer of aid to Mrs. Davis. She wished to consult you about the possible chance of having her book published in England, not with a view to one farthing of profit, but as an introduction there that might aid her in her future works. Have you or Messrs. Sheldon any opportunities of inquiry which we have not?" He assured the editor, "Mrs. Davis and I will both be glad to do what we can for our old friend the *Galaxy*."[8] The Churches did not secure English publication for *Waiting*, however, and Rebecca maintained a more peripheral connection with the periodical thereafter.

As with the *Atlantic* and the *Galaxy*, Rebecca's entry into a new publication, this time *Lippincott's*, was soon followed by Clarke's appearance in its pages as well. He was a talented journalist and nonfiction writer; his forays into fiction were of mixed quality but grew in strength over the next few years. "The Wreck on the Shore," which also included a female con artist, appeared in the same issue as Rebecca's ongoing serialization of "Dallas Galbraith." It was a good beginning for Clarke's minor career in fiction, and it demonstrated the ways in which themes crossed Rebecca and Clarke's works even as they were presented in quite different styles. They had truly melded their careers and support for one another's work by this time—Rebecca aided Clarke's entry into major periodicals, and he promoted her work in newspapers through soliciting notices and reviews. They forged mutual friendships with publishers and editors out of genuine affection but also to mutual benefit. The Davises had become an extraordinarily well-oiled machine of talent and marketing.

In March Davis received a letter of praise for "Dallas Galbraith" from the Southern poet and critic Paul Hamilton Hayne and a book of his poems. She received "much pleasure" from his letter and analyzed the differences in their styles, which he had remarked upon:

> I can understand how, to you in your "fields of purpling flowers" a picture of the bleak fishing village or the strongly-featured life of Western Virginia should have given a surprised pleasure from contrast. But I am glad that you told me that it did. The only recompense to a woman who utters her voice outside of the seclusion of her own home, is the occasional sincere and friendly call, which otherwise she never would have heard,—*not* of praise, but recognition.

Although Rebecca would soon be traveling extensively, she nurtured for Hayne the image of herself as a homebody, "My husband and I, with our two little boys, live in as quiet a little house in a great city, as yours under the pines."[9]

She responded to the book of poetry Payne had sent as well, "Sincerely, there is a truth in your expression of Southern scenery which touches me as though the subtle atmosphere and sensuous sunshine had at last found a real voice. This is especially true, (to *me*) in the poem Renewed and after that in Under the Pine." In addition to presenting herself as a homebody, Davis insisted she had "not a spark of the divine critical faculty and like and dislike things from the most womanish, personal, unreasonable causes"—even though she had been writing reviews for several years. Perhaps most surprising, when she explained why she was not reciprocating with a book of her own with her letter, was Rebecca's assessment of the impact of *Waiting for the Verdict* in spite of its critical praise: "I have but one copy of each of the other novels I wrote, or I would gladly send you Margret Howth, the other I think *not*. I tried, being from a border state Virginia, to sketch representative people North and South, and every one says their own likeness was badly done. The book was a failure."[10] That certainly was not true financially or critically, but no critic was harder on Davis than she was on herself.

Writing as prolifically as she did at this point in her career meant that letter-writing became less and less attractive, as Rebecca explained to Annie Fields in a long-overdue letter in March. "I'm not lazy," adding in the rhetoric of Spiritualism, "I only dislike pen and ink. . . . In some of those worlds to come, there will be a sort of spiritual telegraph attached to everybody's brain, and mine shall rap out 'Boston' once a day, at least." Yet letters allowed Rebecca and Annie to continue to share their opinions of contemporary authors, this time Charles Dickens. Rebecca had attended Dickens' reading in Philadelphia in January, and she freely expressed her ideas on his performance, though she knew that few authors were so idolized by the Fieldses as Dickens. She liked

> the genial half of his humour as much from his voice and actual person as ever I did from his pen. There is a certain emotion which I do believe never was wakened in anybody since the world was made until Dickens got hold of the key and let it out; a sense—a mixture of the comic and pathetic at once which brings a tear and a laugh at the same time. His reading had the same power as his words in that he was, I fancied, more human than any actor in expressing happiness.

However, there were aspects of his performance that disappointed her, "But when it comes to simple pathos—unmixed with any comic element, his voice and manner had no effect upon me—one was metallic and the other artificial.

Others felt differently, so the fault was perhaps in myself. But of course I tell you honest what it was to me personally."[11]

It was not at all the norm for *Atlantic* authors to be out of line with the Fieldses' preferences in literature or people,[12] but as they had come to expect, Rebecca always expressed herself honestly with them. She also reiterated to Annie a promise to herself she made many times in her career but rarely kept, "You ask me what I am doing? Writing a story for 'Lippincott' which you have seen, no doubt. I never will begin to publish another long story until it is quite finished—it is too great a tax on one's endurance." She also revealed the challenges of working with Lloyd Smith, "And then the horror of being sick with an infuriate publisher waylaying the doctor to know the chance of 'copy'!!"[13] Rebecca would be pleased when Smith stepped down the next year and John Foster Kirk became editor of *Lippincott's*, as she developed a much better relationship with Kirk.

It was a wonderfully productive year for both Rebecca and Clarke. She published a five-part serial, "The Tragedy of Fauquier," in *Peterson's* in April. An extension of the John Page stories, this well-told mystery was primarily an exploration of the dangers of Spiritualism and the complexities of what constitutes insanity. Davis's reflections on concepts of insanity in the novella—whether born or bred, partial or full insanity—were attuned to current medical debates, and her narrator insisted that a belief in Spiritualism was itself a form of insanity, reflecting proclamations of many orthodox physicians.

In May Rebecca took a very different approach to the question of what constitutes insanity, as the Davises began a new political campaign against the abusive asylum system in the US, and specifically in Pennsylvania, with Clarke's publication of "A Modern Lettre de Cache" in the *Atlantic*. This campaign also marked a new stage in their collaboration as political-activist writers, in which they joined ranks, using articles, fiction, editorials, and political appointments to fight for reform. At the time, the system for institutionalizing someone was fraught with abuse in Pennsylvania; as in many states, it required only the signature of a single physician to incarcerate the individual who was assumed to be mentally ill, and the incarcerated person had no recourse to challenge the assessment.

As Clarke observed in "A Modern Lettre de Cache," although the treatment of mentally ill patients had changed from abject cruelty to the building of asylums in which patients, though rarely cured, could receive care, "our statutory laws regulating these institutions, and the forms of consignment to them, have remained precisely as they were fifty years ago.... No matter how unknown, how criminal, how ignorant or besotted, how old or how young, the physician may be, if he is armed with that mighty weapon, the diploma of a medical school, he holds us at his mercy." He specifically cited Dr. Thomas Story Kirkbride, head of the Pennsylvania Hospital for the Insane and founder of the Association of Medical Superintendents of American Institutions of the Insane, who had proudly asserted "that to him alone 'is confided the general superintendence of the establishment,—the *sole* direction of the medical, moral, and dietetic treatment of the patients, and *the selection of all persons employed in their care*.'" Clarke argued, "we cannot fail to see the capacity for evil with which he is clothed, since every officer of the institution, from the physician to the scullery-maid, depends upon his favor to maintain position under him." This practice exposed the dangers of private "mad-houses" to which the doors were closed to the public. Clarke insisted that the "treatment" inmates had to endure would have driven many a sane person insane.[14]

When a reviewer in the *Round Table* charged Clarke, in a lengthy response, with writing a "sensational" piece, implying his instances were exaggerated, Clarke responded with an equally lengthy letter to the editor denying "Modern Lettre" was at all sensational and documenting more thoroughly the basis of his argument. Although the magazine published his rebuttal, it followed with a detailed editorial response mocking the idea of having each case of insanity determined by a jury, for which Clarke had argued. The editors insisted "Dr. Davis" had responded with too much fervor and too little judgment.[15]

His article for the *Atlantic* raised vehement responses from physicians as well, whom he also countered in print. When a Dr. Howe insisted on the right of physicians to declare insanity without outside influence, Clarke cited a recent case in which a well-to-do man had been abducted from a hotel and placed in Dr. Kirkbride's asylum with only the signature of a physician who had never seen the patient. Clarke insisted Kirkbride had affirmed in writing that the man was insane, but it was revealed at trial by Kirkbride's own testimony under cross-examination that he had no knowledge of the man personally or of his insanity. The man in this instance had been held without cause in the asylum for over five months. "And this is the law," Clarke concluded, "that the asylums defend; that they dare not denounce, lest they find their well-paying wards depopulated."[16] This was a cause that the Davises passionately believed in and were unwilling to abandon in spite of significant criticism from those who profited by the system. Within a few months, Rebecca would join the fight to change state laws, and she and Clarke would continue their efforts on behalf of the wrongfully institutionalized over the next several years.

The Davises were especially ready for their summer retreat in 1868. While at Point Pleasant, Rebecca observed how thoroughly Charley—or "Boysey" as they often called him—had recovered from his early ailments. Boysey was "strongly built," she wrote in her diary, and "a rosy little fellow with a manly open face full of expression, and voice full of feeling"; at "any instant" his hot temper could burst forth. "I dont know if he is brighter than other children," she added, "but he has a frank boy way about him that wins everybody at once—." Yet Rebecca abhorred obesity, and she often worried that he was becoming "as fat as a little pig."[17] Charley would struggle with his weight—and his family's criticism of it—throughout his life.

As a mother, Rebecca loved the time spent with her boys. She worried about their moral development and rejoiced in their achievements, memorializing the moments, large and small, in her diary. She was delighted to observe Hardy's development as a storyteller and was amused when he spent an entire afternoon on "the never to be forgotten subject of the Pantomime" after one of his trips to the theater: "I never saw Hardy as animated or lively as he was tonight, full of life and festive, telling about the circus & pantomime & imitating every thing from [Columbia?] to the elephant." She was proud of him, too, when a veterans' parade passed the house and he shouted "Hurra" from the window for "the Boys in Blue."[18]

One of her favorite ventures was taking the boys out into the surf while at the shore to watch them laugh as they jumped in the water. She was distressed, however, when she discovered Hardy had told his parents a lie. "I'd rather see him dead I think than a liar," she dramatically confided in her diary, but she quickly rescinded such a harsh judgment: "He is too young to know the difference between a lie and 'a story' & I never saw a child with the imagination that he shows." Charley, still quite young, received close attention as well, and Rebecca cherished being able to see him grow "every day, strong as a little bear and running over with life but with the lovingest little heart in the world." She worried sometimes about how she was educating her sons religiously. Her mother and Clarke questioned her training of Hardy early on "because it makes him speak familiarly of 'the Lord.' But I hope I am right."[19]

Rebecca also recorded in her diary intimate details about her relationship with Clarke that never appeared in letters. His long work hours and frequent travels were repeated causes for notations—"Pet did not go out until after dinner & then was gone till 10"; "It was a happy day although clouded by the thoughts of old Pet's going"; he was all day at the "office & we had dinner all alone & now he is gone again." But she also recorded how closely they worked together. When she received a proof for the second number of one of her serials, she remarked that it "kept us both busy, as it all had to be rewritten, almost." But her frustration with diary-keeping was also evident as she recognized the inability of words on the page to fully capture certain feelings:

> After all what is the use of a diary? I can put down every little trifle every day, to the bill of fare for dinner, but I cant put in words the happy sense of home, and love that is under and over all. The thousand little ways in which my Darling shows how strong and tender is his love. I cant paint Hardy['s] bright face or funny antics.... I can't catch the look of Charleys earnest blue eyes. So my diary is a poor map of the country.[20]

When the family returned to Philadelphia in the fall, *Dallas Galbraith* appeared in book form and continued to receive high praise. The Philadelphia *Evening Bulletin* remarked with the serial's conclusion that it

> will be a source of regret to the large circle of readers whom that lady has held spellbound by the deploy of her varied resources for so long a time. Mrs. Davis's style—need we describe it at this date, when it has become one of the familiar enchantments of literary art in this country?—is almost unique in its faculty of revealing profoundness in the ordinary plot of common life. In other words, this woman of genius, while confining herself to pure and humane themes, can find in them such a wealth of color as must be sought by lesser writers ... in blood, atrocities, or historic crises. As a specimen of her wonderful intensity and passionate sympathies, this sustained and wholly noble romance is equal or superior to any previous achievement.[21]

The reviewer asserted in a second review that *Dallas Galbraith* "will remain a classic in American literature."[22] Similar enthusiasm appeared in reviews in *Godey's*, which declared it to be "a powerfully written story" that "entitles [Davis] to a prominent place in the very first rank of American novelists." The *American Literary Gazette* also viewed it as "a novel of unusual power and originality."[23] The novel would continue to be ranked prominently in American literature for the next several decades, including the *Independent*'s assertion in an 1881 review of American literature since the war: *Dallas Galbraith* "is one of the most powerful novels that any American has written."[24]

In November Rebecca made her first major contribution to the cause of asylum reform, a contribution that would significantly impact her career for the next two decades. She and Clarke had made the acquaintance of a patient, Malcolm Maceuen, at Dr. Kirkbride's state institution; they believed Maceuen was sane. Clarke sought publication in the *Galaxy* of a poem written by the patient about his treatment, but since it had been privately printed and distributed, the magazine declined to publish the poem.[25] But the Davises continued to support Maceuen's efforts for release and to indict current asylum practices. Rebecca's first effort was to publish an article in the *New-York Tribune* on "Asylums for the Insane." Citing three recent cases in which men and women had been unjustly imprisoned in asylums, including Dr. Kirkbride's, Davis detailed the wrongs committed against all patients, including those erroneously incarcerated; the profit that was made from such imprisonments by unscrupulous physicians and those building the numerous asylums that were appearing all over the country; and the duping of visitors who were shown only lovely carpeted halls and fountains but not the dark cells and horrific treatment of the patients. She concluded with a call for regulatory laws so that these institutions could not function without oversight.[26] It was Davis at her indignant best, in a voice she employed for numerous reforms throughout her life.

Choosing the *Tribune* under Horace Greeley's editorship as the vehicle to advance the cause meant Davis's article reached a circulation of 200,000. Soon after, she was invited to become one of about twenty editorial correspondents at the *Tribune*. Since her apprentice years with the *Wheeling Intelligencer*, Davis had harbored a strong desire for an editorial voice, and for the next two decades she would be a powerful force in the *Tribune*'s editorial pages. She had met Greeley in his early abolitionist days, and she came to know him well during her tenure at the *Tribune*. "Anecdotes of Horace Greeley's absurd and childish doings circulated widely during his life," she noted years later in her autobiography. "Any vulgar scribbler or cartoonist could point them out with giggles and hisses. Only those who worked under him or knew him well understood how great and sincere was the soul beneath them."[27] Moses Purnell Handy, a widely recognized reporter and later newspaper editor, noted that Davis's "editorials on social topics" for the *Tribune* "made them one of the popular features of the paper."[28]

Within four months, Clarke would become managing editor of the *Philadelphia Inquirer*, the beginning for him of a renowned career as a nationally recognized newspaper editor. With their work on asylum reform through editorials, Rebecca and Clarke shifted their careers dramatically into journalism. It would be Clarke's lifelong focus, while Rebecca would combine journalism and authorship for the remainder of her career. Together, they fought for many reform causes over the decades, crusading to improve conditions for the downtrodden, the oppressed, and the impoverished.

In 1869 Davis began another new avenue of writing—temperance fiction—and in a new periodical, *Hearth and Home*. "The Tembroke Legacy" was serialized from January through mid-April. *Hearth and Home* had begun publishing the previous year and sought a diverse readership of men and women; while it included patterns and recipes like most women's magazines, it also published market information and national and international news. Among its editors at the time Davis became a contributor was Harriet Beecher Stowe. In the late 1860s when Davis penned "The Tembroke Legacy," the temperance movement was just beginning to be revitalized after the war. The movement's leaders continued to view alcoholism as a moral issue and much of the temperance literature of the period looked to instantaneous religious conversion as a solution. The Women's Christian Temperance Union (WCTU) would not be founded until 1873 when it would advocate many forms of women's rights on the basis of the ties between domestic violence and the abuse of alcohol. Davis emphasized her narrative was a "domestic story" but rather than creating abused women, she focused on a female character who was a model of "true womanhood." For Davis, the term included having the courage to work outside the home, helping her husband overcome his addiction and supporting her family. More important to Davis was refuting the religious-conversion idea of temperance with her preference for newer theories from the medical community, certainly influenced by a book she was reading at the time, Dr. Charles Elam's *A Physician's Problems*.

"The Tembroke Legacy" was widely advertised by *Hearth and Home*, promising the usual "genius of Mrs. Davis in its intensity and somberness." The story was published under the name of "Mrs. R. H. Davis, Author of 'Life in the Iron-Mills,' 'Dallas Galbraith,' etc." Reviews of the serial were strongly positive, often describing it as "the best piece of writing" in the periodical.[29] This magazine was an apt venue for Davis's growing interests in temperance and in expanding occupations for women. Yet once again, she had to face an editor who wanted to shape the plot of her story into her own desired conclusions. When Harriet Beecher Stowe received the second installment of the story, she feared it would follow Davis's predilection for tragic endings. In a thirteen-page letter to Davis, Stowe included pages and pages of laments about what alcohol did to families and pleaded with Davis for a family-oriented outcome.[30] Davis did save the main character's life but concluded the essay with an emphasis on alcoholism as a disease, drawing on her reading of the latest medical theories.

In February Davis added another periodical to her publishing repertoire, *Putnam's Magazine*, which had resumed publication for the first time since the late 1850s. Although this latest version of the magazine would only survive for two years, it enticed several notable authors to its pages, including Davis, Elizabeth Stoddard, and William Dean Howells. Edmund Clarence Stedman was editor when Davis published the essay "Men's Rights." Although her name did not appear with the article, she was identified in the index as "Mrs. R. H. Davis" and her name was used when a segment of "Men's Rights" was reprinted in the *Saturday Evening Post*. The *Post* was clearly following Davis's work, and they excerpted her writings fairly often in these years; it would be several decades, however, before she would become a regular contributor for the popular magazine. The Philadelphia *Evening Bulletin* also reprinted a section of "Men's Rights" under her name, terming it a "stinging article" for its strictures on contemporary culture.[31]

It was a particularly important essay, though not in the way Davis intended. Revealing her conservative reaction to the suffrage movement, especially the "rages" of its leaders, the essay was notable for its revelation of the paradoxical struggle Davis, and many women, felt in the postwar resurgence of the women's rights movement. Three months after the essay appeared, the first national women's suffrage association would be founded by Susan B. Anthony and Elizabeth Cady Stanton. Davis had built her career on exposing the wrongs, or "needs" as she preferred, of the impoverished and oppressed; but she also had been educated to a traditional relationship between men and women, a tradition she at once embraced and rejected. Strong-willed, she had always gone her own way, building a career before marriage, not marrying until she was thirty-one, and establishing an egalitarian marriage that was as fulfilling as it was unusual for its time. She also absolutely loved being a mother, and that role became an integral part of her identity.

As "Men's Rights" suggested, she wanted both worlds—for herself and other women—but she did not want that change to come through powerful public outcries for women's rights. Just as she would have preferred slavery to be abolished without a war, so too did she want new kinds of work and opportunities for women to come without war between the sexes. It was the "rages" of women's right leaders that most offended Davis, and she spent pages rationalizing her position. Although she only hinted in this paper at her rejection of woman's suffrage, it was a position she maintained throughout her life, even as she argued for women's rights in other venues. The conflict Davis felt over these issues was repeated in a story she published in *Peterson's* a few months later, "Lois Platner," which was part of the anti-Mormon literature of the period. Davis was not alone in these conflicting attitudes about the rights of various groups. The nation was undergoing an extraordinary shift in values, and even writers such as Davis, who often led the call for change, struggled to accept some of the consequences.

Rebecca and Clarke were continuing their publishing partnership with what was now their usual pattern: Rebecca's entry into a new magazine, followed by Clarke's publication in the periodical shortly thereafter. His serialization in *Putnam's* of "A Stranded Ship" began the month after "Men's Rights" was published. It would be his most popular fictional work. As was common in Rebecca's writings about shipwrecked lives, Clarke traced the consequences of one tragic moment in an otherwise good man's life. As a lawyer, he was able to capture the tense suspense of courtroom scenes and cross-examinations. The reviews for "A Stranded Ship" were mixed, though most were positive. One of the reviews suggested a sense of competition between Clarke and Rebecca, claiming Clarke's romance "will make the laurels on the brow of his gifted wife tremble with apprehension."[32] Nothing could have been further from the truth in their exceptionally supportive relationship. Clarke also followed Rebecca into the pages of *Lippincott's* in May with "Dick Lyle's Fee," a legal narrative.

That spring Clarke essentially ended his legal career when he became managing editor of the prestigious *Philadelphia Inquirer*. As Sam Hudson, a reporter for the *Inquirer*, attested, Clarke was a "brilliant editor" and one "of the pleasantest" to his coworkers.[33] His skill would cast him as one of the foremost newspaper editors of the nineteenth century. This new position also dramatically helped to change the Davises' lives. It moved them ahead financially, to the point that they were living a comfortable life in Philadelphia and would be able to buy the cottage at Point Pleasant that they had rented for several seasons. This change in Clarke's status combined with Rebecca's national reputation as an author also advanced their inclusion in Philadelphia's high society circles; initially introduced into these circles by Charles Peterson, their standing was now based on their own reputations. Although neither of them was particularly interested in society for its wealth and notoriety, it did offer them access to a vast roster of internationally recognized politicians, artists, scientists, and celebrities.

The Stranded Ship was published in book form in June, and Clarke's novella served to peripherally reconnect Rebecca and Louisa May Alcott. Clarke sent the book to Alcott via a mutual friend, reminding her of their brief meeting once at the Fieldses when he had been traveling for work and Rebecca's recollection of Louisa's hospitality many years before. Alcott replied that she had received the book in the morning, sat down on the doorstep, and did not move until she had finished reading it. "The first part, somber & magical," she noted, "reminded me of Hawthorne, & the latter part of Winthrop, for every word *tells* & the story sweeps one along like a fresh sea-breeze." She had passed the novella on to her mother and knew she would like it because "the dear old lady" has a heart "as full of romance as a girl's. Do write some more strong, sweet, breezy tales," she encouraged Clarke, preferring his work to "the unwholesome trash we have had so long." She was surprised that Rebecca remembered her "bit of hospitality" of many years earlier and assured Clarke that using Rebecca's name meant a welcome reception. She invited them and their sons to visit her, asserting she would love to meet their boys.[34]

As always, the summer offered both Rebecca and Clarke time for revitalization, which would be needed in the very active months to come. Formerly Rebecca had used this time to write long letters to friends, but she had so immersed herself in the culture of the Manasquan shore that she did not respond to two letters from Annie Fields until after she returned to Philadelphia in September. She described their life on the shore in an attempt to entice the Fieldses to join them some summer:

> there is [a] pretty farmhouse imbedded in thick woods with some simple nice people who come every year & of whom we can see as much or as little as we choose. That is for eating purposes. We have a little cottage of two rooms. Inside—low beams, white paper a great open chimney and andirons where we can have a log of wood kindled on stormy days: Outside, a low porch with easy chairs a horse-shoe shaped stubble field edged by pine-woods a dead poplar & osprey's nest—& the inlet with the white sailed boats flitting up & down. Mr Davis has a very Dexter of a boat yclept the Vagabond & somebody has painted Vagabond's Rest over the eaves of the cottage. The sea is on the other side from the inlet. We have spent every summer there since we have been married & it seems like home to us. So I welcome you to it."[35]

Writing Annie also allowed Rebecca to continue one of her favorite activities, critiquing recent literature. She had just finished Joaquin Miller's *Joaquin et.al.* (1869) and was not impressed; it was a "noisy effort in which there seems to me as much music or meaning as in a blast from a trombone." She thought it was a "hodge-podge of Alexander Smith, Byron & Swinburne," adding, "I don't know why I vent my disgust on you—only that I just laid the book down. This Ouida school in style and aim is so lame and so wearisome!"[36]

Rebecca then turned to an issue of continued importance to her: temperance. Davis suggested to Annie that Fields and Osgood publish an American edition of Dr. Charles Elam's *A Physician's Problem*, which was published by Macmillan in London. "It is a book which has had a curious fascination for me," she told Annie, "and which I believe would accomplish great good by its mode of meeting the problems of constitutional inebriety. Whether it would be a *selling* book of course I cannot judge. I have written two or three articles for the Tribune trying to have it republished and would push it in that paper and any other way I could. The subject is one that troubles me constantly, it seems so general a disease and the remedy at hand and yet unknown. Ask Mr Fields to think of it. Dr. Elam is a personal friend of Dr. Holmes, I think. He will know all about the book."[37] James Fields agreed with Rebecca's assessment of the book's value, and *A Physician's Problem* was published with an introduction by Holmes; it proved profitable, going into several editions. It was also one of the major sources for Davis's belief that alcoholism was a disease.

The fall saw Clarke working arduously at the *Inquirer*, "still driving" as Rebecca remarked, "with his usual overplus of energy,"[38] while she published "Charity's Secret" and "Captain Jean" in *Peterson's*. Davis always distinguished what she viewed as her serious literature from romances and mysteries written largely for money. In *Peterson's* she made this distinction by the use of different authorial pen names. Romances such as "Charity's Secret" appeared with the authorial identification of the "Author of 'The Second Life'" while more realistic stories or those Davis viewed as more serious literature, such as "Captain Jean," were identified as by the "Author of 'Margret Howth.'" The identification of "Margret Howth" would be dropped in few years in favor of her own name for this class of stories.

In November Davis returned to *Hearth and Home* with a series of articles titled "Open Doors" in which she detailed employment opportunities for women outside the home. She sought to encourage women who were either insufficiently educated for teaching or disinclined to sew for a living, realizing that some women who were near starvation feared having to turn to prostitution to survive. The five-part series suggested opportunities that could be pursued in the city or country. Women need not wait, she argued, for suffrage to clear their path or depend on charity. In the first three "Open Doors" essays that ran through December, Davis revealed her discovery of opportunities when she visited a Quaker-run home that boarded and trained women as nurses for no fee; a well-known herbalist, Mother Kiehl, who explained her own path to growing and selling herbs for a good living; and tuition-free training at the School of Design, with details by a female graduate as to how a student could make additional money while taking courses.

It was about this time that both Rebecca and Clarke became contributing editors to the Philadelphia *Evening Telegraph*. Like Clarke, the managing editor, Watson Ambruster, had earned a law degree at the University of Pennsylvania but had turned to journalism. Initially a reporter for such papers as the *Chicago Republican* and the New York *Citizen*,[39] his liberal politics and earnest belief in the importance and integrity of journalism undoubtedly led the Davises to agree when he sought them as editorial correspondents.[40] Davis was still writing for the *Tribune* as well. Although her editorial articles were unsigned, a short story under her byline appeared on the front page of the *Tribune* on Christmas Day. "A Homely Story of Home" was a typical Christmas story about finding faith and a better life, but with Davis's insistence on addressing the working classes, an embittered washerwoman was the protagonist. The story's byline, for the first time, publicly associated Davis and the *Tribune*.

In the winter of 1869/70, the Davises moved into the first home they owned. The three-story, brick Greek Revival row house, located at 230 South Twenty-first Street, would be their home for the remainder of their lives. It had white stone steps and trim and, to Rebecca's joy, a deep backyard where the Davises maintained a large garden and planted an abundance of trees and flowers. It was nearer the office Clarke maintained at 607 Sansome Street and not far from the offices of the *Inquirer*. They were also only three blocks from the prestigious Rittenhouse Square, and the park there was the perfect place for rambunctious boys to play. Rebecca and Clarke did not force their children into adult behavior, as was the custom in middle and upper-class homes of the time. They allowed Dick and Charley to explore, run, play, climb, and often joined the boys in their spirited play. The new house was also an easy walk to the Episcopal Academy that Clarke had attended and where they planned to send their sons in a few years.

The family was now closer to the cultural center of the city as well, with the South Broad Street, Walnut Street, and Chestnut Street Theatres and the Academy of Music readily accessible. Dick and Charley decorated their new rooms with cabinet photographs of famous actors and actresses, many of whom were family friends. The boys liked to perform melodramas on rainy days when they were housebound, and Rebecca noted that Dick always cast himself as the hero who defeated Charley, the villain.[41]

In mid-January Rebecca learned that Ralph Waldo Emerson would be coming to Philadelphia the following month to present a lecture at the Academy of Music. She wrote immediately, inviting him to stay with her and Clarke while he was in the city. He declined, as he did several other friends' invitations, preferring to reside in a hotel. It was common practice for the Davises to invite visiting dignitaries—literary, theatrical, and political—to stay with them; the invitations were regularly accepted, and their home on Twenty-first Street quickly became known as a haven for artists in Philadelphia. Visiting dignitaries and members of the literary and theatrical worlds could often be found at the Davis home in the evenings, as it came to constitute one of the most notable literary salons in the city. Rebecca, Clarke, and the boys called it the "Centre of the Universe," and to them and their never-ending guests, that is what it remained throughout their lives. As an adult, Charles recalled the "hard endeavor and unusual sacrifice" his parents made to purchase the home and fill it "not only [with] the comforts and the beautiful inanimate things of life, but to create an atmosphere which would prove a constant help to those who lived under its roof."[42]

Dick and Charley were now at an age when they loved stories about nature and stories of adventure, especially those that included young boys. Sophisticated children's periodicals were proliferating in the postwar environment, and Rebecca began another new stage of her writing career, turning to children's literature. It was a turn she would embrace for the remaining thirty-five years of her career, and the last story she published before her death would be a children's story for *St. Nicholas*. More than one hundred children's or young adult stories would appear under her name prior to that final entry.

She began this phase of her career by publishing "Old Thorny" in *Our Young Folks*. The magazine was published by Fields and Osgood, offering Davis a marginal reconnection to James T. Fields. The editors, John Townsend Trowbridge and Lucy Larcom, were authors themselves; Trowbridge began his career with an antislavery novel and Larcom with writings for the *Lowell Offering*. The editors were able to draw notable authors to the magazine, including Davis, Elizabeth Stuart Phelps, and Edward Everett Hale. Davis's entry into children's literature was anything but conventional. The main characters of "Old Thorny" were West Indian birds, Senor and Senora Ruta Max, and their young ones who lived in a mill town. In this cold, sooty environment, they often talked of the grand balls they had attended at home, and Senor Max related the story of his child, White Wing, meeting Old Thorny, a talking bush. It was the beginning of many wonderfully imaginative stories as well as historical narratives Davis wrote for children.

The days when Davis aligned herself with one periodical were long over. She continued in the early months of 1870 to publish in *Peterson's*, *Hearth and Home*, and *Putnam's*, wrote editorials for the *New-York Tribune*, and agreed to publish in Horace Elisha Scudder's *Riverside Magazine for Young People* with "The Shan Van Voght," a historical study of the conflict between the English and Irish. Rebecca had become adept at balancing home and work, though it was easier when Clarke was home in the evenings to help with the boys. On February 2, for instance, she noted in her diary that he had surprised her by coming home early, which allowed her to finish a story she was working on and then to enjoy her time with the family afterward and be in bed by ten o'clock.[43] Her pattern of writing in the evening as well as during the day continued through the years when her children were young.

As prolific as Davis was in these months, she and Clarke still attempted to find time to be together, and this year they romantically planned an evening at the opera for Valentine's Day. When the day turned damp and rainy, however, Rebecca persuaded Clarke to spend the night at home, and they celebrated the day with the boys.[44]

In spite of having two young children, Rebecca still made time as well for charitable work with some of the Quaker activists in Philadelphia, especially Mary Grew and Margaret Burleigh, whom she had become acquainted with when she first arrived in Philadelphia and learned of their antislavery activities. Rebecca was with Grew and Burleigh in early February when they received news that the Fifteenth Amendment had been ratified. Years later Rebecca still recalled the moment they heard the news: "The hope of their lives was accomplished. But they were silent for a long time. 'What will thee and I do now?' one said to the other drearily. 'There is prison reform? Or we might stir up women to vote?' They could hardly wait until the next day to begin."[45]

Another friendship shaped Davis's return to the pages of the *Galaxy*. She knew through her continuing friendship with William Church that the brothers were struggling financially and in repeated arguments with the publisher Sheldon and Company over contract issues. Several years earlier the brothers had entered into a contract that was decidedly in the publisher's favor, and they tried at this time to abrogate the contract, to no avail.[46] Undoubtedly in an effort to help, she returned to the *Galaxy* with two stories, "A November Afternoon" and "Hand to Hand." The former presented fictionally the arguments of the "Open Doors" series, and "Hand to Hand" was the first of several stories Davis would write about contemporary journalism. "Hand to Hand" blended journalism, religion, and crime—themes that served as daily fodder for the newspapers themselves. The story was very popular and was reprinted several times over the next two decades. Davis was also writing for *Lippincott's*, where she now published annually. "Leonard Heath's Fortune" was a historical narrative but captured the realities of life in a metropolis: "the contract-houses, in the middle of the network of sewers and gas-pipes, with butcher and baker and friend and critic, pushing in on every side of Turner's Lane."[47] This story also would be reprinted several times between 1870 and 1890.

Most of Rebecca's attention in the spring of 1870, however, was devoted to her ongoing concerns about the need for asylum reform. In many ways, a significant portion of Davis's writings fit the category of "investigative fiction," beginning with "Life in the Iron-Mills" and *Margret Howth*, a form of fiction that explained her natural draw to journalism.[48] It was through asylum reform that she would next offer an important contribution to investigative fiction. Nearly 45,000 Americans had been institutionalized by 1870.[49] After the publication of Clarke's "A Modern Lettre de Cachet," the Pennsylvania legislature had passed an act that only surviving guardians could commit a person to an asylum; but if the guardian was deceased or absent, friends or relatives could commit the individual if they had the signature of one or two *reputable* doctors, depending on the state.[50] The system was widely abused, however, and Davis intended to reach the widest possible audience by publishing a novel on the theme to draw support for legislative action. As she told Paul Hamilton Hayne, her novel had been delayed because of the "bitter battle" that followed the publication of "A Modern Lettre," proudly adding that Clarke had fought the battle "single-handed through press and legislature" against "virulent opposition."[51] It was not quite single-handed, since Davis had written on the subject for the *Tribune* where she reached a far wider audience than the *Atlantic* article, but Clarke's endeavors were indeed significant.

In May Davis serialized in *Peterson's* her political novel calling for asylum reform, "Put Out of the Way." By publishing the novel in *Peterson's*, Davis was assured of a readership of nearly 150,000 as opposed to the 30,000 to 50,000 readers of most high literary magazines. The novel pushed beyond the well-appointed lobbies of the asylum, which were the only areas most visitors saw, into its depths of cruelty and depravation as it explicated the legal and punitive horrors faced by a sane man who was committed so his relatives could gain access to his wealth. Asylum reform would remain an issue to which both Rebecca and Clarke were dedicated; she would publish other stories on the subject, while Clarke continued his legislative campaign.

It was May before Rebecca responded to Annie Fields's wedding anniversary letter, sent in March. Even then Annie had questioned Rebecca's silence. Rebecca's apology insisted on the difficulty of writing letters when one writes for a living. "If pen and ink were *your* tools, through which you uttered all the something or nothing that was in you," she tried to explain, "you would wish your friends who wrote to you and suffer *you* to stretch out dumb hands of greeting to them in some higher sort of intimacy than scribbling—Seriously, I do grow so weary of writing that to those I love (if I cannot talk to them) I feel as if absolute silence was the freest expression. I'm afraid you will think my excuse overstrained—But it is a real feeling with me." The explanation did little to bridge the growing distance between the two women, but Rebecca tried to personalize the letter by sharing with Annie her love of gardening and the pleasure she took in having "a good deal of ground—for town" in which she could plant her favorite flowers; "I have never had such a chance to root in the earth, since I was married."[52]

Knowing James Fields had been publicly chastised by Gail Hamilton for his unequal treatment of female authors,[53] Rebecca had contacted him, offering to write an article for the *Atlantic*. She told Annie she intended to start the article, apparently a commentary on Catholicism, the following week, but she professed to feeling a bit "Cowardly" about undertaking the subject: "The Catholic system is such a mail-proof coat of armour . . . and I am growing old—which means with most of us that we are more apt to shiver a lance against dread evils or pour oil into our brother's wounds. Cui bono—is oftenest our motto after thirty—But as to the article I hope to send it soon and hope our good friend 'J.T.F.' will like it. *He* is the Atlantic editor for me."[54] Her offer of support was a kind gesture, but no such article ever appeared.[55]

Instead Davis published another story, "Two Women," with the *Galaxy* in June. The tale was notable for the depiction of a woman who had cross-dressed as a man in order to spy for the Confederacy. Davis continued her attention to gender fluidity in "A Hundred Years Ago" for the *Riverside Magazine*. Willy Lewis is "so like a girl" with his pretty face, blue eyes, and yellow hair that men at the tavern call out "Hi, Miss Molly!" whenever he passes, using the common nineteenth-century epithet for homosexuals. It was a surprising choice for a young adult magazine. The story did not embrace homosexuality, nor did it suggest that Willy's identity should be altered.[56]

Near the end of June, Rebecca was shocked to receive word that her youngest brother Henry had died. Barely thirty years old, Henry had gone to Louisville, Kentucky, on business when he became seriously ill and telegraphed his brother Wilse for aid. Wilse left immediately and was able to see Henry briefly before he died. Telegrams were then sent to the rest of the family on June 21 while Wilse prepared to bring his brother's body home. It was a tragic role Wilse would have to undertake several times for his siblings. Henry was buried in the Washington Cemetery next to his father.[57] His grave marker was etched with the same "Sacred to the Memory Of" heading as his father's tombstone. Unlike any of the other Harding headstones, however, Henry's had a towering spire atop, perhaps because his youth necessitated special recognition.

Rebecca was devastated by the loss, as she revealed in a letter to Annie Fields. Charles Dickens had also died recently, and in the August issue of the *Atlantic,* James Fields published an essay on his memories of Dickens. When the Davises received their copy in mid-July,[58] Rebecca was prompted to write to Annie, "thank your good husband for me for one of the sincerest pleasures I have enjoyed this many a day." The tribute, she felt, captured Fields's genuine admiration, "but it is the power by which in these simple facts he places Dickens before us who did not know him—genial and loveable—*as strongly as any of the great master's own work could do.*" Then she partially revealed her own loss to Annie: "I have had a great sorrow since I wrote to you last—of which I cannot yet brave to speak. I have not been able to write cheerfully to any one and gloomy letters are so tiring." Rebecca's emotionalism was evident in her signature, "My dear friend—yours always."[59]

The Davises were leaving in a couple of days after this letter was written for Point Pleasant. Dick and Charley had been sent ahead with their nurse to give Rebecca time to grieve without disturbing the boys. Traveling to the shore was still complicated in these years, hardly something that a grieving person could easily face, but it had become routine by now to take the steam ferry from Philadelphia to Camden and board a train there that would take them as far as Jamesburg. At this small town they changed to another train, the Agricultural Railway, that traveled into Freehold. From there, they booked passage by stage that took them over an old plank road to their destination.[60] It was one thing for Rebecca and the boys to make the trip in July and return in September, but Clarke made the trip weekly since he needed to be in the *Inquirer* office several days a week even during the summer.

The time at Point Pleasant was exactly what Rebecca needed this summer to recover. Often the Davis family would be joined by others staying at the Curtis

House or nearby as they rode in farm carts along the sandy road to the beach. They spent the days swimming in the ocean, rowing, playing croquet, reading, and, for Rebecca, writing. The concern Rebecca had felt in earlier years about members of the community who wanted to see Manasquan turned into a major resort area was already becoming a reality. This year Captain John Arnold, a retired seaman and the major proponent of creating Point Pleasant as a resort, was building a roadway to the ocean.[61]

Nonetheless, the Davises determined to buy the cottage in which they had spent every summer since 1863. Clarke used his carpentry skills to add two bedrooms, creating a two-story cottage to accommodate their growing family. The Davises took their meals at the Curtis House, starting with breakfast around seven in the morning, and then they spent the day in constant activity until they dropped, exhausted, into their beds at night.[62] It was a wonderful change for Rebecca and Clarke from their over-scheduled lives in Philadelphia, and an especially healthy and adventurous time for two young boys. In spite of traveling between Philadelphia and Point Pleasant, these summer days were restorative for Clarke as well. Rebecca recorded in her diary the joy of being at the shore and their ability to capture romantic moments together, noting Clarke had been on the water all day and she joined him that evening on "the inlet to see the moonlight on the water. A good happy day."[63]

The return to Philadelphia in the early fall meant a significant increase in productivity for Rebecca. In rapid succession she published "A Heroine" in *Peterson's* and serialized "Natasqua" in *Scribner's Monthly Magazine*. "Natasqua" appeared in the inaugural issues of the new publication, which was edited by Dr. Josiah Gilbert Holland. Davis would become a frequent contributor over the magazine's decade-long existence. *Scribner's* merged both *Putnam's Magazine* and *Hours at Home* into its pages and prominently employed Davis's name in its announcements of the new periodical.[64]

"Natasqua" was a well-written story, rich in detail of the seafaring life and environment of the coast, and it satirized the capitalist as well as the state of journalism. Yet the novella received almost no critical attention. Perhaps this was because *Scribner's* was a new, untested periodical, competing with many others, but "Natasqua" was the first story in a long time that Davis had concluded without a romantic resolution. The tragedy of the conclusion may not have appealed to the reviewers of 1870, but by the 1880s and into the twentieth century when tragedy and realism were again more popular, "Natasqua" would be remarked upon as an important contribution to *Scribner's* success and noted for its strong storytelling. At this time, reports also began to emerge in newspapers and magazines that Davis was an editorial contributor to the *New-York Tribune*. Some notices of the fact were brief, "Mrs. Rebecca Harding Davis writes some of the editorials of the Tribune," but word of the significance of her contributions would soon circulate even more widely,[65] and she would become recognized as one of the journalists who helped open doors for women at national newspapers.[66]

Surprising news arrived at the end of the year: James Fields announced his retirement as editor of the *Atlantic Monthly* and William Dean Howells as his successor. Rebecca wrote to Annie, adding best wishes to James and hoping retirement would mean they could finally visit the Davises in Philadelphia. Fields's retirement marked the end of an era in publishing, one that embraced the gentleman publisher, a style of editorship that had faded already from most periodicals. Yet it was a model Davis appreciated in many ways, and she would nurture friendships with many subsequent editors. The Davises and Fieldses would remain friendly, the Fieldses would finally return to Philadelphia for a visit, and all would remain quite cordial. But cordiality was not the same as the deep friendship they had once shared, and Davis's signature for her congratulatory letter was revealing—"Always cordially yours."[67]

Chapter 6

A Conservative Progressive (1871–1875)

The early 1870s were a volatile period in Philadelphia. After wresting control from the conservative Democrat William McMullen, Republican Mayor William Stokley's law-and-order leadership sought to enact his goals of racial equality and centralized government. The number of police officers was increased to curtail gangs that had taken over the streets of the city, and Stokley installed a city-run fire department in place of volunteer fire companies that were the vehicles for political cronyism. The mayor proclaimed central control of the police, fire fighters, and the judicial system was essential to create a safe city environment. Reactions to his new policies, however, led to violence and rioting prior to the October 1871 city elections. An African American man, Jacob Gordon, was killed on October 9 for no reason other than his race, and the next night a meeting of African American and Euro-American Republicans at Union Hall was shut down by a rock-throwing mob still opposed to the political mixing of the races. Prejudice against African Americans and the Irish was at its greatest since before the war.[1]

As a supporter of Radical Republicanism and a voice for the national responsibility of providing greater opportunities for African Americans, Davis seemed to be an author who could enter into this period of turmoil with a vision for right actions, class advancements for all citizens, and racial tolerance. Her writings of this period did examine class inequalities, race, disabilities, history as a means of understanding the present, and women's roles in society; yet they also exposed her own conflicted attitudes on many of these issues.

In the spring of 1871, Davis expanded the repertoire of periodicals in which she published with her first contribution to the Boston-based *Youth's Companion*, the leading young adult and family magazine of the era. Her writings for *Youth's Companion* evidenced a disparate collection of progressive ideas and some of the best children's literature of the period, yet also some that were laced with blatant racism. As editor, Daniel S. Ford had imaginatively marketed the magazine and increased its circulation. By joining the rank of *Youth's Companion*'s regular monthly contributors, Davis's stories reached the widest readership of any magazine for which she was writing in the 1870s, and Ford drew many other well-known writers to the magazine at this time, including Harriet Beecher Stowe, Grace Greenwood, Edward Everett Hale, Louise Chandler Moulton, and Louisa May Alcott. After publishing one story in *Peterson's* in January, Davis concentrated for the next eleven months primarily on writing children's stories.

With two young boys who loved to be read bedtime stories, she had a ready audience for initial responses to her children's fiction. Often in the first person, these stories, like her adult fiction, were notable for the effective use of dialect to signify the educational, racial, ethic, and class variations of characters. Historical settings were popular in these stories—from the War of 1812 in "Senor" to the Civil War in "Hard Tack"—and they expanded the historical narratives that would be a major marker of Davis's writings. As requisite with children's literature, the stories were moral tales about brotherly love, the dangers of bragging, the importance of taking advantage of opportunities to advance oneself while continuing to help others, the consequences of teasing a "simple-minded" boy, and city boys who visited rural cousins and learned about outdoor life. As with her adult literature, physicians played a large role in the stories as community leaders and especially as individuals who could offer young men from rural areas or the shore an opportunity for a better life as apprentices; "shore stories" again abounded, such as "Lost and Found" and "Senor." Characters recurred as well, including the Widow Matmoth and her sons in "The Deacon's Surprise" and "Lost and Found."

A series of stories Davis published this year about Charley Gray and his pet monkey, Jack, however, were racially charged. Full of adventures and wild disruptions caused by Jack at home, at parties, and even at a traveling "freak show," the stories appealed to young boys of her sons' ages. Yet this set of stories inscribed racial stereotypes that had not appeared for some time in her adult fiction. Davis's depictions of race and analyses of racial issues in these years were far more problematic in terms of African Americans than any other race or ethnicity. In the Charley Gray stories, the Gray family's servant, Pete, an African American child whose race is identified through his dialect, played with Charley and his friends. But it was he who called the monkey a "mizzabel little niggah"—sometimes with pride, when referencing Jack's adept actions, and at other times with frustration as Jack caused havoc. Pete also referred to "Master Charley" and adult white males as "massah."[2]

It was not only this series that presented such ideas. In another comic story, "How Jack Went Tiger-Hunting," young Jack Leigh has been reading the work of anthropologist Paul Belloni du Chaillu, whose books had appeared in the US in the1860s and who had lectured recently in New York, London, and Paris. du Chaillu was a frequent visitor to Philadelphia, and Davis knew him personally. The year before, she had read to her boys sections of the anthropologist's books alongside *Alice in Wonderland*.[3] du Chaillu was instrumental in popularizing the dehumanizing belief in the similarity of Africans and gorillas. In Davis's story, Jack decided he would be a better hunter with du Chaillu than "those negroes" who were "poor stuff for hunters."[4] The laugh was on Jack, however, for when a tiger escaped a traveling show, he thought he had corralled it in his backyard—only to learn he has captured the neighbor's dog. If he proved a worse hunter than "those negroes" who traveled with du Chaillu, the story's racial markers were unambiguous.

Accepted by *Youth's Companion* and its large readership, Davis's stories that implied an alliance between primates and Africans reflected the extraordinary level of racism still prevalent in 1870s America. That Davis would replicate those values for the next generation, however, was in direct contrast to the more progressive attitudes she rendered in her writings for adults. Her disparate attitudes toward race were evident when the Charley Gray stories were followed by a much more progressive trend in her writing through what was often a highly racialized cultural code: "blood." In her annual Christmas story, "The Mountain Shanty," in *Hearth and Home*, for example, Davis traced the life of an arrogant and wealthy young man who publicly belittled his servants and who thought they were too ignorant to feel humiliated. The story's moral was uttered by his mother who argued that whites and blacks were the same—"of one blood."[5] As significant as the "one-blood" argument was during Reconstruction (and would continue to be, as Pauline Hopkins demonstrated at the turn of the century), the simultaneous publication of these works revealed Davis's ongoing struggle with racial equality.

Davis focused a series of stories for adults on class differences that were far more progressive in content. Beginning in April with "Compensation," one of many two-contrasting-women stories for *Peterson's*, she presented a psychological study of a well-to-do, pampered woman who meets her double, her "shadow," in the figure of a wretchedly poor woman. "The Pepper-Pot Woman" published in *Scribner's Monthly* in 1874, captured Davis's interest in the working street-people of Philadelphia and included a biting class analysis through the lens of upper-class society and American art. Turning to nonfiction, Davis's

"Two Women" for the *Independent* in 1875 examined the different attitudes of society toward the lady of New England birth who was down on her luck and forced to live in poor quarters versus the huckster woman who lived next door but was of no interest to society. For the former, "the Christian Church finds a place and work. But what of the other? She is the type of a class who stand in every great city, not avowedly criminal, but suspected, tainted—like lepers, without the gate. Yet it was a woman of her kin . . . whom the Master of us all chose first to bless with the certainty of eternal life."[6] Analyses of class differences and class biases would continue to be a vital aspect of Davis's repertoire throughout her career.

At this time Rebecca and Clarke were trying to keep family-only holidays whenever possible, and on April 1 they spent the day on a family outing, after which they returned home to be entertained by a play the boys performed. Clarke brought candy, and "we had such a fun happy time," Rebecca confided to her diary. After the boys were put to bed, she and Clarke played backgammon, their new favorite game for the evenings.[7] In May Mrs. Cyrus Dickson and her daughter visited from Baltimore, staying overnight, which allowed Rebecca to catch up with her friends from their Wheeling days.

In the summer of 1871, the Davises plans included a special bonus: her twenty-nine-year-old sister Emilie married the Washington, Pennsylvania, lawyer John L. Gow, Jr. on July 7. Gow was a member of a leading family in their community. His father was a judge, a position to which John had also ascended. Like Rebecca, Emilie married late but established an enduring marriage. After attending the wedding in Washington, Rebecca and family settled in at Point Pleasant for the summer. While there she published another story for *Peterson's*. Although seemingly on a mundane subject, "How We Spent the Summer" was an avenue for examining changing class structures in America. By the 1870s a new employment trend of offering middle-class workers one week's vacation was spreading rapidly, and Davis supported the trend. More affordable travel due to the increase in railroads had also changed attitudes about labor. Many once-exclusive summer resorts were increasingly populated with middle-class vacationers.[8] As Davis observed in this story, the pattern quickly devolved into the middle-class attempting to emulate the wealthy families at the resorts, creating desires for fashion and an expensive way of life that they carried back to their city lives.

Several years earlier in "The Clergyman's Wife," Davis had used the format of a journal kept by a distraught woman to reveal her inner thoughts about her family and her own needs. Replicated in "How We Spent the Summer," journal entries revealed the woman's desire for a summer out of the sweltering city, but the resorts and popular farmhouse vacations were far beyond the means of her family. Davis employed the character of a physician to lend authority to the idea of the health and economic benefits of camping at the shore: "I wish there was some way for me to make this [possibility] known to the thousands of poor men and women sitting in the city, for whom a week or two of rest and return to the simple out-door life would give strength and courage for a year of drudgery."[9] Although the Davises could now afford to go to one of the fashionable resorts, they had grown to love the Manasquan area and its people, and they would continue to summer there for many years.

In the fall, Rebecca burned through ideas for stories. By December she had produced several new works. In addition to *Youth's Companion* pieces, she published "A Thanksgiving Story" in the *Massachusetts Ploughman*. In spite of its agricultural title, this Boston periodical published by George Noyes attracted many well-known writers in the mid-nineteenth century, publishing both original works and reprints. Davis's story was simultaneously published as "The Conductor's Story" in *Hearth and Home*, and, as was common practice, it was reprinted by several newspapers, including the *Hartford Courant* and the *New-Hampshire Patriot*.[10] Although such reprints popularized Davis's work even further, there was no compensation to the author for the use of her work beyond the initial publication, a practice that would further writers' interest in changing copyright laws in the coming years.

It was at this time that Davis also returned to the issue of Native American rights with a new zeal, and her major contributions to this subject were far more progressive than some of her commentaries about African Americans in these years. In March, the US government had passed the Indian Appropriation Act. Not only did the Act deny sovereignty to any tribal society, regardless of previous treaties designated as between nations, it cast every individual Native American as a "ward" of the federal government. The combined language ensured greater access to tribal lands by the federal government as it served to infantilize all Native Americans.

In response, Davis published "Barred Acres—The Doctor's Story" in *Peterson's* at the end of the year. Presented as a frame-narrative ghost story that also critiqued the genre, the outer frame of "Barred Acres" was narrated by a physician and broadly lamented the loss of much western folklore: "there may yet be found remnants of strange traditions and superstitions, which have never found their way into books, but which in any other country would have been carefully guarded as folk-lore, out of which the germs of national creeds and customs might be defined. Many of the superstitions, in their relentless fatalism, betray their Indian origin."[11] The inner narrative was related by a local woman who recalled part of the lore that might tragically be lost. It was the tale of a chief named Gray Wolf and his family who had been murdered by a white family, the Cresaps, so they could usurp his land. The Cresaps and anyone else who has tried subsequently to live on the land had died or simply disappeared without a trace. "The Gray Wolf," the story concluded, "still keeps his land undisturbed."[12] Returning to the outer frame, a curmudgeonly old judge insists the story is a tale of "Indian vengeance," but the narrator counters this attitude, defining the story as a cautionary tale against the usurpation of Native lands. This was Davis at her best in exposing injustice through fiction.

In early 1872, Davis continued her prolific production schedule. In January her works appeared in *Peterson's*, *Youth's Companion*, and *Our Young Folk*. The children's stories Davis published in these months dissuaded dreaming of fanciful lives ("Pot of Gold") and imitating fashionable society ("The Boy Who Was Himself") in favor of hard work and being one's best self. The latter was Davis's last publication in *Our Young Folk*. Though the magazine would continue publication through 1873, she preferred *Youth's Companion* both for its exceptional circulation and its better pay. In 1874, *Our Young Folk* would merge with *St. Nicholas*, which would become another of Davis's favorite places to publish her children's literature.

Her adult literature turned to a very different issue at this time. "The Other Side" for *Peterson's* was fictional, but it addressed an issue Rebecca knew about all too well. In the story, a young family was troubled by the husband's frequent bouts of depression, even though he has succeeded in his profession after years of hard work. Rebecca had long faced the dilemma of Clarke's chronic depression. Even though Clarke was a kind and gentle man with many talents and a strong moral compass, as well as decidedly successful in his profession, he nonetheless was prone to severe depressions, as their eldest child would also eventually be. The wife in "The Other Side" struggled with how to help her husband through these periods: "She had never given up so long as there was any tangible trouble to fight—poverty, or debt, or sickness. But this formless chimera . . . what was she to do with that?"[13] Although Rebecca could craft characters who confronted the basis of the husband's depression and overcame it, no such solution was available to her family. It was a struggle the Davises faced throughout their marriage.

During these years, the Davises were actively continuing their support of the Academy of Music, both for its musical contributions to the city and for its support of lectures by leading speakers of the day. Thomas Burnett Pugh, a publisher and bookseller in Philadelphia known for his ardent abolitionist stance in earlier years, had founded the "Star Course" at the Academy in 1870. This annual lecture had quickly become the leading intellectual event in Philadelphia[14] and was the series through which Emerson had presented his lecture the previous year. The Davises were delighted when James T. Fields was selected as speaker for the 1872 lecture in April. After retiring as an editor, lecturing offered Fields a new outlet, and the Davises were likely responsible for suggesting him for the Academy of Music series.

With the announcement of his selection in February, Rebecca wrote to Annie with great enthusiasm:

> Of course you will come and of course you will both come to us during your stay. We are living downtown now where Mr Fields will be *convenient* to Mr Pugh . . . and you and I can go back to the old friendship or begin a new one on a new basis. You shall be just as free to come and go as in a hotel, for you will soon find that we live in such a pic-nicy way that *irregularity* is the normal condition. I tell you this because I know men who have business to attend to—dislike to be cramped by visiting in a private house. Mr Davis says tell them it is settled for them. All you have to do is to write that you think it is well settled.

She was excited that Annie would finally see her boys and concluded her letter with a heartfelt desire to see her once-special friend, "Say you will come dear Annie and afterward you will always think of this house as one of your many houses—."[15]

Rebecca assumed Annie would be as excited to meet again as she was, yet a month later no reply had been received. Rebecca wrote again: "Only a line to ask you *when* you are coming? Every day when Clarke comes home I look for the letter to say you will be here. . . . I can give you a real summer welcome in more ways than from our hearts." Though it was February, they had the doors open for a surprisingly spring-like day, and it heartened Rebecca's sense of Annie's visit, "Oh so much I have to say when you do come." Although she only hinted, "I have grown so restless lately that all the time I must be walking or writing to hold myself down so I'm afraid I will talk to you after the manner of an escape of steam," the real news was that Rebecca was pregnant with the Davises' third child. She ended her letter with "love to Mr Fields" and "au revoir I hope" to Annie.[16]

Her disappointment was palpable, therefore, when she finally received word from Annie that they had decided to stay in a hotel. The Fieldses had several friends in the area, and this was probably the most diplomatic choice, but it had taken Annie nearly six weeks to inform Rebecca of their decision, and the delay felt like neglect. In the interim Annie had sent a book to Rebecca, who replied immediately with a note of thanks. When the note was not delivered by the carrier company, it seemed that Rebecca had been negligent of Annie's gesture. Rebecca's frustration with the entire situation burst forth for a moment—"Your carrier must be stupid not to know where you live"—but she shifted tone, adding, "I am so sorry if you thought me careless to any sign of affection from you." She tried to turn to brighter issues, talking about a short trip to the shore the family had taken due to the uncommonly warm weather,

> We & the boys—all three, that is and I—have just been having a holyday at the sea shore and such a holyday! It only lasted four days, but it was so bright and windy and full of fun and foolishness and woodfires, and hungry glorious dinners—that it was worth all the summer. We all send our love to you and the coming man whose praises the Inquirer ceaseth not to sound, with every morning's note.[17]

As implied, Clarke had widely promoted James's lecture in his newspaper.

Rebecca's disappointment in Annie's response resulted in a restless energy that she used to enact a period of great productivity with an emphasis on major cultural issues of the period. In April alone, she published "A Story of a Shadow" in the *Galaxy*, "Jack Graham" and "Jenny's Hero" in *Youth's Companion*, and penned "Gertrude" for a New York benefit. Returning to the *Galaxy* after another two-year gap allowed Davis to write again the long short stories she preferred, and "A Story of a Shadow" was a sophisticated and nuanced example. Unlike Davis's earlier stories about Spiritualism, this one embraced the possibilities of "shadows" that impact people's lives. It also explored several cultural issues of importance to Davis—the struggles of alcoholism, reflections on American nervousness, aiding convicts' reentry into society, the scheming of party politics, and the idea that economic difference does not signify a difference in human beings. It was a rich story that captured the complexities of US society in the 1870s. "Jack Graham" for *Youth's Companion* was a temperance story. Unlike in "The Tembroke Legacy" in "A Story of a Shadow," however, there was no redemption. The conclusion indicted social drinking as the alcoholic's downfall.

Prison reform again emerged as a theme in "Jenny's Hero." The late 1860s had seen a resurgence of interest in prison reform, largely due to Theodore Dwight and Enoch Wines' study of the overcrowding of prisons nationwide, which had led to calls for reform, and a number of women were instrumental in founding the American Prison Association (APA) in 1870 with the goal of penal reform. The APA's Declaration of Principles identified its primary purpose as the moral regeneration of convicts so they could return to society as productive citizens.[18] It was a philosophy Davis clearly embraced through her fiction. She was also becoming more active in local benefits, albeit active through her pen since she still abhorred joining organizations. In April 1872, New York supporters of homeopathy held a benefit for the Homoeopathic Surgical Hospital, which included printing *The Similibus*, an eight-page pamphlet of advertisers' endorsements, identification of society women and physicians' wives who were hosting tables at the fair, and physicians' testimonials. Its literary content was poetry, poetical translations, and excerpts from fiction. Davis's "Gertrude" was the only original story in the pamphlet. It examined the life of the title character, Gertrude, Hortense de Beauharnais's classmate who was stricken with a disease that left her "horribly, hopelessly deformed"; in spite of the loss of her lover, Gertrude educated herself, becomes the host of a Paris salon, and is known always to attend to others' ailments.[19]

Davis continued to write editorials for the *Tribune* as well; although the editorials were unsigned, items began appearing in newspapers and magazines about her role on the newspaper. As a reporter for the *Lowell Daily Citizen and News* remarked, with Horace Greeley's withdrawal "from the control of the *Tribune*, it may well be considered as under the immediate direction of young persons. Whitelaw Reid, the managing editor; John R. G. Hassard, John Hay, Noah Brooks, Lucia Gilbert Runkle, Rebecca Harding Davis, all editorial writers; . . . and many others who contribute regularly to the columns of that journal range from thirty to forty."[20] At forty, Davis was remarkably accomplished: a nationally recognized author and journalist, a rising figure in Philadelphia's cultural life, successful in her marriage, the mother of two healthy and happy boys, and three months' pregnant with her third child.

The Davises attended James Fields' lecture at the Academy of Music, but as matters finally evolved, Annie did not come to Philadelphia. Although Rebecca was having "sick headaches," she wrote to Annie in May to acknowledge how much they had enjoyed James's visit. She made only a gesture toward his invitation to visit them in Boston, "I *would* like to see Boston again as I would like to go to a thousand places, but I am firmly rooted in Philadelphia & likely to remain so for years to come as if I were a sponge or oyster on a rock." She also mentioned her friendship with Elizabeth Stuart Phelps and concluded with her appreciation of James's lecture, "A Plea for Cheerfulness," signing off, "Yours always."[21] Both women's refusal to travel to see the other certainly shaped this breach in what had been a longstanding friendship, but in reality two factors were already undermining it—Annie's typical adoration and then abandonment of friends, and Rebecca's very different life in Philadelphia with children.

Davis continued her productivity in the months leading up to the family's departure for their annual trip to the shore. In May she published another caustic critique of journalism, "In the Chronicle Office," in *Peterson's*, and in July *Lippincott's* published one of her most popular stories, "Balacchi Brothers," an unusual version of Davis's "one-blood" stories.[22] The inner story also detailed George Balacchi's loss of a leg in a circus accident and his strength in adapting to his disability. "Balacchi Brothers" would be reprinted numerous times in the nineteenth and early twentieth centuries in collections of national and international "best works."[23]

The representation of individuals with disabilities was becoming a touchstone of Davis's literary repertoire. From "Life in the Iron-Mills" to "Balacchi Brothers" and throughout her career, she employed the motif of disability to reflect Americans' attitudes toward anyone who was supposedly "different." "A Thanksgiving" (*Youth's Companion*, 1873), for instance, addressed blindness, while "Tom Gillet's Fortune" (*Peterson's*, 1873) lauded the title character for abandoning his capitalistic pursuit of wealth through speculation in order to focus on his creative abilities. When he designed a chair that offered greater comfort for invalids, his actions were recognized for constituting true productivity. In adult and children's literature, Davis would continue to explore the implications of national responses to disabled people as a means of defining the American character itself.

Beginning in July, Davis also published a serial, "A Wife, Yet Not a Wife," in *Peterson's* in which a woman married a man, knowing his supposedly dead wife was still alive. In stories like "The Mountain Shanty" and this one, Davis abandoned the romantic endings with which she had concluded many stories in recent years, returning to stark studies of human nature that had marked her earliest fiction.

At the same time, the Harding family was delighted to learn that thirty-seven-year-old Hugh Wilson Harding had been appointed Professor of Physics and Mechanics at Lehigh University. Wilse would begin his new position in the fall, and he would remain at Lehigh until he was eighty-three years old. He developed and chaired their program in Electrical Engineering and established a reputation as a devoted teacher. His lectures, described as "lucid, fresh and admirable," quickly drew students, as did his reputation for a love of challenging received opinions.[24] Rebecca's pride in her brother never faltered, and he would become an influential guide for her two sons.

Davis was writing at a fast pace in the summer and early fall of 1872 in anticipation of the birth of her third child. She produced "The Messenger" and "Annie's Mother" which would appear later in the fall in *Youth's Companion*; and "Elise" which would appear simultaneously in *Massachusetts Ploughman* and *Peterson's*. Although literature of the 1870s was demonstrating a renewed interest in immigrant communities, it tended to focus on urban settings. In "The Messenger" and "Elise," Davis turned to immigrant communities in isolated regions of the Midwest—both those of longstanding Dutch-German traditions, as in "The Messenger," and new French immigrants in "Elise." Her fame as a children's author was growing, and in October, *Youth's Companion's* announcement of major contributors listed Davis at the top of a compendium of authors that included Louisa May Alcott, Kate Sanborn, "Sophie May," Grace Greenwood, and others. It was now on a par with *Peterson's* as one of her major vehicles for publication.

On October 16, 1872, Rebecca gave birth to her third and last child, daughter Nora Davis. Dick and Charley would be two of the most loving brothers a sister could hope to have. Like her brothers, however, Nora was a fussy baby in the early weeks of her life, affording her parents little sleep. For the next two months Davis wrote a number of stories for *Youth's Companion* and *Hearth and Home*, but they were very short pieces.

Her Thanksgiving story for the former, "Through Rough Ways," was one of Davis's many historical narratives of this period. She had used historical settings in her John Page stories of the 1860s as a means of reflecting on Southern racial attitudes while the US was in the midst of a Civil War fought for the abolishment of slavery. Historical narratives allowed Davis to offer readers a distance from present troubles in order to more fully reflect on their causes and consequences—and to suggest the long scope of the nation's failure to rectify them. Many of her historical narratives in this and the coming decades would return to the Civil War in recognition of the importance of the unfinished business of the past.

Although Rebecca had returned to her normal routines of work and family life as much as possible, with a seven-week-old infant, she was unable to attend

Horace Greeley's funeral in New York City in the first week of December, even though Whitelaw Reid, the new editor, asked Rebecca, William Winter, George Ripley, E.C. Stedman, Noah Brooks, and Kate Field to attend as members of the Editorial Department.[25] Clarke attended, representing Rebecca and himself as a fellow newspaper editor. Thirty-five-year-old Whitelaw Reid and Rebecca would form a good working relationship that lasted more than fifteen years, but it was purely a business relationship and never a friendship. In these late years of Reconstruction, Reid developed the *Tribune* into one of the nation's leading Republican newspapers, and he would significantly expand Davis's editorial contributions shortly after he became editor.

Rebecca traveled home to Wheeling and to Washington, Pennsylvania, in January 1873 to introduce baby Nora to her mother and other relatives in the area. Once again she was shocked at the changes she saw in Wheeling. The iron and steel mills that had proliferated along the banks of the Ohio River may have made the city the "nail capital of the world," as it liked to boast, but the soot and grime coated everything with even heavier layers than in previous years. It was a lament she would return to whenever she visited the region.

Also in January Davis turned to a new major focus in her fiction—corrupt capitalists—as in "Tom Gillet's Fortune" for *Peterson's*. The topic would culminate the next year in the novel *John Andross*. This month Davis also returned to the pages of the *Atlantic Monthly* for the first time since 1867 with a powerful historical narrative, "A Faded Leaf of History," her only publication under William Dean Howells' editorship. The story began with a first-person narrator who related discovering "a curious pamphlet" dated 1698 she found one snowy afternoon while working in the Philadelphia Library. The pamphlet and the subsequent story described the experiences of immigrants to the New World who were "part of that endless caravan of ghosts that has been crossing the world since the beginning."[26] Based on the experiences of the Quaker John Dickinson, the narrative foreshadowed the many essays Davis would write about immigration in the coming years. The "curious" story received strongly favorable reviews. As the *Literary World* reviewer remarked, it was typical of Davis's style: "written with force and fervor."[27]

In the spring Rebecca was delighted to have Josiah Gilbert Holland, poet and editor of *Scribner's Monthly*, visit her in Philadelphia. Their acquaintance had begun prior to their association through *Scribner's*. She recalled Holland rejecting one of her submissions, most likely to *Hours at Home*, when he was its editor. Rejection was such an unusual experience that Davis had replied immediately—not to chastise his decision but to indicate "how very much I would like to know you personally. I have had a wide experience of publishers and editors, and the man who rejects a *Ms* with such tact and cordiality as to satisfy the author quite as much as if he had accepted it, I would be very glad to welcome under my roof."[28]

In March 1873, Holland was finally able to make the trip and told Rebecca she was his first choice of the author he wanted to stay with if the invitation was still open. She was delighted and invited Mrs. Holland to join him as well. Rebecca promised they would "find a Virginia welcome."[29] Holland quickly became a family friend. Years later she would recall his "clarity of self-insight," more so "than any of our other writers," and found him to be "as kindly and wholesome as his poetry."[30]

After Holland's visit, Rebecca returned to her prolific writing schedule. In the postwar years, a body of literature began to appear with women physicians as either the protagonists or as the subjects of ridicule, and Davis's "Berrytown" serial for *Lippincott's* was one of the earliest and most provocative of the responses to the cultural change women physicians emblematized. With the publication of the first chapters of the serial, the critical response was enthusiastic. As the literature reviewer for the *Boston Daily Advertiser* exclaimed, "These opening chapters are full of promise for a powerful and graphic story," and he continued to praise it throughout its publication.[31]

The main character, Dr. Maria Haynes Muller, symbolized the advancements for women physicians as well as the costs of such progress while addressing several major issues of concern in the medical profession at mid-century, including the New Woman versus the domestic woman, homeopathy versus allopathy, and women doctors and marriage. "Berrytown" depicted a domestic woman, Kitty Guinness, as living a manipulated and manipulating life in contrast to the sometimes difficult but largely fulfilling and independent life of the New Woman. As an extension of her disabilities analyses, Davis's serial drew on medical theories about neuralgic disability and rest cures set forth by Drs. Johann Müller, Charles Elam, and John Vansant. There was no triumphant romantic conclusion to the novella but rather a suggestion that the woman physician would be able to recover from her neuralgic disability, whereas the scheming domestic woman would never escape her moral shortcomings.[32]

"Berrytown" marked the cultural issue Davis explored most broadly in these years—in fiction, essays, and editorials—women's changing roles in society. In some ways, this theme began in *Margret Howth* with the title character undertaking an office position in a manufactory. In the 1870s it would reveal Davis's conservatism as well as her progressivism. She believed, not surprisingly, women who had an egalitarian marriage and children were the happiest; and while she continued to abhor the outspokenness of suffragists, she embraced work outside the home for women as well as new forms of remunerative work that could be done from home, especially for rural women. No subject so engrossed Davis or so clearly revealed her own conflicted attitudes toward this momentous change in US society.

Clarke was continuing his many contributions to the cultural world of 1870s Philadelphia as well and was instrumental in founding the Aesthetic Club. The club's interdisciplinary goals brought together painters, architects, sculptors, musicians, engravers, journalists, literary *men* (as specified in its founding documents), and those who supported the fine arts. As would become evident in numerous events in the last half of the nineteenth century, regardless of the success of many women authors, nationally organized literary clubs remained exclusive to men—even when one of its founders was married to an internationally recognized author. Although Rebecca was known for refusing to join any organization, being a member of such a club was an unusual reliance on patriarchal traditions on Clarke's part.

In these years Clarke also maintained his passion for the theater and contacted William Church at the *Galaxy* to inquire about publishing another essay on actors. The editors' enthusiastic response resulted in "Gossip About Actors, Old and New" in the May 1873 issue, in which he examined the challenges for women actors such as Sarah Siddons, the power of male actors such as Garrick and Kean, and especially the rise of Adelaide Neilson. The article had a lasting impact on theater criticism. Thirty years later it would still be recognized as important for its valuable analysis of Neilson's particular talents.[33]

This summer Rebecca limited her writing to four stories for *Youth's Companion* that appeared in August and September. "Swift's Comet" was a humorous piece about a man who inherits a telescope; members of his community in a small New York village come to believe they have discovered an opening into the heavens when they peer into the night skies. There was a renewed public interest in science in the early 1870s after the English physicist John Tyndall delivered lectures to large New York City audiences in 1872. The *Tribune* had devoted a special edition to Tyndall's visit that sold in excess of fifty thousand copies. Davis was one of the notable writers who increasingly infused her storylines with scientific themes.[34]

Most unusual among her works at this time, however, was "The Doctor's Story," a tale that advanced her more progressive perspectives about African Americans in this era. The protagonist was Dr. Fetridge, "one of the many educated colored men in Philadelphia, who constitute there a class set apart and distinct from any to be found elsewhere. In no other city, North or South, does the freedman carry himself with such grave self-respect and real social equality as among the quiet Quakers."[35] With a large, successful practice, Dr. Fetridge "had that peculiar grave, even melancholy reticence of bearing which marks the best of his race."[36] Yet, Davis noted, this man could not ride in the city's street-cars, which sometimes necessitated walking miles to conduct his business.

It was a particularly timely commentary. Although Philadelphia streetcars had been legally desegregated in 1867, it remained common practice for African Americans to be excluded from first-class cars where white physicians of Dr. Fetridge's status would have ridden.[37] In 1873 the streetcar system was in the planning stages for significant expansion in preparation for the upcoming Centennial celebration,[38] but integration on the cars remained a volatile issue in the city. Davis's story clearly called for integration. It also revealed that Fetridge had been born a slave, was separated as a child from his family, and sold to a white physician who trained him in the profession. In *Waiting for the Verdict*, written immediately after the war, she had concluded the black physician's story with his death—a heroic death, but one that seemed to suggest she could not yet imagine how a black man could continue to practice once he no longer passed as white. Here, however, Dr. Fetridge thrives and was not an exception but part of a class of successful black professionals. Unlike the often offensive Charley Gray stories, penned only a few years earlier when Davis first started writing for *Youth's Companion*, "The Doctor's Story" educated young readers to the rise of the black professional class.

Davis's reputation as a children's author was garnering considerable attention in the early 1870s, and in the fall, Mary Mapes Dodge invited her to become a contributor to *St. Nicholas*, a competitor of *Youth's Companion*. Dodge had known Davis from her days as a co-editor of *Hearth and Home*, and she was seeking to build a notable league of authors to contribute to the new periodical from Scribner's publishing house. Within a year, Dodge would build the magazine into one of notable acclaim and one that subsumed *Our Young Folk* and *The Children's Hour*.[39] Some authors, including Louisa May Alcott, initially remained loyal to *Youth's Companion* and did not publish with *St. Nicholas*, but Dodge was able to entice a number of writers to join her, such as William Cullen Bryant, Donald K. Mitchell, Lucy Larcom, and Davis. Writers new to children's and young adult literature joined Dodge's cadre of writers as well, including Bret Harte, Charles Dudley Warner, and Celia Thaxter. Davis published her first story, "The Enchanted Prince," a delightfully fantastical story, in the inaugural November issue of *St. Nicholas*.

When Rebecca received a copy of the first issue of *St. Nicholas*, she wrote Dodge with warm congratulations and reflected on the status of children's literature: "Where you found all the good things to go in [the issue] in these days when writing for children is so over-done, I can not guess. The Magazine ought to be a success—if all boys approve of it as mine do." Dodge had asked about one-year-old Nora, and Rebecca admitted the baby "keeps me busy" and had brought about "such terrible arrearages of sleep that I write and talk with my eyes half shut." Rebecca closed her letter with an invitation for Dodge to visit her in Philadelphia.[40] Although publishing was definitely a business for Davis, she continued to enjoy friendships with her favorite editors, and Dodge, like James Fields, William Church, Josiah Gilbert Holland, and others, would remain a family friend throughout their lives.

That winter, Rebecca and Clarke had a brief reconnection of a few hours with Annie and James Fields who were visiting in Philadelphia. Although they had sporadically continued their correspondence, each woman had moved on to new facets of her life. Rebecca could hardly have forgotten the Fieldses' earlier rebuff of her invitation to stay at the Davises' home when James was lecturing in the city or Annie's decision to forego the visit completely. It had been several years since the two women had seen one another. Rebecca complemented Annie on how little she had changed, but Annie, in a bit of a snit, chose to see it as a "rebuke" since she had not been feeling well. As always, Annie tried to cast women she cared for in conventional "true woman" categories, and her only remark about Rebecca was that she represented "a fine type of tender loving self forgetting motherhood."[41] Rebecca *was* a remarkable mother, but she was equally a highly accomplished artist, albeit one who had left the *Atlantic Monthly* fold, and thus Annie's good graces as well. It was the last time the Fieldses and the Davises would see one another.

During these months when Davis was publishing primarily children's literature, she had been working on two novels for adults. *John Andross* would appear early the next year, but "Earthen Pitchers" began serialization in the November issue of *Scribner's Monthly Magazine*, which had garnered a circulation of 40,000 in its first year.[42] Davis wrote numerous short stories and novels over her career about women's stifled lives, especially about women artists. Perhaps none of these so poignantly captured the sense of personal and cultural loss as did "Earthen Pitchers." It compounded the tragedy of these women's lives by demonstrating the psychological damage incurred when a woman artist must choose, as society and her upbringing dictated, between domestic happiness and a career. Whichever path such a woman chose, she was compelled to long for the other path as well. Whereas many of Davis's earlier stories resolved such conflicts with a happy marriage, "Earthen Pitchers" avoided easy solutions in favor of depicting the soul-wrenching costs when women internalized society's assumptions of their subordinated cultural status. It was a powerful contrast to Davis's censorious assertions about women's roles in "Men's Rights."

In spite of having a young baby and two active boys, Davis continued to write with fervor. In November and December 1873 alone, she published, in addition to the installment of "Earthen Pitchers" and the *St. Nicholas* story, fiction in *Peterson's*, the *Galaxy*, a second story in *St. Nicholas*, and three stories in *Youth's Companion*. The range of interests revealed in these stories was equally notable. "Madam Bourne" for *Peterson's* represented her studies of class differences in America, and Davis's stories of the 1870s increasingly included working-women characters, often those who were forging careers for themselves. Madam Bourne, for instance, hosts a tea for the head of a newly founded female seminary and its young women teachers. "One Week an Editor," for the *Galaxy*, underscored Davis's interest in representing the challenges of journalism and included a woman character who works in a newspaper office.

This was Davis's last publication for the *Galaxy*, although the magazine would continue publication until 1878. The *Galaxy* had managed for a period of time to attract a respectable number of subscribers and had seemed to be on the verge of becoming the latest major literary periodical, but its circulation had peaked at 23,000 in 1871. With the emergence of *Scribner's Monthly* and, perhaps most importantly, the *Galaxy's* failure to compete in the new marketplace of extensively illustrated magazines such as *Scribner's, Lippincott's, Every Saturday*, and *Harper's*, its circulation quickly dropped to around 6,000.[43] Davis and many of their former contributors were in demand and thus could choose to go with the larger magazines that paid better and would reach a truly national audience.

The coming year brought Rebecca new opportunities and renewed connections with family and friends. She still tried early each year to visit her mother and relatives in West Virginia and eastern Pennsylvania. When she made the trip in January 1874, she especially lamented the extraordinary changes in the lives of the Scotch-Irish farmers she had known as a young woman. She was struck particularly by the erasure of their old ways; with the discovery of oil in the region, their lives had been completely altered. The Scotch-Irishmen she had grown up with were as important to national values, she believed, as New Englanders or Virginians, having "contributed to the national character his shrewd common sense, his loyalty to his wife, his family, and his country."[44] When she again visited these successful farmers in the 1870s, however, "The orchards, the yellow wheat fields, the great silent woods, were all swept away.... The farmhouse was gone; in its stead were the shops and saloons of a busy drunken town. My old friends had struck oil; their well was one of the largest in the State. Money poured in on them in streams, in floods. It ceased to mean to them education or comfort or the service of God. It was power, glory. They were drunk with the thought of it."[45]

Davis's second serial of this year, "John Andross," depicted a similar change in urban Philadelphia. In spite of Mayor Stokley's efforts through a centralized government to break the power of ward politics in the city, a massive and corrupt system of saloon politics emerged,[46] and Davis exposed the system's brutality and cunning in this novel. Serialized in *Hearth and Home* beginning in December, "John Andross" was part of the larger exposé of Whiskey Rings in New York, Washington, St. Louis, and Philadelphia, and Davis drew both on accounts of the New York ring that appeared in the *Tribune* and her own keen knowledge of Philadelphia politics. Published in book form after its serialization, the novel was recognized as one of the pioneering works of political fiction that analyzed the dangerous machinery of corporate capitalism. This was not the battered but "epic hero" business tycoon that Henry James would celebrate in 1898,[47] but the precursor to later works such as Hamlin Garland's *A Spoil of Office* (1892) and Upton Sinclair's *The Jungle* (1906).

The *Tribune* excoriated Boss Tweed's Whiskey Ring in New York. Davis was writing many editorials for the *Tribune* at this time, and she may have penned some of their commentaries, as her novel did much the same for Philadelphia's ring that was run through the city's saloon politics. As with the *Tribune*'s exposés, Davis's novel was received, both in its serialization and book form, as powerful fiction but as an exaggeration of the corruption by reviewers for the *Atlantic Monthly* and the *Galaxy*. Other reviewers, however, recognized what she had accomplished in this novel, especially those reviewers in Pennsylvania where the corruption had played out. The *Huntingdon Journal*'s writer, for instance, declared "Mrs. Davis is one of the very best story writers in America" and *John Andross* was "one of her best works," while the *Philadelphia Inquirer* advised that "cultured and refined readers" would be attracted to the novel's themes and its "keen, analytical studies of human nature." As an author of "refined and elevating fiction," the reviewer remarked, Davis had presented "an excellent illustration of the class of novels we have endeavored to indicate. Such are rapidly becoming recognized not only as a grateful source of intellectual recreation, but as an important if not an essential element of the fullest mental culture."[48]

It was the *Scribner's Monthly* reviewer, however, who articulated the most astute assessment, not merely of *John Andross* but of Davis's body of work up to this time:

> There is a class of novels which invites the same censure that French criticism brings against English painting—that it is employed to point a moral more than to display an art. Of the American writers who use the weapon of fiction to attack an evil or defend a theory no one succeeds better than Mrs. Davis in combining a special object with simplicity of plan and naturalness of character. Most of them set up some abstraction, some ideal embodiment of right or wrong, controlling the persons it concerns like puppets. With her, human nature in its exposure to temptation or its efforts at duty is the chief study, and moral generalities do not usurp the first place. She does not describe institutions or abuses as making or unmaking human beings, nor men and woman as colorless, bloodless images through which a principle acts. We sympathize with her heroes of either sex, because they display natural wills and natural weaknesses, neither erring by rule nor right upon system.
>
> "Waiting for the Verdict," for instance, was written to combat a prejudice. But the prejudice turns out to be an instinct, and, in spite of herself a strife of emotion, and repulsion, and sadness gathers about it which makes the novel a thoroughly human lesson instead of the Civil Rights essay which it probably set out to be. So the story of John Andross involves the scheme of a tract against legislative corruption, yet the least important of the thoughts its suggestive pages excite is the fact that an enormous evil of the sort exists, and deserves attack. This is far from being a failure on the author's part. It only proves that she is greater than her subject, and that her power of analyzing mental operations and portraying shades of feeling carries her far beyond and above the narrow limits of didactics.[49]

As the reviewer recognized, in addition to exposing the city-wide corruption, Davis also analyzed human nature and the lure of seemingly easy money in *John Andross*. This aspect of the story was based on a real but minor figure involved in the New York scandal, Mr. Bailey, collector of the Thirty-second District, whose life was destroyed by his involvement. Overwhelmed by personal financial difficulties, Collector Bailey, whose story had been part of the *Tribune*'s reporting, became complicit in the very illegalities he was supposed to be policing. In Davis's novel, Bailey's embezzlement and subsequent attempts at a cover-up mirrored the manner in which the ring gained a grip on John Andross. Part of the power of the novel was that it examined both the financial and moral corruption inherent in the system.

In the spring, baby Nora was ill,[50] but Rebecca for the most part maintained her writing schedule. She and Clarke were successful enough in their careers to afford household servants and a nurse for the baby. Rebecca was a hands-on mother, but she valued the assistance from the nurse which allowed her to write steadily. In "Between Man and Wife" for *Peterson's*, she poignantly returned to a theme she had explored earlier in "The Clergyman's Wife" and "How We Spent the Summer": a marriage in crisis. In April Davis also returned to the mystery genre with a three-part serial, "The Saar Secret," for *Peterson's*. Its themes had become important to her cultural critiques of this period—mixed-race "blood" (Caucasian and Native American) and inherited insanity. But the story was also a return to Davis's negative depictions of Native Americans as cunning, savage, and barbaric in contrast to the Philadelphia-raised "white" heroine of the story. Davis's sardonic humor emerged in this story as well, but it could not overcome the racial biases that grounded the narrative.

In April, newspapers announced that Davis had agreed to write two-page stories for *Scribner's Monthly*, "a new departure in magazine literature, and no doubt will be very popular with newspapers," which could now reprint complete stories rather than excerpt them as had been their pattern.[51] This may well have been Richard Watson Gilder's suggestion; within the next few months, he would become the dominant editorial figure at *Scribner's* as Holland reduced his workload. Holland had often let his friendship with particular writers influence his acceptance of their work, but Gilder was much more in tune with shaping a periodical with high-quality literature, and Davis was one of the authors he worked to retain. They became lifelong friends as well.

There was a certain irony to Davis's agreement to write two-page stories, since she was constantly in negotiations with her publishers for more space in which to express her ideas. The first of these short-short stories to appear included "The Best Fellow in the World," "The Doctor's Wife," and "The Pepper-Pot Woman." Each of the short-short stories actually spread slightly onto a third page even in the beginning, but the format allowed Davis to craft several notable character sketches. Gilder recognized the changing trend toward realism rather than the moralist literature that Holland had preferred, and these three short-short stories by Davis were important transitional features as he turned the magazine in that direction.[52] The first of the genre analyzed "the Major," a figure known in any part of the country but especially in the South and West; and "The Doctor's Wife" depicted a nondescript woman who died as she lived, quietly and having had little impact on the world. "The Pepper-Pot Woman" was a terse representation of Davis's biting class analyses.

As the summer of 1874 began, Rebecca received an invitation to attend a reunion at the Washington Female Seminary commemorating Sarah Foster Hanna's retirement. She declined but wrote an editorial, "A Woman's Work," for the *New-York Tribune* honoring Hanna's contributions to female education and social reform. Noting that Margaret Fuller had recognized the importance of Sarah Foster's work in *Woman in the Nineteenth Century*, Davis praised her former teacher for her "power towards unveiling the hidden intellect" of her students and for her enduring efforts to advance female education. As was common in Davis's writings about opportunities for women, she admired the woman who discovered "precisely what she could and could not do." This was part of Davis's theory of supporting women who sought work outside the home—they must not assume they were brilliant at every endeavor; they needed to find their distinctive talents and appreciate them, whether it was as a seamstress or a physician. Thus Hanna "was not meant to be an artist or author, or even a teacher *par excellence*; but she had an exceptional executive ability," at one time running three separate females seminaries.[53]

One section of Davis's *Tribune* editorial was excised, however, when it was reprinted in the *Commemorative* pamphlet after the reunion. In that section she criticized "so-called progressive reformers" of the day; this was becoming an increasingly bitter note in her commentaries about women's cultural progress—she did not object to reformers, being one herself, but rather to the emerging New Woman who castigated earlier women for their less radical ways. In this article Davis also revealed Hanna to be one of the major influences on her own life as a reformer:

> The so-called progressive reformers would claim no doubt that such training as here was calculated to increase the number of Domestic Women in the country; but in one point her teaching was more broad and catholic than their own. Long ago, before humanitarian doctrines became the fashion, her pupils were brought close to every species of

suffering in any part of the world which they could help to relieve. Whether it was the Southern slave, the famine-wasted Frenchman or Hindoo, or the needy soldier in Federal or Confederate prison, she made them real men and brothers to her girls—not vague ideas. In her way—not the newest or most scientific way, perhaps—she tried to teach these women whom she sent out into the world a sincere love for God and their fellow-man.[54]

At this time, Lippincott's Publishers issued a volume of Davis's work, *Kitty's Choice: A Story of Berrytown, and Other Stories,* that included "The Balacchi Brothers" and "Leonard Heath's Fortune" as well as "Berrytown," here retitled *Kitty's Choice,* thus emphasizing the domestic woman rather than the woman physician. Although the collection received favorable reviews, the *North American and United States Gazette* was not unusual in its misreading of Kitty, asserting "her merit was pure and simple womanliness"; not surprisingly, the reviewer thus found the story's conclusion and Kitty's choice of a husband quite perplexing—and no mention of the woman physician was made in the review.[55]

Changing the title to emphasize the domestic woman was an odd choice, considering the story's engagement with a heated contemporary issue. Typically, a book would appear more rapidly after the publication of a serial novel; but the decision to publish "Berrytown" with its woman-physician protagonist in 1874 was likely a response to the publication in the fall of Dr. Edward Clarke's *Sex in Education* and the responses opposing his opinions, including Julia Ward Howe's collection, *Sex and Education*; Elizabeth Bisbee Duffey's *No Sex in Education*; George Fisk and Anna Manning Comfort's *Woman's Education and Woman's Health*; and Anna Callender Brackett's collection, *The Education of American Girls.* Davis's depiction of the uneducated domestic woman as a simpleton who could only find power in dominating her household versus the woman physician who faced numerous struggles professionally and romantically but thrived in the end as a women's rights lecturer was an important complement to the nonfiction opposition to Edward Clarke.[56]

In August Rebecca left her family at Point Pleasant and traveled to North Carolina. Part of her trip involved lengthy travel on mules into the high mountain country, as she would describe in "Qualla." Davis had always believed in research as integral to her writing, and she wanted to explore the purported New South and especially the mountain life of the North Carolinians. Newspapers commented on Davis's every move, though they erroneously reported her trip to North Carolina was research for a novel.[57] However, she did publish a number of stories for *Scribner's* and other periodicals that drew on the materials she gathered during this sojourn, beginning in October with "The Rose of Carolina" for *Scribner's Monthly*. In the postwar publishing boom, *Scribner's* wanted to attract a Southern readership again and thus was drawn to New South themes.[58]

In the fall Davis also published stories in *Youth's Companion*, *Peterson's*, *St. Nicholas*, and *Scribner's*. Although her stories for boys were often adventurous, they paralleled the stories for girls in their cautionary arguments, calling for trust in parents and especially appreciation of one's mother ("Phonz," "At the Race," and "Hetty Fanning" for *Peterson's*). Her stories for *St. Nicholas*, such as "Chip," included the cautionary narrative but were typically more adventurous and imaginative. Mary Mapes Dodge clearly encouraged this difference as an editor, and Davis always preferred writing for Dodge but felt compelled to publish the majority of her children's and young adult stories in *Youth's Companion* because she could make more money doing so. For all that she was an artist, she was also a partner in the family's income—at times its greater contributor—and had to market her work where she could earn the most.

It was not only for monetary reasons, however, that she retained a decades-long association with *Youth's Companion*. She admired its editor, Daniel S. Ford, immensely: "One of the most remarkable men I ever knew," she wrote in her autobiography. "He was set apart from all other men by his total lack of self-appreciation. He sincerely believed that that paper was a lever which would uplift the minds and souls of American children."[59] Likewise, her stories for *Peterson's* in these months, "George Frost's Madness" and "The Ledoux Crevasse," had a similar if more subtle moral message: learning to judge the character of a lover. George Frost was one of several "coming" young men who attended the theater and men's clubs and treated women as objects in a marketplace, whereas Andrew Maull in "The Ledoux Crevasse" must resist his controlling mother in order to find happiness with the woman he loved.

On the other hand, Davis's story for the November *Scribner's*, "Dolly," satirized an artist's idealization of the title character who was from Bethlehem, Pennsylvania's Moravian community. The artist was completely disillusioned when years later he found her in a P.T. Barnum show, but Dolly was an "unrepentant Magdaline" who was happily married to a judge, while the artist was left with his illusionary "aesthetic sensibilities."[60] The Moravian community in Bethlehem was one Rebecca had often observed when visiting her brother Wilse, professor at Bethlehem's Lehigh University, and it would appear in several stories in the coming years. The Sister's House, where Dolly's aunt had retired after many years of service, was a fixture of the Moravian community.

In spite of the industrialization of the city with the founding of Bethlehem Steel Corporation in 1857, the Moravians' old-world ways remained an integral part of the city's attraction for Rebecca. The productivity Davis achieved in the fall of 1874—writing for numerous adult and children's periodicals—would be, with only rare exceptions, the pattern for the rest of her life.

At the beginning of 1875, *Appleton's Journal* published its annual assessment of the state of literature in the United States. It was not "particularly encouraging" at present, they concluded, with a few good books, yet also several that "dallied apparently within a few steps of the accomplishment of a good novel, but have not been strong enough to reach it." This included works by John DeForest, Louise Chandler Moulton, Julian Hawthorne, and others, but in Davis's case it was not the quality of the work that suggested its classification in this category: "Mrs. Rebecca Harding Davis made a by no means indifferent contribution in 'Kitty's Choice,'" but it "did not seem to us to attract sufficient attention."[61]

The new year, however, would move Davis in several new directions in her career and expand on themes she had been exploring in recent years, including her attention to the experiences of Native Americans. "A Fox and A Raven" for *St. Nicholas* and "Taneo" for *Youth's Companion* were both in this category. Each seemed to be well-meaning in their acknowledgement of the long tradition of white men duping Native Americans out of their land, but the solutions were assimilationist and gendered, treating Native women as redeemable but not most Native men. As yet, Davis had no real understanding of tribal culture or a consideration of its value. Only when she experienced indigenous life firsthand would her attitudes change.

In addition to Native American characterizations, temperance was a common theme in this year's stories. Davis explored this national problem in several works for *Youth's Companion* and *St. Nicholas*, such as "The Story of Ann" and "The Negro's Ring." The woman artist continued to be a theme of great interest to Davis as well. "The Poetess of Clap City" for *Scribner's* reimagined the theme of the woman artist whose talents are subsumed by marriage and motherhood. This was a topic Davis had edged around from numerous angles—here, it was a tragedy and one understood by many women; in other stories, marriage and motherhood were held as the greatest opportunity for women. Undoubtedly, Rebecca viewed her own life from these and many other perspectives—she loved her family and the life she had chosen, but there was always the crush of obligations, personal and economic, that pushed against her artistic ideals. At times the artist won out; at others, family did. She would not have given up either, and it was a struggle of emotions many nineteenth-century women writers understood intimately.

At this time the Davises were delighted to meet new neighbors who would soon become lifelong friends. John, Ethel, and Lionel Barrymore began visiting their grandmother, the actress and theater manager Louisa Lane Drew, in Philadelphia while their parents, Maurice Barrymore and Georgiana Drew, performed in tours. Eventually the Barrymores would reside in a house very near that of the Davises,[62] and it was not long before the Barrymore children were playing with Dick and Charley Davis in Philadelphia and at Manasquan as well when the Davises enticed the Barrymores to join them on their summer vacations.

Before leaving for the shore in 1875, Davis penned several works for late spring and summer publication. Her short-short stories for *Scribner's Monthly* now regularly ran three pages; she simply could not contain her writing, even in pithy character studies, to two pages. The three-page story better fit her artistic needs, and she produced several notable sketches in this format. One of her stories, "The Knight and The Castle," ironically foreshadowed problems that would soon face the Davis family. It was a touching and very contemporary story for *St. Nicholas* about a young boy who was placed in a boarding school to toughen him up; the boy, who was not a good scholar, faced harsh treatment and studies at a level for which he was not prepared. His lack of scholarly ability resulted in whippings and his ardent longing for home. A kindly uncle rescues him. Davis could not have known how prescient this story would be to her elder son's life. In just a few years, the family would have to face the reality that Dick, who they viewed as having so much potential, was struggling with academic life. Rebecca and Clarke would turn to her brother Wilse to rescue Dick's academic career.

In May Davis also published her only story for *American Homes*, a magazine "Devoted to All Classes & Ages." "The True Story of Wolfenden" began with a reference to the infamous Charley Ross kidnapping the previous year that had stunned the nation as it became the first kidnapping for ransom in the US. The incident was used by Davis as a means for exploring "other mysterious disappearances." She had descried many popular beliefs in the supernatural, yet she also turned frequently, as in this story, to the uncanny and unexplainable to explore race relations in America. Wolfenden was known to have had only one enemy—a former slave, "a half breed, *black and red skin*."[63] Wolfenden had been such a brutal master that he finally killed the man. Before dying, however, this man had charged his children and grandchildren to avenge his death, and the story revealed the ways in which the vestiges of slavery continued to haunt the nation and the inescapability of consequences for one's actions.

Over the summer two major events occurred. First, Davis returned to *Lippincott's* with another of her North Carolina stories. She had not published in *Lippincott's* since the serialization of "Berrytown" in mid-1873, but "The Yares of The Black Mountains" was another strong story that was highly praised at the time of publication. Davis again drew on her travels through North Carolina for the regional details of the story, in which she examined the Civil War's effect on these mountain people. With the distance of time and nearing the end of Reconstruction, the Civil War was regaining interest as a topic for literature, and this was one of several stories in which Davis exposed the costs of war. Many of her recent stories had sympathized to varying degrees with southern ways, but "Yares" was a story of North Carolinians who would not join the Confederacy and of the life-threatening penalties they paid for holding to their moral decision.

While the Davises were at the shore in the summer of 1875, the second major event of the summer unfolded: Rebecca began a major new phase in her career as an author and editorial writer in the pages of New York's *Independent* magazine; she would have a thirty-three-year association with the periodical. Founded in 1848 as a religious newspaper aligned with Congregationalism, the *Independent* was under the editorship of Henry Chandler Bowen when Davis joined the paper as an author. In 1870 the *Independent* had boasted a circulation of 75,000, but the Henry Ward Beecher-Theodore Tilton adultery scandal of that year cost the newspaper dearly. Both men had been editors of the paper at the time, and it could not escape the public backlash.

After the scandal, Bowen again assumed the editorship of the paper he had helped to found, seeking the affiliation of nationally recognized authors and journalists such as Davis as a means of reestablishing the paper's national standing; in these efforts, he built a periodical that, in fascinating ways, blurred distinctions between newspapers and magazines. Bowen was successful in these endeavors, and by the 1880s the *Independent* would again have a strong circulation. With the talented William Hayes Ward as his assistant, Bowen established the magazine as one of the few religious periodicals to have a nonsectarian audience, especially as it turned to analyses of important issues of the day. This was the area in which Davis was a major contributor. Her commentaries on public events for the *Independent* received national attention, and she was instrumental in maintaining the paper's popularity for the three decades of her affiliation.

Davis began her association with Bowen's periodical with three cultural commentaries: "Gossip on the Jersey Beach" in August, "Mother and Baby" in September, and "Two Women" in October. The first two were published on page one, signifying to the readership the arrival of Davis as a major contributor to the paper. Although most of Davis's writings for the *Independent* could be clearly classified between commentary and fiction, she often blended the genres, beginning a piece with a seemingly factual and often first-person commentary and then almost indistinctly gliding into a fictional story that represented the concepts of the initial commentary. This refusal to adhere to genre restrictions became a trademark of her writing, making the "story of to-day" both real and representative.

Periodicals in the mid-1870s were drawn to stories about various kinds of sectional reconciliations; as it became increasingly evident that Reconstruction was a failure, many magazines used such stories to fight against the idea that the goal had been largely defeated.[64] *Youth's Companion* was one such magazine. Davis, Louisa May Alcott, Harriet Spofford, Rose Terry Cooke, and a few others were touted as major contributors in all of the magazine's advertisements, and Davis adhered to Daniel Ford's goals for an uplifting magazine but equally so to the national call for at least seeming reconciliation. In the fall Davis published "The Break in the Sand," which configured reconciliation of city people and Jersey shore mariners as well as the educated with those of little formal education. Yet, as with many of the purported reconciliation stories of this period, Davis's narrator followed the pattern of depicting the North as the superior region.

In November Davis published one of her most important works of the period in *Lippincott's*. "Qualla" combined her interests in Native Americans and North Carolina. It also importantly signaled a change in her attitudes, informed by her firsthand exposure to Native American life and by the tensions between the Cheyenne and the US government that would develop in the next year into the Great Sioux War. General George Armstrong Custer's expedition into the Black Hills of Dakota Territory in 1874 set the stage for increased tensions, which had been exacerbated by the economic panic of 1873 as thousands of US citizens turned to mining in the Territory as a means of making a living (and for a few, of making great profits). Although there was some attempt to halt the incursion, the Grant Administration soon buckled under pressure from interests who wanted the Black Hills to be taken from the various tribal societies, especially the Cheyenne, even though their rightful ownership of the land had been granted under a treaty with the US government many years earlier.

In May 1875 delegations from the Sioux, led by Spotted Tail, Red Cloud, and other Native leaders, met with government officials in Washington. The Sioux refused, however, to sign a new treaty that would have forced their removal to Indian Territory. It was this same month that Davis began writing the account of her travels to the Cheyenne community of Qualla in the North Carolina mountains, and it was an impassioned plea—parallel to *Waiting for the Verdict*—for readers to recognize their obligations to aid and accept the people of Qualla.

Although Davis initially described the town's residents as reduced to extreme poverty and dirty, she shifted in this story from depicting drunken and ignorant savages. Rather, she indicted the white men who supposedly loved the Cheyenne but treated them like slaves, taking their lands and forcing them into an abusive system of labor. In one episode, concluded with an example of her most pointed irony, she described how their white guide, whose Indian name was Tallalla and who professed to love the Cheyenne, tried to justify his actions to her and the other travelers as they traversed a waterway in the mountains:

> "Do you mean to say," queried the skeptic of the travelers, "that the keeper of that country store [who stole the Cheyennes' land] ruled over a thousand people from behind this counter?"
>
> "Absolutely...."
>
> "And that from the profits of that miserable little shop he clothed and fed them for thirty years, and bought the land of three counties?"
>
> "The profits were larger than in ordinary trade," stammered Tallala. "We always expected to make one hundred or a hundred and fifty per cent, on every sale."
>
> "Who were your customers?"
>
> "The Indians, necessarily."
>
> "Oh!"
>
> The water was growing too muddy for further fording.[65]

When the travelers met the people of the village, however, they were struck most notably by the difference between reality and Tallalla's depiction of them as children who needed to be ruled.

Davis and her companions stopped at the home of Oo-tlan-o'-tch and his wife Llan-zi. The latter "was not the terror of a savage animal, as Tallalla and his like rank her; she was a clean-minded, womanly woman—without ideas, probably, but whose fault was that? There was in her face, and in the face of every Indian but one whom we saw in Qualla, that heavy, hopeless sadness which belongs to races to whom God has given a brain for which the world has as yet found no use."[66] Yes, their huts were miserable, but "the faces of these people, I am bound to confess were of a far higher type than those of the same class of whites, American, English or Irish, would have been in like condition. They were neither vicious nor vulgar in a single instance. On the contrary, they were grave, thoughtful, self-possessed."[67] The narrative demonstrated these traits through the Cheyenne's ability to determine what would be best for their community. They most wanted the opportunity for an education; twice teachers had come to the community, but they stayed only a couple of months. Rather than send white teachers, the Cheyenne suggested, why not take one of their brightest young men and train him as a teacher who could return to the village and share his knowledge?

Llan-zi and her people were "not savages," Davis insisted, but "placable, industrious, eager for knowledge"; and then she explained forthrightly her goal: "I honestly acknowledge that my motive in writing this paper has been to ask the question, What can be done in the North for Llan-zi and her people?"[68] After detailing the recent success in the lawsuit the community had brought against the white men who had stolen their land, receiving $15,000 and the hope that schools would be built, Davis expressed her reservations about the fact that part of the reconciliation of the lawsuit was to place the tribe

> under the direction of the Commissioner of Indian Affairs. . . . We, who are more conversant with the management of the Western Indians by government agents, shall not probably be so sanguine as to these speedy beneficial results as is the North Carolinian. Government surveys of Indian lands are usually followed by white squatters and whisky much more promptly than by schools or model farms.[69]

Rather than sending missionaries or money abroad, Davis suggested the vast army of "unmarried or childless women [of the North], with both culture and money, whose sole complaint is that there is no standing-place in the world in which they can use their talents" should envision what they could do for Llan-zi and her people. "I have great faith," she concluded, "that some strong and kindly men and women, reading these pages, may suddenly perceive that these are their own kinsfolk needing their help."[70] Two factors altered Davis's attitude from easy slurs about Native American "savages" to this newer perspective: the injustice of the government against the Cheyenne, and perhaps most important, meeting and getting to know the people themselves. It was an important lesson for Davis, and one she would build upon in the next few years.

Ironically, Davis's final publication of the year was a two-part commentary for the *Independent*, "American Convents," that employed distinct anti-Catholic biases. The December 23 section of "American Convents" recounted the tale of a young woman from Pennsylvania who was duped by a priest and forced into a nunnery where she was groomed for the sisterhood. Davis insisted it was a true story, adding, "It does not at all matter whether such outrages or any outrages are practiced in convents. The point is that outrages should be made impossible; that the barred sister-houses and nunneries, as well as the barred gaols and insane asylums, should be open to regular legalized examination and their immured inmates given the chance of complaint as well as the madman or felon."[71]

Although anti-Catholicism raged throughout the nineteenth century,[72] the December 30 conclusion of her commentary revealed that she was also engaging a hotly debated contemporary topic that had an international basis: the Tory MP Charles Newdegate's demands in the British parliament for the passage of a bill to inspect convents. This conservative attack was bound to the fictional renderings of nunneries as either brothels or chambers of torture, but Davis wanted to insist it was an issue of human rights:

> No illegal power, as every American will grant, should be permitted, uncurbed, to immure human beings behind prison bars. In the case of insane asylums, the helplessness and the violence of the patients and the presumed skill and philanthropy of the medical superintendents were held for many years as a justification of this unrestricted power of confinement, until it was proved that the power was abused and subordinated to the basest purposes. Insane asylums and every other house where personal duress is practiced, are now under legal surveillance, except the so-called convents."[73]

As with her change in attitudes toward Native Americans, Davis would later come to moderate her anti-Catholicism.

At present, this newly heightened interest in human rights, for Native Americans as for all people she considered incarcerated and/or abused, was a marker of Davis's increasingly overt and prolific political stances, which she would pursue over the next decade.

Chapter 7

Centennial Celebrations and the Failure of Reconstruction (1876–1879)

As the 1876 Centennial Exposition preparations moved toward completion, Philadelphia was filled with excitement for hosting the national celebration and its international audience. Family and reunion were frequent themes in the advertisements employed to enhance anticipation throughout the country. *Reunion* was intended to emphasize a mythology the North held dearly—that the past fracturing of the nation could be forgotten as the country turn to its glorious and harmonious future.[1] *Family* was also a key element of reunification theories, which fit well with Davis's interests. Family had been a theme of increasing importance to her over the past several years, and it became even more so as she turned in the late 1870s to publishing in a number of family-oriented magazines.

Clarke's involvement in the development of the Centennial celebration was through very public and influential roles. In January he was elected vice president of the Press Club of Philadelphia with Stephen N. Winslow, editor of a commercial newspaper, as president. These were coveted positions since the club was formed to help shape commentary about the Exposition. The Press Club moved into new and larger headquarters, elegantly furnished to acknowledge its influence and to serve as a centralized location for visiting journalists who would number in the hundreds during the run of the fair.[2] Rebecca joined in public events occasionally but, as usual, preferred to represent her ideas and goals through writing. Hers was not a minor role; she would become the go-to person for several major literary magazines that wanted to capture the history of Philadelphia in its Centennial year.

In spite of finding their Twenty-first Street home even more popular than usual during these months, Rebecca continued to write. "Effie," a light romance for *Peterson's*, was set at the Warm Springs resort in Virginia, while fiction for *Lippincott's* and *Youth's Companion* returned to two of her favorite locales, the Jersey shore and Tarrytown, New York. The former locale became a key feature of two influential essays she published in the first months of the year: "The House on the Beach" and "Life-Saving Station," both for *Lippincott's*.

The former was an extensive history of coastal life-saving stations.[3] She followed it in March with the second essay. Having learned about the life-saving service from a guide, she could proclaim she left the shore with "a sense of protection and trust in the government."[4] Newspapers across the country excerpted sections of this second, more popular article; it was included in editions of the *Encyclopedia Britannica* for years to come, including the landmark 9th edition in 1889, typically referred to as the "Scholar's Edition" for its outstanding analyses.

When writing for *St. Nicholas*, Davis sometimes turned to religious themes, such as "Herod," published in March. The story depicted an elderly slave in prewar Virginia who modeled a Christian life truly lived. It was part of a special issue devoted to "Talk with Boys" that included works by Davis, Charles Dudley Warner, John Greenleaf Whittier, and Lucretia Hale. Through children's literature Davis began to find her work published in England—not through her efforts or to her profit, but increasingly in reprints or excerpts, including an excerpt of "Herod" that appeared in the *Manchester Times* just days after it was published in the States.[5]

Davis was also exploring in more depth and with greater criticism the phenomena of young women with little training or experience but a great desire to see themselves in print, a theme to which she would frequently return. The young women who had exaggerated beliefs in their ability to make a living by their pen often met with tragic results that Davis explored at this time in "Marcia" for *Harper's New Monthly Magazine*.

Harper's was another new and important affiliation for Davis. She would write for the magazine for more than twenty years and guide both her sons to its pages. Fletcher Harper was the chief editor until his death in 1877; he and his brothers, James, John, and Joseph, had founded Harper's Brothers Publishing in 1850. By the mid-1870s it was the country's premier literary magazine with a circulation of 135,000. Leading the way in recognizing the marketability of highly illustrated magazines, *Harper's New Monthly* was the greatest competition for *Scribner's Monthly*, *Lippincott's*, and the *Atlantic Monthly*. In spite of the efforts of all of the magazines to retain major authors like Davis solely for their own periodicals, those days had passed, and the competition for the leading American literary artists was sharp, in part due to the sense among editors that there were only a small number of authors who truly fit the category. *Harper's* and *Scribner's* were usually able to attract this group of writers with significantly higher payments than other literary magazines could offer.[6]

Like its competitors, *Harper's* intended to make full use of the Centennial year as subject matter to promote the periodical. Davis was becoming known for her historical narratives as well as contemporary cultural critiques, and these strengths served her well in this period. She produced a two-part narrative, "Old Philadelphia," for *Harper's*. It began in April, one month before the fair opened. A sixteen-page illustrated history of the city, the essay ranged from Penn's time to the present day and detailed important historical sites and their foundings; it served as a guide for tourists who visited the city during the fair.

At the same time Davis produced two stories for Mary Mapes Dodge at *St. Nicholas*: "The Strawberry Girl" and its sequel, "About The Painter of Little Penelope." Historical essays such as these would become a staple of Davis's contributions to *St. Nicholas* as she sought to educate as well as entertain its young readers. "Gilbert Stuart," which continued the tradition, created some unforeseen difficulties, however. The story was well received critically—"a capital biographical sketch"[7]—but shortly after its publication Davis received a letter from Dodge indicating a living descendant was upset by the depiction. It was a policy of Davis's, one that she adhered to even when she wrote her autobiography in 1904, not to write about living people, viewing it as an invasion of their privacy. But selecting historical figures had seemed to avoid any difficulties. She replied to Dodge, "I certainly did not know that Stuart had any descendants living. The facts I gave have been in print often before, with others much more discreditable, which I passed over in silence. But if I had had any idea that he had a relative who could be hurt by the article I assuredly never should have written it." Dodge was apparently satisfied, and the issue ended without further ado.[8]

Rebecca had other worries at the moment. Nora was very ill. As Rebecca explained in a short note to Dodge, "my poor little girl is sick and scarcely leaves my arms—Maybe *you* are the fortunate woman to have no daughter— you don't have so many heartaches—."[9] When their children were young, the Davises had changed family physicians, turning to Dr. Louis Starr, a renowned Philadelphia physician on the staff of the Episcopal Hospital and a member of the highest social circles in the city. He would continue as the family's physician for the rest of their lives. Under Starr's treatment, Nora recovered in a few weeks, and her health improved to the extent that she was rarely ill in her later childhood.

The Centennial Exposition opened on May 10, 1876, with a cacophony of celebration by the ringing of bells from the Independence Hall tower, the

Liberty Bell, and numerous churches around the city. As the first international fair since the 1851 London Exposition, the Centennial Exposition's goals were lofty; national wounds that would not heal and the lingering effects of the 1873 economic depression made reaching those goals tenuous, but the fair proved to be a successful diversion.[10] The opening ceremonies included a welcoming address by President Ulysses S. Grant that had an audience of over 100,000. Clarke was one of the city leaders who was invited to join Grant on a short ocean trip after a reception that was held for him in Philadelphia. These first brushes with the nation's most powerful leaders would become common events in both Clarke's and Rebecca's lives, and a future president would become one of their closest friends.

The fair also allowed threads of friendship to be reconnected. At the Exposition's opening, Clarke was one of about two hundred men who attended a reception at the Penn Club for the former Speaker of the House, James G. Blaine. A private men's club for city leaders, the Penn Club had been founded the previous year to help promote the Centennial. Unlike some of the other social clubs, its founding documents included the recognition of women, although not as members: "The purposes for which the Corporation is formed are the association of authors, artists, men of science and the learned professions, and amateurs of music, letters, and the fine arts; and by receptions given to men or women distinguished in art, literature, science, or politics, and other kindred means, to promote social intercourse among its members."[11] Since Blaine was Rebecca's relative and a childhood friend from her Washington, Pennsylvania, days, it was a welcome opportunity for them to see one another again. Clarke became as fond of James as Rebecca, and the Davises' path would cross with his periodically in the coming years as Clarke's fame as an editor grew and Blaine's advancing political career occasionally brought him to Philadelphia.

It was only a month later that Clarke began his very public support of Blaine, although the family connection was not recognized by Blaine's critics. As Speaker of the House, Blaine was an adept politician and was used to bipartisan recognition that, one colleague observed, was extraordinary: "Other leaders were admired, loved, honored, revered, respected, but the sentiment for Blaine was delirium"—and that included members of the press.[12] Not surprisingly, then, his opponents grasped the opportunity to denigrate Blaine when rumors began to circulate that he had been bribed with railroad stock before becoming Speaker;[13] the rumors cost him the party's nomination for the Presidency.

The editorial in Clarke's newspaper praised Blaine for his prompt congratulations to the nominee, Rutherford B. Hayes, "actually before it had been announced by the clerks in the convention" and thus foregoing internal party strife. "Not only does the great leader [Blaine] rejoice that Governor HAYES has been selected, but he promises to labor in [his home state of] Maine [on Hayes' behalf].... The act is in keeping with Mr. BLAINE's record, and through it he will gain in respect."[14] Blaine wrote Clarke from Washington, D.C., thanking him for his "cordial support of me in these trying weeks—I can never forget it—You have a warm place in my affections though so lately an acquaintance—To my fair cousin [Rebecca], give my warmest regard—I feel that I have caught again one of the golden threads of life—broken these many years but never to be lost again I hope."[15]

Meanwhile, competition increased among the major literary magazines for Davis's historical narratives that complemented the fair. Following *Harper's* was *Scribner's Monthly Magazine*. Published in June, "Old Landmarks in Philadelphia" was a twenty-two-page addition to her historical accounts of "the city of the Friends, as she opens her gates to entertain the world this summer."[16] Here, however, she emphasized the affordable housing for laborers in the city compared with most metropolitan areas and detailed the ethnically diverse immigrants who helped settle the city. Native Americans were briefly mentioned, but they were termed "savage guests" when they visited Philadelphia.[17] The article's strongest points were its attention to Quakers and to women who helped forge the city's growth.

Not to be outdone, *Lippincott's* asked for an essay on the city, and Davis complied with a two-part serial, "A Glimpse of Philadelphia in July, 1776," that ran through the popular summer months of the fair. In spite of all that Davis contributed literarily to the fair's success, she professed to have attended for only one day, though as she told Annie Adams Fields in a rare letter, it was "for many reasons of which lack of interest was not one."[18] But the claim of having attended for only one day was suspect, since she wrote numerous and highly detailed accounts of several aspects of the fair over its seven-month run.

What Rebecca particularly enjoyed about the fair was that it meant an increased number of friends from Philadelphia joined the Davis family at Point Pleasant for the summer to escape the crowds, and out-of-town visitors combined a visit to the fair with time at the shore. Beginning at this time and over the years, the Davises were joined at Point Pleasant at various times by an amazing group of artists and intellectuals, from the painters George Lambdin, Margaret Ruff, and Milne Ramsay to celebrities such as the spirit medium

Madame Blavatsky and her patron Henry Steele Olcott, whom the Davises had met many years earlier. In a few years Frances Hodgson Burnett and Joseph Jefferson would be numbered among their visitors, and their longtime friend Horace Howard Furness, the premier Shakespearean scholar in the US, became so enamored of the region that he built a summer house near the Davises' cottage. Burnett was just at the beginning of her fame, and the Davises' younger son Charley recalled her love of "millinery finery. One day my father took her out sailing and, much to the lady's discomfiture and greatly to Richard's and my delight, upset the famous authoress." In spite of being doused in the ocean, Burnett remained friendly with the Davises.[19]

In addition to Joseph Jefferson, many actors who had become intimate friends of the Davises migrated to the Point Pleasant, most importantly the Drew-Barrymore clan. Louisa Drew (actor John Drew's spouse) and her daughter, Georgiana Drew Barrymore, spent their summers at a nearby hotel. Georgie, as she was known, made a distinct impression on young Charley, "I can remember Mrs. Barrymore at that time very well—wonderfully handsome and a marvelously cheery manner. Richard and I both loved her greatly, even though it were in secret." Georgie's daughter, Ethel Barrymore, became a particular friend, and she remained close to the Davises throughout their lives as their celebrity grew in the literary and theatrical worlds. Charley's early memories of Ethel were "as she appeared on the beach, a sweet, long-legged child in a scarlet bath-suit running toward the breakers and then dashing madly back to her mother's open arms." Dick and Ethel "became great pals. Indeed, during the latter half of his life," Charley asserted, "through the good days and the bad, there were very few friends who held so close a place in his sympathy and his affections as Ethel Barrymore."[20] Many such lifelong friendships were solidified during the long summer months at Point Pleasant.

Along with her historical accounts of the city, some of Davis's Centennial writings were overt guides to the fair and critiques of contemporary culture. Before she left for the shore in the summer of 1876, Davis contributed to one of several "Extras" that the *New-York Tribune* published to commemorate the Centennial, and this seventy-two page "Guide to the Exposition" was one of its most impressive Extras. Selling for twenty-five cents, it included a fold-out map of the grounds. Several of the newspaper's editorial correspondents contributed essays on major sections of the Exposition from "National Exhibits" and "Woman's Work" to "Scientific Features" and "Machinery Hall" where the mammoth Corliss steam engine was on display. Davis's section of the Guide was "Education." She asserted that educational exhibits most attracted women because these fair-goers wanted to find "the odd phases of human nature in every sort of national expression, the broad contrasts and subtle likenesses among them; the unexpected stage effects and their suggestions." Visiting the education exhibitions of Japan, Sweden, Belgium, France, Austria, Hawai'i, and several others, Davis attempted to distinguish the great private educations from those of government schools and the differences in educating students of varying classes.[21] The essay was well received and led some newspapers to again proclaim Davis was among "the first order of newspaper writers."[22]

If the fair was focusing on the national family, Rebecca was thoroughly enjoying her own at the shore, and especially her children. Dick (as he now preferred) was twelve, Charley ten, and Nora three. Although Nora was old enough to enjoy the sand and dip her toes in the ocean waters, the boys had added new sports to their summer activities, including baseball and football. Having become acquainted with so many of their parents' actor and playwright friends, Dick and Charley naturally began to emulate these heroes. They had been very young when Clarke first took them to plays, and a ritual had soon developed in which the boys periodically met Clarke at his office and, after lunch at a nearby chophouse, they would all go to one of the first-class theatres in Philadelphia. There they saw Edwin Booth, Joseph Jefferson, Adelaide Neilson, Charles Fletcher, Lotta Crabtree, John McCullough, John Sleeper Clark, and the elder Sothern.[23] It created a wonderful bond between father and sons, and it afforded Rebecca blocks of quiet time for her writing. Soon the boys were spending rainy afternoons in the upstairs front room of their Philadelphia home enacting melodramas written by Dick as starring vehicles for himself. Filled with action and most often great scenes of hand-to-hand combat between the brothers, these plays were wonderfully imaginative outlets.

Not all of their experiences with actors were quite as favorable, however. A few years earlier, just before the great tragedian Edwin Forrest ended his career, Rebecca was delighted to discover he was on the same streetcar as she and Dick. Her desire to impress her son with the great actor's importance was diminished, however, in an untimely incident that Charley recorded. It captured Rebecca's joy at telling humorous stories that became part of the family legend. "At the moment Forrest was suffering severely from gout and had his bad leg stretched well out before him. My brother," Charley wrote, "being very young at the time and never very much of a respecter of persons, promptly fell over the great man's gouty foot. Whereat (according to my mother, who was always a most truthful narrator) Forrest broke forth in a volcano of oaths and for blocks continued to hurl thunderous broadsides at Dick, which my mother insisted included the curse of Rome and every other famous trade in the tragedian's repertory which in any way fitted the occasion."[24]

Rebecca rarely returned from a summer at Point Pleasant without penning a story set at the seashore for the fall magazines, and this year it was "The Races at Shark Bay" for *St. Nicholas*. The gathering of artists at Point Pleasant this celebratory year had been too nourishing intellectually for it to be relegated to a once-a-year event, so increasingly over the years family friends from the national theatrical world would join the Davis family's salon of writers, artists, and theater people at their Twenty-first Street home. Among their associates were the drama critic Augustin Daly and actors Ada Rehan, John Drew, and Joseph Jefferson, who often discussed the great Shakespearean actor Edmund Kean. Their salon was a renowned part of Philadelphia's cultural life.

The fall in Philadelphia was alive with national political tensions as the Presidential election moved into high gear and became one of the most contentious elections in recent history due to contested Electoral College votes. Clarke had begun his editorial campaign for the Republican Party in the pages of the *Philadelphia Inquirer*. On October 3, he asserted the premier issue of 1876 was "whether the Rebel Democracy are to be victorious over the loyal Republicans at the polls, after they were beaten by loyal Republicans in the field."[25] Clearly, for all that the Centennial hoped to emphasize reconciliation, the wartime differences remained heatedly present for many Americans.

Even as the Centennial was coming to a close in November, requests for articles about the fair continued to arrive in Rebecca's mail. She crafted two such articles for *Harper's Weekly*: "A Rainy Day at the Exposition" and "Odd Corners of the Centennial," her only publications with this periodical. Almost every writer in the country had written about the exposition's features, but what interested Davis were the visitors themselves; some were cheerfully crowded into the Main Building, eating brown-bag lunches and seeking shelter from the rain. Most notable to her mind was "the number of women who have come alone to the Exposition.... Thousands of poor teachers, farmers' daughters, young girls from the West and New England, with eager brains and almost empty pockets." She assured readers that at the fair the single young woman of any class was "as secure of protection and courteous treatment as though she were the daughter of a millionaire out for an airing with her attendant *bonne*." She admitted that she began the day doubting she would find "universal brotherhood" at the fair; however, when she watched how everyone cared for a blind woman at each exhibit and allowed her to run her hands over the displays so she, too, could "see" the fair, Davis was forced to rethink her pessimism. "Turk, Christian, Jew, they were all kinsmen of this poor blind woman. The day began to seem sunshiny and cheerful in the great World's Fair, although without the night was falling and it was raining heavily."[26]

"Odd Corners" examined national character based on what each country chose to exhibit—showing only its skill in manufacturing or informing the world about its people as well. Thus Davis sought out the exhibit from China. Not only was this display placed at a great distance from the Main Hall and other favorite attractions, the racial hostility toward the Chinese at the Exposition had been vicious. In contrast to the American working woman who, according to Davis, visited the fair and was protected by the courtesy of all, individual Chinese visitors were followed by crowds of men and boys who shouted at them and treated them like strange beasts that needed to be corralled for the safety of others.[27]

By turning her attention to the Chinese exhibit, Davis immediately entered into a broiling political controversy. The Page Act of 1875 had begun the legalized exclusion of Chinese immigrants, under the argument that the US must exclude "cheap Chinese labor and immoral Chinese women," as Representative Horace Page had argued, creating class- and gender-based arguments purportedly to protect American laborers and to suggest all Chinese women were prostitutes.[28] That Page was a Republican indicated how drastically some segments of the once radical Republican Party were shifting.

In response to the nationwide denigration of the Chinese, Davis reported a different view: if the man from China "and one of the master-mechanics yonder in Machinery Hall could find language and possible space clear of prejudice on which to meet, they would differ but little in the scope and culture of their intellects, in their experience of men, or their treatment of women." On the other hand, she was put off by the dirt and grease of the Esquimaux in their Exposition hut, she reported, but when two Danish men confronted her about this attitude by revealing the history and legends of the Inuits, she concluded, "After all, what does it matter—Esquimaux hut or the palaces of the Exposition, with their treasures of science and art? The man and his friend are the same every where."[29] The Exposition essays for *Harper's Weekly* presented some of Davis's heartfelt arguments for the universal value of all human beings.

In December 1876 Davis published a powerful story, "How the Widow Crossed the Lines," in *Lippincott's*. The tale returned to the opening months of the Civil War in Wheeling and was particularly notable for the rare autobiographical allusions that were sketched in its opening pages. In the story, Mrs.

Potter holds radical abolitionist ideas, which she publicly expresses, while her brother has secretly sided with the Confederacy and is waiting to sneak out of town and join his troops. Because of their political differences, "the alienation between them had been growing more bitter," but they still loved one another.[30]

In a humorous and timely conclusion to the story, the narrator assured readers that one character, the die-hard Southern rebel Mrs. Van Pelt, survived the war "for she visited the Exposition in October. . . . She is still a rebel at heart, sniffed the air as she passed West Virginia's noble exhibit and building, and would eat nowhere but at the Southern Restaurant." Davis also humorously captured both sides of Southern attitudes that were revealed at the fair: Mrs. Potter's Confederate brother, "General Pomeroy, on the contrary, hobbled about on his wooden leg (he lost one in the Wilderness), full of zeal for 'our reunited country.' He was a Southern commissioner, and so has been dined and wined into hearty good fellowship with his Northern brethren."[31] In all, the nation's grand celebration had been a notable year for Rebecca as well as for the country.

The following year was as remarkable as the Centennial year had been, if in entirely different ways. In 1877, Rebecca would again expand her places of publication and continue to argue on behalf of universal brotherhood—and sisterhood. However, she and Clarke would face new challenges with Dick's educational experiences, and the city of Philadelphia, like the nation, would find that reunion and a reconciled society were far from an achieved reality. Labor disputes erupted throughout Pennsylvania, and economic inequalities became more evident as the nation entered the Gilded Age in which great wealth would be made but extraordinary levels of poverty would also develop; as industrialism forged ahead, many workers and especially immigrant laborers and African Americans faced new levels of inequities. As much as anything, the Gilded Age confirmed that most of the questions of Reconstruction remained unresolved.

Economic and class inequities had long interested Rebecca, and as the disparities in society spread in this era, she addressed the realities of life rather than mythologies. For *Youth's Companion* she countered the mythology of the poor as lazy in "Did His Best." Davis continued her indictment of the increasingly stratified American society with "The School-Boy's Story" for the *Independent*. Narrated by a boy attending Beebe Academy, the story was a stringent critique of the class and racial barriers that remained a part of American education. At the time the story was published, Henry Ossian Flipper, who had been born a slave, was the most notable of the first four

African American cadets at West Point, and Flipper would be the first to graduate from the institution. "The School-Boy's Story" initially seemed to be about the ways in which class structures pervade private academies, but the story exposed racial biases at the school like those Flipper and other cadets had faced, and Flipper is referred to in the story as "the West Point cadet."[32]

In "The School-Boy's Story," when Joe da Costa, the most talented boy, revealed his mixed-race heritage, his wealthy friend Pack immediately denounced him and declared he would not return to school if Joe was allowed to attend. The school's proprietor, Dr. Beebe, professed his abhorrence of "mixed" schools, "even in the case where the Government has authorized one. The West Point cadets have nobly shown their disapproval of the plan. I am informed the colored cadet is not recognized by them as a human being." So Joe must leave the school, even though Beebe knows he is a far superior scholar to Pack. The final lines of Davis's story indict the prevailing discriminatory practice that propelled the continuation of social inequities in the country: "We must consider the skin!" Dr. Beebe absurdly cries, "We must consider the skin!"[33] Whereas Davis's stories of the early 1870s had been some of her most racist, narratives such as "The School-Boy's Story" suggested a more progressive turn.

Rebecca had been able to draw on her own experiences as the parent of two boys now at private academies for "The School-Boy's Story." Dick had been sent to the Episcopal Academy, his father's alma mater. He would complete the year's studies in May, graduating in the middle of the class, and that would be the highest academic standing he would ever achieve. Charley was sent to a different academy, the William Penn Charter School, which proclaimed its fame for "developing great men."[34] There were good reasons for this separation of the boys. Charley was a top scholar, and Rebecca and Clarke likely realized how difficult it would be for Dick if Charley was to outshine him so publicly. On the other hand, Charley had always been in Dick's shadow, and being at a different school allowed him to become an independent "Charles Davis" rather than "Dick's little brother."

The life of another child and the economic and class implications of its death once again led Rebecca to identify herself publicly in the *New-York Tribune*. Although her editorials remained unsigned, she did sign a letter to the editor that was published on January 2, 1877. In December, the *Tribune* had reported on a woman whose child had died while she was on the street, "driven out of doors by a drunken husband, and the child had literally frozen to death while she sat there asking for help in vain from Christian people who passed by." The item acknowledged people might argue that there were numerous charitable institutions to aid such families, but it concluded, "The people responsible are those who passed her by."[35] This assessment set off a firestorm of responses from varying perspectives. The two most notable came from Josephine Shaw Lowell and from Davis herself—and became key arguments in the "indiscriminate charity" debate of the period.

Lowell insisted that to give money indiscriminately to beggars was only to encourage more beggary. This was part of a national debate surrounding questions of poverty and charity. The development of the American Charity Organization movement, begun in 1873, was founded on the argument that indiscriminate charity should be replaced with a "scientific" system that would include the elimination of street beggars through an intricately structured organization designed to investigate and counsel, but it would not offer material relief. Although some good was certainly done through these organizations, central to their thinking was the development of the notorious "Ugly Laws" that sought to remove from the vision of the average American citizen anyone on the streets with disabilities or anyone who revealed the extraordinary breadth of poverty in America.[36]

The position Lowell had taken deeply offended Rebecca, and she sent a lengthy rebuttal letter to the *Tribune*, which was published under the headline, "Indiscriminate Charity." In the previous year, Lowell had been appointed Commissioner of the New York State Board of Charities, becoming the first woman to hold the commission. As Davis recognized, Lowell had the position and power to enact her ideas of poverty reform. Davis had always argued against large charitable institutions, preferring direct charity by any individual in a position to aid another human being. She began her assessment of the published responses to the child's fate as "more comfortless" than the original article itself, horrific as it had been. There was much good will by those who had the means to aid others in need, she felt, "but the connecting link is lacking."[37]

In spite of temperance and prison reform movements and the newly developed large charitable institutions, statistics from those sources had not revealed a lessening population of the "so-called dangerous classes," Davis observed. The people who passed the mother and child, and who daily passed numerous others, were not enacting their Christian values; they could not blame charities or the police, she argued, but must look to their own failed actions.[38] Lowell and other respondents had used the term "dangerous classes" for the impoverished, with implications of violence or an economic malingering; these respondents were drawing on Charles Loring Brace's widely read *The Dangerous Classes* (1872), which supported large organized charities and the transportation of poor New York children to the West via orphan trains. Davis abhorred the belief that it was the right of the wealthy and of political leaders to dictate the lives of the poor, including separating families; her preference was to find economically viable work for the poor.

Two days after Davis's letter appeared, the *Tribune* continued the discussion by responding with an editorial on "Charity." Acknowledging Lowell and Davis were "well known to philanthropists," the editorial attempted at first to present a balanced assessment, but ultimately sided with Davis: "Indiscriminate almsgiving" should not be discouraged because it disarranges "corporate schemes of relief" and should not "strive to limit the workings of universal brotherhood to an affair of State taxation."[39] It was an issue Davis would return to numerous times in her life, and although major cultural figures such as Herbert Spencer and John D. Rockefeller would argue against indiscriminate charity and in favor of large charitable organizations, it was a perspective Rebecca never accepted. The reference to Davis's philanthropy was notable as well. Her generosity was noted periodically by national leaders, but never by Davis who would not allow her name to be used to promote her financial aid to many in need.

Discussions of women's fate in the hands of a society that thought more about the law and organized philanthropy than about individual women's lives began to turn Davis's thoughts again to novel-writing. It had been over three years since she had published a novel, and early in 1877 she conceptualized a new work on women and the law. Once again Davis longed for a broader, international audience. Although *Lippincott's* would serialize "A Law Unto Herself" and publish it in book form, they, like her previous publishers, would not push for English publication. This time Rebecca turned to a sister journalist and author for advice. She had first met Kate Field in 1862 during her visit to Boston. She admired Field and had followed her career over the years; recently they had been reunited as editorial correspondents for the *Tribune*. Field was lecturing and living in England at this time, and Rebecca felt Field might be more forthcoming than Davis's publishers had been.

Rebecca tread lightly as she began her letter to Field, since her purpose was to ask a favor: "I know how many people there are in the world who ask favors and are bores. In consequence, it is with a good deal of reluctance I add myself to the number. But I really need some information and can only think of you as the most capable person of giving it. I am sure you will be willing." Having cleverly praised *and* insisted on a response, Davis continued, "To plunge *in media res* at once I want to write for an English magazine—one of the best class, of course." Listing a number of questions she had about the matter, she asked Field if it was likely she could have her new novel "published simultaneously there as *Black's*[,] *MacDonald's* etc. are here? And, thirdly, I am absolutely ignorant of the whole matter, and know that in all probability you have the *carte du pays* of the literary world in your hand, and can advise me what to do." She closed her letter, however with advice to Field, "I have been heartily glad to hear of your great success in England. Don't come home just now, if you are happy there. You can have no idea of the stagnation of all business and life here. The country is like a man whom somebody is holding by the throat. Once more—don't think of me as a nuisance. I have strong dislike to myself while writing this letter—for I know that I am one."[40] In spite of Davis's efforts, the novel was not published in England.

In the spring Davis added another new periodical to her repertoire of publishers, *Appleton's Journal*. "Doctor Pajot" was a notable contribution to her extensive body of fiction in which physicians represented varying cultural attitudes. Although the story satirized publishers' marketing practices, its primary focus was on the title character, a Virginia physician who believed he was intellectually far superior to almost everyone he meets and who was supported in his ideas by an idolizing wife. Disdaining periodical literature, Dr. Pajot only wrote books, but they were never accepted for publication—because his brilliance could not be understood by his inferiors, he was sure. It was his wife who finally saved the family—by becoming a writer for the publishers who rejected his work—while he died in obscurity. Satirizing arrogant writers was a notable, and clearly enjoyable, part of Davis's literary repertoire.

In June her new novel began serialization in *Lippincott's*. "A Law Unto Herself" continued her exploration of the political novel, in the tradition of *Waiting for the Verdict* and *John Andross*, this time examining women's legal status at mid-century. Several national events compelled Davis to turn to the theme of women and the law—the enactment of a number of married women's property laws in recent decades that seemed to offer progress toward legal equality; the infamous *Bradwell v. Illinois* case that demonstrated the ephemeral nature of this supposed progress; the Centennial Exposition's exposure of the lack of equality for all people in the US; and her continuing concern about the best charitable means to address poverty.[41] The experiences of the novel's protagonist, Jane Swendon, exemplified the complicated legal machinations a single woman must negotiate. Although the other two main female characters—Charlotte, a

Spiritualist medium and confidence woman; and Cornelia, a bohemian New Woman and author—were contrasts to Jane, they also demonstrated that living outside the law and conventionality offered a means for financial gain and survival. To transgress boundaries, then, was neither celebrated nor denigrated; rather, the novel suggested the practicality of such actions in the face of biased legal restrictions for women.

Davis was writing in the aftermath of *Bradwell v. Illinois* in which the US Supreme Court denied Myra Bradwell's right to be admitted to the bar. As a married woman, the court determined, she could not enter into contracts without her husband's permission, thus negating any possibility of practicing the law. If women could not be lawyers, Davis and many other reformers recognized, it was unlikely that laws would be changed to benefit women or that laws relating to married women's property rights would be enforced in any widespread manner. Through the character of Jane Swendon, Davis demonstrated what these limitations meant realistically for a woman who wished to determine how her inheritance would be used or was swindled out of her inheritance entirely.

If Davis did not participate in the public demonstrations by suffragists at the Centennial, she used her pen in these years to support many of their ideas, especially to expose gender inequalities under the law and the inequalities in legal thought—but never to support women's right to vote. "A Law Unto Herself" also allowed Davis to dramatically retell the beliefs she had iterated in "Indiscriminate Charity." To emphasize the legal support the large corporate charities were receiving, the character of Judge Rhodes voiced the opinions Josephine Shaw Lowell had expressed in her debate with Davis in the *Tribune*. The judge referred to the impoverished as "the dangerous classes" and rejected the idea of the Good Samaritan as a model for individual aid to those in need. He shockingly responded in regard to a poor man, "Let him starve. He will have self-respect. The Good Samaritan knows nothing of political economy."[42] In contrast, Jane Swendon purchased a large farm and created "a colony of Philadelphia paupers."[43] The novel both argued for women's legal rights and against the belief that poverty was caused by laziness. What all citizens needed was work that paid a living wage.

Initial reviews of the serial were positive, but as the story unfolded and when it was published in book form the following year, it was considered too grim. *The Capital* acknowledged its "clear, realistic word-setting" but found it "a disappointment."[44] In fact, the assertion that Davis and other realist writers were "morbid" had become so common that a critic for *The Evolution*, a New York weekly that reviewed politics, science, and literature, wrote an article on the subject. "When any literature tends toward a loss of catholicity," he wrote, "it gives signs of debasement, if not decay there is no doubt that a critical demand for 'cheerfulness' in fiction is eminently *in conjunction with* realism in the depiction of women's status under the law." When critics such as Henry James, and a few others who reviewed *A Law*, denigrated Davis's work, as James had in *Waiting for the Verdict* and *Dallas Galbraith*, he did so on the basis that she brought emotional responses (in her characters and her readers) into realism,[45] failing to recognize this treatment of the subject as one of intent by a *reform realist* rather than a failure to adhere to male-defined literary conventions. A few reviewers comprehended that Davis was not writing "tea cup" realism nor attempting the supposed "objective" narration of some realists. As a reviewer for *The Nation* remarked, "she succeeds in giving a truer impression of American conditions than any writer we know except Mr. Howells, while there is a vast difference between his delicately illuminated preparations of our social absurdities and Mrs. Davis's grim and powerful etchings."[46]

With the novel completed, Rebecca and Clarke spent the summer and early fall of 1877 on their first trip to Europe. With Dick and Charley in academies and Nora ("Nolly") now five years old, they could comfortably make the trip. Being out of the country at the time meant they were not in Pennsylvania when the Great Railway Strike of 1877 began in mid-July, a topic both of them would have been likely to write about if they had been able to study it firsthand. They stopped for a short time at the Jersey shore on their return from England, and Clarke published a letter in *Scribner's Monthly* about the London stage that came to be known as "Joe Jefferson in London," his first and only publication in the periodical. He had met Richard Watson Gilder, now the primary editor, through Rebecca, who had been publishing in *Scribner's* since 1870, and the Gilders and Davises were close friends. The Davises had seen Jefferson in his triumphant performance of "Rip Van Winkle" on the London stage, and Clarke would return to London periodically to view its latest offerings.

Rebecca ended 1877 on a strong note of publications in *Peterson's*, *Youth's Companion*, *Harper's*, and *Appleton's* and entered into a new kind of publication for *Scribner's Monthly*, an occasional nonfiction piece published under her initials in what essentially was the editorial page of the magazine. "A Market for Art-Work" was the first entry of this type. She reported on the group of wealthy women who were opening fine-art salesrooms in New York to aid struggling artists. Davis noted, "the finest work on the Minton and Doulton ware is done by women. . . . There is no reason why this career should not be opened to American women of talent and skill.... The plan was at first intended to benefit only women; but the Society has wisely, as we think, declined to acknowledge any distinction of sex in art."[47]

In December two works appeared. "A Night in the Mountains" of North Carolina was Davis's second and last publication for *Appleton's*. In earlier years *Appleton's* had been a strong competitor of *Harper's Weekly*, but it had waned in its attention to contemporary events, and Davis turned to other periodicals. Her second story, "The Man in the Cage," was a powerful contribution to *Harper's Monthly*. The story had first appeared in the *Wheeling Intelligencer* on November 24; the *Intelligencer* had long followed Davis's career and periodically reported on her activities, and she had maintained a distant friendship with its editor, Archibald Campbell. The story was another instance of her reform work, this time in opposition to the death penalty. As she and Clarke had argued against false incarceration in asylums, she now turned to the death penalty for similar reasons of concern.

"The Man in the Cage" depicted a person wrongfully charged with murder in North Carolina, cruelly imprisoned, and chained in his cell for over a year. In the 1870s several states were challenging the mandatory death penalty for murder in favor of life imprisonment,[48] and Davis's story strongly supported this perspective when, five years after the prisoner's escape, another man confessed to the murder. The Davises had been friends of George Leib Harrison and his wife Lucretia Mitchell Harrison since their earliest married years. Although Rebecca was more radical in her thinking than George, they had a mutual interest in questions surrounding the death penalty—she advocated its abolishment while he was greatly concerned with humane practices if a convicted felon was to be executed. In two years he would be appointed inspector of the Eastern Penitentiary in Pennsylvania. The question of the treatment of prisoners would continue to resonate in Davis's reform writings in the coming years.

Davis's pen was in constant action in these months, but as the year ended, the masculine dominance of publishing in America—in spite of the extraordinary popularity of many women writers—was blatantly demonstrated. The *Atlantic Monthly* under William Dean Howells's editorship sponsored a banquet on December 17 at Boston's Hotel Brunswick to celebrate John Greenleaf Whittier's seventieth birthday and the accomplishments of the periodical itself. To the surprise and disdain of the many women who had helped to secure the magazine's reputation for high literary quality, the banquet's guest list included men only. Rebecca tended to take such events in stride, but no one spoke more eloquently on the injustice of women writers' exclusion than Frances Willard, who published a letter of protest in the *Boston Daily Advertiser*.

In the era of national calls for women's rights, Willard asserted, "In the Republic of Letters, if nowhere else, woman is a citizen." She named writers who had been instrumental in the success of the periodical: "who had *earned* a seat at Whittier's own right hand? Who but Harriet Beecher Stowe, one of the chief contributors to the *Atlantic*? and Harriet Prescott Spofford, Rebecca Harding Davis, Gail Hamilton, Elizabeth Stuart Phelps, Mrs. Whitney, and Louisa M. Alcott—were they not 'the manner born'?" Willard concluded the letter with a simple but pointed declaration, "My brethren, these things ought not so to be!"[49] For all that Davis and the other named women writers had accomplished, it was not a propitious ending to the year. The path to literary equality remained a rocky one. That these women attained and held national status as authors attested to their willingness to fight on in the battle for professional recognition and to collapse "any distinction of sex in art," as Davis had remarked.

It was also around this time Rebecca reconnected with Louisa May Alcott when the Bostonian visited her in Philadelphia. The young woman who had been so impoverished but passionate was older, but she remained a favorite of Davis's. As Rebecca recalled, when Alcott arrived, "I hurried to meet her. The lean, eager, defiant girl was gone, and instead there came to greet me a large, portly, middle-aged woman, richly dressed. Everything about her, from her shrewd, calm eyes to the rustle of her satin gown told me of assured success." Yet her character had not changed: "I am sure fame and success counted for nothing with her except for the material aid which they enabled her to give to a few men and women whom she loved. She would have ground her bones to make their bread. Louisa Alcott wrote books which were true and fine, but she never imagined a life as noble as her own."[50] The meeting demonstrated the support women writers had for one another, just as Willard's December remarks had.

The coming year of 1878 would have certain family challenges but generally would be a happy and productive time for Rebecca. She would continue to publish in *Scribner's Monthly*, *Harper's*, *Lippincott's*, *Peterson's*, and *Youth's Companion* and add *Sunday Afternoon* as a new regular place of publication. The year would also bring new travels and a renewal of old friendships.

She began the year with a three-part serial for *Peterson's*, "The November Night." During and after the Civil War, Davis's John Page mysteries had revealed the racial abuses that marked the South and which it had attempted to hide under customs of chivalry and honor. A Page cousin appeared in "The November Night," and the story asserted that in the postwar years the Southern plantation families still destroyed lives through their insistence on hiding the reality of crime and avarice in order to maintain a family mythology. This story was the last serial Davis would publish in *Peterson's* for several years and the last of her longer stories for them. By mid-year she had turned to a maximum of four to five pages per tale for the magazine, which allowed her to continue to contribute to the periodical that, for more than fifteen years, had offered her a steady income and a lasting friendship with its editor, Charles Peterson, but which also allowed her to write more prolifically for other magazines.

In February Davis contributed a temperance story, "A Sunday in Limeburgh," to *Scribner's Monthly*. She also began contributing to the newly founded *Sunday Afternoon*, published by E. F. Merriam and under the editorship of Washington Gladden. Gladden and Davis had many values in common; previously as editor of the *Independent*, he had exposed the corruption of Boss Tweed's organization, he used his editorial position to support workers' rights, and in 1877, he had been a founder of the Social Gospel movement. Although Davis never overtly joined that intellectual movement, its goal of bringing Christian ethics to the nation's social problems was a practice she had followed her entire career. *Sunday Afternoon* was a monthly Congregationalist "household magazine" from Springfield, Massachusetts. It focused on religious writings and literary offerings and was considered a "high-grade magazine" that attracted writers such as Edward Everett Hale, Horace Elisha Scudder, Rose Terry Cooke, and Sarah Orne Jewett. In its goals and quality, it was an apt periodical for Davis.[51]

Davis's writings for religious periodicals were typically no more overtly religious than her publications for major literary periodicals, as they focused on family and community, on ethics and personal responsibility, and were set in Virginia, West Virginia, and Pennsylvania. For instance, her first contribution to *Sunday Afternoon*, "Nicholas Harbour's Work," paralleled "A Sunday in Limeburgh" for *Scribner's Monthly*. In these regional and thematic preferences, Davis sought to expand American literature's geography to underrepresented regions as she had from the beginning of her career. This story was set in the hills of Pennsylvania in a small community that idolized its preacher and had as many class-based ideologies as any urban metropolis. "Nicholas Harbour's Work" was also a temperance story that exposed class biases within the clergy as well as the congregation. The publishers included Davis's story in the gift book, *Sunday Afternoon 1878*. This was the first major religious periodical for which Davis became a regular contributor; within a few years she would expand her repertoire in that field and continue to write for religious periodicals for the rest of her life.

It was March before Davis published her first story of the year with *Youth's Companion*. "Seventy-Seven" extended her prison reform writings to children's literature. She followed the next month with "Brave," one of her rarer stories set in Philadelphia's upper-class society—or those who pretended to be of that class while running up unpayable debts to maintain that lifestyle. Such people were contrasted with the young man who worked for a living and paid his own way. The story was reprinted as "Brave Dick" by several labor-oriented periodicals, including the *Miners' Journal* and the *National Labor Tribune*.[52] This month Davis also published an editorial in the *New-York Tribune* about West Virginia and its resources, encouraging people in need of work to look to her home state. A West Virginian sent a letter to the *Tribune* editor a month later asserting that the article had "done more to draw attention to our State than all the advertising of years," and the *Wheeling Intelligencer* reported that the Governor had received several letters from people who read the article and were interested in moving to the state.[53]

Davis returned to the pages of *Sunday Afternoon* in April with "St. Matthew's and St. Mark's," in which she offered "biographies" of the two churches. "Why should not churches have their biographies as well as individuals?" she asked. "They have their characters, even to idiosyncracies and hobbies . . . precisely like an exaggerated type of human being."[54] She most admired St. Matthew's because, unlike St. Mark's, it did not expend its funds on building a magnificent church but rather to help the poor. She followed in June with a companion piece on "The Charities of St. Matthew's."

In the early summer Rebecca was delighted to briefly host James G. Blaine, now a US Senator. He was in Philadelphia to speak at the opening of the Centennial's permanent Exhibition in Fairmont Park. At the ceremonies he reiterated his position on the debates over tariff laws, arguing for greater international trade by the US. Clarke had written an editorial in support of Blaine's position the previous month: "Mr. BLAINE, who is an old Pennsylvanian, is upon the right side of the tariff argument. . . . Mr. BLAINE is not only thoroughly informed upon this particular feature of political economy, but he has the necessary force of character and controlling influence in the Senate to compel attention to and respect for his arguments." During his speech in Philadelphia, Blaine expressed sentiments that paralleled those of Rebecca: "the country is always happiest and most prosperous when labor is honorably employed and amply compensated at home."[55] Although Blaine could spend only a few hours with the Davis family on this trip, it was sufficient to reinforce the bond that would be both personally and politically beneficial. He began to make these brief visits more regularly, finding the Davis home a refuge from public attention.[56] Clarke remained interested in James's political theories and would continue to support him in the pages of the *Philadelphia Inquirer.*

In the spring of 1878, the family had to admit Dick was not succeeding in his studies at the Episcopal Academy. As Charley revealed, "his weekly report never failed to fill the whole house with an impenetrable gloom and ever-increasing fears as to the possibilities of his future."[57] Two years short of graduation, Dick was withdrawn from the Academy. Rebecca and Clarke arranged for him to be tutored by her brother Wilse in Bethlehem, Pennsylvania. In the fall Dick was to move in with his uncle for a year's trial to see if he could improve his studies enough to enter college, but it also meant that he and Charley would be further separated. Instead of just weekdays apart, they would now only see each other when one or the other could travel between Philadelphia and Bethlehem. Like all of the family, they would write frequently.[58] In spite of the many challenges with Dick's education, his parents' sense of his extraordinary talents never diminished.

Rebecca's summer plans this year were slightly different than usual. Wilse met Rebecca and the children at Cheat Mountain, part of the Alleghenies in eastern West Virginia that had been the setting for many of her Civil War stories.[59] From there, they all went to Point Pleasant and were joined by Clarke. More than previous summers, Rebecca could see the ways in which their once isolated spot was becoming a tourist resort. A four-story hotel, the Resort House, had just opened, the first of many hotels that would be developed in the coming years; and now, instead of the usual wagon ride to the beach, a horse-drawn trolley shuttled hotel guests to and from the sandy beaches.[60] The Davises would continue to summer at Point Pleasant for many more years, but its quaint atmosphere was gone.

While at the shore, another of Davis's commentaries for *Lippincott's* "Our Monthly Gossip" editorial column was published. "A Lost Colony" connected to the increased international interest in exploring the North Pole. There had been a longstanding story about a lost colony of Norwegians that Dr. Isaac I. Hayes of Philadelphia had written about after his 1860 exploration. Davis interviewed Dalton Door, who had accompanied Dr. Hayes, and reported, he "tells me that among the Esquimaux there is a tradition that a colony of foreigners once owned the land, and about five centuries ago emigrated in a body northward."[61] She called upon American antiquarians, historians, and novelists to examine the theory. "I know no mystery made of such nightmare stuff as this in history; and mysteries are growing scarce now-a-days . . . we cannot afford to lose one of them."[62]

She also published "A Day with Doctor Sarah," in *Harper's*. This quixotic tale was her only other depiction, besides "Berrytown," of a woman physician. At the same time, Davis published "His Great Deed" in *Lippincott's*, drawing on the Norse legend of Grimmel, the youngest of three brothers who must undertake all adventures, confront the Devil, and win the pot of gold in the end. Davis transposed the legend to the Black Mountains of North Carolina. The story also included the characterization of a woman alcoholic, a rare instance in fiction at this time.

Clarke wrote an important theatrical review while at the shore as well. The Davises attended the various theaters in Philadelphia, and when the company of *H.M.S. Pinafore* had come to Philadelphia's Broad Street Theatre in the spring, they attended. Clarke wrote a glowing review of the performance that was reprinted by the producers and credited with the play's success throughout the winter: *Pinafore* was so popular it ran in five Philadelphia theaters simultaneously.[63] Rebecca and Clarke took the children to see the play, and Uncle Wilse joined them; it was the "grand point" of the family's outing that day, Rebecca noted, after which they all went out for a "jolly dinner."[64]

In the fall, Dick was settled into his uncle's home where Wilse also had the company of seventy-year-old Rachel Harding. The fourteen-year-old Dick's letters to his parents and to Charley reveal his poor spelling skills but also a delightful sense of humor; he often added sketches in the margin to illustrate whatever he was describing, from Philadelphia friends at the skating rink to a man who was found dead in the streets of Bethlehem. Occasionally signing the letters with his childhood name of "Hardy," he most often used "Dick" now, and he reported to his parents that he missed them but was getting on well. To Charley, he wrote with great comradery and often about the girls he met, but he lamented that his invitations to social events were as yet few. After a very active social life with many friends in Philadelphia, living where he knew no other boys his age was a difficult transition, but he gained a bit of cache with a local college student when the young man learned he was related to "Harding Davis, the author." Dick was being tutored by several teachers, but his French teacher, Mr. Ringer, was the bane of his existence and received ample attention in his letters to Charley, or "Gus" as the family sometimes called him.[65] Uncle Wilse worked closely with Dick throughout the fall and winter, overseeing the tutors and encouraging his young nephew to work diligently. The family still hoped that Dick could attend college—their dream for both boys—and this year would be the telling point.

As the winter set in, Rebecca published in *Peterson's*, *Youth's Companion*, and *Sunday Afternoon*, and after a nearly two-year gap, returned to the pages of the *Independent* with "The Conards." The story presented very grim perspectives on changes in contemporary society. The Conards lived in one of the new housing projects that were appearing in cities at the time, "a mass of six hundred cheap, tawdry little houses, alike to the very door-bells, built by a stock company by contract, and dubbed Elysium Place, on one of those whims of sentiment peculiar to the American mind. . . . The gay, lace curtained windows and silver-plated little doors turned the same jaunty, well-to-do front to the world, no matter what crime or misery lurked behind them."[66] The story critiqued ward politicians, American education, and the ways in which women's labor is undervalued in society and in the family.

In the first two months of 1879 Rebecca published seven stories, one each for *Lippincott's*, *Harper's*, and *Sunday Afternoon*, and two each for *Peterson's* and *Youth's Companion*. "The Colonel's Venture: A Story of Old Virginia" for *Lippincott's* continued the story of a Page family member. In spite of her critiques of the Old South, Rebecca loved traveling through the North Carolina mountains almost as much as spending summers at Point Pleasant. Riding through the hills on mules, camping out, and the breathing the invigorating mountain air offered the perfect get-away for her, and she raised her children to love the outdoors as well. Mountain vacations (in North Carolina, West Virginia, and Georgia) became a frequent means in her short stories to explore a wide variety of cultural issues. "Landry's Strange Story" for *Peterson's* followed this pattern, as it examined the cultural dangers of ignoring poverty and persecuting non-whites.

Davis's extensive attention in the late 1870s to the South was a response to the North's postwar representation of the region as backward and decaying, due in part to the yellow fever outbreak in the Mississippi River Valley that claimed nearly 20,000 lives.[67] Although Davis had used similar arguments during the war, she often countered this stereotypic designation in her later stories. In February 1879 she directly addressed epidemics in "A Story of the Plague" for *Harper's*. As with her Civil War stories, Davis used the past as an analogy. Set during the cholera epidemic of 1832, Davis's story seemed to confirm the image of the South as a mix of "dirt and splendor."[68] Yet the story traversed from the iron mills on the Ohio River to the plague-ridden South, connecting northern capitalists who profited from the resources of the South to the horrors of cholera outbreaks.

This month Davis also published the lead story in *Sunday Afternoon*. "In Re Silas Rhawn" continued her critiques of regional biases, examining New Englanders who felt only disgust for people from the South and West. Here it was the Southern man who personified true humanity. The juxtaposition of "The Colonel's Venture" and "In Re Silas Rhawn" revealed the ways in which Davis worked to defraud stereotypes of Southerners—there were Old Southerners like the Colonel who represented the failures of the South, and just as many people of the region, such as Dr. Rhawn, who demonstrated the progressive character of some Southerners. Davis liked writing for *Sunday Afternoon*, which in its third year was drawing many famous American writers to its pages, including Elizabeth Stuart Phelps, Edward Everett Hale, Caroline Dall, Rose Terry Cooke, Octave Thanet, Sarah Orne Jewett, and Edward Bellamy.

Both Rebecca and Clarke were traveling more often now that their children were older. They went to Bethlehem as often as possible to see Dick and Wilse and sometimes met Rebecca's mother there as well. Rebecca occasionally traveled to New York for the *Tribune*; and Clark traveled even more than usual for his editorial work with the *Inquirer*. He frequently visited Washington, D.C., at James Blaine's invitation and stayed at the Riggs House in the capital, a favorite of politicians such Presidents Garfield and Harrison and those hoping to influence politicians, including Elizabeth Cady Stanton and Susan B. Anthony. On March 26, Blaine sent a note inviting Clarke to join him for dinner that Friday to "meet a few friends of both parties & all ages—quite informally—."[69] Through such invitations, Clarke was able to meet many influential men, but he maintained a reputation for asserting his own opinions in the *Inquirer's* editorials, and as President Rutherford B. Hayes let Clarke know in June, they did not always please the politicians.[70] In a few years, Clarke's life among the Washington elite would lead to one of his most enduring friendships—with Grover Cleveland.

During the summer, works by both Rebecca and Clarke appeared in the magazines. She published in *Peterson's* and *Lippincott's*, and Clarke continued his interest in theater criticism with "At and After the Play: Jefferson and Rip Van Winkle," also in *Lippincott's*. Summer, however, was a time for family. Although Rebecca's sister Emilie and her husband John Gow only occasionally came to Point Pleasant, Rebecca stayed in close contact with Emilie, who also maintained a relationship with her niece and nephews via letters. Wilse Harding was sometimes able to entice Rebecca and Clarke to events at his college as well, and he used that pretext in the summer of 1879 to aid Clarke when he was again struggling with depression. Undoubtedly planned with Rebecca, Wilse invited Clarke and Dick to attend Lehigh's commencement ceremony before they left for their summer at the shore. Wilse's pride in his brother-in-law was evident when he brought Clarke up on the commencement platform and had a "grand dinner" in his honor afterward. Clarke returned to Philadelphia tired, but he assured Rebecca he would go again the next year. Upon his return she wrote in her diary about her "Darling": "Oh it was so good to see him a little happy once more!"[71]

The family went to Point Pleasant earlier than usual this year, in late June. Clarke had encouraged a friend, Mr. Kirk, and his bride to join them. "Such a daring experiment," Rebecca reflected, "for a middle aged man with a family to marry a woman of the same age & no money to speak of any where. But such a wise thing to do."[72] It was not an easy summer, however, since the Davises were having the cottage remodeled. There were workers in the kitchen, in the boys' room, and knocking out a section of a wall to add a doorway.[73] To his parents' relief, however, Dick was doing much better in Bethlehem. "He is so full of fun & happiness bubbling over with it," she recorded in her diary, but lamented, "He told me how when he was at that wretched school [the Episcopal Academy] he had once made up his mind to kill himself. . . . And we never knew." Dick could be very dramatic, but Rebecca was well aware that he suffered from despondency much like his father, and she condemned herself and Clarke as "blind fools" not to have seen how extremely unhappy their eldest child had been.[74]

To Rebecca's surprise, August brought a letter from Annie Adams Fields seeking to reconnect and inviting the Davises to spend a week with the Fieldses in Boston. Writing from Point Pleasant, Rebecca responded warmly to the reconnection but declined the visit:

> Indeed dear Annie I should be glad to take up the dropped thread again. But a week's visit with my three young Berserkers would be too tough a knot to tie them with, I think. For other reasons, too, it is impossible for me to accept your tempting invitation. Mr. Davis left us in May,[75] and since then I have been traveling through my old camping ground, the North Carolina mountains, and have just settled down to rest. This has been our summer home for thirteen years, and it has grown in to a habit for my mother, brothers, and other friends to meet us here every August. The gathering of the clan is now in

progress, and of course I can not go away. Mr. Davis expects to join us the middle of September.

She offered an alternative to a trip to Boston,

> Can you not spare time for a letter? Consider it one of the talks we might have had, if I had gone, and let me have a glimpse of you both—and your seaside home of which I have heard pleasant things. Cordially yours R. H. Davis.[76]

As the signature suggested, Rebecca felt cordial toward Annie, but the thread had, in fact, been broken. Perhaps most notable in this letter, however, was Rebecca's brief reference to "brothers." She and her estranged brother Richard Harding had reconciled, and though Rebecca did not mention him again in her letters, she would dedicate a children's novel to him and Wilse in 1892.

Over the summer Rebecca had determined to take something of a break from her non-stop schedule by declining to make long-term publishing commitments for a while. She would focus on short stories and journalism for the next few years, writing prolifically but without the constant pressure of novel and serial commitments for a number of publishers that often meant she could not take on new venues. Over the fall and winter, Davis published several short stories in *Peterson's*, *Youth's Companion*, and *Good Company* (formerly *Sunday Afternoon*). *Good Company* had been able to retain the major writers who had written for *Sunday Afternoon*, and Davis's first contribution to the revised magazine was "Tom Hardy," one of the longest stories she published in the late 1870s at sixteen pages, and certainly the most overtly political. The story, which began in the prewar years, addressed the popularity of Henry Clay's and William Henry Harrison's "Whiggism" in the small coal town of Powhatan, Virginia.

Rebecca was also pleased to learn at this time that Dick had now made many friends in Bethlehem; he had been invited to a party and attended a wedding in the fall with a guest list of more than 300 people. She enjoyed her son's delight in having new clothes for the event. "He was happier than even the bride," she wrote bemusedly in her diary. "For she did not know how the new husband might turn out. But there was no doubt about the new clothes"![77] Her elder son would remain a clotheshorse for the rest of his life, garnering both praise and condemnation for his dramatic attire.

The year ended on a positive note for women writers as well. William Dean Howells and the *Atlantic Monthly* had learned two years earlier the very public consequences of excluding women when they held the banquet in honor of

John Greenleaf Whittier. Thus when they organized a similar banquet of recognition for Dr. Oliver Wendell Holmes in December, the women writers who had helped establish the magazine's reputation were invited, including Davis. Julia Ward Howe spoke at the gathering, and several people who could not attend sent letters that were read at the event.[78] Davis was among the latter and wrote, "I am sincerely sorry that I cannot accept your invitation to be present at your pleasant celebration of Dr. Holmes's birthday. I must content myself to be one with all the rest of the world who delight to honor your good poet every day in their own homes."[79]

It had been a highly successful decade for Davis. She had published major political novels, continued to expand the repertoire of magazines that published her work, she and Clarke had sustained the strength of their marriage, and their three children were healthy and developing into distinct individuals. The next decade would bring increased opportunities for Davis in journalism, she would again expand into a new realm of reform writing, and she would travel even more widely than she had in the past. As the nation experienced a decade of renewed industrialization and became even more materialistic in the Gilded Age, Davis would be at the forefront in assessing the rapid changes in US society and examining its excesses as well as its possibilities.

CHAPTER 8

Exposing Government Corruption (1880–1884)

As the new decade began, Rebecca was at the height of her career. She was nationally recognized as one of the premier writers in the country, sought after by all of the major literary magazines, and had established herself as one of the most influential women journalists through her work with the *New-York Tribune*. Nearing fifty, she was in excellent health, physically active and adventurous. Clarke was successful in his career and recognized as one of the leading newspaper men in the nation. Their sons were old enough to be thinking about their futures, and their daughter was healthy and active. Nora, at seven, was being educated at home. Dick continued living in his Uncle Wilse's home in Bethlehem,[1] where he was tutored, and Rebecca's mother, Rachel Harding, lived alternately with Wilse and Rebecca. Dick reported to Rebecca how carefully Rachel attended him when he was sick, which eased her mind about being separated from her son.

During this time, mother and son began a process of writing to each other numerous times a week, a pattern they would continue for the remainder of their lives whenever they were apart. The bond between Rebecca and her children was extraordinarily strong. In the winter of 1880, Rebecca and Clarke were still worried about Dick's academic abilities, but they were relieved that he had adjusted well to life in Bethlehem.

Charley was thriving at William Penn Charter School. A private Quaker institution, Penn Charter was a feeder school for some of the nation's Ivy League universities. The brothers remained close and supported and praised each other whenever possible. When Charley sent Dick an account of a cricket match he had attended, Dick told his mother that it was "supreme," and Charley "ought to be a reporter."[2] Everyone anticipated at this point that Charley would become an engineer, but Dick already recognized his brother's writing talents.

The Davises were now prosperous enough to have four live-in household servants: Eliza McNeil, a thirty-nine year old Irish woman; Mary Jones, a thirty-year-old mulatta from Virginia; Louisa Mann, a sixteen-year-old from Pennsylvania; and William Wilson, a twenty-five-year old, who came from Maryland originally.[3] With a constant stream of people to be entertained—friends (the artists who always populated their evenings, and local friends such as the Motts, Dr. S. Weir Mitchell, the poet and former diplomat George Henry Boker, and the Shakespearean scholar Horace Howard Furness), family, and dignitaries—the household was a demanding part of Rebecca's life as well. Instead of viewing the 1880s as a period to rest and enjoy the comfortable life she and Clarke had built together, however, Rebecca extended her interest in certain reforms, expanded her journalistic endeavors, and became a regular contributor to new periodicals.

Lippincott's magazine published a column, "Our Monthly Gossip," devoted to contemporary cultural events, and Davis began 1880 with a contribution to the column, "Such Stuff As Dreams Are Made Of." The essay was part of an increasing body of anecdotes and scientific records in the new field of psychical research. William James and several British scientists were studying the phenomena, attempting to take such issues of memory, dreams, and thought transference out of the realm of popular mediums and séances and into the realm of science.[4] Davis had written about this new field in "The Captain's Story" in 1866, and in the new essay she recounted two related incidents from her years in Washington, Pennsylvania. The first was of a young woman of notable intelligence who, after a fever, awoke into a new "soul" or personality completely different from her former self; through the remainder of her life, she moved back and forth between her two selves, Davis reported, without being aware of the alternative self.

The second instance she recounted in the essay related to the murder of a young woman, Rachel Plymire. As Davis learned, a woman who lived forty miles away from the Plymire farm had a dream in which she saw the murder; she identified two perpetrators, but since dreams could not be used as evidence in a trial, the men were not convicted. Davis lent credence to the account of the woman's dream by indicating that Rev. Charles Wheeler, a highly respected Baptist clergyman, and Ephraim Blaine, a magistrate and father of Senator James G. Blaine, were among those who examined the woman. Although Davis's instances were anecdotal, the phenomenon was given much more credence than she would afford mesmerism in a story published the following year. Davis's interest in psychical possibilities came from her habit of reading medical journals where the topic was receiving considerable attention, and she was always interested in the uncanny and unexplainable.

In these years Davis remained interested, too, in developing women characters who understood their legal rights. "The South Branch Farm" in *Peterson's*, for example, traced the horrific life of a widow whose husband had been miserly and whose son was even more oppressive than his father had been. Rather than a romantic solution in which the women were rescued, typically through marriage, Davis depicted the seemingly meek daughter as rising from her oppression and legally claiming her and her mother's shares of the family estate from her brother's domineering control, after which she bought a homestead of her own where she and her mother lived in comfort. Davis also retained her dual signatures for *Peterson's*: a romance used "By the Author of 'The Second Life,'" whereas more realistic cultural analyses such as "The South Branch Farm" appeared under her own name.

Late in the spring of 1880, James G. Blaine wrote Clarke, thanking him for his support during the difficult period in which he was seeking the nomination of the Republican Party for President of the United States. When Rutherford B. Hayes decided not to run for reelection, Blaine seemed to have a good chance, but as prospects began to turn against him, Blaine told Clarke, "I have deeply felt the worth and value of your friendship in these trying months now coming to an end—You have been true, zealous, [cap]able & farsighted. . . . No pen has been mightier than yours in making public conscience & fixing public thought—Thanks from my heart—And from my heart I send love to my good cousin [Rebecca]—and lasting gratitude to you—Ever faithfully, J. G. Blaine."[5] By the convention in June, the votes would swing to James A. Garfield.

Meanwhile, Rebecca's powerful story, "Walhalla," set in an isolated German colony in the North Carolina mountains, appeared in the May issue of *Scribner's Monthly*, but it was her last publication with the magazine. It ceased publication in 1881 and would soon reappear as *Century Illustrated Magazine*. The shift was a business change, with Scribner selling his interests in the magazine, and Richard Watson Gilder taking charge. The quality of fiction and the keen attention to political and social issues remained hallmarks of the new magazine. With this change, Davis focused on short nonfiction pieces for the *Century*. It would be 1895 before she again published fiction in Gilder's magazine, preferring instead to contribute pithy cultural analyses.

At the same time, Clarke worked with Putnam's to reissue a collection of his fictional writings from the late 1860s for their "Knickerbocker Novels" series; the collection included "A Stranded Ship," "Dick Lyle's Fee," and a new story "A Queen of Burlesque." The collection received mixed reviews; the reviewer for *Appleton's* captured the change in fiction in the decade since Clarke had first published his stories: the reprints came from an older era when "animation of narrative" ruled rather than "the modern subtleties of character analysis and portraiture"; it was, the reviewer concluded, "a good species of its class."[6] This collection was the last fiction by Clarke for nearly a decade. He concentrated thereafter on journalism and an occasional article about the theater.

Rebecca continued to publish in *Good Company* in the early 1880s as well. The magazine had gained a reputation in England, where, according to *Trubner's*, it was considered second only to the *Atlantic Monthly* for its talented group of "native writers," including Davis.[7] Her first publication of the year for the magazine was "A Homely Story of A Home." Although titled nearly the same as an 1869 *Tribune* Christmas story, this was a new piece that encapsulated one of her favorite themes—the commonplace man or woman who never gains the limelight, even in their own communities, but whose work and goodwill support everyone in their family and town.

Over the summer, Rebecca again traveled in the North Carolina mountains, writing as she traversed the area. In spite of her insistence that she would avoid serials, she returned to that format for a novella, "By-Paths in the Mountains," that ran from July through September in *Harper's New Monthly Magazine*. Perhaps as much as any other of Davis's blended-genre stories, "By-Paths" melded a seemingly nonfiction beginning with a fictional story. The long narrative offered insights into the less-traveled mountain regions of West Virginia and North Carolina and satirized the popular idea of summering in the South to recover from overwork by "getting back to nature." "By-Paths" demonstrated that truly journeying in nature's less-traveled regions was arduous, at times dangerous, and often exhausting, even when it offered pure air and magnificent scenery. When the story's travelers—a white physician Dr. Mulock, his wife, and a single woman, Sarah Davidger—have been roughing it for several weeks, they come to the resort at Highlands, North Carolina. Samuel T. Kelsey of New York had founded several cities in the South but none had the commercial success of the Highlands, which he promoted for its healthful climate and arable land. The narrator concurred on the benefits of its climate but soon exposed the sense of class and cultural superiority of the New England travelers who want to impose their own cultural values on locals. Davis also criticized the resort's use of African Americans as little more than remodeled slaves, a common Southern resort practice in the postwar years to present a façade of the Old South for tourists.

As the travelers once again moved on, an image was presented in stark contrast to Edward King's imperialistic view of *The Great South*, which had appeared in *Harper's* after the war and had argued African Americans were incapable of self-sufficiency. In Davis's travel-narrative story, all through the mountainous region of the South the travelers find little cabins and "'own patches' of the freedman, which show that, like all other human beings, he puts more intelligence and energy into his work when it is for himself than for others."[8] Davis's descriptions of the African Americans' cabins contrasted sharply with the many filthy homes of impoverished white mountain men and women the travelers had encountered, and it rejected the idea of race inferiority.

Of particular importance was the challenge of "By-Paths" to the practice of brutal convict labor. In the 1880s the convict lease system was established to build railroads in North Carolina, Alabama, and other states. Black legislators had curtailed the convict lease system in the early 1870s,[9] but it was again thriving in 1880 after African Americans had been forced out of their congressional seats and after several miners' strikes in the mid- and late 1870s gave Southern Democrats the ability to enact new convict labor laws. Davis exposed the government's whitewashing of housing and labor conditions for the convict laborers. Leaders such as North Carolina Governor Thomas J. Jarvis sought to present the system as humane, rehabilitative, and progressive since much of the convicts' labor was employed in building railroads in the state.[10] Part of a series of laws passed in the 1880s to restrict African American mobility, the Convict Lease Act allowed states to arrest any black man deemed a "vagrant" or for other (often falsified) charges; the "convicts" were then hired out to white men looking for cheap labor, and the profits for state and local governments were considerable.[11]

Against this propaganda, Davis exposed the realities of the system in "By-Paths." In North Carolina the travelers stayed at a rustic lodging in the woods. In the evening Mrs. Mulock and Sarah were sitting on the porch when "half a dozen camp fires started into light, and the gorge swarmed with hundreds of wretched blacks in the striped yellow convict garb. After their supper was cooked and eaten, they were driven into a row of prison cars, where they were tightly boxed for the night, with no possible chance to obtain either air or light." The travelers learned that recently one African American man had been sentenced to life for stealing a mackerel, "But the South must have convict labor, to finish her railways." All of these actions were conducted under cover of night. When the travelers prepared to leave the next day, "the prison cars had vanished, the world was all so bright and pure and splendid that Sarah began to think that cars and convicts had only been a malarious vapor of the night."[12]

The indictment of the inaction of the white travelers was represented when they simply moved on and forgot they had ever seen the brutalization of these men.

In the fall, Rebecca and Clarke saw the benefits of their decision to have sixteen-year-old Dick tutored for the past two years when he was admitted to Swarthmore College Preparatory School, designed to offer additional preparatory training for students before entering college.[13] Rebecca's mother had come to live with the Davises at this time as well. Rachel Harding's health was declining, and she could no longer live alone.[14] Amidst these family changes and holiday preparations, Rebecca managed to publish three stories at the end of the year: in November, "The Fire Opal" for *Youth's Companion*, another story in the saga of the Colonel Page family; and in December "La Barrone" in *Peterson's* and "Only Father" in the *Independent*.

In these years, the *Independent* was one of the most important religious magazines of the day; it had become an interdenominational periodical that was adept at covering cultural events, supported Republican presidential candidates, and was able to draw some of the best writers of the day. Along with Davis, its core of writers included author-activist Helen Hunt Jackson; Rev. Theodore L. Cuyler, one of the nation's leading religious writers in the 1880s; reformer and author George William Curtis; and many others. It would soon become one of the periodicals in which Davis regularly published, though her road to status as a regular contributor would not be smooth.

In addition to the alterations in her family, holiday preparations, and writing fiction, the major issue that occupied Davis in the final months of the year was the US government's policies toward Native Americans. The government's corrupt acts to dupe the Poncas into signing a treaty that usurped all of their lands had been publicly exposed and outraged many people. In an effort to garner broad support, several of the Ponca leaders toured the metropolitan centers of the East Coast, giving lectures and meeting with prominent legislators and supporters. Davis attended a dinner at which Inshata Theumba ("Bright Eyes," also known as Suzette La Flesche) was the guest. In support of Native American rights, Davis followed the meeting with one of her commentaries for *Lippincott's* "Our Monthly Gossip" editorial column in December. "An Unfinished Page of History" opened by celebrating America's cultural diversity—by traveling down Seventh Street in Philadelphia, Davis noted, you could easily come across Russian Jews, Negroes who had escaped slavery and built a new life in the city, Fenians, Huguenots, and many other races and ethnicities that were far worthier of study, she argued, than the ancient ruins of Europe.

It was the meeting with La Flesche that had the greatest impact on Davis, however: "I met at dinner not long ago a lady who was introduced to me under a French name." She had "a mind of great original force" and a presence that commanded the respect of everyone present. Yet she and her people were treated worse than the Russian serf, Davis thought: "They are held legally as the slaves not of individuals, but of the government, which has absolute power over their persons, lives and property." After detailing the way in which this barbaric government was starving these "enlightened and refined" people, Davis emphasized the dignity of her dining companion. Here La Flesche was not named outright, but Davis knew readers would easily identify her when she mentioned the woman had dined with President Hayes, as the event had been widely discussed in newspapers. Davis concluded: "My readers understand my little fable by this time. It is no fable, but a disgraceful truth. The government under which a people—many of whom are educated, enlightened Christian gentlemen—are denied the legal rights of human beings and all protection of law is not the absolute despotism of Siam or Russia, but the United States. . . . The legal disability under which the Indian is held is as much of an outrage on human rights, and as bald a contradiction of the doctrines on which our republic is based, as negro slavery was."[15]

Davis again supported the Poncas in an editorial for the *New-York Tribune* at the end of the month. National attention had been drawn to the broken treaties with the Poncas by a debate between Helen Hunt Jackson, writing for the *New-York Tribune*, and Secretary of the Interior Carl Schurz, in the *New York Times*. Schurz published another letter on December 9 in response to Massachusetts Governor John D. Long's sympathy with the Poncas. In his response Schurz declared the Poncas should not be returned to their homeland,[16] even while admitting the fraudulence perpetrated by the government. Earlier in the year Chief Standing Bear had successfully sued the United States, arguing before the US District Court in Omaha that Native Americans were persons under the law and thus had the right of *habeas corpus*, but the US government was still trying to justify their actions and delay the return of the Poncas to their homeland.

As the debates went back and forth, Davis entered the fray on December 24, with a *Tribune* editorial, "Secretary Schurz's Apology." As Davis recognized, Schurz's response to Long was an act of "justifying himself, not to Governor Long, but to the country." Not a single wrong that the Poncas had charged was contradicted by Schurz, she noted. After indicting the Secretary by using his own statements to condemn his actions, Davis asserted the correct legal and moral actions that should be taken: "The red man living in Dakota should have the same rights to the land he owns or the house he has built as the New-Yorker or the German naturalized on our soil. . . . the land in Dakota has been adjudicated theirs by the United States Court, and the Indian Department has no further discretion in the matter. It is their right to return to it when they choose. It is the duty of the Department, and its sole duty, to furnish transportation to them to their homes."[17]

Helen Hunt Jackson was delighted with the editorial. She and Rebecca had known one another for several years, through their writings and through their editorial work for the *Tribune*, and she was aware Davis intended to go to the nation's capital in support of the Poncas. Earlier Jackson had asked Davis to review *A Century of Dishonor* for her. For unknown reasons, Davis declined. "I'm sorry you can't 'do' the notice of my book," Jackson replied from New York a week after Davis's editorial appeared. "I counted on you bringing out the facts as I want them brought out. . . . the thing I want most is that the notices of the book shall help to circulate the real *knowledge* of the Indian Question. Can you do anything about getting it well noticed in Phila?—I'll see that you have one of the advance copies." She then complemented Davis on the editorial, calling it a "superb shot."[18]

Jackson detailed in her letter the wrongs committed by Indian Commissioner Ezra A. Hayt over the years, asserting he had lied in his recent statements when compared with comments he had made earlier in the Annual Reports of the Departments. "I wish you could continue to give him a sharp prod about this, & show up the lie," she encouraged Davis. "I shall try to publish a set of extracts showing it.—Bright Eyes is in Washington now—Her address there is Metropolitan Hotel,—but how long she will stay, I don't know.—I'm afraid I shall not be here when you come . . . but if I am here, it will be at the Brevoort—& how glad I shall be to see you I need not say.—Yours ever, Helen Jackson."[19] They continued to correspond on this topic during the coming year,[20] and Native American rights remained one of Davis's most outspoken avenues of reform writing in these years.

At the same time, Davis was engaged in a new venture. Moses Purnell Handy had moved to Philadelphia in 1876 to take the position of associate editor of the *Philadelphia Times*. In 1880 he became managing editor of the Philadelphia *Press*. A former reporter who had worked with Rebecca on the *New-York Tribune* editorial staff for many years, Handy immediately sought contributions from Davis. Though the *Press* was known as one of the leading Republican newspapers in the state, it was in decline when Handy became managing editor; circulation had waned to 10,000, and he sought Davis and several other writers to help him revitalize it.[21] In the four years he ran the newspaper, its circulation increased to 60,000, due to his strong editorials and to his skill in bringing first-rate journalists such as Davis to its pages.

In the first six months of 1881 Rebecca focused on her contributions to Handy's newspaper and the *Tribune*, publishing only occasionally in other periodicals. After a gap of many years, she did return in January to the setting of the Bethlehem, Pennsylvania's Moravian community in "A Comedy in a Garden" for *Peterson's*, but then she did not publish fiction again until May when "David Conn and His Wife" appeared in *Good Company*; this was another study of the meaning of charity. Davis also published one story in *Youth's Companion* in June, "Marty's Cabbage Crop," with a mulatta as the protagonist, but the majority of her work until the summer was in journalism.

In spite of the Davises' busy schedules, they continued to work mutually to support one another's careers. Just as Rebecca opened the door to many literary periodicals for Clarke, he reciprocated in early 1881 when he attended a reception at the Penn Club for the author, editor, and jurist Albion Tourgee. Clarke apparently used this opportunity to connect Rebecca and Tourgee. The two authors had much in common, both having written scathing critiques of the South's racial politics during and just after Reconstruction (Davis's *Waiting for the Verdict* in 1868 and Tourgee's *A Fool's Errand* in 1879). Tourgee would publish fiction by Rebecca in his literary magazine, *Our Continent*, in 1882.

Rebecca's introduction of James G. Blaine to Clarke continued to have equally mutual benefits. Now Secretary of State in Garfield's administration, Blaine's political favor was even more powerful. He invited Clarke and Rebecca to breakfast with him while they were in Washington, D.C., so he could talk with them about several political issues.[22] As Clarke left for Europe in July, Blaine prepared a letter of introduction for him to the Honorable Levi P. Morton, American Minister in Paris. Clarke sailed on the *Indiana* on July 9, heading for England and then France. At the same time, President Garfield, under the encouragement of Blaine, was preparing to nominate Rebecca's old friend and editor of the *Wheeling Intelligencer*, Archibald Campbell, to the post of minister to China.[23] The assassination of Garfield ended the process, since Campbell had opposed President Arthur's earlier selection as Vice President. The process revealed, however, the many ways in which the group of activists who had matured in the volatile atmosphere of early 1860s Wheeling had each risen to positions of prominence twenty years later.

With Clarke traveling, Rebecca was able to focus on her writing. In July she published "Across the Gulf" in *Lippincott's*, the first of several stories she wrote about the "gulf" between people—culturally or self-imposed. In July she also published "Mesmerism vs. Common Sense" in *Peterson's*. Although mesmerism had reached its peak in the US during the Civil War, it had resurged in the late 1870s and 1880s, only to come under attack again by the medical community and others. Davis's story was part of this trend, but she emphasized women's agency in rejecting a con man's use of mesmerism to try to control women sexually and financially.

This summer Rebecca and Clarke had to face once again the fact that Dick was not succeeding in his studies. In spite of his desire to excel at Swarthmore, he had failed many of his courses; as Charley later remarked, Dick's transition from the Episcopal Academy to Swarthmore had been "anything but a success." Charley often visited Dick at school in the hope of encouraging him, but "they were not very joyous occasions, as Richard was extremely unhappy over his failures at school and greatly depressed about the prospects for the future."[24] Dick withdrew at the end of his first year.

Rebecca and Clarke learned at this time that their eldest son was developing an interest in writing. Under the signature "D.D.," he had published a short story, "The Hat and Its Inmate" in the *Judge* while at Swarthmore, and after he and Charley returned from a hunting trip in July, he presented his parents with a little pamphlet he had written. "The Boys in the Adariondacks" was light and entertaining, full of misspellings (including the title), and autobiographical in nature. These traits would define Dick's writings for many years, and the autobiographical gesture would remain a staple of his body of work, whether he was writing fiction or working as a journalist. Clarke returned from Europe on August 19 and joined the family at the shore. While there, Rebecca and Clarke determined that Dick would return in September to his uncle's home in Bethlehem to attend Ulrich's Preparatory School, a feeder for Lehigh University. In spite of Dick's failure at both the Episcopal Academy and Swarthmore Preparatory, his parents would not give up their dream that both of their sons would receive a college education.

In the fall, with Dick and Charley back at school and Nora being educated at home, life returned to its normal, constantly busy pace. An assessment of Rebecca's career and distinctive style appeared in *Good Literature*, a New York-based magazine of literary criticism. The article asserted that the best writers of the day included Thomas Bailey Aldrich, Edward Everett Hale, Elizabeth Stuart Phelps, Elizabeth Spofford, Davis, and Frances Hodgson Burnett: "No discriminating reader would ever confound their tales or sketches with anybody else's."[25] At this time, Rebecca also lost a longtime friend, Rev. Cyrus Dickson, who died on September 18. Dickson had been a stalwart friend during her Wheeling years, and they had remained in touch since. Newspapers across the country marked his passing. It was probably Rebecca who wrote the obituary for Dickson in the *Tribune*.

As the fall progressed, Clarke was busy as a member of the Citizens' Reception Committee, preparing for a visit to the US by British Minister Lionel Sackville-West on his way to Washington, D.C., while Rebecca published several works of fiction in these months, beginning with "The Great Kean Estate," a romance for *Peterson's*. "Christina" for *Youth's Companion* addressed a theme common to Davis's class: the mistress-maid relationship. Like many of Davis's stories for young adults, "Christina" purported to teach a lesson of tolerance, but the opening commentary about free negro servants "who invariably decamped," Irish servants who drank, and Christina as "faithful and imitative as a Chinaman" inculcated racialized attitudes into the narrative.[26] Davis never overcame this paradoxical attitude toward non-white races and various ethnicities: she could create stereotypic characterizations such as these at the same time she spoke out on behalf of the Chinese at the Exposition or the Poncas in their battles with the US government.

In December, Rebecca was surprised to receive a letter from William Hayes Ward inquiring when he would receive a story from her. He had earlier requested her to write again for the *Independent*, but she had declined because they offered only twenty-five dollars for short stories. In response to his letter, she explained,

> I did not understand that I was to send you a story. When you asked me for one I declined to write it, for the very low price paid by the Independent and asked you if you were willing to pay more, to write to me. I received no answer of any kind. I am very busy at other work, but if you have counted on my help I will try and send you a short story by Saturday Dec 14—the price to be $50 *paid on receipt of Ms*. If this will suit you please write by return mail. Respectfully, R. H. Davis.[27]

Ward agreed to the higher rate, and "Next Door" appeared in the January 5, 1882, issue of the *Independent*. In addition to this story and "Mesmerism vs. Common Sense," Davis published a number of stories in this period in which young women were depicted as independent and quite capable of discerning people's true characters.

In the early months of 1882, Davis contributed more to magazines than she had the previous year. She published "A Rainy Day" in *Peterson's* under her own name and returned to longer stories for Charles Peterson's magazine. She also began in these months a long-term association with the *Congregationalist*, with "A Woman's Message" in March, "John Copley" in May, and "On Sunday Afternoon" in November. Her pattern in the first few years of her association with the *Congregationalist* was to publish three stories a year, significantly increasing her annual output for the periodical in the late 1880s. Davis would contribute short stories and essays to the Boston weekly for more than twenty years.

In the summer Davis published two articles in *Youth's Companion*. "Vacation Sketches Among the Alleghenies" suggested travelers looking for a new experience take the five-hour train ride from Pittsburgh into the Pennsylvania hills that were populated with long-established German communities, especially the Amish. "Homely Hints on Homely Occupations," on the other hand, returned to a topic she had written about periodically since she penned the "Open Door" series for *Hearth and Home* in the 1860s: "industries which women can pursue profitably at home . . . which require no long or costly education or training."[28] She would periodically return to this subject throughout her career.

Most of the summer, however, was devoted to two quite different events—the expanding artist colony that Point Pleasant had become, and preparations for the Davises' elder son to enter Lehigh University. The Manasquan village now drew numerous artists to its shores, and the Davis family formed close bonds with a wide range of artists. Regular visitors included the Barrymore acting families, Horace Howard Furness, and Frances Hodgson Burnett, and old friends and family from Washington, Pennsylvania, now joined the Davises as well. Dr. Julius LeMoyne's daughter Madeleine brought her family, and Rebecca's cousin Clara Wilson Baird and her husband visited occasionally. The Davises could always count on Wilse Harding to join them, often bringing university friends, and he eventually purchased lots on the river as the Davises had done.[29]

The Davises rented out their two extra "cottages" on the Manasquan River when they did not need them for friends or family. As Rebecca notified one potential renter who had been recommended by her friend, the author Frank Stockton and his wife, the residences "were *not* Queen Ann cottages but old fashioned farm houses. One which Admiral Marsden occupied for many years has 10½ acres about it. There are eight rooms and a kitchen, barn, and porches back & front. The other has about seven acres—nine rooms, porches, etc." They rented unfurnished for $150 each per year, although, she noted, they would consider a multiple-year rental with furnishings for a higher rate.[30]

Before coming to Point Pleasant that summer, Dick had been in Newport and Boston. On his way home he visited Rebecca's old friend Rev. Cyrus Bartol whom she had known since her first visit to Boston in 1862. Dick also stopped to see another old acquaintance of his mother's, Dr. Oliver Wendell Holmes. "He talked a great deal about mama . . . ," Dick reported to the family. "We got along splendidly. He asked me to stay to dinner but I refused with thanks, as I had only come to pay my respects and put off to Dr. Bartol's. Dr. Holmes accompanied me to the depot and saw me safely off. Of all the lovely men I ever saw Dr. Bartol was one."[31] This was only the beginning of important literary connections that his mother's fame would afford Dick.

In spite of the problems Dick had with his studies at Episcopal Academy and Swarthmore Preparatory, he had improved under his tutelage at Ulrich's Preparatory, and in September he entered Lehigh University where Wilse was a professor. He was enrolled under a "special student" category, still preparatory in nature, in the Latin-Scientific course. Few students at Lehigh were in that particular field since nearly ninety percent of the student body majored in engineering.[32] He continued to live in his uncle's house on Market Street, near the Moravian settlement across the river from the university.

Wilse was an active and gregarious man, and his personal charm filled his home with a wide circle of intellectuals who his precocious nephew cultivated as well. Though only seventeen, Dick made several friends through Wilse's introduction, including William W. Thurston, president of the Bethlehem Iron Company, and Jefferson Davis Brodhead, who had just been admitted to the bar and would later become a congressman. Dick's pattern was to stay in Bethlehem during the week and return home to Philadelphia on most weekends.[33] He (and Charley when he also entered Lehigh) made some lifelong friends at the university as well, including Mark De Wolfe Howe, who would become an influential literary editor, and Kenneth Frazier, a future internationally recognized portrait painter.

Even with frequent visits, the family kept up a steady correspondence with Dick during the week. It was typical for Rebecca to write her son on Monday nights after he had returned to school and after she had completed the usual batch of business letters needing responses. She detailed for Dick the various receptions Clarke had to attend in the evenings and the typical image of Charley "hard at work at his desk." Nora, who turned ten this year, was a frequent companion of her mother's, and Rebecca recounted the long walks mother and daughter took around the city and their social visits. The letters were always encouraging and filled with good humor and advice. Rebecca knew Dick had the same tendency toward melancholy and depression as his father, so her advice was often similar to what she wrote in a letter shortly after he had started at Lehigh:

> when you feel as if prayer was a burden, stop praying and go out and try to put your Christianity into real action by doing some kindness. ... you will go home with new light on your own relations to Him and a new meaning for your prayers. You remember the prayer 'give me a great thought to refresh me.' I think you will find some great thoughts in human beings—they will help you to understand yourself and God, when you try to help them God makes you happy my darling. Mama.[34]

Even with her mother now staying with her and a visit from her sister Emilie and sons,[35] Rebecca managed to write a number of stories in the fall for *Peterson's, Our Continent*, the *Independent*, and *Youth's Companion* as well as an article for *Century Magazine*. For Albion Tourgee's *Our Continent* she contributed "The Story of a Newspaper." Tourgee had successfully drawn some of the best writers of the period to his magazine. "'There is always room at the top' seems to have been kept constantly in view by the publishers of *Our Continent* in preparing the first number of their magazine ... ," the *Philadelphia Inquirer* reviewer wrote. "The brilliant list of contributors is the first that strikes the eye."[36] In addition to Davis, the early contributors included Oscar Wilde, Donald G. Mitchell, George Henry Boker, Harriet Beecher Stowe, Julian Hawthorne, Joel Chandler Harris, Kate Field, Helen Campbell, and others.

Davis had first submitted "The Story of a Newspaper," an analysis of the eighteenth-century French newspaper *Journal Politique* to the *Independent*; they rejected it, probably because it was very short and she had asked thirty-five dollars for it.[37] So when Albion Tourgee contacted her for a submission, she sent the story to him. In spite of the connections through Clarke, Rebecca did not feel obligated to continue writing for *Our Continent*; it was her only story for the magazine, and Tourgee remained editor for only two more years.

Although she had covered several home occupations for women in her August article for *Youth's Companion*, Davis returned to the subject in "Home Industries for Women" in November with a detailed account of beekeeping. The extent to which such articles spoke to the needs of her audience was evident when a woman who was disabled wrote Davis several months later with additional questions. Davis took the time to reply in some detail but also with realistic cautions,

> The article on Bee-Keeping was written several months before it was published. The prices given were those sent to me at that time by the leading apiarists in the country. Probably the price in your neighbourhood is exceptionally high. The manuals you mention cost from $1 to $1.50. Before purchasing bees you would do well to study the subject a little and determine whether, being an invalid, you could undertake the work. They are like babies—require constant steady care and will not bear neglect. Yours truly, R. H. Davis.[38]

Davis liked writing for the *Independent* because she could publish some of her most outspoken commentaries and meaningful fiction in the magazine. But when editor William Hayes Ward sought to formalize her relationship as a regular contributor, she resisted while keeping her commitment to the periodical evident; equally evident was her own struggle with the decision: "I do not see," she responded, "the use of any 'definite agreement.' If I can find time I will send you a story before Dec. 5th and I am quite sure you will send the money for it. As I may not—possibly—be able to do it (though I have no doubt I shall)—it would be safer for you not to announce the story until you had the *Ms* in hand."[39] Having several other "definite agreements" with magazines and newspapers, Davis was loath to commit to the expectation of additional scheduled obligations. Ward would continue to push for Davis's commitment, since the ability to advertise her as a "regular contributor" was beneficial to the magazine. Davis met the deadline and published "Aglae," a story of two North Carolina sisters, in the *Independent* in December.

Davis also published "Teddy," a short story in *Youth's Companion* this month. However much Wheeling reveled in claiming Davis as one of their own, the city residents could hardly have appreciated the way in which she described the area in the opening paragraph of this story: "In 1853 we lived in one of the hill-towns on the upper Ohio. It was a dingy, disheartening place. The streets along the river were lined with glass and steel mills, and the hills walling in the back of the town were honey-combed with coal-mines. The air was heavy with the rolling bituminous smoke, and the low brick houses were streaked with soot."[40] Yet, for all that it was a "commonplace and ignoble spot," there were heroic people living there. Unlike Mrs. Sprout, "a lady who controlled her own family so well that she had time to manage the lives of all of her neighbors," Honor Neal, the Irish laundry woman employed by Mrs.

Sprout, was the true heroine of the story. Davis had long written about class differences, and she penned several short stories in these years with heroic working-class protagonists.

At the same time, Davis returned to short nonfiction pieces for *Century Illustrated Magazine*. "To Americans Seeking New Homes," published in the "Home and Society" section, offered advice to people contemplating moving West, which had become popular due to the high unemployment rates in the large Eastern cities during the economic depression of the early 1880s. Davis liked writing these short commentaries and would continue to do so for several years.

Both Rebecca and Clarke received public attention as the year closed. Clarke was acknowledged as one of the "celebrated people" invited to attend a reception at Philadelphia's Academy of the Fine Arts for Sir Dr. Francis Seymour Haden, renowned London surgeon, author, and painter. For Davis, the attention revealed the extent to which she was responsible for editorials in the *New-York Tribune*. The *Boston Evening Transcript* published a history of the *Tribune* and its editorial staff at the end of the year. Commenting on the creation of a Sunday edition beginning in 1870 and continuing to the present, the article noted,

> Perhaps, as an offset to the more worldly and frivolous contents of the Sunday Tribune, its readers, as well as those of the week-day issues, have been favored with an occasional lay sermon in the guise of an editorial. The Sun has been in the habit of attributing these productions to Whitelaw Reid but whatever credit is due for them belongs to Mrs. Rebecca Harding Davis.[41]

Davis continued her steady output of fiction and editorials in 1883, but she would pace her writing more than she had typically done in the past. It was a year in which Clarke would increase his cultural activities in the city and in which Dick would attempt a writing career. In January, Davis published "The Poem That Never Was Written" in *Peterson's* under her own name and an article in the *Congregationalist*. The *Peterson's* story was an unusually tragic tale of missed connections between people and of lives gone astray, ending with the suicide of a young, unmarried woman who left no message as to why she chose to end her life. "A Brand Left to Burn" for the *Congregationalist* returned to the idea of indiscriminate charity, but with an ironic twist. A few years before Dr. Josiah Gilbert Holland's death, Davis recalled, he forwarded to her a letter he had received from a Philadelphia woman in need of aid. Holland "was, theoretically, at that time sternly opposed to indiscriminate charity. . . . But, practically, his heart melted, and his hand was in his pocket at the first cry from a hungry woman."[42] He sent money, asking Davis to deliver it to the woman—an old friend of his, she had claimed, though he did not recall her.

Seeking out the woman, Davis discovered "a professional beggar"; clearly fascinated with the con artist, Davis followed the woman's schemes for several years until she died a tragic death. The odd narrative offered two disparate lessons—first, "I pity the man who does not take an especial interest in the adventurers who 'live by their wits' in our large cities," and a condemnation at the woman's death: "Aloya Ocloff was buried in the Potter's Field. The brand, which had once life and strength and sweetness in it, was burned and charred into ashes and trodden under foot. Could society, could the Christian church, find no other use for it than that?"[43] Davis continued to write about "adventurers" and con artists as late as 1904 when a section of her autobiography was devoted to that extraordinary class of people. She recognized their failings, yet she could not help being fascinated by their skills of manipulation. Nor did the experience deter her commitment to indiscriminate charity.

Following in his mother's footsteps, in early 1883 Dick began writing for his school's literary magazine, *Lehigh Burr*. As editor of the magazine, he had great opportunity to publish his own work, sometimes a necessity to fill the *Burr*'s pages. In January he began a series built around the character Conrad Maur. Running through several issues, the Maur figure was clearly autobiographical,[44] but Dick had learned somewhat to sublimate his life into a fictional character, a practice that would serve him well when he became a professional writer. If the pieces were mostly light, they were humorous and these early experiences in writing and editing gave him an excellent opportunity to hone his writing skills.

While Rebecca and Dick were pursuing their writing endeavors, Clarke was increasingly active in the city's various civic and men's clubs at this time. These activities were a requirement of his position as managing editor of one of the city's prominent newspapers, but occasionally they also gave him a unique opportunity, such as the chance to attend a reception for the Italian tragedian Tommaso Salvini in January. Clarke's passion for the theater never waned, and his reputation in the US and England warranted his designation as Salvini's host for the formal event. The occasion to meet someone of Salvini's stature made up for the many nights Clarke spent away from home at such receptions.[45]

In February he participated in the inaugural dinner of the Five O'Clock Club; it was an early attempt at an interdisciplinary intellectual organization.[46]

Clarke was also appointed by the Pennsylvania House of Representatives to the Board of Trustees of the Pennsylvania Museum and School of Industrial Art (later the University of the Arts and the Philadelphia Museum of Art). The institution had been founded in 1876 in conjunction with the Centennial, and Dr. William Pepper, founder of the *Philadelphia Medical Times*, was its president. As with Philadelphia's fine arts museum, both Rebecca and Clarke strongly supported these cultural institutions throughout their years in Philadelphia.

The late 1870s and the 1880s saw publishers turn to studies of American literature with assessments of past and contemporary authors in early attempts to canonize the nation's literature, and inevitably Davis was discussed in these studies. Charles Francis Dickson's *A Primer of American Literature* appeared in its second edition in 1883, for example, and it praised Davis as one of the country's "female authors of merit": "Mrs. Rebecca Harding Davis . . . has great power in the delineation of the sad and solemn sides of life, especially in the lower classes."[47] Her inclusion in similar canon-making texts continued throughout the century. She was so well known as a writer at the time that she was sometimes used as an example in other writers' fiction, such as Emily Hewitt Leland's "A Little Money of Her Own" in which the central character sadly discovered that she could never write with the talent of a Rose Terry Cooke or a Rebecca Harding Davis.[48]

Although most of Davis's stories of this period were set in the South or on the mid-Atlantic coast, she turned periodically to life in the East Coast's large metropolitan centers. In February she published in *Lippincott's* "A Wayside Episode," a scathing critique of high society. The same month Davis published two short stories in *Youth's Companion*. The extent to which Daniel S. Ford had the ability to draw first-rate authors and to innovate new marketing techniques for the magazine was evident by the mid-1880s when the *Companion*'s circulation rose to 400,000. He had begun years earlier promoting premium offerings, from stationery to sewing machines, based on the number of new subscriptions a person could bring to the magazine. Perhaps most important, however, was that Ford refocused the magazine's content so it would appeal to the entire family. Children's stories still prevailed, but as Davis's writings attested, fiction and nonfiction for adults were now staples of the magazine as well.[49]

The spring brought three other publications for Davis. An historical romance engaging mixed-race heritage, "At Kittery," appeared in *Peterson's*. Davis still frequently developed characterizations of physicians for her fiction, but often in the 1880s, as she wrote for more religious periodicals, she turned to ministers and their families as the focus—or, as in the case of "John Sorby" in the *Independent*, combined the two professions. Countering the popular belief in hereditary insanity, "John Sorby" argued that much of what seems like mental disability was the result of overwork, and the story condemned the ways in which some congregations asked their ministers to do the work of three men while paying near-starvation wages. "Uncle Abel" in the *Congregationalist*, on the other hand, returned to the locale of Tarrytown, which Davis had used in several stories in the 1870s. Uncle Abel symbolized Tarrytown and all small, rural communities: "All the bigotry, the intolerable self-conceit, and the kindly feeling of that mountain village, lived and moved in the lean figure of the old bachelor."[50] This story was indicative of Davis's view of Christianity: it was lived, day by day, rather than confined to an elaborate church building.

The summer months were productive for Davis as well, and September brought a highly praised and frequently reprinted story for *Harper's*, "A Silhouette." Termed by critics as one of her typically "powerful stories," "a singularly clever and vigorous Southern sketch," and "one of the best [short stories] that has appeared in 'Harper's' or any other magazine for a long time,"[51] "A Silhouette" combined several themes, including the talented young Northern woman who goes South to teach and believes she understands a community from a brief observance, and a Hatfields-and-McCoys type of generations-long feud. Most importantly, however, this story captured Davis's aesthetic interest in the concept of a "silhouette," a term she preferred to "sketch." It symbolized the way in which people see one another only in silhouette, regardless of how much they think they know someone or how keen they believe their perceptions of a situation to be. The silhouette became a genre Davis developed further in future writings.

In the fall of 1883, Charley joined Dick at Lehigh University. An accomplished student, Charley thrived at university even though he was always viewed as "Dick's brother." These were wonderful months for Charley and Dick, as they were again together and sharing their beloved uncle's home. Later that fall Dick sent good news to their parents: his summer studies had proved worthwhile, and he had received a pass in Latin.[52] He continued to write stories and articles for the *Burr*, although he was learning that poetry was not his forte.

Clarke also returned to article-writing in the fall with "These Our Actors" for *Lippincott's*, a study of Augustin Daly's Fifth Avenue Company in New York with special attention to the actress Ada Rehan. Whenever the Davises were in

New York, they attended the theater, and whether there or at home in Philadelphia, they could count the leading actors and theater critics of the day among their friends.

Rebecca followed in November with another "Author of 'The Second Life'" story for *Peterson's*, "In an Inn." A common feature of Davis's fiction in these years was to begin with a brief commentary on contemporary culture and then to develop the fictional story around that issue. In this mystery, she began,

> It is part of the creed of all well-bred Americans now-a-days to contemn American hotels and the class that use and are happy in them. And yet there is so much to be said on the side of the hotels, if the traveler chooses to become a quiet spectator, and watch the fragments of tragedy and comedy played for him by the pretentious crowds he meets there. One of these fragmentary dramas comes back to me now, with the irritating persistence of an unguessed riddle. I will give it to my readers to solve.[53]

Davis had embraced this style of the "quiet spectator" who creates art from her observations throughout her more than twenty years as a professional author.

At the end of the year, Davis published her annual Christmas story, "David Evans' Christmas," in the *Christmas Traveller*, a collection published by the semi-weekly *Boston Traveller*. The editor had approached Davis in October about writing a new story for the collection. She asked $125, considerably higher than she was paid for a story by the periodicals in which she regularly appeared, but the editor readily agreed.[54] The story, another in her series of critiques of large charitable organizations, opened with an account of the Philadelphia Orphanage for girls, run by a wealthy woman who treated her wards, "the dangerous classes," like prisoners, identifying them by numbers instead of names. Once they were old enough to be placed in some form of labor, Davis observed, they were informed "this Institution does not hold itself responsible for you any longer. You must shift for yourself."[55] Indicting the approach, the story traced the arduous fate of "Number Forty."

In contrast, the Davises themselves could celebrate Christmas with great joy. Their careers were successful, they were financially well off, and everyone was healthy. Nora was progressing in her studies, and Rebecca's mother, though weak, was doing well. The boys seemed to be developing their skills in ways that would allow them to succeed in whatever fields they chose, and both Rebecca and Clarke continued to see their national reputations grow. The family celebrated the holiday, thankful for the immensely good fortune they had received.

The following year would largely continue this pattern of good fortune and professional success, though the fall would bring great sadness to all their lives. In January 1884, however, Rebecca was feeling strong and ready to return to writing a serial for *Peterson's*, her first since 1878. "The Elk Heights Tragedy," under the "Second Life" signature, centered on an orphaned girl bound in labor to her cousin. Davis was also approached at this time by Charles Scribner who wanted to include "Balacchi Brothers" in a new series they were preparing, *Stories by American Authors*. Rebecca agreed and received what she felt was very liberal payment for the reprint. Each of the volumes in this series contained only six stories, deemed the best of the year by American writers. For the first volume, Davis's story appeared with the following selections: a story by Bayard Taylor, a travel and adventure writer; a co-authored story by Brander Matthews, who wrote about theater life, and H. C. Bunner, humorist and editor of *Puck*; a story by William Henry Bishop, author and political essayist; and the final story by Albert Webster, best known for his "Boarding-House Sketches."

Among Davis's publications in January was a short story for the *Independent*, "Paul," that continued her reflections on American attitudes toward insanity and extended her joint efforts with Clarke in the crusade against maltreatment of mental patients. Late in 1883, the legislative committee assigned to study practices of asylums, of which Clarke was a member, had finished its work and submitted a report to the governor. The recommendations and the subsequent legislation, "An Act Relative to the Supervision and Control of Asylums or Houses in which Lunatics are Detained," sought to lessen the ability of unscrupulous individuals, physicians, and asylum directors to admit persons as insane without careful regulation and documentation; all such facilities would now have to be licensed by the state. The Act also established an oversight commission to be responsible for practices in both public and private facilities and to propose legislation as they examined the system. Importantly, the commission explicitly allowed for women to be appointed to the oversight boards. Much work remained to establish safe and effective asylums, but the committee had ensured progress at present and for the future.[56]

After publishing "Paul," Davis took a break from the *Independent*. She was frustrated with how slowly her submissions were published, and she always had to negotiate the rate of pay. It would be two years before she returned to its pages, but taking a break proved effective, for both sides. The editor realized the potential loss for the *Independent* and wooed her, and in two years, she would finally agree to become a regular contributor, a position she held until 1908.

As Rebecca and Clarke were building a life of notable success on their own terms, they were very proud of their children's efforts, in whatever form they took, as long as they were upstanding and acted for what was right. So when Dick, at nineteen, decided he wanted to collect his stories from the *Lehigh Burr* and publish the collection under the title *The Adventures of My Freshman Year*, they were happy to fund the printing. Though at first no sales appeared, before long the book had sold out, and Dick was abashed when his parents declined to fund a second printing. What he would not know for many years was that his collection had not sold a single copy; to avoid his great disappointment, Rebecca and Clarke had secretly bought all the copies, so it was little wonder they declined to support a second printing. As Dick would later joke, after he was an internationally recognized author, the book did so poorly "because someone must have read it"![57] But their secret purchase was indicative of the support they offered all of their children.

One of the items Davis published in May was for the *Century's* "Open Letters" column. She had been saddened to see so little attention given to the death of the Southern novelist and religious writer William M. Baker. From her perspective, "Mr. Baker stood more alone, probably, than any American author since Hawthorne. He was outside of all literary cliques; he had no following of influential friends, of sect or party, and hence had none of that professional backing and advertising which counts for so much with the public." In this long letter, Davis revealed her own literary preferences as she detailed Baker's life and writings. He cared little for plot but wrote "startling portraits of powerful, strong-featured characters, such as are common in the States. The oily politician, the clergyman whose nature is higher than his petty sectarian creed, the statesman slowly sinking into a drunken sot, the educated half-breed, at war with God, man, and himself—there they are, live men, whom we meet face to face, and love or hate ever after. They are . . . photographed upon the page with a single electric flash."[58]

Over the summer, Rebecca published only one short story for *Youth's Companion*, as she spent most of the season again traveling in the South, gathering material for future writings. It was late summer before she arrived in Point Pleasant. Newspapers continued to print items about her work and travels in the popular "personals" columns—snippets about famous people that populated the pages of most newspapers. The idea of "revealing" that women were among the *Tribune*'s key editorial staff members was almost an annual event now, and in August the *Daily Alta California* proudly asserted, "The three ladies on the editorial staff of the New York Tribune are Mrs. Rebecca Harding Davis, Miss Nelly Hutchinson and Mrs. Lucia Runkle."[59] It would have been difficult by this date *not* to know of Rebecca's work as an editorial writer for the newspaper, but such a position, especially on a major national paper, remained so unusual that announcements of the fact would continue for several years.

A difficult political situation arose for Rebecca and Clarke in the summer and fall of 1884. Rebecca's cousin, James G. Blaine, whom Clarke had publicly and privately supported, determined for the third time to run for the US Presidency and finally was nominated on the Republican ticket. But his opponent, Democrat Grover Cleveland, had become a friend of the Davises as well. With the end of Reconstruction, the Republican Party disappointed many reformers with its seeming abandonment of the rights of African American citizens, and some Democrats had turned to more liberal perspectives. It was a time of political upheaval and transitions for both parties. Painful to the Davises were the charges of corruption that emerged against Blaine by reform-minded Republicans, many of whom became Cleveland supporters. It was a particularly ugly campaign. The old story of Blaine's special favors for the railroads resurfaced, and new correspondence emerged that seemed to question Blaine's denials of wrongdoing. On the other side, Cleveland's opponents revealed documents to prove he had apparently fathered a child out of wedlock years earlier. The popular vote in the fall was very close, but the Electoral College clearly gave the victory to Cleveland.

In spite of the revelations of the election, Rebecca maintained a fond relationship with Blaine: "During his busy years of public life when on his way from Washington to New York he would dodge committees and crowds at the Philadelphia station and come to us for a quiet hour or two of—'Do you remember?' or 'What has become of' this or that old comrade. He kept sight of all the poor, obscure friends of his boyhood, and as I learned elsewhere, he never, with all his burden of work and worry, failed to help them or their children when they needed help." She knew that Blaine had mixed feelings about the loss of the nomination: "I heard him say the week before the convention met which meant to nominate him:—'I am sick to the soul of the public and of public life. I want a quiet home, my children, and peace for my old age.'" As Rebecca recognized, "He meant it—on that day."[60] The Davises remained in contact with Blaine, but it was with Cleveland that they developed an intimate and enduring friendship, in spite of Clarke's lifelong dedication to the Republican Party.

In the midst of the political upheaval of the final months of 1884, Rebecca had continued to publish, though less than usual. One of her works at this time was "The Weed in the Wheat" for the *Congregationalist*. The story critiqued philanthropists who seek from their recipients public admiration and gratitude for their "generosity" and insist their names be attached to the charities they endow.

This kind of publicity was something Rebecca abhorred. Several people who knew her well attested to her philanthropy, but her name appeared nowhere in the public record. "The Weed in the Wheat" was popular among the magazine's readers to the extent that the chaplain of the Clifton Springs Sanitarium, Lewis Bodwell, had it reprinted as a "tractlet," a popular means of more widely distributing some of the *Congregationalist*'s best stories. Bodwell reported that he found it to be "one of the very best things he has seen to slip into a letter and scatter it various ways."[61] It was not the last time one of her writings for the magazine received tractlet status.

New friendships, such as with Grover Cleveland, made these years especially enjoyable. Another such new friend was Dr. William Osler. On October 1, Dr. Osler, who had been successfully lured to Philadelphia, gave his inaugural lecture at the University of Pennsylvania Medical College. Already renowned, he would become one of the most influential physicians of the nineteenth century. The Davises probably met Osler through the college's president, Dr. William Pepper; Clarke had worked with Pepper during the organization of the Centennial and on civic committees. The Davises' acquaintance with Osler would last through his attendance at Nora's wedding the year after Rebecca's death.

Amidst the happiness of new friends and thriving careers, a great sorrow settled on the family. On October 9, Rebecca's mother, Rachel Leet Wilson Harding, died at the Davis home in Philadelphia. Rachel had been an integral part of the Harding and Davis families. A warm, intelligent, and generous woman, her loss left an indelible mark on the lives of her children and grandchildren. Rachel Harding was buried next to her husband and son Henry in the Washington Cemetery. The gravestones of Rebecca's father and brother Henry had begun with the carving "Sacred to the Memory Of," followed by their names and dates, but Rachel's tombstone read "Entered Into Life" carved over the date of her death, followed by "Rachel L. Harding / Widow Of / Richard W. Harding / Aged 76 Years. / "She Loved Much." She was the person who first taught Rebecca about storytelling and about the importance of history, who had encouraged her children to see education as a lifelong endeavor, and who proudly supported her daughter's professional life. The absence left what Rebecca defined as a "cypher" in her life.[62]

CHAPTER 9

An Era of Nonfiction (1885–1889)

The late 1880s were years of notable professional changes for Rebecca and her family. She turned to a far greater emphasis on nonfiction and journalism, and if the early 1880s had entailed a particular focus on US government policies toward Native Americans, the late 1880s were a time for analyzing the cultural status of African Americans twenty years after emancipation. It was also an era in which Rebecca and Clarke worked arduously to ensure their elder son attained a foothold in journalism, replicating their own history of creating professional access for one another. As Clarke had introduced Rebecca to Charles Peterson and Rebecca had enabled Clarke's publications in the *Atlantic*, the *Galaxy, Scribner's Monthly,* and *Lippincott's*, they would open doors for Dick to several Philadelphia newspapers.

Rebecca's first publication in January 1885, "In St. Paul's Place" for *Peterson's*, captured the special atmosphere of that section of Philadelphia where the residents were "young people who are starting in life, old ones who have lost their fortunes and have drifted in here for repairs, adventurers, and all the rest of us who put on gentility as you would a domino at a masquerade—to hide behind." The young doctor-narrator felt "a contagion of success" the moment he opened his office in the district and discovered the ways in which the people in the community tried to help one another.[1]

The Davises were hoping for a similar "contagion of success" for Dick, as he struggled to finish his studies that winter. Clarke arranged an extraordinary opportunity for his son to serve, on a one-time basis, as a reporter for the *Philadelphia Inquirer* and accompany Alexander K. McClure, publisher of the Philadelphia *Times*, as he traveled through the South to inspect changes in the era of the New South. Their final destination was the World's Industrial and Cotton Exhibition in New Orleans, which was designed specifically to demonstrate the industrial changes and future developments of the South into a new economic force. With a leave of absence from Lehigh, Dick made the journey and published three accounts from the trip in the *Inquirer*. The experience offered him an opportunity to see what reporting actually involved and, perhaps equally important in his parents' mind, to meld his association with McClure.

Surprisingly, Dick signed his pieces for the *Inquirer* "R.H.D.," a signature his mother had used in *Hearth and Home, Scribner's Monthly,* the *Century,* and newspapers since the 1860s but which she thereafter abandoned for a period of time. Since Dick was writing about the South, an area in literature and journalism Rebecca was known to cover, there must have been some confusion among readers as this transition in signatures occurred, especially since she would soon publish a series of works on the New South as well.

By February Dick was back at Lehigh, devoting most of his time to writing for the *Lehigh Burr.* Over the winter, Rebecca also headed south, extensively traveling through the Gulf States where she interviewed Southerners about their perspectives on the transitions the South was undergoing. It was probably on this trip she visited the actor and Davis family friend, Joseph Jefferson, who had settled on a plantation in Louisiana after the war. Jefferson entertained her at his home and took her by carriage to the New Iberia area.[2] She liked experiencing firsthand different regions of the South, and Louisiana would appear in some of her later writings.

As the close of the school year at Lehigh approached, Rebecca and Clarke again were confronted with Dick's poor academic performance. The brothers had enjoyed their extracurricular activities, however. At Charley's suggestion, they had founded the Mustard and Cheese Club, a theater group that performed farces and musical comedies. Dick wrote plays for the club and Charley performed in many of them, both receiving high praise from local newspapers.[3] Dick and Charley were in the General Literature track at this time. Charley found the university a natural fit, with his talents in writing and soon through his shift to studying civil engineering.[4] Although Charley was thriving in his studies, Dick had decided by the end of the term to leave the university.

The type of relationship the Davises had with their children was evident in a letter Clarke sent Dick a few months earlier for his birthday, when it was apparent he would be withdrawing: "My Dear Boy, You are to be nineteen years old on Wednesday. After two more years you will be a man. You are so manly and good a boy that I could not wish you to change in any serious or great thing. You have made us very happy through being what you have been, what you are. You fill us with hope of your future virtue and usefulness."[5] Such support, rooted more in their character than their accomplishments, allowed the Davis children to weather crises and continue to explore new adventures in life.

Having decided to forego long-term commitments of serials and novels, Davis could explore new magazines for publication in these years. Over the summer her published works included "What John Found" in a new children's magazine, the *Golden Argosy*; a reprint of "The Story of a Newspaper" in the *Congregationalist*; and in September, another article about "Women as Beekeepers," this time in the *American Apiculturist*. Although Charley returned to Lehigh for his sophomore year, Dick decided he wanted to be a writer and enrolled in a special course of study at Johns Hopkins University he believed would help develop his skills.[6]

This was not the route Dick had originally anticipated. Over the summer, Clarke had taken him to see Talcott Williams about a job on the Philadelphia *Press*. Rebecca had been an editorial contributor to the *Press* for many years, and both parents believed it would be a good place for Dick to start his reportorial career. But Williams, as managing editor, was not interested in a young, inexperienced writer. He recommended a few years of study in the social sciences at Johns Hopkins and then four to five years apprenticing as a reporter. Dick would never succeed in lengthy scholarly study, but the course with an emphasis in writing at Hopkins seemed a possibility. While in the program, Dick began sending out his poems and stories for publication, and a few minor pieces were accepted.

Meanwhile, Rebecca was crafting her work in two directions—the usual stories and articles for *Peterson's*, the *Congregationalist*, and *Youth's Companion*, and more overt politically engaged writing for the *Atlantic Monthly*, the *Independent*, and other periodicals. Over the summer Rebecca had been contacted by the current editor of the *Atlantic Monthly*, Thomas Bailey Aldrich. It had been twelve years since she had published in the magazine, then under the editorship of William Dean Howells, but because Aldrich expressed interest and because he was willing to publish nonfiction by Davis, she sent him an essay on a topic that dominated her thinking during these years—the advances of and continuing challenges for African Americans in US society. She told Aldrich when she submitted "Some Testimony in the Case," "I really think it is impartial."[7] The article was the result of her interviews with Southerners over the past winter. Although she clearly believed it was impartial, Davis's writings about social issues were always partial and often paradoxical, insistent on creating a more democratic society and, though well meaning, not always without racial or ethnic biases.

The article appeared in the November issue. It was widely excerpted and analyzed. A "great game" was being played out in the South, she argued; "the result of this struggle, if not a matter of life and death to either race, will certainly affect permanently their domestic relations, their commercial property and the place which the South will hereafter hold in the scale of civilized peoples."[8] After traveling through the Gulf States the previous winter, she realized that each person felt he or she had the only clear perspective and rarely understood their neighbor's thinking on the issues. So she gathered testimony from conversations she had and from letters sent to her in order to expose the multiplicity of perspectives and the challenges confronting the South—voices from Alabama, Virginia, Mississippi, Louisiana, Georgia, and North Carolina.

Some of the attitudes were extraordinarily racist, others more balanced and contemplative. The typical assertion by white male planters was that all African Americans were lazy. The extent to which the plantation owners saw the issues only from their own perspectives, however, was emphasized by the subsequent testimonies of an African American couple. They presented a carefully rendered assessment of the present situation until the issue of slavery arose, and then the pain and abuse of that system was captured in the husband's response. Davis followed his comments with a pithy summary: "It is impossible to see the present of the negro in its true light without the background of the past."[9]

The pattern of multiple perspectives in the article continued across a wide range of issues, including education, economics, convict labor, segregation, and political rights. Davis concluded two facts from her discussions with Southerners that she felt deserved further consideration: the great demand for skilled labor in the South and the lack of training opportunities for African Americans in this area. At the New Orleans Exhibition, she claimed, "their schools and colleges made creditable displays of [African Americans'] intellectual progress. But the work of their hands was almost invariably the work of willing but untrained hands."[10] Notable exceptions came from the Hampton Industrial School. She concluded, therefore, training in skilled labor was African Americans' greatest need; they could then fill the demand in the Southern industries that were at present being "surrender[ed] to foreign capitalists and foreign laborers."[11]

The *Friend's Intelligencer and Journal* published both an excerpt from the article and a lengthy analysis of its implications, which it found "not only most true, but deeply important at the present time." Although the missionary spirit had declined in recent years, the journal asserted, here was "a field so very suitable for Friends and friendly people." The *Literary World* claimed none of the article's perspectives were "very hopeful. But we think that Mrs. Davis touches upon a radical defect in the education of the negro when she urges the necessity of industrial training." The *New York Freeman* also recommended Davis's article to its readers, concluding, "she draws important inferences" from the testimonies gathered.[12] Davis's emphasis on industrial training was important, but it would soon lead her into controversial positions as greater numbers of African Americans sought advanced educations and professional careers.

At the end of the year, Davis's story "Dominique" for *Youth's Companion* drew on her travels through Louisiana and the fears of leprosy that were circulating through the region.[13] She also began a series on "Forgotten Worthies" for the *Congregationalist*, examining the lives of the Quaker John Woolman; David Zeisberger, the colonial Moravian clergyman from Bethlehem, Pennsylvania; and Dimitri Gallitzin, the Russian-born priest known as "The Apostle of the Alleghenies." Though Woolman was a standard figure in religious histories, Zeisberger and Gallitzin were not; this tactic was typical of Davis's writing in any genre—explore the familiar, and rethink its implications through the less familiar. The series' range of religious figures reflected the *Congregationalist*'s openness to articles on all sects. Another quasi-autobiographical piece also appeared in *Youth's Companion*. "The White Peddler" drew on Davis's own family history, in which many tales of the White Peddler of Munster had been related to her and her siblings by her father. The main character in the story, Thomas Hardy, was clearly modeled on her paternal grandfather, Thomas Harding.[14]

In mid-January 1886, Rebecca was delighted to receive word from the author Rose Terry Cooke that she was coming to Philadelphia and wished to interview Rebecca for an article. Rebecca warmly responded, noting she had long meant to write Cooke about the high regard she held for an early book of poetry Cooke had published. "But I never could summon courage," she insisted. Although Rebecca had so many engagements scheduled she had to put off the visit for a week, she enthusiastically set the date for after the 30th of January. "You shall have all the dates you choose, and even if they will not be enough for you to make an article, come,—not as an interviewer but a friend to discover two friends who have admired and honoured you for twenty years. Let me know on what day and train to expect you and come directly to the house and spend the night with us." In a postscript she added, "If you have a copy of that book with you bring it and we will go over it together. Don't forget. To think I should read 'Done For' with Rose Terry herself!"[15] Rebecca managed, as always, to sidestep an actual interview. Cooke published no article about Davis, and whatever occurred during their day together remained private.

Shortly thereafter, however, a lengthy article appeared in the Fort Worth *Gazette* noting the influential English critic Edmund Gosse had expressed surprise at a recent suggestion that readers gave the highest place among short story writers to Henry James and William Dean Howells "while the superior claims of Rebecca Harding Davis are comparatively overlooked." Gosse insisted the oversight had to be due to manipulation of readers by publishers who, "like fashion designers," shape this kind of response—and always in favor of New England writers. In comparison to the attention to the external person in James's and Howells's characterizations that slowly moved inward, Gosse noted that Davis "begins from the interior and builds outward. Her men and women move, breathe, their hearts beat, their blood flows. They are endowed with passions, not mere mental tricks." The critic, after detailing a long list of Davis's outstanding stories and novels, also noted, she "has been one of the principal editorial writers on the staff of the Philadelphia Press, the two non-political leading editorials appearing in the Sunday number of that journal being usually from her pen."[16] Gosse's assessments of Davis's writings would appear several times in the coming years.

On a sadder note, J. B. Lippincott died in January. Rebecca had not published in the magazine for three years, but Lippincott, known for the personal relationships he developed with authors, was a longtime friend. The *Literary World* published a lengthy review of his life and impact on the field of literature, noting the group of popular writers he brought to the magazine, including Anthony Trollope, Ouida, and Davis.

At this time Rebecca also joined a significant roster of American authors who published letters in support of international copyright laws. Contributors included James Russell Lowell, Lyman Abbott, the presidents of Cornell, Columbia, Johns Hopkins, Yale, and Washington and Lee Universities, the president of Williams College, George H. Boker, Hjalmar H. Boyesen, Phillips Brooks, Frances Hodgson Burnett, George Washington Cable, George William Curtis, Frederick Douglass, Mary Mapes Dodge, Theodore W. Dwight, Edward Eggleston, Julian Hawthorne, Thomas Wentworth Higginson, William Dean Howells, Elizabeth Stuart Phelps, Louisa May Alcott, Thomas Bailey Aldrich, and numerous others; it was a compendium of Who's Who in the literary and academic world.

The letters appeared in the February issue of the *Century Magazine* and most argued for the justice of the law and the rights of authors. Davis, as was typical, took a somewhat different tactic: "I am afraid that all of the arguments of authors and publishers in support of International Copyright are as hackneyed to the public ear as the eighth commandment, of which they necessarily are only variations." She argued that the law was to the advantage of readers as well as authors and publishers, revealing the extent to which she believed in the role of what she termed morality in literature; copyright laws "would serve to keep the lower mass of worthless literature in each country at home where it originates. If the experiment of publishing a foreign book cost more here, we should be spared much that is puerile and poisonous. Unfortunately, we cannot now keep out these printed paupers and criminals, nor send them back, as we do their human kinfolk. In every way, therefore, this, our late effort at honesty, would help our morals."[17]

In April the *Brooklyn Magazine* ran an article about women and marriage. In what was an increasingly popular format, the magazine asked several women writers to comment on the question of when a woman should marry. Respondents varied somewhat, but most attempted to give a particular age: Madeleine Vinton Dahlgren thought by twenty a young woman had "seen enough of the social atmosphere in which she lives, to be able to discriminate wisely," while Lucy Stone rejected the idea of early marriages. Helen Campbell thought neither sex should enter marriage before thirty; Julia C. R. Dorr insisted it depended on the maturity of the woman rather than a particular age, which was similar to Davis's assessment. "It seems to be as impossible to lay down any general rule with regard to the proper age for a woman to marry," she wrote, "as to prescribe a universal diet which shall agree with all stomachs." She concluded with the most explicit rendering of her belief in marriage for women, though the idea had been imbedded in many of her stories over the years: "I am old-fashioned enough to believe that marriage, provided it be based on pure, strong affection, is better for a woman, even under the worst circumstances, than a single life under the best; and I think, therefore, that the time for a girl to marry is when she meets a man who heartily loves her and whom she heartily loves, if she is old enough to be a helpmate to him and not a dead-weight."[18] In addition to these collective endeavors, Davis was finalizing negotiations with Cassell and Company Publishers to bring out a new edition of *Natasqua* in their "Rainbow Series" of inexpensive editions.

Rebecca had curtailed her fiction publications during the winter of 1886–87, in part because preparations for the publication of the *Natasqua* edition took a significant amount of her time. When the edition finally appeared early in 1887, there was debate among critics about an author of Davis's caliber publishing in the Cassell editions: "So good a writer as Rebecca Harding Davis deserves a better setting for her work than cheap and gaudy paper covers,"[19] *Life*'s reviewer proclaimed. The highly decorated cover was awash in flowering vines and had the logo of "Cassell's Rainbow Series of Original Novels" with a classic Grecian profile. Although the story was, in fact, not a new novel, that point was not mentioned by critics; it was the association with the series itself that drew the most attention. A reviewer for *The Critic* remarked: "NATASQUA, by Mrs. Rebecca Harding Davis (Cassell), has dropped into the vivid and florid Rainbow Series like a cool pearl into the midst of flame. It is a hopeful sign to see the standard of the Rainbows thus suddenly raised; for 'Natasqua' is a story of fine and genuine merit, with rare delineations of curious human nature, and a moral as clear-cut as a cameo, standing out in fine relief from a background of interesting story."[20]

In the spring of 1886, Dick again ended his academic studies and returned to Philadelphia. He wanted to be out in the field, not in a classroom, he insisted, and everyone now agreed this was probably the best solution as it was evident he would never graduate from college. He had made friends with William W. Thurston, president of Bethlehem Steel, through his Uncle Wilse and, though Dick had intended to take the first job offered to him, quickly agreed when Thurston invited him to go to Santiago de Cuba with him. Dick fell completely in love with Cuba—"a love," Charley observed, "which in later years became almost an obsession with him, and for the rest of his life, whenever he could, he would set sail for Santiago."[21] Dick returned to Philadelphia later in the summer, having decided he wanted to be a journalist. Clarke repeated the pattern of introducing Dick to a newspaper managing editor, this time at the Philadelphia *Record*, where Dick was hired to write "'chance' work."[22]

In September, while worrying over the fact that her elder son seemed to be perpetually adrift, Rebecca published in *Youth's Companion* "The Pawned Watch" about a poor boy's struggles to gain a college education. She also published a long story in the *Atlantic Monthly*. "Mademoiselle Joan" invoked the supernatural as the title character cursed her corrupt sister with her dying breath and the curse was realized. That the story began with the schoolmaster narrator having been ordered to take a rest cure was not coincidental. That year, three of Davis's close friends, Drs. S. Weir Mitchell, William Pepper, and Horace Furness were part of a commission funded by the University of Pennsylvania to study Spiritualism. Henry Seybert had bequeathed the university $60,000 for the investigation of "All systems of morals, religion or philosophy which assume to represent the truth, and particularly of modern spiritualism."[23]

Although the commission's report largely concluded they were all too busy to give proper time to the study of Spiritualism, its authors did not hesitate to devote much space to the ridicule and denial of the phenomena.[24] Although Davis had raised questions about Spiritualism in early works, she also had published several stories similar to "Mademoiselle Joan" that suggested she was more open to the possibilities than her medical colleagues. The story was her last publication in the *Atlantic Monthly*.

Rebecca was also helping Dick as he worked on an article about his experiences in Santiago while he was working at the *Record*.[25] The newspaper assigned him a wide variety of stories, but it took little time for it to become evident that Dick, with his dandyish attire, was not fitting in with the other reporters. He still carried the cane he had adopted as a prop when he was at Lehigh, and he now added a long yellow ulster with green stripes and kid gloves. He was not happy with the work he was assigned either. As Dick recognized, the *Record* was letting him do even this much reporting "to oblige Dad" or, he hoped, "giving me a trial trip before making an opening."[26] It was a shock, then, when he was fired in late October, but it was also an important indicator that he needed to take his work responsibilities more seriously. Years later he admitted he had been fired for incompetence although he felt it was impossible to be competent when he was given eighteen assignments a day.[27]

Worries about Dick continued to dominate the Davis home and surely impacted both Rebecca and Clarke's low productivity over the winter months. The only story Davis published this year was another "Second Life" romance for *Peterson's*, "The Story of Hetty." Dick assured his parents he would not again be cavalier about work after the humiliation of being fired, so Rebecca introduced him to Mary Mapes Dodge at *St. Nicholas*, and Dodge accepted his submitted short story for the December issue. Reviews immediately linked Dick's name, appearing for the first time, with Rebecca, and at least one reviewer felt that he gave "fair promise of being no unworthy son of his mother."[28]

Dick was soon learning the realities of a writer's life, however. He had had a story accepted by *The Current*. However, the publication had never appeared and he sought his mother's advice. "If it has suspended publication," she suggested, "be sure and get your article back. You must not destroy a single page you write. You will find every idea of use to you hereafter." She also offered a cautionary note:

> I know it would be better if you would not publish under your own name for a little while. Dr. Holland—who had lots of literary shrewdness both as writer and publisher—used to say for a young man or woman to rush into print was sure ruin to their lasting fame.... Now my dear old man this sounds like awfully cold comfort. But it is the

> wisest idea your mother has got. I confess I have *great* faith in you—and I try to judge you as if you were not my son. I think you are going to take a high place among American authors, but I do not think you are going to do it by articles like that you sent to *The Current*. . . . A lasting, real success takes time, and patient, steady work.

Rebecca attempted both to soften and reinforce her advice as she closed the letter: "I don't say, like Papa, stop writing. God forbid. I would almost as soon say stop breathing, for it is pretty much the same thing. But only to remember that you have not yet conquered your art. You are a journeyman not a master workman. . . . The future is what I look to, for you."[29]

Dick, however, had quite different goals than his parents: they sought to reform society and to gain recognition through the quality of their writing and their intellectual engagement with issues; Dick sought fame, immediate fame. He was coming of age in an era that popularized both the "cult of personality" and the "cult of celebrity." Dick embraced these avenues to fame not only as a young man but throughout his life. Perhaps nothing spoke so fully to the differences in these generations of writers. Although Rebecca would continue to have national recognition as one of the nation's notable writers and Clarke would thrive through his newspaper editorials, which were nationally recognized for their astuteness, Dick would gain international fame as a flamboyant writer, reporter, and man about town, known as much for the power of his personality as the quality of his writing.

Clarke preferred that Dick look to journalism, and once again the Davises helped their son find a position with a Philadelphia newspaper, the *Press*, which now agreed to hire Dick. This time the fit was much better, and Dick kept his promise to make a serious effort. As Charley confirmed, his brother "did his first real work and showed his first promise" during the three years he would remain with the *Press*. He honed his skills, reporting on sports, taking undercover assignments, and working as a general reporter in any capacity the paper required. The position allowed him to meet several famous people who lived or visited the city as well, including the actresses Helena Modjeska and Sarah Bernhardt and the poet Walt Whitman. After Dick left his meeting with Whitman, the poet remarked to Horace Traubel, who was also present, "So you say that was the son of Rebecca Harding Davis? I thought him an Irish boy: I liked him—he was so candid, interesting."[30] The acceptance by the literary world through the affiliation with his mother was typical in the early years of Dick's career and served him to great advantage. At last, Rebecca and Clarke could breathe a sigh of relief that Dick seemed to have found his footing.

A major loss occurred for both Rebecca and Clarke in early 1887 when Charles J. Peterson died on March 4. He had been a family friend and Rebecca's editor at *Peterson's* for more than twenty-five years. His death came after Rebecca had suffered a period of serious illness during the early months of the year; she was only beginning to recover when the news of her friend's death reached her.[31]

Perhaps as a result of her illness and grief, Davis published only three stories, all in *Youth's Companion*, during the first six months of the year, probably choosing that periodical because it paid well and required only short contributions. Rebecca was also spending a considerable amount of time with Nora. Rebecca guided her fourteen-year-old daughter's education and social contacts. Amid her illness, Peterson's death, and attention to her daughter, however, Rebecca was considering the directions of her career. It would be the end of the year before her new plans became evident.

To the joy of Rebecca and Clarke, Charley graduated from Lehigh University in the spring. They aided Charley in finding employment as they had Dick, although he needed far less patronage with his degree in civil engineering and his strong work ethic. Within a short time he had secured a position at the Union Pacific Railroad. He would also work for the Philadelphia and Reading Railroads, and it seemed he would not follow his parents into the field of authorship and journalism. Yet it was Charley who all the other members of the family believed had great talent as a writer, based on his letter-writing skills. Amusingly, an article, "Children of Literary Women," ran in the *Chicago Times* in the spring. It insisted women's writers' children did not typically replicate their talent. The author asserted Davis was "one of the strongest story-writers of the day, and has children, not one of whom is in the least likely to follow in her authorial footsteps"—a prediction that was already proving false.[32]

It would not be the first inaccuracy about Davis in these years and was indicative of the dangers of the cult of celebrity, in which critics, with little knowledge of individuals in the public eye, felt free to ascribe all kinds of unfounded traits or actions to them and their family. For instance, there was the St. Louis critic who wrote about the slender, physically active Davis's supposedly "chubby fingers" and what she looked like, without any knowledge of her. However, a few periodicals were more consistently accurate in their coverage of Davis, such as *The Critic*, based in Philadelphia. But many falsehoods were circulated and would become even more extreme when Dick gained national fame as well.

Soon after Charley's graduation from Lehigh, Rebecca undertook a long trip through the South in preparation for another serial about the region. Just as she was about to depart, Ida Tarbell published an article on "Women in Journalism" in which she cited Davis as one of the "representative women" in the field.[33] This recognition continued in the fall with an article in *American Magazine* that identified Davis as not only a leading fiction writer but "an accomplished lead-writer, and a frequent editorial contributor to two or three influential American newspapers."[34] The *American Magazine* was an illustrated monthly published in New York that set its goal as being "Representative of American Thought and Life," and the article was written by Moses P. Handy of the Philadelphia *Press*, who had served as Davis's editor there and as a co-journalist at the *Tribune*. He was one of Davis's greatest admirers when it came to her work as a journalist. While she was traveling, the *St. Louis Globe-Democrat* ran an article on "Literary Marriages" that highlighted the melding of Rebecca and Clarke's private and professional lives. The Davises' marriage would continue to attract discussion. Soon, they would be noted as a "literary family" as the Davises ensured their sons' opportunities in the profession as well.

Upon returning from the trip south, Rebecca settled in at Point Pleasant and devoted her energies to a five-part serial, "Here and There in the South," for *Harper's*, to be illustrated by William Hamilton Gibson. *Harper's* was publishing a number of pieces about the South in these years, beginning with Edward King's "The Great South" and later included Charles Dudley Warner's "Southern Sketches." In "Here and There in the South," Davis refuted King's perspectives more extensively than she had in "By-Paths," especially in terms of his view of a conquered and lazy South. In her novella, Mr. Ely—an invalided clergyman who embraced Dr. George M. Beard's theory of overwork by Northerners ("We wear out brain and body in our haste to be rich, at the North"[35])—traveled South for his health with his wife Sarah. Ely was nostalgic for the Old South's nonindustrious life and its eschewing of the "money getting" that had come to define the North. What he found, however, was a new and productive South that was making its own way financially and culturally.

Passionately defensive about the complacency with which Northerners habitually stereotyped Southerners, Davis specifically satirized the views of Harriet Beecher Stowe and Albion Tourgee by having a train passenger from the North remark: "We all know the South. Some of the best books in American literature are descriptions of these people. Did you ever read *Uncle Tom's Cabin* or *A Fool's Errand*? They show you that a more indolent, incapable, pig-headed race never breathed.'"[36] The travelers learned, however, that there were many industrious southerners who modeled prosperity in spite of devastating losses during the war.

In the 1860s and early 1870s Davis had depicted the South as a decayed and debilitated region, devastated by its own refusal to let go of its past prejudices and false sense of honor.[37] By the late 1880s when she traveled through the region in order to write "Here and There," she realized a significant change had been enacted by the younger generation. Major Pogue, a prosperous southerner who befriends the Elys, voiced this alteration: "But it is the men who were children in '65 that have their hands on the lever now; they make no mistake about issues. Where their fathers dreamed of reopening the slave-trade and of conquering Mexico and annexing Cuba, to form a great empire, they talk of new cotton-gins, and a thousand other ways of developing our resources. It is the young men who are the New South. I fancy you Northern people know little about the New South."[38]

Davis sought to distinguish the diversity among southerners not only through her depictions of its white residents but through its African American citizens as well. Some African Americans depicted in "Here and There" were lazy, but they were an exception: "the 'Black Belt' . . . is full of rich plantations under scientific cultivation." As the narrator emphasized, "the 'new town'—[has] streets of cheerful rose-covered cottages belonging to the colored people. Nowhere in the South have the freedmen made more steady and swift progress to thrift and intelligence than here" in Montgomery, Alabama.[39] Yet Davis did not skirt the fact that racial prejudices could not be easily overcome, nor did she avoid exposing the way in which the northern travelers could only reconstruct their thinking to a certain degree. With travels through North Carolina, Alabama, and Louisiana, Mr. Ely recovered his health but retained the stereotypic ideas of the South with which he began his journey; the South, concluded the Northerner, was an alien nation.

After returning to Philadelphia from Point Pleasant in September, one of the first and certainly most enjoyable events the Davises attended was a reception for Frances Folsom Cleveland at the home of George W. Childs, publisher of the *Public Ledger*. Frances had married President Grover Cleveland in early June. The reception's guest list was a Who's Who of Philadelphia's social and political leaders. In spite of the fact that Frances was the same age as their elder son, she and Rebecca and Clarke became good friends as well. Rebecca liked the intelligent, warm First Lady. Although the friendship with the Clevelands would solidify over the next couple of years, perhaps the most notable aspect of this first evening's events was that Clarke was dining with the publisher of the *Public Ledger*, the major competitor of his own newspaper. At the time, the *Ledger* was the most prestigious newspaper in Philadelphia. Childs had become its editor in the early 1860s and changed the newspaper politically to align with the Union; under his guidance, the paper had become one of the most influential in the nation. Two weeks after the reception at Childs's home, Clarke resigned his position on the *Inquirer* and became an associate editor for the *Public Ledger*.

It was a momentous decision. At fifty-three years old, Clarke had been with the *Inquirer* for nearly twenty years, but he knew this was an extraordinary opportunity to have an even greater influence on the political and social values of the nation, and he had Rebecca's strong support for this new venture. The news of his move to the *Ledger* was well received in Philadelphia and beyond. As the *North American* noted, "Mr. Davis is one of the most cultured as well as one of the most agreeable men in the profession of journalism. He is a forcible and incisive writer, with thorough earnestness of convictions, the vigor of whose work is adorned by a graceful and scholarly style that is charming and unusual." The *American* asserted, "the *Ledger*, always a well written paper, will have an acquisition of mark in him."[40]

Throughout the fall, even with these significant family changes, Rebecca returned to her usual productivity. She published "From Door to Door" in the *Congregationalist* in October; "Defeated" in *Peterson's*, "Tirar y Soult" in *Scribner's Monthly*, and "Two Hunted Men" in *Youth's Companion* in November; and in December, she published for the first time in *Harper's Bazar*. Davis's contribution to *Harper's Bazar*, "At Noon," was a biting assessment of the elite classes. Jane Fitch was a wealthy and indolent woman. Once a "milkmaid beauty," she had "grown gross and vulgar" and was alienated from her only child because when he was born she had determined she "could not give up Society to be the servant of that little bald, toothless creature." Realizing her status in society was slipping, Jane killed herself with an overdose of laudanum. Her death was mentioned merely in passing in the society columns, and only the maid cared about the boy left behind.[41] It was an extraordinary indictment of those who only value social standing.

Harper's Bazar had long been edited by Mary L. Booth, who would die only two years after she brought Davis to the magazine. It would be nearly a decade after "At Noon" before Davis would again appear in the magazine's pages, but the success of the *Bazar* reflected the popular new emphasis on society's elite class. The first US social register was founded in 1887, and attention to the lives of the American aristocracy became a fervent national pastime. "At Noon" had observed the inaccuracies of society pages, and in spite of Rebecca's preferences to remain out of the society and gossip columns of newspapers, which were instrumental in building the cult of celebrity, she was too well known to avoid such scrutiny. In December one newspaper noted that, in spite of writing stories with "a melancholy turn," Davis was in fact "a thorough optimist" and "a vivacious body." "She and her husband, L. Clarke Davis," the report continued, "are a home-loving couple, and their house is full of sunshine."[42] Many such items would appear over the years, when people who knew Davis only through her fiction were surprised to find she was an active, outgoing, and affectionate personality, one who loved to tell humorous anecdotes.

In 1888, Rebecca wrote for the usual range of magazines and newspapers, including *Peterson's*. Charles's widow, Sarah Peterson, had assumed the editorship of the magazine, and Rebecca remained loyal to it. Davis also added three new periodicals to her repertoire, but she published slightly less in quantity than had been her typical pattern. She was at a point in her career and in her life when she could be more selective and write more overtly about political issues than she had at times in the early years. This year also evidenced some important changes for the Davis family as their sons advanced their careers and their friendship with the Clevelands developed more fully.

In January, Davis began a three-part serial for the magazine, "The Kennairds." A well-written romance, the story incorporated many contemporary issues, including the private use of detectives to find missing family members, the female con artist, and the debunking of the idea that any newly wealthy young American woman could find a titled husband in Europe, regardless of how vulgar her family was. Davis also published two stories in the *Congregationalist* at this time, where her conservative strain was more evident, especially on the issue of women's duty to create a comfortable home life for her family, but as always, she would shift back and forth from her conservative to her progressive side.

In the spring, Rebecca and Clarke attended the wedding of Morton McMichael, Jr., son of their late friend, the former mayor and owner of the *North American*. McMichael, Jr. married Louise Godey Seeger, the granddaughter of the founder of *Godey's Lady's Magazine*, for which the senior McMichael had been an editor before purchasing the *North American*. Although *Godey's* was one of the nation's most popular women's magazines and had been published in Philadelphia for most of its existence, Rebecca never wrote for the periodical since it was the competitor of *Peterson's Magazine*. As part of the society circles of Philadelphia, however, the Davises and the Godey relatives often met.

Although Davis had published steadily throughout the winter and spring, she had submitted only one story to the *Congregationalist* the previous year, instead of her usual two or three contributions annually. In 1888, however, she made a major shift in her relationship to the periodical, more than doubling her usual output for the magazine. Sophisticated religious periodicals such as the *Congregationalist* were successful in drawing many well-known writers in this period; in spite of the shift to a greater secularism in many major literary magazines in the postwar years, Christianity remained central to most Americans' lives. The *Congregationalist* joined *Peterson's*, the *Independent*, and *Youth's Companion* as one of Davis's most noteworthy literary alliances, and she continued her prolific newspaper work as well. In the spring, Davis had also contracted with the *Watchman and Southron* to have her story "Hand to Hand" reprinted. The *Watchman* was starting a new series of what they termed novelettes to appear periodically; in addition to Davis's story, the series included Henry James's "The Story of a Masterpiece," Robert Louis Stevenson's "The Treasure of Franchard," and others. The transposition of stories between literary magazines and religious periodicals remained an accepted aspect of many writers' careers in these years.

In June Rebecca participated in a national literary event. A series of "Authors Readings in Washington" were held in support of the American Copyright League. Readings were given at the Congregational Church in the capital, hosted by the League's vice president Edmund Clarence Stedman. The League's members regarded it as a "moral movement."[43] The readings coincided with the bill the League was trying to pass through Congress in support of American authors and publishers. The President and Mrs. Cleveland were in attendance, and when a souvenir book was published the next year, a copy was presented to Frances Cleveland. The supporters whose comments appeared in the book were a "Who's Who" of US authors, including Davis, Thomas Bailey Aldrich, Mark Twain, George Washington Cable, Mary Mapes Dodge, John Hay, Marion Harland, Thomas Wentworth Higginson, Oliver Wendell Holmes, William Dean Howells, Henry James, and numerous others.[44]

Before the Davises left for their annual summer vacation, Rebecca published her first and only article in *The Fireside Teacher*, a magazine "Devoted to Home Culture and Literary Improvement." "Despondency Cured" addressed an issue Davis had faced several times in her own family—a "young man had made his first plunge into disappointment, so common in life, and the chill of it struck to his heart."[45] The means of recovery, she advised, was to engage in challenging work that employed the young man's best talents, as reiterated the next month in a contribution to the *Congregationalist*, "Cured by Active Work." Though she rarely spoke openly about this family issue, several times in recent months Rebecca had nursed Clarke and Dick through periods of despondency. Charley and Nora, like their mother, seemed to have escaped that familial pattern.

In the summer of 1888, the Davises made a major transition in their summer retreat. Although they would continue to spend some time at Point Pleasant in coming years, they shifted to Marion, Massachusetts, and it would become their primary summer retreat for many years. Marion had been developed as a resort in the 1870s, but its fame came through the large artists' colony that had developed there in the 1880s, primarily through the influence of Rebecca's editor at the *Century Magazine*, Richard Watson Gilder. Marion was a small village on Buzzard's Bay, about sixty miles south of Boston, and traveling there each summer required the Davises to engage a circuitous system of trains, a boat, and the stage. By the time they joined the community, regular members included Marianna Schuyler Van Rensselaer, who wrote numerous articles for the *Century Magazine* on contemporary art; the actress Bessy Harwood; the illustrator Charles Dana Gibson; the actor Joseph Jefferson and his son Charles; as well as occasional visitors such as Henry James, Mark Twain, the Arctic explorer General Adolphus Greely, and the sculptor Augustus Saint-Gaudens, who was working on his most memorable work, the Robert Gould Shaw Memorial, a bronze bas-relief that commemorated Shaw and the African American soldiers of the Fifty-fourth Massachusetts Volunteer Infantry. Some of these visitors, like Saint-Gaudens, eventually became regulars as well.

Gilder's spouse, Helena de Kay Gilder, was a talented artist who drew other artists to the community, many of whom became friends of the Davises over the years. Among the wealthy summer people in Marion were the Chicagoan Louise Clark and her teenage daughter, Cecil. Cecil's fame as a portrait painter would come in future years—as would her marriage to Richard Harding Davis. The Gilders lived in a large, ramshackle homestead, and there was a small building on their property that became Helena Gilder's studio; the "Old Stone Studio" was renovated by the architect Stanford White and became the site of theatricals performed by the summer residents each year. Over the years, participants in these performances included many of the literary artists and painters in the community as well as renowned actors such as Jefferson, John Drew, Ethel Barrymore, John Barrymore, Evelyn Nesbitt, and Maude Adams. It was in Marion that Nora Davis developed a life-long friendship with Adams.

It was in Marion, too, that the Davises would deepen their friendship with Frances and Grover Cleveland. At Richard Watson Gilder's invitation, Frances summered in Marion for the first time in 1887 and drew the national press to the village; the activities of the artists' colony would thereafter be followed by the national press unceasingly. This first summer when the Davises joined the community, Frances and her mother had returned, and the following summer Grover would join them. The "cottage" that the Davises rented each summer was a massive estate on Buzzard's Bay (see Figure 5). Three stories with an extensive porch and balconies, the cottage was surrounded by well-groomed lawns and lush flowers and was located next to the even larger cottage-estate of Judge James Austin.[46]

As Rebecca returned to Philadelphia in September and was preparing manuscripts for submission, the *Ladies' Home Journal* published a lengthy, multi-authored section on Philadelphia, which assessed the political, economic, and social status of the city. The British author and literary critic Edmund Gosse assessed the literary life of the city for the issue and once again identified Davis as "the best of living American story writers."[47] A new periodical, *Current Literature,* also contacted her requesting information for a profile. She replied to the editor, "Dear Sir, There really is nothing to be said about me for Current Literature. I am not writing any book and do not expect to publish one soon. With many thanks for your kindly interest. I am, yours sincerely, Rebecca Harding Davis."[48]

In fact, she was quite busy writing both fiction and journalism at the time, but this refusal to assist in personal or even professional biographies was a typical response. Famous throughout her lifetime, she would fade from literary annals for a period of time after her death, in part because she was a woman writer but perhaps even more so because she did not leave the requisite body of personal commentaries, photographs, and critical biographies so popular in magazines of the day and that were essential to the establishment of the canon of American literature in the next century. She was anti-celebrity to an almost self-damaging degree.

Davis continued to write for the *Congregationalist* with such stories as "The Pragues' Ambition" in October, a cautionary tale about a young minister's wife who becomes obsessed with fashion and society. But Davis turned to a far more serious issue in the magazine that month as well, one that had long concerned her: prison reform. Brief assertions about the need for prison reform had appeared in earlier works, such as her depiction of the abusive treatment of contract-labor prisoners in "Here and There in the South." "Prisoners' Sunday" detailed what it was like in a large city prison, most likely drawn from her knowledge of Philadelphia's Moyamensing Prison, which she referenced in several of her works. She humanized the prisoners by selecting three men's stories to relate and offered two ways in which readers could make a difference in their communities: first, work with others to develop crime-prevention methods; second, like the charge about slavery she had made to the nation in *Waiting for the Verdict*, take responsibility to aid released inmates so they could become valuable members of society again.

The Presidential election of November 1888 thrust Rebecca into a brief public position she surely did not seek when the *Reno Evening Gazette* ran a long article on which candidate famous women would support if they could vote; it asserted she favored Benjamin Harrison. It is doubtful Rebecca actually indicated her choice, but the election revealed the dilemma of friendships and politics. She had sided with the Radical Republicans after the end of the war. With the changing nature of both Democratic and Republican parties, however, many Americans were shifting their alliances, but it remained a period of fraught transition. There had been some effort by the Republicans to induce James G. Blaine to run again, but when he refused, Harrison became their candidate. He ran against the Democratic nominee—and the Davises' friend—Grover Cleveland.

If Rebecca did not voice her party preferences, Clarke did so as a newspaper editor. During this election, the *Public Ledger* retained its commitment to American labor. Republican leaders argued protective tariffs would aid labor, and the *Ledger*'s editorials supported that position to the extent it was credited with helping to sway two swing states, New York and Indiana, to the Republican side.[49] Harrison won the election. Regardless of their political differences, the Davises and the Clevelands remained friends. As that friendship grew, however, Clarke would powerfully and publicly align himself with Cleveland.

In spite of the political turmoil of the fall, Davis had a very productive period at the end of the year. In November she published in the *Congregationalist* "Losing Her Hold," the story of a fifty-five-year-old woman who regains her vigor for life by working with the poor and taking in three orphans. Davis also published two stories this month in the *Independent* and one in *Youth's Companion*. The *Independent* was increasingly drawing renowned US writers to its pages. This issue included works by Davis, John Greenleaf Whittier, Joel Chandler Harris, Harriet Prescott Spofford, and several others. One of Davis's stories for the *Independent*, "Low Wages for Women" was an ardent front-page assessment of women and labor.

In December Davis turned to her third new periodical of the year, *Scribner's Magazine*. She had worked with Charles Scribner on *Scribner's Monthly* for many years; the magazine had published some of her major works, including the novel *John Andross*. Scribner insisted that *Scribner's Magazine* was not a revival of the *Monthly* but a new effort to publish the best political and literary works of the day. In spite of competition with *Harper's* and other already highly successful magazines, *Scribner's Magazine* made its mark under the editorship of Edward L. Burlingame with outstanding writers and the inclusion of color illustrations. It had begun publication the year before, and Davis's first contribution, "At the Station," was one of her North Carolina stories.

Scribner's Magazine joined a group of periodicals, like the *Century*, that had decided to forego the reprinting of English serials, a mainstay of most literary magazines in the US. *Current Literature*'s reviewer asserted, the "outburst of mental energy that followed the Civil War" made such a transition possible as "American writers began to develop. Dr. Holland himself, Rebecca Harding Davis, Bret Harte, Edward Everett Hale, Miss Trafton, Frances Hodgson Burnett, W. D. Howells, Edward Eggleston, and Mr. Boyensen were among those who furnished continued stories for the monthly." The reviewer noted that the success of the magazines that pursued this emphasis on American literature "was immediate."[50]

At the end of the year Dick was also immersed in writing, having started a weekly magazine, *The Stage*, with the younger Morton McMichael, for which they wrote every article. Dick's primary contribution was a column about theater manners, public relations, props and costumes, and notably, celebrity.[51] Once again Clarke could be proud of the early introduction he had given his children to the world of theater. Although the weekly would be short-lived, it helped Dick develop critical skills and learn the ins and outs of publishing from all aspects of the process. Although still writing for the *Press*, Dick now spent a great deal of time in New York City as well; he loved the theater life there, dining at Delmonico's, and the vibrant atmosphere of the city. But when he became ill in September, he returned home to be nursed by his mother. The pattern of returning to his parents' home when he needed nurturing and sustenance was one that would recur throughout Dick's life.

The year ended with a profile of Rebecca appearing in Laura C. Holloway's *The Woman's Story as Told by Twenty American Women*. One of the early contributions to the new genre of collections by and about women writers, the volume received good reviews, but the section on Davis had apparently been published without her perusal as it included a number of errors, which was surprising because Davis did, atypically, supply Holloway with some details for the book.[52] Also notable, as a review in *Good Housekeeping* observed, each biographical sketch included a portrait of the author, "all but one case (that of Rebecca Harding Davis, who will not permit her portrait to be taken, even for relatives)."[53] Holloway had tried to persuade Rebecca to send a photograph, but she replied, "I am sorry to spoil the symmetry of your book, but I cannot send you a vignette. One of the idiotic spaces in my brain of which Dr. *Holmes* tells us, is filled with a dislike to seeing my own face. As even my children have pleaded in vain, you will not I am sure, think me ungracious when I refuse you."[54]

Perhaps the most significant change in Rebecca's life during the late 1880s came early in 1889 when she resigned her position as editorial correspondent for the *New-York Tribune*.[55] Davis had been writing a series of editorials about abuses perpetrated by several Northern industries. She focused on their monopoly of chemicals needed for their manufacturing. Their monopoly depleted an important source of chemicals needed for medical treatments of patients in the southern states. She had accurately detailed the practices of the manufacturers, but they were major advertisers in the *Tribune*; when they protested the editorials, Davis was ordered to desist. She was shocked by Whitelaw Reid's intrusion.[56] Although the two had worked together amiably enough, she had never developed a friendship with Reid. In later years, she would reveal in private letters the disdain in which she held him.[57]

In spite of her disassociation with the *Tribune*, Davis was not without opportunities for editorial work. After twenty years of writing anonymously for the *Tribune*, she had finally been persuaded by William Hayes Ward to become a regular editorial contributor to the *Independent*. Davis would continue to publish fiction in the *Independent*, but she would also publish some of her most important political commentaries as signed editorials for the New York periodical. She retained her editorial affiliation with the *Independent* for twenty years, until shortly before her death.

She began her new role with the *Independent* in January 1889 with two commentaries—"Our Creditors" and "What About the Northern Negro?"—and in February, "The New Religious 'What Is It?'" The first commentary examined the new system of credit between household managers and tradesmen, while "What About the Northern Negro?" demonstrated the two styles of editorials Davis wrote for the *Independent*: the moral commentary and the political commentary. An article by the same title had recently appeared in the paper detailing the difficulty African Americans had in gaining well-remunerated employment while paying high rents for shabby housing and finding doors shut to avenues of advancement. "These are facts concerning his condition in the city of New York," Davis agreed in her front-page assessment, "but do they fairly index his status in the whole North?" Outside of New York, the majority of African Americans who had turned to farming had succeeded, she argued; although the trade unions in the North had excluded African Americans as well as whites in favor of foreign skilled laborers, in the South "he will find the trades almost wholly in possession of his race, and abundance of work and wages waiting for the sober, industrious man." In Philadelphia, she noted,

> the colored people in this city form a large, influential community. They earn their money not only as 'cooks, waiters and barbers,' the employments to which they are said to be doomed, but precisely as their white brethren earn it. They are dealers in groceries, coal, wood, dry goods; they are doctors, clergymen, teachers, caterers, brokers, tailors, dressmakers; they have their churches, their schools, from the highest to the lowest grade; their clubs—dining, dancing, Shakespearean; their charitable and literary societies, their newspapers.[58]

Although she did not argue against this segregation of restaurants and literary societies, such assessments were yet in advance of many Americans' attitudes at the time.

"The New Religious 'What Is It?'" responded to Mary A. Ward's recent attack on orthodox Christianity in the pages of the *North American Review*. Acknowledging she found Ward's novel *Robert Elsmere* "a brilliant success," Davis nonetheless took umbrage with Ward's desire to see Christianity eradicated. Secularism was gaining ground in American culture, a fact that Davis found deeply disturbing. She asserted, "this clever novelist is thoroughly imbued with the unconscious lofty self-sufficiency of the Arnold clique in England, of which every member, whatever his equipment as to brain, speaks like a dictator in the realm of thought. Mrs. Ward is not guileful enough to see the disadvantage at which this amusing assumption of superiority places her before her reader." "But what is this new doctrine of unbelief" that Mrs. Ward espouses, Davis asked. It is "only the insular habit of thought. . . . known only to a few secluded thinkers [of] the hackneyed dogmas of the Hicksite Quakers and of other branches of the Unitarian Church in this country. That is it and nothing more."[59]

Davis's scathing indictment did not go unanswered. An editorial comment a few weeks later from a member of the Hicksite Quakers took exception to her comments about their hackneyed beliefs and their alliance with the Unitarians.[60] The protest letter to the editor was reprinted in the *Friends' Intelligencer*, with equal disdain for Davis's charges.[61]

Like Rebecca, Clarke was immensely busy and productive in the early months of 1889. In addition to his editorial role at the *Ledger*, he also managed to write occasional theater reviews for the newspaper. The Davises had attended the New Year's Eve performance of "Romeo and Juliet" starring Julia Marlowe. Clarke wrote a glowing review, asserting he had seen all of the great performances of Juliet in the last thirty-five years and Marlowe's was among the finest. The review gave a significant boost to the attendance of the play by Philadelphians.[62]

Praise for Rebecca came at this time as well—from one of the great activist-writers of the era. Frances Willard published her autobiography, in which she cited the importance of Davis's attention to the commonplace people and events of life and to the importance of her status as a writer. Working against those critics who saw "Life" as Davis's best work, Albert Henry Smyth also published a survey of *American Literature* in which he asserted she was among the women writers who had done their best work since the Civil War, especially in her portraits of "the lower classes of society."[63] As the assessments of American literature continued to proliferate in the late nineteenth century, Davis always received such attention for her large and influential body of work. *Current Literature*, which offered similar assessments on a monthly basis, followed her career closely. She was among the authors, their literary reviewer observed, who offered readers "much mental food of the most nourishing description."[64]

Throughout the spring, Davis continued her editorial work for the newspapers and her work appeared in the pages of *Harper's*, the *Independent*, the *Congregationalist*, and *Youth's Companion*. Among these publications was a powerful political statement, "Ned Moxon's Grievances," that received strong support from the *Independent*'s editorial staff: "If there be sermons in stones there are also sermons in stories. A better one has not been printed in our columns this many a day than Rebecca Harding Davis preaches this week. Read the story, and if the text applies, if you have confused your affections with your self-love, find a cure at once and do not wait for bankruptcy or death."[65]

"At Our Gates" appeared in the *Independent* one week later; also a type of sermon, it raised vital questions for contemporary Christians. Drawing on an incident in Connecticut in which a poor man who had civilly asked a farmer's wife for a cup of coffee was arrested and tried for begging for food, fined thirty dollars, and sentenced to one month's imprisonment, Davis again questioned the efficacy of organized charity. Although she acknowledged the Board of Charities and the Society for the Suppression of Beggary did some good work, she qualified her assessment—"unless [the donated money] happens to fall into the hands of mercenary, tricky men, as it sometimes does." Her particular concern was the Society for the Suppression of Beggary because it assumed "every man who asks for food is a scoundrel and fraud until he proves himself otherwise." She admonished Christians who simply give their money to large charities "and henceforth wash your hands of all care of your needy brother."[66]

Among Davis's many publications in the summer of 1889 was "Some Significant Facts" in the *Independent*, a highly xenophobic essay built around the purported scavenging of corpses and mistreatment of the victims in the aftermath of the Johnstown flood by "German and Irish toughs" and "gangs of Hungarians." Davis asserted, "Bishop Potter in his noble Centennial sermon told us, in effect, that our national character had been lowered in the last hundred years by the incessant drainage to our shores of the lowest classes of Europe. . . . If we are to continue to offer 'a refuge for the oppressed of every nation,' we have the right to exact that the standard of law, manners and morals in that refuge shall be American, not Hungarian, German nor Irish."[67]

The so-called "New Immigration" of the 1880s had struck Philadelphia particularly, with large numbers of Catholics and Jews coming from Italy and Russia, and Davis's commentary represented the nativist perspective that these immigrants would be unable to assimilate socially or economically into US society. It was yet again a paradoxical response from Davis, since her own father had emigrated from Ireland, and in so many other instances, she argued against classist attitudes. As with her perspectives on racial equality, she could be ardent in her arguments against class and ethnic biases even as her xenophobic response to immigrants recurred periodically over the rest of her life.

That Rebecca published only two items in June was undoubtedly due to the time spent nursing Dick, and in July, though she published three pieces, only two were written in the spring months. "The Modern Phyllis" in the *Congregationalist* debunked the idea that modern licentiousness, crime, and drunkenness were urban phenomena, but Davis's argument also continued her concern about the freedom that young women now had, whether they lived in the country or the large cities. She concluded that excessive freedom for women was "neither modest, safe nor decent. Where are the mothers of the girls who carry on flirtations in the cars, or who go driving in buggies with men whom their parents have never seen, or who plunge into the surf with a promiscuous mob every day in the season?"[68] As the mother of a daughter who was now fifteen, Rebecca was clearly facing renewed concerns about how young women were being encouraged to new and different types of activities that held far less parental oversight than in the past.

This year, the Davises combined Point Pleasant and Marion for their summer vacation. Frances and Grover Cleveland rented a small cottage in Marion for the summer and, like the Davises, they again joined the gregarious group of artists, authors, and theater people who populated the village for the summer. Clarke fished nearly every day, in the company of Grover and the actor Joe Jefferson. While in Marion, Dick's story for *St. Nicholas* appeared; it drew on his youthful experiences at Point Pleasant. Dick had written to his parents when the manuscript was accepted; he was joyously excited about being paid for a story in a national magazine. Rebecca had responded enthusiastically, "Well done for old *St. Nicholas*! It took me back to the day when I got $50. for 'Life in the Iron Mills.' I carried the letter for half a day before opening it, being so sure that it was a refusal." She also encouraged him in relation to a manuscript he had sent to her: "Have you done anything on Gallagher? That is by far the best work you have done—send that to Gilder. In old times *The Century* would not print the word 'brandy.' But those days are over."[69] The pattern of reading Dick's manuscripts, offering critiques and sometimes editing them, became a common pattern for Rebecca.

In the fall, an important change for the Davis family came to fruition. Dick, unhappy with the lack of advancement in his journalism career in Philadelphia, decided to move to New York City. Although he had no position when he settled in the city, he soon ran into an acquaintance, Arthur Brisbane, the newly appointed editor of the *Evening Sun*. Brisbane hired Dick as a reporter for his newspaper at thirty dollars per week. For the first time in his life, the twenty-five-year-old Dick had found employment without his parents' intervention. He rented a room with board in a small house on Waverly Place, though he would continue to spend many weekends in Philadelphia at his parents' home.

Charley began to make frequent trips to New York to visit his brother and immerse himself in the newspaper and theater worlds there. The comic opera was particularly popular in New York at this time, and Dick and Charley became friends with two of its stars, Francis Wilson and DeWolf Hopper. Charley sought an economic pattern for the brothers of eating cheap dinners in order to afford the theater. On the other hand, Dick had learned generosity from his parents, if not the art of budgeting his money. At his most advanced, he made less than fifty dollars a week at the *Evening Sun*, but he spent money without reserve on everything from parties to helping struggling authors and artists to donations for every beggar who asked. Charley felt "this habit of giving Richard must have inherited from his father, who gave out of all proportion to his means, and with never too close a scrutiny to the worthiness of the cause"; both father and son thought it better to give to all the possible fakers rather than "refuse one worthy case."[70]

Life in Philadelphia continued much the same for Rebecca and Clarke. Throughout the fall Davis published a number of stories and articles, including "A New National Trait." The editorial indicted the practice of publishing gossip about famous people's personal lives. Does the American actually believe "that notoriety is elevation and an vulgar exposure of his affairs to the public is distinction?"[71] She tried to instill these distinctions in her sons' minds as well, but it was a generational divide she could not alter.

At the end of the year, Rebecca published one of her most notable indictments of US racial prejudices. "Our National Vanities" responded to a recent cultural commentary she had read. Murat Halstead had published "a brilliant article" in the *North American Review* about "little vanities in which the American delights to wrap and warm himself and to strut before the world." As insightful as Halstead was, Davis thought he was far too gentle in his critique. She offered additional assessments of American vanities, noting that Americans liked to travel the world, proclaiming their nation adhered to personal freedoms. "And then," she wryly observed, "the happy boastful American comes home and helps to make laws which rob certain of his fellow citizens of their property; which deny their right to earn or hold property at all, or to appeal, like other human beings, when their houses are burned or their wives outraged, to the law for justice. Why? ... Because their skins are red." Further, "in the free, enlightened, charitable Northern States," citizens who are typically well educated and striving to earn a living are thwarted at every turn: "The reason is—their skins are darker than his own. Our other American conceits are laughable," she concluded, "but there is something tragic in our vanity on our national freedom and justice, when we see that they now depend wholly on the color of a skin."[72] This was Davis at her progressive best.

The year ended with the public announcement that Rebecca was now not only a writer for *Youth's Companion* but one of its "salaried editorial attachés."[73] Another writer, Alexander Young, published an article about the *Companion*, noting its circulation was now

> more than 430,000. The annual premium number of the paper (1889–90) has an edition of 600,000 copies. ... *The Youth's Companion*, as is

well-known, has a small army of distinguished special contributors; it has ten office editors and a large number of salaried editorial attachés, among them being James Parton, Rebecca Harding Davis, George Makepeace Towle, Clarene Pullen, Edward Stanwood, Bradford Torrey, and Thomas H. Clay, a grandson of Henry Clay.

Young noted, too, that every manuscript received four readings before the editor-in-chief made the final decision on its publication.[74] Davis's dual role of editorial writer and author for the magazine was one more expansion of her editorial interests she had been able to undertake since she was no longer writing for the *Tribune*. If there had been an unusually significant number of transitions in Rebecca's life over the past five years, she embraced these changes with vigor and was looking forward to the decade that would mark the end of a most amazing century.

1. Rebecca Harding, c. 1860 (Rachel Loden Collection)

2. Nora Davis, prior to 1887 (Rachel Loden Collection)

3. Charles Belmont Davis, 1893 (Rachel Loden Collection)

4. (Top) Richard Harding Davis wedding, 1899. Front row, right to left: Louise Clark (Cecil's mother); Rebecca Harding Davis; seated in the wicker chair, L. Clarke Davis with Richard Harding Davis at his feet; Cecil Clark Davis.

5. (Above right) The Davis cottage at Marion, Massachusetts (Sippican Historical Society)

6. (Above left) Hope Davis, Rebecca Harding Davis's only grandchild, sitting on the lap of her mother, Bessie McCoy Davis (Charles Scribner, NY, 1917)

Chapter 10

"A Message to Be Given" (1890–1893)

In the 1890s the Davises became one of the most prominent literary and journalistic families in the nation. As Rebecca's and Clarke's fame was joined by recognition of Dick as a writer, Charley turned from his engineering career to writing as well, and Nora became a rising figure in Philadelphia's and New York's society circles. As the Davises numbered among their friends not only actors, artists, and authors but also presidents, they became popular figures for discussion in gossip and society columns. Newspapers such as the *Boston Globe* and the *Philadelphia Inquirer* frequently reported on their travels and personal activities as well as their work. Although Rebecca continued to abhor the invasions of privacy and the assessments of her life rather than her work, Dick adored the celebrity status beginning to come his way. The family members were also traveling much more than they had in the past. Rebecca occasionally and Clarke frequently visited Dick in New York where the family dined at Delmonico's or the Madison Square Garden roof-top restaurant and attended numerous Broadway openings.

Rebecca continued regularly to write fiction for *Harper's*, *Peterson's*, the *Independent*, *Youth's Companion*, the *Congregationalist*, and other literary magazines, but much of her time was devoted to editorial work for several periodicals. Some, such as the *Independent*, were under her signature, but a majority (including for the *Century*) was unsigned. Though Rebecca would publish only two stories in *Peterson's* in 1890, she returned to writing longer pieces for the magazine. "A Reporter's Work," for example, was a tribute to a Philadelphia reporter, F. Jennings Crute, who had recently died. Although many people knew and disdained him only for his probing into societal fashions and secrets, "they forget that the public are hungry for this meal of personal gossip or it would not be served to them," Davis wrote in a signed remembrance. Crute was devoted to his profession and had been the first Philadelphia reporter on the scene of the Johnstown floods, risking his life to report on the disaster; it was time, she asserted, "we understood the work of the class to which he belonged, and recognized its wide and often heroic service."[1] Dick responded in a private letter to the tribute, "I cannot tell you how it pleased me except to say that loving him as I did I would not have changed a word of it. It was so nobly written and so well written because it was just the truth beautifully told. There is nobody can write as you can mother. It made me cry—and rejoice over it at the same time."[2]

In addition to writing, Rebecca was frequently active in cultural events in Philadelphia. In early February, she was one of four patrons sponsoring a series of Tennyson recitals at the Academy of Fine Arts.[3] When Clarke was managing editor of the *Philadelphia Inquirer*, the newspaper rarely mentioned Rebecca's civic activities, limiting itself to reviews of her writings. Once he moved to the *Public Ledger*, however, the *Inquirer* frequently reported on her activities.

Clarke, on the other hand, had long been an active member of the city's elite clubs, and his attendance at various events was always reported in detail. He liked many of the club associations required for his work, since they afforded him an opportunity to meet many renowned literary, scientific, political, and philanthropic people from around the country and abroad. In February he gave a speech at Philadelphia's Harvard Club on the importance of advanced training for journalists in the changing world of that profession and the need for universities to consider such training as part of their mission. The following month Clarke was a guest speaker at the Fellowcraft Club with both the *Ledger* publisher George C. Childs and Alexander Graham Bell in attendance.[4] Immediately after notices about the lecture appeared, Dick wrote Clarke to say how proud he was of his father.

Soon Clarke traveled to New York to join Dick for the American dancer Carmencita's debut in "The Pearl of Seville."[5] This year, too, Dick was admitted to the theater profession's famous Players' Club, which welcomed people from literature and the arts who supported the theater. Founded by Rebecca and Clarke's friend Edwin Booth, the club was where Dick would meet the architect Stanford White. Dick also began at this time to date Helen Benedict whose father, Elias C. Benedict, was a millionaire New York stockbroker, banker, and yachtsman.[6] These associations moved him into very different circles in New York than he had previously experienced.

March of 1890 was an extraordinarily busy month for the Davises. Rebecca published an essay in the *Congregationalist* and fiction in the *Independent*. At nearly fifty-nine, she was experiencing the pangs of a life that was rapidly changing as her children became adults and she found herself often sidelined in decisions about their lives. In reality, she was far more involved in their lives than many mothers, but the transition was startling to her. In "As We Grow Old" she reflected on such changes. Following a series of articles on aging that the eighty-year-old Oliver Wendell Holmes had recently published, she questioned the "cheery" perspective he took. Literature itself does not explore her generation, she noted: "Poets and painters see nothing picturesque or dramatic in our role in life, and leave us unhonored and unsung. The novel stops when the young people marry." Further, young people look at "the flat delta of middle age" as a barren space in which love and fancy no longer grow. She reflected that having a career brought solace when children left home and recommended those who did not have that outlet should pursue the dreams of their youth as a means of finding joy in life again.[7]

The fictional "Polly's Venture" continued this theme, exploring another generation of women seeking to fulfill their dreams in the years immediately after the war. A young quadroon, Polly, had been raised and educated with her mistress's daughter; she refused to become a cook or laundress, and her former mistress would not help her to receive an advanced education. But through her mother's highly regarded cooking skills and Polly's hard work, she graduated in four years. When no one would hire her, Polly opened her own shop in her mother's house, and the two women built a sustaining business of their own. Davis concluded, "Many of Polly's sisters in both the South and the North, educated, modest, intelligent girls, are seeking eagerly for work now outside of the kitchen. Can they learn nothing from her story?"[8] Concluding her essay with a question was a notable marker of Davis's style, demanding thought and action from her readers.

The other side to these uplift stories was a series of narratives about women's wasted lives, written over the breadth of Davis's career. One of these tales, "An Ignoble Martyr," appeared in *Harper's Monthly* in March. She had not published in the magazine for nearly a year, and it would be another seven years before she returned to its pages with a short story, but Harper's would become the publishers of her novels thereafter. At the same time "An Ignoble Martyr" appeared, Dick published the first of his Van Bibber stories in the New York *Evening Sun*; the stories would escalate his popularity. But he was also writing "slum stories" for the paper, such as "A Vile Den to Be Closed" and "Young Ladies in the Tombs."[9] "Slumming" had become a popular activity and a part of American slang in the mid-1880s; in part for charity but largely out of curiosity, it became popular to tour disreputable or impoverished sections of the city.[10] When Jacob Riis published *How the Other Half Lives* this year, slumming became frenetically popular.

Nothing could have been further from the kind of stories and articles Davis wrote about the poor, but newspapers such as the *Sun* profited from this new cultural phenomenon. She wanted Dick to aim for higher types of writing, and thus she sent one of his manuscripts to Horace Elisha Scudder, her old friend from Houghton Mifflin who was the new editor of the *Atlantic Monthly*. She insisted he not give Dick preferential treatment as her son; though she had hopes that Scudder would be interested in Dick's work, he rejected the story—and she learned to withhold her request that an editor not consider the author was her relation when she promoted her son's work. Although Dick would never publish with the *Atlantic*, two humorous series he was writing would soon gain extraordinary popularity—his Gallegher and Van Bibber stories. Thereafter many magazines would clamor for his contributions.

At the end of March, Clarke travelled to Washington to meet with President Benjamin Harrison. James G. Blaine wrote a letter of introduction for Clarke, noting his high character and that he was a respected editor and "justly distinguished in the field of Literature. My personal interest in Mr. Davis," Blaine explained to Harrison, "is greatly enhanced by the fact that his wife—the well known Mrs. Rebecca Harding Davis—is a family connection of mine for whom I have entertained a sincere regard since boyhood days."[11] Blaine explained to Harrison that he did not know the subject for Clarke's requested meeting, and its content remained between the President and the journalist.

In April Rebecca published "An Old Legend" in the *Independent*, which called for the preservation of regional historical documents, a theme she would return to periodically. She also returned to her concerns about living conditions for Native Americans in an article for the *Congregationalist*. "Needs of the Reservations" addressed readers who were zealous in their efforts to Christianize Native Americans. Davis met several times with Native activists over the years, as she announced at the beginning of her essay: "I have been asked by both whites and educated Indians on the reservations to bring these facts before the Eastern public as far as I could."[12]

The list of needs was presented with discussions of the challenges to their fulfillment as well: the need for industrial training on the reservations. Davis again indicted the US government's treatment of Native Americans, reporting that white farmers appointed to teach Native Americans new technical practices in farming were instead using their positions for personal profit. They used "the red men to dig and plow like beasts of burden" rather than teaching them techniques that would ease their labor and create more productive lands. New positions were also needed for young tribal members who were educated in the East and returned to the reservation; they could not all be teachers, she insisted: "Only work, lucrative work and plenty of it, can reconcile young people to their anomalous position" and aid in the elevation of their tribes.[13]

Revealing of Davis's attitudes, both practical and assimilationist, was her insistence that it was right to send missionaries to the reservation, "But the capitalist who will establish industries among them, who will teach them the meaning of 'work' and 'wages,' will do more than any other man to make their religion real." In this article, she claimed to support some aspects of the Dawes Act, but asserted it had not addressed the need for Native Americans to be taught the "morality" of legalized marriage (as opposed to the practice of polygamy that had been ascribed to some tribes) so the Native Americans could inherit the land from generation to generation rather than have it escheat to the State.[14] While her concern was for inheritance rights, the article revealed Davis's ever-paradoxical attitudes toward non-white Americans.

The following month Davis published a story in the *Independent* with autobiographical implications. "In the Ore" was a story of two brothers that traced the means by which the one who demanded attention from the moment he was born always overshadowed the quiet but more loving brother. Intentional or not, the story paralleled the flamboyant Dick's constant demands to be the center of the family's attention, while Charley was forging a quieter but solid base for his writing career. Rebecca was trying, too, to guide Dick, both in his writing and in his life choices. He, in turn, wrote many playful, entertaining letters to her in response to her advice against "hack work."[15]

On the other hand, Dick necessarily sought to establish his own boundaries as well. In late May he expressed appreciation of her positive criticism of a story he had recently published, "Goddess in Mid-Air." But as to her objections to the story's implicit sexual content, he added,

> it was not a bit necessary to add the *moral* from a *mother*. I saw it coming up before I had read two lines and a very good moral it is too with which I agree heartily. But of course you know it is not a new idea to me Anything as good and true as that moral cannot be new at this late date.... I have no doubt but that the Methodist minister's daughter would have made Hiram [the story's protagonist] happy if he had loved her but he didn't. No doubt Anne Cummins, Nan Webb, Katy Shippen and Maude Hoyt [friends from Wheeling] would have made me happy if they would have consented to have me and I had happened to love them.[16]

Although his criticism of what he viewed as his mother's outdated moral preferences was a rather typical, if biting, response of a young man who did not want to be quite so thoroughly under his mother's guidance as in the past, his letter also revealed the honesty with which the family members read each other's work and received criticism from one another. They always combined such disagreements in overall praise of each other's talents and thereby maintained the ability to serve as critics for one another throughout their writing lives.

As the summer began, Mary Mapes Dodge again asked Davis to contribute to *St. Nicholas*. It had been fourteen years since Rebecca published in the magazine. She preferred the quality of *St. Nicholas* to that of *Youth's Companion*, but the latter paid better and her editorial role kept her tied to the periodical. Instead it was Clarke who published in the children's periodical at this time. "With Stick and Thread" was a fishing adventure story and was well received in the press,[17] but it marked the end of his fiction writing. He would focus on journalism and theater criticism thereafter.

As the family headed to Point Pleasant and then Marion for the summer, two works by Davis were published. Her stories for the *Congregationalist* in the late 1880s and early 1890s were always featured on page one, as she had become a prominent draw for readers of the magazine. "A Common Fault" voiced in fiction Davis's lifelong frustration with New Englanders' arrogance: "What have you done—what have you thought—to make you Brahmins, while all the rest of the world are Pariahs?"[18]

At the same time, a piece for the *Independent* continued her series of commentaries on current cultural and political issues. "The Modest Naturalized Citizen" turned to Fourth of July celebrations. Davis proclaimed her appreciation that people across the country celebrated the day in styles that differed from region to region and ethnicity to ethnicity: "The gorgeous floats and poetic effects which please the holiday-making Latin Americans in the far South" might puzzle a New Englander and contrast with the drums and flags preferred by the Midwesterner, but that was all good "provided [the day's] object is borne in mind—to make the American more an American than he is now. . . . Teach the native-born child and the foreign child, the Indian and the Negro, to have a saving sense of the dignity of their position, not as Irish-Americans or German-Americans, black, reds or whites, but—*Americans*."[19]

In spite of celebrating diversity, the article was in fact a response to the vast influx of immigrants into the United States and especially into Philadelphia in the 1890s. Known as the "Workshop of the World" because the city offered newcomers access to industry and a thriving field of maritime jobs, Philadelphia had seen a large increase in its Irish and German immigrant population in recent years.[20] Davis's article called for "more modesty" from naturalized citizens to demonstrate their appreciation for the gift of freedom. It was time, she insisted, the American "reminded his guests who refuse to submit to his laws and customs that here, the majority rules. . . . and that he has still the power of wholly closing the door against him"![21]

Although Davis emphasized people who did not "submit to laws and customs," the call for gratitude from immigrants would echo through her writings in the coming decades and would mark the beginning of her late style as an artist. As with many authors, Davis's "late style" reflected the depth of wisdom gained over a lifetime of reflection and experience, but it also imbued a kind of intransigence in some areas and unresolved contradictions that could not be suppressed.[22] The paradox of this later transition in Davis's writings was that it coexisted simultaneously with her progressivism. She could neither abandon nor reconcile the two sides of her cultural philosophy.

After a short stay at Point Pleasant, the family settled into Marion, which was a wealthier shore area but not yet as commercialized as the New Jersey resort was becoming. The Clevelands summered in Marion again as well. Dick was still dating Helen Benedict, and he introduced her father to Grover Cleveland. The two men, each wielding extraordinary cultural power, became close friends,[23] and soon they would draw Clarke into a great controversy about Cleveland's health.

When Dick published "Gallegher: A Newspaper Story" in *Scribner's Magazine* in August, he seemed, like his mother, to be distinguishing between popular stories such as those in the *Sun* and more sophisticated but still highly entertaining fiction for the literary magazines. The story had been rejected by seven other periodicals before *Scribner's* accepted it; it was an educational process for Dick, who had largely ignored the considerable criticism of the story from his mother.[24] He would always acknowledge when his mother's critiques had been correct, however, especially after receiving the same response from magazine editors. On the positive side, the publication brought an unexpected re-acquaintance with Charles Dana Gibson when Gibson was hired to illustrate the piece. It was the beginning of a long collaboration and friendship between the two men.

The connections Rebecca had established with major literary magazines opened the door for Dick, not just to *Scribner's* but also to *Harper's* where he published "A Walk Up the Avenue" in August as well. This latter connection was one of the most important his mother ever made for him, as it would soon lead to the offer of an editorship with *Harper's Weekly*. "A Walk Up the Avenue," however, once again raised concerns from Clarke. "It is far and away the best thing you have done," he wrote his son, but added,

> I am not afraid of Dick the author. He's all right. I shall only be afraid—when I am afraid—that Dick the man will not live up to the other fellow, that he may forget how much the good Lord has given him. . . . Don't let the world's temptations in any of its forms come between you and your work. Make your life worthy of your talent, and humbly by day and by night ask God to help you to do it.

He reiterated how proud he was of Dick and signed off, "Lovingly, Dad."[25] Both of his sons cherished Clarke's praise, but humility was a trait Dick would never learn.

At this point in his career, virtually any recognition Dick received was accompanied by notations that he was the son of Rebecca Harding Davis.[26] It was one of the benefits of being part of the increasing fame of The Davis Family, as they were often called in literary criticism of the day, and one of the drawbacks of trying to establish his own style and reputation. He seemed, however, to handle the constant alliance with grace, recognizing the benefits outweighed the comparisons. It was an alliance the periodicals would make throughout their lives, as The Davis Family became increasingly famous as a literary entity.

At this time, Rebecca contacted her publisher and friend Richard Watson Gilder about a new novel she was writing. "My boys have been anxious for a long time," she explained, "that I should write one and to please them I gave up newspaper work two years ago and rested before doing it—The novel is now well begun." She explained to Gilder she had another offer for the novel, but added, "I would rather see it in the *Century* than anywhere else. I suppose your arrangements for next year are made. But the next. I would rather finish it outright before publishing."[27]

Kent Hampden was an excellent young adult novel set in pre–Civil War Wheeling. Gilder passed on the novel, perhaps because the *Century* rarely published young adult literature. Davis would serialize the novel in *Youth's Companion* the following year and then publish its book version with Scribner's publishing house. It was perhaps not the wisest decision by Gilder, since all of Davis's major works thereafter went to other publishers, although she would write editorials for the *Century* for many years. *Kent Hampden* was the beginning of her return to novel-writing. It would be very well received, and the transition back to longer fictional works would result in one of Davis's best novels four years later—and it would go to Gilder's greatest competitor, Harper Brothers' publications.

The summer of 1890 ended with weeks of relaxation and the opportunity for Clarke and Grover Cleveland to spend many days fishing on Buzzard's Bay. The link between the two men was now public knowledge and covered in newspapers and magazines across the nation. Though Clarke was known in journalism circles for his lack of biases or favoritism, his writings about Cleveland were the exception, and after this summer's excursions, amid rumors of Cleveland's ill health, Clarke reported, "For five weeks, during nearly every day except Sundays, which Mr. Cleveland went to church, I was his constant companion with rod and reel in Capt. Ryden's or Capt. Hathaway's boat, and generally afterward at supper and I never passed a month with a healthier, cheerfuller, more genial, entertaining man, or with a more patient, hard-working, persistent and enthusiastic fisherman." The item was picked up by national and local newspapers across the country.[28] Its significance carried national weight, since Cleveland, who had ended his first term in office the previous year, was contemplating a second run for the presidency. Clark's testimonials for his friend, however, would lead to the first charges of editorial bias he had ever received.

The 1890s would see a significant rise in attention to women's contributions to literature, especially through critical studies and encyclopedic collective biographies, with Davis well represented in these assessments. In October, for instance, Helen Gray Cone included Davis among the important women writers she identified in an article for the *Century*. Cone was a poet, literary critic, and professor at Hunter College who wrote numerous articles on women's advancements. "Woman in American Literature" was a history of writers but emphasized nineteenth-century authors. Cone assessed the quality of Davis's longstanding impact on American literature: "The hopeless heart-hunger of the poor has seldom been so passionately pictured. A distinguishing characteristic of the work of Mrs. Davis is her Browning-like insistence on the rare test-moments of life. If, as in the complicated war-time novel 'Waiting for the Verdict'—a work of high intention,—the characters come out startlingly well in the sudden lights flashed upon them, the writer's idealism is tonic and uplifting."[29] Cone's comments began a critical mythology that would last for the remainder of Davis's career—that she had produced, "perhaps, nothing stronger than 'Life in the Iron Mills.'"[30] Critics who knew Davis's large body of work never made such an assertion; in fact, they often argued her later work was more important, but many other critics would repeat Cone's assessment over the years.

With the publication of "Nicholas Cleever's Money" at the end of 1889, Davis had concluded her use of "The Author of 'The Second Life'" as a signature for *Peterson's*, and "That Akers Girl," published in November 1890, and all of her subsequent writings for magazine identified her by name. "That Akers Girl" was one of Davis's powerful sibling stories, capturing the dangers of gossip in a small town. "For Sale?" in November and "Hetty's Christmas Gift" in December for the *Congregationalist* exposed the pressure many a young woman faced from her family and community to marry a wealthy man she did not love in opposition to her true, if poorer, love. It was a theme Davis would return to several times in the coming years as economics seemed to rule American ideas about "successful" marriages. These arguments, against what Davis viewed as the contemporary marriage-market for young women, were always intertwined with critiques of the class-based values inherent in such a system.

At the end of the year, announcements about Davis's forthcoming novel began to appear. *The Critic*, for instance, announced, "Mrs. Rebecca Harding Davis has written for next year's *Youth's Companion* a serial story for boys, the scene of which is laid in Virginia fifty years ago, when she was a child there. Mrs. Davis is also writing a novel of the present, the scene being laid partly in Pennsylvania, and Louisiana."[31] *The Critic*, largely through Jeannette Gilder, who anonymously wrote the magazine's literary column, "The Lounger," kept Davis's work constantly before the public and generally offered strong reviews for her fiction. The reference to where Davis spent her childhood for *Kent Hampden* was in keeping with the autobiographical interests of the reading public. Though the boys' novel would soon be published, the adult novel, to be titled *Doctor Warrick's Daughters*, would not appear for several years. Davis would take longer to craft this novel than any other in her career.

In December Clarke traveled to New York for the opening of the Pulitzer Building on December 10th. The *New York World*, Joseph Pulitzer's newspaper, was thereafter housed in the building, and the opening drew the top journalists from around the nation.[32] Although it was Clarke who attended the event, a decade later it was Rebecca who became affiliated with the *World*.

A major transition in Dick's life occurred at this time as well. The connection Rebecca had made for him by introducing him to the Harper brothers and Clarke's exchange of letters with editor George William Curtis during the previous year paved the way for an offer that stunned the publishing world. It was announced that Richard Harding Davis had been selected as associate editor of the extraordinarily popular *Harper's Weekly*. All the announcements noted that Rebecca was his famous mother and several included Clarke's reputation as well. Although at age twenty-six Dick had only minimal editing experience, his Van Bibber and Gallegher stories were reaching a very wide audience and his socializing in both literary and theater circles in New York made him a recognizable name for the public.

Perhaps nothing in these years so fully confirmed the nation's—and Dick's—belief in the power of the cult of personality. He envisioned a younger audience for the magazine and quickly removed many established writers in favor of new and popular younger authors and journalists, including *Sun* reporter David Graham Phillips and the *Press*'s star reporter A. E. Watrous. Although his relationship with the Harper brothers would be constantly at odds, the position would establish Dick's influence in the literary world. His salary increased significantly and, as Charley noted, so did his spending, a trait that would always be an issue for Dick.[33] His appointment, with the announcements' alliance of his name with that of his parents, further flamed the interest in The Davis Family as a notable writing collective.

The publishing world experienced several changes in 1891 that would significantly impact the direction of literature in the US. In addition to Dick's new position with *Harper's Weekly*, William Dean Howells left the *Atlantic Monthly* for *Cosmopolitan*, both of which marked the literary shift from Boston to New York. This year also saw the beginning of the publication of the *Cyclopedia of American Biography* with Davis included in the volume on famous women. Equally important to the literary world was the passage in Congress of the international copyright law, enacted to end pirating. The literary world and the nation also became eminently aware that they were entering the last decade of the century, and *fin-de-siècle* themes circulated everywhere, including in the appearance of a new though short-lived magazine devoted to the concept, *Century's End Magazine*. A story by Davis appeared in the second issue of the new periodical.[34]

The new year began with an exciting social whirl for the Davises as they hosted Frances and Grover Cleveland's visit to Philadelphia beginning on January 7. Frances opened the Charity Ball that evening at the Academy of Music. Grover was in Philadelphia to attend the Young Men's Democratic Association the following day. The Clevelands spent three days with the Davises, during which every move by both families was recorded in the national newspapers. Clarke had met Cleveland in Jersey City and, with other prominent figures, rode the train to Philadelphia with him. Frances came separately, and Rebecca and Clarke met her at the train station. The greeting was "very warm," the papers reported, and Frances took Rebecca's arm as the two were seen "conversing rapidly." They dined that evening at the Davises' home. Rebecca and Nora attended the Charity Ball with Frances, and the following morning they and Clarke joined Frances for a breakfast that included George W. Childs. Frances attended the annual Jackson banquet with Rebecca and Nora, and the following morning the Clevelands attended breakfast at the Davis home "in company with personal friends of both gentlemen."[35]

When Frances was presented to the Prince of Wales on the evening of the eighth, Rebecca was in her company. The following day Rebecca hosted a tea for Frances at the Davis home, with Nora in attendance as well; two hundred people had been invited to the tea, and guests came and went throughout the afternoon. Rebecca and Frances were together in a box for the evening performances at the Academy of Music, and Frances was reported as "chatting pleasantly in her characteristic way with Mrs. Davis. . . . The part of debutantes included . . . Miss Nora Davis." At a dinner for the Clevelands held at George Childs' home before the performance at the Academy of Music, Dick and Nora joined their parents, as did Clarke's longtime assistant at the paper, F. Percival Farrar. Dinner guests also included Pennsylvania's governor-elect Robert E. Pattison, and numerous business leaders in Philadelphia including Anthony Drexel and John C. Bullitt.[36]

Dick and Nora were given the honor of accompanying Frances to the train station when she left Philadelphia; they joined her in Vice President Thompson's private railcar on the journey to New York City.[37] It was a whirlwind few days of events, and the Davises were prominently identified throughout the national reports of the Clevelands' activities. This was an especially important transitional moment for Nora. She had been moving in the society circles of Philadelphia and peripherally in New York, but her prominent status at the events with the former First Lady and identification as a "debutante" secured her position in these circles.

Charley had been notably absent from the Clevelands' visit, since he had just moved to New York City. Having determined to give up his career in civil engineering and turn to journalism, Charley moved in with Dick at 10 East Twenty-eighth Street; they would share these rooms until Charley moved to Italy two years later. Here they established a wide range of friends, including Charles Dana Gibson; Robert Howard Russell and Albert La Montagne, two of the young writers Dick had brought into *Harper's Weekly*; Helen Benedict; several actors, including Ethel Barrymore and Maude Adams; and Arthur Brisbane from the *Evening Sun*. Charley had found work as a reporter for the *New York*

World, notably not long after Clarke had attended the opening of its new home at the Pulitzer Building. The *World* would soon be identified as the leading newspaper in New York,[38] and it was recognized for its support of the Democratic Party.

More than their public lives, however, the Davises were focusing on their careers, and in spite of their immensely busy schedules, they continued to offer critiques of one another's work, as Rebecca did when Dick published a short story "How Hefty Burke Got Even" in the *Evening Sun* in January. They continued to freely debate their ideas, as Dick defended his literary choices against his mother's critique, "I could not understand why you did not like 'Hefty' because if I understand you it was his being such a tough that you objected to."[39] A few days later he wrote Rebecca to say he had finished another story and would bring it with him "to have it criticized—I do'nt want you to think that I wrote it but to judge it as some hated rivals effort. I think you were all too lenient about the gambling story, for all three editors of Scribners said the motive for the change in the youth's determination was not strong enough. So I want a rigorous talk over this as I hate to make corrections after a thing is written."[40] The story was "The Other Woman," published in *Scribner's* in March.

Charley was also an astute critic for Dick's work, as was demonstrated with another story. Charley had suggested making cuts to the final paragraph, but Dick submitted it without incorporating his brother's suggestion—only to have the editor insist the final paragraph be significantly shortened.[41] At the end of the month Dick also wrote his parents to report on a tea he attended in Boston with William Dean Howells, Oliver Wendell Holmes, and the society doyenne and art patron Isabella Stewart Gardner. He had been invited to the tea because they were a group of people who admired Rebecca, he noted, as was the case with evenings he spent at Julia Ward Howe's home and that of Margaret Deland. At the tea, "they all spoke of mother and so very dearly that it made me pretty near weep."[42] He joked that no one in Boston had read his stories![43]

By February, 1891, Rebecca decided not only to travel to Europe in the summer but to take a break from writing for the *Independent* and the *Congregationalist*. As she wrote William Hayes Ward at the *Independent*, "I hope to go to Europe in May and shall not be able to do any occasional work for a year—afterwards. Would you like me to write you before I go a short story for Thanksgiving and one for Christmas? The price of each would be $100 *to be paid on receipt of Mss.* If you wish to have them please let me hear from you at once. And let the people in the office understand the arrangement." She added a postscript, "Why do you never come to Philadelphia? I know your son and daughter-in-law—Mrs. [Elizabeth Stuart] Phelps-Ward so well that I should know you."[44] Ward responded immediately, confirming his desire to have her write stories that could be published in her absence—and agreeing to visit her in Philadelphia, staying in her home for the visit.[45]

While the rest of her family was busy with their writing careers, Nora, now nineteen, was actively involved in the whirlwind of teas and parties among Philadelphia society leaders. In February she attended a society tea hosted by Dr. and Mrs. William P. Smith, Jr. Dr. Smith was a physician and on the Board of Directors of the Commercial National Bank of Pennsylvania. Nora was friends with his daughter, Elizabeth, who cohosted the tea; the daughter of the Davises' longtime family physician, the wealthy Dr. Louis Starr, was also in attendance. This was typical of the events Nora was attending after having finished her education. She did not pursue a career and seemed to love this life of fancy balls and society weddings that occupied her time. For all that Rebecca had criticized the vacuous nature of much of society life—and its biases against the working classes—she did not attempt to curtail any of her children from entering these circles, and she accompanied Nora to many such events. Yet nor did her affiliation with upper-class society change what she wrote about the elite class.

In early 1891, Clarke was also turning his hand again to writing about the theater, publishing "A Play and an Actor" in *Century Magazine* in April. The article addressed the smash hit the English actor Edward Smith Willard had made a few months earlier in the Henry Arthur Jones play, *The Middleman,* at New York's Palmer Theater. Grover Cleveland wrote Clarke to convey his admiration for the article, adding that he and Frances had enjoyed having Dick and Charley to dinner the previous week.[46] With both sons in New York, Clarke was spending even more time in the city now, and he attended the celebratory dinner in April of the American Authors' Copyright League in New York, held at the famous Sherry's restaurant.[47] Typical of her resistance to public literary gatherings, Rebecca did not attend, though she was the author in the family who had signed the bill when it was sent to Congress.

Just before leaving for Europe, Rebecca had another of what were becoming frequent debates with William Hayes Ward about what she was being paid for her work. He asked her to contribute a short article for a collective piece in the magazine, for which she asked thirty dollars. Ward was facing increased pressure from the publisher to lower their rates, and he replied to Davis that they would only pay twenty-five dollars. She acquiesced, as she often did in negotiations with Ward; yet it exacerbated her frustrations with the periodical. Her appreciation of the magazine's readership kept her with the *Independent* for the rest of her life, but not without constant editorial negotiations.

The article was "Women in Literature," part of a special group of articles in the *Independent* on "Woman's Enlarged Sphere." Other articles in the series included Julia Ward Howe on the progress of women, Grace Dodge on working girls' development, Mary Livermore on the New Womanhood, Frances Willard on temperance, and Lucy Stone on the advancement of women. In writing on the status of women in literature, Davis articulated her philosophy of what constituted good literature and identified writers she felt met her high standards. It was one of her first signed essays of literary criticism. The next generation would give rise to even more women writers, she predicted, and some would be drawn to the profession through a "desire for personal notoriety with which the American soul, both male and female, seem of late to be so fatally tainted." Yet a few talented women "will write for other reasons than these, simply because there is in them a message to be given, and they cannot die until they have spoken it." She hoped none would attempt the Great American Novel: what novel could grasp "our national life, from the New Yorker in Wall Street to the Navajo Indian; the Virginian, rich only in forefathers and good breeding; the lepers in Acadia; the nihilist, the already dominate Jew, the Catholic, and the German anarchist, each biding his time; the educated Negro still under the ban; the red man; the Mafian and Molly Maguire brethren; and the Chicago millionaire!"[48]

Davis's preference was "genre pictures of individual characters in our national drama." She identified the most talented contemporary women writers' genre pictures, emphasizing the turn to more realistic themes and characterizations: Marion Harland's old Virginia plantations, Mary Murfree's Tennessee mountaineers, Mary Dean's rural New York, Mary Hartwell Catherwood's and Mary Hallock Foote's Western men, Constance Fenimore Woolson's Southern women, Elizabeth Stuart Phelps' educated Puritan woman, and Sarah Orne Jewett's and Mary Wilkins' soul-and-body-hungry New Englanders.

Davis declared French writers had so dominated the memoir that it was a field yet open to American women writers. In all, "I have a hope that this body of women who have the habit of broad and accurate thought will not always be content to expend their force in society, or even in charitable work. They will be stirred by the ambition to leave something more permanent behind them."[49] This last comment captured the distinction Davis made between the desire for *personal* notoriety and high-quality work that so encompassed the realities of the human dilemma as to have an impact from generation to generation.

Rebecca had conveyed in recent months to Dick her frustrations with publishers, and shortly before leaving for five months in Europe, she indicated she was having serious problems with headaches. While stress may have been part of the case, it was more likely the headaches were an early symptom of the eye problems that would soon plague her. He replied with sympathy, offering to try to save enough money to help ease the costs of the trip, if it would help.[50] This was rather ironic, since Dick had never managed to save money, but the gesture was heartfelt. In late May Rebecca and Nora sailed from New York City on the *City of Paris*. They traveled to England, Ireland, and several European countries. Clarke would leave in July and travel with them for the latter part of their journey. He returned in early September, followed by Rebecca and Nora a month later.[51]

While Rebecca was abroad, her works continued to appear, and Dick's first collection, *Gallegher and Other Stories*, was published by Scribner's with the dedication "To My Mother." These were the stories Rebecca had suggested Dick send first to Gilder at the *Century*; though Gilder had rejected them, Dick still dedicated the British edition to Gilder's daughter Francesca and her godmother, Frances Cleveland. The ability to distinguish between personal and professional lives was important for editors such as Gilder who maintained friendships with many of his regular authors. They could remain close friends, as the Davis and Gilder families did for many years, even when some of their work was rejected.

As always, Dick thought nothing of spending money on an elaborate party at Delmonico's to celebrate receiving $900 for the collection. It was at this time that he also became close friends with the British actors Seymour Hicks and Ellaline Terriss who were visiting the States. Both Dick and Charley continued to be drawn to the theater world and formed many friendships among the younger generation of actors and playwrights who they, in turn, introduced to their parents. The Davises were key players in the integration of the literary and theater worlds in these years, a connection that would eventually be solidified with the rise of the moving picture industry in the early twentieth century, for which both Dick and Charley would develop screen plays from their novels and short stories.

In the summer of 1891, the Clevelands purchased a large estate in Marion. "Gray Gables" would be their summer home for many years. It was close to the Davises' summer cottage, and the two families moved freely between the houses throughout their summer sojourns. As Clarke was preparing to leave for Europe, Grover wrote a critique, in the extreme discourse of a politician who will neither confirm nor deny his actions but subtly encourages his friend to continue writing editorials about his activities:

> For a man that is "a good deal in the dark" you get the situation, so far as it relates to me, just about as it is. Of course all the talk about any conference between my friends and myself, and the representation as to what took place at such a conference, is baldly imaginative; but what you reproduce on the subject comes nearer what *might* have been said at any such conference, than much else that has been published concerning my position. . . . I cannot imagine how much harm can be done—at least within the party to which I belong. I am trying to keep my temper and, as long as the fish bite well, shall succeed. That reminds me. Why cannot you come to us for a few days before you "cross the briny deep"? . . . Mrs. Cleveland sends her affectionate regards to you and through you to Mrs. Davis and Nora; and I join just as strong as I possibly can."[52]

Clarke met Rebecca and Nora in Europe in mid-July. He had missed joining Rebecca in the celebration of her sixtieth birthday on June 24. At sixty, Rebecca could reflect on a life well lived. She had created with Clarke a loving and supportive family life, her children were thriving, and she continued to be recognized as one of the leading writers of the era. With financial security, Rebecca could write what and when she preferred, including taking as much time as she wished to craft her next novel.

Having Clarke join her and Nora in Europe was a welcome reunion, but one that caused some difficulties as well. Unlike other members of his family, Clarke was not an easy traveler; he often became agitated at his inability to speak the language when he was in Italy and Switzerland. He worried that Rebecca and Nora would not have as good a time as he hoped under these restrictions and felt responsible if they did not enjoy their trip.[53] But the two women were having a wonderful time; they had already managed both London and Paris on their own, where in the latter Rebecca's fluency in French served them well. They probably relaxed more once Clarke had returned to the States, as did he.

Rebecca had needed rest and to get away from the pressures of constant writing, and the trip was an effective antidote. She also learned how small the world was when she met two young women from Wheeling, Ann and Elizabeth

Cummins, while she was in London. Rebecca graciously introduced the sisters to her longtime friends, the actors Henry Irving and Ellen Terry, when she visited backstage after attending their performances.[54]

Before leaving for Europe, Rebecca had made connections for Charley with the *Independent*, just as she had for Dick with various newspapers, magazines, and the Harpers brothers. Charley had published stories in the *Evening Sun*, but he also wanted to place his work with more prestigious journals. Rebecca encouraged her younger son's interest in literature as well as journalism. Dick was gaining praise for his Gallegher stories, but it was Charley who would become much more his mother's literary legatee. Dick had talent, but he always preferred fame and any means of earning more money above the craft of his profession. Charley was more interested in the quality of his writing, whether in fiction or journalism, and carefully worked to craft his talents.

Set in the western mining territories, Charley's story for the *Independent*, "The Last Chance," foretold a successful future for the young writer. Dick was proud of his brother, too. As he wrote Clarke, "I am so pleased he has succeeded.... We did not count enough on his fast training, at least some of us did not. What has surprised me the most is his quickness in writing. He is confident and clever over it as he can be and he already disagrees with me as to how a story should be handled and with reason." These differences were acknowledged in Dick's comment that Charley was "like a child" about writing because he "takes the keenest interest in every line and paragraph."[55] Charley, like Rebecca, wanted to craft every word, while Dick loved the broad stroke and abhorred making revisions.

Clarke returned from his European trip in early September, and at the end of the month Dick sailed for England for a short stay. He met Rebecca and Nora there and traveled home with them in early October. Once at home, the Davises' lives returned immediately to their usual hectic paces. With the retirement of William McKean from the *Public Ledger*, Clarke advanced to the position of managing editor as George Childs became the editor-in-chief. His former employer, the *Philadelphia Inquirer*, reported graciously on Clarke's promotion, noting he was an "editorial writer on the [Philadelphia] *Evening Telegraph*. He is a brilliant journalist, of genial character, well equipped for his work. In politics he is an independent Republican and is a close friend of Grover Cleveland."[56] Dick and Charley knew this change in position would grant Clarke greater latitude on the newspaper, so in a letter to his mother, Dick advised, "Tell Dad not to introduce his new feature in the Ledger until he talks with Gus [Charley] as Gus and I have ideas about it we want him to consider."[57]

The exchange of ideas about their careers now moved smoothly between the generations of the Davis family.

Over the summer Clarke had also been appointed by Governor Pattison as Manager of the Education and History Committee and the Public Institutions Committee for Pennsylvania's World's Fair Commission in preparation for the upcoming Columbian Exposition in Chicago, and the following month he would be added as a member to the Transportation and Electricity Committees as well.[58] Another of Clarke's appointments reflected his and Rebecca's opposition to war: in September he was appointed to the Philadelphia Press Committee of the Pan-Republic Congress; the Congress aimed "to abolish slavery and do away with guns and gunpowder and bring about a resort to arbitration in all questions of international law, that heretofore have plunged countries into war and caused incalculable bloodshed."[59]

While Clarke was immersed in his work at the *Ledger* and on the various civic committees, Rebecca was working on her first collection of short stories since *Kitty's Choice: A Story of Berrytown, and Other Stories* appeared in 1874. She would delay work on her novel to devote much of the next year to preparing the collection, often altering her decisions on which stories to include. She also published several works over the winter—some written before she went to Europe and others after her return. "Mrs. Loper's Ambition," published in a September issue of the *Congregationalist*, dramatized the social ambitions of a Pottstown woman who outdid the upper classes in her all-consuming social snobbery. "The Slave in Algeria," in the November 1891 issue of *Youth's Companion*, continued her stories based on materials she discovered in local archives.

The Thanksgiving and Christmas stories she had written for the *Independent* before leaving for Europe appeared this winter as well. "In a Way She Knew Not" distinctly captured Davis's interest in how the crises of our lives creep upon us unknowingly. This idea would become increasingly popular in realist literature, such as the "night crises" of characters in Henry James's *Portrait of a Lady* or Lily Bart's slow descent in Edith Wharton's *The House of Mirth*. As Davis observed, "The supreme moments of life come to us heralded by no signs or wonders. The soul, when it is to be tried, is conscious of no mysterious forebodings casting their shadows before. Tragedies, as a rule, put on paltry disguises to us and grimace as burlesque." Although the story ended with the requisite happy conclusion for holiday stories, even then Davis hedged. The main character could reflect that "God always answers our prayers," but not without adding, "tho in a way that we know not—almost always in a way that we know not."[60] Her other publication in November, "The Leroy Gold Mine," was a temperance story that addressed the dangers of financial speculation.

As was becoming far too common, Davis was forced to write Ward about delayed payments from the *Independent*, which grated especially when she had agreed to accept less than her usual fee for a story.[61] It was a problem she never had with the *Congregationalist*, and she published "The Modern Irishman" in their December issue; the essay drew on her recent travels in Ireland. Beginning with an indictment of the lack of interest the Catholic Irish had for their country and the failure of Parnell to lure their support, the essay ended with a twist that forced the reader to consider his or her own nation's economic policies: Ireland, "rich, beautiful and empty, seems to be waiting for the energetic, modern farmer to enter in and make himself wealthy. I said this to a landlord in the south of Ireland. He shook his head. 'It is not Parnell we have to fear nor the boycotter, it is you, the American. We cannot fight against your cheap meat and wheat. That is the real ruin of Ireland now.'"[62] If her nativist attitudes arose at times, so too did her opposition to America's sense of superiority and imperialism, as in this story.

Just before Thanksgiving, Dick met with Grover Cleveland, seeking advice about going into politics. He told Cleveland he had been thinking about the possibility for some time, but the response was not what he had expected. "To say he discouraged me in so doing," Dick wrote his parents,

> would be saying the rain is wet. He seemed to think breaking stones as a means of getting fame and fortune was quicker and more genteel. . . . I do not know as what Cleveland said made much impression upon me—although I found out what I could expect from him—that is nothing here but apparently a place abroad if I wanted it. But he thought Congress was perfectly feasible but the greatest folly to go there.[63]

Cleveland undoubtedly tried to let Dick down as easily as possible, in spite of Dick's audaciousness of suggesting he could *start* his political career in Congress. It was, in fact, Charley who soon would receive Cleveland's assistance with a political appointment.

At the same time, Clarke was hosting Secretary of State James G. Blaine for his visit to Philadelphia. It was a short visit, with only two meetings scheduled—first, with two businessmen who sought time with Blaine, and second, with George Child for an interview. Clarke accompanied him for the latter meeting. But even with limited time, Blaine made the effort to visit Rebecca, which was fortunate as he died two years later. The year ended with a visit from Rebecca's sister, Emilie. It was a fitting end to an extraordinarily busy year for the entire family.

Although Davis had told William Ward in May that she would want a year off from her responsibilities at the *Independent* after she returned from Europe, she was publishing with the periodical again as early as January 1892. "Old Lamps for New" asked people of all faiths, as they turned to new methods of religious teaching, to remember what was effective in some of the older traditions—especially the use of symbolism to convey Jesus's life and teachings. Although all of the Davises held Christian beliefs and values and defined themselves as Christians, Rebecca and Clarke deepened their faith as they aged while their children adapted to a more secular world. Rebecca clearly found solace and a like-minded audience in writing for periodicals such as the *Independent* and *Congregationalist*.

In February, Clarke was once again struggling with severe depression. Writing to Dick, he advised, "Don't be afraid to preach the truth and above all the religion of humanity." But the letter soon revealed his state of mind when he told Dick he had brought "sweetness and joy to a life that has had little of either in it."[64] These episodes always meant considerable worry for Rebecca as she tried to navigate how best to help her husband through his depressive states. This episode was shorter than usual, and by March, Clarke seemed to have recovered.

An article appeared that month in *Art in Advertising*, a businessman's monthly, focusing on Clarke's excellent work as editor of the *Public Ledger*, one of the first articles to begin what would be a major transition in the coming years—Dick and Charley would continue to be identified at times in relation to their parents, but their parents would soon also be identified through their successful sons. The article also noted the contributions of Clarke's chief assistant, Percival Farrar, "a young man hardly twenty years of age, who labors under the disadvantage of being the son of a distinguished parent, the name of Archdeacon Farrar, of London, reaching to the uttermost bounds of the world. Mr. Farrar has a smooth, boyish face, speaks with no English accent at all, and seems happy in the situation in which he finds himself."[65] Farrar had been at Lehigh University when Dick and Charley attended, and he was a close friend of the family as well as Clarke's assistant. Years later he would marry Nora Davis.

Letters that arrived from Grover Cleveland throughout the early months of 1892 revealed the former President was also struggling emotionally at this time and talking with Cleveland about their concerns helped Clarke regain his equilibrium. Many of Cleveland's letters were about fishing or his travels, but in early March he revealed to Clarke his personal frustration at the life of an ex-President.

> I am in a miserable condition—a private citizen without political ambition trying to do private work and yet pulled and hauled and importuned daily and hourly to do things in a public and a semi-public way which are hard and distasteful to me. . . . I am afraid you will suspect me of cant when I say to you that I am honestly trying to do some good in the world—within political lines or otherwise. But so it is. I often have a pretty blue time of it and confess to frequent spells of resentment, but I shall get on in a fashion. Give love to your dear wife and the children.[66]

Although both men were highly successful, each felt at times a vacuum in his life that left him frustrated and burdened by depression, what the medical community at the time termed "nervous exhaustion." In spite of Cleveland's claim to having no political ambitions, he would soon run again for President.

In the spring Clark was in better health, and Rebecca was able to return to writing, though not as prolifically as usual. She had to miss a tea honoring Mary Mapes Dodge, but the event offered Rebecca an opportunity to reconnect with the *St. Nicholas* editor. She sent her regrets on April 2:

> I cannot content myself with sending cards to show how sorry I am not to be able to go to your tea. How long it is since I saw or heard from you! Do you never come to this quiet corner of the earth? We live in the same old house at 230 South 21st street. *Do* come. I heard you had a boy in town, but I suppose he would be bored by an old woman. If I ever go to New York I shall find the Cordova [Hotel] and claim friendship with you.[67]

While their reconnection correspondence was warm, it would be eight years before Rebecca returned to the pages of *St. Nicholas*.

Dick traveled to London in early May, where he wrote numerous articles about his impressions of English culture for *Harper's Weekly*. While there, he met many celebrated Brits, including Lady Brownlow and her nephew Harry Cust, who became a friend. Cust was a Conservative nominee for Parliament at the time, and Dick worked on his campaign during his stay in London. Charley joined Dick at the time of the election; when Cust won by a narrow margin, the Davis brothers were there to celebrate his success.[68] Charley also supported his trip by writing a series of articles on English life for the New York *World*. Nora did not join her brothers on this journey, as she often did; she was active in several charities in Philadelphia that occupied much of her time.[69]

The family kept in constant contact via letters, however, and Dick often commented on his appreciation for his mother: he wrote that he could just imagine her, "brooding over all of us with love for each. There was never such a good mother."[70] While her sons were in England, Rebecca had been steadily working on the collection of short stories she wanted to publish, and in June, she finalized the contract with Scribner's to publish *Silhouettes of American Life*. Finally, after years of seeking transatlantic publication of her books, Scribner's aligned with Osgood-McIlvaine to publish *Silhouettes* simultaneously in London.

Preparing the collection took considerable time as Rebecca worked with the publisher to make the final decisions about the collection's contents. She went to Marion earlier than usual, in mid-June, to devote herself to the project and corresponded from there with Scribner's on the final contents. Originally, she had planned to include "A Homely Story of a Home" but the editors suggested its withdrawal. She agreed and decided she also wanted to exclude "A November Afternoon" and substitute "Mademoiselle Joan." She negotiated a ten percent royalty and insisted they confirm in writing the royalties would be "on all copies sold however bound."[71]

While at Marion she also published two articles in the *Independent*—"Out of Sight" and "The Alien Brothers." The latter was of particular interest, addressing the failure, three decades after the war, of white Americans to "give the Negro his rightful place among us. . . . When will the colored man cease to be a stranger among us? and when will we put an end to the shying of stones at him—of persecution and of advice?" Yet this final question did not stop Davis from offering her own advice "to my colored friends—the friends I may say of my whole life." Develop cohesion among yourselves, she advised, and "that pride in blood without which no race has ever succeeded."[72]

She opposed recent calls for classical education for all African Americans, however, and argued that training "to fit the Negro to take his place in the carpenter shop in the factory, and, above all, behind the counter as a tradesman, are surely needed now, as the steps to his real immediate progress, more than classical schools and universities." Unlike earlier essays, she now envisioned African Americans as shop owners, not just laborers. She was not speaking of the well-educated African American, she explained, but of field hands and household laborers: "To prescribe Latin and Greek to Louisiana field hands is as apt advice as to urge a man drowning in the midst of the

Atlantic to put on a dress suit." The essay's allusion to "a Northern professor" undoubtedly referred to W.E.B. DuBois who had recently published *The Negro Problem* (1888) and *The Philadelphia Negro* (1889). She felt Professor DuBois was "familiar with the highest class of dark gentlefolk in Washington and Philadelphia" but implied he was less so with the field hands who she argued needed a different level of education and practical training. The essay was both an important call from a white writer for equality and an act of racial hubris.[73]

At this time, Charley published in another of the literary magazines in which Rebecca was a recognized contributor, *Century Magazine*. "A Friend of the Family" was the first of Charley's stories drawn from his time in London. Unlike Dick, whose London essays focused largely on the upper classes, Charley's story was that of a young boy who sold newspapers on the streets of London. As one reviewer observed, "if present prospects hold good it is not unlikely that the fourth of this literary family will eclipse the light of the others." The *Portland Oregonian* reviewer added, the "Davis family is destined to be prominently before the reading public this autumn and winter," asserting Charley was the better writer of the two brothers.[74]

In October *Silhouettes of American Life* was published. The concept of "silhouettes" had long interested Davis as a literary genre. In 1883 she had published "A Silhouette" in *Harper's New Monthly Magazine*. As with that earlier contribution, she preferred silhouette to the term "sketch" because the latter implied one had captured a moment or individual in a brief glance while the former implied we can only know people in the outline of a silhouette, never fully. More complexly, the concept required the reader to understand that every person has hidden depths of thought and character. It demanded readers look beyond the surface of a character's nature and yet denied any person could have full knowledge of another.

The collection received high praise from critics. "This volume of impressionistic tales," the *Current Literature* reviewer reported, "will add to the writer's justly won reputation, great as that is" and defined "The Yares of the Black Mountains" as "a prose idyll of great beauty and strength." Chicago's *Inter-Ocean* reviewer noted that the collection reflected Davis's usual strengths; she "always draws with insight, feeling, and humor the type of humanity characteristic of American life and customs." Reviewers deemed Davis as representative of the best story writers of the day, but an interesting debate emerged over the "modernity" of the collection.[75] In opposition to those who thought it a model of modernity, *Life*'s reviewer insisted the stories are not very modern in manner, and that may be counted in their favor. To read a short story nowadays which is not the evident vehicle for parading the smartness and knowingness of its author, is refreshing.... You feel that she is interested in people because of their affections; that she sees the nobility of unselfish affection in all grades of life, and circumstance; that she believes in that sort of charity which is simply human kindness; and that she sees many people in the world more admirable than "superior persons."[76]

Because Dick's *Van Bibber and Others* appeared at the same time as *Silhouettes,* the *Literary World* reviewer insisted on comparing Rebecca's and Dick's writing. His was "characterized by a dash and manly vigor which at the same time [was] so thoroughly youthful in its scope and point of view that we find ourselves constantly wondering whether he will go on writing." Though the reviewer felt Rebecca's "signposts 'to the moral' [were] a bit too dominant," he found the collection representative of a mature writer. *Art Amateur,* on the other hand, thought it was "one of the best of the many good books of short stories that are now before the public."[77] The collection, dedicated to Dick, would go into three editions over the next year.

The publication, in conjunction with books Dick was publishing and the stories Charley was beginning to publish brought numerous joint assessments of their work and continued to fuel the idea of The Davis Family of writers. As the *Roanoke Times* observed, Rebecca, Dick, and Charley had all retained their popularity, had excellent sales records, and were paid well for their work.[78] All three authors were doing exceedingly well in a difficult business. Scribner's used this moment of high praise of Rebecca's collection to announce it would publish *Kent Hampden* at the end of the year, which garnered additional anticipation from reviewers.

In November *Art in Advertising,* which several months earlier had published an article about Clarke, presented an essay purportedly on the Davis brothers but was primarily about Charley. With a photograph of the dashing young man, the article suggested he was better than working with the *New York World* would suggest, citing "A Friend of the Family" as more indicative of his talents. As was the custom, the article was as much about the Davis brothers' personalities as their writing. Noting that Charley lived with Dick in New York, the magazine asserted he "looks enough like him to cause much confusion. They frequently pay each other's debts, for instance. He does not say 'to-doi' for 'to-day' as his brother Richard does, and in other respects is quite an improvement on the original Great and Only." Similar criticisms of

Dick's pretentiousness would haunt him for years, but the article concluded it was fortunate for the public that they would undoubtedly see further contributions from "these bright young men."[79] These light biographical articles filled with photographs and supposed "inside" information demonstrated the ways in which Rebecca's sons were integrally part of the cult of celebrity that she had so long rejected.

At Thanksgiving, Clarke traveled to Exmore Island in Virginia to join Grover Cleveland and Charles Jefferson in a hunting and fishing jaunt. This was in large part a celebration of Cleveland's reelection earlier in the month to the Presidency of the United States. In addition to the Presidency, the Democrats gained control in both houses of Congress, setting the stage for a significant shift in the American political scene. Clarke and Cleveland remained close friends in the coming years, but the President would draw Clarke into a scandal during his second administration.

At the end of 1892 a major transition impacted *Peterson's Magazine* when Sarah Peterson stepped down as editor, replaced by the novelist and poet Frank Lee Benedict. Rebecca remained with the magazine and connected Charley to the periodical as she had earlier with the *Independent* and *Century* magazines. Announcements that the *New Peterson's Magazine* would begin publication in January noted it was bringing in a new generation of contributors—Charles Belmont Davis, Gertrude Atherton, Ella Higginson, and Julian Hawthorne—while retaining their stable of major writers—Rebecca Harding Davis, Thomas Wentworth Higginson, and Hamlin Garland, among others. For Rebecca and Charley to be publishing in the same magazine again raised the image of The Davis Family as a unique literary entity.

Two events in early December caused great alarm for the Davis family, however. Clarke was still fishing with his friends in Virginia when he appeared to have a stroke. Because he was with Cleveland, Clarke's "stroke" was reported on the front page of newspapers across the country. It was the next morning before it was confirmed by doctors that he had actually suffered from the extreme cold during a day on the water, not a stroke.[80] Rebecca received the news through the newspapers and telegrams, leaving her stressed for news of Clarke's fate for more than twenty-four hours. Then, two days later, just as renovations were being completed on the offices of the *Public Ledger*, fire struck. It damaged a large part of the building, including their business office and they were forced to move their typesetting rooms into another building.[81] No one had been hurt, but the fire caused considerable hardship at the paper for several months until the renovations could be completed.

Finally, good news arrived with the publication of Rebecca's young adult book, *Kent Hampden*, a political novel set in preindustrial Wheeling. The book was dedicated to her brothers, Hugh Wilson Harding and Richard Harris Harding. This was the first mention of Richard since his visit with the Davises at Point Pleasant several years earlier and it suggested old wounds had at last healed. *Kent Hampden* received high praise from reviewers. The appeal of the sixteen-year-old protagonist was universal. The *Atlantic* termed it "a skillful story of adventure,"[82] and reviewers agreed that the novel was "among the very best" boy's stories of the year.[83] Within a few years it became part of several school curricula's recommended reading for seventh graders along with Twain's *The Prince and the Pauper*, Stowe's *Uncle Tom's Cabin*, Alcott's *Eight Cousins*, and Weir Mitchell's *Hugh Wynne*.[84] With the notable, back-to-back successes of *Silhouettes of American Life* and *Kent Hampden*, Davis's reputation as a fiction writer again surged to the forefront of American literature.

As the year ended, the Davis and Cleveland families seemed to be constantly intertwined. In addition to the reports of Clarke's trip to Virginia with Cleveland, an editorial he wrote that was highly critical of President Harrison's policies was widely cited negatively by Republican papers as being an iteration of the President-elect's views and suggested that Clarke was simply his mouthpiece.[85] This was an extraordinary shift for Clarke, who had always been recognized for his fair and balanced editorials. On a brighter note, Nora went to New York to spend time with Dick and Charley. While there, they dined with Helen Benedict's family and visited the Clevelands.[86] Grover and Frances had warmly accepted the Davis children as family friends and often invited them to their home.

Rebecca was one of the longtime contributors whose work appeared in the first edition of the *New Peterson's Magazine* in January 1893. "A Grumble" was Davis's reflection on the loss of individualism in US culture. In pithy observations, she captured late-nineteenth-century life: "A man does not think or act now: he cooperates; his baby is not trained in its mother's arms, but in a kindergarten; his daughter does not choose a husband to please her own soul, but her 'set.'" She recognized, however, the "protest is as vain as the chirp of the sandpiper against the incoming tides of the ocean."[87]

Grumble as she might, the world was changing; if not in ways she wished, it did so in ways that her children often embraced. At this time, Dick entered another phase of his writing career. He had taken the managing editorship of *Harper's Weekly* largely because he wanted to make more money than he was able to do by publishing his own stories. With several books and one or two plays now published, he was seeking new ways to advance his career. Thus, he set out in late January for Egypt where he would report on the region for the *Weekly*. The trip whetted his appetite for international travel. He would soon realize there was more money in journalism and serving as a war correspondent and would largely turn to those means of writing in preference to fiction.

This trip established for Dick a popular pattern that was economically beneficial: publishing articles about his travels in periodicals and then collecting them for book publication, more than doubling the income he could initiate from each trip. He was never a good businessman in terms of his personal finances, consistently spending more than he made, but he was very adept at marketing himself and his work in viable ways. Nora had wanted to go to Egypt with Dick; to her surprise, he declined. He wrote Rebecca a month later that, though he felt "miserably mean" about denying Nora the opportunity, it had turned out to be a good thing as the trip was far more arduous than he had expected. In reality, he wanted to be on his own, as a young man free to travel as he wished. "I feel sure we can have another holiday together later," he told his mother, "that will satisfy her as well and in the meanwhile I shall have had my fling—So, I know she will forgive me."[88]

Nora was in that awkward limbo so many young women of her generation faced: she was young, healthy, and financially capable of taking on new adventures, but not so much a New Woman as to embark on her own. And Dick did have the need of proving himself. Rebecca and Clarke were extraordinarily supportive parents, but their very high standards seemed daunting at times to a young man trying to make his way. Things had seemed to come much easier to Charley. Dick had never completed college, had been fired from an early job as a reporter, and although he was now well known, his brother's seemingly easy success had to grate a little.

Although Dick constantly verbalized only positive appreciation of his younger brother's successes, one telling note about his own self-doubts was evident, if subconscious. The more successful Charley became, the more Dick addressed him as "Dear Kid" in the numerous letters he wrote his brother. The family continued to be supportive, however, and while Dick was traveling, Rebecca served as editor of his articles before they were forwarded to *Harper's*. As he told Charley, "She is a great copy editor."[89] She certainly had enough of her own writing to complete, but this, too, was a pattern mother and son would continue for years to come, and both Dick and Charley would offer critiques of her and each other's work as well. It was part of the family writing enterprise.

Rebecca and Clarke's sons had learned the lesson of a familial hand-up very well. For the remainder of their lives, they would reenact their parents' endeavors. Thus, in February, Charley published his first, and only, article in *Harper's Weekly*, "The Vaudeville Club," which observed the changes in admittance of women to vaudeville. As with Dick, Clarke's love of the theater and of vaudeville was well invested in Charley. Clarke told Edward Robins, drama critic for the *Public Ledger*, that his dream was to retire to a farm and write the definitive life of the great British actor Edmund Kean; he would never fulfill this dream, which Robins felt "was really a pity, for with his tastes he should have left a scholarly book behind him to immortalize his love of the stage and its players. He was the intimate friend of Augustin Daly, Ada Rehan, John Drew, the Jeffersons, John S. Clarke and many more Thespians of distinction, some of whom I used to meet at his house."[90]

Even though Charley published only one item in Dick's magazine, it gave him a new audience and attracted much attention from other editors and publishers. Charley was advancing well in his writing career, but behind the scenes, he and his parents, with the help of President Cleveland, were developing plans for a significant change in his career direction.

While waiting to hear about the possibilities for Charley, everyone continued with their writing routines. Rebecca persisted in her editorial role for *Youth's Companion*,[91] and she continued to write commentaries and publish fiction. "Two Methods" appeared in the *Independent* in March at the same time that Charley's "A Freak's Midsummer Night's Dream" appeared in *New Peterson's Magazine* and Dick's first publication from his trip, "American in Africa," appeared in *Harper's New Monthly Magazine*. Davis had actually written "Two Methods" earlier, but when it had not appeared by mid-March, she wrote Ward, "I sent you about a month ago a short article on Miss Marsden's appeal for the Liberian lepers. You usually are so prompt in publishing my articles that I was surprised not to see it. Do you not want it? If not, I must send it elsewhere while it can do any good."[92] It was quickly published.

In March of 1893 Rebecca and Clarke traveled to Washington to attend the inaugural ceremonies for Cleveland's swearing in, and Clarke served as a member of the Reception Committee. As newspapers reported, the Davises were among the small number of "absolutely intimate friends who surround the President."[93] They were barely home from the inauguration before Clarke left again for New York to attend a dinner in honor of the architect Daniel Hudson Burnham who was being feted for his endeavors as Director of Works for the Columbian Exposition.[94] Rebecca could not accompany Clarke to New

York this time because she was recovering from influenza; "the grippe" had been rampant in Philadelphia this spring. As she wrote to Howard Allen Bridgman of the *Congregationalist*, the illness had delayed work on her novel and she was so far behind it would be September before she again published in his periodical. But she invited him to visit her and Clarke in Philadelphia. "You shall have a hearty welcome when you do."[95]

In April the three Davis literary writers were again tracked in the national magazines and newspapers. As Davis published "University Extension in Canterbury" in *Harper's Monthly*, the *Literary World* was proclaiming the promise of Charles Belmont Davis as a writer, and Dick had a play produced in New York based on his story "The Other Woman." The coinciding of their work, which would now occur with increased frequency, set off even greater interest in the gossip and society columns. The *Kansas City Times* was typical with its article "Gossip of the Authors": "Rebecca Harding Davis is at work upon a new novel, to be issued next autumn. In the meantime, her eldest son, Richard Harding Davis, is loitering in Tunis on his tour for the Harpers, while his younger brother, Charles Belmont Davis, is writing a series of short stories for the *Century*."[96]

Other assessments of the renown of The Davis Family also circulated. With Charlie's publication in the *New Peterson's Magazine*, he tended to be the lead interest. As the *Literary World* observed, his "curious and vigorous story . . . gives promise of repeating the remarkable success as a writer which his brother, Mr. Richard Harding Davis, has had and is still having." The article asserted that Nora "has already done some clever things" and "may win distinction in the future," a claim that was most likely a misattribution; Nora never published essays or fiction. Clarke was briefly cited for his editorial and literary work, and Rebecca was defined in a way she would have found ghastly: "Mrs. Rebecca Harding Davis, is a well-known celebrity in fiction." The conclusion captured the notoriety that now encompassed the family: "It is not often that so many members of a literary family take to authorship."[97] The Davis Family had hit its stride.

Writing from Athens, Dick revealed to his father he had not abandoned his political ambitions (or his unspoken competition with his younger brother),

> I hope I shall hear about Charley, it has been so awfully long in being decided. I have just write [sic] to Harper suggesting a series of articles for the weekly on Washington and the new administration before I settle down to chair work again. I think the more American things I write the more people will take an interest in my foreign things and I have a good many friends in Washington now on one side or the other

and I want to make more. I will be want[ing] a Cabinet position soon myself.[98]

He was going to remain in Paris for a while, as he had contracted with *Harper's Monthly* to write a series of articles about the city.

While the rest of the family was receiving praise from the literary magazines, Clarke was facing continuing critiques of his role now as Cleveland's "mouthpiece." In an article syndicated widely in newspapers, Clarke's editorial talents were acknowledged, but the piece lamented his blatant support of Cleveland since "Mr. Davis nor the Ledger has ever been reckoned as political elements to any great extent."[99] This was not quite accurate; during his years at the *Philadelphia Inquirer* Clarke had been known for his ardent support of Republican causes, but with his well-publicized friendship with Cleveland, he came under scrutiny for partisanship, albeit primarily from Republican-oriented newspapers.

In early May the *Ladies' Home Journal* published another of the popular collective-response articles. Purportedly about women's changing roles in society, such articles were typically quite conservative in terms of the questions they posed. "Under Which Name?" asked how should a married woman be addressed? Ella Wheeler Wilcox, Harriet Prescott Spofford, Amelia Barr, Elizabeth Stuart Phelps, and others joined Davis in responding. Adeline Whitney thought it imperative for a woman to take her husband's name, but Frances Hodgson Burnett said she could not give a definitive answer, and Phelps preferred a woman use "Mrs. Sarah Smith" rather than "Mrs. John Smith." Davis's lackluster response was simply, "As it is the name of John Doe which appears in a town directory, and in tradesmen's book, and not that of his wife before her marriage, I should think that her letters, purchases, and inquiring friends would reach her more certainly if directed to Mrs. John Doe than to her maiden name. I do not see any room in the matter for either logic, or sentiment; or, indeed, for anything but expediency."[100]

The excitement of this month, however, was Rebecca and Nora's trip to Chicago to attend the World's Fair. Magnificently constructed by Daniel Burnham and Frederick Olmstead with canals and lagoons, the "White City" covered more than six hundred acres, marked the 400th anniversary of Columbus's expedition, and promoted the future of American exceptionalism. While at the fair, Rebecca and Nora attended a luncheon hosted at Pennsylvania's building. Numerous publications emerged from the Fair era, including *The National Exposition Souvenir: What America Owes to Women* in which Davis was named one of the nation's important women writers. "This vigorous and brilliant writer," the editor, Lydia Hoyt Farmer, wrote of Davis, "with a strong grasp of the political situation could handle the greatest problems of the day and find in them a chance of free play for her artistic and literary skill."[101]

While Rebecca and Nora were in Chicago, Clarke and Charley attended a gala at the Edwin Forrest Home sponsored by Augustan Daly's actors and other professional stage performers, with Ada Rehan as the premier performer of the evening. The Home, once the residence of the famed tragedian, was a favorite cultural effort of Clarke's; in future years, he would become its director.[102]

Rebecca and Nora returned to Philadelphia in time to attend a dinner with Clarke for the Grand Duke Alexander and other Russian dignitaries. The dinner was covered in the society section of newspapers as thoroughly as front-page articles that focused on the political nature of the visit. Shortly thereafter, Rebecca and Nora were again in the society pages, as guests at the opening of the "suburban season" at an event to benefit the Bryn Mawr Hospital. If Rebecca had aided her sons' writing careers, she equally ensured Nora's success in Philadelphia's elite society.[103]

Clarke left a few days later to again join Grover Cleveland for a week of fishing off Hog Island in Virginia. Photographs of the two fishermen appeared in numerous newspapers across the country. There was some criticism of the President for taking a vacation, which apparently upset him to the extent that he castigated Dick about a *Harper's Weekly* photographer having covered the outing. Dick sent a heated letter to Rebecca: "I have seen the photos of the fishing party and they are quite impossible. I am only sorry there should have been so much doubt as to my judgement in using them should they turn out undignified. I should not in any event have submitted the proofs to Cleveland or anyone else. If he does not think I have sufficient taste to run this paper in his interests he should give me credit for being able to run it on my own." Calming down, he asked if Rebecca had read his latest book, *The Englishman in Paris*. "You must at once," he asserted. "I would send it [to] you but that I am too poor as I am SAVING MONEY. But buy it and read it for me."[104] Rebecca could not resist counseling her son repeatedly about the need to save money, as his response pointedly acknowledged.

In spite of Rebecca's busy schedule this month, she made time to critique Dick's second article about Egypt, sending suggestions for revisions. He wrote a letter of appreciation at the end of the month, "You are a dear critic and know me too well not to know my bad work as well as what is good—."[105] The article appeared in *Harper's Monthly* the following month and was part of his collection *Rulers of the Mediterranean*.

Although he published frequently, Dick's works received mixed reviews in these years. The *Philadelphia Inquirer*'s literary reviewers greatly admired Rebecca's work, but they were consistently Dick's harshest critics—and it would only become harsher when he became a war correspondent. His articles and stories often appeared alongside Mary Wilkins Freeman's fiction and rarely to his benefit. They were writing very different kinds of literature, but the *Inquirer* reviewer was unsympathetic with Dick's style: "Richard Harding Davis describes the Derby, the Ascot and the boat race at Henley, subjects which have been done so often by magazine writers that the hope of conveying a fresh impression must be rather slight."[106] In spite of several book publications, Dick was still searching for a unique style; the Gallegher and Van Bibber stories had been popular but subsequent works seemed to fade from public attention quite quickly. When he turned in a few years to a career as a war correspondent, he would find his best fit.

As most of the family prepared to leave for Marion this summer, Nora traveled to Paris to visit Dick, which he now welcomed. But he remained dissatisfied with President Cleveland's lack of attention to his wishes for political appointment and wrote Rebecca in June insisting that she and Clarke use their influence with Cleveland on his behalf: "Dad is I suppose too proud to speak to anyone now that he is consorting with Cleveland. Tell him to tell Cleveland to appoint me Ambassador to either Paris or London if he is nominated ... see that my application gets in first—there is nothing like being first in the field. And I do'nt want any funny business about it either I want a definite answer in writing or I shall home him up."[107] The letter went on in a similar vein for some length. Clearly meant to be humorous, the underlying meaning was less so.

Dick had corresponded often with his parents about their working behind the scenes to gain a diplomatic appointment for Charley, and he clearly could not forget that Cleveland had refused his own earlier efforts to garner a position. Charley's appointment had been in process since the election, and the entire family was anxiously awaiting word. As would become evident, Cleveland felt Charley was a more viable diplomat than Dick. He liked all of the Davis children, but he would not appointment the flamboyant Dick, who frequently changed directions in his careers, to any position that represented his administration. Cleveland had come to know Charley well while he was working as reporter for the *World*, following Cleveland to Marion on his fishing trips, through which Cleveland had an opportunity to see Charley in his professional role as well as a family friend.[108]

If Rebecca did not like the cult of celebrity that had overtaken the literary world, she was not at all above participating in new forms of publication, from "cheap edition" series to books marketed for specific events. Thus "Tirar y Soult" was included in Scribner's collection of *Stories of the South* in July. Other stories in the collection were authored by Joel Chandler Harris, Thomas Nelson Page, and Harrison Robertson. It was produced for the now highly mobile reading public "in an attractive little volume, which can readily be carried in the pocket," meant to coincide with travel to the World's Fair.[109] Reviewers embraced this form of publication. The New York *Sentinel*, for instance, was fascinated with the delicacy of the volume's production: "There is a tempting air of mystery about these little white-bound books, gold sealed in a fold of tenuous parchment through which the palmetto leaves on the cover are dimly discovered." They were perfectly produced for travel or for reading while lying in a hammock, the reviewer asserted. His comments were favorable for all of the entries in the collection but thought readers would prefer Davis's story, "one of her best."[110]

When the Davises went to Marion in mid-July, Mark Twain was visiting Richard Watson Gilder and Grover Cleveland. This was the last summer the Gilders would spend at Marion, although they had been the magnet that drew so many friends. The Davises, Clevelands, and many of their political and artistic associates would continue to summer on Buzzard's Bay for several years.

During the summer Charley was also honing his assessments of the popular theater with an article on "The Rise of the Dancing-Girl" in the August issue of *New Peterson's*. Under Benedict's editorship, the magazine was attending much more to theater and the arts, and Charley's interests fit well with the new focus. Dick also received an unusually positive review for his *Harper's Monthly* story, "His Bad Angel," from the *Philadelphia Inquirer*. It was "as good a thing as Mr. Davis has ever done," the reviewer surprisingly remarked.[111]

For all of the success the family was having with their writing, an explosive issue developed in early September. Rumors had been circulating that Grover Cleveland was in ill health. Years earlier Dick had introduced Cleveland to Elias Benedict and the two men had become close friends. In an attempt to keep secret his ailment, a noncancerous growth on his palate, Cleveland had his physician perform the surgery on Benedict's yacht, away from prying photographers and reporters. But rumors about his health quickly circulated; to counter them, Clarke sent a dispatch to George Childs at the *Public Ledger* indicating he had often seen the President over the summer and he was in good health.

Clarke's comment made front-page news across the country, and his reputation for honesty and unimpeachable integrity worked to reassure the nation. However, critics of the closeness of the editor and the President pounced, suggesting he was covering for Cleveland.[112] One astute reporter in Topeka, who apparently had inside information on the Davises' efforts to have an appointment for Charley in the Cleveland administration, printed Clarke's comments, but bitingly added, "Let's see; have all the first-class foreign missions been filled yet?"[113] It was a stunning public humiliation for Clarke, but he remained loyal to Cleveland.

In the early fall Rebecca published stories in the *Congregationalist* and *New Peterson's*. Reports that her time-consuming editorial work for the *Youth's Companion* would result in a reduction in her productivity were in part true, but she maintained a steady output of writings for other periodicals. Mother and daughter characters in "Without Foundations" for the *Congregationalist* were used to contrast personal and organized charity. "What Did Not Happen" for *New Peterson's* centered on the idea that "if the most commonplace life were laid before us in its bare truth, stripped of disguise, we should find in it something wonderful and strange."[114] After more than thirty-one years as a regular contributor, this was Davis's last story for *Peterson's*. The new directions of the magazine did not interest her. In 1898 it would be purchased by Frank Munsey and incorporated into his popular *Argosy* magazine. Ending her association with the magazine allowed Rebecca more time both for writing editorials and to work on her novel; it also offered a reprieve from having to write so prolifically while traveling—and she would travel much more in the coming years than in the past.

The economic depression that began in 1893 had a significant impact on the country and enlivened the fears of everyone about the state of the nation. Two major societal responses occurred, and the Davis family demonstrated their cultural and political differences through their individual responses. One response was to celebrate the nation's accomplishments, as was demonstrated at the World's Fair, and all of the members of Davis family embraced pride in the US exhibits at the Fair and its general success. The alternative response was a vast outbreak of Populist agitation and often violent labor disputes. In addition, there was a general malaise and a sense that the moral integrity of the nation was collapsing. Surprisingly, Rebecca, who had been so vocal about labor issues throughout her career, voiced no opinions on the subject at all.

Dick's pattern was to embrace the first alternative of negating a sense of cultural disruption by writing positive stories and articles for *Harper's Weekly*, often about football and other activities.[115] The Gibson Girl illustrations by Charles Dana Gibson also embraced this perspective by focusing only on the upper-class young woman who was dressed in the finest clothes and physically active, always on display to a public that could not be satiated in its desire for images and stories of the privileged classes. As the primary male model for the Gibson Girl illustrations, Dick embodied the former response to the national crises, and his modeling catapulted his fame as much as did his writings and editorship. In opposition to such features, however, a more graphic realism began to fill the pages of literary magazines, and Charley would turn in the coming year to writing about strikes and follow in his mother's footsteps of interest in the working classes.

When Dick returned to New York after covering the World's Fair, the tensions he had long experienced with the Harper brothers came to the forefront over his constant travel and what they felt was a neglect of his editorial duties. The result was that Dick was demoted to associate editor, a part-time position that paid seventy-five dollars per week.[116] He put as positive a spin on the situation as possible for his parents, suggesting it would give him much more time for his writing and travel, but to Charley he conveyed how unhappy he was with the demotion.[117] Perhaps as a result, Dick suffered a severe depression. Their family physician, Dr. Starr, indicated Dick's nerves were "completely shattered."[118] Starr continued to monitor Dick's depression while he was at his parents' home; his depression would recur periodically into the following spring and deeply worry everyone in the family.

In October 1893, after nearly a year of anticipation, the Davis family was informed that President Cleveland had forwarded to the US Senate Charley's nomination for the position of American Consul to Florence, Italy; it garnered immediate Senate approval. With Cleveland's support, Charley had hoped to be posted to London or Paris, but these were prime appointments and senior ambassadors resisted an untested appointee receiving such a coveted position.[119] Florence was still a highly sought-after location, and Charley and all of the Davises came to love the city during his tenure there. His annual salary would be $1,500 with slightly over $2,300 for expenses.[120] Although many newspapers noted the alliance of the Davises and Clevelands, there was a general sense, as the New Orleans *Times-Picayune* observed, that Charley was "eminently fitted by education and natural gifts to adorn the position."[121] He had a few weeks at home before leaving for Italy, during which he accompanied Nora to a reception at the home of Mr. and Mrs. Harry C. Cook for a coming-out party for their daughter Rosalie.[122] When Charley went to Italy, Rebecca would return to attending such events with Nora.

Over the winter months, Davis published a number of stories and essays. One drew a very different response than she expected. "The Newly Discovered Woman" in the *Independent* continued her practice of responding to other articles about new cultural issues. Helen Watterson Moody had published "Women's Excitement over Woman" in the September issue of *The Forum*. Davis found her arguments about women moving into the professions and the trades to be an excellent discussion, especially as it noted "a false note in their rejoicing. There is too much sex consciousness in it, and a great deal too much boasting." Although asserting that "active sisters'" accomplishments were valuable, Davis clearly preferred the quiet woman who did her work without seeking acclaim. It was in Chicago over the past summer that the New Woman "seized on the World's Fair as an opportunity to exploit herself," she wrote. What seemed the basis of Davis's unhappiness was her sense that the "graduate of Vassar or Smith has a pitying contempt for her grandmother whose life was spent in her nursery and kitchen."[123] It was an issue about the New Woman to which Davis would frequently return.

Not surprisingly, the article drew a response two weeks later when a "Smith Graduate" took exception to Davis's comments about women's colleges. Asserting that Davis offered no evidence of this "pitying contempt," the Smith Graduate recounted the acknowledgement of women's past accomplishments from women she knew and concluded the essay with a charge: "It is often said that we convict ourselves of a fault by our very ardor in denial of it; but in the case of a college girl's feeling I demand more conclusive evidence than any Mrs. Davis has yet produced."[124] Davis did not respond.

In November Charley prepared to leave for Italy, and Nora would soon follow, spending a few weeks with him as he settled into his new position as Consul.[125] Before leaving, Charley had written a long story, "Out of Her Class," that would be published the following year, but at this time he sent it to Rebecca and Dick for critiques. Dick wrote a long response that revealed the family's differing ideas about literature. As Dick explained,

> I have read your long story and think it fine, up to the last three pages. Mother and I disagree about the end, I think he ought to win out the girl from her low ideals and you ought to show the danger American girls run without making a horrible example of anyone of them.

Mother thinks the story ought to end with the girl being unable to go back to the old ways.

After numerous other minor suggestions, Dick added,

> The first part of the story is excellent and masterly and I enjoyed the scene at the ball and at the dinner immensely but I think it is a pity to waste such a good chance and I would add a little to it and end it by showing the danger the girl is in.... The only criticism I have to make on it is that you are to [sic] inclined to *your* friend Guy de Mauppasant [sic] and to his cold blooded view of life. You want to put in a little more of the humanity of which you are full.... You will say that is not art.[126]

Charley had become a very talented writer, and he retained his own preference for the ending—realistic rather than romantic.

Although Dick had been well enough to return to New York, he suffered a renewed bout of depression shortly before Christmas and was encouraged by his parents to return home over the holidays so he could recover more quickly under their care. By the end of December, however, he was becoming anxious to return home. As he wrote Charley, "I have been manfully sticking it out here in Philadel. having agreed to stay from Christmas to the second of Jan. I feel as though I had been here a *month*. I don't know how you stood it... I'm so blue I cant eat over here. I love my family but I don't care much for their city. Dad is more jolly than I ever saw. I suppose it's relief at getting you fixed and though mother is quiet she seems happy."[127] Unlike Dick, Charley loved Philadelphia as much as New York and spent a good deal of time in his hometown whenever possible. Dick visited the city and his parents less in the coming years.

At the end of 1893, under increased criticism in other newspapers, the *Public Ledger*'s publisher, George Childs, insisted the newspaper sever its support of the Cleveland administration, which had been largely shaped by Clarke's editorials. Although Childs generally admired Cleveland's efforts, he was distressed by the Wilson-Gorman Bill,[128] also known as the Revenue Act. The bill only slightly reduced the US tariff rates from the 1890 McKinley tariff bill, but it added a two percent income tax. Child's insistence on curtailing support of Cleveland and his policies in the *Ledger* left Clarke in a very awkward position. In two months, however, Childs would be dead and Clarke would have even greater control over the paper's editorial content, and he would return to his open support of Cleveland.

Only a few years into the new decade, the Davis family was in one of the most productive and critically acclaimed periods of their careers. Rebecca had published a critically and popularly acclaimed collection of her short stories as well as one of the most successful novels for boys in recent years, and she was continuing her editorial work for the *Independent, Youth's Companion,* and some Philadelphia newspapers while writing her next novel. Clarke's dear friend was now President of the United States and his own career was flourishing, in spite of criticism of his alliance with Cleveland. Nora was well accepted in Philadelphia and New York society circles and was involved in many charities. After publishing several books and serving as managing editor of one of the most influential periodicals of the day, Dick returned to journalism and expanded his horizons both geographically and literarily. And Charley was now hailed as an important new writer on the American scene and had achieved his dream of becoming a US ambassador. If the sons were on the verge of their greatest fame, the parents were still at the top of their respective fields and looking forward to the opportunities ahead. It seemed as if nothing could stop the incomparable "Davis Family."

Chapter 11

A Return to Novel-Writing (1894–1896)

The mid-1890s was a less productive period for Rebecca in terms of publishing. She turned most of her attention to completing the novel, *Doctor Warrick's Daughters*, which would appear to critical acclaim in 1896. Two issues thwarted her opportunities to write: family illnesses and, more positively, extensive travel. In her early sixties, she was financially secure and the break in quantity of publishing was not a crisis. She published no fiction or essays until May of 1894.

Dick was healthy enough to return again to New York at the beginning of the year, and, after spending the holiday with his family, Charley returned to Florence in late January. Letters between New York and Florence maintained the brothers' bond and allowed Dick, in particular, to express frustrations he sought to hide from his parents. He also revealed many aspects of the Davis family life in the early months of 1894. Perhaps most rewarding for Charley was Dick's acknowledgement, "The family are delighted at your going in for Art." In spite of admitting that all of their New York friends had only high praise for Charley's "Out of Her Class," Dick again stressed his different view of literature: "I think it is bully but too serious which is a quality I find in all you write and one which you ought to avoid not because it is unpopular but because it is not your real strong point you can be very amusing and you ought to be."[1] Dick's assessment of Charley's ability to write humorous and insightful cultural commentaries was accurate, but the younger brother wisely recognized "seriousness" was one his best qualities as a fiction writer.

Dick did understand, however, that seriousness was precisely what made his brother a successful consul. When Charley described his early experiences in Florence for his family, Dick responded: "Your letter was so mature and so broad that all that I expected would result from this position has come true." Dick also reported to his brother that he had visited the Clevelands in Washington in mid-January and revealed his own continuing political aspirations: "I consider Washington holds great chances for me some day."[2] He would never achieve that dream.

Almost as soon as Dick returned to New York on January 3, Clarke succumbed to another bout of nervous exhaustion. These periods of stress and depression were debilitating for Clarke and extremely stressful for Rebecca, both emotionally and physically as she attempted to care for her family and ease their difficulties. However, by late January Clarke was well again. Through all of this care, Rebecca continued to critique and proof Dick's work.[3]

On February 3, the *Public Ledger*'s publisher George W. Childs died. Although his death was not unexpected, it again sent Clarke into a period of stress. What impact would this have on his own position? In spite of his excellent reputation, at fifty-nine, he did not feel in a position to make a major career change again. Dick attempted to encourage both Clarke and Rebecca in a letter sent to his mother "I am afraid Dad is still worried and bothered and I do wish I could do something to help. All I can think of is to assure him that in spite of outward changes in the *Ledger*, the insides are what count and he takes care to keep them healthy!"[4] Shortly after sending his letter, Dick was struck by a severe case of sciatica, followed by severe depression, and he once again returned to his parents' home to recover.

It was a grim household that Rebecca sought to manage in these months. When the twenty-five-year-old George W. Childs Drexel, who had just inherited a fortune from his father Anthony Drexel, was announced as the next publisher of the *Ledger*, Clarke seemed to have reason to worry. Drexel immediately began making innovations at the newspaper, and Clarke feared an older editor would not be to the publisher's liking. Finally, to his delight and relief, Clarke was assured that Drexel wished to retain him as managing editor of the newspaper. In fact, for decades only George Childs' name had appeared on the editorial page, but now Clarke's name and the Managing Editor title were placed at the head of the paper's editorial columns.[5] All of the changes received considerable public attention and gave rise again to charges that, through Clarke, the *Ledger* was "the president's personal organ."[6] This time, however, a counter opinion came from the *World*; Clarke was familiar with the *World*'s editor and publisher and Charley had worked for the paper for a few years, so they had strong support from that quarter. The New York paper insisted that, if there were any truth to such assertions, it was the President who was echoing Clarke because he so highly valued the editor's opinion.

As life at the *Ledger* began to return to normal and Clarke regained his health, Rebecca continued to nurse Dick whose sciatica kept him largely bedridden. Nora had sailed for Italy on the *Genoa* on February 18. Dick acknowledged to his siblings that having his leg in splints "will give mother a lot of

[work] but I really think she will enjoy it for [she] is blue now that Nora is out of the house."[7] While Dick was bedridden, Charley's life in Italy was busy and all he had hoped. In spite of the responsibilities of his position, Charley continued to write, and nothing more fully demonstrated his commitment to serious writing than the article he published in the March issue of the *Century*. "The Great Sympathetic Strike," although set in New York, was probably based on the recent Philadelphia stonecutters' strike.[8] The main character was a non-union man whose actions led first to a small local strike and then to a nation-wide strike of dozens of unions that crippled the country. Although the ward leader of the local union was criticized, it was the capitalists who received the brunt of criticism in the story: "It was absurd for capitalists to employ the non-union men. For the first time the workmen showed what the possibilities of organized labor could accomplish."[9]

Published only two months before the great Pullman Strike did, indeed, cripple the nation, Charley's story sought to suggest the role President Cleveland *should* take. It concluded with the joyous moment when a message arrives for the strikers: "The worst is over. The President has joined the strike!"[10] In reality, Cleveland would send in federal troops to break up the Pullman strike, but in Charley's idealistic vision, his friend took on the heroic role of supporting the strikers over the capitalists who sought to break the unions. Charley also wrote numerous consular reports as part of his new position, and one on the benefits of cultivating eucalyptus in the US, including its potential use in treating malaria, had wide influence within government publications for several years.[11]

Dick began a tradition at this time that the entire family would continue for the rest of their lives: mapping each other's travels so they could assess where the traveling member of the family was at a given moment. He began the process to ease Rebecca's worry about Nora as she crossed the ocean and to give himself something interesting to do while recovering. On March 1, Nora arrived in Florence. She immediately sent a cable with the news. As Dick told Charley, knowing Nora had arrived eased Rebecca's mind as nothing else really could. But Dick, who occasionally praised one of his mother's works, never acknowledged the importance of her *career* and the time and effort it demanded: "I guess she was very lonely until I came for Dad is busy and the house seemed empty. My taking possession of Nora's room has made it more lively."[12]

Dick also revealed in his letters the freedom the servants in the Davis household had to express their opinions. Much to Dick's frustration but to the delight of the rest of the family, when John Drew visited Dick at his family's home and apparently made some untoward comments, Drew had to leave because it created what Dick termed "a race war" with the servants. Dick himself complained that Edwin, the male servant in the household, was not at his beck and call, but Rebecca insisted Edwin had his own duties before he could consider running errands for Dick. Although Dick insisted he was joking, the difference in attitudes between mother and son was always evident around such issues.[13] Rebecca viewed household employees as individuals whose lives mattered to her, and she often criticized in fiction and the mistress-and-maid essays the arrogant matron who viewed her relationship with servants as ending at their paycheck.

After settling into the consulate, Nora sent a long letter to her parents describing the meeting with Charley. "Mother read it about eight times," Dick reported, insisting it was "quite providential" their mother had him to take care of since she so dearly missed her other children. Although it was undoubtedly true that Rebecca wanted to help care for her son, having to give him medication three times a day and negotiate between him and the servants took a considerable—and unacknowledged—toll on her own work in these months. In a funny aside to Charley, however, Dick perfectly assessed the level of pride Rebecca had in her children: "I take the greatest comfort in the way you are distinguishing yourself and you have no idea how proud the Governor is and mother of course—If one of her sons was in Sing Sing she would be proud of his making better shivs than Billy the Bilk!"[14]

At the end of March, Dick returned to New York and immediately immersed himself in his social life, including dinners with friends at Delmonico's. He wrote Charley that their father was "at *last* perfectly happy about you and Noll [Nora]. He just really delights in it and is only fearful lest he does nt give Noll enough money to enable you to keep up your dignity—." He added in the way only an older brother could, "But who are you any way. *You* have 'nt been in bed one month and N.Y. two hours with Mrs. Freddie Gebhard on one side and Com Vanderbilt on the other and the establishment bowing to you and you not paying your bill for three months—."[15] For Rebecca, Dick's return to New York meant that at last she could return to her usual writing schedule and respond to a large stack of correspondence that had accumulated during the time she was caring for her son. Most of her letters this month began with an apology for the long delay in responding.

In May Davis's first publications of the year appeared, beginning with a story in *Romance* magazine, which was edited by the journalist and novelist Gilson Willetts; as the *Hartford Courant* noted, the issue included "three realistic stories among the sixteen . . . and Rebecca Harding Davis, Elizabeth W. Champney, Justin McCarthy, and Alphonse Daudet help to make the number attractive."[16] Her second publication this month was "The Outlook for the Boys" in the *Independent*. The essay lamented the large number of well-educated young American men who were accustomed to luxurious lives but in contemporary America were discovering it difficult to find work that would provide them the opportunity to continue that lifestyle. For many Americans in the Gilded Age, following every detail of the lives of the wealthy was a source of constant desire for more, but Davis worried about the consequences of a dream that, for most people, could never be realized.

In June Charley published "The City of Homes" about Philadelphia in *Harper's Monthly*, alongside works by Constance Fenimore Woolson, Hamlin Garland, and Owen Wister. The illustrated article distinguished the "two cities" of Philadelphia—the quiet old part of the city and the new bustling section; the article also highlighted the many famous writers living in the city at this time as well as society figures, including Wister, Agnes Repplier, S. Weir Mitchell, Charles Leland Moore, and Richard Harding Davis—but not one word about his famous mother, undoubtedly at her own insistence, since the authors' photographs were included as were illustrations of some of their homes.

The publication was another example of Davis family members opening the door of a distinguished periodical for other family members, as Rebecca had published in *Harper's Monthly* for many years, and Dick was becoming a regular contributor to its pages just as Charley began publishing there as well. Not only did his essay receive high praise from critics but, as Dick proudly informed him, also from family friends such as Maude Adams, Clara Wilder (Bowden), and the actor Eddie Coward. Even more impressive was the letter of high praise Charley received at the time from US Minister to Italy, Wayne McVeigh, for his ambassadorial work over the past several months.[17] The same month, *McClure's* ran an article about Dick, including numerous photographs of him from age five to the present. Rebecca could truly be proud of her sons. Each was rising in the world in their own distinctive way.

As Rebecca returned to her regular routine of writing, she was confronted with the differences that were reshaping publishing in the 1890s. Although some publishers of newspapers such as Joseph Pulitzer and William Randolph Hearst were beginning to offer astonishingly high rates to fiction writers, the more traditional literary periodicals in which she regularly published had tightened their budgets in the aftermath of the economic crisis of the early 1890s.

Unlike in the age of the "gentleman editor" when editor and author often developed friendships, the new era of editors and publishers often bore a much tougher attitude toward their authors. For many authors, this transition had occurred in the post-war years, but Davis had been fortunate in maintaining strong friendships and financially equitable relationships with her publishers and editors for decades. The *Independent* editors William Hayes Ward and his daughter, Susan Hayes Ward, wanted to pay Davis as high a rate for her stories as possible, but administrator Henry S. Chandler insisted all authors should be paid on the same scale, based on the number of columns needed for a story.

Letters flew back and forth between Chandler and the Wards in mid-June when Davis submitted the manuscript of "Achill" and asked her usual $100. Susan Hayes Ward had sought approval of that rate, arguing that Davis wrote some of the strongest fiction in the magazine. Chandler was unmoved, "'A story is a story' and business is business," he responded. "The idea that writers for newspapers and magazines are not supposed to do business in a business way, it seems to me, ought to be exploded. The only way to treat with R.H.D. or any other writer is from a business standpoint. If they write for money they enter the business arena and they must treat and be treated accordingly."[18]

The presumptuousness of assuming an author of thirty years did not know she was in a business market seemed to escape Chandler, who had been given authority over the editors by the publisher Henry Chandler Bowen, and he continued, "It is directly in the line of business to write to R.H.D. and tell her we would be very glad to pay her $100 for a story but we must first know whether the length of the story will be in accordance with our ideas as to how much $100 should pay for. If it isn't, I should not be willing to pay $100 to her. I would not pay her $100 unless the story were certainly ten columns in length." Davis had good cause to ask for $100, as it was the rate she had consistently been paid by the *Independent* for stories in recent years, which Chandler acknowledged even as he sought to reduce the rate of payment. Her asking price was quite reasonable; by contrast, in December *Scribner's* would pay Dick $400 for a story.[19] But Chandler's goal of paying authors not on quality or name recognition but per column meant he would offer only $50 to "R.H.D. or any body else."[20]

William Hayes Ward had the unfortunate duty of informing Davis he could no longer pay the $100 rate, adding, "I wish I could do it."[21] She had intended the story for the *Independent* and had sent the manuscript over the summer to Ward, noting she thought he would like it as "it has a new idea in it." When Ward responded with the news, Davis wrote, "That is a pity, especially as I have near finished the story with a view to 'Independent' readers."[22] "Achill" was published in the August issue of the *Independent*, presumably for the lower rate. Davis, however, was unwilling to be treated as she had been by Bowen, and "Achill" was the last story or editorial she would publish with the magazine for the next three years—until after Henry Chandler Bowen's death in 1896.

"Achill" was one of several articles Davis wrote in these years about conditions in Ireland, but in this instance she argued in favor of the restrictions on Irish immigration to the US as part of her broader criticism of immigrants that appeared periodically in the last decades of her life. She insisted it was England's responsibility to act on the behalf of the people of Achill. Better they should be fed and clothed and allowed to stay on their own island than be relegated to the tenements of Boston and New York, she argued, but she went further, turning to a xenophobic assessment: the recent Pullman Strike was due to "the anarchical principles and methods imported with foreign immigrants amongst us."[23] Philadelphia had embraced immigration in the past; with a population of approximately 1.5 million, the city was one of the most diverse cities in the nation. More than a quarter of its residents were immigrants, and the largest segment was Irish. The violence of the Pullman Strike, however, had frightened many Americans. Although xenophobic comments were common in the US at this time, they were in direct contrast to Davis's earlier celebrations of Philadelphia's diversity and her championing of the downtrodden.

Not surprisingly, the article drew a quick response from John J. O'Shea, an Irish American journalist in New York, who "indignantly repudiate[d]" the categorization of Irish immigrants as paupers and anarchists, suggesting instead that political independence for Achill and all of Ireland was the better solution.[24] Davis would return to her former, more liberal beliefs at times in her remaining years, but in her sixties and seventies her writings took on a more conservative tone.

In early June Rebecca and Clarke traveled to New York to see Dick. The three Davises drew national attention when they dined at Delmonico's, including an article about the "Three Davises" by Moses Purnell Handy for the *Mail and Express* that was widely reprinted. He noted what a "remarkable family group" had gathered that evening, missing only Charles Belmont Davis to make the literary family complete. Handy focused on Rebecca, observing that, in addition to novels and stories, she was responsible for "literally thousands of columns of the best editorials, from a literary point of view, printed in her day and generation." He had been on the *New-York Tribune* staff when she was an editorial correspondent, and he repeatedly praised her editorial work over the years. Here he revealed she had written editorials that

> vied in popularity with those of [Isaac Hill] Bromley, [John] Hay, [John R.G.] Hassard and [Charles Taber] Congdon, and she may be said to be the pioneer in the editorial discussion of social topics in daily newspapers.... After Harriet Martineau ... I know of no other woman who is entitled to more honor as a journalist than Rebecca Harding Davis. The anonymity of the editorial page has alone prevented her from the general recognition of the distinction which she has so well deserved.[25]

Handy was not the only insider to acknowledge Davis's extraordinary contributions to journalism. At the International Sanitary Conference in the fall, Margaret Welch gave a paper on "Is Newspaper Work Healthful for Women?" in which she asserted that, although some newspaper women did suffer from nervous exhaustion, "Mrs. Rebecca Harding Davis, Mrs. Lucia K. Runkle, Mrs. Margaret Sullivan are in full physical vigor after twenty-five years of brilliant newspaper work."[26]

The family reunion in New York was very brief, however, as Dick left the next day for London, and when French President Marie François Sadi Carnot was assassinated, he continued on to Paris to cover the story.[27] In early August, Charley arrived in the States for a summer visit,[28] to his parents' joy, though once again Clarke was ill, curtailing the family's travel until he recovered. Over the summer, in addition to "Achill," Rebecca published "Unto the Least of These" in the *Congregationalist*, her first story for the periodical in 1894. The item examined the complacency that could settle over a congregation when it became too self-satisfied.

By August Clarke was again healthy and Dick was back in the States, so the entire family was finally able to convene in Marion. Rebecca's sister, Emilie Harding Gow and her family had moved recently to Seattle;[29] although they would remain in close contact, the sisters were no longer able to visit at least yearly as they had in the past. While in Marion, the Davis children lunched with Frances Cleveland, reported first by the *Boston Globe*.[30] Associating with the President and First Lady meant that even something as innocuous as a luncheon was reported in national newspapers, further establishing the celebrity status of Dick, Charley, and Nora. Charles Dana Gibson also began summering in Marion at this time, and Dick, who was then thirty years old, introduced him to a Marion regular, Irene Langhorne of Virginia, whom Gibson would marry the following year.

Boston newspapers were particularly interested in covering The Davis Family in these years, and an article in the personal columns of the *Boston Daily Advertiser* was representative: "Rebecca Harding Davis, herself a famous tale writer, is responsible for the career of two others well known in literature. Her son, Richard Harding Davis, thanks her for his literary career, which she encouraged by getting all his first good stories in print, and destroying others that would not add to her son's reputation. This she did until he could 'go alone,' as one says of a child." Dick obviously had not revealed that his mother was still his best critic and copyeditor, but the article also recognized Rebecca's role in Clarke's success: "Then there is her husband, Clark [sic] Davis of Philadelphia, one of the first editors of the country, and one who thanks his wife for her advice on all knotty editorial points and questions of literary judgment."[31] As news reports suggested, and family correspondence confirmed, Rebecca was the driving force in her family's lives, personal and professional.

In late September Charley left for Florence, and Rebecca and Clarke returned to their normal work routines in Philadelphia. Dick offered his brother astute advice as he returned to Florence: begin creating a body of work now, so when his political position ended he could easily step back into his literary career.[32] It was advice Charley followed closely. Rebecca finished the year with a contribution to "When Is a Woman at Her Best" for the November issue of *Ladies' Home Journal*. Another of the jointly authored articles by women writers, Davis was joined by Julia Ward Howe, Amelia Barr, Octave Thanet, Mary Mapes Dodge, Mary E. Wilkins, Gail Hamilton, and others. The general consensus was that a woman's best years were between thirty and forty. Davis insisted, however,

> that every woman is at her best in body and mind at the age when she is most fully occupied with her true work in the world, whether that be art, cookery, lecturing or child-bearing, provided that she goes to it simply and humbly. It is not their work that prostrates the nerves of women or vulgarizes their natures. It is the incessant squabbling and posing and boasting about their work. No body or mind at any age can be in healthy condition which is perpetually busied with examining and exhibiting itself before the public.[33]

This response was typical of Davis's views in her later years—a refusal to homogenize women and yet a sweeping resistance to women's new, more public roles in society.

Clarke started 1895 by attending President Cleveland's annual state dinner in Washington with cabinet members and selected senators,[34] and he was appointed by the President to the Assay Commission for the US Treasury Department.[35] In contrast to his parents' preferences, Dick was now part of New York's young social elite—designated as the "Swell Set"—and the newspapers often depicted his stylized socializing.[36] But Dick was adept at combining his social life and his work. In February 1895, for instance, he and two friends left for a three-month trip through South and Central America that would be the basis for articles he serialized and then collected in *Three Gringos in Venezuela and Central America* the following year.

Dick wrote lengthy letters to Rebecca and other family members as he traveled, but a private comment by Dick to Charley as he prepared to leave for his trip suggested the arrogant disdain he had for a periodical in which his mother had published dozens of works and been an editor. "It is very important," Dick wrote, "that you should keep your mind in the way of constantly seeing 'stories' in everything. The Youth Companion or the Harper's Young People take anything about child life and that rot you could write for practice and there must be good stuff all around you"![37] Rebecca had curtailed her writings for *Youth's Companion*, not having published a story there since 1891, but his denigration of a periodical with which she was so well identified was shocking. Such comments also discredited the many talented writers who published in the magazine at this time, from Oliver Wendell Holmes and Kate Cleary to Harold Frederic and Justin McCarthy. In spite of Dick's repeated insistence that Charley turn to popular topics and magazines, Charley preserved his own literary values and choices about publications.

In February Rebecca published a powerful article in the well-paying *Century Magazine*, a piece that might well have gone to the *Independent* had Chandler not insulted her with his reduction in pay. Davis sent the manuscript to Richard Watson Gilder with the note that "The only merit of this is that it is a fact—to me a very strange one. I don't know whether I have shown how strange."[38] Unlike Chandler, Gilder agreed to Davis's requested $100 rate.[39] "In the Gray Cabins of New England" examined women who lived isolated, tragic lives due to nervous exhaustion and years of self-repression. Davis's nonfiction images were similar to the powerful characterizations in fiction by Mary E. Wilkins. Davis suggested remedies for such women to extract themselves from their morbid lives by finding a new, more meaningful way of living. This was Davis at her non-conservative best, and it demonstrated she could still champion the downtrodden. The story received strong critical praise.

In March Charley befriended the American pianist and composer Ethelbert Nevin and his wife Anne who had recently settled in Florence. Since Charley was a bachelor, Anne soon became his official hostess for social events at the consulate and his home, except when Nora visited and she took on that role. Many prominent Americans who lived in or visited Florence found their way to Charley's home as it quickly became a favorite gathering place for artists and writers, much like his parents' Philadelphia home. Among the regulars for the winter seasons were the English politician and writer Henry Labouchère, Charles Dana Gibson, the American politician Henry Brereton and his wife, the sculptor Thomas Ball, the Parkman Blake family of businessmen from Boston, and the German dramatist Gerhart Hauptmann.[40]

Dick wanted very much to join Charley in Florence in April, but while he was traveling in South America he had unwisely asked Rebecca to handle his mail. "She read all of my bills that happened to be very large," he reported to Charley, explaining why he would not be coming to Europe. "I could not make her understand that the people to whom I owed them never cared when they were paid and that they always let them run as long as I liked." Rebecca had been raised in a family that constantly struggled for solvency, and she had married a man whose generosity often exceeded the reality of their income in the early years of their marriage. She had learned to be a wise economist for the entire household, and she was appalled at her elder son's lackadaisical attitude toward paying his bills. "She got it fixed in her mind that I must pay off those bills first," Dick lamented in a lengthy letter written from his parents' home that sought to justify his actions, but he finally concluded he had better not anger his parents and agreed to forego the trip to Italy.[41]

The following month the *Boston Daily Advertiser* highlighted another difference between mother and son. Rebecca, they reported, "is said to have spent six years on her novel, Dr. Warrick's Daughter. If the talented Richard Harding Davis would spend six years on everything he writes we would like him ever so much better."[42] Rebecca did not like the slightest criticism of her children's talents, however, and as Dick could attest, she was known to toss all bad reviews of his work in the wastebasket.[43] In spite of her agreement that Dick needed to hone his craft much more than he was wont to do, she would not have appreciated the negative comparison of their writing styles.

To redeem himself in terms of his finances, Dick wrote Rebecca at this time, insisting he could contribute to the costs of Rebecca and Nora's planned trip abroad; he had received royalties from three of his books that would more than tide him over for the summer. The offer was typical of Dick: generous in spirit, but shortsighted in any sense that he might save some of his income for the future. "We are all one family," he wrote, "we can help ourselves."[44] And they always had.

Rebecca declined Dick's offer, preferring to wait another year when she and Clarke could pay for the trip. They spent the summer of 1895 in Marion, and Charley spent a few weeks with them. Like his mother, Dick found Marion an amenable environment for writing, and this summer he spent much of his time working on another novel. He, Charley, Nora, and their friends were enamored with the new craze of bicycle riding, and the Davis siblings were seen bicycling around the area during the long summer days with Cecil Clark, Maude Adams, Charles Dana Gibson, and Ethel Barrymore.[45]

"Doctor Warrick's Daughters," Rebecca's first novel for adults since *A Law Unto Herself* in 1878, began serialization in *Harper's Bazar* while she was at Marion and ran through November; the book would be published early the following year. *Harper's Bazar* had been established with an audience of women in the middle and upper classes in mind and, under the editorship of poet and author Margaret Sangster, had attracted major writers to its pages. In this year alone, Harriet Prescott Spofford and Thomas Wentworth Higginson, like Davis, had published several stories or articles. Through the rest of the 1890s Davis would contribute a second novel and several articles to the magazine, which paid her $2,500 for the serialization of "Doctor Warrick's Daughters."[46]

Back in Philadelphia in mid-October, Rebecca was surprised to see a notice in *The Critic* that she was a contributor to *Frank Leslie's Pleasant Hours for Boys and Girls*, a children's magazine in competition with *Youth's Companion*. Though she would write only two more items for *Youth's Companion*, she had no contract with the Frank Leslie publications. She wrote to Jeannette and Joseph Gilder, editors of *The Critic*, asking them to retract the statement and to indicate that she had no plans to write for the Leslie publications. Arthur Conan Doyle and Edmund Gosse had written similar letters of protest when their works also appeared in Leslie publications.

When the Gilders published the authors' complaints, the editor of *Pleasant Hours* brusquely responded that his publishing house had purchased the stories and could publish them when and where they wished.[47] In spite of new copyright laws, Davis and the other writers were experiencing the new patterns of publishing that often cost the authors while becoming more profitable for publishers. Newspapers, many of which were syndicated by this time, could readily reprint authors' works, such as the republication of Davis's 1888 story

"Elizabeth's Thanksgiving" in the *Galveston Daily News* this year. It was a rather sour end to the year.

Early in the winter of 1895, political tensions in the US were evident as Cuba sought independence from Spain. Clarke attended a meeting of the Philadelphia Brigade Association, a Civil War veterans' society populated with many onetime abolitionists; at the meeting, Indiana Governor Claude Matthews spoke in support of Cuba's independence. Clarke signed the Association's resolutions that were then presented to President Cleveland and the US Congress.[48] The Cuban War of Independence would lead to the Spanish-American War, a conflict that reflected the imperialist desires of both the US and Spain at the expense of the island nation's independence. It was also the beginning of very different political allegiances within the Davis family and among their friends and extended relations. Like the Civil War, the Spanish-American War often pitted family members against one another in a battle for the future direction of the nation. The next three years would be a period of increased tension within the Davis family as the years leading up to and during the Spanish-American War exposed the disparate philosophies about war held by each member.

In the interim, Dick invited his mother to meet him in Jersey City for "lunch and a good talk," and when he returned home he regaled her with tales of dining with his long-time friend Helen Benedict and the actress Maude Adams in New York. He had such fun, he reported, "Maude Adams sang to us after dinner, and then went off to see Yvette Guilbert at a 'sacred concert' to study her methods."[49] Rumors had circulated that Dick would marry Adams, but they were merely great chums who both loved the nightlife and the theater. The same was true of his relationship with Ethel Barrymore. He escorted her to the wedding of Charles Dana Gibson and Irene Langhorne on November 7 in large part, he explained to her uncle and his friend John Drew, so she could meet people of her own age. Maude and Ethel were also friends of Nora Davis, and Ethel traveled with Nora to the wedding in Richmond, which was one of the major events of the Richmond social season.[50] The Gibsons honeymooned in Europe, visiting Charley in Florence.[51]

The year ended with warm and friendly letters between the Davises and the actress Ellen Terry, with whom they had maintained a close friendship for many years. Rumors had circulated in *Life* magazine's gossip column that Dick did not like Terry, but their letters proved the falsity of such claims. In a playful letter written on Christmas Day, she wrote him:

> Why my dear Mr. Dickey Davis how 'sweetly pretty' of you to send me your pleasant †mas greeting & *the*-very-thing-I was-so-much-in-need

of!! (for I brought no travelling clock with me—) I thank you *very much*—Next time you are at the Play do come round—or better still come & eat with us—we could all go home in Sir Henry's Shay—Chay!?—It's surely sending 'Coals to Newcastle' to wish you happiness—for on Monday evening I thought you appeared to be the happiest person I had ever looked upon—but I do wish you a happy new year, for one can't, they say, have too much of a thing that is good! Your sincere friend *Ellen Terry*.[52]

More soberly, she also penned a note to Clarke, thanking him for a recent visit. Rebecca, Clarke, and Dick had seen Terry in the American tour of *Macbeth* earlier in the year, and she added, "Your little boy 'Dickey' sitting at the Play with his Mother, was a never-to-be-forgotten sight—He is quite a Dear—To you and yours Peace & Content in the New Year."[53]

1896 would prove to be a very good year for Rebecca professionally and for the family as well, but it also brought increased rumblings of international tensions about Cuba's demands for independence. Both Rebecca and Clarke were opposed to war; he took public action, and she would soon take to her pen to argue against the US entering the war. In February a conference was held in the Universal Peace Union's (UPU) rooms at Independence Hall at which arguments were set forth in favor of international arbitration. Clarke had sent a letter of invitation to "representative men" to attend the conference, which would be covered by Henry Clubb, editor of *The Peacemaker* and attended by Albert Love, the founder of the Peace Union. The conference produced a resolution seeking "the creation of a permanent Court of Arbitration for the peaceful adjustment of difficulties that may arise between the United States and Great Britain," signed by Clarke, Love, and others.[54] The UPU also sent a letter to Spain in support of Cuban autonomy, but a letter that Albert Love sent to the Queen was intercepted. Published in a corrupted form, Love's letter created outrage to the extent the UPU was forced to move its headquarters out of Independence Hall and Love himself was burned in effigy.[55] It was decidedly not a popular time to crusade for peace in the US.

In March Rebecca and Nora set sail on the *St. Paul* for England,[56] where they would visit with old friends, travel through Europe, and spend considerable time with Charley in Florence. Rebecca always used the Brown Brothers investment bank in London as the place for all of her correspondence to be sent while she traveled in Europe. Nora would do the same years later when she lived there. While staying in Siena, Italy, Davis wrote Richard Watson Gilder at the *Century* with an enthusiastic account of the ancient city, which she felt was "less altered from mediaeval days than Rome or Florence." She wanted to publish an article about a "curious affair" she had seen there—the Palio de Siena, a horse race in which each of the *contrade*, or city wards, were adorned in representative colors. She was fascinated by the preparation and passion of the people for the biannual event.[57]

While Rebecca was traveling, the book version of *Doctor Warrick's Daughters* was published, with a dedication to Charley. Like the serial, the book received very strong reviews. Many commentators remarked on the realistic depiction of Southern customs and dialects; as the *New York Observer* suggested, the novel included "bright descriptions of town and country life, and witty dialogue on Southern themes." "The book itself is one of sharp contrasts—of the North and South, of wealthy and poverty, of husband and wife, of sister and sister, of brother and brother and of two lovers for each of the heroines. . . . Davis has made a strong and interesting story," the *Congregationalist*'s reviewer observed, adding, "the book brings a well-reasoned and enjoyable study of American life to a definite end in which the moral is obvious enough—if any reader nowadays cares for a moral." The Philadelphia *Press* asserted Davis "has done few things of a finer literary quality," a statement that Harper's used thereafter in its advertising of the novel. More extensively, the reviewer for the *Literary World* described the novel as

> not only set[ting] forth the workings of retribution and the crisscross ways of human life, but the admirable narrative power of its authoress holds throughout its pages the interest of its readers. She deals alike with the contrasts in locality (Pennsylvania and the extreme South) and in character. . . . How retribution works the reader shall learn for himself, rejoicing, as he closes the book, that if the love of money is the root of all evil, home-keeping hearts are the happiest.

The *San Francisco Call* was particularly effective in articulating the contrasts Davis drew in the novel:

> One of the doctor's daughters—Mildred—carried away with the vanity of riches, marries a man whose poverty of mind she had often scorned. But he has become one of the money kings and she sells herself for his gold. . . . The other daughter, Anne, strives to improve her mind and is sought after for her intellectual attainments. She chooses a husband of honest worth, after proving his character, and they live humbly and happily. The millionaire's wife brings her husband close to the brink of ruin by stock gambling. She dies in Paris, leaving a son,

who is made to profit through the father's consciousness of his own life's mistake.

Similar ideas were articulated by the *Philadelphia Inquirer* as well.[58]

The only exception to these positive reviews was *The Churchman*, which did not approve of her failure to have a character interpose at the end of the novel to correct wrongs. Davis had returned in her novels, as in her articles, to a much more realistic, even harsh sense of the impossibility of such interventions. The general consensus, as *The Dial* remarked, was that the novel was "one of the best of the season."[59] It was also one of her most popular novels. She had negotiated fifteen percent royalties and she retained the copyright. The book paid royalties to her and her heirs until 1923.[60]

Rebecca's story "At the Foot of the Class" also appeared in *Youth's Companion* while she was in Europe. She had written many stories about the seemingly dull student who rises to achieve great success in life, in this story she emphasized the difference between being a scholar and a teacher. It was the first story she had published in the magazine in five years.

Other news about Davis was circulating as well. With the disclosure that Harriet Martineau had contributed editorials to the *London Daily News*, the interest in women journalists continued to build, and in May of 1896, the Chicago *Times-Herald* and *San Francisco Call* asserted "there are other women . . . scholars, patriots, students, imbued with an absorbing love of science and humanity, who, constitutionally devoid of personal ambition, have thus contributed to the progress of the age which, unseen but not unheard, they have adorned. Among these are Margaret Fuller, Rebecca Harding Davis and Lucia Calhoun Runkle."[61] The newspapers continued to recognize the importance of women journalists' contributions to national commentaries on the state of the nation and to American thought.

Clarke joined Rebecca and Nora in June, traveling to Europe for the first time in many years. Dick, who had been covering the Russian coronation, met the family in Florence. The city was abuzz this summer with literary figures and artists. The poet Edith Thomas and the author-editor Charles Godfrey Leland were among the visitors, and several celebrated artists had taken up permanent residence in the city, including the sculptors Thomas E. Ball, Longworth Powers (son of Hiram Powers), and Larkin Mead (William Dean Howells' brother-in-law).[62] Their studios offered a rich assortment of artwork to view, and the city offered the Davises a continual round of socializing. Returning to New York in August ahead of the rest of the family, Dick described this time as "the happiest in my life," a sentiment shared by all the family.[63]

Just before Clarke left for Europe, William McKinley was nominated the Republican candidate for President. With Grover Cleveland no longer a candidate, Clarke returned to his Republican roots. Issues of currency and tariffs dominated the election in which McKinley would soundly defeat the Democrats' candidate, William Jennings Bryan. As part of his campaign materials, McKinley's camp published a collection of congratulatory letters sent to the candidate upon his nomination, *The People's Choice*. Included in the collection was Clarke's letter to McKinley: "Your Letter of Acceptance is certain to become a powerful influence for intelligent, conscientious voting. The financial issue has never before been presented in form so direct, clear, simple and convincing to those to whom it is so desirable, essential even, that the truth shall be made manifest. As a citizen and Republican, I thank you for its presentation."[64] In addition to politicians and businessmen, several newspaper editors joined Clarke in praising McKinley, including William Penn Nixon of Chicago's *Inter-Ocean*; Frank McPhillips of the Bay City, Michigan, *Tribune*; R. C. Alexander of New York's *Mail and Express*; and Charles Emory Smith of the Philadelphia *Press*. In a few years, Clarke's support of McKinley would be greatly challenged, but at this point, he admired the man.

The family's true enthusiast for McKinley, however, was Dick. His support at this time of America's imperialism and sense of national superiority had been blatantly revealed in *Three Gringos*. As the *San Francisco Call* noted in its review of the book (appearing in the same issue as their review of *Doctor Warrick's Daughters*),

> One of the conclusions that he reaches is that "the Central American citizen is no more fit for a republican form of government than he is for an Arctic expedition, and what he needs is to have a protectorate established over him either by the United States or another power, it does not matter which so long as it leaves the Nicaraguan canal in our hands. Away from the coasts, where there is fever," Mr. Harding says, "Central America is a wonderful country, rich and beautiful, and burdened with plenty, but its people make it a nuisance and an affront to other nations, and its parcel of independent little States with the pomp of power and none of its dignity are and will continue to be a constant danger to the peace which should exist between two great powers."[65]

Dick would soon transfer this attitude to Cuba as well, in contrast to his parents' antiwar stance.

The Davises returned to the States and spent a short time at Marion in September. When Rebecca, Clarke, and Nora returned to Philadelphia in late September, they reestablished the salon that included brunches before matinees and post-edition gatherings for their artist and actor friends.[66] As fondly as Rebecca and Clarke were held within the social and artistic communities of Philadelphia, Dick was not. His ego became the topic of numerous satiric commentaries that appeared in various *Philadelphia Inquirer* columns at this time, such as "Poor, Poor Richard," "Too Much of the Czar," and "He's in Moscow" in which the newspaper collected a bevy of negative comments published by other papers. "Dicky" was a nickname fondly used by his friends, but the newspapers used it to satirize Dick's immaturity. "It must be lovely to be as wonderful as Richard Harding Davis," the papers commented, and "Dicky Harding Davis . . . may not be royal, but he can give the Czar points on aristocratic prejudices."[67] It was earned to a degree and largely the cost of celebrity. Within his own social circle, however, Dick was well liked and maintained many friends throughout his lifetime.[68]

The winter months of 1896 brought a number of tensions to the family. Dick was becoming increasingly interested in war correspondence, a development in his career that Rebecca would come to admire but which caused her even more worry than usual about her elder son because of the dangers he would face. It also raised the specter of Rebecca and Clarke's anti-war associations with a son whose career would find its greatest heights of fame while he was covering war zones. The election of William McKinley pleased Clarke and elated Dick. Dick and his friends celebrated in the streets of uptown New York all night, while the "plain people," as he termed them, went downtown,

> cheering all the time and trying to find a Bryan man to lick, but everybody was the other way—Dana and I marched in the Sound Money Parade. It was a great sight the Republicans adopted the flag as their emblem and American flags were hung from the battery to 42nd Street up Broadway and 5th Avenue and on *every cross street* east and west completely blocking the view. It was the most effective campaign trick I ever saw.[69]

The election of a Republican president meant that Charley's appointment as consul would end with the new administration, and he would have to return to the States, find employment, and rebuild his literary career.

The aftermath of the election, however, brought devastating news to the family: the death of Clarke's nephew, Almyr Cooper. It was a haunting echo of

Dick's joking about finding "a Bryan man to lick." The family believed the circumstances of Cooper's death were suspicious and not likely to have been an accident. Clarke joined Almyr's wife, the actress Isabelle Evesson, in questioning his death after Cooper purportedly walked into a saloon and collapsed. Although some accounts claimed he had fallen and hit his head, an autopsy revealed he had a fracture at the base of his skull that could not have been caused by a fall. His death occurred the evening after McKinley's election. A William Jennings Bryan supporter, Cooper was known for his outspoken harangues against McKinley, and speculation was that he may have been attacked on the street after voicing such opinions and then stumbled into the saloon. The family was never able to gain a satisfactory accounting of what had happened that night or who may have murdered Cooper.[70]

The event cast a dismal pall over the holidays that was not lifted for Rebecca and Clarke when, in mid-December, Dick and Frederick Remington left to cover the Cuban war for independence for the New York *Journal*—not because his parents opposed Cuban independence (they did not) but because Dick left without telling them. Rebecca was stunned to receive a letter from him while he was at Key West waiting for transport. He explained he had been in too much of a hurry to let her know, but it was more likely he did not want to hear her concerns. She and Clarke worried endlessly about Dick while he was gone. Dick regarded war as "a senseless wicked institution"—not because, like his parents, it was brutal and often immoral, but because of the makeshift nature of travel and accommodations during wartime.[71] Little could the Davises or the nation know what great part war was about to play in their lives.

The next few years would be transitional for the family. In early 1897 a second novel Rebecca was crafting would appear, and later that year she would return to the *Independent* under a new publisher and on her own terms. Clarke continued his successful work on the *Public Ledger*, but he would have increasing bouts of illness and overall declining health to the extent that he and Rebecca began to spend much of January and February each year in Florida as a reprieve from the harsh Philadelphia winters. Dick would turn seriously to war reporting at the end of the century, and Charley would end his term as consul in Italy and return to the States to build his literary career. Nora would continue her life among the socially elite but depend largely on her brothers to expand her horizons through travel and entertainments. The last years of the century would also bring death to a family member, and for Rebecca, a slowing of her productivity but a honing of her critical commentaries as the nation moved to war with Spain.

Chapter 12

War Years (1897–1899)

At the end of 1896, Davis's novel "Frances Waldeaux" had been serialized in *Harper's Bazar* with strong praise by critics. Davis always preferred a high-literary periodical with a sophisticated readership, but she had felt compelled her entire career to couple that desire with a consideration of how well the magazine was willing to pay her for her artistic work. Thus, she had first approached Richard Watson Gilder at the *Century* about publishing the novel in his magazine: "I have done a foolish thing—written a novel—and finished it—without saying a word to any magazine publisher about taking it. Now, of course, you all have serials engaged for many years! Still—will you look at it? Nobody has a word of it but Dick, who thinks it the best work I have ever done. All I know is that it is very unlike anything else I ever did. Please let me hear from you soon."[1]

The novel was indeed "unlike anything else" she had written. It was set almost entirely in Europe, and it more forthrightly considered the complex sexual and familial relationships of her characters. Gilder asked to see the manuscript, promising to read it himself. When she sent it, she added, "It is heroic in you to offer to read it yourself. But as you have undertaken it, may I ask you, if the first chapters seem slow to you—*to finish it?*"[2] Gilder wrote across the top of Rebecca's letter a note to acknowledge receipt with a special letter, but he apparently passed again on publication of a novel by Davis, or he offered too low a price—either of which was surprising since her last novel, *Doctor Warrick's Daughters*, had garnered both critical and financial success, and it had been only two years since it appeared, which meant she had a strong novel-reading audience ready for another book from her. For whatever reason, Davis placed *Frances Waldeaux* with *Harper's Bazar* for serialization and book publication with Harper's Brothers in early 1897. Harper's was dedicated to British publication of Davis's novels as well, and again a London edition appeared simultaneously.

Frances Waldeaux was dedicated to Nora with the salute, "A Remembrancer of Brittany for the Best Fellow-Traveller in the World." Although the main characters were a doting mother, Frances, and her condescending son, George, this provocative novel was more broadly about the impact of family secrets, both in their keeping and in their revelation. Everyone believed Frances had inherited wealth, but she secretly worked to put her son through Harvard and fund their voyage to Europe. She began earning money in the manner Davis had long advocated for women who wanted to work at home—raising fine fruit and flowers that she sold in the Philadelphia market and then trading in high breeds of poultry and cattle. But Frances had always had a desire to write and a distinct talent for amusing critiques: "Her fun was not vulgar, but coarse and biting enough to tickle the ears of the common reader. The editor offered her a salary equal to her whole income for a weekly column of such fooling." She feared that George would discover "his mother is the 'Quigg' of the New York——, a paper which he declared to be unfit for a gentleman to read."[3]

The novel offered an insightful character study of a middle-aged woman; it was more realistic and overt about sexuality than Davis's earlier works as well, including Frances's short but brutal marriage, after which she eschewed another relationship in favor of an extreme devotion to her son. As Frances admitted, her obsession with George had left her "like one of those plants that have lost their own sap and color, and suck in their life from another. It scares me sometimes."[4] Equally overt was Davis's depiction of Frances's daughter-in-law Lisa, whose life of being used by and using men to survive resulted in a desire for sexual and emotional revenge. For all of the cruelty in the battle between mother and daughter-in-law, the novel's conclusion specifically affirmed the importance of professional work for older women. When a friend reminded Frances she was getting old and suggested she stop working, Frances resisted. She would continue to work and exercise her mind as long as she could and asserted, "'But *I* am not growing old. . . . Even out in that other world I shall not be only a mother. I shall be me. *Me!* After a million of years—it will still be me.' There stirred within the lean body and rheumatic limbs depths of unused power, of thought, of love and passion, and deeper than all, aw[e]ful possibilities of change."[5] The last line could have been written about Davis herself.

Many reviews recognized the change in Davis's writing in this novel, which was much more modern in theme and style. That change led to the few negative reviews the novel received, primarily from religious periodicals. The *Western Christian Advocate* was representative of this perspective, when its reviewer asserted concern for the "very sordid set of lives" examined in the novel; "it is scarcely above the level of a newspaper 'sensation,' and gives nothing to conscience, heart or mind." The *Portland Oregonian* reviewer felt Davis was a better short story writer than novelist and that this novel would have made a "capital" short story because after beginning "brilliantly," the last part of the novel became "commonplace." *The Outlook* also offered a mixed review; it praised her characterizations but felt there was "a tinge of melodrama in the crisis of the plot which seems a little out of Mrs. Davis real province as a novelist. The fun of the book, on the other hand, is natural and effective."[6]

The majority of reviews, however, positively embraced the "distinct departure from [Davis's] early style." As the *Literary World* noted, "Of old she was wont to write, so to speak, enigmatically. It was not easy, always, to make out exactly what her sentences were meant to say; but a process of clarification has taken place, analogous to that produced by dropping the albumen of eggs into a clouded jelly, and what was turgid has become brilliantly clear. *Frances Waldeaux* ... is a fresh and entertaining story ... and we commend it to readers." William Morton Payne in the *Dial* agreed it was "an exceptionally strong piece of literary work," and several reviewers agreed with the Lexington *Morning Herald* that the novel was "brilliant."[7]

Harper's paid Davis $700 for this shorter novel; and though their standard contract for novels paid ten percent royalties for the book publication after the first one thousand copies, they agreed to her demand for fifteen percent royalties on all copies.[8] With again strong sales, the lesser pay up front in favor of royalties on all copies was a wise choice. In spite of the success of both *Doctor Warrick's Daughters* and *Frances Waldeaux*, they were Davis's last novels. She would devote the remaining decade of her career to a few short stories and a significant body of nonfiction cultural commentaries. At sixty-five and with the income from these novels, Davis remained both professionally and financially secure enough to be as selective as she wished about how much she wrote and where she placed her work.

Rebecca was enjoying the success of *Frances Waldeaux* when news arrived that her brother Richard had died of Bright's disease on January 19, 1897. Richard Harris Harding had been living in St. Augustine, Florida, in recent years, and Rebecca may well have visited him when she and Clarke traveled to Ocala for the winter months. After Richard's death, Wilse went to St. Augustine to bring Richard home at last. He was buried in the Harding family plot. In a perhaps unwitting reminder of the pain Richard's charge of treason had caused the family, his burial site was not next to his parents' and brother Henry's graves, but in a separate row in front of them, forever near and yet isolated from the rest of his family, as he had been in life.

While coping with the loss of her brother, Rebecca was also anxious about Dick while he was in Cuba covering the war. In actuality, he was still having a difficult time even reaching the war zone and was stuck in Key West for a period of time.⁹ On the other hand, when he finally arrived in Havana, he received an encouraging letter from his father with assurance that he felt his son had made the right decision to cover the war.¹⁰ Dick recognized this was both an opportunity to make "a *lot* of money" because Hearst wanted his byline for the New York *Journal* and to discover "a great knowledge of myself and many new ideas on War which strikes me as being the damnest fool proposition still existing."¹¹ It was only the beginning of discussions the Davis family would have about the merits of war, and Dick's letter gave an inkling that his own beliefs were in flux, especially when he saw the cruel treatment of the Cubans.¹² At that time, however, he was an ardent advocate for US intervention.¹³

Dick always put himself in the center of his reporting, which inevitably led to derogatory commentaries about his self-focused war reports; the *Philadelphia Inquirer* gleefully collected and published the commentaries with notable frequency, including snipes such as "The Cuban war cannot end at present. Richard Harding Davis hasn't collected enough material for a novel down there yet" and "A baby wolf in the Boston zoo has been named after Richard Harding Davis. It is hard to tell why the honor was not bestowed upon a magpie."¹⁴ These personal attacks angered and hurt Rebecca; though she threw all of them in the trash, she could not ignore such constant criticism of her elder son. It was what she abhorred about the celebrity status of authors, because adulation inevitably turned to criticism at some point and did not reflect the work as much as opinions about an individual's personality.

By the first week in March, Dick was back in the States to cover President McKinley's inauguration. He stayed with Thomas Nelson Page and cavorted with the Vice President's son, which he reported only to Charley.¹⁵ A month later, Dick was again on his way to Europe for work and to visit Charley in Florence. While abroad, he sent his article about the inauguration to Rebecca, who was still his most effectual critic and copyeditor. He asked that she edit it, have Clarke read it to fact-check his various assertions about past elections and the number of votes for Bryan, and then send it on to Harper's.¹⁶

In the early spring of 1897, the brothers had works appearing simultaneously; Dick's essay on Budapest was published in *Scribner's* at the same time Charley's story "La Gommeuse" appeared in *Harper's*. While in London, Dick dined with representatives of the generation of realist writers who, like Rebecca, combined careers in journalism and fiction: Stephen Crane and Harold Frederic.

Shortly after Dick left for Europe, Clarke became so severely ill that Dick offered to come home, but his parents discouraged him from doing so. Before Clarke recovered, Nora also became ill, and the family designated Rebecca "dear Mother Head Nurse." Weeks later, when everyone had finally recovered, the parents' discussions with Dick again turned to finances. Rebecca and Clarke had taken over the "stewardship" of Dick's finances, and he thanked both of them when they reported he now had several thousand in savings.[17] This shift was immensely important for his future.

Rebecca devoted much of the spring to her family, caring for them while they were ill and aiding their career plans. While Charley was preparing to return to the States, he was in negotiations with R. H. Russell, a publisher of theatrical works, for an editorial position. In April, while visiting Charley, or "Gus" as the family often called him, Dick had written his mother. "Everyone is so kind to Gus and he is so popular. . . . Gus is looking better than I have ever seen him and he is very much delighted with . . . his getting congenial work with Russell—I am sure when Russell comes he will make him senior partner."[18] Russell was impressed with Charley's knowledge of drama and his critical abilities, but negotiations would take several months to conclude.

While following her sons' activities and caring for Clarke, Rebecca had managed to write two pieces, both published in April. The first was a historical narrative for *Youth's Companion*, "President-Making in Old Times." This was her last contribution to the magazine, the culmination of twenty-six years of writing for *Youth's Companion*. Though she would never forego seeking the best rates for her publications, her ability in these years to choose the quality of a magazine over its payment rates allowed her to place her children's literature hereafter exclusively in *St. Nicholas*.

Davis's second work this month, "Some Hobgoblins in Literature," appeared as the lead item of the *Book Buyer* and represented Davis's most overt challenge to the cult of celebrity. Critiquing both the idolization of Margaret Fuller and Walt Whitman as well as the demonizing of Edgar Allan Poe, she asked, "Why should we not give up our habit of throwing Roentgen rays into our men of genius to discover abnormal vices and virtues in them? It is time that we understood that the light of genius may burn in a man, and yet that he will be in no sense a god or a fiend, but remain a very ordinary fellow."[19]

Reprints of Davis's recent and earlier works also appeared in numerous periodicals in the 1890s, including in *Zion's Herald*, the *Christian Observer*, Chicago's *Manford's Magazine*, London's *Ladies Treasury* and *Christian Commonwealth*, Australia's *Traralgon Record*, Wales' *The Cambrian*, as well as in numerous American and British collections of the best literature of the year or decade. It was in these years that the canonization of American literature was gaining force, and while Davis was typically included in the various tomes that canonized US and world literatures, when she was not, the oversight was quickly noted by critics. For example, when *American Authors, 1795–1895* was published, *The Critic*'s reviewer welcomed the bibliography but admonished the publisher for the failure to include Davis.

This year the Davis family dominated *Harper's Monthly* with publications by Rebecca, Dick, and Charley. In May, Rebecca published "The Education of Bob" in the magazine. As she aged, reminiscences about her childhood years in Wheeling increasingly entered her writings. "Some Hobgoblins" had begun with a recollection of her first meeting with a woman author as a schoolgirl, and "The Education of Bob" was set in post-war Virginia and populated with characters from her earlier stories, such as Colonel Champernoun, who had appeared years earlier in "A Story of Life-Insurance" (*Peterson's*, 1862) and elsewhere. But this story also embraced newer ideas, such as young Lizzy Yorke becoming a telegraph operator, which allowed her to bring news from all over the world to her small community. Typical of Davis's romances, the story concluded with a happy marriage and the gaining of unexpected wealth, based on Lizzy's decision to act in an honest rather than self-serving way. It was one of the few short stories Davis published in these years, and it blended the old and the new about American culture.

Davis had again reached her stride in producing significant works on a regular basis. If she was more likely in these years to publish one and occasionally two works each month rather than the four to six per month that had appeared in her most productive years, the steady output and the quality of her work, as well as the frequent reprints of her stories and articles, kept her before the public as one of America's premier writers.

At the same time "Hobgoblins" appeared, Charley published "La Gommeuse" in *Harper's*, and Dick's *Soldiers of Fortune* soon appeared as well. It was one of his most successful novels and continued his enamored celebration of US imperialism, with the hero triumphing over supposedly lazy and corrupt Latin counterparts.[20] The Davis Family of writers seemed to be everywhere in the publishing world in the late 1890s.

After the tumultuous spring, by summer everyone in the family was healthy again, and Nora served as one of the hosts for the Archaeological and Paleontological Department of the University of Pennsylvania when it held an elaborate opening for Dr. William H. Furness's exhibit of his photographic and artifactual collections from Borneo, which served as the department's founding collections. Son of the Davis family's friend, Howard Horace Furness, Dr. Furness's travels were financed by his father, a trustee of the university, and his heiress mother.[21] The connections that Rebecca and Clarke had with Philadelphia's elite culture afforded Nora frequent opportunities to participate in these kinds of events and to find a means to be active outside the home.

In June, the family celebrated when Rebecca's brother Wilse retired as a professor of engineering and physics from Lehigh University. He had been responsible for expanding the university's engineering studies into a four-year course that became recognized for its quality and the caliber of students who graduated from the program. A beloved professor, tributes came from faculty and students, and the university acknowledged that his retirement meant the loss of a "distinguished man of science" and a dedicated teacher.[22] Sometime after his retirement, however, Wilse moved to Seattle to live near his sister Emilie. With his move, Rebecca was the last of the Harding siblings in the east, and she particularly felt Wilse's absence.

The entire Davis family gathered at Marion this year as Charley prepared to return permanently to the States. Part of the national fame The Davis Family now attracted was to be tracked regularly in the *Social Register*, which announced the summer plans of the elite of New York, Philadelphia, Chicago, Boston, and Baltimore.[23]

At the same time, Dick continued to be flagrantly satirized in newspapers. *Life* magazine published a satiric poem by Carolyn Wells that acknowledged the entertainment of the Van Bibber and Gallegher stories but concluded, "But from his war-notes, the saints save us."[24] The *Philadelphia Inquirer* renewed its barrage of criticism as well, yet the newspaper also accurately captured the cult of personality that nurtured his fame, often at precisely the cost that Wells' poem revealed: "regardless of the individual or personal criticism of Mr. Davis," the *Inquirer*'s reviewer observed, "the latter has the satisfaction of knowing that he cannot be ignored, that he has a personality that thrusts itself forward in a most persistent way."[25] In contrast, Rebecca made a rare public appearance this month when she presented two addresses before the Unitarians at the Isles of Shoals where they were holding meetings and a memorial service for the poet Celia Thaxter, whom Davis had known and admired for many years.[26]

This summer the Davises began to add Warm Springs, Virginia, to their summer haunts. Warm Springs was not as fashionable as Hot Springs, but it was a spot where the well-to-do gathered as well. It attracted primarily the old aristocracy of the South and the West while Hot Springs attracted the newly wealthy. Hot Springs could be reached by rail, but continuing on to Warm Springs required another five miles of travel up the mountains. Undoubtedly, part of the appeal for Rebecca was its locale in the mountains where she loved walking, its genuine Virginia cooking, and that it provided "the atmosphere of a first-class southern home." But it also retained the post-war resort practice of having only African American servants who aided in establishing a sense of the Old South, a resort trait she had criticized in "Here and There in the South."[27]

In these years Rebecca continued to write unsigned political and social commentaries for Richard Watson Gilder's *Century Magazine*. At one point Gilder asked her to flesh out a point and questioned a comment she made in one submission, and she replied from Warm Springs: "Here is my little screed. I have tried to fill it out but I have little straw for my bricks.... Please send the cheque—a big generous cheque—to me at the Warm Springs."[28] It was rare that editors asked for more than minor revisions of Davis's submissions, and this humorous defense of the way it was written was typical. Someone at the *Century* had written "How long?" across the top of her letter, but the check must have been generous enough because she continued to write for the magazine.

Change could be beneficial as well, however. The previous year the *Independent*'s publisher, Henry Chandler Bowen, had died. Although the Bowen family would continue to control the magazine, William Hayes Ward had been made editor-in-chief upon Bowen's death and thus had greater control over efforts to meet Davis's requested fees for fiction and articles. Though financial relations would remain frustrating at times, Davis liked the magazine's audience and she liked working with Ward. So in August she wrote him from Warm Springs: "It is a long time since I sent you any comments on the world and its ways. So I hope you will welcome this little paper. It is something which I thought somebody ought to say *now*. If you do not want it please let me know *at once*." Ward had always admired Davis's work and immediately accepted "Two Points of View," which appeared in the September 1897 issue.

In this essay, Davis assessed W.E.B. DuBois's *Atlantic Monthly* article on prejudice in the US. In a nuanced argument that revealed how closely she followed leaders of the civil rights movement at the end of the century, she quoted liberally from DuBois's arguments and agreed with his assessment of prejudice against the race, "No candid white man can deny the justice of this passionate arraignment of the dominant race. The prejudice against the Negro in the

Northern States has been as unjust and cruel in its effects as was slavery. We opened our schools and universities to him, and when he was ready and eager to earn his living we barred every way before him except those which led to the kitchen and the barber-shop," and she cited Frederick Douglass as an example of the struggle.[29]

Yet Davis also peppered her positive race commentary with xenophobic comparisons, "This prejudice is as silly as it is cruel. Slavery at least had its advantages—for the slaveholder. But the angry whim which bars a large class of educated, able, moral, native American citizens out of the professions and the markets of the country because of the coloring matter in their skins, while it admits the lowest output of European slums, is blind and suicidal."[30]

It was the despair with which DuBois, Booker T. Washington, and Bishop Benjamin Tanner expressed their sense of progress to date and the future that Davis resisted, preferring the attitude expressed in the report published by the General Negro Conference at Hampton that had been authored by Douglass and others. It "shows that there is another side; that a spirit which is neither that of despair nor defeat animates this struggling people. The paper is a message from their leaders, men and women of acknowledged high culture and ability to the whole Negro race." Yet she continued to use terminology such as "the dusky clans" and to assume that she could offer better counsel than leaders such as DuBois:

> The Negro should remember, however that his progress depends, not on his affiliation, political, mercantile or social, with the whites, but on the development of his own people. The time that he spends in striving for recognition by the paler race, in denouncing them or upbraiding them, is only so much time wasted. He should remember, too, that he suffers from no more cruel prejudice than did the Goth in Italy, the Moor in Spain, and the Jew in all Christendom.

What mattered, she concluded, was how far up the hill he would go, the hill which every man must climb.[31] The article was representative of Davis's complex, hybrid conservative and progressive ideas that marked her thinking in these years.

By fall when Rebecca and Clarke returned to Philadelphia, they still hoped Charley might be reappointed as Consul in Florence by McKinley, but when that did not happen, he returned to the States, arriving in October. R. H. Russell, the premier publisher of plays in America, finalized an offer to him of an editorial position in his New York office, to begin in January. Announcements asserted that Charley had resigned his position in Italy to take the editorship, which cast a polite veil over his reasons for returning home.[32] The Russell publishing house, formerly the prestigious DeWitt Publishing, was internationally recognized for the quality of its theatrical publications. In the relationship Russell formed with Charley, Russell would become the head of the division of art and other books, and Charley would be the head of the division that published plays.

Charley's new position was an extraordinary high-water mark of the Davis family's long passion for the theater, from the days when Clarke took his young sons to plays, to the family's alliance with many playwrights and actors, to Dick's move into writing plays, to Charley's opportunity to shape the field of theatrical publications in the US. Charley would extend this influence in later years when he became the theatrical reviewer for the *New-York Tribune*. His immediate roster of playwrights included Henrik Ibsen, Edmond Rostand, Arthur W. Pinero, and Augustus Thomas. Charley and Dick would support one another's efforts in the field of dramatic publications just as the family had in all of its literary and journalistic endeavors. In New York, Charley settled into an apartment at 34 West 13th Street.[33] He could look to the future with great hope for a successful transition into the literary world as both writer and publisher.

That fall, Rebecca returned to writing for the *Independent* with enthusiasm, and "The Passing of Niagara" appeared in late November. The narrative "I" was unidentified by race, gender, or age, but the preference for sitting in "our little library" with other intellectuals who like "poring over old histories, or sipping poetry as if it were rare wine, or speculating on religion" was very much like the salon evenings at the Davis home, as was the narrative's rejection of the culture's current adoration of the commercial world. "The Passing of Niagara" was a parable about the dangers of materialistic capitalism and an example of Davis's interest in preserving the environment. The businessman in the story, Herr Wahn, insisted Niagara should be abandoned as a national example of environmental glory and instead be used as a water source for "turning machinery." Yet the parable was rooted once again in xenophobic comments, which placed much of the blame for the changing culture on the "incoming flood of ignorance and brutality. But the flood brought cheap labor." On the other hand, in this contribution, Davis did not denigrate Catholicism, as was so common in these days by non-Catholic authors and as she had done in the past. Rather, she equated Catholicism with patriotism and the good. The concluding moral was overt: the nation was "sacrificing now to the practical prosperity of the country not only a waterfall but our old-fashioned ideas of patriotism and honor and religion. We sell our votes, our offices and our creeds."[34]

Over the fall, Rebecca was also delighted as Clarke's health improved and he returned to his usual level of work and participation in civic events. He gave a lecture at Philadelphia's Art Club and was involved in the development of plans to host an international exposition of manufactured goods in the city. After months of organization, the event would be held from September to early December 1899 with great success.[35] He also attended a Gridiron Club dinner in Washington, D.C., as one of the "eminent guests" with Hawaiian President Sanford B. Dole as the honored guest of President McKinley's administration. Numerous foreign ambassadors and US senators attended. But Dole's imperialist policies were under strident attacks, and Queen Lili'uokalani had been calling for Hawaiian independence since her dethroning by the US in 1893. As an editor, the dinner was part of Clarke's business obligations, but the guest list was not compatible with his antiwar proclamations.

Early in January 1898 newspapers also ran an assessment of authors' pay rates, noting Arthur Conan Doyle, Rudyard Kipling, and Anthony Hope could name their price and that Mary E. Wilkins was almost on a par with her English contemporaries. The majority of the article, however, was devoted to Richard Harding Davis, who was now one of the highest-paid writers in the country. As much as newspapers liked to mock his war reporting and his self-aggrandizement, it had made him a celebrity of the first class with book sales to support that status. For the majority of authors, the article noted, rates had remained the same for the last decade,[36] and this was true for Rebecca as well.

On February 15, the *USS Maine* exploded in Havana harbor. President McKinley had been moving toward involvement in the war between Cuba and Spain, not for Cuban independence but so the US could purchase the island nation where American sugar interests had already bought large tracts of land that, along with changes in tariffs on sugar, had helped to foment the revolution. The sinking of the *Maine* gave McKinley the impetus he needed to enter the war. Dick had headed to Cuba earlier, hired by the *New York Herald* and the *London Times* to cover the war. When news of the sinking of the *Maine* arrived, Rebecca and Clarke had heard nothing from him for several weeks, and their fears were at full height until word arrived that he was safe.[37]

In spite of war in Cuba, life in the States continued much as usual. This year brought a notable—and short-lived—change in Rebecca's attitude toward publicity when she agreed to an interview with the literary critic and essayist Julia R. Tutwiler for the collection *Women Authors of Our Day in Their Homes*, edited by Francis Whiting Halsey. Davis knew Tutwiler from time spent together at Warm Springs and evidently felt assured that Tutwiler would present an honest representation of her beliefs and values. The collection included studies of Marion Harland, Agnes Repplier, Margaret Deland, Frances Hodgson Burnett, Harriet Prescott Spofford, Mary E. Wilkins, Edith Wharton, and others. In spite of her decision to grant the interview, Davis had changed little else about her policies toward publicity; most of the entries included photographs of the author and her home, but Davis declined both.

It was a revealing interview in which Davis had an opportunity to reflect on her career. She was often self-effacing about her publications, but in this interview she expressed sincere and amusing reflections on her past works. She insisted her first novel, *Margret Howth*, was "A funny little book in which I hammered my readers with the views and opinions smouldering for years in me—and forgot to tell a story," but she felt *Waiting for the Verdict* had retained its power and still reflected her attitudes toward the problems inherent in US culture. Tutwiler noted that *Waiting*, like everything Davis had written from *Dallas Galbraith* to *Frances Waldeaux*, invoked diverse opinions about its subject matter from readers, yet everyone agreed "as to the interest of the story and the quality that makes the interest."[38]

Tutwiler asked Davis which was more important in *Frances Waldeaux*, a man's love for his mother or his wife, to which Davis quickly responded, "That is for you to decide." This was a significant part of what Tutwiler admired about Davis: the author's "willingness to leave questions open, to acknowledge that every verdict must be an individual verdict; and an equally pronounced unwillingness to talk about herself, either as an individual or as an author, are distinctive traits of a writer who was one of the first American women to win international recognition as a thoughtful interpreter of American life and human nature."[39]

The collection as a whole was invested in the cult of personality, and Tutwiler admitted that her goal was "to bring Mrs. Davis's personality before her readers." She faithfully captured Davis's nuanced personality—"high-minded, persistent devotion to the profession of letters" and a great pride in her sons' literary success with a recognition that "maternal love is almost passion with her, and blending with it in scarcely unequal parts is love of country." Necessary to this type of writing about authors, Tutwiler added a personal description of Davis ("a square-cut face with strongly marked features, a reticent mouth, and earnest, dark brown eyes ready to kindle into merriment—the face of a woman who has thought and lived deeply and wisely—and a sense of right that refuses to bend to any sophistries about beauty or art for art's sake") before returning to specifications about Davis's "large sympathies" and a recognition of her keen sense of humor.[40]

Tutwiler also noted her subject's "simplicity and vividness of expression [that] make her a delightful companion." Having spent much time with Davis at Warm Springs, Tutwiler revealed her routine while at the resort:

> ...during the summers she spends at the Warm Springs, at the end of an hour's talk, she always manages to escape from the shady veranda, and the friends and acquaintances who would detain her there, to the little white weather-boarded one-story cottage, built flat to the ground, and overlooking a lawn beautiful with close-cut, freshly springing grass and noble trees. Here she writes all of the morning and most of the afternoon—what, she will never say, any more than she will discuss what she has already given to the public. Silence, stony in its impenetrableness, is her refuge from admirers who want to talk over her books.
>
> "But *why* won't you tell me anything when you know I have read and loved you ever since I was a little girl?" a young writer demanded one day.
>
> "Because when you are mad about a thing you should never talk about it," she returned, and fled incontinently to her cottage.[41]

Davis revealed to Tutwiler, however, two principles that had guided her writing throughout her career: "'There is no such thing as a generality that covers the ground it takes,' and 'If you want a reader to see a thing you must slap him in the face with it.'" In a final image of Davis, Tutwiler captured the author's broad interests: "Mrs. Davis's intellectual outlook is not confined to her home and literature. She is abreast with the thought and movement of the day, entering into the life around her with the enthusiasm which is one of her most helpful and inspiring qualities and which is tempered and individualized by the habit of reflection."[42] It was an honest and revealing interview, one that rewarded Davis's trust in Tutwiler's understanding of her attitudes toward her work and that captured the author and a life well lived.

Davis's next publication returned to the issue of race relations in America that she had discussed with Tutwiler. As with all of Davis's essays on race in these years, "Two Methods with the Negro" for the *Independent*'s March 1898 issue was a combination of insight and blindness. A facet of Davis's later style was that she became more personal in her commentaries, which was evidenced in this essay as well. Her insight was projected in a concern that the public had largely ignored Booker T. Washington's International Conference on the Negro at Tuskegee "with the noise of the 'Maine' explosion in its ears. . . . I know of no more important or dramatic action in contemporary history than the slow upgrowth of this nation within the American nation." The blindness came in her repeated insistence that W.E.B. DuBois and others undermined their effectiveness with bitterness, even while she admitted they had "naturally been made bitter and resentful by the cruel injustice of their treatment by the whites."[43] In many ways, Davis was far ahead of the majority of her white contemporaries in registering the full rights of African Americans and the injustices they faced, but she could not forego the sense of her own right to tell them what was the correct path to follow.

However much the Davises and other Americans tried to carry on their normal routines, the strife in Cuba hovered over everything, and on April 25, 1898, the US declared war on Spain. In spite of how frequently the *Philadelphia Inquirer* had lambasted Dick in the past, it proudly announced in late April that it had reached an agreement with the *New York Herald* to supply readers with news of the war from the *Herald's* war correspondents, first of whom was Richard Harding Davis. Suddenly, the *Inquirer* described Dick as "a brilliant and graphic writer."[44]

This association, however, put the *Inquirer* in direct competition with Clarke's *Public Ledger*. Clarke was furious that the *Inquirer* had been able to publish news of the bombardment of Matanzas before the *Ledger*. The *Inquirer* gloated and made the issue bitingly personal in an article about the competition: "What covers the Ledger with particular shame is the fact the Inquirer printed in full the graphic description by Richard Harding Davis, son of the managing editor of the Ledger, although a little amount of energy and newspaper sense would have made it possible for the Ledger to have used it also."[45] The war between Philadelphia newspapers, adding significantly to Clarke's stress, was becoming as intense as that on the battlefield.

At the same time, Charley was attempting to finalize a contract with the dramatist Robert Hilliard who had written a play based on Dick's short story, "Her First Appearance." The brothers developed a pattern at this time of integrating their professional lives that would last throughout their lifetimes. Responding to Charley's explanation of the negotiations, Dick added, "By all means close with Hilliard—I think I can place the play in London and we get you something out of it there. I call it a very good contract indeed and reflects much credit on your powers as a manager."[46] The negotiations would take considerable time, but finally *The Littlest Girl* was produced by Russell Publishing. Charley retained all copyrights for the plays he published under his own name, as with this play by Hilliard. In June, Russell Publishing moved to new offices at 34 West 30th Street, and *Publisher's Weekly* announced the move with a notice that Charles Belmont Davis was now the active business partner in the enterprise, which was dedicated to publishing all new plays as soon as they appeared in the US and England.[47]

Rebecca's entry into discussions of war at this time began with "Women and Patriotism" in the May issue of *Harper's Bazar*. The essay reflected her conflicted attitudes about the Spanish-American War. Promoted as a war to aid Cuban independence, she declared it to be "holy and just," but she cautioned women against their tendency to be "more intemperate haters than men." This tendency destroyed many homes during the Civil War, she recalled; it was a destructive behavior that often lasted long after a war's end. She also addressed the New Girls—a popular public term that in itself diminished the New Woman movement's quest for independence and new professional and political opportunities. Davis disdained some tactics by the New Girls to enter into the war itself, but she praised those who wished to perform hospital or sanitary work, traditions for women that had been acceptable during the Civil War and that Davis still held as the "proper" roles for women in wartime. Conservative as her perspective was, it had wide appeal, and "Women and Patriotism" was reprinted in several other magazines and newspapers in June as troops landed in Cuba.[48]

Davis continued writing children's stories as well. Mary Mapes Dodge was pleased to have Davis as a contributor again, and she published many of her stories in the coming years. In May 1898, Davis's "In Old Florence" marked her return to the magazine. Against her anti-immigrant commentaries, this story exposed Americans' hubris. Drawing on her knowledge of Florence from her visits there when Charley was consul, Davis used the history of the city and congeniality of its people to demonstrate how an arrogant young American who had just graduated from an academy and thought he would "Americanize . . . the 'Dagos'" when he settled in Florence learned that he was the one who needed a lesson in living a better life.[49]

In June Rebecca also published a tribute to Frances Willard in the *Ladies' Home Journal*. Willard had died in February, and Davis felt that the tributes published to date had looked at the public woman; she wanted to write about the private woman whom she had known. Willard was "one of the foremost women in the world," Davis asserted, not only for her activism and scholarship but for her maternal side as well. She was a kind and generous-spirited woman, and Davis noted she still had all of the letters Willard had written to her. In this tribute she wanted to present the ideal of Willard that she held, a woman who wielded "a lance . . . not a battle-axe." Davis never abandoned her preference for the "womanly woman," and Willard was the ideal of this image: the woman who retained her femininity while confronting the wrongs of the world.[50]

Rebecca, Clarke, and Nora had gone to Marion in late May for a month's stay before they returned to Philadelphia briefly and then travelled on to Warm Springs. They just missed crossing paths with Dick who returned to Marion in the summer to recover from malarial fever that he had contracted while reporting on the war. This time Rebecca did not nurse her son. Her concerns were directed toward Clarke. Although he was only sixty-three, Clarke's health was gradually deteriorating and the recent debacle with the *Inquirer* had not helped his constant battle with depression. She hoped the time at the Springs would help him recover his equilibrium. They were at Warm Springs in time for the Fourth of July celebrations. Julia Tutwiler's interview had captured an earlier moment of Rebecca's intense patriotism at Warm Springs: "Those who saw her when, at the Fourth of July dinner, the orchestra struck into 'The Star Spangled Banner' will never forget her. She was the first person on her feet, and as she faced the length of the large dining-room, her hands crossed on the chair in front of her, her head a little thrown back, she could have stood for Love and Renunciation—the model of the Christian mother and the Greek patriot."[51]

Charley took his summer vacation in August to join them. Nora and Charley loved the socializing that defined Warm Springs, and they attended numerous gala parties during the season, including an allemande, which the society reporter for the Richmond *Dispatch* was careful to note was an evening "of quiet grace and refinement." The reporter admired Nora's beautiful outfit of a "black satin and sixteenth-century silver girdle" and added that Charley had won the prize of a Russian leather and silver card case.[52] Rebecca participated as well, and as the season was coming to an end, she hosted a dance, a "flower german," for the summering crowd.[53]

Throughout their summer travels, Rebecca had continued to write, publishing "The Death of John Payne" in the *Independent*, one of the few short stories she published this year. Many stories and commentaries published during these months turned to the Civil War as a means of reflecting on the current war. Davis's story, however, entered into the current debate over pensions for veterans who were not seriously wounded, which she opposed. While this story clearly had implications for the Spanish-American War, it was in August that Davis turned specifically to that conflict with an article for the *Independent*, "The Surprises of War." Davis had not been among the Americans on the left who initially opposed the war; in the early stages of the war, she had believed the government's argument that its motive was Cuban independence, which she deemed "the purest and most unselfish that ever caused a war."[54]

By this point in August, however, she recognized the horrific mismanagement of the war. She offered a damning assertion that the management of the war had been "a stupendous failure," both in military actions when the soldiers did not have ample artillery and in the brutal treatment of troops, camped in "fever-haunted swamps," and the wounded who were left in such conditions, "dying of fever [with] no bandages, no medicines, no tents to shelter them from the incessant storms . . . The War Department refused to bring them home, because the transports were needed to carry troops to Porto Rico, on a picnic parade, intended to gratify the military pride of certain States whose vote was uncertain in the next campaign." The story was known, she acknowledged, but *knowing* was not sufficient: "Well, what do you make of it? Were the mistakes due to a lack of practical ability . . . or to the political corruption which would sacrifice scores of human lives to keep inefficient men in office and insure success in a coming campaign? The true answer to that question," she concluded, "is of more importance to us than the acquisition of Cuba or the Philippines."[55]

When the peace treaty was signed in December, Cuban independence was granted, but Puerto Rico and Guam were ceded to the US, which was also guaranteed the right to purchase the Philippine Islands for $20 million. Three thousand men lost their lives in the four-month war—only ten percent from battle; ninety percent died from infectious diseases.[56] Although Dick also abhorred the treatment of soldiers, the war exposed the differences of opinion mother and son held about war and imperialism. She increasingly exposed the underbelly of imperialistic endeavors, while he returned from covering the war more ardent than ever in his belief in US imperialism.[57]

During these late summer and fall months, Rebecca returned to publishing more broadly following the pattern of her most productive years. In addition to the *Independent*, the *Ladies' Home Journal*, and *St. Nicholas*, she published in *Harper's Bazar* and the *Congregationalist*. "In Proof of To-morrow" for the September *Harper's Bazar*, Davis recorded her meeting with a mulatto woman she had met while at Warm Springs. As she came to know the woman, talking privately with her about her life, she felt there "is no work in this country which seems to me so urgent as the uplifting of the negro race." The woman and her husband were, to Davis's minds, models of the good lives many African Americans were leading. As missionaries to the Congo, the family had faced great losses and, while they had been unable to convert any adults, the woman insisted, "The hope is in the children."[58]

While Rebecca was articulating her opinions in the *Independent* and *Harper's Bazar*, Dick continued to write about his Cuban experiences, turning to *Scribner's* as well as newspapers, and preparing collections of his writings for book publication. But the most exciting news for the family was the publication of Charley's first book, *The Borderland of Society*. Published by Chicago's H. S. Stone publishing house, which included Harold Frederic and Henry James among its authors, it was an act of independence from Charley, breaking with the family's usual places of publication to place the book on his own. If he wished his work to be assessed on its own merits, however, it was a losing battle. The advertising for the book played on the notion of The Davis Family of authors, and most reviewers used that theme to assess the collection. As the Lexington *Herald* simply put it, "kinship" would assure attention for the book.[59] Similar reviews based on the famous Davis Family name appeared in *Current Literature, Current Opinion*, the London *Academy*, and *Munsey's*. Although the *Philadelphia Inquirer* insisted that Charley had modeled his writing style on neither that of Rebecca nor Dick, writing from the borderlands of society was precisely how Rebecca had established her own career in the 1860s and thereafter.

The winter of 1898 in New York offered the Davis siblings a whirlwind of parties with many friends who were in the city again in the post-war season. Nora was particularly enjoying the social season, often joined by Dick. In early November they went to Delmonico's with Helen and Stanford White, Louise Clark, Ethel Barrymore, and others, arriving in a special car to great fanfare. The Davises knew the architect White from his days at Marion when he was remodeling the Gilders' home.[60] The siblings partied through the night, arriving back at Dick's apartment at forty-thirty in the morning. Dick knew his mother would not approve, especially for Nora, so when he wrote her, he focused only on Charley's success and their brotherly comradery: "Dear Mother, Here I am in Charley's office with all his pretty things about me and each of us is smoking a fine segar. I am having a grand time and getting the book done. I see the Scribner's nearly every day and they are sure the war book will be a great 'money maker'—Charley is so dear over his work and so happy and everyone likes him so much."[61]

The next year would prove to be a much happier one for the family with the war over, Rebecca's continued writing, Charley's success in publishing and writing, and Dick's marriage. It was a year of many transitions for The Davis Family of writers, both in their careers and their personal lives. The first item Rebecca published in January was a lengthy review for *Harper's Bazar* of Inshata Theumba's (Susette La Flesche) book. Davis recalled her instant admiration of Inshata Theumba when they first met nearly twenty-five years earlier. She found the Native American woman's book of little historical value but of "great human interest." The review focused primarily on the ways in which, despite cultural differences, Inshata Theumba's people were so "very like our own." "Some of the men and women introduced to us" by the author, she added, "are of so high a caste that we feel that we have found a red-skinned Sidney and Sir Roger, and think the better of ourselves that we have been keeping such good company."[62] Davis had rarely signed book reviews in the past, but in the next decade she would publish a select number of signed reviews or book-cover blurbs for Native American and African American writers to help promote their work to a wider reading public.

Davis published a second essay in January, "The Work Before Us," in the *Independent*. It was inspired by news from England of Lord Kitchener's success at the Battle of Khartoum, also known as the Battle of Karari.[63] The Sirdar had announced that, with funds from the British, they would establish the Gordon Memorial College in Khartoum. With a highly acerbic tone, Davis commented, "Having successfully avenged Gordon's death by the slaughter (planned for fourteen years) of tens of thousands of Dervishes and negroes, [the Sirdar] now proposes at once to elevate the miserable conquered residue." Her primary goal, however, was to force Americans to reflect on their own moral failings, rooted in capitalistic greed and imperialistic desires:

> What condition is the American in just now to become the controller and guide of an alien brother? Is his own domestic life clean and unselfish and noble with content and simplicity, or is it tawdry with vulgar display and mean ambitions? Are his public men working for their country, or for the next election? Is the press just and dignified and free from scurrility and filth? Does he really at heart worship God—or money?[64]

The magazine's editors chose to publish Davis's essay but add their own disclaimer. Agreeing with her argument that religion should not be excluded from education, they went on at length to discredit the rest of the article, including disdain for her argument that instruction at the College should use the people's own language rather than English.⁶⁵

The Critic's editors, Jeannette Gilder and her brother Joseph Gilder, had always been effective promoters of Rebecca's work, and in January Charley joined the magazine as an "occasional contributor" with an article about Charles Dana Gibson's art. The article clearly demonstrated the effects of The Davis Family's networking to support one another's careers—not only was Rebecca's influence used to benefit Charley's connection to the magazine, but he extended this pattern to support their friend Gibson. The intricacies of this network, begun by Rebecca and Clarke and adapted to include their author-sons, had created a dynamic force in publishing throughout the last half of the nineteenth century.

As Charley was learning, however, family connections sometimes led to bad publicity as well. Although Dick received most of the personalized negative press, Charley's book publication began to align him more fully with his brother and not always in complementary ways, as evidenced in an item published in the *Broadway Magazine*. After briefly noting the publication of *Borderlands*, the reviewer turned to an ad hominem attack against Charley, who always struggled with his weight: "Mr. Davis is a big, thick gentleman with small grace and large feet.... His face usually carries that appearance of vivacity and geniality displayed by a sleeping Newfoundland.... I cannot help expressing surprise that Richard Harding Davis and Charles Belmont could possibly belong to the same family."⁶⁶ If Rebecca privately fretted over Charley's weight, this public attack would have outraged her, as any criticism of her children did.

As Rebecca and Clarke were preparing to leave for several weeks in Florida over the winter,⁶⁷ she was contacted by the dramatist, novelist, and a *St. Nicholas* editor, Albert Bigelow Paine. Indicating he had admired *Kent Hampden*, he explained his desire to publish another novel for juveniles if she had a project available. She responded with interest in a collection of short stories for girls; Davis envisioned the collection's stories would all be set in the same village like her friend Margaret Deland's *Old Chester Tales*. Whether it was because Paine did not want a collection of stories for girls or they could not reach an equitable agreement over the rate of pay, no such collection appeared. Davis would, however, publish several girls' stories in *St. Nicholas* over the coming years.

When Dick left for London on a work assignment in February, Rebecca sent him a letter demonstrating the love and admiration she had for her elder son:

I have been reading lately steadily over two shelves of my favorite author. I've been reading for[?] trying to be a critic. But somehow you always get your hand on one's heart & give it a squeeze and there's an end of criticism! It's too human. People may criticize this or that writer & applaud—usually stupidly. But they just love *you*. Do you know—do you begin to guess what it is to me that you have written them? You struck your great decisive blow before you were forty. And *it is struck*, and I'm your mother. God has been good to me.[68]

While in London, Dick decided to propose to Cecil Clark. In his usual quest for publicity, he hired a fourteen-year-old boy, William Jaggers, to fly from London to Chicago with a ring to cement the proposal he had earlier made to Cecil, who had not yet given him an answer. Though he tried to profess shock at the international clamor made by the adventure of Jaggers, he undoubtedly had informed the papers of what he was doing. He asked Rebecca to take care of Jaggers while the boy was in the States, "I am sure you will make the poor little chap comfortable—I do regret having sent him on such a journey especially since the papers have made such an infernal row over it. However, neither of us will lose by it in the end."[69] After a period of resisting Dick's overtures, Cecil's acceptance set in motion plans for the first marriage among the Davis siblings.

Amidst all of the excitement, Rebecca managed to pen another timely discussion for the *Independent*'s April issue. "Two 'Servants of the Republic'" was a political, environmental, and social indictment of national and local governments' practices. It also demonstrated that Rebecca still advocated cremation in opposition to the Philadelphia Council's allowing drainage from cemeteries and cesspools into the water system, which caused daily deaths. The essay also continued her attack on the federal government's mismanagement of the Cuban campaign and the harm they had done to their own ailing soldiers; it also condemned national and local politicians' attempts to cover up their actions in order to be reelected, including their dubious granting of Civil War pensions.

Davis did not reject pensions for men who had truly served their country but those "who were bounty-jumpers, who were drafted and sent substitutes, still others who, being drafted, escaped by pleading incurable ailments. None of these men ever saw a day's service or came in sight of the battle-field." On the other hand, she argued for a civil pension list as well as a military one, so civil servants who had worked their entire lives and were injured on the job would not have to rely on the kindness of strangers or die of want. Pensions should be granted to those men in the military or civil service who were injured or lost the ability to work, "*and to such men only*," she concluded.[70] In this instance, the *Independent*'s editorial commentary explicitly supported Davis's position.[71]

Much of the spring was devoted to plans for Dick and Cecil's wedding, and on May 4, 1899, the elaborate ceremony took place in Marion at St. Gabriel's chapel with the Boston Episcopalian minister Rev. Percy Browne presiding. Browne had frequented Marion over the years and had become a friend of the Davises and the Clevelands. Ethel Barrymore, as maid of honor, was Cecil's only attendant, while Dick had Charley as his best man and several groomsmen, including Charles Dana Gibson. The groom and attendants walked to the chapel, but Cecil arrived in a surrey covered with ribbons and drawn by two pure white steeds. After the ceremony, the guests returned to the Clarks' estate for a reception on their vast lawn.

It was at the reception that a photograph of the attendees was taken for the *Boston Sunday Journal*, which had exclusive rights for the wedding. For the first time in more than thirty years, Rebecca appeared in a photograph; it was the one time she could not refuse, but she turned to the side, so as little of her face as possible is visible (see Figure 4).[72] Seated next to Clarke, with Dick at their feet, a trim-figured Rebecca with her hair in a thick twist gazes with a smile at Cecil. Others in the photograph included Charley in the center of the group; Nora, seated near Cecil; and friends from New York, Boston, Philadelphia, and Washington, D.C., as well as the very wealthy Clarks' Chicago friends.

Rebecca adored her daughter-in-law. Cecil was a charming, athletic, and politically astute woman who would travel with Dick to Africa, South America, England, Europe, and Japan. Though Rebecca would worry about their safety when they were in war zones, she loved the dynamic energy and willingness of Cecil to create an egalitarian marriage. Cecil was also a show-dog breeder, but most importantly, she was developing her own career as a portrait painter, and in the coming years she would be a highly regarded artist whose portraits of Charles Lindbergh, numerous society figures, and the actress Dai Turgeon revealed her remarkable talent. Cecil also made extraordinary efforts to assure Dick's siblings and parents that nothing about their close relationship would change, and she included them in everything she and Dick did for the remainder of their marriage.[73] Cecil also became a first reader of Dick's work and an astute critic. In all ways, Cecil quickly became an integral part of the Davis family.

While Dick and Cecil honeymooned in France and London, Rebecca published an article on education in the *North American Review* that became one of her most controversial publications. "The Curse of Education" was her only article in the conservative periodical. The article elaborated on an idea that had appeared in passing in Davis's works over the years—that people should be educated to their appropriate level and not taught that they will all be great scientists or writers or the President of the United States. The rhetoric with which she expressed this fullest sense of her ideas rightfully brought outrage from some quarters. Xenophobic and racist allusions undermined the seriousness of her argument. She tried to emphasize that she was not suggesting there could be "too much education," only that it was the nation's responsibility "to develop [each student's] individual capacity and to fit him for his especial place in life"; to do so was actually doing the best for each child, she insisted. She concluded, "When will Americans see that there is no blessing like the education which we can use; but that the education of which we cannot use is a curse?"[74]

Davis seemed to have forgotten how much she had benefited from a higher education and how hungry she had been as a young woman for better educational opportunities than the culture thought was appropriate for a female living in a small industrial town. Although the federal government embraced her remarks, reprinting them in the *Report of the Federal Security Agency: Office of Education* and as "Education and Crime" in the 1899 *Report of the Department of Interior–Education*, the general reaction was quite different. Among the first publications to condemn the article was the *Independent*: "That our public school system is not perfect, and that sometimes it is badly administered we may admit, but it is perfectly futile for Julian Hawthorne or Rebecca Harding Davis or the Southern Presbyterian Assembly to denounce it as a whole or to create prejudice against it."[75] Although the *Independent*'s editorial attacked Hawthorne and others at length, this was their only reference to Davis, cautiously seeking to disagree while maintaining her as a regular contributor.

The rare voice of support among periodicals came from the *Literary Digest*, which quoted liberally from her article and proclaimed "it is not often that we find any one who has the temerity to face the American people and tell them that its pet idol, its universal solvent for all ills, is in most instances no better than a curse."[76] By far more typical and deeply reasoned was Mrs. M. G. Schuyler Van Rensselaer's rebuttal in the *North American Review*. Van Rensselaer, who the Davises knew from Marion's art colony, agreed that schools could do a better job, but she cautioned, "It is dangerous to exaggerate the share of blame [for social ills] that should be laid upon the public schools."[77] Rebuttals lasted for months and were reprinted widely.

At this time Clarke also made a remark that would become one of the most reprinted comments about their famous literary family: "I used to be known as the husband of Rebecca Harding Davis. Now I am known as the father of Richard Harding Davis." When Charley's work as an author grew, Clarke amended it to "now I am known only as the daddy of the Davis boys."[78] Clarke loved repeating the joke, but its implications were more broadly emblematic of the change in literary generations taking place at the turn of the century.

In July Rebecca published one of her most important anti-war articles. As controversial in a progressive way as her education essay had been in a conservative vein, "The Mean Face of War" appeared in the *Independent*. Her powerful opening paragraph set the tone for an indictment of US imperialism under the guise of advancing Christianity and the nation:

> Of all the gods on Olympus Mars is always the most popular figure. Especially is he heroic in the eyes of a nation which is just about to set the crown of Imperialism on its brows, to gird a sword on its thighs and drive another nation into civilization and Christianity—at the point of bayonet.

Davis admitted her own reassessment of the Spanish-American War:

> Our campaign last summer, for instance, loomed before us in June a glorious outburst of high chivalric purpose and individual courage. But when we looked back at it in September war had come to mean polluted camps, incompetent officers appointed by corrupt politicians, decayed meat and thousands of victims of disease and neglect.

She reflected on the Civil War's similar false front: Union flags on every house in Wheeling but dissension in almost every family with many young men crossing the lines to join the Confederacy. Her concern was that, "After thirty years of peace, a sudden effort is now being made by interested politicians to induce the American people to make war its regular business." While the government talks of glory and heroism, she observed, "What is really intended, of course, is the establishment of a uniformed guard to police the Philippine Islands in the interest of certain trusts."[79] Davis no longer felt the need to temper her political commentaries as she had as a younger woman, and she raged against the abuses of government she felt were rapidly expanding in these years.

Hamilton Holt had become the publisher of the *Independent* in 1897, and he and the weekly's editors had already disagreed with Davis on the issue of education, which she had published in another periodical. She had long been one of their most popular page-one authors, and they were not willing to lose her as a regular contributor, so they cautiously inserted a disclaimer in their editorial columns:

> We know hardly any one who can write more brilliantly than Rebecca Harding Davis, and we are very glad to publish her article, "The Mean Face of War." Yet we cannot consent by any means to her statements that Mars is a god "whom we are about to make our tutelary deity," and certainly not to her assertion that what is intended by our Government "of course, is the establishment of a uniform guard to police the Philippine Islands is the interests of certain trusts." We would like very much to know what those trusts are that are thus hoodwinking our Government.[80]

If the *Independent* resisted Davis's perspective, the *Advocate of Peace* embraced it and reprinted "The Mean Face of War" in its entirety in their September issue.

In the meantime, Dick and Cecil decided to make Marion their permanent residence for a while so each could pursue their artistry. Dick was doing well as a popular author and journalist, but Cecil's father subsidized them so she could continue to live in the style in which she had been raised, with a lady's maid and a cook and, when they returned to New York, a full staff as well as a kennelman and a chauffeur. Financial pressures would be significant in Dick's decision to turn more fully to playwriting where he could make more money than in his other writing venues.[81]

In the fall Rebecca, Clarke, and Nora were able to return to their normal routines after the hectic months of preparations for the wedding, but the normalcy and routine that the Davises valued was not to be long-lived as both of their sons pursued new directions. In this lull, Rebecca published "A Royal Procession" in the September issue of the *Independent*, a reflection on the differences in law enforcement in the US and England. Even with a royal procession the figure of the English policeman was sufficient to signify "incarnate Law. *He never carries arms.*"[82]

Also during this time period, Charley had been approached by the owners of Weber and Fields' Music Hall in New York with an offer to become their new manager. Weber and Fields was a high-class burlesque venue the Davis brothers often attended—high class, but nonetheless, a burlesque hall. Charley's initial reaction had been to turn down the offer, but Dick encouraged his brother to reconsider: "I think you owe it to yourself and to all of us who are interested in your success to do. Cecil was very keen that you should do it, and I think you should take it. . . . Leave it to me to square the family."[83] Since his return from Italy, Charley had struggled to find the right foothold. His writing was well received but not yet sufficiently established to support him; the position at Russell Publishing was prestigious but meant that he put all of his time into other writers' careers. The Weber and Fields position would pay well, but both sides procrastinated for several months.

Of greater concern to the family was the news from South Africa of conflicts, which would develop into the Boer War. By the end of the year Dick and Cecil were making plans to cover the war, although they had not yet told Rebecca and Clarke.[84] Their plans to leave for South Africa were delayed in December, however, when Nora was stricken with a severe case of pneumonia and doctors cautioned the family she might not survive the illness. The Davises rallied around her and supported one another until she recovered a few weeks later.

Nora's illness and the fears surrounding the family at this time may have been why Rebecca declined an offer from Paul Reynolds, a literary agent, when he contacted her about publishing some of her novels in England. In the 1860s and 1870s this had been her dream, but now she simply declined and continued to publish social commentaries. In reality, she no longer needed an agent to internationalize her reputation, as her most recent novels had already appeared in London as had several of her shorter works. She turned to other interests.

In the last decade of her life, Rebecca would decidedly assess the nation's progress and failures, nurture her children's careers, care for Clarke whose health was more fragile than ever, and thoroughly enjoy her life as she continued to travel, write, and embrace the opportunity to become a part of the life that Cecil and Dick would create at their home in Mount Kisco in a few years. The 1890s had not been easy years, but no one in the family was more resilient than Rebecca, and she looked forward to the new century with her usual enthusiasm for life and its many divergences.

Chapter 13

Transitions (1900–1904)

The new century loomed with uncertainty for the nation. Having barely recovered from the Spanish-American War and still engulfed in heated debates about US imperialism, the nation swayed between the nineteenth-century image of itself as a democratic nation with its hand out to the poor and exiled versus the newer, less idealistic image of itself as an empire that could conquer and dominate other nations. Rebecca swayed between the older values and the new as well, though never foregoing her powerful sense of moral right and never embracing imperialistic endeavors. Though fully aware that her values were largely those of the past, she turned in the first years of the new century to an invigorated engagement with the policies and values of the newer generation. Both her political commentaries and personal reminiscences reflected this transitional period. The early years of the century were lively and engaging for the entire family, as its members entered into new career paths, including Rebecca's associations with a mass-audience magazine and with a major newspaper. The family traveled widely and yet maintained the extraordinary closeness that had always marked their relationships. The early years of the century would end, however, with an extraordinary family loss, one that would demand from Rebecca a new phase in her life.

The household on Twenty-first Street in some ways remained much the same. Although both Dick and Charley had their own homes, they frequently visited their parents in Philadelphia, while Nora, who still lived at home, was traveling more often, mostly to visit her brothers but occasionally on her own with friends. Clarke continued to work long hours at the *Public Ledger*, though he somewhat lessened his commitment to civic activities and professional clubs. With only the three Davises now living at home, they had reduced their staff to one live-in servant—Mary Perry, a cook who had long been with the family and who, at fifty-six, was now widowed; like many of the Davis's long-term household employees, she was a Virginian by birth.[1] Undoubtedly additional staff was brought in for the frequent evening gatherings of artist friends and for special events, but the household in these years was a quiet space in which Rebecca could write without interruption and know that the house was being run efficiently.

In February of 1900, she published "Under the Old Code" in *Harper's New Monthly Magazine*. This was her first piece for the magazine in nearly three years, and it was her last publication for the Harper's publishing house. Between the monthly and *Harper's Bazar*, she had serialized two novels and published dozens of stories and articles over the years with the Harper brothers. It had been an enduring and mutually beneficial relationship, but Rebecca was about to begin a far more lucrative association with another periodical that would demand most of her writing time.

"Under the Old Code" looked back to her early years in Big Spring (Florence), Alabama, and the strange sense of honor the South sustained through duels— "This washing of reputations clean by blood was going on perpetually"—and the communal power structure of the Old South that cost more lives than it elevated. "Under the Old Code" also began a theme that would run through several of her writings in the early 1900s: variations of American hospitality. If the cotton plantation people of Big Spring fought duels, they also readily showed their generosity by welcoming strangers "with ardent kindness."[2] This and several other reminiscences Davis penned in the early years of the new century formed the basis for an autobiography she was writing.

Accounts of The Davis Family of writers continued to appear in newspapers and magazines and held great interest for the reading public. The *Ladies' Home Journal*, for example, ran an article titled "A Family of Writers" that identified the work of Rebecca, Clarke, Dick, and Charley.[3] Along with Rebecca's *Harper's* publication, Dick was appearing in *Scribner's* and Charley was still receiving recognition for his collection of stories and his work as a publisher with Russell publishing house, although much of his writing drew on memories and ideas that emerged from his time in Italy. It was impossible to be aware of the literary world and not be familiar with the network of writings from this famous and famously productive family.

As always, for Richard, this status had a downside. In a scathing critique, Willa Cather summed up his blending of writing with a personal flamboyance; his rendering of the newspaperman in fiction, she suggested, had thwarted the development of that character into a figure which "languished under that gentleman's chaperonage until he has come to be regarded as a fellow careful of nothing but his toilet and his dinner."[4]

The family's differing attitudes about war and imperialism were about to emerge once again. Dick had been commissioned by the *New York Herald* and the London *Mail* to cover the Boer War, and he would also publish a series of articles in *Scribner's* (and, notably, this time also for the *Public Ledger*[5]) that would become the basis of his next book. He and Cecil had left for Cape Town in late January. Cecil stayed with Rudyard Kipling and his family when Dick headed to the warfront. On their way to Cape Town, they had stopped in England, and Dick gave an interview in which he supported British imperialism against the Boers and indicated his disappointment in not being able to travel with Lord Kitchener in South Africa.[6]

Ultimately, Dick was able to cover the war with Winston Churchill; while doing so, he wrote frequent letters home that detailed his experiences, though he attempted to assure his parents he was not in any danger. If Dick admired British imperialists such as Kitchener at this time, his attitudes would change, as his political views often did; but it was Rebecca who would write one of the most damning indictments of Kitchener and the British command's scorched-earth policy in the coming months. By the summer, after time in South Africa, Dick reversed his position and was speaking publicly in opposition to the British efforts against the Boers, which alienated him from some of his British friends.[7]

In the fall of 1900, the national announcement was made of Charley's new position as manager of Weber and Field's Broadway Hall.[8] Whatever his parents' private feelings about this new path of work, they publicly supported Charley. He would retain the position for several years, bringing many of the greatest performers of the time to the theater, including Lillian Russell, Fay Templeton, DeWolf Hopper, and Marie Dressler. Dick had hoped by this time to have the dramatization of his Van Bibber stories opening in New York; he had worked throughout the summer and early fall on the project. Although the four-act play was purchased by the theatrical manager Henry B. Harris, Dick refused to make changes that Harris felt were necessary, and the play was never produced. This early experience, however, would not deter Dick from his decision to turn to the more lucrative playwriting business now that *With Both Armies in South Africa* had been published.

At this time Rebecca entered into another new commitment: to write editorials for the *New York World*. Joseph Pulitzer's newspaper was one of the leading national papers and was explicitly aligned with the Democratic Party. This was the era in which Pulitzer was reducing his work at the paper, and within a year, Frank Irving Cobb became editor; Cobb would become famous for editorials that supported liberal Democrats and for its crusades in support of various reforms.[9] The liberal political position of the newspaper at this time was undoubtedly part of its appeal for Rebecca, but so was the opportunity to return to editorial writing for a major national newspaper, which she had not done since leaving the *Tribune* in 1889.

This new editorial role curtailed her contributions to periodicals for which she had long written, including old standbys like the *Independent* and the *Congregationalist*. Initially, she continued her contributions, but they would be reduced once she turned more fully to writing for the *World* and she soon added the *Saturday Evening Post* to her repertoire as well. With the *World*, as with the *Post*, she could reach a far larger audience than ever before: the *World* had one million daily readers in the late 1890s.[10] For a woman who had earned a national reputation for her editorials in the *New-York Tribune* in earlier years, this was an opportunity to continue to represent her ideas to a wide audience and to demonstrate her extraordinary political and cultural knowledge.

Rebecca continued to write cultural commentaries for the *Independent*, if fewer in number. Two articles appeared in October—one about the field of literature and the other about race relations in the US at the turn of the century. As with many of Davis's commentaries, she began "The Temple of Fame" with a general maxim about American habits and then traced a specific instance of its application. The article analyzed the American obsession with a "short cut to truth, which we use on every occasion. No matter what the subject in doubt may be, we vote on it. The majority, we assume, must be right. . . . The voting habit is a chronic disease now among Americans." This was especially true, she noted, with the call every few months from some magazine or newspaper editor for readers to vote on who was and always would be the best poet or artist.[11]

Davis was responding specifically to a recent proclamation by the University of New York on the establishment of a Temple of Fame for Americans, based on the decision of one hundred eminent men as judges. She presented a thoughtful critique of the American obsession with fame: "But how can [the judges] give a dead man *Fame*? If the temple had been one of Honor—yes."[12] The extent to which Davis's critique threatened the growing literary and cultural canonization of white male figures was evident in the lengthy justification for the Temple of Fame that quickly appeared in *Current Literature* in response to her critique.

"Two American Boys," on the other hand, was another of Davis's attempts to draw attention to writers whose work she admired: the Native American author Francis La Flesche who had just published his memoir, *The Middle Five: Indian Boys at School*, and Booker T. Washington, whose work in industrial training for African Americans she had written about on several occasions. Her recommendation of La Flesche's memoir was immediately picked up by his publishers and used to advertise the book. Her conclusion to "Two American Boys" presented the other side of her resistance to the Temple of Fame:

> The stories are very human—both of them. One boy was an Indian, the other a negro. But in their thinkings and doings, in their loves and dislikes, their ambitions, their struggles to be manly and brave and like their idea of God—they might have been white as you are, your brothers or your sons. And yet you put them outside the gate—because of the color of their skins![13]

Once again this was a mutual effort by Rebecca and Clarke, one that had long held great concern for them and for which they had worked to support in a variety of ways. The following spring, for instance, Clarke would join a number of distinguished Philadelphia clergymen, rabbis, lawyers, physicians, and activists in developing a conference to address ways in which they could assist in the "Improvement among the Colored People of the North," as the conference was titled.[14]

In November Davis published two works, "On the Jersey Shore" for the *Independent* and "A Little Gossip" for *Scribner's Magazine*. The *Independent* piece was the beginning of a series of articles she penned that revealed her astute knowledge of the wars and political machinations of her time on a global scale. She turned to her beloved New Jersey shore as a site of overlooked history to offer sustenance in a time when readers were overwhelmed by "the Boer War and the doings of the Boxers, and of the Germans in China, and of our army in the Philippines, and . . . the sudden and thorough debasement of politics at home."[15]

"A Little Gossip," on the other hand, was part of the autobiographical writings she was preparing. It was reviewed, reprinted, and excerpted in numerous periodicals. Retitled in her autobiography as "Boston in the Sixties," the narrative captured her memories of meeting the Alcotts, Hawthorne, Emerson, Holmes, and many others when she visited Boston in 1862. The article offered touching reminiscences of revered American authors; the revised autobiography version that would appear in 1904, however, would include an assessment of their weaknesses as well as their strengths. "A Little Gossip" was Davis's last publication with *Scribner's*, but her sons were both writing for the magazine and would carry on the family connection. Rebecca's reminiscence was well received, but even then the family could not escape comparisons of their writing. As the *Cedar Rapids Republican* proclaimed the article "deliciously entertaining," they concluded with the snide remark, "What a wonderful writer Richard Harding Davis ought to be with such a mother!"[16]

The end of the year saw Rebecca's continuing burst of writing and a visit from old friends. While writing for the *World*, she also published "An Unwritten History" in the *Independent*. In "On the Jersey Shore" Davis had admonished historians for producing innumerable reiterations of the Puritans or of the history of Florida while neglecting the rich and unique past that New Jersey had to offer. Readers had responded in significant numbers to that charge, and so in "An Unwritten History" she traced several other notable events from the state's past and concluded that she had only tapped the treasure trove of history that was waiting to be uncovered.

Shortly before Christmas, Frances and Grover Cleveland again stayed with the Davises when Grover came to Philadelphia to give a commencement address for the Pierce School of Business, held at the Academy of Music. It had been a while since the two couples had had the opportunity for this kind of close and relaxed reconnection, and it made a particularly enjoyable end to the year. At this time Dick and Cecil also decided to move back to New York City from Marion so Dick could be closer to Broadway in order to promote his plays. They rented a Manhattan townhouse at 172 West Fifty-eighth Street near Central Park as well as a nearby studio for Cecil. It was a joyful change for Charley, who could once again be close to his brother. Dick, however, soon discovered he was not adept at translating his novels into plays and he wisely hired playwright Augustus Thomas to prepare a version of *Soldiers of Fortune*.[17] It seemed that the entire family was settling into their new paths with enthusiasm and success.

With the beginning of 1902, Rebecca renewed her commitment to publishing. "An English Passion Play" appeared in *Century Magazine*, and her most radical political indictment in years, "Lord Kitchener's Methods," was published in the *Independent*. Although Davis had published several unsigned cultural commentaries in the *Century*, this was her first signed work in the magazine since 1895. "An English Passion Play" looked back to one of her European trips when she and a traveling companion, most likely Nora, learned humility among the faithful Cornish villagers they met by chance.

"Lord Kitchener's Methods," on the other hand, was an explosive indictment of the British command's genocidal scorched-earth policies against the Boers. Reflecting on the "abnormal traits" that nations had recently been demonstrating, Davis engaged international politics. "What was there in the character of the French people," she asked, "to prepare the world for the Dreyfus case? What American, ten years ago, could have conceived of his country as at war with the Filipinos, or as again a slave owner? . . . It is our

English cousin, however, who has startled us most of late." She wondered how the English public could be so silent in the face of its military's tactics to end the war, specifically their decision

> to starve out the Boer soldiers and force them to subjection by burning their farm houses and growing crops; by driving their women and children and aged folk out homeless to "live like baboons among the kopjes." This kind of warfare proved effectual in Ireland under Raleigh and Lord Gray; in Burma during the war with the dacoits, and it is being tried in China now, where the Russians and Germans are dealing with the heathen.[18]

Davis carefully cited the eleven reasons given by English leaders for their actions, adding the specific military or political leader's assertion and the date each order was given: "1. Because it would cow the enemy [Colonel Pilcher's devastation of thirty square miles of the Free State, January, 1899. . . . 3. Because a whole district had to be devastated.—[See proceedings of General Campbell in Ficksburg, September 14th, General Rundle in Free State, General Paget in the Transvaal, Lord Methuen in Zeerust]. . . ." The information of the scorched-earth policy had been revealed to the English public, as well as "the secret instructions issued by Lord Kitchener to the army," which she also detailed. It was the lack of any outcry, indeed of any effect at all on the public, that astonished Davis. They proclaim themselves "defenders of the weak," she concluded, "Yet when Lord Kitchener is let loose on Boer mothers and children they are silent."[19]

Once again, the editors refuted Davis's claims, in spite of her careful documentation of the facts. Insisting they had heard stories of such abuses on both sides of the war, they concluded that "from the best of information that we can find it appears that both British and Boers have respected their opponents and treated them when prisoners with as much gentleness as the conditions would allow"![20]

In mid-February 1901 Rebecca and Clarke arrived in Ocala, Florida, and stayed at the Ocala House Hotel for several weeks. In spite of his continued business and civic activities, Clarke's health continued in severe decline, and he could no longer tolerate the cold Philadelphia winters. The Davises had started spending winters in Ocala in 1897, and they would continue to reside at the hotel each January and February for the next few years in an effort to ease his health problems.

During this year, Rebecca would see several of her works reprinted in large collections of "literary bests," including an excerpt from *Doctor Warrick's*

Daughters in the ten-volume *The World's Great Masterpieces* published by the American Literary Society. These works were intended to create a history of US and world literature not only for contemporary readers but for future readers as well. It was another piece of the canonization process, and in these years Davis was always included as an integral part of contemporary American literature. She did nothing to promote her status, however. In March, for instance, when Charles Wells Moulton contacted her to request a photograph with a sketch of her life, she offered no assistance: "You are very kind. But I have not had a likeness taken for thirty years and I assure you: the public do not care to see a sketch of my life. Nothing ever happened to me which would give point to an item. And I have a dislike to seeing anything about myself (personally—) in print. But I quite appreciate your compliment."[21] Moulton was preparing the multi-volume *Library of Literary Criticism of English and American Authors*, and this was the rare collection of the period in which Davis was not included.

The following month, however, when the *Youth's Companion* marked its 75th anniversary, the editors acknowledged Davis's importance to the success of the magazine even though she was no longer a contributor. They recognized writers such as Davis, Harriet Beecher Stowe, Elizabeth Stuart Phelps, Lucy Larcom, and Louisa May Alcott as instrumental in turning the once-flagging magazine for youth into one of the most popular family magazines in the nation.[22] It was a fitting tribute to both her literary and editorial contributions to the magazine.

In May Davis published another reminiscence, "A Quiet Half-Hour," in the *Independent*, but this was of a different sort. Like many of her homages to the past, it suggested that people of earlier eras—Antoine Bénézet, John Woolman, a young Delaware Indian chief renamed Johnny Wilson by his white neighbors—had higher aims and greater generosity to others than the moneygrubbers of the present generation. In this instance, however, Davis called a halt to herself and other older people who made such proclamations. Citing several recent instances of moral and physical courage enacted for the benefit of others that one could find almost daily in the newspaper, she concluded, "so we old people may put an end to our grumblings. The saving leaven is still at work in the world when the hero blood shows itself in elevator boys and the negro cleaners of iron boilers" whose stories she recounted.[23]

On June 24, 1901, Rebecca turned seventy years old. Although the celebration was, as she always wished, a quiet one, Dick sent her a loving letter to mark the day:

Dear Mother:

In those wonderful years of yours you never thought of the blessing you were to us only of what good you could find in us. All that time, you were helping us and others, and making us better, happier, even nobler people. From the day you struck the first blow for labor, in *The Iron Mills* on to the editorials in *The Tribune*, *The Youth's Companion*, and *The Independent*, with all the good the novels, the stories brought to people, you were always year after year making the ways straighter, lifting up people, making them happier and better. No woman ever did better for her time than you and no shrieking suffragette will ever understand the influence you wielded, greater than hundreds of thousands of women's votes.

We love you dear, dear mother, and we *know* you and may your coming years be many and as full of happiness for yourself as they are for us.

Dick[24]

It was a letter any parent would cherish.

After time at Marion, Rebecca and Clarke headed to Warm Springs where Nora, and Charley joined them. The family continued to host events such as a moonlight ride that Charley sponsored in August. While at Warm Springs, Rebecca published "An Unlighted Lamp" in the *Independent*. Perhaps no author so thoroughly analyzed the American character as did Davis in her essays of the 1890s and 1900s, and this long essay incorporated numerous assessments, some that she had addressed several times in her commentaries and others that elaborated her sense of what the highly celebrated and often self-congratulatory New American was truly like. These were not cynical assessments; rather, Davis pointed out to readers the inconsistencies and sometimes unrecognized consequences of well-meaning but often ill-advised social and political policies. Her assessments included highly progressive ideas about what changes were needed in US culture as well as some conservative underpinnings that leavened the impact of her remarks. In this now common paradoxical mix, Davis herself represented, more than she realized, precisely the traits of the New American.

Once again Dick and Clarke followed Rebecca into one of her major places of publication, the *Independent*. Dick's article on the Boer general Christiaan de Wet had appeared in January, while Clarke's "Different Points of View" in

September countered claims about the decreasing influence of religion in American life, asserting it had never been "so potent."[25] Rebecca's and Clark's essays, published within weeks of one another, captured the very different outlooks they held about the current state of the nation. In some ways, she saw beneath the surface while Clarke remained the idealist. His extraordinary idealism was, of course, part of what had drawn her to him for the past forty years. For both Clarke and Dick, these would be their only publications in the *Independent*.

On September 6, the nation was shattered by the news that an assassin had shot President McKinley shortly after he had given a speech at the Pan-American Exposition in Buffalo, New York. The President died from complications of gangrene the following week, and Theodore Roosevelt became the new president. The shock reverberated throughout society, and many Americans worried about the fate of the nation in this moment of violence and disruption. In late October, Davis expressed her sentiments in the *Independent*. "Is It All for Nothing?" was her deeply moving acknowledgment of having lived through three presidential assassinations. The blame rested with the individual assassins, who were all seeking notoriety, *and* with the nation, she declared: "We are responsible for the vanity, for the mad longing for notoriety which has become a national disease."[26] This assertion went beyond just her usual dislike of the cult of celebrity; it examined the ways in which such personal fame dictated individuals' character development.

Davis also captured the poignancy of a nation brought together by tragedy. As McKinley's funeral train passed through the country, "The richest and the poorest, in masses side by side, in the cities; mountaineers with their guns in hand, the old sects of the Amish and Dunkards; thousands of grimy mill-hands; little children" all sang "Nearer, my God, to thee," as the casket passed. It was the song that McKinley purportedly attempted to sing on his deathbed. She did not support McKinley's policies but respected him as "a tender husband, a kind, honest man, a faithful servant of Christ," and concluded, "Is it for nothing that the people have . . . gone back to their old beliefs in the homely virtues of a good man and tried with him to stretch out their hands to God?"[27] Davis wanted to believe this moment would be transitional, that a nation driven mad by the lust for money, that viewed the domestic woman as a thing of the past, and in which young college people rejected Christianity would maintain the moment of national unity and faith it had expressed at the President's death. She would feel within a few short months that it had been a lost opportunity.

By November the nation had not recovered from the assassination of its leader, but daily life returned to a semblance of normalcy, and Rebecca published her first essay in a new periodical, *Success Magazine*. Founded in 1897 under the editorship of Orison Swett Marden, the magazine promoted his New Thought philosophy, which encouraged positive thought and personal development as a means to a successful life. At its height under Marden, the magazine had a circulation of nearly 500,000. Davis's first publication in *Success* was "The Olden Type of Woman and The New." It was included under the title "Girls—Then and Now" in the *Success Library*, a ten-volume compendium of articles and stories from the magazine that was published this year as well. It was another of Davis's insistences that the New Woman has lost some of the power and love that the Domestic Woman retained, though the New Woman thinks she is far above her progenitor.

Of particular interest, however, were the changes made from the magazine article to the essay in the collection. "Woman" was erased from the title in favor of "Girls," and the Advanced New Woman became "Advanced New Girl"; a similar change appeared in the essay by Julia Ward Howe that followed Davis's. Although Howe used "woman" and "women" throughout her essay, its title was converted to "The Highest Type of *Girl*."[28] For all that *Success* viewed itself as progressive and a guide to new avenues for a successful life, the old gendered distinctions remained more within the editorial system than among the women writers who contributed to the magazine's success.

At seventy, Rebecca entered 1902 with a burst of productivity. She continued to publish frequently in the *Independent*, was contributing editorials to the *New York World*, and would occasionally contribute to the *Congregationalist*. In this year, however, she also began one short-lived and one long-term association with new magazines. At the same time Dick and Charley would forge a beneficial alliance with *Collier's Weekly* magazine. Clarke continued his role as managing editor of the *Public Ledger*, but for health reasons, he was beginning to curtail a good portion of his civic and club commitments. Spending their winters in Florida meant they missed the wedding of Secretary of State John Hay's daughter Helen to Payne Whitney in February. It was considered the society wedding of the year, and Cecil and Dick attended with a long list of renowned guests.

Rebecca's first publication for the *Independent* this year was "The Black North" in February. It was her most extensive comparison of W.E.B. DuBois and Booker T. Washington. Davis focused on the unending advice that African Americans were given in this era: "our poor black brother is the most advised man in Christendom." The essay was a classic example of Davis's conservative-progressivism, with a concluding assessment of the recently published novel by Paul Laurence Dunbar, *The Sport of the Gods*, "No man is the sport of any god. The negro leaders do irreparable damage to their people by their incessant melancholy wails of complaint and defeat."[29]

At this time Dick was having success with his dramatization of *Soldiers of Fortune* at the Hyperion Theatre in New Haven, Connecticut, after years of trying to convert the novel into a play; it would open in New York at the Savoy Theatre in mid-March. He would never give up writing for periodicals, but the lucrative stage was his primary focus. This is also when he and Charley began writing for *Collier's Weekly* with nonfiction contributions: Dick's "Inside Stories of Recent History" and Charley's "The American Pantomime Season." Both brothers would contribute fiction and essays to the magazine over the next two decades, and in a few years, Charley would become fiction editor of the magazine.

Perhaps most important for the future of the family, in ways they could not yet foresee, was Dick and Cecil's decision to buy a 204-acre farm in Mount Kisco, New York, about an hour outside New York City. The area was popular with society figures and artists. It offered Dick the convenience of being near the city for his theatrical productions and being able to see Charley often, and it gave Cecil the space she needed to breed her show dogs and to paint.

Building the house would take much longer than they originally anticipated, but it would become a replica in spirit of the home Rebecca and Clarke had established in Philadelphia as a place for family to gather and artist friends to congregate. Even as Dick was beginning to oversee the work on the house, he wrote lovingly to Rebecca that he envisioned her in Philadelphia in "the library or your own room or at the parlor window," the places where she liked to write. He added a cautionary note, however, "I do not like your sitting out on the porch in the rain,"[30] but Rebecca had liked nothing more than being outdoors her entire life, even if it meant only on the porch, and that would never change.

In May the *National Magazine* ran a lengthy review article on Weber and Fields' Music Hall's upcoming season, adding that the Hall was

> quite unlike any other in this country or England. With a clever short story writer, Charles Belmont Davis, for its manager; one of New York's best composers, Mr. Stromberg, always at its command; a playwright under contract to supply so many burlesques a year and an "all star" cast whose salaries would frighten any ordinary manager, Weber and Fields have succeeded where others would have been involved in financial ruin.[31]

Charley was an astute financial manager, both for the business and for himself. He not only lived well and within his means, he was also a trustworthy financial adviser for Dick.

In April Dick and Cecil left to cover the coronations in Spain and England. His novel *Ranson's Folly* was published by Scribner's while he was out of the country. He would also become a popular author in Harper's and Scribner's cheap book series, both of which published collected volumes of his work. These well-paying cheap editions allowed him to regain some financial stability. The royalties from the Scribner edition alone would reach $20,000 by 1905.[32] Dick had clearly tapped into the new literary model of popular and highly lucrative writing. Charley continued to prefer what he termed "serious" writing, but he was gaining recognition as a short story writer, if not the extraordinary financial success Dick achieved.

In May 1902 Rebecca published her second article with *Success*. "The Return to the Soil" was an analysis of why so many well-to-do Americans had left the cities for the country in recent years. Davis loved to collect old books, histories or memoirs of early America, and she drew on one such book to suggest why the country environment had such an appeal. It was a subtle extension of the argument she had made in the post–Civil War years: that the city dwellers who were driven to the streets and starving because they could not afford to live there, or anyone whose health was being destroyed by the pollutants of the city, could thrive if they would move to the country or the shore. The article obviously hit a chord of desire in the reading public at the beginning of the twentieth century, as it was reprinted widely in newspapers over the next two months. One newspaper asserted it was one of the magazine's "important articles showing the upward trend of the world."[33]

In May Davis also began an affiliation with the well-paying *Saturday Evening Post* that would last for the remainder of her writing life. Davis's decision to become a regular contributor to the magazine marked a significant change in her career, as she aligned herself with one of the new mass market magazines rather than popular but more elite literary and religious periodicals. Cyrus H. Curtis, publisher of the *Ladies' Home Journal* with whom Davis had worked occasionally in the 1890s, had wisely hired the talented and ambitious thirty-one-year-old George Horace Lorimer to reshape the *Post*. When Lorimer began his editorship, the *Post*'s circulation was a mere 2,000 subscribers; Lorimer sought Davis and other major writers of the day in order to transform the failing magazine into one of the most influential national magazines with the nation's top-tier writers appearing in its pages. Less than a decade later,

Lorimer had increased the circulation to one million, and Davis's signed articles and unsigned editorials and literary reviews were integral to the magazine's success.

Curtis, and especially Lorimer, had very distinct goals for the *Post*: while the stories and essays where to be entertaining, they were to convey specific values—not simply to reflect the culture, but very explicitly to shape its readers' values.[34] Those values were imbedded in nineteenth-century codes of fairness in business, individual initiative, hard work, and sensible finances that included saving money, and a deep sense of the responsibilities of citizenship. Curtis and Lorimer were committed to the goal of making the *Post* the vehicle of an American consciousness.

The *Post*'s stories and essays were initially aimed primarily at the up-and-coming young businessman who would bring the best values of the nineteenth century into the present. These were not the businessmen of the elite professions, but the middle-class men working to better themselves and their families. It was rather ironic, then, that Davis's first item for the *Post*, "Some Modern Buccaneers," explored "those disreputable folk; the half-starved, scampish adventurers who haunt the outer edge of the field of literature and journalism" whom she had known. "I must plead guilty," she admitted, "to a liking" for this group because "there was not one who did not have some honest fibre in his soul . . . some rag of white flag to hold up to God's sight as he went down."[35] This article, too, would be slightly revised and included in Davis's autobiography as "The Shipwrecked Crew."

In June, Rebecca published four articles. The first appeared in the *Congregationalist*, which had combined with *Christian World* and was now published under the dual titles. The article was a reminiscence of George W. Childs. She had declined to write about the famous publisher immediately after his death in 1894 because of her close friendship with his wife, Emma Peterson Childs; she had felt that to write about Childs at that time would have intruded on Emma's grief and seemed to be using his death for Davis's own benefit.

It had long been Davis's policy not to write personal remembrances of living people, but with his death, she now felt it was both timely and appropriate to discuss her views about her friend and her husband's employer. She recalled Childs' ability to "make charity a fine art . . . the half-starved clergyman had his three months in Europe, the clerk received a paid-up life insurance for his children, the penniless bride was made happier for life by a pretty trousseau, a good stock of napery and silver to carry into her new home."[36] His actions, of course, were so appealing to Davis because they replicated her charitable preference of helping individuals rather than donating to large charities.

"On the Uplands," a short item about the generosity of a wealthy Jewish businessman and another example of one-on-one charity, was also published in the *Congregationalist and Christian World* and reprinted in several religious periodicals. "The Disease of Money-Getting" for the *Independent* was an articulation of the contemporary lust for money that she had lamented for many years; however, Davis drew on her readings in the new field of sociology for her argument in this article:

> Our recent writers on sociology recognize the recent change in the values which we set upon the things of life. Our old idea of a higher class to be imitated, men and women of honest parentage, of gentle breeding and high purposes, is, we now hear, stale and fantastic. Our House of Lords, we are told "is already incorporated. They are the Plutocrats of New York. They soon will give us a syndicated Presidency."

It bordered on a national insanity, she insisted.[37] The essay hit a chord of recognition with physicians and was reprinted in full in the August issue of the *Journal of Medicine and Science*. Her fourth essay of the month, "A Boy's Flight" for *Success*, received strong reviews, describing it as a "dramatic, gripping story, which cannot fail to interest all lovers of good literature."[38]

Although the rest of the family continued to thrive in their literary careers, Nora still demonstrated no interest in following that path. She had found her own niche in the social circles of Philadelphia and New York and at the famous summer resorts, where she was known for her tasteful style and fun-loving personality. She filled her days with horse-riding and society events, such as a luncheon she attended at Mount Pleasant, the country home of Mary V. Crawford. Crawford was a graduate of Bryn Mawr in history and political science and represented the changing face of high society in which the old customs of society events continued but in which young women were much more highly educated and looked to a very different future than previous generations.

Rebecca supported Nora's interests in society life. Her public commentaries on young women were quite different from the life her own daughter was living, however. In July, for instance, Davis published "Country Girls in Town" in the *Independent*. She understood why so many young women were coming to the large metropolitan cities of the East Coast: "On most Western ranches the woman is overworked, and the loneliness of her life is intolerable; while in the smaller Southern towns the monotony, the pettiness of events in the slow-going hours and days and years stifle and kill an active brain, just as the creeping gray moss smothers a living plant." But they come, having read Augusta Evans's *Beulah* or some other popular novel, with the expectation of making a fortune through authorship or journalism when they know "no more of either kind of work than [they] do of ship-building." Many of these young women end up in prostitution as a means of survival, Davis insisted, and she wished they would remain at home to preserve their minds and bodies against the harsh realities of city life.[39]

A backlash quickly followed as newspaper columnists were outraged at the suggestion that some good country girls turned to prostitution,[40] in spite of the rampant numbers of prostitutes in the major cities all along the Atlantic seaboard. Using Davis's article as a base, the magazine *Womanhood* reported on new US Department of Labor studies that asserted only three percent of prostitutes in a study of over three thousand such women were found to have been shopgirls, most of whom were originally from the country. *Womanhood* was dedicated to a positive representation of women—with illustrations of women bicycling, playing chess, and so on—and rejected any sense of women's immorality. The author of the review, in spite of her insistence that the public image of immoral shopgirls was inaccurate, defined Davis as "a well-known writer on sociology," a common inscription of Davis's cultural commentaries at this time.[41]

This month Davis also published "New Traits for New Americans," her only article for *Outlook* magazine. At the turn of the century, *Outlook*, the *Nation*, and the *Independent* were ranked as the top three weekly journals of news and opinion, so it was a natural fit for Davis's interests, and her reputation as an author and journalist adept at deciphering the news and opinions of the day would have appealed to the editors of the *Outlook*. Whether she decided she preferred the *Independent* or they made an effort to ensure she wrote only for them after this article appeared in their competitor's magazine, she returned to the *Independent* thereafter and maintained it as her primary news and opinion magazine for the remainder of her life.

"New Traits of the New American" provocatively assessed the changes in the national character over the past fifty years. On the positive side, citizens were more tolerant of governments and religions that differed from their own, and they believed a poor man could rise to lead the nation. Yet she felt, with forty thousand immigrants coming into the US every year for the last sixty years, there was no longer among American citizens a belief in the "vital idea of the Republic." Many new citizens were not naturalized; they knew more about the politics of their homeland—in Ireland, Italy, France, or England—than they did of their new nation's practices or of the delegates in their own trade unions, she insisted. Yet, she acknowledged, another notable trait of the American was "his kindness, his eager, good-humored charity." The saddest new trait, however, was the alarming increase in nervousness due to money-grubbing and status-seeking, and it would be beneficial, she concluded, for people to "take stock of its powers."[42]

While Rebecca was thriving in her renewed productivity, Clarke was facing a potentially devastating change, once again, at the *Public Ledger*. In spite of his illnesses, Clarke was by no means ready to step down as managing editor, but he feared he would be forced out of his position when Adolph Ochs bought the *Ledger* from George Childs Drexel in July. While the Davises were at Marion and Warm Springs over the summer, speculations about potential changes under the new publisher were being played out very publicly in front-page newspaper articles across the nation.

With the purchase of the *Ledger*, Ochs had determined to combine it with his other newspaper, the *Philadelphia Times*, under the title of the *Public Ledger and Philadelphia Times*. Two managing editors would now be consolidated into one, and though family members tried to reassure him, Clarke knew it was possible he could lose his beloved editorial position. With the appointment of a relative, George Ochs, as general manager, Clarke felt even less sure about the stability of his position, but finally, in August, Ochs announced that Clarke would be editor-in-chief of the combined newspapers and the former *Philadelphia Times* editor, A. C. Lambdin, would be his associate editor.[43]

At Warm Springs, Rebecca could relish the southern traditions she still loved and a mix of guests that represented every section of the US. Yet even in the new century, Warm Springs remained representative of the Old South like so many of the southern resorts. Warm Springs's advertisements liked to boast that it had been "patronized by the aristocracy of the South for generations" and that all of the "help" were African Americans. Even much of the entertainment relied on "old-time concerts." And while guests did come from the West and North, many, like Davis, had roots in the South. Among the "notables," as travel writers observed, who were at the springs this season were "Fighting Joe" Wheeler, who had served in the Confederate Army and had later served as a US Representative from Alabama, and the historical novelist Mary Johnston, who was both a native Virginian and a women's rights activist. The old, often racist traditions and the inroads of newer ideas exemplified the atmosphere at the Springs.[44] Davis's writing this summer included "What Does It Mean?" for an August issue of the *Independent*. The article was an indictment of the public's relish for crime as entertainment; she lamented that such articles were no longer part of yellow journalism but standard stock in all newspapers and recent novels.

Returning to Philadelphia in September, Davis published an article and an editorial in the September 20th issue of the *Saturday Evening Post*. The signed article, "As I Remember," was another of her popular reminiscences. The essay drew Dick's attention, which he termed "the best writing in America," though he also revealed that he rarely read her work—in spite of the fact she read everything he wrote.[45] Davis also published an unsigned *Post* editorial in September, "The Best of Company."[46]

George Lorimer, who approved every editorial, essay, and story that appeared in the *Post*, created an editorial page designed to educate, perpetuate the broader values of the magazine, and especially create a sense of an ongoing conversation between readers about what they had read that week in its pages in order to invest readers with a nationalistic zeal and a belief in the exceptionalism of the American reader. It was, in this way, an odd fit for Davis whose anti-exceptionalism was well recorded. But the editorial values of the magazine were in line with many other of her own beliefs, and she was allowed to express her ideas without interference, in spite of Lorimer's known control of content. Part of the conversation the editors wanted to invigorate was designed to include a group of major literary writers and national leaders who would be discussed publicly as writers for the *Post*. In addition to Davis, these writers included Frank Norris, Harold Frederic, Paul Laurence Dunbar, Joel Chandler Harris, Bret Harte, Hamlin Garland, and political leaders such as Grover Cleveland.

As Davis was building her association with the *Post*, Dick published his last novel, *Captain Macklin*, and dedicated it to his mother. Although it had a short-lived success, Dick always identified it as his favorite among his novels, while Rebecca, in her incomparable pride in her children's accomplishments, declared it "immortal."[47]

The *Saturday Evening Post* editors continued to appreciate Rebecca's contributions, and in October, they contracted to have her write weekly commentaries for the magazine. A few would be signed, but most constituted unsigned editorials. She immediately jumped into contemporary issues for the *Post* with articles such as "Coal, Fifteen Dollars a Ton," "The Human Dippers," "The

Religion of Things," "Two Kinds of Charity," "Prescriptions for Trouble," "The School for Hustlers," and many others.

Politics were shaping the thoughts of other family members as well. Through his reporting, Dick had helped to create the public image of Teddy Roosevelt and his Rough Riders during the Spanish-American War when Roosevelt supported Cuban independence, and Dick tried to maintain contact with Roosevelt as the latter rose in his political career. But it was Clarke's opinion that Roosevelt valued, and once again, Clarke began a correspondence and association with a president of the United States. His influence as an editor was as important to politicians as ever, and they courted his good favor while he sought their responses to political issues that plagued the nation at particular moments during their administrations. Although the two men would never have the close relationship that Clarke and Cleveland had established, he liked Roosevelt's actions in the early years of his presidency.

The year ended with strong publications from Rebecca. The first, "Ingenuity in Earning a Living," was for the *Interior*, a Chicago weekly that was considered one of the three most important weeklies to emerge in the years after the Spanish-American War.[48] The article extended Davis's earlier writings about ways to earn a living without having to spend years in apprenticeships or at college and was especially directed at women in rural areas who had less opportunities to earn a living outside the home. Davis also published five unsigned editorials for the *Post*, including another on the topic of American hospitality and a call for greater public civility.

It had been a wonderfully productive and invigorating year for Rebecca, but just as the new year began, she learned of the death on December 27 of her old friend Jessie Benton Frémont. In tribute, Davis published remembrances of Frémont in the *Independent* and (unsigned) in the *Post*. The country, Davis noted sadly, "apparently had forgotten the woman who during the critical period of last century, was one of its foremost and most picturesque figures. We are not a grateful people; our memory of our most popular favorites is apt to be short lived. But now that she is dead, no doubt there will be many skilled pens ready to do her justice." Davis did just that, detailing Frémont's life and her contributions to the nation as well as adding anecdotes about General Frémont that had not been previously in print. Davis personalized her relationship with Jessie Frémont as well: "she was a friend to me. I cannot be altogether silent now that she has gone. It seems as if this eager, money-making generation ought to be told how warm and living a fire went out in the world when her heart grew cold."[49]

Davis's signed article for the *Post* in January 1903, "A Peculiar People," was a reminiscence that would be revised for her autobiography. With this recollection of the abolitionists she had known, Davis once again employed the genre she described as a "silhouette" because "the inattentive eyes of a young girl could not discern depths of character or heights of motive."[50] Yet the remembrance allowed her to write a fuller picture of her friendship with Dr. F. Julius LeMoyne, the leading abolitionist figure of her childhood and a man who had greatly shaped her own thinking. In her autobiography, she would extend her account to many other famous abolitionists she had known. Perhaps nothing so clearly marked the changing landscape of American literature than the juxtaposition of Davis's remembrances and the serialization of Frank Norris's *The Pit*, about the Chicago futures market, that followed on the next page of the *Post*.

The entire family was concerned when Clarke was struck with a severe case of influenza in January of 1903. Rebecca and Clarke had been preparing for their trip to Ocala, but he was not well enough for travel. Grover Cleveland wrote to Rebecca from Princeton about his concern for his dear friend, noting that "the grippe" was a "treacherous enemy." He invited the Davises to visit before they went to Florida, signing his letter, "We send our love to you and him and to Norah; and you know I am, Faithfully your friend, Grover Cleveland."[51] As much as Rebecca and Clarke would have enjoyed spending time with their friends in Princeton, it was imperative Clarke be in a warmer climate as soon as possible, and they headed directly to Florida when he was well enough.

With Clarke's illness and the time it took to travel, Rebecca published only two articles in the *Saturday Evening Post* in February: "Cheating the Children," about the dangers in wealthy families of glutting their children's lives with luxuries, and "The Blot on The Great Man's Name," a response to Edward Everett Hale's debunking of the myth that Daniel Webster had been a drunkard. Although everyone rejoiced to learn this new information about Webster, Davis observed, there was another side to most people's responses in which they did not rejoice: "Why is this?" she asked. "Are we at bottom a kind of malignant animal? . . . Or is it only that the ordinary man and woman are chilled and stifled by these faultless ruling folk. . . . The dazzle and shine of an archangel awes us, but a dab of coal-soot on his wing makes him human at once."[52]

When they returned from Florida to Philadelphia, Rebecca published only unsigned essays in the March issues of the *Post*, including "A Rope of Sand," in which she argued that the prevalence of divorce in America was true for the upper classes but not among other Americans, and "Hard Times for an Old

Man," in which she acknowledged both sides of corporations' insistence that men retire at age seventy. Many men want to continue to be productive, Davis acknowledged, yet many older Americans, women even more than men, were worked incessantly in old age by their own families. It is "the crushing out of the individual by the Juggernaut Community." As the nation saw itself progressing steadily through industry, she asked people to stop and consider: "Can we afford to lose out of life the calm, the significance of leisurely old age?"[53] It was a rather ironic question, coming from a woman whose productivity at nearly seventy-two was as prolific as ever.

Other than the memorial of Jessie Benton Frémont, Davis had not published an article with the *Independent* since the previous August. The *Post* paid significantly higher rates than the *Independent*, and more importantly, the ability to publish unsigned cultural analyses, as she had for the *Century*, gave her a freedom of expression she wholly embraced. She did not, however, completely abandon her affiliation with the *Independent*, publishing "The Old Black Teapot" in the April issue and thereafter an article about every two months throughout 1903. "Old Black Tea Pot" was significantly revised and retitled "The Scotch-Irish" for Davis's autobiography.

Of particular interest among her unsigned editorials in the *Post* in April were "The Man in the Iron Mask" and "The Rage for Writing." The former critiqued the manner in which people were still creating iron masks to wear throughout their lives. In one way this implied "a certain *esprit de corps* among all us poor children—white, yellow, and black— ... a showing of the best that is in us to the man next to us." Alexandre Dumas's man in the iron mask "was buried in his mask. Shall we, too, wear ours—out yonder into the dark?"[54] In "The Rage for Writing" Davis observed that the literary profession had come to consume young men and women; it was a fact every editor in the nation understood as his desk was flooded with manuscripts. With the recent success of a few historical novels, these young writers had been pouring out replicas, with little success because they were full of errors; the authors did not know their subjects thoroughly. She suggested they turn to their own towns and acquaintances; write every day what they saw around them. If they recorded certain events, such as the actions of a local trade union, their writings would "be correct and vivid, and forty years hence of great significance and value."[55]

By late April Clarke was well enough to accept Grover Cleveland's invitation to join him and Elias Benedict on a train trip to St. Louis where Cleveland was to present the opening address for the Louisiana Purchase Exposition.[56] While in St. Louis, Clarke joined a number of political dignitaries, including Cleveland

and ambassadors from France and Mexico, at a dinner for President Roosevelt.[57] In spite of Clarke's recent illness, he was fully back into the swing of his editorial and political endeavors.

While he was away, Rebecca had time to return to her weekly writings for the *Saturday Evening Post*, including several powerful critiques of contemporary issues, including "The Bogey Man Banished," which examined the change in cultural attitudes toward criminals. Where once a convicted man would be seen as different from ourselves, Davis noted, today judges acknowledged sympathy with those they were condemning, and the public had to ask how different this person really was from every other citizen. It was necessary, then, she concluded, to show children and young adults the convict in the dock or on the gallows "and say, 'You, too—but for the goodness of God and the power of fight that is in you."[58] While the item refused to separate criminals from the rest of humanity, it also insisted on personal responsibility.

Davis returned to the *Independent* in late June with "Lost," which began with the same image as "The Old Black Tea Pot": the old person, sitting in the chimney corner, contemplating life, and remembering the past. For the *Post*, however, she turned to a different kind of remembrance. "Friend Paul" was a tribute to the French-American anthropologist Paul du Chaillu who had died on April 29. du Chaillu's first African expedition had been sponsored by Philadelphia's Academy of Natural Sciences, he had often visited the city, and Davis knew him personally. He became a highly popular lecturer in Philadelphia and elsewhere based on his discoveries of tribes of pygmies and giant gorillas in Africa.

In spite of du Chaillu's fame, she insisted, "Friend Paul, as those who knew him loved to call him, remained the same clean-minded, affectionate, eager boy, always finding depths of goodness or power in his friends which nobody else suspected." Davis viewed du Chaillu as a man who "had a curious liking for the negro, the red man—for all wild races."[59] This essay captured the difference in du Chaillu's contemporary standing and the subsequent recognition of his strongly racist ideologies; it also captured the ways in which Davis herself could be a promoter of equality at one moment and in the next view Africans and Native Americans as "wild races."

This paradox was especially notable when "Friend Paul" was read next to Davis's subsequent essay for the *Post*, "Red Names for Red Men." Several tribal chiefs had recently protested the insistence by white educators at Carlisle and other schools for Native American children who were requiring their children be renamed. Davis did not object to the missionary attempts to

Christianize Native Americans, but she fully agreed with the protest against having their names anglicized: "The name which is given a boy when he comes into the world, by the time he has carried it for a dozen or fifteen years, has become as much a part of him as his head or his hand; it is his property; it is he. What right have we to take it from him?"[60]

Rebecca's productivity and Clarke's renewed health meant their summer weeks at Marion were especially happy this year. Cecil and Dick were living there while Dick worked on his next play and while their home at Mount Kisco was being built. Dick walked over to see his parents every morning. Nora was with them, and Charley visited frequently. They did not forego their time at Warm Springs later in the summer, however. This year Charley and Nora did not join the family at the Springs. Nora was traveling abroad with the actress Maude Adams, with whom she had long been friends. They went to Egypt, traveled up the Nile, and then to Jerusalem for five weeks; thereafter they spent a few weeks in the Libyan Desert camping, sleeping in tents, and riding horses all day, accompanied by a local cook and guide.[61] It was a wonderful adventure for the young women and expanded Nora's travel experiences. Charley also went abroad over the summer and connected with Nora along the way. Like Dick, Charley used his travels to advance his publications, contributing "A Few Stray Thoughts on Ocean Travel" to *Outing* magazine.

Over the summer and fall of 1903, in addition to the weekly cultural commentaries for the *Post*, Davis began to contribute to the magazine's regular feature, "Literary Folk—Their Ways and Their Work." The column included signed and unsigned articles about the world of literature and many well-known authors of the day contributed to the feature. Davis wrote three of the columns between July and September. The first was on the topic of "Race Books" and was published on the Fourth of July. "Race" was used in this instance to designate "a people," not simply a skin color. "There is a certain kind of strange book which appears at long intervals here and there in the world that ought not to be read or judged like any other," Davis wrote. "Each of these strange books we are talking of was born, not made. . . . It is red with human blood." They "paint a portrait of his race." There are always imposters who insist they are speaking for their race, but only four or five "true geniuses" who truly can do so. She considered Émile Zola for the French and Sir Jonah Barrington for the Irish as being among such geniuses. Other works qualified, such as Grace Rhys's *The Wooing of Sheila* because it offered "the genuine voice of the Celt." American readers today liked flash, not substance, she argued. They prefer Mrs. Humphrey Ward's "carefully compounded waxwork show" to the artistry of Rose Terry Cooke.[62]

Two other books that met her standards of a "race book" were by Native Americans. The first was Francis La Flesche's *The Middle Five*, which she had reviewed when it first appeared and again praised highly. The second was *Oo-mah-hah Ta-wah-thah*, "a thin little yellow volume, printed on a private press in Lincoln, Nebraska. A white woman has edited it, and a white man has inserted some poems of his own making upon diverse subjects, but between these inanities are a few papers by native Indians which open to us the life and the character of the red man as we find them nowhere else." Rather than the "bloodthirsty savage" of James Fenimore Cooper's pen that Americans had accepted as indicative of Native character, in this volume Davis found "the original grave, thoughtful owners of the continent, the families who dwelt on the same land for centuries, who trained their children up to habits of kindness, of high-bred courtesy, of reverence for the old and of obedience to the Great Spirit."[63]

She also noted Inshata Theumba's (Suzette La Flesche or "Bright Eyes") involvement with the project, "the Omaha girl . . . who pleaded the cause of the Ponca tribe in the East in Washington, and won it." While she praised this work, she felt that, in spite of the proliferation of depictions of African Americans in US literature, no one had yet written that race's book; when they did, "they would take a place in the foremost rank of men."[64] For someone who had eschewed literary criticism for most of her career, Davis now gave explicit voice to her wide ranging opinions in her "Literary Folk" columns over the next several years.

In July Charley's publication of a story in *Red Book* signified his growing fame as an author as well. *Red Book* was regarded as one of the premier periodicals for new fiction at this time. He would soon publish in *Ainslee's Magazine* and the *Smart Set* as well as *Outing* and *Red Book*. As a single man, Charley was often identified as dating eligible young women, and this summer it was the actress and singer Lotta Faust who the gossip columns reported to be his latest girlfriend.[65]

With Rebecca, Dick, and Charley all publishing in major literary magazines and newspapers, there continued to be no escaping reporters who wanted to write about The Davis Family as a literary phenomenon. Although originally a literary magazine, *Town and Country* in recent years had turned to covering society events and the people whose names appeared in the *Society Register*, and Rebecca and Clarke had long been listed in the *Register*. Thus it was only natural that *Town and Country* would eventually cover the Davises, as it did in July. The magazine highlighted Rebecca and Clarke's home as a longstanding salon for intellectuals of the various arts.[66] For nearly forty years the Davis home had been known among a wide group of artists, authors, and actors as the best gathering place in Philadelphia, but the Davises had never publicly talked about this aspect of their lives. The people who populated their home in the evenings came to talk about art, literature, and politics in an intellectually invigorating environment, not simply to be seen at a popular spot as the Swell Set sought. The difference was indecipherable to the society gossip columns but essential to Rebecca, Clarke, and their guests.

While in Warm Springs in August, Rebecca continued to write weekly editorials for the *Post*. "The Porch Climbers" insightfully noted that historians who write only about wars as a means of defining a nation miss the true nature of its people. They ought to study the masses of people who leave cities each year for resorts or the shore and congregate on the porches of inns. The best aspect of this "porch culture," she observed, was that it brought different classes together and "made us a more homogenous people."[67] Davis argued in "A Lesson from France" that Americans would do well to emulate the French practice of the *dot*, supplying a dowry to a daughter, regardless of her class. With a *dot*, a young woman would be able to marry whomever she chose because she could contribute to the establishment of her home; if a woman never married, she would not be a burden on someone else but could live independently. On the other hand, "The Cave-Man" addressed physical abuse of women; her solution was a return to Christ in contemporary culture in order to change society's increasing immorality.

At the same time Clarke was immersed in a heated exchange of letters with President Roosevelt and Lieutenant-General Nelson A. Miles. Clarke had sent a letter of recognition to Miles in early August when the general was retiring. Like many newspaper men, Clarke had written an editorial in honor of Miles, especially when there was a sense that he had been booted out of his position by the President. Though they corresponded occasionally, Clarke was surprised to receive a letter shortly thereafter from the President who took exception to Clarke's assertion that Miles had been a loyal soldier. "To speak of Miles as 'loyal,'" Roosevelt wrote, "is to use a fairly comically inappropriate word. He has, during the last few years, when head of the army, been as disloyal to the President and to the army, and therefore to the nation, as any man ever has been. . . . He has been in unscrupulous intrigue for his own political advancement."[68]

The President went on at length explaining his sense of Miles' disloyalty. When Clarke replied thanking Roosevelt for his explanatory letter, the President again replied at length: "I thank you for your very kind and manly letter. It was because I had such a high regard for you that I wrote to you alone of the various critics of my actions." He clearly hoped Clarke might publish something about Miles' disloyalty, asserting it was not something that only the administration should be privy to, but he wrote again on August 27 to counter that suggestion, insisting now that he did not want any of this information made public because he did not want to enter into a public debate on "an issue of personal veracity," knowing that Miles would only deny his charges.[69]

With all of this political intrigue, it was a welcome alternative when Clarke and Rebecca could turn their attention to more enjoyable events. Whatever they originally thought of Charley's association with Weber and Fields, the recognition of his accomplishments from newspaper accounts and from friends went a long way to assuage their concerns. One of those friends was Ethel Barrymore who returned to New York City in August for rehearsals of the play "Cousin Kate."

Barrymore joined Charley and other friends at the Music Hall one evening and could not offer enough praise of his production: "Weber and Fields . . . put on a perfectly wonderful show—this is one time when that word is exactly right—in which they always had a terrifically funny takeoff on some current success." She recognized the talents of the comedic actors in the company, including Lillian Russell, Peter Daly, Willie Collier, May Irwin, and David Warfield. Charley, as manager, was "all dressed up every night in white tie and tails, making a magnificent front and enjoying himself immensely."[70] Charley's experiences at Weber and Fields were beneficial to his writing career as well, as he was becoming known as an author who was particularly talented at presenting realistic contexts about the theater for his readers. He remained manager until Weber and Fields ended their partnership in 1904.

Davis's second contribution this year to the *Post*'s "Literary Folk" column was "Human and Inhuman Books" in September. Although evolution was as yet only a theory, Davis noted, there were enough animals from dogs to monkeys and even plants that seemed to have human qualities to suggest the truth of evolution, and books could have this "abnormal human quality" as well, she insisted, whether or not they were well written. The hotly debated recent publication of *More Letters of Jane Welsh Carlyle*, a reflection on the marriage of Jane and Thomas Carlyle, was one such book, she asserted. The same was true of several recent books about Sir Richard Burton, in all of which he was revealed to be "a learned brute." She detailed several other comparable revelatory books, recommending them even if they challenged the romantic images built up around some famous figures.[71] Davis also published several other works in

September, and she contributed to another of the popular collective articles by women writers for the *Ladies' Home Journal*, a short story for the *Independent*, and two editorials for the *Post*.

In October, Davis yet again opened the door to a periodical for a family member, with Charley's publication of "Miss Marr's Lovers" in the *Post* at the end of the month. On their own social front, Rebecca and Clarke continued their friendship with the Clevelands, and in mid-October, Grover contacted Clarke to ask if he knew anything about the merits of a Philadelphia artist by the name of Thomas Eakins. He had had so many bad portraits painted of himself, he explained, that he did not want to sit for Eakins unless Clarke had a strong recommendation for him. The assurances were apparently strong enough to convince Cleveland, as Eakins' painting became one of the best-known portraits of the former president. In Cleveland's many letters to Clarke, Frances always sent her love to Rebecca and Nora as well; although they saw each other less often than when the Clevelands summered at Marion, they maintained a warm acquaintance.

On October 5, the current president was again asking for Clarke's guidance, this time in relation to the labor problems he was facing. Roosevelt insisted to Clarke in an eight-page letter that Samuel Gompers, founder of the American Federation of Labor, had misrepresented Roosevelt's remarks in recent weeks. As was typical of their correspondence, the President would not issue denials but offered correctives to Clarke's editorials and used these private communications in an attempt to receive positive press in the *Public Ledger* during national crises by creating a sense of intimacy with phrases such as "for your private information" and by inviting Clarke to Washington so he could personally discuss the labor trouble with him.[72]

Roosevelt wrote again two days later to encourage Clarke to come to Washington for lunch as soon as possible, with the enticement of showing him some letters written by Abraham Lincoln. Roosevelt frequently compared himself to Lincoln, and in this instance, the letters were to demonstrate that the earlier president had also chosen to accept misrepresentation rather than endlessly attempt to explain his positions. Clarke accepted and traveled to Washington that week, and at the end of the month, Roosevelt asked him to come to the White House after the election so they could talk about the postal investigation that had so long plagued his administration. The envelope for this final letter was marked "Personal," another means Roosevelt used to create the sense that Clarke was receiving inside information no one else should know.[73]

While Clarke was involved in political discussions with Roosevelt, Rebecca turned to a new place of publication. In November 1903, she published "The Man Who Came Back" in *Metropolitan Magazine*, a sophisticated New York magazine edited by John Kendrick Bangs intended for theatergoers; it included quality fiction and articles about urban life. This was Davis's only publication for the *Metropolitan*, but in a few years both Dick and Charley would become frequent contributors.

Davis published only one article in the *Saturday Evening Post* in November, "A Shelf of Idols." The weekly contributions were becoming onerous with her editorial work for the *World* and her other publications, so, with occasional exceptions, she reduced her contributions to the magazine to one or two items a month. In a "A Shelf of Idols," using the Biblical tale of the golden calf, Davis asserted that contemporary Americans "have little metal calves of our own whom we worship every day," beginning with Society, especially the so-called Four Hundred. Another "calf" was the mass of novels that young people were reading, mistakenly calling them "American literature": "Our ideal literature now is only a gilded calf—it is not even gold." There were many other "calves" as well—"the voluble club-woman; the young victor in the Stock Exchange or Grain-pit; the modern Jove wielding his millions in his fist instead of arrows." She concluded, "Are these real Powers in life or only poor little gilded calves of our own making?"[74]

At the same time as Davis's article appeared, Charley published a nonfiction sketch in *Smart Set* that demonstrated how fully he had duplicated his mother's talents. While at the consulate in Florence, he had met John Bradford, who as a boy had sold crabs to Rebecca and Clarke when they summered at Point Pleasant. Bradford had a superb operatic voice, and he came to Florence to study with the masters. Although he greatly admired the ancient architecture of the city, he also came to know the people on the street where he lived and to immerse himself in the local culture, falling in love with a young woman from the area. The sketch was not a romance, however, as Bradford had to leave his dreams and his love behind to return home when his father had a stroke. As Charley concluded, the romance of Florence has ennobled some, but it also has a tragic side; it "sapped the life and destroyed the virility of others, and left them as they did Bradford, mere wrecks on the shores of their high ambitions."[75] The tragedy of Bradford's wasted life clearly haunted Charley.

At the end of the year Rebecca was included in a volume of "great thinkers of the day" as part of the twenty-volume *Consolidated Encyclopedic Library*. Dick was not faring as well in the public at present. A scathing satire of his "crimes against literature," casting him as "one of the worst literary criminals of all time," was published across the country in syndicated newspapers.[76] For Rebecca, however, 1903 had been a happy and productive year. She always had a remarkable spirit and a talent for endurance through difficult times—and she was going to need both for the coming year.

The year of 1904 began well, and Davis would publish four editorials in the *Saturday Evening Post*: a New Year's article, two cultural critiques, and an analysis of current trends in writing. She also published four "Literary Folk" items for *Saturday Evening Post* this year. She was moving forward with vigor in her career, and it seemed as if it would be one of her best years for writing and for her family's progress in their own careers.

In early 1904, Dick was approached by Robert Collier to cover the Russo-Japanese War for his magazine; in spite of Dick's earlier insistence he was going to focus only on stage work, he could not forego another opportunity for war reporting. The investment *Collier's* made in publicly promoting its war correspondents helped to ease the critical attacks against Dick's literary work. As he and Cecil were preparing to leave for Japan, Dick attempted to ease Rebecca's worries by insisting that this would be nothing like the dangers of the Boer War; it would be simply "a trip of cherry blossoms and Geisha girls."[77] Rebecca knew well enough what war was really like and undoubtedly what her son was doing, as well as the kindness that was intended. The assignment meant that Dick was out of town when his first original farce, "The Dictator," opened in New York and was a smashing success, confirming his hope that he could successfully commit to writing for the stage.

Clarke's health again took a turn for the worse creating concern for the entire family. Rebecca published nothing between February and April, and then only a short piece, "A Text for a Sermon" in the *Churchman*, a tribute to the Quaker Charles Caleb Pierce whose ministry took him to the mining camps of El Dorado. The following month she returned to the *Post* with only one signed article, "In the Debatable Lands: What the Civil War Meant to the Non-Combatants of the Border." This reminiscence would make its way into her autobiography as well, as she recalled the families split by differing alliances, reflected on her great admiration for Lincoln as a leader and an everyday man, and acknowledged the difference between the statistics of war and seeing a neighbor draped over the coffin of a loved one.

In spite of her limited contributions to the *Post* at this time, Davis was continuing to contribute editorials to the *World*. Samuel E. Moffett contacted her in April; he was an editorial writer for the *New York World* who was filling in for the managing editor, William Bradford Merrill, and he asked if she could contribute additional items for the paper. She responded with several editorials, including one on "drunkenness."[78] Although Davis's editorials for the *World* typically appeared in the Sunday editions, "Unhappy International Marriages" was an exception. Preceding Edith Wharton's *The Buccaneers* by many years, the piece covered similar territory. Davis noted that wealthy young American women who sought to marry a titled European were unprepared for the reality of such a marriage. They would never truly be accepted by the rank-conscious societies of their husbands.

Clarke appeared to have recovered enough strength by May to undertake a long train journey. He had always been involved in the international expositions, and he felt well enough to travel to St. Louis for Press Week at the World's Fair where the American Newspaper Publishers' Association was meeting. The event was headline news in the *St. Louis Republic*, which listed Clarke as one of the "prominent members" of the Association.[79] By July, with Clarke's continuing improved health, Rebecca was as productive as ever, with articles in the *Saturday Evening Post*, *Success*, and the *Interior*.

Writing while she, Clarke, and Nora were at Warm Springs, Davis contributed her second "Literary Folk" essay for this year to the *Post* in July, asserting certain books that lie outside the norm of literature could not be assessed within the normal parameters of criticism, such as recent books that purported to present an inside view of anarchism in England or the inside perspective of the poorest classes in that country. In contrast, Jack London's *The People of the Abyss* was written by a professional observer, she argued, and although his suggestions for reform were extreme, the study did not mock its subject as the book on the English poor did. It was, however, the authors who looked to why such conditions existed that Davis preferred to those who merely exposed shocking conditions.

Rebecca spent much of the summer working on her autobiography, revising published essays and adding new ones. It was one of the more enjoyable books she had written, as it allowed her once again to think back to the many people and places she had known intimately. It was her major book project of the 1900s, and she had been working on it diligently throughout the early years of the century, but she continued to write other items as well. In September, Davis returned to Philadelphia and to the pages of the *Independent* with a short story, "A Middle-Aged Woman." It was her first publication for the weekly since her 1903 Christmas story. Davis would continue to publish stories and articles in the *Independent* until 1908, but starting this year, she reduced her output for the magazine typically to two items a year.

Davis published her only article for the *Smart Set* this month as well. Charley had become a frequent contributor to the magazine, and, reciprocating the pattern of his parents, it was undoubtedly he who encouraged her to submit an article to the New York magazine that had instantly become the rage among the social elite. Its founder, William d'Alton Mann, sought to perpetuate the values of that class and to publish sophisticated literature for a well-educated audience. When Charles Hanson Towne became editor, he particularly sought to bring in young authors as well as the famous, and Charley continued to contribute to the magazine as did his friend O. Henry and others who came under Towne's tutelage. The magazine's circulation was over 300,000 at this time. Davis's contribution, "The Inside Story of It," invoked the dangers of relying on appearances. The popular wife of a presidential candidate who seems to be a quiet, unpoliticized woman was revealed to be the manipulative power behind her husband and a woman with a scandal in her own past. Although this story was her only contribution to the magazine, it was included in the publisher's ten-volume *Library of American Fiction*, which appeared at the end of the year.

Davis addressed political issues from a historical perspective in another contribution to the *Saturday Evening Post* this month. She rarely wrote about specific political campaigns (though many articles about Clarke's work suggested that she contributed ideas to his editorials), and she never publicly endorsed a candidate, but "Presidential Campaigns of To-Day and Yesterday" looked across the decades of her life to the alterations in how Americans had conducted presidential campaigns: "The Nation, every four years, still goes through the same convulsion, but with more outward calmness and dignity." But that is the outward presentation; inside the political machines something quite different occurred: "An enormous fund is now quietly raised by each party; a Cortelyou and a Taggart are chosen to conduct the war; secret orders are given to officials, from State bosses down to ward leaders. Nobody asks what is done with the money; nobody interferes with the tactics of the commanders."[80] Davis's article appeared just two months before the next presidential election in which Theodore Roosevelt ran on the Republican ticket and Alton Parker on the Democratic ticket; she named both in her article, without indicating a preference. Rather, she suggested, the voters mattered little with the vast machinery running the campaigns.

Davis's first book reviews had appeared, unsigned, in the *Atlantic Monthly*, in the early 1860s and she had published a few other reviews over the years, but it was the *Post*'s "Literary Folk" columns that honed her skills in the genre. In the September column, she acknowledged her admiration of the French journalist Octave Uzanne but admitted it was not a common American response. The French reading public's interest in scientific writings and well-crafted literature was not representative of the American reading public. Americans were largely noncritical and bored by Lamb's or Stevenson's thoughtful works, she lamented. American readers "are decent folk" but "want to be driven to vigorous laughing or crying, to be jerked violently for an hour out of their weary daily grind."[81]

Clarke's struggle with his health came to a crisis in October when he became seriously ill. Dick and Cecil were on their way home from Europe via British Columbia and immediately left for Philadelphia when they received the news. There was no quick recovery this time. The family tried to continue their normal routines, although it was most difficult for Rebecca to do so. She published only her annual Thanksgiving story in the *Independent*. She and Clarke barely marked the presidential reelection of Theodore Roosevelt.

While the family consulted with their physician and sought to comfort Clarke as much as possible, Rebecca received the news in early November that her beloved sister Emilie Harding Gow had died suddenly while in California. Emilie and her family had moved to the San Juan Islands near Seattle a few years earlier, which meant Rebecca had been able to see her far less than usual and their summer reunions at the shore were a thing of the past, but the close relationship of the sisters had lasted a lifetime. Their brother Wilse had moved to Seattle to be near Emilie's family,[82] and he was again responsible for arranging a sibling's funeral and burial.[83] In spite of the distance, Emilie's and Rebecca's children would remain in close contact. As late as 1952, Nora wrote to Amy Gow and enclosed a copy of the family history that Rebecca had written before her death.[84]

The shock of her younger sister's death meant Rebecca had no time to celebrate the publication of her autobiography, *Bits of Gossip*, which she had been working on for several years. It was an unusual autobiography in that it was full of reminiscences, as expected, but they were about the people she had known and the changes she had observed over the course of her lifetime rather than a chronicle of her own experiences.[85] The book drew on many of the memoir articles she had published in the last two years and added new chapters as well. In the preface to her autobiography, Davis explained her belief that "each human being, before going out into the silence, should leave behind him, not the story of his own life, but of the time in which he lived,—as he saw it,—its creed, its purpose, its queer habits, and the work which it did or left undone in the world."[86] True to her creed, *Bits* did not present her life story in dates and revelatory events; her own beliefs filtered through the pages, however, as she wrote about the extraordinary people she had known.

Her reflections were a compendium of the changes that had evolved over her lifetime, from a childhood when there were few railways and no automobiles, to the turn of the century when the US had become a money-obsessed, empire-building nation. "My easy-going generation," she acknowledged, "did not push the world's work on very far perhaps; we did not discover wireless telegraphy, nor radium. But neither did we die of nerve prostration."[87] Although the cultural autobiography was that of an older person who lamented some of the changes she had witnessed, it was also an important reflection on the realities of those past times rather than the romanticizing of bygone days that had become so popular in US culture. Davis demythologized New England and praised the heartiness of the Scotch-Irish in more detail than she had in her earlier writings. She especially appreciated that the Scotch-Irish were willing to go into Pennsylvania and West Virginia to settle in the lush hillsides where earning a living was easier than in the rugged landscape of New England. "It was no doubt a very poetic, picturesque thing to land on Plymouth Rock," she reflected, "but surely it was a stupid thing to stay there."[88] Yet even the hearty Scotch-Irish, she admitted, could take their beliefs too far, demanding a level of self-denial among their children that went beyond any purpose it could serve.

One of the most important chapters she added to her previously published memoirs was on the Civil War, and it was in this section that she particularly sought to deromanticize: "The histories which we have of the great tragedy give no idea of the general wretchedness, the squalid misery, which entered into every individual life in the region given up to the war. Where the armies camped the destruction was absolute."[89] She captured the naiveté of most Americans when the war began: "The newly-made surgeon of a newly-made regiment came to bid us good-by before going to the field. 'Yes,' he said exultantly, 'we're off to the front to-morrow. My men are ready. I've vaccinated all of them, and given every man a box of liver pills"![90] They had no idea of the brutalities they were about to face, nor how some soldiers might act.

"There were phases of the long struggle familiar enough to us then which never have been painted for posterity," Davis added. "There were, for instance, regiments on both sides which had been wholly recruited from the jails and penitentiaries. This class of soldiery raged like wild beasts through the mountains of the border States. They burned, they murdered men, women, and children, they cut out the tongues of old men who would not answer their questions."[91] Further, while some men served out of patriotic fervor, many men, especially in the late years of the war, enlisted because if they did not, their families would starve. She insisted on the necessity of exposing these realities, since hiding them has allowed "our young people . . . to look upon war as a kind of beneficent deity, which not only adds to the national honor but uplifts a nation and develops patriotism and courage." Although that is true in some ways, she argued, "it is only fair, too, to let them know that the garments of the deity are filthy and that some of her influences debase and befoul a people. . . . A man cannot drink old Bourbon long and remain in his normal condition. We did not drink Bourbon, but blood."[92] Perhaps more than anything, Davis's recollections of the Civil War revealed the extent to which the war had remained a vivid memory to the generation that had experienced it firsthand.

Davis significantly revised the earlier reminiscences of the abolitionists she had published in the *Saturday Evening Post*, determining that odd and zealous as they were, single-minded in their goals, they believed in the righteousness of their cause. She also added a new chapter at the conclusion of *Bits of Gossip*. "Above Their Fellows" detailed some of the most extraordinary people she met over the course of her life. "The only hero known to my childhood was Henry Clay," she recalled with affection, and he clearly remained a noble figure to her mind. James G. Blaine was another of her heroes; her cousin had died in 1893, but she remembered him fondly and the large circle of friends who were drawn to him. Others who remained vivid in her recollections were Charles J. Peterson, Edgar Allan Poe, Walt Whitman and his great admirer William O'Connor, and two editors who left a lasting impact on her: Josiah Gilbert Holland and Daniel S. Ford. If these two editors were not geniuses, such as she categorized the former group, they acquired great influence over their generations and each had a notable sense of self-recognition.

She included several women in this group of people "above their fellows" who had influenced the nation at varying times. "The South always chose its reigning favorite, first for her power to harm, and next for her beauty," and such women as Sallie Ward and Winnie Davis were representative. The same traits were valued in the North, "with the addition in most cases of some intellectual force." At the beginning of the Civil War, the most notable nationally beloved woman was Jessie Benton Frémont, and later Frances Willard garnered a greater following than any other woman of her time.[93] "The world is crowded with brave and friendly souls," Davis concluded her autobiography, "though they may be slow in recognizing one another. And of all the good things for which, in the evening, I have to thank the Father of us all, the best is, that I have known so many of them, and for so long have kept them company."[94]

The reviews of *Bits of Gossip* were excellent. The *Washington Times* reviewer best captured Davis's accomplishment when he noted, "Mrs. Davis' personality shines through and illuminates all she writes with a bright kindliness, which in no way dims her keen vision."[95] These were the traits with which Davis had inclusively critiqued US society for more than forty years, and they remained integral to her autobiography. It was her "strong and convincing individuality" that reviewers appreciated as shaping her reminiscences, and because of the strength of her personality "these sketches leave an impression far more lifelike and distinct than one expects from such recollections."[96] The *New-York Tribune* praised her "brilliant pen" and wished the book were even longer.[97] Many reviewers felt the title was too modest for the serious content of the volume; as *The Spectator* insisted, "this is most decidedly a book to be read."[98] The popularity of *Bits of Gossip* was reflected in the many excerpts from it that were reprinted in collections about US literature and culture in the coming years.

Sadly, all of the excitement about her autobiography was veiled by Emilie's death and Clarke's failing health. Rebecca had published her last "Literary Folk" column for the *Post* in early December. It continued her lament about the proliferation of trite novels and praised a handful of writers, including Edith Wharton. But she published little else at this time.

By early December it was clear that Clarke could not live much longer. As they had always tried to face issues directly and thoughtfully, they had prepared for Clarke's death—determining the division of his estate, what to do with his vast library, where he would be buried, and every other necessary detail. Dick, Cecil, and Charley came home as often as possible, and on one visit, Dick wrote Charley, "Dad is the same but greatly depressed in spirits. We are allowed to see him for only a few minutes as it excites him greatly."[99]

Clarke died from heart disease on December 14, 1904. Rebecca's faith and personal strength sustained her through this heartbreaking loss. For forty-one years she and Clarke had built an extraordinarily strong and egalitarian marriage in which their love never abated and in which they supported one another personally and professionally while creating a family life for their children that was a model of love and generosity.

The national sense of loss was equally strong, with obituaries appearing in newspapers across the country. The Philadelphia newspapers, where he was intimately known, were able to capture the personal side of Clarke's "simple and beautiful" home life as well as his "fearless integrity and intense abhorrence of every form of public or private wrong. His high ideals of human duty and destiny appealed to his readers because of the nobility of his thought, the force of his expressions and the purity of his diction."[100]

Clarke had prepared his will in 1891, and the extraordinary love he had for Rebecca was reflected in his bequeathing to "my dearly beloved wife . . . absolutely, as if it had been hers from the beginning of the world, all and whatsoever property, estate or belongings of which I may die possessed, whether Real, Personal, or mixed." To Dick he left his gold watch and chains "and my Dante Ring"; to Charles, "my set of antique buttons, also my cameo set, and my intaglio Ring"; and to Nora, "the sum of fifty dollars with which to buy a ring to be worn by her in loving remembrance of me."[101]

It was during family crises that Nora's extraordinary personal strength always came to the forefront. She was a practical and astute manager, and although Clarke had designated Rebecca as executrix, the administration of the estate was handed over to Nora. The codicil to the will was attested to by Clarke's longtime assistant, F. Percival Farrar.[102] Clarke's estate was valued at a modest $4,000. Always one to donate or give away money, his generosity had always made finances a matter that needed careful attention. By far the more frugal and practical of the two, Rebecca would amass more than ten times Clarke's estate by the time of her death six years later.

Now the sole breadwinner for herself and Nora, Davis continued to publish. She had contributed "Some Old-Time Christmases" to the *Saturday Evening Post* a week before Clarke's death, and by the end of the month she published another essay on "Old-Time Hospitality" in its pages. Rebecca would spend the last six years of her life as a widow, but one with exceptionally loving children who were even more attentive than usual in her final years. She did not, however, abandon her career. If she felt as a young woman that she "must write or die," the same passion for her art remained with her until the end. But from this point on, she would do it without the great love of her life beside her. Never again to hear his voice. Never again to share ideas or read aloud together in the evening. Never again to travel together to Europe, Marion, Warm Springs, or Ocala. Never again to feel his touch, to smile at one another with the intimacy of forty years together. It was to be a new chapter in her life, and the final one.

CHAPTER 14

The Widowed Writer (1905–1910)

One of the first tasks Rebecca undertook after Clarke's death was to prepare his extensive collection of theater memorabilia for auction through the Anderson Auction Company in New York. The collection included rare dramatic books, playbills, and portraits of numerous actors the Davises had known over the last several decades.[1] This process brought her close to one of Clarke's most beloved activities and kept her busy enough to contain her mourning. Her abiding faith was of utmost help during this period of loss, and writing was both her income and her salvation. She wrote extensively for the *New York World* and *Saturday Evening Post* as well as publishing in a wide range of periodicals, both old standbys and new magazines. She still had a great deal to say about contemporary US culture, and in 1905, her pen flew across paper. Rebecca and her sons had always written to one another several times a week as well, and even within those terms, she increased her letter-writing in the aftermath of Clarke's death.[2] For the woman who "must write," her career and her family helped her navigate loss and the coming years without Clarke.

Numerous family members, friends, and acquaintances sent condolences, the famous and the familial. Her cousin Clara Wilson Baird's letter of condolence was a welcome voice from the past. "I know you appreciated Clarke and loved him," Rebecca responded. "Who could help loving him? As you wrote to me 'Nobody ever knew him to do a selfish thing.' I was glad too to have a loving word from you after our long silence. We are too near the shore of the great river to forget our deep affection of the past."[3] Rebecca asked Clara to respond to their other cousins for her; she needed to limit her writing to her work at present because of problems she was having with her eyesight. For the next few years she would struggle with eye strain before finally agreeing to surgery.

Throughout her career, Davis had occasionally written about her profession, but her alignment with the *Saturday Evening Post* opened a new avenue for critiquing the state of literature and publishing. In 1905, she nearly doubled the number of "Literary Folk" columns she wrote for the magazine, beginning in January with a column in which she turned to the rapacious English and

American appetite for memoirs, recognizing the genre helped to feed the desire to learn the intimate details of celebrities' lives. Assessing the content of four works about the lives of Lords and Marquesses, she ultimately preferred Charles A. Eastman's *Indian Boyhood*. Recognizing that the customs of so many Native Americans were being lost through assimilation, Davis believed the Santee Sioux author's story would "hereafter be of great historical value."[4]

Dick and Cecil were longing for a warmer climate, but they debated traveling so soon after Clarke's death. However, Rebecca encouraged their desire to undertake a trip to Cuba, Panama, and Venezuela in February. While they were traveling, Charley took care of their estate and finances, a practice he would continue for the remainder of his brother's life. He also made sure to visit Rebecca most weekends. Although Rebecca had always been the core of the family, supporting all of them personally and professionally, Charley was a close second in the role, and after Clarke's death, he was the family member who cared for everyone, financially and personally. A generous and loving man, Charley may have been overshadowed publicly by his older, flamboyant brother, but everyone in the Davis family knew his strengths and depended on him.

In late February, Davis published two "Literary Folk" columns in the *Post*. The second one included a recommendation of *The Life of Dean Farrar*. Davis had long known Frederic Farrar, Dean of Canterbury, and, though acknowledging he deserved credit for his public service, she appreciated him as "the gentle, cordial host and friend, apt to be excited about trifles ... but eager to do good to every living thing." Dean Farrar's son, Percival, was a longtime family friend and had been Clarke's assistant for many years. Davis reviewed several other works in these columns, concluding with Lady Gregory's *Gods and Fighting Men* in which the stories were simple but had "a strange power" over the reader. "To read this book, after the modern novels," Davis concluded, "is like going out of city streets on a noisy Fourth of July to keep company with the silent mountains or the sea."[5]

Although the majority of Davis's writings in these years were nonfiction essays and journalism, she and Dick had recently been identified as two of America's "prominent novelists" in Henry William Elson's *History of the United States of America*. Charley was also gaining greater attention and high critical praise. The quality of his publications in *Collier's Weekly* and elsewhere had earned him an offer to become the fiction editor of that magazine, which he readily accepted. He continued to publish fiction and essays in a wide range of periodicals, including new publications such as *Everybody's Magazine*,

All-Story Magazine, and *Reader Magazine*, as well as standards such as *Munsey's* and *Outing*. Charley's editing of dramas earlier in his career and now of fiction at *Collier's* had lasting influence on literature at the turn of the century.

Rebecca's prolific writing in the early months of 1905 helped her transition into life as a widow. In addition to an article in *Success*, she published another lengthy "Literary Folk" column in April that reviewed several books about the problems in the slums of metropolitan areas, including Jacob Riis's *The Battle with the Slum* and *Children of the Tenements*. She acknowledged Riis's expertise but felt he made the error common to many reformers, assuming "that fresh air and cleanliness are synonymous with virtue, filth with vice." She added praise, but with her continuing xenophobia, "Still it is impossible not to sympathize with Mr. Riis in his triumph as he writes the history of the long fight for decent dwellings in the worst quarters of New York. The fight was won. Five Points is gone, Baxter Street is purified, and the hordes that tenanted them are now made comfortable if not less vicious."[6] She wrote favorably of Washington Gladden's *Social Salvation* and Maud Ballington Booth's *After Prison—What?* because both valued Christianity as the most important offering for the poor man.

As always, Dick continued to send Rebecca drafts of his stories for her to critique. In late April, the bluntness with which the family critiqued one another's work was evident as she declared that the characters in his latest manuscript were neither attractive nor interesting. Dick responded, "I thank you very, very much for saying just what you did. You always are my true friend and helper. One result of your letter is that I love you more than ever, which is quite untrue, because it is quite impossible. God bless you dear, dear mother."[7]

Davis published an essay in *Success* and two reminiscences in the *Post* between May and July. It had been two years since she contributed to the *Ladies' Home Journal*, and she returned to its pages with "The Story of a Few Plain Women." It was a contemplative article: "One thing is sure in this strange world of ours, and that is, that every human being that comes into it has his or her load to bear." The Queen who resides in luxury may harbor cancer in her body while the poor laborer "has a hunger gnawing in his heart for noble music which he never can hear."[8]

The latter image was part of a theme that had coursed through Davis's work since "Life in the Iron-Mills," and in this essay she delved into the ways in which each individual bears that burden as the mark of character and occasionally of true greatness. Notable to Davis were the lives of a few ordinary women rather than the famous political or religious figures. Among the women she acclaimed were Mary Willard of Chicago, whose early death inspired her sister Frances and others to found the Women's Christian Temperance Union, and the Irish American Margaret Haughery of New Orleans, an orphan who could neither read nor write but who was industrious and wise in business. Haughery left all of her considerable estate to the Orphan Asylum in her hometown. What Davis admired in these women was their means of thwarting life's burdens in favor of "a healthy heroic spirit of self-sacrifice," a trait that always held high rank in Davis's hierarchy of greatness—and one, she observed, that could be found "in almost every home."[9]

In the summer of 1905 Rebecca and Nora returned to Point Pleasant for the first time in several years. Rebecca had always loved the area, and it was where she and Clarke had spent so many happy summers when their children were young. She enjoyed writing while at the shore as well. Dick and Cecil joined them before traveling on to Marion.[10] The *New York Times* tracked Rebecca and Dick's movements over the summer as part of the trend of reporting on the travels of authors, celebrities, and the socially elite.[11] For someone who had eschewed literary criticism for much of her career, this summer Davis relished such writing. She published "Literary Folk" columns in the *Post* in June and July. The June column was of particular interest as she discussed a strange phenomenon in literature: women writing about what they did not know—"women of the protected classes" wrote about the slums while working women like Charlotte Brontë wrote about noble women, and she critiqued the title character of Kate Douglas Wiggin's *Rebecca of Sunnybrook Farm,* who "does not seem more real to us than a talking doll upon a Christmas tree." Edith Wharton was clearly a highly intelligent woman, Davis acknowledged, and someone she had previously praised, but she found that once she had closed the pages of her novels, she never thought about them again. The characters "are tired of life, tired of themselves, of each other. Nothing happens. There is no hint of character, thought, passion, or purpose in [any] of them. . . . Is the American fiction then, so far as our women writers are concerned, to be purely a matter of style?" She longed for writers like Sarah Orne Jewett whose Mrs. Todd and Captain Littlepage were as real as any neighbor; only Margaret Deland continued to create such characters in this era, Davis concluded.[12]

Although Rebecca continued writing throughout the summer, first at Point Pleasant and then in Warm Springs, she was having considerable problems with her eyes. Through the fall, she published several articles in the *Post* and one in the *Independent* and continued to write editorials for the *World,* but she would soon have to confront the fact that her eyes were severely strained. The exciting family news, however, was that over Labor Day weekend, Dick and Cecil were able to move into their new home, Crossroads Farm, at Mount Kisco. They had built a lake at the foot of the hill on which the spacious house stood. Located in a richly wooded area, Crossroads Farm was not visible to neighbors and afforded them a quiet place of retreat from New York City. Much more than her summer retreats, Crossroads Farm would become Rebecca's second home. Cecil was generous in welcoming her mother-in-law and encouraging her to come as often as possible. The two women were quite different—Rebecca preferred the older ways of the domestic woman, and Cecil was a decidedly New Woman—but they loved and greatly admired one another. Rebecca could not have been more fortunate in a daughter-in-law.

Rebecca was especially prolific in the last months of the year. She published three essays in the *Post* and stories in the *Independent*, wrote for the *World*, and returned to writing for *St. Nicholas* for the first time since 1899. The magazine was under new editorship; Mary Mapes Dodge had died in August, and William Fayal Clarke, Dodge's longtime associate editor, became the magazine's new editor. Rekindling her interest in children's literature, Davis would continue to write for the renowned children's magazine for the remainder of her life.

Her sons were active at the end of the year, too. In the winter Dick was involved in the production of his new play, "The Galloper," scheduled to open in Baltimore in mid-December. Charley had been recuperating from ill health at Crossroads Farm, but the exercise he engaged in as he recovered and his enjoyment of playing pool in the evening had restored his health to the extent he could join Dick in Baltimore for the opening. Nora and the Charles Dana Gibsons were there as well.[13] The play was a success and would open in New York in January. Nora was now moving in high society circles in Baltimore as well as in Philadelphia and New York, and Charley was keeping notable company, as the *New-York Tribune* reported; he and Mark Twain were guests at the Society of Illustrators' dinner in late December.[14]

As the year 1906 began, Rebecca remained committed to a steady writing schedule, though her eye problems caused occasional delays. "The Love Story of Charlotte Bronte" appeared in the *Post* in January as Dick's play opened in New York. He had a second play on Broadway as well. "Miss Civilization" starred the longtime Davis family friend Ethel Barrymore. Later in the year when Ethel was starring in "Alice Sit-by-the-Fire," Charley and Ethel dined together. He tried to explain that a woman using the term "assignation" was considered inappropriate by US audiences even though it was not in England. As always, they had a good friendly argument about it, neither changing his or her opinion. The next day, however, Charley sent Ethel a leather engagement book—but he had "Engagements" on its cover changed to "Assignations"![15]

It was March before Rebecca again published, but two items appeared that month. "An American Family" in the *Independent* looked to the common American family and the way in which its successes and differences could tear members apart. A signed essay, "Religion in the Days of Our Father," for the *Post* continued Davis's turn to the past for her subject matter in these last years of her life. She also published a review of Hamilton Holt's *The Life Stories of Undistinguished Americans*, a collection of sixteen autobiographies of immigrants, for the *Independent*. She praised its originality, asserting it was the first such effort "to show in detail how the experiment [of immigration] has succeeded; how the incomers have seized and used the chance." Concluding her appreciation of the accomplishments of this racially and ethnically varied group of new Americans, Davis seemed for an instant to return to her xenophobia. Common to them all, in addition to the successes they have made of their lives, was that "there is not in a single one of these histories of life, a word of acknowledgment or gratitude to the country which gave them the chance and the success." This time, however, she pushed her thinking about why that might be: "Was there anything lacking in the gift?" she asked as a conclusion.[16] The concluding question continued Davis's pattern of using this method to force readers to contemplate the question's implications.

Shortly thereafter, Davis reviewed the African American poet James E. McGirt's latest volume of poetry. Although she was not a poet herself, Davis had immersed herself in the study of poetry since she was a teenager, and in letters to friends and family, she often critiqued the latest volumes of verse. This was the first collection she had reviewed in print, however, and a line from her assessment of McGirt's talents was used to advertise the book: "I find in Mr. McGirt's verses a meaning and accent which belong only to the true poet."[17]

In the spring, Rebecca and Nora decided to travel to Europe again. Nora was recovering from a lingering illness and felt the trip would help restore her health, and Rebecca knew this would probably be her last opportunity to travel abroad. Dick had urged them to go and financed the trip, a gift Rebecca did not refuse this time. When he was flush (and often even if he was not), he was as generous as his father had been; Crossroads Farm would leave him always fretting over his finances, but his plays on Broadway were very profitable. The trip was a gift Rebecca and Nora thoroughly enjoyed. On April 20, 1906, they departed from New York City and traveled to England, Germany, and Italy.

Three days later Rebecca described the first stage of their trip to Dick and Cecil: "nothing could be finer. The sea is not much more uneasy than our lake [at Mt. Kisco].... Neither of us has missed a meal." She admitted that her thoughts were more with home than their destination, "I just lie & wonder about you children," and she pummeled Dick with questions about his plays and activities and about Cecil's work. "When you write," she advised, "don't ask about us—We shall job on like everybody else. But remember that I am all the time wanting to hear of you both. Whatever you do Dick, remember there is an audience of one old woman waiting to hear."[18] Crossroads Farm had become a place of comfort and solace to Rebecca, and she wrote later in the sea voyage that "I am coming back *sure* to the farm to sit in my chair & look at the lake & play pool. One of the best & most loving things ever you did was to take me in for these last days. It is all very nice here & we are not a bit seasick."[19] Though it might have surprised some of her friends, Rebecca was an avid and competitive pool player when with family at Mt. Kisco.

Before leaving for Europe, Davis had submitted what would be her last publication for the *Saturday Evening Post*, though both Dick and Charley would publish there in the coming years. By the time she returned from her travels, Rebecca would have to admit that her eyes were considerably worse, and she would not be able to write for more than six months. Thereafter she focused on writing newspaper editorials and items for the *Independent* and *St. Nicholas*. In the interim, she thoroughly enjoyed her travels.

As they neared Gibraltar, she could report that they had had smooth sailing the entire way. Rebecca recounted an anecdote purportedly about Nora but in reality about her sons. "We are most of the time in our room & did not think anybody knew anything about us," she wrote to Dick.

> "But the other evening Noll was in the salon & the officers & all were there & . . . the woman who was managing—there always is one—came to Nora & said wont you play for us. 'Thank you I don't play' Noll said. 'Then you sing?' "No I don't sing.' Perhaps you recite?' 'I can't recite'—'Oh, then you will tell a story. 'No I cant tell stories.' 'And yet' said the woman turning to the listening room, 'and yet she is Dick Harding Davis' sister!' Then every one talked & said how they had read every word you wrote . . . Noll came down laughing at them. But I saw she was very much pleased. Ever since when I go up somebody comes & talks to me of you boys—[20]

Undoubtedly, Nora did not want to be commanded to perform, but the anecdote revealed how intrusive the fame of The Davis Family could be.[21]

By early May, Rebecca and Nora were ensconced at the Santa Lucia Hotel in Naples, which offered them views of the bay and Mount Vesuvius. The eruption of Vesuvius in April had devastated the city, though Davis found the people there "as noisy & happy as ever but the eruption was a hard blow to them. The whole city lies under the gray dust from Vesuvius. It covers the palaces & the trees & flowers. The mountain itself looks to me as if one third of it were gone—a big hollow in the top."[22] They left a few days later for a four-week stay in Rome where they enjoyed sightseeing and exploring the famous sites of the city, including a visit to the Vatican.[23] While traveling, Rebecca quietly celebrated her seventy-fifth birthday.

When the travelers returned in the fall, Rebecca headed to Crossroads Farm for an extended visit rather than immediately returning to Philadelphia; Nora joined her for a few days but then went ahead to Philadelphia to get the house ready. While Rebecca was abroad, Charley had taken up her mantel of publishing in the *New-York Tribune*. One of his first pieces for the newspaper, "Coccaro the Clown," appeared in November and was highly praised. As one critic observed, "There are not many great short stories in the broad field of the world's literature, and the critics are accustomed to count on the fingers of one hand all the truly good stories that appear in the American publications in the course of an entire year. Mr. Davis' short story, 'Coccaro, the Clown,' comes very near winning a finger in the count."[24] Charley would continue to write stories for the *Tribune* for the next five years.

Demonstrating why The Davis Family was such a popular subject for literary columns, at the same time, Dick published *The Real Soldiers of Fortune*, including individuals he had known such as Winston Churchill, and he, too, received good reviews of the book. Rebecca was contacted at this time by H. E. Rood at Harper and Brothers, who requested contributions from her, but the one piece she did write at this time was for *St. Nicholas*, a study of Benjamin Franklin that would be one of her most popular reprints in both England and Australia.

While she was at Crossroads Farm, Rebecca's brother Wilse traveled from Washington State to join the family for a visit as well. No one could know at this time of laughter and enjoyment that it would be their last time together. On December 12, 1906, Rebecca's beloved brother Hugh Wilson ("Wilse") Harding died at a friend's home in Bethlehem, Pennsylvania, where he had stopped on his way home from Crossroads Farm. He had visited the Davis family regularly in Philadelphia and most summers since the 1860s, until his move a few years earlier to Seattle, he had joined them at Point Pleasant and Marion; he was truly part of their family.

This time it was Rebecca who arranged for a sibling's funeral. Wilse was buried near their parents and two brothers in the Washington Cemetery. In loving tribute, Rebecca had his tombstone inscribed, "The Pure in Heart Shall See God." Although Wilse had appointed his Davis and Gow nieces and nephews as his executors, it was again Nora who actually performed these duties. Wilse owned a good deal of property, and his properties in Seattle and the San Juan Islands were left to the Gow siblings and Nora Davis. His Point Pleasant lots were willed to Rebecca. He had kept a storage vault in Bethlehem in which furniture, books, rare china, and other items were stored; these were left to Dick, Charley, and Nora.[25]

Unfortunately, Nora had plans to travel shortly after Wilse died, and Rebecca felt terribly alone. Dick sent a letter to console her: "Dear Mother— You have lost dear old uncle and the erring child wanderer [Nora] but you have me and Gus [Charley] and your adopted daughter [Cecil] within call."[26] Although she was the eldest sibling, Rebecca was now the last surviving member of her Harding family.

As 1907 began, Rebecca's children were frequently traveling. Charley went west on business, while Dick and Cecil left on January 25 for the Belgian Congo where he was to report on the war for *Collier's*. Rebecca worried about Dick's assignment because of its dangers and because he had studied nothing about the war before leaving. As was the family custom, she and Nora, joined by Maude Adams, posted a map of Africa in her Twenty-first Street home so they could track Dick and Cecil's travels. Rebecca wrote to them, keeping them updated on the trial of Stanford White's murderer and reporting on Charley's activities in the west where he was overseeing the out-of-town premiere of one of Dick's plays.

Dick's dependence on Charley in these years grew multifold; in town or out, he relied on his younger brother to manage his contracts, oversee theater productions, and handle his finances. He also offered Charley a welcoming second home at Crossroads Farm, and it was a place that meant as much to Charley as to their mother. In her letters, however, Rebecca cautioned Dick to become better educated about the situation in the Congo. She recognized that, due to US investments in the rubber trade there, the situation was fragile and a highly volatile subject in the States. She wanted him to "relish the African adventure," but insisted, "Be awfull careful of [] facts about the Congo matter. It's a burning subject here."²⁷ Dick adhered to her advice and began studying the bases of the fighting while he was onboard ship.²⁸

Charley returned from the west in mid-February and reinstated his frequent visits with Rebecca. She appreciated his visits as much as she relished her sons' literary and journalistic successes, observing to Dick, "I do thank God for the help you & Charley have given to the under-dogs in this life and that you weren't lawyers or shopkeepers or brokers—good respectable folk as they are."²⁹

Although Charley visited often, he had an extraordinarily busy life in New York and attending to Crossroads Farm while Dick and Cecil were traveling. Nora visited him at the farm on the 20th of the month. Rebecca could not help feeling lonely without her daughter as a constant companion, but as she told Dick, Nora had been "very tired & we thought three days at the farm would be a glimpse of Paradise to her."³⁰ Although Nora traveled more now, she was the abiding source of support for her mother in her old age, as she had been for decades.

By March Rebecca was able to write again, and she published "Girls in Business" in the *Churchman*, praising the idea of teaching women "the ordinary rules of business" so they would never be subject to impoverishment and desperation due to dependence on a man's ability to earn money.³¹ At this time Charley was writing a great deal about theater life, taking up his father's mantel both in fiction and nonfiction, and Rebecca was handling proofs for *The Real Soldiers of Fortune* while Dick was in Africa.

She was feeling better about Dick's trip after receiving a letter from him about his experiences. He had taken the assignment, "hoping to root out stories of massacre and torture," but the letter suggested he had come to have more sympathy for the situation after seeing the war-weary soldiers.³² She replied, "what is best is what *you* are getting out of this. This letter to me today shows that. Seed into your brain & sun and rain and all together your going was one of the best moves of your life & the wisest."³³ She could not help but add two other comments—that Charley was rested after his short visit to Crossroads Farm, but that he was "growing fat," a constant concern about her youngest son. She added, however, that *he* was saving money, a pointed comment against Dick's infamous overspending. She could report from Charley a few days later, that the play was doing well and that he would have a "nice purse" waiting for Dick. In spite of her criticisms of Charley's weight problems, she recognized his strengths: "Today dear old Gus is here—he is so loving and watchful of his old Mother it makes me quite young again."³⁴ Unless he was out of town, Charley now came every Sunday to be with Rebecca.

In spite of a snow storm that had blanketed Philadelphia, her longtime friend and author Margaret Deland spent a few days visiting Rebecca in March. Deland's visit was followed immediately by one from Frances Cleveland and Caroline Jayne. Both women delighted Rebecca by praising Dick's recent publication, "The Scarlet Car," and hoped to see the story continued. A Philadelphia friend, Maria, came to see her every day as well.[35]

In addition to visiting with old friends, Rebecca continued to engage with contemporary events even as she immersed herself in remembering her earlier life. She had always attended Easter services and as she wrote Dick after attending this year,

> No day is like Easter for me—not even Christmas. Just sixty years ago I went to the communion for the first time on Easter—and then Dad [Clarke] cared so much for it—And just now at church hundreds of people were crowding to the altar. Men—old men—women, poor and rich one little deformed boy and I remembered that this was but one little church in the town and that there were thousands of towns in the country and that all over the world they were rejoicing because He rose from the dead—and were trying to live like Him. Not doing it maybe. But the trying is something—for us, isn't it? Forgive me dear. But I feel as if I had to tell somebody the thing concerned the whole world.

Rebecca also included in the letter a note about her pride in Nora's efforts as a Sunday School teacher: "there were five poor little girls who came to speak to Noll as we went out. I knew them—for she has taught them since they were tiny children and all they knew that is good came from her. But I wouldn't dare to say it to her. I *must* tell you for I do like to talk of what my children do."[36]

Dick and Cecil stopped in London in April for a rest after covering the Congo. It had not been a successful trip in terms of reporting, though it would afford Dick enough articles to collect in a book. He sent Rebecca the first of his Congo articles, and she could at last relax, knowing he would not embarrass himself with his reporting on the subject: "I must confess I have been awfully anxious about these articles. . . . the whole subject was so gruesome! But I'll never be uneasy about your work again. This picture is vivid & horrible from beginning to end—It has grim touch that is like nobody else's touch. . . . the whole thing reeks of horror. . . . Well I'm a foolish old woman I suppose but I never can get used to the power in your work or stop rejoicing in it as if it were something quite new to me."[37] Rebecca was always most proud of Dick's writings when he exposed the pathos of a people's situation.

By April, Rebecca and Nora had decided to close the Philadelphia house in early May this year and head to Point Pleasant, where Charley and his frequent companion, the actress Margaret Fraser, would join them. Rebecca had hoped to see Dick and Cecil in New York before going to the shore, but the travelers had determined to stay in London for a while longer. She was sorry to miss out on time at Crossroads, both for herself and Charley. "If the farm did no good to anybody but Charley," she conveyed to Dick, "it has already been worth the price. But when you think what it is to *me*—I can't tell you—At night I lie sometimes & think of my seat on the terrace the view down to the lake and how it is *yours*—my boy's—."[38]

It was to the *New-York Tribune* that Davis turned, publishing three articles with the newspaper in the spring and early summer of 1907. They were her first publications in the *Tribune* since leaving her role as editorial correspondent in 1889. The first article, "Unpublished Tragedies," was a recollection of how everyday tragedies have an impact on ordinary people's lives. The following month she published "Some Strange True Stories" in which she conveyed accounts of real-life stories she had been privy to over her life, stories that "equal many of the most extravagant plots to be found in modern fiction."[39] Her third piece for the *Tribune*, "A Strange True Story," was a return to the genre of the mystery. She and Charley were now both appearing in the *Tribune*'s pages, as he continued to publish articles about theater life in the newspaper. At the same time, Dick published *The Scarlet Car*. The Davis Family was as productive as ever.

One of the first articles Dick published about his experiences in the Congo appeared in June. Rebecca wrote to him from Point Pleasant as soon as "My Brother's Keeper" appeared, asking for extra copies to distribute to her friends there. "Isn't it strange to think that you over here can strike a big blow for thousands of negroes who never heard of you and never will know that you can save them from torture and death!" she wrote. "Such a strange world! And God behind it! Sometimes I wonder we stay sane with the awful mystery of it all. But then one remembers that 'the world is full—*full* of the *goodness* of God.'"[40]

It was Nora who now made all of their travel arrangements; as Rebecca observed, "She is the finest manager!"[41] Before leaving Philadelphia for the summer, Rebecca had agreed at last to undergo eye surgery, but not until fall. The oculist had determined that the worst eye would be operated on and if the second one needed surgery by the time the first eye had healed, they would do both. But for the summer, Rebecca was free to make her usual journeys, and she turned again to writing, in part because she could think of writing again with the relief that Cecil and Dick were now safely out of the war zone.

Nothing hindered Davis's frequent travel in these years, in spite of her eye problems. In mid-summer she returned to Philadelphia for a day to see friends, and then she traveled to Washington to meet Nora who had gone there from Point Pleasant to visit her friends. They traveled together to Warm Springs, staying at Mrs. Eubank's establishment. During her travels, Rebecca sent an article, "One Woman's Question," to the *Independent* for the July issue. What disturbed Davis was the "growing vulgarity, dishonesty and vice in the country" that symbolized "a creeping paralysis which threatens us almost undetected." She also noticed, after returning from Europe, "certain suggestive small changes" in the country "to which the governing American seems to be blind."[42] Her charges about these changes were centered, once again, on the influx of immigrants to the US, though she specified no particular race or nationality.

Rebecca had admitted to her sons that she could not write them as frequently as usual; her eyes were bothering her too much. But they visited her as often as possible. Charley joined her and Nora for part of their time at Warm Springs, filling his days with activities ("Charley is the king of the place here," Rebecca proudly noted), but he always stopped by Rebecca's cottage with "a kiss and loving word" several times a day. The time at Warm Springs was restorative, as she reported to Dick:

> I must tell you something which pleased me very much. There is an old Doctor here—very old who has always practiced through this part of the state & has a great reputation for wisdom and skill through the South. He and I have been friends for years. Yesterday we were talking & he said suddenly 'Do you know that you are in a very different state of health from when you came? *Very much* better.' I was glad to hear it and know you will be too.

By late summer, Rebecca and Nora were planning to visit Dick and Cecil in Mount Kisco before returning to Philadelphia. "I do hope it will be dry there," she wrote, "so that I can walk through the woods a lot." She had never lost her love of the outdoors or of walking as her favorite exercise.[43]

In the fall, Rebecca's eyesight had improved somewhat and her surgery was postponed. She was able to return to a steady if lessened pace of publishing, typically one item a month. In September another of her short stories, "Elizabeth's Romance," was syndicated in the newspapers through Joseph B.

Bowles' Syndicate Service, and she published an essay in support of professionally trained nurses in the *Independent*. At the same time, Charley's talents as both an editor and a fiction writer were acknowledged by Sinclair Lewis in an article for *Life* on "Editors Who Write."[44] Charley was finally receiving the recognition he deserved.

As the fall passed, Rebecca struggled with depression for the first time in her life. Receiving letters daily from Dick and Charley "helps me stay alive," she admitted, but added, "You see the worst thing in growing old is that you feel that it is all over you are out of it." She recovered quickly, at least in her letters, "But you children convince me every day that I am in it. It is so good—you can't guess *how* good. . . . Noll & I are looking forward to Thanksgiving & [Cecil's] dog show when you both will be here," she confided to Dick. She did not forego analyses of the culture concerns about the state of the country, but the tinge of melancholy was there as well: "I am thankful you boys have nothing to do with stocks—New York seems like a huge gambling pit."[45]

One of the most difficult aspects of her failing eyesight for Rebecca was that by late fall she could no longer take the long walks that had been a staple of her active life. She only managed to be outdoors by taking carriage rides—a poor substitute for a walk, to her mind. When she was most depressed in the last years of her life, she did not hide her feelings from her children. She was so self-deprecating at one point, however, that Dick responded in a rare instance of anger with her:

> You must not write me letters saying you are useless, and a burden, unless you do it as a jest. Because, it makes me mad. And someday, while in a rage, I might explode, and it would be your fault. When you tell me it gives you pleasure to go riding, and that you are taking others with you to whom it will give pleasure; that makes me happy. I cannot write *seriously* in answer to such awful statements. We love you so, that you are conscious how we need you, how greatly we need you. There was never any woman of as *much* use to her family, and less of a 'burden' and *more* of a blessing! So, remember *that*!"[46]

The pattern of feeling isolated and morose, followed by a period of reinvigoration marked Davis's last years, and it was often when she returned to writing or family members visited that she was again her lively self.

By December of 1907, Rebecca was feeling better and returned, when she could, to writing. She published her annual Christmas story in *St. Nicholas* this year. Charley had embraced this family tradition as well, publishing

"Carmichael's Christmas Spirit" in the *New-York Tribune*. As the new year began, Nora and Charley travelled to Washington for a society dinner hosted by Jefferson Davis Broadhead and his wife at their home on Connecticut Avenue; other guests included Major General William Mason Wright and his spouse, and Republican congressmen Peter Porter and Marlin Olmstead.[47] Just before they left for the capital, Rebecca had written a birthday letter to Charley, in which she acknowledged how bad her eyesight had become:

> I have a good deal of time now when I can't read or write—just shut my eyes and think and I find myself jogging back in the old track—the old home days. And if you only knew all the things you did to show your love for me—that I remember. I want *you* to remember those little things. Daddy wrote to me once 'Gus sure is a grand noble gentleman' and you were. But you were our dear good son too in every little homely way, remember.[48]

She also commented to her sons that she was deeply comforted by their love for Nora,[49] knowing she could count on her children to support one another after her death. Because of her eye problems, Rebecca hired a live-in nurse, but in the spring she changed nurses, which pleased her children as they felt the first nurse was "capable but not tactful."[50]

In spite of her bouts of melancholy, Rebecca was far too practical to let any important matter go unattended, and she began preparing her will in March. She appointed Dick and Charley as executors, although Dick would relinquish his role and, as always, leave the responsibility of managing everything to his younger brother. Recognizing that Nora had no income of her own and would need to cover basic expenditures before the estate could be distributed, the will stated that immediately upon Rebecca's death Nora was to be given a sum of money equal to Davis's total income for six months. The New Jersey property Rebecca had inherited from her brother Wilse was to be divided equally between the three heirs, while Davis's own property at Point Pleasant was bequeathed to Dick and Charley. Following family tradition, Rebecca left the family home solely to her daughter, and Dick and Charles were bequeathed her stocks, bonds, and personal securities; the rest of her real estate went to the three children equally.[51]

In June Rebecca made a long visit to Crossroads Farm. It was a happy time for everyone in the family, in part just from being together and in part because Rebecca was planning several new stories and Dick and Charley were seeing publications appear at the same time. Dick published his first novel in six years,

Vera the Medium, to generally good reviews. Charley's collection of short stories, *The Stage Door*, was published with the dedication "To Mother." "There are some exceedingly interesting stories in Charles Belmont Davis's 'The Stage Door,'" one critic wrote, noting the author "is able to see [the theater's] good as well as dark side. The volume is really a study of a phase of our modern life, as well as being exceedingly interesting reading."[52]

Like his mother, Charley wrote entertaining stories but always pushed to place entertainment in conjunction with a critique of modern society. Other critics deemed his collection an "excellent work ... The stories are keenly alive with the spirit of New York and the glitter of its great white lane," while another noted his "originality, plot-invention, and unusual skill in narrative."[53] Scribner's, publisher of both Dick and Charley's books, took advantage of the interest in The Davis Family of writers and placed large ads in numerous periodicals that jointly promoted the brothers' books. Even the family now jokingly referred to Davis as "the firm name."[54]

In the summer Charley also picked up Rebecca's mantle at the *Saturday Evening Post*, publishing his first of several stories in that magazine. Dick would join him the following year and publish occasionally in its pages for several years. It was a family tradition that lasted throughout their lifetimes, and one that was recognized by literary critics. In July, *Putnam's* ran an item with photographs about Dick and Charley as Rebecca's sons, noting they not only looked like her but had inherited her talent. The piece was reprinted in several newspapers as well. During this time, Rebecca had decided to write a family history, meant only for her children. In separate sections, she recorded the history of the Wilson, Leet, and Harding families. The section on the Hardings was the longest, and as Nora observed years later, she learned a lot by reading the account, especially about Rebecca's father who had died before Nora was born.[55]

As usual, Rebecca spent the late summer at Warm Springs, and while there, Dick sent her a novel he was writing, *White Mice*, for her critique. No matter how difficult reading was for her, she would not forego the opportunity to read her sons' works in progress and offer suggestions for revision. Nor would she abandon writing letters to them that were filled with her assessments of contemporary life. At one point when Dick was thinking of going to London again, for example, she wrote from Warm Springs,

> I know how homesick you are for Pall Mall. But if you go to the Ritz I will disown you. It was too much for the vulgar Americans—Drexels & Astors & the likes—to seize on that part of London and make it

their own. It was alive before with Steele & Lamb and the Regent—there were great ghosts still in every house and now—Whitelaw Reid & Tony Drexel tramp them down. You will think I am quite foolish. But I hate to read the London news now—really.[56]

It was one of the rare comments she made about her former editor at the *Tribune*, Whitelaw Reid, but he was the exception among her editors as one with whom she did not form a friendship.

In September Rebecca went to Crossroads Farm to spend a few weeks, as did Nora. Charley often joined them, and the family loved to play billiards and cards in the evening. As Cecil noted frequently in her diary, she always seemed to lose the most money at card playing, but she was an expert billiards player. The family members had a wonderful time exploring the farm during the day, and Rebecca watched from her chair on the terrace. Dick, Cecil, and Charley played tennis often, and all of them competed with one another in games for the evenings. Cecil had begun also to study socialism, becoming increasingly fascinated by its premises, and the family engaged in many lively political discussions as well.[57] Rebecca was full of good spirits this fall, as she usually was when at the farm, and when she returned home her letters were rife with references to "the dear old farm" and "especially the terrace" which was her domain.[58] Cecil and Dick were preparing to go to London again, and it was there that Cecil would meet and study with John Singer Sargent.[59]

Rebecca remained at Crossroads into mid-October; when Dick had to go into the city, she and Cecil dined and read a novel together in the evenings.[60] Cecil always made sure that her mother-in-law had time and a quiet space in which to write, and this fall Rebecca was again able to do so. She published "One or Two Plain Questions" in the *Independent*. If future weather conditions could be predicted, she asked, why not the moral character of the nation? Certain traits such as self-confidence were evident; all men were free and unions had given workers new powers; and reporters looked to the future optimistically. Though she noted these changes, Davis pessimistically saw the world's corrupt nature as well, and she denied women's suffrage was a form of progress.

On the 19th of October, Cecil took Rebecca to the train station; in spite of her age, Rebecca was still spry enough to travel. She was headed to Point Pleasant for a two-week stay. Cecil went the next day to New York where she and Dick dined together and then went to see Bessie McCoy, a stage performer who was gaining fame as the "Yama Yama Girl," based on a song in the play.[61] Cecil had no idea at this time that Dick's frequent trips into New York were actually because he was having an affair with McCoy. Cecil's world—and that of all of the Davises—was about to change drastically and painfully. Rebecca knew nothing of the situation at this time; Dick and especially Cecil would make every effort to conceal their marital troubles from her for as long as possible. In the interim, her writing stamina had returned.

In November she published three articles. "In the Old Days" for the *Independent* added to her collection of studies about the past, this time examining American attitudes toward marriage in the post-Revolutionary era and asserting that "love and marriage counted for more in the life of Americans in those days than they do now."[62] Davis published her annual Thanksgiving story in *St. Nicholas*. Her popularity remained as strong as ever among the magazine's readers, and *St. Nicholas* touted her "bits of wisdom and timely suggestions" as a contributor in their advertisements.[63] She was also invited this month to contribute to the popular *Women's Home Companion* (formerly *Ladies' Home Companion*). Her recollections of past times were very popular with family magazines, and the editors asked that she analyze "Old-Time Political Campaigns," extending her previous thoughts on the subject.

At the same time, Dick was struggling with the out-of-town openings of the four-act play he had written based on *Vera, the Medium*,[64] and Charley published an extremely popular essay in *Lippincott's*, "The Cost of Transporting Big Shows," which was reprinted in newspapers across the country in their theater pages. The essay advanced his reputation as a major voice in analyzing the culture of modern theater. He was instrumental in aiding Dick's work in the theater as well, from creating potential cast lists, to overseeing out-of-town productions, to editing proofs of Dick's plays, to profitably negotiating contracts and managing Dick's royalties.[65] The brothers would continue their lives in the theater for the remainder of their careers.

This month, Cecil wanted to go to London with Dick, but he encouraged her to go alone, insisting the play meant he could not leave. She was not enthusiastic about going alone—"sounds kind of foreign & lonesome"—but she finally decided to do so, sailing on the *Lusitania* at the end of the month.[66] She could not have known that her decision to leave New York at this moment allowed Dick to fully embrace his affair with Bessie McCoy.

As the year ended, Rebecca published an article in the *Century*, "An Old-Time Love Story." Drawing again on materials she found at historical societies, Davis recounted two stories from early America that "give us a glimpse of the ideas which our forefathers had of love and honor. After the stories of modern marriages and divorce to which we are accustomed lately, they have to me a queer and welcome flavor, something like an Arab meal of figs and bread and water after a dinner at a Paris café."[67] That two of her articles in these months discussed problems in marriages suggested she may have been more aware of the tensions between Dick and Cecil than they realized.

At seventy-seven, Rebecca was feeling as well as she had in some time, enjoying her writing and thankful for her children's close attention, yet always with the sense of loss after Clarke's death. At these moments, her faith was her greatest comfort. As she expressed to Dick, "I've been sometimes so awfully alone—I oughtn't to feel that way. It is wicked. I have you & Charley & Noll—And God has come so close since I was left alone just like my Father—that is the way He seems now—No creeds nor theories—Just our *Father*. . . . Oh I know now in whom I have believed."[68]

For Cecil, the year ended with Dick's painful revelation of his affair. He arrived in London on December 10. At first they followed their usual pattern while in the city, visiting friends such as the Kiplings, going to the theater, and dining out. But the day after Christmas Dick told Cecil he wanted a divorce. "So I suppose I must," she sadly reflected in her diary.[69] She turned to painting for solace, and she found her true niche in this field of endeavor in the coming years. Rebecca was not told of the pending divorce. Her correspondence with Dick remained the same always; in one letter she told him, "Some day you must go to Oxford for me & go sit in the garden of New College and up by the fence where the deers come at Magdalen. I used to sit there hour after hour. Give my love to dear Cecil. I do hope her painting will please her."[70]

While Dick and Cecil worked out their pending separation, the new year brought a steady weakening of Rebecca's health. Nonetheless, she published two articles in January of 1909, "What We Can" in *St. Nicholas* and "The Coming of the Night" in *Scribner's Magazine*. "What We Can" embodied Davis's philosophy of life: each of us may never write a poem as brilliantly as one by Keats, nor discover radium, but we can rise every morning with the knowledge that we have the ability "to help the men and women in [this world], to make them better and happier." Plant a garden that brings joy to your neighbors, she suggested, or start a night school to help educate workers who have no access to schooling; whatever it is your skill to do, do it. She concluded, "God has filled our hands with good seeds, which if we plant them will go on yielding fruit throughout the ages."[71] The article was reprinted widely in magazines and newspapers, suggesting she had touched an ideal that many still valued. "The Coming of the Night" continued this positive view of life, focusing on the importance of keeping active in old age.

Shortly after these articles appeared, however, Rebecca became bedridden. She occasionally managed to write letters, however, and by March she had improved enough that Nora was able to leave her with the nurse and go to New York to dine with friends on Park Avenue. Nora could also rely on Alice Selby Lilly, an African American woman who was now a member of Rebecca's household staff.[72] At forty-five, Lilly efficiently ran the household, relieving Rebecca of much of the everyday concerns. It was April, however, before Rebecca could again come downstairs and receive visitors. By that point, Dick was back in New York as well; he wrote his mother about his long walks around Crossroads Farm, and she replied, "Don't you ever think that I am tramping beside you in your walks? I *am*. My knees & eyes will be new some day and then what walks I'll take!"[73]

Still in London, Cecil was struggling with the best means for pursuing the divorce. She consulted her attorney but was dismayed at his response. "Apparently it's impossible to do this thing decently—for Illinois [where her parents lived] it means two years residence for desertion—& Dick regrets every second—& in New York it must be infidelity. So its up to Dick. Oh how squalid & degrading & futile it all seems. I trust he may be happy, but its hard on the rest of us."[74]

Finally, in mid-April, Dick told Nora he was planning to divorce Cecil. He cabled Cecil with Nora's response. "She said it would be very serious for his mother," Cecil revealed in her diary, "so that things were indefinitely postponed."[75] No one knew if Rebecca's recent health issue was a temporary state or if she had only a short time to live, and all of their lives teetered around her condition until she recovered. Meanwhile, Charley was successfully pursuing his career, as yet unaware of Cecil and Dick's planned divorce. In May he published another collection of stories, *The Lodger Overhead and Other Stories* to good reviews. Dick also published a novel, *The White Mice*, to mixed reviews, though better than he had lately received.

Cecil returned to New York in early May, and around that time, Rebecca was well enough to publish "Three Little Stories" in *St. Nicholas* in which she recounted the accomplishments of ordinary people—an English printer, the Quaker Eliza Turner (whom Davis had long known), and a Birmingham teacher Rowland Hill—as examples of people who, "when they saw a huge heap of evil on the road, were not disheartened.... They went to work at it ... There are huge evils in our way, and each one of us has his little spade. Are we going to use them? Or shall we pass by, daunted on the other side?"[76]

Shortly thereafter, however, her eyesight again worsened. After consulting an optician in June, she agreed to have surgery on her eyes, but again put it off until October, insisting she wanted to rest at Warm Springs over the summer before undergoing surgery. Unbeknownst to Rebecca, her decision was a frustration for Dick. He wanted to push his divorce forward in the early summer, but Cecil was adamantly against the idea. "Dick goes to N.Y. tomorrow to see his lawyer," she noted in her diary on June 7. "I refuse to *do* anything until after the operation on his mother's eyes in October."[77] Throughout the summer and early fall then, a strange pattern developed in which Dick would spend time in New York City with Bessie and then go out to Crossroads Farm to see Cecil.

In July Rebecca and Nora left for Warm Springs. Nora had said nothing to her mother or Charley about Dick's situation. The time in Virginia was refreshing for Rebecca, and she enjoyed talking with other authors who were there, including Mary Johnston and Ellen Glasgow, and she relished the warmth of a Virginia summer. Rebecca continued to correspond frequently with her sons, writing at one point to Dick,

> In these last years when there have been such big empty spaces round me, I find it helps me to go back & think of all that our Father has done for us . . . everything in the big world and our love for each other & your and Charley's power— & Daddy—waiting yonder—and all. The Gibsons all are devouring [*The White Mice*] & sending delighted messages. I don't look on them as high literary critics. But whatever their friend does is the best that ever was done & they are proud of being your friend.[78]

Restored strength in the late summer and early fall allowed Rebecca to write two more pieces for *St. Nicholas*, "Stones of Power" in August and "Homely Hints for Everyday" in September. Then she had to lay her pen down and undergo eye surgery, which was successful in restoring her eyesight. She was heartened during this time by Charley's publication of "The Conquerors" in *Collier's* on a theme that echoed one dear to her heart and about which she had often written: the story of a young woman and man who came to New York and were destroyed when they were caught up in the mad race for money and recognition. Charley also received notable acclaim from George Jean Nathan, a theater critic and editor who had helped to make the *Smart Set* a prominent literary magazine. "There is to my mind," Nathan wrote, "only one writer today who knows how to paint true pictures of stage women with his pen, and . . . that man, [is] Charles Belmont Davis."[79] During this time, Cecil moved out of Crossroads Farm and into her own place in New York City, but as yet Rebecca and Charley remained ignorant of the planned divorce.

In early January 1910, rumors began circulating in the newspapers about Dick's plans for a divorce and that he would marry Bessie McCoy. Rebecca was so shocked and distraught over the news that she suffered a minor stroke. Not a word of Rebecca's thoughts about the divorce appeared anywhere in public or private. Charley, on the other hand, was furious with Dick for his infidelity; a deep rift emerged between them, in which Charley felt betrayed both for Cecil and himself, and Dick felt humiliated by Charley's vocal accusations. It nearly destroyed their lifelong bond. In public, Rebecca maintained a dignified presence, refusing to discuss the issue.

Rebecca was well enough in April to speak at a luncheon honoring Horace Howard Furness for his contributions to the dramatic arts. It was an event she would not have wanted to miss. Furness had been friends with Clarke since before he and Rebecca met, and after Clarke's death, Furness had remained a close friend to Rebecca, visiting her often.[80] The news of Dick's divorce would not fade, however, and in May Clarke's former newspaper, the *Public Ledger*, published a detailed account of the divorce for all of Philadelphia to read.

Rebecca maintained as much distance from the situation as possible, but her seventy-ninth birthday was overshadowed by the disintegration of her elder son's marriage. For a woman who envisioned her children as beacons of morality and goodness, who truly believed in the sanctity of marriage, and who loved her daughter-in-law as well as her own children, it was a devastating period. National newspapers and magazines recognized her birthday, allowing her to appreciate in her final year the national standing she still maintained, and by summer Rebecca had rallied. Her children could not know that in a few months, they would lose their beloved mother.

Nothing could restrain Rebecca from writing if her health permitted, and in July she published "Two Brave Boys" in *St. Nicholas*. It was her last publication, and it appropriately embraced her belief in the importance of unselfish behavior as the true reward of life. Rebecca spent this last summer at the New Jersey shore, where she could see old friends and remember her days there with Clarke and her young children as they learned to swim and explore the wild coastline. Rebecca knew she would not be able to travel for very much longer, so she determined to make an extended visit among friends on her way to Crossroads Farm where she was to spend the late summer. She stopped in Germantown and again in Connecticut to visit old friends before arriving at Dick's home.[81]

The travel had been exhausting, however, and she became ill shortly after arriving. She wanted to return to Philadelphia, and Dick promised he would accompany her as soon as she was well enough, but at 5:00 p.m. on September 29, 1910, Rebecca Harding Davis died at Mount Kisco.[82] The cause of death was recorded as oedema of the lungs, caused by heart disease.[83]

Rebecca had been preparing for her death. She had let her children know that she wanted to die in Philadelphia where she and Clarke had built their life together, and so they returned her body to the city in which she had lived for more than forty years. A private funeral was held at the family home, conducted by Dr. Floyd Tomkins who read the Episcopal burial service.[84] Rebecca's preparations had included purchasing a burial plot in Leverington Cemetery; she had had Clarke's ashes moved from their first place of burial in the Roxborough Baptist cemetery where his parents had been interred.

Rebecca and Clarke's plots in the Leverington Cemetery overlooked the Wissahickon River where they had fallen in love while rowing on the river in the early mornings. Rebecca had also determined what she wanted on her gravestone as well, simply "His Wife." Even in death, Rebecca wanted no public attention, no marker that might lure fans to come and pay homage to one of America's most talented and long-admired authors. Her work was to stand for itself; her private life was built on a marriage to a man she had loved and respected until she died.

Rebecca left an estate of $50,000, half in real estate and half in personal property, and the will she had earlier prepared divided the estate between her three children.[85] The accolades and remembrances came swiftly, in newspapers and magazines, and this time Rebecca could not escape personal attention on a national scale. Most of the obituary commentaries recognized her work both as an author and as a journalist, and many encompassed the inevitable Davis Family tradition as part of her bequest to literature. She was remembered as "a long-time favorite" who was "a prolific, but never careless writer, and her name in a magazine meant quality and interest. It seems almost unthinkable that there is to be an end to her contributions."[86] One of the most thoughtful commentaries came from the *New-York Tribune*:

> It is worth loyal remembrance of auld lang syne that many readers, and especially readers of The Tribune, bid farewell to the admirable American writer who has just died, Mrs. Rebecca Harding Davis. It is long since she was a constant contributor to our editorial columns, but the memory of her work therein is still fresh. She was a woman of character and mind, writing wittily and forcefully with a wholesome human purpose. . . . She cared for the things about her, for the familiar inter-

ests of daily existence, and this sterling material she handled with a personal, beguiling and stimulating touch.

Among our native authors she ranked as a realist, keen upon the truth, preferring the portrayal of types that she knew to the invention of fantastic plots and the fabrication of romantic figures. But it was not her way to make a fetich of mere fact. Just as in her persuasive Tribune articles, she enriched her observations of current topics with fancy and humor, so in her fiction she was wont to build up a good story from her sincere and sympathetic stories of men and women and to give a narrative of homely events the higher literary value of a work of art. She had a keen instinct for drama, a fact of importance in her novels and perhaps having even greater weight in her short stories. For well pondered and yet not at all forced simplicity, for a kind of natural picturesqueness and honest power, it would be hard to surpass a brief sketch like "On the Trapeze." Everything that she did was sound and workmanlike. The thoughts of grateful friends will follow her to her rest.[87]

In December, the *Washington Herald* ran an article about the many notable men and women who had died in 1910. In addition to Davis, the list included Julia Ward Howe, Florence Nightingale, Samuel Clemens, and Leo Tolstoy. It marked, the newspaper declared, the end of a remarkable period,[88] and it was an era that Rebecca Harding Davis, as an author and journalist, had played a remarkable role in shaping.

Chapter 15

Final Pages: Richard, Charles, and Nora

The Davis family personified the changing literary landscape of the nineteenth century, and it was a change that Rebecca fully recognized. She was, as the editors of the 1911 *New International Yearbook* remarked shortly after her death, "one of the best known contributors to American magazines" in the nineteenth and early twentieth centuries.[1] Part of what established and maintained her reputation as a writer was her ardent insistence that literature was an artistic endeavor that needed to be honed and nurtured as well as her belief that literature might well entertain, but it also should engage its cultural moment. Yet she had admitted to a guilty liking "for those disreputable folk; the half-starved, scampish adventurers who haunt the outer edge of the field of literature and journalism." More importantly, she recognized that by the turn of the century these fields—the adventurers who sought fame and the artists who viewed their work as a craft to be honed throughout a lifetime—"march together now and the fence between them is almost broken down."[2]

What was perhaps the most notable difference between the generations of Davis family writers were their approaches to literature: the secular writings of the sons were in contrast to Rebecca's enduring incorporation of faith into much of her literature, especially in her later years. Although her sons approached their writing careers from quite different perspectives, both generations were experts at negotiating this new literary landscape. It was Rebecca's non-writing child, Nora, who best retained her values of faith and endurance.

Richard Harding Davis

Both Dick and Charley demonstrated the radical changes in literature through their synthesis of fiction writing with the burgeoning field of motion pictures at the turn of the century. Dick was the first to enter this new field with his story "The Romance of Hefty Burke," which was made into a moving picture in January 1911, and another story which was filmed as "The Disreputable Mr.

Raegen" in March; many others followed. It was a profitable and exciting new adventure that both Dick and Charley embraced enthusiastically.

Dick continued magazine writing for periodicals such as *Scribner's* and *Collier's* and added new places of publication, such as the *San Francisco Call* and the *Saturday Evening Post*. At times he again turned to journalism, beginning with the outbreak of World War I, when he reported for the *New-York Tribune* and other newspapers. He also published several books, both fiction and nonfiction, in the years after his mother's death.

In spite of Charley's disappointment in Dick's affair and pending divorce, the brothers were able to mend their differences and remained close. It was not an easy recovery of the bond they once had, but in July 1911 they traveled together to Europe, where they spent the summer and tried to reestablish happier times.[3] Dick's and Cecil's divorce was long and drawn out, in part because of a required waiting period and because at one point, for unknown reasons, Cecil withdrew her suit. The divorce remained a major story for newspapers across the country.[4] It was finally granted on June 18, 1912, and two weeks later articles began to appear in newspapers about Dick's intention to marry Bessie McCoy.[5]

On July 8 Dick and Bessie were married by a justice of the peace. Dick was 48 and Bessie was 24. Rather than a traditional wedding reception, they hosted a party for 500 poor East Side mothers and their children.[6] Although this gesture received praise with the *Washington Times*, which asserted the reception "should be held up as a model" for society couples,[7] it did little to diminish the gossip about their seemingly quick marriage.

Nor was this union the joyous relationship Dick had envisioned. Bessie proved to be a challenging partner, as Dick himself undoubtedly was, and they did not find the happiness they had hoped. The hardest part for Dick and his siblings was that Bessie made every effort to separate Dick from Charley and Nora, refusing whenever she could to have them at Crossroads Farm. The joy of this marriage was in the birth of a daughter, Hope, in January 1915. She was Rebecca's only grandchild, one she did not live to greet into the world.

Shortly after spending a long stint reporting on the war, Dick returned home in 1916. He was still publishing articles about the war, having some of his stories produced for film, enjoying his young daughter, and looking forward to a productive life to come when, on April 11, after a short illness, he unexpectedly died. It was just days before his fifty-second birthday. His funeral was held in his beloved Mount Kisco home with a few close friends in attendance and conducted by an Episcopal minister, after which Charley, Bessie, and Hope accompanied the body to Philadelphia where he was cremated, as Rebecca and Clarke had been.[8]

Obituaries for each member of the Davis family inevitably turned to the powerhouse publishing family they had been, but an especially touching connection at this time captured the family's deep bond. "During the short illness that preceded my brother's death," Charlie recalled, "although quite unconscious that the end was so near, his thoughts constantly turned back to the days of his home in Philadelphia, and he got out the letters which as a boy and a young man he had written to his family. After reading a number of them he said: 'I know now why we were such a happy family. It was because we were always, all of us, of the same age.'"[9]

The bond of Dick's family with Bessie was far less strong. Although he loved his daughter immensely, his relationship with Bessie had been strained in the years before his death. Bruce Clark, Cecil's brother, and his wife Nancy had remained friends with Dick after the divorce. On April 13 Nancy Reagan Clark wrote Cecil a revealing letter to notify her about Dick's death and to give her impressions of his second marriage:

Dear Cecil:

I am just back from Mt Kisco and I dont know quite how to write you, whether you want to hear all I can tell you or not, but I feel that you you [sic] wd. like me to tell you if I cld. sit down and talk to you so I am going to write it. Poor dear old Dick, it was a fine end for him and all of us that have loved him are glad that he did not live to suffer as he wd. have, his illness was only of about two weeks, angina pectoris, heart disease, which is absolutely fatal, but also apt to last for years with frequent attacks of great suffering, I dont think he believed he had anything serious and he was only in bed for two or three days, and was up on Tuesday and as the papers say was found dead in the telephone closet about midnight by Bessie, he had been dead three hours and they all believe what the doctor says that he never knew when he was stricken, that we all have to be thankful for.

The house is just the same as it always was, I have not been there in years, but nothing has been moved or changed except the panel room, and nothing has been put in there since yr. things were moved out, I felt exactly as if walking amonst [sic] ghosts and though I had every intention of going out to the funeral I was much relieved when Dai [Charley's wife] telephoned me that Bessie wanted me to come. Poor

Charlie, he has not been able to go out and see Dick while he was sick for during the past year or two Bessie has forbidden Charlie to go there, her poor foolish insane jealousy has tried to separate those devoted brothers they have of course met in town and Dick used to go out to Charlie's sweet little place, but it is a bit late now, but Charlie and Dai are fine and are doing all they can. Dai had the news of Dick's death at one o'clock a.m. by telephone and got a foolish motor and started for Mt Kisco, she told Charlie of Dick's death en route and they arrived at Mt Kisco at 7 a.m. they are taking Dick to Philadelphia tomorrow to be cremated and he will be buried Saturday

... Poor Charlie ... asked if you knew today, he has a tough road to hoe now, after it is too late to help Dick any, Bessie is filled with repentance and only wishes Charlie had been asked oftener to Mt Kisco and now the hard part of straightening out Dicks affairs are on Charlie's shoulders, he is of course broken hearted but only wants to do what he can for Dick ...

Good night dear Cecil I wish I might see you, my heart is very full of love and sympathy. Dick came to see me about two weeks ago and wanted to know all about you and hoped you were well.

Always affly.
Nan.

I saw the baby, a dear sweet little girl, looking like Dick & his mother. Poor little soul, I wonder what her future will be——[10]

Dick left his entire estate to Bessie and Hope, but with a stipulation that if Bessie remarried before Hope was twenty-one, she would forfeit her share of the estate,[11] perhaps to ensure that most of the money would go to Hope. Personal property was bequeathed to Nora and Charley. Cecil learned that she was entitled to a life interest in the widow's third of the estate, but she directed her lawyer to release her right to the inheritance.[12] Although it had initially been claimed by several newspapers that Dick's estate was valued at $250,000, it was, in fact, just slightly over $50,000.[13] Bessie tried in the years after Dick's death to maintain a public role, writing about her appreciation of Dick and insisting that she was in communication with his spirit, but her fame was short lived.[14]

Charley and Nora were devastated by Dick's untimely death; the closeness of the siblings was part of their extraordinary sense of loss and yet also the source of the support they were able to offer one another at this time. Cecil had remained close to both of them as well, and she immediately wired her sympathy to Nora, who was living in England. Nora's responding letter revealed a great deal about the love between the siblings and their former sister-in-law and about Cecil and Dick's relationship from Nora's perspective:

> My very dear Cecil—
>
> Thank you so much for your cable—and for all the love and thought—
>
> I wish I could see you and say all I want for letters are never much good—and mine are so abrupt when things go deep and this does—for I know it is what Dick would want me to do—and it is the last direct thing I can ever do for him—to try to tell you truly and fully how deeply he loved you. He was in London for a week in January and we just had parties by ourselves—I felt then that although I had not seen him for so long, and that although we had such different kinds of lives—that in it all we had only been coming closer together and I know that I never was so near to Dick as in these last days. In a way from one time to another through the week, he summed up all his life—Of what father and mother were to him—and of the old house—and of all they had given him in it—and of you—Oh Cecil it was such a great love and humble and simple as a childs and it is too big for me to tell you—
>
> He spoke of his life simply as a matter of course—since the divorce as maimed through his own fault and as his idea of life was to now "gather up the fragments that remain" for he said once I have had so much in life in every way—and in Cecil who gave me the best I know or have—that now it would be ungrateful for me not to be thankful for any happiness or work or any chance of doing than good that may still be left me—He said he must have been the hardest man in the world to live with—and of how he had seen and taken life [] and of how differently you had and had taught him too, now—
>
> One day at the Savoy he said how much he got in living over the good days he had had and how many there had been there with you. I am sure he went to look at the house at Chelsea [where Cecil and Dick were living when he asked for the divorce] and he stayed at Greenslades and the day he sailed I went with him from there to the station—he asked me what rooms you had when you were there last winter, and as the cab turned out of the street he turned back to look at them—

I feel that caring for you as he did—your being to him all the big and best of life—and in accepting what he felt were his responsibilities to Bessie, from his own madness—that he suffered so much that for I have not one single regret that he has gone—The terrible thing was that there was noone who could help him. I am so afraid I have given you the idea he complained—he never did—he made the best of all things—and took up with the truest courage I have ever seen the consequence of his fault—and with such infinite unselfishness. It was his bravery that hurt me most—I told him of Percivals [Nora's husband] and the British volunteers being transferred and he was so proud of you for doing—[15]

He wanted to hear all about you and told me two or three times that your mother wrote him sometimes—

I seem to have got the big and little things all mixed up—but to him they weren't big or little. They all meant you—and you were the April of his life—

Dear Cecil if there is anything more I can say you will ask me wont you for I know he wants you to understand—

The news came as a great shock to me and I thought I would put off writing until I could think more clearly but then it seems only right to tell you at once

With great love
Nora
123 Pall Mall[16]

Charles Belmont Davis

Charley lived much of his life in his elder brother's shadow, but he was the child who most fully inherited his mother's writing talents. At the time of Rebecca's death, he was coming into his own as a writer and gaining international recognition in the literary world through his position as fiction editor for *Collier's Weekly*. In addition, his short stories were appearing in both literary and popular magazines to consistently positive reviews. One of the most popular was a novella, "The Octopus," which was serialized in *Cosmopolitan* in December 1910. At this time *Cosmopolitan* was one of William Randolph Hearst's magazines, recognized for its first-class fiction and investigative reporting, and to be showcased in the magazine was a major step forward for Charley's recognition as an important writer. He continued as well to publish in *Scribner's, Collier's*, the *New-York Tribune, Metropolitan Magazine*, and many other periodicals. He wrote about cultural changes, covering British and European coronations, new crazes for aeroplaning and bicycle marathons, and many other topics of the day.[17]

Most influential in fiction and nonfiction, however, were his studies of theater life. His keen abilities to capture behind-the-scenes realities as well as the glamour of the stage and the lives of actors—and those who only dreamed of fame among the lights—marked him as a unique talent, and his reputation in this arena grew throughout the remainder of his career. He published four collections of his writings after Rebecca's death, including *Tales of the Town* (1911) and *Her Own Sort, and Others* (1917), as well as a novel about theater life, *In Another Moment* (1913).

Charley also continued to be the man-about-town captured in the images of New York's Swell Set, and he never lost his love of the summer society at Warm Springs. He added Palm Beach, Florida, to his social circle as well, as it became a popular winter gathering place for society and political leaders in the early twentieth century. In an essay for *Collier's*, he reveled in Palm Beach as "gloriously unpuritanic."[18] It was in Florida that he discovered the upper-crust's fascination with hydro-aeroplanes, thanks to the stage and film actor William Collier who had introduced him to Palm Beach society.[19] The change in US culture was nowhere so evident from Rebecca's generation—as a child, she had watched the Conestoga wagons passing through Wheeling, while he was thrilled at demonstrations of the hydro-aeroplane.

As a notable figure in New York's literary and theater cultures, Charley was a very eligible bachelor. Since he haunted the theaters as a cultural critic and fiction writer, it was not surprising he dated many actresses. George Jean Nathan who wrote regularly for the *Smart Set* magazine noted Charley's attraction to the beautiful women who populated the international traveling musicals: "Neither the transparent hauteur nor the spurious devilishness of the American chorus jade will be hers. . . . And, beholding her, Charles Belmont Davis will abruptly sit him down and write a lengthy poem. . . . And it will, in due time, be published in *Collier's Weekly*."[20] In the fall of 1912, however, rumors began to circulate that his romance with the beautiful young actress Dai Turgeon was becoming serious.[21]

In January 1914, Charley married Dai in London at St. James's Cathedral in Piccadilly.[22] Just as in Dick's second marriage, Charley was 48 and Dai 24. Dai was French Canadian and had only recently begun to receive attention on the New York stage for her performance in the "Girl from Montmartre." Their wedding party was filled with Charley's friends from his days as an ambassador. Hallett Johnson, third secretary of London's American embassy, served as best man, and Dr. David Jayne Hill, former US ambassador to Germany, walked Dai down the aisle. Many prominent members of the American colony attended as did Charley's friend, British author Anthony Hope Hawkins.[23] Their wedding made headlines in newspapers across the US. Cecil Clark Davis, who remained in touch with Charley throughout their lives, painted a stunningly beautiful portrait of Dai several years later. Charley and Dai honeymooned in a castle in northern England,[24] returning to the States on the *Oceanic* at the end of April. The marriage would last for seven years; in 1921 they quietly divorced. Charley never remarried.

By mid-1915 Charley was actively involved in the exciting new enterprise of film. He had left his position as fiction editor at *Collier's* to concentrate on his own work, and this year his short story "Countess Veschi's Jewels" was adapted as an Essanay two-act drama in May. Essanay Studios was an early Chicago film company that opened a California studio this year, producing Charlie Chaplin films. The first film company to have a California production company was Selig Studios, and a few months after the Essanay film appeared, Selig produced an adaptation of Charley's novella *The Octopus* as "Mother O' Mine," to great popularity. The filmmaker Archibald Selwyn (whose Selwyn and Company would soon be renamed Goldwyn Pictures Corporation) was known for throwing extraordinarily lavish annual dinners, and at the end of the year Charley was a guest at the event, along with Douglas Fairbanks, Mary Pickford, and others.[25]

Charley's fame as an author was advancing as well, and in July 1915, the journalist and author Joyce Kilmer interviewed Charley about "The Financial Aspects of Story Writing" for the *New-York Times*. Kilmer began with reference to Charley as Rebecca's son and Dick's brother, but quickly turned to Charley as an authority on the financial realities of a writing career, both from the perspective of a former editor and as an author. Setting aside the myth of the "Neglected Genius" whose work is too good to be published, Charley asserted, "If a man can write good fiction, he'll find a market for it" in either the leading magazines or the second tier: "A really good short story is never lost." In spite of this optimistic assertion, Charley did not advise young men to give up other work to devote themselves to writing under the assumption they would easily be able to make a living in the profession. It was a long road to financial success, he explained; even if a writer was able to write twelve publishable stories a year, at an average rate of $250 for a story, he would not soon become rich.[26]

In early 1916, Charley published his only novel, *Nothing a Year*, which was dedicated to his niece, Hope Davis. This work was also adapted for film, appearing under the title *A Woman's Business* in 1920. Charley would never escape the alliance of being Rebecca's son and Dick's brother—and it was a connection he never sought to sever. After Dick's death and with his own established name in literature and film, however, he was a recognized writer in his own right and became a talented theater critic and screenwriter.

He was becoming a go-to person for film producers as well, not just for his stories but as a person who had necessary contacts in the profession. In the summer of 1916, for instance, he was approached by a film producer to locate a playwright for a proposed adaptation of Harold Frederic's *The Damnation of Theron Ware*, and within a few years Charley, unlike Dick, would begin to write original screenplays. At the end of 1919, Myron Selznick hired Charley as a screenwriter for his film production company, and within a few weeks Charley was being touted as one of the lead writers for Selznick Pictures.[27]

The 1920s saw Charley's role in theater and film expand. In 1923 he became dramatic editor for the *New-York Tribune*, overseeing a staff of reviewers, and his own reviews were published in newspapers throughout the country. By 1925 the *Literary Digest International Book Review* classified him as one of the "moderns of high rank" for his work in fiction as well. Ironically, in spite of his success in literature and film, Charley would be best known in later years only as the author of *Adventures and Letters of Richard Harding Davis*, a loving tribute to his brother, published in 1917 by Scribner's. On December 10, 1926, while traveling in North Carolina, Charley died, apparently from heart disease. He was sixty years old.

Nora Davis Farrar

For all that Nora was little more than a side note in the fame of The Davis Family enterprise, she was the one involved in the greatest scandal, claiming international attention. In many ways, Rebecca was closest to Nora, who traveled and lived with her mother from her birth until Rebecca's death—thirty-eight years—and she was the one who had the responsibility of seeing her mother through her final years. Immediately after Rebecca's death, Nora pursued her lifelong love of music by studying in Dresden.[28] Whether she had postponed her engagement due to the responsibility of caring for her mother or whether her relationship with F. Percival Farrar emerged while she was in Germany, it was less than seven months after Rebecca's death that Nora and Percival became engaged.[29]

Percival was the son of Rev. Frederic William Farrar, Dean of Canterbury in the Anglican Church—the Dean Farrar about whom Rebecca had written a few years earlier. Percival had been a Davis family friend since his days at Lehigh University, and he had been Clarke's personal assistant at both the *Philadelphia Inquirer* and the *Public Ledger*. Percival had lived with publisher George Child's family while he was attending Lehigh, after which he had been a reporter for a short time before taking the position with Clarke. Percival's father had encouraged him to return to London and study for the ministry, and after Clarke's death, Percival entered into this new phase of his life. It was a goal he took on heartily, and by the time he and Nora became engaged, he was Rev. Farrar, rector of Sandringham and domestic chaplain to King George and honorary chaplain to Queen Mother Alexandra.[30]

Like her mother, Nora had a deep and abiding faith, and this life as the wife of a royal chaplain perfectly suited her. It combined her two loves—religion and a life in high society. Percival was highly favored by the royal family, and rumors of his elevation to a bishopric were circulating at the time of their engagement.[31] Their future seemed to be filled with the possibilities of happiness and good fortune.

A month after her engagement, Nora sold the Davis family home on Twenty-first Street in Philadelphia for $20,000; she planned to make her life in England with her husband.[32] On the symbolic day of July 4, 1911, Nora married Percival Farrar in St. Andrew's Church, Westminster. Her years in society circles of Philadelphia, New York, Baltimore, and Warm Springs, as well as the family's many connections in Europe, made for a who's who of attendees at the wedding. Rebecca's and Charley's former editor and now US Ambassador to the Court of St. James, Whitelaw Reid, and his wife were in attendance, as was the internationally famous physician and a family friend from his days in Philadelphia, Sir William Osler. Gifts arrived from King George, Queen Mary, Queen Mother Alexandra, and other members of the royal court.[33] The wedding was reported across the US and in England as one of the principal society events of the season.

Both Charley and Dick attended the wedding. Charley's work demanded he return to the States immediately after, but Dick stayed in London for a while visiting friends and motoring to Sandringham to see Nora.[34] For four months, Nora and Percival were gloriously happy. He seemed to be thriving in his work and she was settling in to her new life. But in November, only days after officiating at Sunday services for the royal family, Percival was asked by King George to resign amid charges of a scandal; when he refused, he was dismissed as the king's chaplain and from all Court appointments on November 21.[35]

Such a scandal could not be contained, in London or America. Reports flew around the metropolis and across the Atlantic that he had been charged with drunkenness, immorality, and leading a double life (implying homosexuality). Accounts insisted that "powerful friends" had helped him escape before the dismissal was publicly announced, and soon Scotland Yard was employed to try to locate Farrar.[36] A few newspaper reports came to his defense with the assertion that there had never been "a breath of suspicion" connected with Farrar, "though disgraceful things have been going on for some time at Sandringham, of which church Mr. Farrar was rector." It was reported he had fled to British Columbia, France, or Austria.[37]

Nora wired Dick and asked that he or Charley come to London at once. Dick arrived on November 29 and was immediately besieged by the press. For once, he wisely refused to feed the press, telling reporters only that he knew nothing.[38] Nora clearly wanted to avoid publicity, but that proved impossible. The moral atmosphere of Sandringham had been questionable for many years and new leadership sought changes; within a short time the charges against Farrar were described as having been brought by individuals identified only as "certain persons" and some people claimed they reflected the bitter rivalries at play in Sandringham.[39]

By the end of the year, for unstated reasons, the royal family insisted the search for Farrar be abandoned by Scotland Yard; the scandal "is being forgotten by royal command," newspapers reported.[40] In spite of initial assertions in the newspapers, Nora did not abandon Percival. After weeks of daily reports in British and US papers, she joined him in Europe; they later settled for a while in Canada.[41] Whether Percival himself had been caught in some immoral act or blamed for a failure of oversight was never clarified. Publicly, it mattered little; he was disgraced.

It was assumed by most people that Nora would apply for a divorce, but that was not her intention.[42] She simply disappeared from all of her old circles. Very few friends ever had contact with her again, and she faded from public attention. She did not, however, abandon her marriage or the family and handful of friends who stood by her. In May 1912 when she returned to the States, she was bombarded by reporters at the pier.[43] Both Dick and Charley met her there, and she only commented briefly to the reporters that there had been so much talk already "and it has been so distressing that I do not care to say anything about it."[44] The three siblings went to Crossroads Farm where they could be together without public attention.

It was not until late 1916 that Percival and Nora again garnered international attention when he drew reporters' notice—not, however, for a scandal this time. He had joined the French Foreign Legion during World War I, and as papers reported in Europe and the States, he was considered to have restored his reputation when he was decorated for valor during the war. As a consequence, he was offered a commission in the British army, but he declined in favor of remaining in the Foreign Legion. Not surprisingly, the lengthiest account of Percival's restored honor appeared in Philadelphia's *Public Ledger*, where Clarke had been managing editor and Percival his assistant.[45]

After the war, Nora and Percival settled in Italy, a country she had come to love when she visited Charley during his years as consul. They lived a quiet life until Percival's death in 1946 in Lima, Peru. His "beloved wife" was with him at his death.[46] Sometime after her husband's passing, Nora settled in England, in Kent, where she died on July 18, 1958, at the age of eighty-nine, after a long illness.[47]

In spite of the quiet, almost invisible life she had led against the landscape of the famous members of The Davis Family writing enterprise, it was she who became the subject of one of the great international scandals of the early twentieth century. Yet she also was the only Davis sibling who, in spite of the extraordinary challenges of its first years, built a lasting marriage. In many ways, Nora's strength of character and determination emulated her mother's.

Notes

PREFACE: THE REAL REBECCA HARDING DAVIS

1. Moses Purnell Handy, "Three Davises," *Mail and Express*; rpt. *New Haven Register* (7 June 1894), 2.
2. Ida Tarbell, "Women in Journalism," *Chautauquan* (7 Apr. 1887), 393ff.

CHAPTER 1: SOUTHERN ROOTS (ANCESTRY TO MID-1861)

1. The following family history is drawn from Rebecca Harding Davis's (hereafter RHD), "The Wilson Family" in *Rebecca Harding Davis: Writing Cultural Autobiography*, eds. Janice Milner Lasseter and Sharon M. Harris (Nashville, TN: Vanderbilt UP, 2001); *Commemorative Biographical Record of Washington County, Pennsylvania* (Chicago: J. H. Beers, 1893); Alfred Creigh, LL.D., *History of Washington County* (Washington, PA: Alfred Creigh, 1870); Boyd Crumrine, *History of Washington County, Pennsylvania* (Philadelphia: L. H. Everts, 1882).
2. RHD, "The Wilson Family," 137.
3. My thanks to Rachel Loden for the original spelling of this name, RLC.
4. RHD, "The Leet Family" in Lasseter and Harris, eds., *Rebecca Harding Davis*, 140.
5. Ibid.
6. This property would later become the Leet Burying Ground of Washington County, Pennsylvania.
7. RHD, "Wilson Family," 137.
8. RHD, "Leet Family," 141.
9. RHD, "Wilson Family," 137–38.
10. The exact familial relation between RHD and Blaine is unclear, but he referred to her as his cousin in letters. "Cousin" was a loosely used term in the period for close and distant relations.
11. Today the Old Stone House, as the family called it, is known as the Bradford House, after the original owner David Bradford of Whiskey Rebellion fame.

12. Creigh, *History of Washington County*, 196, 199.

13. Richard William Harding's birth date is given in various documents as 1792, 1796, 1798, and "about 1799." Even though 1796 was carved on his gravestone when Rachel was still living, 1792 is probably correct as the family historian Rachel Loden (RLC) has located records in Ireland that give his birth date as February 8, 1792.

14. This assertion is made in RHD's family history, but it is more likely family mythology than fact, as no verification can be located.

15. RHD, "The Harding Family," in Lasseter and Harris, eds., *Rebecca Harding Davis*, 142.

16. Ibid., 142–46.

17. Ibid., 148.

18. *The Encyclopedia of the Stone-Campbell Movement*, Douglas A. Foster, ed. (Grand Rapids, MI: Wm. B. Eerdmans Publishing, 2004), 295. Campbell also founded Bethany College in Bethany, Pennsylvania, in 1840, and the Pleasant Hill Seminary for women in 1847, for which his sister Jane Campbell McKeever served as the first principal (Harriet Branton, *Focus on Washington County*, vol. 1 [Washington, PA: Observer Publishing Company, 1980]: 95–96).

19. RHD, "Wilson Family," 138.

20. Otis K. Rice and Stephen W. Brown, *West Virginia: A History* (Lexington, KY: U of Kentucky P, 1993), 67.

21. RHD claimed Rachel's father "had doubts of all handsome foreigners" ("Wilson Family," 139).

22. Washington, PA, *Examiner* (21 Aug. 1830); *Washington County, PA, Marriages, 1780–1857* (Apollo, PA: Closson Press, 1987): 3.

23. RHD, "Bits of Gossip,"(hereafter "Bits")in Lasseter and Harris, eds., *Rebecca Harding Davis*, 53; RHD, "Under the Old Code," *Harper's New Monthly Magazine* 100 (Feb. 1900), 399.

24. RHD, "Bits," 55–56.

25. US Census, Alabama, 1830.

26. *Abstracts of Washington Co., Pa. Will Book #5 (1832–1841)*, n.d., n.p. (Washington County Historical Society).

27. RHD, "Bits," 23.

28. Ibid., 24.

29. Ibid., 25.

30. *Bradley v. Knox*, et al., "The Federal Cases," 1837, https://law.resource.org, 6 March 2015.

31. Washington, PA, *Examiner* (21 Aug. 1830).

32. Advertisements in *Wheeling Times and Advertiser 1839* and *Wheeling City Directory, 1839*.

33. In my earlier publications and elsewhere, Emilie's name has been given incorrectly as "Emilie (or Emelie) Berry Harding"; her correct name was Emilie Mary Harding per records held by Rachel Loden, RLC.

34. Two other daughters, Ellen and Florence, were born to the Hardings but died in infancy (RHD, "Bits," 139).

35. RHD recalled her uncle as a "very lovable and also scholarly man" ("Harding Family," 145).

36. This building is now the McLure Hotel on Market Street.

37. Deed records, Ohio County Deed books or indices, Book #24, 1840, pp. 209–10. I am indebted to Dan Bonenberger for this information.

38. US Census Records for Wheeling in 1840, 1850, and 1860 indicate live-in servants, their place of birth if they are Euro-American, and whether they were free or enslaved if they are African American. The Hardings' servants were all Euro-American. Richard Harding's business partner, Reddick McKee, however, had two "male colored persons (free)" and two "male colored persons (slaves)" in his household (US Census, Wheeling, Virginia, 1840).

39. RHD, "Bits," 26.

40. Ibid., 27.

41. Ibid., 31.

42. Ibid., 27.

43. Ibid., 28.

44. Ibid., 36.

45. Ibid., 25, 28.

46. RHD, "Some Hobgoblins in Literature," *Book Buyer* 14 (Apr. 1897), 229.

47. The church, though badly in need of repair, is still standing. It is now the Church of God and Saints of Christ and houses an African American congregation. My thanks to Minister Javetta Grey who kindly showed me through the building and pointed out the area to which slaves had been relegated during RHD's childhood.

48. Rice and Brown, *West Virginia*, 67.

49. RHD was taken as a child to a Methodist service; she found it alien but felt the faith of the people was genuine. See RHD, "An Unlighted Lamp," *Independent* (15 Aug. 1901), 1903–1904.

50. David L. Holmes, *A Brief History of the Episcopal Church* (London: A&C Black, 1993), 66–67.

51. RHD, "Bits," 30.

52. *Catalogue of the Officers and Members of the Washington Female Seminary for the Year Ending 30th September 1845* (Washington, PA: Grayson & Ruple, 1845); *Quarter-Centennial of the Graduates of the WFS, 1866* (Pittsburgh: Ernett and Anderson, 1866); *The Second Register of the...Washington Seminary, 1837–1924* (Washington, PA: n.p., 1924); *Semi-Centennial Celebration of the WFS, 1836–1886* (Washington, PA: n.p., 1886); J. Simonson Maguire, "The First Washington," *National Magazine* (Sept. 1910), 708–709; Crumrine, *History of Washington County*, 199–200; Branton, "Focus on Washington County," *Observer-Reporter* (15 June 1978–11 Aug. 1979); "Character Studies," *Good Housekeeping Magazine* 52 (May 1911), 583; Sharon M. Harris, *Rebecca Harding Davis and American Realism* (Philadelphia: U of Pennsylvania P, 1991), 23–24.

53. Ibid.

54. Ibid.

55. A photograph of an older, heavy-set woman that has been circulated for years as RHD is, in fact, a member of the extended Harding family but is not RHD. There is only one known photograph of RHD in her later years (see Figure 4), and it reveals her to have been a trim, healthy looking woman.

56. *Catalogue of the Officers and Members of the Washington Female Seminary for the Year Ending 30th September 1845* (Washington, PA: Grayson & Ruple, 1845); *Quarter-Centennial of the Graduates of the WFS, 1866* (Pittsburgh: Ernett and Anderson, 1866).

57. Ibid.

58. Ibid.

59. Letter, RHD to Richard Harding Davis, March 31, 1907 (UVA).

60. Helen Woodward Shaeffer, "Rebecca Harding Davis: Pioneer Realist," (Master's Thesis, University of Pennsylvania, 1947), 30–31.

61. Ibid., 31.

62. RHD, "Bits," 114–17; Maguire, "The First Washington," 707. See also RHD's depiction of Clay in her young adult novel, *Kent Hampden*.

63. Later, Washington and Jefferson College.

64. RHD, "Bits," 117–118.

65. Harriet Branton, *Focus on Washington County Reprints*, vol. 1. (Washington, PA: n.p., 1980),80–81; RHD, "Bits," 99–100; Reinhard O. Johnson, *The Liberty Party 1840–1848: Antislavery Third-Party Politics in the United States* (Baton Rouge: Louisiana State UP, 2009).

66. Phillip J. Schwarz, *Migrants against Slavery: Virginians and the Nation* (Charlottesville, VA: U of Virginia P, 2001), 35.

67. Branton, *Focus on Washington County Reprints*, 80–81; RHD, "Bits," 99–100; Reinhard O. Johnson, *The Liberty Party 1840–1848*.

68. RHD, "Bits," 99–100.

69. Wilma A. Dunaway, *The African American Family in Slavery and Emancipation* (Cambridge, MA: Cambridge UP, 2003), 21–22.

70. RHD, "Bits," 101.

71. RHD, "Bits," 99.

72. US Census, 1850.

73. RHD, "Harding Family," 148.

74. S. J. M. Eaton, *Memorial of the Life and Labors of the Rev. Cyrus Dickson D.D.* (New York: Robert Carter and Brothers, 1882), 105–28.

75. "Spared and Shared 4: Saving History One Letter at a Time," http://sparedshared4.wordpress.com, 26 Feb. 2014.

76. *Laws and Ordinances for the Government of the City of Wheeling, West Virginia* (Wheeling: Intelligencer Publishing Co., 1901), 772.

77. Shaeffer, "RHD," 32.

78. Oren Frederic Morton and J. R. Cole, *A History of Preston County, West Virginia* (1914), 718–19.

79. RHD, "Life in the Iron-Mills," *Atlantic Monthly* 42 (Apr. 1861), 430.

80. Quoted in Shaeffer, "RHD," 33.

81. Advertisement, *Wheeling Intelligencer* (27 Aug. 1858), 2.

82. Ohio County Court House records, Wheeling, WV: Death certificate [for Henry Grattan Harding], Book 1, p. 94, #155.

83. Frederick D. Power, *Life of William Kimbrough Pendleton, LL.D., President of Bethany College* (St. Louis: Christian Publishing Co., 1902), 276.

84. *The Athenaeum: The Story of a Building, 1855–61* (1861; n.p.; a compilation of *Intelligencer* articles).

85. Shaeffer, "RHD," 34–35.

86. "Archibald Campbell," *Wheeling Intelligencer* (14 Feb. 1899), reprinted in "West Virginia Culture," www.wvculture.org, 13 March 2015.

87. "Examination at the Classical Academy," *Wheeling Intelligencer* (25 Apr. 1857), 3; Editorial, *Wheeling Intelligencer* (24 Dec. 1858), 2. The following year's examinations also drew favorable comments for Wilse, "we have often heard of this school, under the management of Mr. Harding, highly spoken of" (22 Apr. 1858, p. 3) and similar comments appeared in December 1858.

88. Archibald Campbell Papers (WVUL).

89. [RHD], "Women and Politics," *Wheeling Intelligencer* (2 Feb. 1859), 2.

90. US Census, 1850. According to the 1860 census, the number had dropped to 100 (42 male and 58 female slaves in Wheeling; 69 were identified as "Black" and 31 as "Mulatto").

91. *Intelligencer*, 1850s–early 1860s, Library of Congress's digital newspapers.

92. RHD correspondence with Archibald Campbell; Letter, RHD to James T. Fields, Jan. 26, [1861] (UVA).

93. A Sad Case," *Wheeling Daily Intelligencer* (29 Aug. 1861), 3.

94. RHD, "Bits," 99.

95. Quoted in Shaeffer, "RHD," 35–36.

96. Gibson Lamb Cranmer, *History of Wheeling City and Ohio County, West Virginia* (Chicago: Biographical Publishing Co., 1902), 177–78.

97. "Archibald Campbell," n.p.

98. David Saville Muzzey, *James G. Blaine: A Political Idol of Other Days* (New York: Dodd, Mead, 1934); Mark Wahlgren Summers, *Rum, Romanism, and Rebellion* (Chapel Hill: U of North Carolina P, 2000), 61.

99. Letter, RHD to James T. Fields, Oct. 25, 1861 (UVA); RHD, "Bits," 121. According to Albert von Frank, the narrative was based on Solomon Northrup's *Twelve Years a Slave* and the Anthony Burns case of 1854, which O'Conner observed firsthand (*Boston Histories: Essays in Honor of Thomas H. O'Connor* [Boston: UP of New England, 2004], 59).

100. Letter, RHD to Richard Harding Davis, August 1888; quoted in Charles Belmont Davis, ed., *Adventures and Letters of Richard Harding Davis* (New York: Charles Scribner's Sons, 1917), 40.

101. Andrew Lawson, *Downwardly Mobile: The Changing Fortunes of American Realism* (New York: Oxford UP, 2012), 47. In addition, the Harding house was worth $1,000.

102. Letter, RHD to James T. Fields, Mar. 15, 1861 (UVA).

CHAPTER 2: TREASON AND FAME (APRIL 1861–MARCH 1863)

1. For an assessment of the impact of these strikes, see William L. Watson, "'These Mill-Hands Are Gettin' Onberarble': The Logic of Class Formation in 'Life in the Iron Mills' [sic] by Rebecca Harding Davis," *Women's Studies Quarterly* 26 (Spring–Summer1998), 116–36. For an analysis of the meaning of work in antebellum America, see Nicholas K. Bromell, *By the Sweat of the Brow: Literature and Labor in Antebellum America* (Chicago: U of Chicago P, 1993).

2. Alan Hyde, *Bodies of Law* (Princeton, NJ: Princeton UP, 1997), 41–42; Watson, "These Mill-Hands," 116.

3. For a study that contextualizes RHD's approach, see Lisa Irene Moody, "Religion and Realism in Late Nineteenth-Century American Literature," Ph.D. Thesis, Louisiana State University, 2009.

4. See "RHD: Complete Works" (http://rebeccahardingdaviscompleteworks.com/) for a comparison of the manuscript and the published version of "Life."

5. Letter, RHD to unknown recipient, undated (bMS Am 1340.2 [1492], HLH). While the recipient is not identified, the content coincides with RHD's descriptions of her letter to Hawthorne and her handwriting is of this period.

6. Elizabeth R. Varon, *Southern Lady, Yankee Spy: The True Story of Elizabeth Van Lew, a Union Agent in the Heart of the Confederacy* (New York: Oxford UP, 2005), 36.

7. Shaeffer, "RHD," 36.

8. Letter, RHD to James T. Fields, May 10, 1861, (FI 1167), HL.

9. Annie Adams Fields was, in essence if not in title, an assisting editor of the *Atlantic*. See Rita K. Gollin, *Annie Adams Fields: Woman of Letters* (Boston: U of Massachusetts P, 2002) and Susan K. Harris, *The Cultural Work of the Late Nineteenth-Century Hostess: Annie Adams Fields and Mary Gladstone Drew* (New York: Palgrave Macmillan, 2002).

10. Letter, RHD to Annie Adams Fields, May 20, [1861], UVA.

11. See, for example, "To the People of North Western Virginia," *Wheeling Intelligencer* (21 May 1861), 1.

12. Rice and Brown, *West Virginia*, Chapter 12; Sean Patrick Duffy, *Wheeling* (Charleston, SC: Arcadia Publishing, 2010); Granville Davisson Hall, *The Rending of Virginia: A History* (1902; Knoxville: U of Tennessee P, 2002).

13. RHD, "Bits," 37.

14. Letters, RHD to James T. Fields, July 30, [1861], and Aug. 9, [1861], UVA.

15. Ellery Sedgwick, *A History of the* Atlantic Monthly, *1857–1909: Yankee Humanism at High Tide and Ebb* (Boston: U of Massachusetts P, 2009), 75.

16. Letters, RHD to James T. Fields, July 30, [1861], and August 9, [1861], UVA.

17. Alexander Campbell, Editorial, *Wheeling Intelligencer* (32 Aug. 1861), 2.

18. Rice and Brown, *West Virginia*, Chapter 13.

19. Rice and Brown, *West Virginia*, Chapter 13; Varon, *Southern Lady*, 36–42; *Wheeling Intelligencer* and *New York Times* accounts, May 1861 through December 1861.

20. See, for example, "John Lamar," "The Second Sight," "The Luck of Abel Steadman."

21. RHD, "Bits," 15.

22. *St. Matthews Episcopal Church of Wheeling, WV* (Wheeling: n.p., n.d.), 4.

23. Letter, RHD to Jim Wilson, quoted in Shaeffer, "RHD," 37.
24. Ibid., 36.
25. "Arrested for Treason," *Cincinnati Daily Press* (31 Aug. 1861), 3.
26. "The Case of Richard Harding," *Wheeling Intelligencer* (3 Sep. 1861), 4.
27. Letter, RHD to James T. Fields, Aug. 17, 1861, UVA.
28. Reviewers in her own time and scholars today have ignored this assertion and continued to insist Howth is both the nucleus and the "heroine" of the novel, perhaps reflecting the power of titles.
29. Letter, RHD to James T. Fields, Aug. 17, [1861], UVA.
30. Ibid.
31. RHD, "Bits," 105.
32. Ibid. At the end of her life, RHD included an odd assembly of men who, to her mind, fit this description: "Lincoln, Frémont, Agassiz, . . . Grover Cleveland and Booker Washington" ("Bits,"105).
33. RHD, "Locked Chamber," *Peterson's Magazine* 41 (Jan. 1862), 42–54; *Waiting for the Verdict* (New York: Sheldon and Co., 1868), 53.
34. Letter, RHD to James T. Fields, Sep. 28, 1861, UVA.
35. Letters, RHD to James T. Fields, Sep. 9, [1861]; Sep. 17, [1861]; Sep. 28, 1861, UVA.
36. Letters, RHD to James T. Fields, Oct. 25, 1861; Oct. 31, 1861, UVA.
37. Letter, RHD to James T. Fields, [c. late Dec. 1861], UVA.
38. Letter, RHD to James T. Fields, Feb. 8, [1862], UVA.
39. Letter, RHD to James T. Fields, Apr. 28, [1862], UVA. Unfortunately, RHD and Wasson's correspondence is not extant, though she references it in several letters to others.
40. Sedgwick, *History of the* Atlantic Monthly, 99.
41. Shaeffer, "RHD," 88. The business records and correspondence of *Peterson's Magazine* have not been preserved.
42. Sedgwick, *History of the* Atlantic Monthly, 74.
43. Letter, RHD to James T. Fields, probably Dec. 1861, UVA.
44. Letter, RHD to James T. Fields, Nov. 16 [1861], UVA.
45. Letter, RHD to James T. Fields, Nov. 26, 1861, UVA.
46. See, for example, letters, RHD to James T. Fields, Jan. 9, 1862 and early Jan. 1863, UVA.
47. Letter, RHD to James T. Fields, c. Dec. 1861, UVA.
48. Letter, RHD to James T. Fields, Dec. 20, [1861], UVA.
49. Letters, RHD to James T. Fields, Nov. 19, [1861], Nov. 26, 1861, UVA.

50. For a comparison of the serial and the book version, see "A Story of To-Day" at "RHD: The Complete Works" (http://rebeccahardingdaviscompleteworks.com).

51. Letter, RHD to James T. Fields, Dec.30, 1861, UVA.

52. Ibid.

53. For more on the Page stories, see Alicia Mischa Renfroe's introduction to RHD's *A Law Unto Herself* (Lincoln: U of Nebraska P, 2014), and on John Page's complicity in the slave system, see Sharon M. Harris, "Rebecca Harding Davis, *Peterson's Magazine*, and the Civil War." *Tulsa Studies in Women's Literature* 30, no. 2 (Fall 2011), 291–315.

54. See also her non-Page stories for *Peterson's* such as a long serial, "The Second Life," in which this theme is reiterated.

55. RHD, "The Murder of the Glen Ross," *Peterson's Magazine* 40 (Nov. 1861), 348, 349.

56. Ibid., 441.

57. See, for instance, RHD's "The Locked Chamber," *Peterson's Magazine* 41 (Jan. 1862).

58. RHD, "The Story of Life Insurance," *Peterson's Magazine* 41 (June 1862), 449.

59. See, for example, Letter, RHD to James T. Fields, Jan. 6, [1862], UVA. Her humor was evident in her response to Fields, who had shared several responses to *Margret Howth*: "We will agree that that clergyman who preached about Margret was a man of taste—won't we? I hope he did not think as some religious critic whose article I saw the other day denouncing me as a Fourierite and wishing 'he' (I) had an engraving of 'The Light of the World' so that I might know who Christ was! I couldn't laugh because he was so sincere and earnest about it—." (Several readers initially believed the story had been written by a man.) She often joked also about not having time to have her portrait taken, adding in one letter "<u>here</u> I am too tender of my beauty to consign its fame to our unfortunate artists!" (Letter, RHD to James T. Fields, Jan. 21, [1862], UVA).

60. Letter, RHD to James T. Fields, Jan. 9, [1862], UVA.

61. Letters, RHD to James T. Fields, Feb. 14 and Feb. 20, 1862, UVA.

62. Letters, RHD to James T. Fields, Jan. 25, 1862 and to Annie Adams Fields, Feb. 14, 1862, UVA.

63. Thomas Woodson, James A. Rubino, and Jamie Barlowe Kayes, "With Hawthorne in Wartime Concord: Sophia Hawthorne's 1862 Diary," *Studies in the American Renaissance* (1988), 291.

64. Letter, RHD to James T. Fields, c. Dec. 1861, UVA.

65. Letter, RHD to James T. Fields, probably Dec. 1861, UVA.

66. Letter, RHD to James T. Fields, Feb. 20, 1862, UVA.

67. "Literary Notices," *Godey's Lady's Book* n.v. (May 1862), 510–11; "Poetry and Fiction," *Christian Examiner* 72 (May 1862), 449–50; "Margret Howth," *North American Review* 94 (Apr. 1862), 553–54.

68. "Review of New Books," *Peterson's Magazine* 41 (Apr. 1862), 343–44; Charles Godfrey Leland, "Sun-Shine in Thought; or, Chapters on the Cheerful and Joyous in Literature and Art," *Knickerbocker* 59 (Apr. 1862), 5.

69. Letter, RHD to James T. Fields, May 1, [1862], UVA.

70. Letters, RHD to James T. Fields, Feb. 20 and Mar. 7[?], 1862, UVA.

71. Sedgwick, *History of the* Atlantic Monthly, 83.

72. Letter, RHD to James T. Fields, Apr. 14[?], [1862], UVA. Charles Zagonyi was a Hungarian who served as Frémont's aide in the American Civil War. "Bob Acres" was a cowardly character in Richard Sheridan's play *The Rivals* (1775); the American actor Joseph Jefferson, who would become a longtime friend of RHD, had made the character famous in the late 1850s on the New York stage.

73. RHD, "Bits," 101.

74. Ibid., 76.

75. Ibid., 103.

76. Ibid., 127–28.

77. Letter, RHD to James T. Fields, May 7, [1862], UVA.

78. Letter, RHD to James T. Fields, May 14, [1862], UVA.

79. Gollin, *Annie Adams Fields*, 36.

80. Letter, RHD to James T. Fields, May 27, [1862], UVA.

81. Jessie Benton Frémont, *The Letters of Jessie Benton Frémont*, eds. Pamela Herr and Mary Lee Spence (Champaign: U of Illinois P, 1993), 324.

82. Ibid., 325.

83. As Sophia Hawthorne wrote in her diary of June 7, 1862, "This afternoon arrived Miss Harding author Margret Howth &c." (Woodson, Rubino, and Kayes, "Sophia Hawthorne's Diary," 303).

84. Ibid., see entries for Jan. 21, Feb. 11, and Feb. 12, 1862.

85. RHD, "Bits," 49.

86. Ibid., 303.

87. Letter, RHD to Annie Adams Fields, Aug. 4, [1862], (Ms Am 1492), HLH.

88. RHD, "Bits," 44.

89. Woodson, Rubino, and Kayes, "Sophia Hawthorne's Diary," 303.

90. RHD, "Bits," 41.

91. Louisa May Alcott, *The Journals of Louisa May Alcott*, eds. Joel Myerson and Daniel Shealy (Athens: U of Georgia P, 1989), 109.

92. Ibid., 119.

93. RHD, "Bits,"47.
94. Woodson, Rubino, and Kayes, "Sophia Hawthorne's Diary," 303–305.
95. RHD, "Bits," 42.
96. Ibid., 38–52.
97. Ibid.
98. Ibid.
99. Ibid.
100. Letter, RHD to Annie Adams Fields, Jan. 10, [1863], UVA.
101 Letter, RHD to Annie Adams, Fields, [mid-June 1862], UVA.
102. RHD, "Bits," 106.
103. Ibid.
104. Letter, RHD to Annie Adams Fields, [mid-June 1862], UVA.
105. Letter, RHD to James T. Fields, June 27, [1862], UVA.
106. Letter, RHD to Annie Adams Fields, Dec. 6, 1862, UVA. Newport would become a locale in some of her later fiction such as "The Wife's Story" (1864).
107. Letter, RHD to Annie Adams Fields, Aug. 28, [1862], UVA. RHD identified Clarke only as "a friend" in the letter.
108. Letter, RHD to James T. Fields and Annie Adams Fields, Aug. 4, [1862], (Ms 1492), HLH.
109. Letter, RHD to Annie Adams Fields and James T. Fields, Jul. 10, [1862], UVA.
110. Letter, RHD to Annie Adams Fields, Aug. 28, [1862], UVA.
111. Letter, RHD to James T. Fields and Annie Adams Fields, Aug. 21, [1862], (Ms 1492), HLH.
112. Ibid.
113. Letter, RHD to Annie Adams Fields, Aug. 28, [1862], UVA.
114. Letter, RHD to James T. Fields and Annie Adams Fields, Aug. 21, [1862], (FI 1168), HL.
115. Sedgwick, *History of the* Atlantic Monthly, 83.
116. Letter, RHD to James T. Fields, July 12, [1862], UVA.
117. Letter, RHD to Annie Adams Fields, Aug. 28 [1862], UVA.
118. Letter, RHD to Annie Adams Fields and James T. Fields, July 10, [1862], and to James T. Fields, July 12, [1862], UVA.
119. Letter, RHD to James T. Fields and Annie Adams Fields, Aug. 21, [1862], UVA.
120. RHD, "Bits," 50–52.

121. Letters, RHD to James T. Fields and Annie Adams Fields, Aug. 4 and Aug. 21, [1862], (Ms 1492), HLH; Letter, RHD to Annie Adams Fields, Aug. 28, [1862], UVA.

122. Letter, RHD to Annie Adams Fields, Aug. 28, [1862], UVA.

123. Ibid.

124. Ibid.

125. Letter, RHD to James T. Fields, Aug. 22, [1862], UVA.

126. Letter, RHD to Annie Adams Fields, Aug. 28, [1862], UVA.

127. Letter, RHD to Annie Adams Fields, Oct. 25, 1862, UVA.

128. Letter, RHD to Annie Adams Fields, Oct. 9, [1862], UVA.

129. Letter, RHD to Annie Adams Fields, Oct. 25, 1862, UVA.

130. Letter, RHD to James T. Fields, May 1, [1862], UVA.

131. *The Letters of Charles Dickens, Volume Ten, 1862–1864*, ed. Graham Storey (Oxford, England: Clarenden Press, 1998): 131–32. For an extended comparative analysis of RHD and Dickens, see Arielle Zibrak's "Writing behind a Curtain: Rebecca Harding Davis and Transatlantic Reform," *ESQ: A Journal of the American Renaissance* 68.3 (2012): 103–128.

132. Frémont, *Letters of Jessie Benton Frémont*, 346.

133. Letter, RHD to Annie Adams Fields, Dec. 6, 1862, UVA.

134. Letter, RHD to James T. Fields, Dec. 30, 1862, UVA.

135. Quoted in Harris, *Rebecca Harding Davis and American Realism*, 78–79; *The Collected Writings of Walt Whitman*, Ed. Edwin Haviland Miller (New York: New York UP, 1961), 1: 77–78.

136. Letter, RHD to James T. Fields, Dec. 2, [1862], UVA.

137. Letter, RHD to Annie Adams Fields, Jan. 10, [1863], UVA.

138. Letter, RHD to James T. Fields and Annie Adams Fields, Jan. 26, [1863], UVA.

139. Letter fragment, Rebecca Harding to Archibald Campbell, WVUL.

140. Letter, RHD to Annie Adams Fields, Oct. 9, [1862], UVA.

141. Letter, RHD to James T. Fields, Oct. 20, [1862], UVA.

142. Letter, RHD to Annie Adams Fields, Dec. 6, 1862, UVA.

143. *Women of the Mountain South: Identity, Work, and Activism*, ed. Connie Park Rice and Marie Tedesco (Columbus: Ohio UP, 2015), section 8.

144. Letter, Jessie Benton Frémont to James T. Fields, Jan. 26, 1863 (*Letters of Jessie Benton Frémont*, 341-42); Fantine, a prostitute, was a character depicted sympathetically in Victor Hugo's *Les Misérables*.

145. Letter, RHD to Annie Adams Fields, Feb. 18, [1863], UVA.

146. Letter, RHD to James T. Fields, Feb. 3, [1863], UVA.

147. Letters, RHD to James T. Fields, [early 1863], UVA.

148. Review by RHD, *"The Story of the Guard: A Chronicle of the War* by Jessie Benton Frémont," *Atlantic Monthly* 11 (Jan. 1863), 142–43.

149. Marriage records, St. Matthews Episcopal Church, Wheeling, WV.

150. Gollin, *Annie Adams Fields*, 49.

151. Biographical information about L. Clarke Davis is scant; my sources for the details here and below are as follows: Untitled, *Friends' Intelligencer* (24 Dec. 1904), 825; "Treemount Seminary" Historical Society of Montgomery County, Maryland, https://hsmcpa.org; Arthur Lubow, *The Reporter Who Would Be King: A Biography of Richard Harding Davis* (New York: Charles Scribner's Sons, 1990), 11; Shaeffer, "RHD," 269; *Philadelphia Directory* (1863, 1864).

152. These transactions were sometimes published in the local newspapers under Clarke's name. See, for example, "For Sale and To Rent," *Public Ledger* (6 June 1860), 3.

CHAPTER 3: A NEW LIFE (MAY 1863–MAY 1865)

1. Letter, RHD to Annie Adams Fields, Feb. 18, [1863], UVA.
2. Letter, RHD to Annie Adams Fields, Jan. 10, [1863], UVA.
3. Letters, RHD to Annie Adams Fields, June 15 and Nov. 9, [1863], UVA.
4. Letter, RHD to Annie Adams Fields, Apr. 21, [1863], UVA. The line was not reinstated, in spite of RHD's wrath.
5. Letter, RHD to Annie Adams Fields, [late April 1863], UA.
6. Letters, RHD to Annie Adams Fields, May 1, [1863] and [May 15?, 1863], UVA.
7. Letter, RHD to Annie Adams Fields, [c. April 1863], UVA.
8. Ibid.
9. Letter, RHD to Annie Adams Fields, June 15 [1863], UVA.
10. RHD, "Bits," Chapter 7.
11. Ibid, 108–111. On the Grew-Burleigh relationship, see Gay Gibson Cima, *Performing Anti-Slavery: Activist Women on Antebellum Stages* (Cambridge, MA: Cambridge UP, 2014), 123.
12. RHD, "Bits," 111.
13. Letters, RHD to Annie Adams Fields, April 21; May 1, 6, 15?; and June 15, [1863], UVA.
14. Letters, RHD to Annie Adams Fields, [late April]; May 6 and 15?, [1863], UVA.
15. Letter, RHD, to Annie Adams Fields, May 1, [1863], UVA.

16. Letter, RHD to Annie Adams Fields, [late April 1863], UVA.
17. Letter, RHD to Annie Adams Fields, June 3, [1863], UVA.
18. Letter, RHD to Annie Adams Fields, May 1, [1863], UVA.
19. Letters, RHD to Annie Adams Fields, May 11, [1863], [May 15?, 1863], and June 15 [1863], UVA.
20. Letter, RHD to Annie Adams Fields, June 15, [1863], UVA.
21. Letters, RHD to Annie Adams Fields, March 12 and May 6, [1863], UVA.
22. Ibid.
23. Letters, RHD to Annie Adams Fields, May 6, [1863] and May 11, [1863], UVA.
24. Letter, RHD to Annie Adams Fields, May 1, [1863], UVA.
25. Letter, RHD to Annie Adams Fields, May 11, [1863], UVA.
26. Letter, RHD to Annie Adams Fields, June 15, [1863], UVA.
27. Letter, RHD to Annie Adams Fields, Jul. 27, [1863], UVA.
28. Sedgwick, *History of the* Atlantic Monthly, 94.
29. Letters, RHD to Annie Adams Fields, July. 27 and [c. Dec. 1863], UVA.
30. Letter, RHD to Annie Adams Fields, Sep. 29, [1863], UVA.
31. Letter, RHD to Annie Adams Fields, Sep. 29, [1863], UVA. The reference is to a character in *David Copperfield*.
32. Letter, RHD to Annie Adams Fields, [late Dec., 1863], UVA.
33. Letter, RHD to James T. Fields, Oct. 20, [1863], (FI 1166), HL.
34. Letter, RHD to James T. Fields, Nov. 9, [1863], UVA.
35. Letter, RHD to Charles Eliot Norton, Mar. 19, [1863], Houghton Library, Harvard University.
36. Letters, RHD to Annie Adams Fields, April 21 and May 11, [1863], UVA.
37. Sedgwick, *History of the* Atlantic Monthly, 87.
38. Quoted in Shaeffer, "RHD," 93–94.
39. Letter, RHD to Annie Adams Fields, [c. Dec. 1863], UVA. Though a Wheeling directory in early 1864 shows Richard as still a druggist in the city, I believe it is incorrect. Both Henry and Hugh were documented in the city for many years after 1863, and I believe it was Richard who moved to Kentucky. A Richard H. Harding lived in Louisville, Kentucky, as late as 1879, working as a chief claims clerk for the Louisville & Nashville Railroad Company (Louisville City Directory, 1879). Richard Harris Harding would eventually settle in Florida.
40. Letter, RHD to Annie Adams Fields, [late Dec. 1863], UVA.
41. Diary, Annie Adams Fields, dated Feb. 7, 1864, Annie Adams Fields Papers, Ms. N-1221, MHS.
42. Letter, RHD to Annie Adams Fields, [c. Feb. 1864], UVA.

43. Letter, RHD to James T. Fields, Feb. 25, [1864], UVA. Because "The Wife's Story" was published after the birth of RHD's first child, Tillie Olsen assumed the story had been written during her illness and its dire content reflected postpartum depression; this interpretation was perpetuated by most RHD scholars until the present. In fact, RHD's letters reveal that the story was not autobiographical; it was written before she gave birth, at a time she was feeling well and hopeful about the future, and there is no record it was revised before publication. The only mystery that remains is why it was not published until July.
44. Letter, RHD to Annie Adams Fields, Mar. 15, [1864], UVA.
45. Letter, RHD to Annie Adams Fields, [Apr. 12, 1864], UVA.
46. Letter, RHD to Annie Adams Fields, [Apr. 12, 1864], UVA.
47. Obituary, Wheeling Intelligencer (22 Mar. 1864).
48. Ibid.
49. Letter, RHD to Annie Adams Fields, quoted in William Frazer Grayburn, "The Major Fiction of RHD," Ph.D. thesis, Pennsylvania State University 1965, 53. Grayburn had access to some of the family papers that have since been lost.
50. Letter, RHD to Annie Adams Fields, [late spring, 1864], UVA.
51. Letter, RHD to Annie Adams Fields, June 27, [1864], UVA.
52. Letter, RHD to Annie Adams Fields, May 17, [1864], UVA.
53. Joan Burstyn, *Past and Promise: Lives of New Jersey Women* (Syracuse, NY: Syracuse UP, 1997), 123–24; Letter, RHD to Annie Adams Fields, June 27, [1864], UVA.
54. Letter, RHD to Annie Adams Fields, n.d., UVA.
55. Shaeffer, "RHD," 163.
56. Letters, RHD to Annie Adams Fields, [early Jul.] and [summer 1864], UVA.
57. Letter, RHD to Annie Adams Fields, June 27, [1864], UVA.
58. Letters, RHD to Annie Adams Fields, [early fall 1864], UVA.
59. Letter, RHD to Annie Adams Fields, [c. fall 1864], UVA.
60. Letters, L. Clarke Davis to RHD, Nov. 1864, quoted in Shaeffer, "RHD," 118–119, 204–205.
61. Ibid. For Seemuller's influence on Henry James via this novel, see Alfred Habegger, *Henry James and the Woman Business* (Cambridge, MA: Cambridge UP, 2004), Chapter 5.
62. My thanks to Alicia Mischa Renfroe for identifying RHD's authorship of these works.
63. Letter, RHD to Annie Adams Fields, [Jan. 1865], UVA.
64. Letter, RHD to Annie Adams Fields, [spring? 1865], UVA.
65. Letter, RHD to Annie Adams Fields, [Jan. 1865], UVA.

66. Letter, RHD to Annie Adams Fields, Mar. 2, [1865], UVA.

67. J. David Hacker, "A Census-Based Count of the Civil War Dead," *Civil War History* 57 (Dec. 2011), 307–48.

68. Letter, RHD to Annie Adams Fields, Apr. 20, [1865], UVA.

69. "The Missing Diamond," *Peterson's Magazine* (May–Sep. 1865), 413.

CHAPTER 4: NEW VENTURES (JUNE 1865–DECEMBER 1867)

1. Letter, RHD to Annie Adams Fields, June 10, [1865], UVA.

2. Letter, RHD to Annie Adams Fields, June 10, [1865], UVA.

3. Letter, RHD to James T. Fields, Jul. 17, [1865], BN.

4. Ibid.

5. Letter, RHD to Annie Adams Fields, Aug. 10, [1865], UVA.

6. RHD, "Bits," 85.

7. Letters, RHD to Annie Adams Fields, "July-Day," [1865] and Aug. 10, [1865], UVA.

8. On the popularity of resorts in the postwar era, see Rebecca Cawood McIntyre, *Souvenirs of the Old South: Northern Tourism and Southern Mythology* (UP of Florida, 2011); Thomas A. Chambers, *Drinking the Waters: Creating a Leisure Class at Nineteenth-Century Mineral Springs* (Washington, D.C.: Smithsonian Institution Scholarly Press, 2002); and Nina Silber, *The Romance of Reunion: Northerners and Southerners, 1865–1900* (Chapel Hill: U of North Carolina P, 1997).

9. Letters, RHD to Annie Adams Fields, "July-Day," [1865] and Aug. 10, [1865], UVA.

10. Letter, RHD to Annie Adams Fields, "July-Day," [1865].

11. Letter, RHD to Annie Adams Fields, Sep. 17, [1865], UVA.

12. Letter, RHD to Annie Adams Fields, Sep. 17, [1865], UVA.

13. Such stories had appeared in *The Knickerbocker* (Mar. 1869) and *Youth's Companion* (Oct. 1869), and were reprinted in *Michigan Farmer*, *The Happy Home*, and the *New York Evangelist*.

14. [RHD], "The Little Street-Sweeper," *Peterson's Magazine* 48 (Oct. 1865), 240.

15. "Editor's Table: Thousand Dollar Stories," *Peterson's Magazine* 48 (Oct. 1865), 291.

16. Kerry L. Bryan, "Civil War Sanitary Fairs," *The Encyclopedia of Greater Philadelphia*, www.philadelphiaencyclopedia.org, Apr. 18, 2015.

17. "Soldiers' and Sailors' Home: Book Department," *Philadelphia Inquirer* (20 Oct. 1865), 3.

18. Letter, RHD to Annie Adams Fields, Nov. 6, [1865], UVA.

19. See, for example, "Aid for the Sufferers," (Philadelphia) *Evening Bulletin* (16 Dec. 1865), 7.

20. Letter, RHD to Annie Adams Fields, [late Dec. 1865], UVA.

21. Nora Titone, *My Thoughts Be Bloody: The Bitter Rivalry between Edwin and John Wilkes Booth That Led to an American Tragedy* (New York: Simon and Schuster, 2010).

22. Letter, RHD to Annie Adams Fields, [c. Jan. 1866], UVA.

23. RHD diary fragments, UVA.

24. Letter, RHD to Annie Adams Fields, [post-Jan. 24, 1866], UVA.

25. Letter, RHD to Annie Adams Fields, [post-Jan.24, 1866], UVA.

26. [Rebecca Harding Davis], "The Stolen Bond," *Peterson's Magazine* 49 (May 1866), 327–28.

27. RHD diary fragments, UVA.

28. William A. Blair, *With Malice toward Some: Treason and Loyalty in the Civil War Era* (Chapel Hill: U of North Carolina P, 2014), 293–96.

29. Frederick D. Power, *Life of William Kimbrough Pendleton, LL.D., President of Bethany College* (St. Louis: Christian Publishing Co., 1902), 276.

30. Letter, RHD to James T. Fields, [c. April 1866], UVA.

31. Ibid.

32. Sedgwick, *History of the* Atlantic Monthly, 91–92; Frank Luther Mott, *A History of American Magazines, 1850–1865, Volume 2* (Cambridge: Harvard UP, 1938), 2: 509.

33. Letter, RHD to Annie Adams Fields, Mar. 30, [1866], UVA.

34. Letters, RHD to Annie Adams Fields, Mar. 30, [1866] and Apr. 21, [1866], UVA.

35. Letter, RHD to Annie Adams Fields, May 20, [1866], UVA.

36. Gollin, *Annie Adams Fields*, Chapter 8.

37. Letter, RHD to F. P. Church, June 4, 1866, NYPL.

38. For a detailed analysis of the rise of the magazine and its importance in shifting the publishing world toward New York, see Justus R. Pearson, Jr., *Story of a Magazine; New York's Galaxy 1866–1878* (New York: New York Public Library, 1957).

39. Pearson, *Story of a Magazine*, 9–10.

40. Letter, RHD to Annie Adams Fields, Jul. 1, [1866], UVA.

41. Letter, RHD to Annie Adams Fields, Sep. 9, [1866], UVA.

42. Letter, RHD to Clara Wilson Baird, Nov. 30, [1866], UVA.

43. Quoted in Shaeffer, "RHD," 100–101.

44. Letter, RHD to Annie Adams Fields, Sep. 9, [1866], UVA.

45. Letter, RHD to Annie Adams Fields, Sep. 9, [1866], UVA.
46. Letter, RHD and L. Clarke Davis to Annie Adams Fields, Sep. 19, [1866], UVA.
47. Letter, RHD to Annie Adams Fields, Oct. 26, [1866], UVA.
48. Ibid.
49. Letter, RHD to Clara Wilson Baird, Nov. 30, [1866], quoted in Shaeffer, "RHD," 102–103.
50. Letter, RHD to Annie Adams Fields, Oct. 26, [1866], UVA.
51. Letter, RHD to William Conant Church, Nov. 1, [1866], NYPL-WCC.
52. Letter, RHD to William Conant Church, Dec. 10, [1866], NYPL-WCC.
53. Sedgwick, *History of the* Atlantic Monthly, 77.
54. Letter, RHD to James T. Fields, Nov. 8, [1866], UVA.
55. Letters, RHD to William Conant Church, Nov. 22, [1866], NYPL-WCC, and RHD to Clara Wilson Baird, Nov. 30, [1866], quoted in Shaeffer, "RHD," 134.
56. Letter, RHD to William Conant Church, Dec. 10, [1866], NYPL-WCC.
57. Letter, RHD to Clara Wilson Baird, Nov. 30, [1866], quoted in Shaeffer, "RHD," 102–103.
58. Pearson asserts that men more easily accepted changes to their manuscripts, but the correspondence with women writers indicates that the editors often changed their manuscripts much more extensively, including altering the conclusions and the meanings of the stories (*Story of a Magazine*, 19).
59. Pearson, *Story of a Magazine*, 19.
60. Letter, RHD to William Conant Church, Dec. 10, [1866], NYPL-WCC.
61. Letter, RHD to William Conant Church, Dec. 24, [1866], NYPL-WCC.
62. Letter, RHD to William Conant Church, Dec. 31, [1866], NYPL-WCC.
63. Letter, RHD to William Conant Church, Jan, 10, [1867], NYPL-WCC,
64. Letter, RHD to William Conant Church, [early Jan. 1867], NYPL-WCC.
65. RHD diary fragments, UVA.
66. Ibid.
67. Letter, RHD to Annie Adams Fields, Jan. 6, [1867], UVA. The reference is to Friedrich Schiller's poem, "Resignation."
68. Letter, RHD to James T. Fields, Jan. 27, [1867], UVA.
69. Martin Delaney's *Blake* (1859–1862) has a black physician as a major character but he is located outside the US.
70. Roger Lane, *William Dorsey's Philadelphia & Ours: On the Past and Future of the Black City in America* (New York: Oxford UP, 1991), 175. Dr. Rossell received his degree in Germany; he served both the African American and German immigrant communities in Philadelphia.

71. RHD, "Bits," 34.

72. Gerald Langford, *The Richard Harding Davis Years: A Biography of a Mother and Son* (New York: Holt, Rinehart and Winston, 1961), 49.

73. Sedgwick, *History of the* Atlantic Monthly, 75.

74. "The New Novelist," (Philadelphia) *Evening Bulletin* (1 Feb. 1867), 1.

75. "The Galaxy," (Philadelphia) *Evening Bulletin* (6 Feb. 1867), 4; "New Publications," *Boston Advertiser* (2 Feb. 1867), n.p.

76. "The Galaxy," *Sunday School Teacher* 2 (Mar. 1867), 95.

77. "The Galaxy," *Medical and Surgical Reporter* (9 Mar. 1867), 195.

78. Letter, RHD to "Miss Chase," Correspondence, Miscellaneous "D," 1864–1875, AAS.

79. Letter, RHD to William Conant Church, Feb. 11, [1867], NYPL-WCC.

80. Ibid.

81. See, for example, Letter, L. Clarke Davis to William Conant Church, Feb. 20, 1867, NYPL-WCC.

82. Letter, L. Clarke Davis to Frank P. Church, Feb. 15, 1867, NYPL-WCC.

83. Letter, RHD to William Conant Church, [early Apr. 1867], NYPL-WCC.

84. Letter, RHD to F. P. and William Conant Church, Apr. 19, [1867], NYPL-WCC.

85. Letter, L. Clarke Davis to William Conant Church, Apr. 28, 1867, NYPL-WCC.

86. Garsed v. Beall, 92 U.S. 684 (1875).

87. Letters, L. Clarke Davis to William Conant Church, Apr. 10, 17, 18, 22, 25, and 28, 1867, NYPL-WCC.

88. Letter, RHD to Annie Adams Fields, May 9, [1867], UVA.

89. Letter, RHD to William Conant Church, May 25, [1867], NYPL-WCC.

90. The editors had begun another serial, Annie Edwards' *Steven Lawrence, Yeoman*.

91. Letter, RHD to William Conant and Frank P. Church, June 4, [1867], NYPL-WCC.

92. Letter, RHD to Annie Adams Fields, June 16, [1867], UVA.

93. Letter, L. Clarke Davis to William Conant Church and Frank P. Church, Jul. 9 1867, NYPL-WCC.

94. Letter, RHD to William Conant Church, Jul. 14, [1867], NYPL-WCC.

95. Letter, RHD to Annie Adams Fields, Jul. 25, [1867], UVA. None of RHD's novels for Peterson's were published in book form. Charles Peterson sought to distinguish himself from T. J. Peterson Publishing, but it was an odd omission since it certainly would have been profitable for him as well as RHD.

96. Letters, L. Clarke Davis to Frank P. Church, June 17 and 19, 1867, NYPL-WCC.

97. Contract dated Aug. 18, 1867, between W.C. and F.P. Church and RHD, NYPL-WCC.

98. Elizabeth Stuart Phelps, "At Bay," *Harper's New Monthly Magazine* 34 (May 1867), 780.

99. Henry James, "Waiting for the Verdict," *Nation* (21 Nov. 1867), 410–11.

100. For an extended analysis of James' review and the Nation's repeatedly negative reviews of novels that addressed miscegenation, see Jean Pfaelzer, *Parlor Radical: Rebecca Harding Davis and the Origins of American Social Realism* (Pittsburgh: U of Pittsburgh P, 1996), 155ff.

101. W. E. Burghardt DuBois, *The Philadelphia Negro* (Philadelphia: U of Pennsylvania P, 1899), 36–37.

102. Quoted in Harris, *RHD and American Realism*, 137.

103. Letter, RHD to James T. Fields, Nov. 26, [1867], UVA.

104. Letter, RHD to William Conant Church, Dec. 27, [1867], NYPL-WCC.

105. RHD diary fragments, UVA.

CHAPTER 5: A NATIONAL AUTHOR (1868–1870)

1. On *Waiting* as the first novel to receive this designation, see Kevin Hayes, "Can the Great American Novel Exist?" Blog. *Huffington Post* (15 May 2012) huffingtonpost.com/author/kevin-hayes.

2. "Literary Notices," *Godey's Lady's Book* 76 (Jan. 1868), 98; "Reviews," *Round Table* (28 Dec. 1867), 433; Dall's book is in the Women's Archives, Schlesinger Library.

3. *Papers and Proceedings of the Eighth-General Meeting of the American Library Association* (Boston: Rockwell and Churchill, 1886), 172.

4. "Philadelphia Photographed," *Lancaster Intelligencer* (15 Jan. 1868), 1.

5. Quoted in Edd Winfield Parks, *William Gilmore Simms as Literary Critic* (Athens: U of Georgia P, 1961), 38–39.

6. Henry James, Jr., "Dallas Galbraith," *Nation* (22 Oct. 1868), 330–31.

7. "Literature and Literary Progress in 1868," *Appleton's Annual Cyclopedia* (New York: D. Appleton, 1873), 8: 408.

8. Letter, L. Clarke Davis to William Conant Church, Feb. 1, 1868, NYPL-WCC.

9. Letter, RHD to Paul Hamilton Hayne, Mar. 15, 1869, Paul Hamilton Hayne Papers, Box 2, Rubenstein Library, Duke University. The quoted lines are from Hamilton's "Renewed."

10. Ibid.

11. Letter, RHD to Annie Adams Fields, Mar. 1, [1868], UVA.

12. Sedgwick, *History of the* Atlantic Monthly, 91. For James Fields' adoration of Dickens, see the chapter on the English author in Fields' *Yesterdays with Authors* (Boston: Houghton, Mifflin and Co., 1896).

13. Letter, RHD to Annie Adams Fields, Mar. 1, [1868], UVA.

14. L. Clarke Davis, "A Modern Lettre de Cachet," *Atlantic Monthly* 21 (May 1868), 589, 591.

15. L. Clarke Davis, "Letter to the Editor," *Round Table* (16 May 1868), 310–11; Editorial Response, *Round Table* (16 May 1868), 311.

16. L. Clarke Davis, "Insane Asylums," *Boston Daily Advertiser* (30 May 1868), 3.

17. RHD diary fragments, UVA.

18. Ibid.

19. Ibid.

20. Ibid.

21. "Lippincott's Magazine for October," (Philadelphia) *Evening Bulletin* (18 Sep. 1868), 1.

22. "New Publications," (Philadelphia) *Evening Bulletin* (10 Oct. 1868), 2.

23. "Literary Notices," *Godey's Lady's Book* 77 (Dec. 1868), 544; "Notes on Books and Booksellers," *American Literary Gazette* (16 Nov. 1868), 41.

24. F. B. Stanford, "American Literature since the War," *Independent* (20 Oct. 1881), 4.

25. Letters, L. Clarke Davis to Frank P. Church, Dec. 3 and 8, 1868, NYPL. For the initial legal decisions in retaining Maceuen, see "Commonwealth ex rel. Malcolm Maceuen v. Thomas S. Kirkbride, M.D." in F. Carroll Brewster, *Reports of Equity, Election, and Other Important Cases…in the Courts of the County of Philadelphia* (Philadelphia: John Campbell, 1869), 1: 541–47.

26. [RHD], "Asylums for the Insane," *New-York Tribune* (28 Nov. 1868), 4.

27. RHD, "Bits," 107.

28. Quoted in "Hay as Journalist," *Scranton Tribune* (19 Mar. 1897), 4.

29. "New Periodicals," (Philadelphia) *Evening Bulletin* (2 Feb. 1869), 2.

30. Letter, Harriet Beecher Stowe to RHD, Jan. 31, [1869], UVA.

31. "The Position of Women," *Saturday Evening Post* (27 Feb. 1869), 3; "L'Opera-Bouffe," (Philadelphia) *Evening Bulletin* (19 Jan. 1869), 2.

32. "The Magazines for March," (Philadelphia) *Evening Bulletin* (23 Feb. 1869), 2.

33. Sam Hudson, *Pennsylvania and Its Public Men* (Philadelphia: n.p., 1909), 16.

34. Letter, Louisa May Alcott to L. Clarke Davis, June 4, [1869], Richard Harding Davis Papers, UVA.

35. Letter, RHD to Annie Adams Fields, Sep. 16, [1869], UVA.

36. Ibid.

37. Ibid. I have been unable to locate a copy of this review. Unfortunately, nineteenth-century editions of the Sunday *Tribune* have rarely been preserved, and those were the issues in which RHD most often published her editorials.

38. Letter, RHD to Annie Adams Fields, Sep. 16, [1869], UVA.

39. "Watson Ambruster," *Michigan Alumnus* 10 (Apr. 1904), 364.

40. "The Press of Philadelphia," *History of Philadelphia*, 3: 1958–2062.

41. Charles Belmont Davis, *Adventures and Letters*, 6–10.

42. Ibid., 1.

43. RHD diary fragments, UVA.

44. Ibid.

45. RHD, "Bits," 111.

46. Pearson, *Story of a Magazine*, 34–38.

47. RHD, "Leonard Heath's Fortune," 5 *Lippincott's Magazine* (Apr. 1870), 398.

48. For a thorough analysis of RHD's work in this area, see Mark Canada, "Stories of Today: RHD's Investigative Fiction," *Journalism Home* 38.2 (2012), 63–73.

49. Davis Dowling, "Davis, Inc.: The Business of Asylum Reform in the Periodical Press," *American Periodicals* 20.1 (2010), 23.

50. Ibid.

51. Letter, RHD to Paul Hamilton Hayne, May 10, [1869?], quoted in Harris, *RHD and American Realism*, 137.

52. Letter, RHD to Annie Adams Fields, May 15, [1870?], UVA.

53. Gail Hamilton [Mary Abigail Dodge], *A Battle of the Books* (Boston: H. O. Houghton, 1870).

54. Letter, RHD to Annie Adams Fields, May 15, [1870?], UVA.

55. One of her "Open Doors" essays, however, also attended at length to Catholicism.

56. "A Hundred Years Ago." *Riverside Magazine for Young People* 4 (Jun.–Jul. 1870): 280, 283.

57. "Death of a Former Wheeling Gentleman," *Wheeling Intelligencer* (30 June 1870), 1.

58. The Davises always received advance copies of the *Atlantic*. This issue was available to the public the week after her July 15 article appeared in the Tribune.

59. Letter, RHD to Annie Adams Fields, Jul. 19, [1870], UVA.

60. Shaeffer, "RHD," 164–65.

61. "History of Point Pleasant Beach," Borough of Point Pleasant Beach, Ocean County, New Jersey, www.pointpleasantbeach.org, May 20, 2015.

62. Charles Belmont Davis, *Adventures and Letters*, 6.

63. RHD diary fragments, UVA.

64. See, for example, Advertisement, *Hearth and Home* (5 Nov. 1870), 727.

65. "All Sorts and Sizes," Bangor (ME) *Whig and Courier* (6 June 1870), 1.

66. Marion Marzolf, *Up from the Footnote: A History of Women Journalists* (Orlando, FL: Hastings House, 1977), 22.

67. Letter, RHD to Annie Adams Fields, Dec. 22, [1870], Huntington Library.

CHAPTER 6: A CONSERVATIVE PROGRESSIVE (1871–1875)

1. Harry C. Silcox, *Philadelphia Politics from the Bottom Up: The Life of Irishman William McMullen, 1824–1901* (Balch Institute Press, 1989), 77–79, 86.

2. See, for instance, RHD, "Jack," *Youth's Companion* (16 Feb. 1871), 163–164.

3. RHD diary fragments, UVA.

4. RHD, "How Jack Went Tiger-Hunting," *Youth's Companion* (25 May 1871), 163.

5. RHD, "A Mountain Shanty: A Christmas Story," *Hearth and Home* (30 Dec. 1871), 1026; reprinted in *Woman's Journal* (13 January 1872), 14–15.

6. RHD, "Two Women," *Independent* (14 Oct. 1875), 6.

7. RHD diary fragments, UVA.

8. Silber, *The Romance of Reunion*, 67–68.

9. RHD, "How We Spent the Summer," *Peterson's Magazine* 60 (Aug. 1871), 123.

10. RHD, "A Thanksgiving Story," *Massachusetts Ploughman and New England Journal of Agriculture* (2 Dec. 1871), 4; reprinted as "The Conductor's Story," *Hearth and Home* (2 Dec. 1871), 946–47; *Hartford Courant* (13 Feb. 1872), 1, and *New-Hampshire Patriot* (10 Jan. 1872), 4.

11. RHD, "The Barred Acres—The Doctor's Story," *Peterson's Magazine* 60 (Dec. 1871), 414.

12. Ibid., 421.

13. RHD, "The Other Side," *Peterson's Magazine* 61 (Jan. 1872), 60.

14. *Mark Twain's Letters. Volume 4, 1870–1871*, eds. Victor Fischer and Michael B. Frank (Los Angeles: U of California P, 1995), 4:240.

15. Letter, RHD to Annie Adams Fields, Jan. 6, [1872], UVA.

16. Letter, RHD to Annie Adams Fields, Feb. 5, [1872], UVA. RHD had all of her mail directed to Clarke's office, and he then brought it home in the evenings.

17. Letter, RHD to Annie Adams Fields, Feb. 21, [1872], UVA.

18. Norval Morris, *The Oxford History of the Prison: The Practice of Punishment in Western Society* (New York: Oxford UP, 1998), 315; Lori Brennan, "American Correctional Association" in Mary Bosworth, ed., *Encyclopedia of Prisons and Correctional Facilities* (Thousand Oaks, CA: Sage Publications, 2004), 32–33.

19. RHD, "Gertrude," *The Similibus* (19 Apr. 1872), 3.

20. Anon., "The Tribune Staff." *Lowell Daily Citizen and News* (24 May 1872), Issue 4929, col. A.

21. Letter, RHD to Annie Adams Fields, May 5, 1872 (UVA).

22. RHD, "Balacchi Brothers," *Lippincott's Magazine* 10 (Jul. 1872), 75.

23. See, for example, *Scribner's Stories by American Authors* (1884); *The International Library of Famous Literature* (1898); *Library of American Fiction* (1904); and Edmund Clarence Stedman's influential *A Library of American Literature from the Earliest Settlement to the Present* (1889).

24. Catherine Drinker Bowen, *History of Lehigh University* (Bethlehem, PA: Lehigh Alumni Bulletin, 1924), 31, 33.

25. Gary Scharnhorst, *Kate Field: The Many Lives of a Nineteenth-Century American Journalist* (Syracuse, NY: Syracuse UP, 2008), 95.

26. RHD, "A Faded Leaf of History," *Atlantic Monthly* 31 (Jan. 1873), 44–45.

27. "January Magazines," *Literary World* (1 Jan. 1873), 124.

28. Letter, RHD to Dr. Josiah Gilbert Holland, May 26, [1870?], NYPL-JGH.

29. Letter, RHD to Dr. Josiah Gilbert Holland, Mar. 30, [1873], NYPL-JGH.

30. RHD, "Bits," 123–24.

31. "Current Literature," *Boston Daily Advertiser* (19 Mar. 1873), 2.

32. For a fuller analysis of this novella, see Sharon M. Harris, "Rebecca Harding Davis's Berrytown and Nineteenth-Century Medical Culture," *American Literary Realism* 44 (2011), 23–45.

33. Lewis Clinton Strang, *Players and Plays of the Last Quarter Century* (Boston: L. C. Page, 1903), 213.

34. John P. Herron, *Science and the Social Good: Nature, Culture, and Community* (New York: Oxford UP, 2009), 25–26.

35. RHD, "The Doctor's Story," *Youth's Companion* (4 Sep. 1873), 281.

36. Ibid.

37. Geoff D. Zulstra, "Whiteness, Freedom, and Technology: The Racial Struggle over Philadelphia's Streetcars, 1859–1867," *Technology and Culture* 52 (Oct. 2011), 678–702.

38. Russell Frank Weigley, et al., *Philadelphia: A 300 Year History* (New York: Norton, 1982), 461.

39. Kelly R. Gordon, *Children's Periodicals of the United States* (Greenwood Press, 1984).

40. Letter, RHD to Mary Mapes Dodge, Oct. 28, [1873], Box 1, Folder 8, PUL-MMD.

41. Annie Adams Fields, Diary, quoted in Gollin, Annie Adams Fields, 85–86.

42. Arthur John, *The Best Years of the Century: Richard Watson Gilder, Scribner's Monthly, and the Century Magazine, 1870–1909* (Urbana: U of Illinois P, 1981), 17.

43. Ibid., 76–77.

44. RHD, "Bits," 64.

45. Ibid., 70.

46. Silcox, *Philadelphia Politics from the Bottom Up*, 22ff.

47. Henry James, "American Letter," Mar. 28, 1898, quoted in *Theory of Fiction: Henry James,* ed. James Edwin Miller (Lincoln: U of Nebraska P, 1972), 53.

48. Review, *Atlantic Monthly* 34 (Jul. 1874), 115; "New Books," *Philadelphia Inquirer* (12 May 1874), 3.

49. "John Andross," *Scribner's Monthly* 8 (Oct. 1874), 753–54.

50. Letter, RHD to Annie Adams Fields, Apr. 15, [1874], UVA.

51. "Personal Gossip." *Hartford Daily Courant* (9 Apr. 1874), 2.

52. John, *The Best Years of the Century,* 54.

53. RHD, "A Woman's Work," *New York Tribune* (19 June 1874), 4.

54. *Commemorative and Farewell Reunion, of the Graduates and Teachers of Washington Female Seminary in Honor of Mrs. Sarah R Hanna, June 25th, 1874* (Pittsburgh: Blackwell and Marthens, 1874), 6–7.

55. "Literary Notices," *North American and United States Gazette* (10 Nov. 1873), col. E.

56. For a fuller analysis of *Kitty's Choice,* see Sharon M. Harris, "RHD's *Kitty's Choice* and the Disabled Woman Physician," *American Literary Realism* 44 (Fall 2011), 23–45.

57. "Personal Gossip," *Frank Leslie's Illustrated Newspaper* (19 Sep. 1874), 27.

58. John, *The Best Years of the Century,* 12.

59. RHD, "Bits," 124.

60. RHD, "Dolly," *Scribner's Monthly* 9 (Nov. 1874), 92.

61. "The Year 1874," *Appleton's Journal of Literature, Science and Art* (2 Jan. 1875), 20.

62. Item, *Oregonian* (2 Apr. 1922), 57.

63. RHD, "The True Story of Wolfenden," *American Homes* (1 May 1875), 6.

64. See Silber, *Romance of Reunion.*

65. RHD, "Qualla," *Lippincott's Magazine* 16 (Nov. 1875), 582.

66. Ibid., 583.
67. Ibid.
68. Ibid., 585.
69. Ibid., 586.
70. Ibid.
71. RHD, "American Convents," *Independent* (23 Dec. 1875), 4.
72. See, for example, Susan M. Griffin's *Anti-Catholicism and Nineteenth-Century Fiction* (Cambridge, England: Cambridge UP, 2004) and Elizabeth Fenton's *Religious Liberties: Anti-Catholicism and Liberal Democracy in 19th-Century U.S. Literature and Culture* (New York: Oxford UP, 2011).
73. RHD, "American Convents," *Independent* (30 Dec. 1875), 6.

CHAPTER 7: CENTENNIAL CELEBRATIONS AND THE FAILURE OF RECONSTRUCTION (1876–1879)

1. See Silber, *The Romance of Reunion*, 63ff.
2. Item, *National Republican* (15 Jan. 1876), 1.
3. RHD, "The House on the Beach," *Lippincott's Magazine* 17 (Jan. 1876).
4. RHD, "Life-Saving Station," *Lippincott's Magazine* 17 (Mar. 1876), 310.
5. RHD, "Primus's Story of Herod," *Manchester Times* (18 Mar. 1876), 2.
6. John, *The Best Years of the Century*, Chapter 2.
7. "St. Nicholas," Newport (RI) *Daily News* (24 Mar. 1876), 1; the praise was reprinted without attribution in England's *Derby Mercury* on April 5, 1876, on its first page.
8. Letter, RHD to Mary Mapes Dodge, Apr.5, [1876], (Author File), HLH.
9. Ibid.
10. For a further discussion of these issues, see Robert W. Rydell, *All the World's a Fair: Visions of Empire at American International Expositions, 1876–1916* (Chicago: U of Chicago P, 1987).
11. Quoted in Cortland van Dyke Hubbard, *History of the Penn Club* (Philadelphia: Winchell Company, 1976), 3.
12. Quoted in Donald A. Ritchie, *Press Gallery: Congress and the Washington Correspondents* (Cambridge, MA: Harvard UP, 2009), 131; 133.
13. Ibid., 140.
14. [L. Clarke Davis,] Editorial, *Philadelphia Inquirer* (17 June 1876), 4.
15. Letter, James G. Blaine to L. Clarke Davis, June 22, 1876, UVA.
16. RHD, "Old Landmarks in Philadelphia," *Scribner's Monthly Magazine* 12 (June 1876), 145.

17. Ibid., 153.

18. Quoted in Tillie Olsen, "Biographical Interpretation," *Life in the Iron Mills and Other Stories* (Old Westbury, NY: Feminist Press, 1985), 147.

19. Charles Belmont Davis, *Adventures and Letters*, 8–9.

20. Ibid.

21. RHD, "Education," *Guide to the Exhibition* (New York: New-York Tribune Co., 1876), 38–43.

22. See, for example, "The Centennial," (Middletown, CT) *Constitution* (13 Sep. 1876), 2.

23. Charles Belmont Davis, *Adventures and Letters*, 9–10.

24. Ibid., 10–11.

25. L. Clarke Davis, Editorial, *Philadelphia Inquirer* (3 Oct. 1876), 4.

26. RHD, "A Rainy Day at the Exposition," *Harper's Weekly* (18 Nov. 1876), 930.

27. Rydell, *All the World's a Fair*, 14.

28. George Anthony Peffer, "Forbidden Families: Emigration Experiences of Chinese Women Under the Page Law, 1875–1882," *Journal of American Ethnic History* 6.1 (Fall 1986), 28.

29. RHD, "Odd Corners at the Exposition," *Harper's Weekly* (25 Nov. 1876), 950.

30. RHD, "How the Widow Crossed the Line," *Lippincott's Magazine* 18 (Dec. 1876), 718.

31. Ibid., 726.

32. RHD, "The School-Boy's Story," *Independent* (18 Jan. 1877), 1–2.

33. Ibid.

34. "A Builder of Character," (Philadelphia) *Public Ledger* (4 Aug. 1917), 8.

35. "A Dead Child," *New-York Tribune* (20 Dec. 1876), 4.

36. Susan M. Schweik, *The Ugly Laws: Disability in Public* (New York: New York UP, 2009), Chapter 2.

37. RHD, "Indiscriminate Charity," *New-York Tribune* (2 Jan. 1877), 2.

38. Ibid.

39. "Charity," *New-York Tribune* (4 Jan. 1877), 4.

40. Letter, RHD to Kate Field, Feb. 3, [1877], BPL. Lilian Whiting's *Kate Field: A Record* incorrectly dates this letter as the summer of 1872; it is clearly dated February 3. Although the letter contains no year, 1877 is the more accurate assumption for its composition based on internal evidence and when RHD was writing a novel. There is no extant letter of response from Field.

41. For an excellent extended analysis of these and other issues in the novel, see Alicia Mischa Renfroe's "Editor's Introduction," in RHD, *A Law Unto Herself*, ix–xlv.

42. RHD, *A Law Unto Herself*, 97.
43. Ibid., 96.
44. "Bric-a-Brac," *The Capital* (2 Feb. 1868), 7.
45. For an analysis of this difference, see Nancy Glazener, *Reading for Realism: The History of a U.S. Literary Institution, 1850–1910* (Durham: Duke UP, 1997), 127ff.
46. "Recent Novels," *The Nation* (18 Apr. 1878), 264.
47. RHD, "A Market for Art-Work," *Scribner's Monthly Magazine* 15 (Nov. 1877), 134.
48. Stuart Banner, *The Death Penalty: An American History* (Cambridge: Harvard UP, 2009), 215.
49. Frances Willard, quoted in *Glimpses of Fifty Years* (Evanston, IL: Women's Christian Temperance Union, 1904), 549.
50. RHD, "Bits," 42.
51. Frank Luther Mott, *A History of American Magazines, 1850–1865* (Cambridge, MA: Harvard UP, 1938), 1:39.
52. RHD, "Brave Dick," *National Labor Tribune* (13 Sep. 1878), n.p.; the NLT noted it had taken the story from the Pottsville, Pennsylvania, *Miners' Journal*. I have been unable to locate a copy of the latter.
53. Letter to the Editor, *New-York Tribune* (20 April 1878), 2; Untitled, *Wheeling Intelligencer* (20 May 1878), 2.
54. RHD, "St. Matthew's and St. Mark's," *Sunday Afternoon* 1 (Apr. 1878), 296.
55. Charles Wolcott Balestier, *James G. Blaine: A Sketch of His Life* (New York: R. Worthington, 1884), 90.
56. RHD, "Bits," 118.
57. Charles Belmont Davis, *Adventures and Letters*, 2.
58. Arthur Lubow, *The Reporter Who Would Be King*, 18.
59. "Washington, PA., Items," *Wheeling Register* (11 Jul. 1878), 4.
60. Jerry A. Woolley, *Point Pleasant* (Charleston, SC: Acadia Publishing, 1995), Chapter 1.
61. RHD, "A Lost Colony" *Lippincott's Magazine* (22 Aug. 1878), 254.
62. Ibid., 252.
63. Andrew Goodman, *Gilbert and Sullivan at Law* (Teaneck, NJ: Fairleigh Dickinson UP, 1982); Lubow, *The Reporter Who Would Be King*, 341n.
64. RHD diary fragments, Mar. 18, 1879, UVA.
65. Letters, 1878, Richard Harding Davis Papers, UVA.
66. RHD, "The Conards," *Independent* (26 Dec. 1878), 4.

67. Molly Caldwell Crosby, *The American Plague* (New York: Berkeley Publishing Group, 2006), 75.

68. RHD, "A Story of the Plague," *Harper's New Monthly Magazine* 58 (Feb. 1879), 443.

69. Letter, Senator James G. Blaine to L. Clarke Davis, Mar. 26, 1879, UVA.

70. Letter, President Rutherford B. Hayes to L. Clarke Davis, June 5, 1879, UVA.

71. RHD diary fragments, June 18 and 19, 1879, UVA.

72. RHD diary fragments, June 30, 1879, UVA.

73. RHD diary fragments, Jul. 8 and 10, 1879, UVA.

74. RHD diary fragments, Jul. 11, 1879, UVA.

75. Clarke had apparently traveled to Europe again, which he did occasionally to attend the London theater.

76. Letter, RHD to Annie Adams Fields, Aug. 15, [1879], UVA.

77. RHD diary fragments, Oct. 15 and 18, 1879, UVA.

78. Clarence Winthrop Bowen, "Threescore and Ten," *Independent* (11 Dec. 1879), 4–5.

79. Quoted in "The Holmes Breakfast," *Atlantic Monthly Supplement* 45 (Feb. 1880), 19.

CHAPTER 8: EXPOSING GOVERNMENT CORRUPTION (1880–1884)

1. Hugh Wilson Harding lived at 113 Market Street in Bethlehem (US Census, 1880) and continued to be a revered professor of physics (Bowen, *History of Lehigh University*, 31–33).

2. Letter, Richard Harding Davis to RHD, [c. early 1880s], UVA.

3. US Census, 1880.

4. See William James, *Essays in Psychical Research*, eds. Frederick H. Burkhardt, Fredson Bowers, and Ignas K. Skrupskelis (Cambridge, MA: Harvard UP, 1986).

5. Letter, James G. Blaine to L. Clarke Davis, May 24, [1880], UVA.

6. "Current Fiction," *Appleton's* 50 (Aug. 1880), 184.

7. Trubner's *American, European, and Oriental Literary Record* 1.1–2 (1880), 130.

8. Ibid., 545.

9. Eric Foner, *A Short History of Reconstruction, 1863–1877* (New York: Harper & Row, 1990), 167.

10. "Craft Revival: Shaping North Carolina Past and Present," www.wcu.edu/craftrevival, 20 Aug. 2015; Cary Franklin Poole, *A History of Railroading in Western North Carolina* (Johnson City, TN: Overmountain Press, 1995), 22.

11. Two years later George Washington Cable also condemned the scope of cruelty he observed in the convict lease system at a national conference on corrections (Edward L. Ayers, *Southern Crossing: A History of the American South* [New York: Oxford UP, 1995], 208); in 1897 the African American author J. McHenry Jones presented one of the most brutal descriptions of the system in *Heart of Gold*.

12. RHD, "By-Paths in the Mountains," *Harper's New Monthly Magazine* 61 (July-Sep. 1880): 360–61.

13. "Students of Preparatory School Who Did Not Enter College," The Register of Swarthmore College (Swarthmore, PA: Swarthmore College, 1920), 273.

14. Letter, Richard Harding Davis to "Family," [c. 1880], UVA; *Commemorative Biographical Record of Washington County, PA*, 1423.

15. RHD, "An Unfinished Page of History," *Lippincott's Magazine* 26 (Dec. 1880), 764–67.

16. Carl Schurz, *Speeches, Correspondence and Political Papers* (New York: G. P. Putnam's, 1913), 4:50–78.

17. RHD, "Secretary Schurz's Apology," *New-York Tribune* (24 Dec. 1880), 4.

18. Letter, Helen Hunt Jackson to RHD, Dec. 30, 1880, *The Indian Reform Letters of Helen Hunt Jackson, 1879–1885*, ed. Valerie Sherer Mathes [Norman: U of Oklahoma P, 1998], 166–67.

19. Ibid.

20. Jackson commented to Charles Dudley Warner in a letter dated Jan. 16, 1881, that "Mrs. Rebecca Harding Davis wrote me the other day" about Schurz; RHD's letter is not extant nor is there information about her activities in Washington. RHD was adamant that no political or philanthropic work she performed be publicly announced.

21. Emily Edson Briggs was also a journalist for the *Press*, where she wrote under the name of "Olivia."

22. Letter, James G. Blaine to L. Clarke Davis, undated, UVA.

23. "Sudden Death," *Wheeling Intelligencer* (14 Feb. 1899); www.wvculture.org, Aug. 24, 2015.

24. Charles Belmont Davis, *Adventures and Letters*, 14–15.

25. "Story Writing," *Good Literature* (24 Sept. 1881), 232–33.

26. RHD, "Christina," *Youth's Companion* (3 Nov. 1881), 405.

27. Letter, RHD to William Hayes Ward, Dec. 6, [1881], BN.

28. RHD, "Homely Hints on Homely Occupations," *Youth's Companion* (17 Aug. 1882), 331.

29. Shaeffer, "RHD," 165–67.

30. Letter, RHD to "Mr. Johnson," Apr. 1, [1880s], Rebecca Harding Davis Letters Collection, NYPL.

31. Quoted in Charles Belmont Davis, *Adventures and Letters*, 19–20.

32. Lubow, *The Reporter Who Would Be King*, 18–19.

33. Charles Belmont Davis, *Adventures and Letters*, 16.

34. Letter, RHD to Richard Harding Davis, quoted in Charles Belmont Davis, *Adventures and Letters*, 17–18.

35. Letters, Richard Harding Davis to Family, [1882], UVA.

36. RHD, "'Our Continent,'" *Philadelphia Inquirer* (9 Feb. 1882), 3.

37. Letter, RHD to [William Hayes Ward], Feb. 22, 1882, Rebecca Harding Davis Letters Collection, NYPL.

38. Letter, RHD to "My dear Madam," Feb. 12, [1883], UVA.

39. Letter, RHD to William Hayes Ward, Oct. 19, [1882?], NYPL-AC.

40. RHD, "Teddy," *Youth's Companion* (7 Dec. 1882), 522.

41. "New York Journalism," *Boston Evening Transcript* (26 Dec. 1882), 6.

42. RHD, "A Brand Left to Burn," *Congregationalist* (25 Jan. 1883), 1.

43. Ibid.

44. Lubow, *The Reporter Who Would Be King*, 22.

45. "Salvini," *Philadelphia Inquirer* (17 Jan. 1883), 3; "Honoring Salvini," *North American* (17 Jan. 1883), 1.

46. J. Hampton Moore, *History of the Five O'Clock Club* (Privately published, 1891), 3; "Notes About Town," *North American* (19 Feb. 1883), 1.

47. Charles Francis Dickson, *A Primer of American Literature* (Cambridge, MA: Riverside Press, 1883), 104.

48. Emily Hewitt Leland, "A Little Money of Her Own," *Wisconsin State Register* (12 May 1883), 1.

49. John Tebble and Mary Ellen Zuckerman, *The Magazine in America, 1741–1990* (New York: Oxford UP, 1991), 60–63.

50. RHD, "Uncle Sorby," *Congregationalist* (28 June 1883), 1.

51. "Fiction in the September Magazines," *The Critic* (8 Sep. 1883), 357; "The Month's Magazines," *Independent* (30 Aug. 1883), 11; "The September Magazines," *Christian Union* (30 Aug. 1883), 172.

52. Letters, Richard Harding Davis to RHD and Family, [c. 1883], UVA.

53. RHD, "In an Inn," *Peterson's Magazine* 84 (Nov. 1883), 407.

54. Letters, RHD to [C. C. Hazewell, Editor], Oct. 15, Nov. 27, Dec. 3, 1883, NYPL-AC.

55. RHD, "David Evans' Christmas," *Michigan Farmer* (15 Jan. 1884), 6; this is a reprint from the *Christmas Traveller* for which I have been unable to locate an original copy.

56. George L. Harrison, a member of the committee, published in January *Legislation on Insanity* (Philadelphia: Privately published, 1884); the committee's report and the Act were appended to his study of US and British insanity laws, pp. 1096–1119.

57. Charles Belmont Davis, *Adventures and Letters*, 18–19.

58. RHD, "William M. Baker," *Century Illustrated Magazine* 28 (May 1884), 151–52.

59. "Personals," *Daily Alta California* (10 Aug. 1884), 4.

60. RHD, "Bits," 118–119.

61. "In Brief," *Congregationalist* (18 Sep. 1884), 3.

62. Quoted in Harris, *RHD and American Realism*, 215.

CHAPTER 9: AN ERA OF NONFICTION (1885–1889)

1. RHD, "In St. Paul's Place," *Peterson's Magazine* 87 (Jan. 1885), 37.

2. Eugénie Paul Jefferson, *Intimate Recollections of Joseph Jefferson* (New York: Dodd, Mead and Company, 1909), 73.

3. Bowen, *A History of Lehigh University*, 73–74.

4. William Ross Yates, *Lehigh University: A History in Engineering* (1992), 82.

5. Letter, L. Clarke Davis to Richard Harding Davis, Apr. 17, 1883, quoted in Charles Belmont Davis, *Letters and Adventures*, 32.

6. Charles Belmont Davis, *Letters and Adventures*, 32.

7. Letter, RHD to Thomas Bailey Aldrich, Aug. 20, [1885], BEPL-JFG.

8. RHD, "Some Testimony in the Case," *Atlantic Monthly* 56 (Nov. 1885), 602.

9. Ibid., 606.

10. Ibid., 608.

11. Ibid., 609.

12. "Colored Industry in the South," *Friend's Intelligencer and Journal* (31 Oct. 1885), 601; "The Periodicals," *Literary World* (31 Oct. 1885), 386; "Magazine Literature," *New York Freeman* (31 Oct. 1885), n.p.

13. RHD, "Dominque," *Youth's Companion* (10 Dec. 1885), 526.

14. See Lasseter and Harris, *Writing Cultural Autobiography*, 144.

15. Letter fragment, RHD to Rose Terry Cooke, [c. Jan. 1886], CHS.

16. Admiral, "Rebecca Harding Davis," *Fort Worth Gazette* (25 Apr. 1886), 6.

17. RHD, et al., "Open Letters: International Copyright," *Century Magazine* 31 (Feb. 1886), 629.

18. "When Shall Our Young Women Marry?" *Parry's Literary Journal* 2 (Aug. 1886), 362–64; I have been unable to locate an original copy of the *Boston Magazine* publication, but the article was widely excerpted in newspapers and magazines.

19. "Bookishness," *Life* (22 Apr. 1886), 234.

20. "Recent Fiction," *The Critic* (1 May 1886), 217.

21. Charles Belmont Davis, *Letters and Adventures*, 35.

22. Ibid., 37.

23. Quoted in Dr. H. V. Sweringen's letter to the *Cincinnati Lancet* (5 Oct. 1901), 380–81.

24. *Preliminary Report of the Commission Appointed by the University of Pennsylvania to Investigate Modern Spiritualism* (Philadelphia: J. B. Lippincott, 1887).

25. Letter, Richard Harding Davis to RHD, Sept. 1886, UVA.

26. Ibid.

27. Charles Belmont Davis, *Letters and Adventures*, 37–38.

28. "Magazine Notes," *The Critic* (30 Oct. 1886), 211.

29. Letter, RHD to Richard Harding Davis, Jan. 1887; quoted in Charles Belmont Davis, *Adventures and Letters*, 33–35.

30. Horace Traubel, *With Walt Whitman in Camden* (New York: Mitchell Kennerley, 1915), 34.

31. "Personals," *Harper's Bazar* (26 Mar. 1887), 215.

32. Quoted in "Children of Literary Women," *Aberdeen Daily News* (5 Apr. 1887), 3.

33. Ida Tarbell, "Women in Journalism," *Chautauquan* 7 (Apr. 1887), 393ff. Tarbell incorrectly identified RHD with the *Inquirer* rather than the *Tribune*. I have found no confirmation that RHD wrote for the *Inquirer*.

34. "Literary Life in Philadelphia," *American Magazine* 6 (Jul. 1887), 311–319.

35. Rebecca Harding Davis, "Here and There in the South," *Harper's New Monthly Magazine* 75 (Jul.-Nov. 1887), 239–40). See George Beard's *American Nervousness, Its Causes and Consequences* (New York: G. P. Putnam's Sons, 1881).

36. Ibid., 236.

37. See Davis's stories in *Peterson's Magazine*; for an analysis of this perspective, see Sharon M. Harris, "The Anatomy of Complicity: Rebecca Harding Davis's 1860s Peterson's Stories" *TSWL* 30.2 (2011), 291–315.

38. Davis, "Here and There in the South," 238.

39. Ibid., 246.

40. "Good Fortune for the Ledger," *North American* (10 Oct. 1887), col. B; "Periodical Literature," *The American* (15 Oct. 1887), 413.

41. RHD, "At Noon," *Harper's Bazar* (17 Dec. 1887), 874.

42. "Literary Men's Wives," *Omaha Daily Bee* (6 Nov. 1887), 14. The irony of the *Bee*'s title is notable in this era in which women writers still struggled with gender biases in the field and in society in general.

43. Catherine Seville, The *Internationalisation of Copyright Law: Books, Buccaneers, and Black Flags in the Nineteenth Century* (Cambridge, UK: Cambridge UP, 2006), 229.

44. "Authors' Readings in Washington," *Publishers' Weekly* (24 Mar. 1888), 517; "The Lounger," *The Critic* (1 June 1889), 273.

45. RHD, "Despondency Cured," *Fireside Teacher* 3 (Jul. 1888), 77.

46. Judith Westlund Rosbe, *Marion in the Golden Age* (Charleston, SC: History Press, 2009); Judith Westlund Rosbe, *Images of America: Marion Art Center* (Charleston, SC: Arcadia Publishing, 2007); Nancy Dyer Milton, *A Romantic Art Colony* (New Bedford, MA: Reynolds-DeWalt Printing, 2000); Pete Smith, ed., *A Picture Post Card History of Marion, Massachusetts* (Sippican, MA: Sippican Historical and Preservation Society, 2007); and Rosamond Gilder, *Letters of Richard Watson Gilder* (Boston: Houghton Mifflin Co., 1916), 139–45.

47. Isaac Pennypacker, "Philadelphia," *Ladies' Home Journal* 5 (Sep. 1888), 15.

48. Letter, RHD to F. M. Hopkins, Sep. 6, [1888], General Ms Collection, CUL.

49. "In the Public Ledger Too," *American Economist* (22 Sep. 1922), 116.

50. Untitled, *Current Literature* 2 (Jan. 1889), 1.

51. Lubow, *The Reporter Who Would Be King*, 35; "Notes," *The Critic* (29 Sep. 1888), 159.

52. Letter, RHD to Laura C. Holloway, Mar. 16, [1888], Letter Collection, Box 7, Folder 279, YUL.

53. "Literary Leaflets," *Good Housekeeping* (17 Aug. 1889), 191.

54. Letter, RHD to Laura C. Holloway, Oct. 20 [1888], Letter Collection, Box 7, Folder 279, YUL.

55. Shaeffer asserted in her thesis, "The end of this association with the TRIBUNE came about because of her sharp and effective denunciation of the practice of keeping certain drugs for use in Northern industries which were sorely needed for the treatment of diseases in the states of the South. Protests were made by the Northern advertisers, and the TRIBUNE advised Mrs. Davis to desist from this theme. She then resigned her position with them, rather than lose the freedom of saying what she pleased, when, where, and how she liked to say it" ("RHD," 271).

Since most of RHD's Sunday *Tribune* editorials are no longer extant, I am relying on Shaeffer's account because she had access to these copies of the *Tribune*.

56. Shaeffer, "RHD," 271ff.
57. Letter, RHD to Richard Harding Davis, undated [c. Aug. 1908], UVA.
58. RHD, "What About the Northern Negro?" *Independent* (24 Jan. 1889), 1.
59. RHD, "The New Religious 'What Is It?'" *Independent* (28 Feb. 1889), 1.
60. "A Hicksite Quaker, Letter to the Editor," *Independent* (21 Mar. 1889), 13.
61. "The Views of Friends," *Friends' Intelligencer* (23 Mar. 1889), 183.
62. Charles Harlen Shattuck, *Shakespeare on the American Stage* (Cranbury, NJ: Associated University Presses, 1987), 253; Charles Edward Russell, *Julia Marlowe: Her Life and Art* (1926), 148–49.
63. Frances E. Willard, *Glimpses of Fifty Years: The Autobiography of an American Woman* (New York: G. M. Smith, 1889), 3:129, 549; Albert Henry Smyth, *American Literature* (Philadelphia: Eldredge and Brother, 1889), 138.
64. Untitled, *Current Literature* 2 (Feb. 1889), 94.
65. Untitled, *Independent* (4 Apr. 1889), 13.
66. RHD, "At Our Gates," *Independent* (11 Apr. 1889), 3.
67. RHD, "Some Significant Facts," *Independent* (13 June 1889), 1.
68. RHD, "The Modern Phyllis," *Congregationalist* (11 Jul. 1889), 235.
69. Quoted in Charles Belmont Davis, *Letters and Adventures*, 40.
70. Charles Belmont Davis, *Letters and Adventures*, 46–47.
71. RHD, "A New National Trait," *Independent* (31 Oct. 1899), 1.
72. RHD, "Our National Vanities," *Independent* (21 Nov. 1889), 1.
73. Letter to the Editor of *The Critic* from Alexander Young, published Nov. 2, 1889, pp. 217–18.
74. Ibid.

CHAPTER 10: "A MESSAGE TO BE GIVEN" (1890-1893)

1. RHD, "A Reporter's Work," *Independent* (16 Jan. 1890), 1.
2. Letter, Richard Harding Davis to RHD, [c. Jan. 1890], UVA.
3. "A Tennyson Recital," *Philadelphia Inquirer* (2 Feb. 1890), 3.
4. "Notes," *The Critic* (22 Mar. 1890), 150.
5. Letter, Richard Harding Davis to RHD, n.d., UVA.
6. Lubow, *The Reporter Who Would Be King*, 49–50.
7. RHD, "As We Grow Old," *Congregationalist* (20 Mar. 1890), 1.
8. RHD, "Polly's Venture," *Independent* (6 Mar. 1890), 26.

9. Richard Harding Davis, "A Vile Den to Be Closed," *Evening Sun* (17 Apr. 1890), 2; "Young Ladies in the Tombs," *Evening Sun* (3 Apr. 1890), 3. The "young ladies" were Davis family friends, the Shippen sisters (Katy, Caroline, and Sophie).

10. Ibid., 54.

11. Albert T. Volwiler, ed., *The Correspondence Between Benjamin Harrison and James G. Blaine* (Philadelphia: American Philosophical Society, 1940), 99.

12. RHD, "Needs of the Reservation," *Congregationalist* (17 Apr. 1890), 1.

13. Ibid.

14. Ibid.

15. Letter, Richard Harding Davis to RHD, May 29, 1890; quoted in Charles Belmont Davis, *Letters and Adventures*, 53–54.

16. Letter, Richard Harding Davis to RHD, [c. May 1890], UVA.

17. See, for example, "Literary Notes," *San Francisco Morning Call* (1 June 1890), 14.

18. RHD, "A Common Fault," *Congregationalist* (24 Jul. 1890), 1.

19. RHD, "The Modest Naturalized Citizen," *Independent* (3 Jul. 1890), 11.

20. Barbara Klaczynska, "Immigration," The Encyclopedia of Greater Philadelphia, www.philadelphiaencyclopedia.org, Oct. 13, 2015.

21. RHD, "The Modest Naturalized Citizen," *Independent* (3 Jul. 1890), 11.

22. For an extended analysis of "late style," see Edward Said, *On Late Style: Music and Literature against the Grain* (New York: Vintage, 2008).

23. Allan Nevins, ed., *Letters of Grover Cleveland, 1850–1908* (Boston: Da Capo Press, 1970), 201.

24. Charles Belmont Davis, *Letters and Adventures*, 47–48.

25. Letter, L. Clarke Davis to Richard Harding Davis, quoted in Charles Belmont Davis, *Letters and Adventures*, 56.

26. See, for example, "Notes," *The Critic* (26 Jul. 1890), 52; "The Magazines," *Christian Union* (7 Aug. 1890), 183.

27. Letter, RHD to Richard Watson Gilder, Aug. 5, [1890?], NYPL-CC.

28. See, for example, "Personals," *Macon Weekly Telegram* (29 Sep. 1890), 4.

29. Helen Gray Cone, "Woman in American Literature," *Century Magazine* 40 (Oct. 1890), 927. A few months later, Annie Nathan Meyer, one of the first Jewish American women to gain national literary recognition, also included commentary on Davis in her book, *Woman's Work*. Meyer simply reprinted Cone's commentary verbatim and in toto, without attribution.

30. Ibid.

31. "Of Making Many Books," *The Critic* (29 Nov. 1890), 278.

32. "Journalists Present," *New York World* (11 Dec. 1890), 2.

33. Charles Belmont Davis, *Letters and Adventures*, 57.

34. "Books and Periodicals," *American Notes and Queries* 6 (3 Jan. 1891), 120; I have been unable to locate a copy of this magazine.

35. On the Clevelands' visit with the Davises, see the front-page reporting in the *Philadelphia Inquirer*, the *Baltimore Sun*, and the *New York Sun*, Jan. 4–9, 1891.

36. Ibid.

37. Ibid

38. Michael Shudson, *Discovering the News: A Social History of American Newspapers* (New York: Basic Books, 1982), 62.

39. Letter, Richard Harding Davis to RHD, [c. Jan. 1891], UVA.

40. Letter, Richard Harding Davis to RHD, [c. Jan. 1891], UVA.

41. Letter, Richard Harding Davis to RHD [?], undated, UVA.

42. Charles Belmont Davis, *Letters and Adventures*, 60–61.

43. Lubow, *The Reporter Who Would Be King*, 257.

44. Letter, RHD to William Hayes Ward, Feb. 12, [1891], BCL.

45. Letter, RHD to William Hayes Ward, Feb. 16, [1891], BCL.

46. Letter, Grover Cleveland to L. Clarke Davis, Mar. 9, 1891, quoted in Nevins, *Letters of Grover Cleveland*, 249–50.

47. "August Gaiety," *The Critic* (18 Apr. 1891), 213.

48. RHD, et al., "Women in Literature," *Independent* (7 May 1891): 1–2.

49. Ibid.

50. Letter, Richard Harding Davis to RHD, n.d. [probably 1891], UVA.

51. "By Way of New York," *Philadelphia Inquirer* (29 May 1891), 4; "Off for Europe," *Philadelphia Inquirer* (9 Jul. 1891), 8.

52. Nevins, *Letters of Grover Cleveland*, 257–58.

53. Lubow, *The Reporter Who Would Be King*, 110.

54. "August Gaiety," *Wheeling Register* (16 Aug. 1891), 5. Irving also mentioned RHD and Clarke as among his London guests at the theater (Bram Stoker, *Personal Reminiscences of Henry Irving* [London: W. Heinemann, 1906], 1:319).

55. Letter, Richard Harding Davis to L. Clarke Davis, [c. Aug. 1891], UVA.

56. "Home from Abroad," *Philadelphia Inquirer* (8 Sep. 1891), 4.

57. Letter, Richard Harding Davis to RHD, [c. fall 1891], UVA.

58. "World's Fair Commission," *Railway World* (22 Aug. 1891), 797; "New Committees Named," *Philadelphia Inquirer* (17 Oct. 1891), 2.

59. "Freedom and Peace to All the Earth," *Philadelphia Inquirer* (17 Sep. 1891), 5.

60. RHD, "In a Way That She Knew Not," *Independent* (26 Nov. 1891), 34–35.

61. Letter, RHD to William Hayes Ward, Dec. 7, [1891], BCL.

62. RHD, "The Modern Irishman," *Congregationalist* (17 Dec. 1891), 1.

63. Charles Belmont Davis, *Letters and Adventures*, 65–66.

64. Quoted in Lubow, *The Reporter Who Would Be King*, 110.

65. "The Philadelphian," *Art in Advertising: An Illustrated Monthly for Business Men* 5 (Mar. 1892), 118.

66. Nevins, *Letters of Grover Cleveland*, 249-50.

67. Letter, RHD to Mary Mapes Dodge, Apr. 2, 1891, Box 1, Folder 8, PUL-MMD.

68. Charles Belmont Davis, *Letters and Adventures*, 82–83, 87–88.

69. Letter, Richard Harding Davis to RHD, n.d., UVA.

70. Ibid.

71. Letter, RHD to Charles Scribner, June 22, 1892, Box 38, Davis folder, PUL-CSS.

72. RHD, "Alien Brothers," *Independent* (7 Jul. 1892), 7–8.

73. Ibid.

74. "The Fourth of a Literary Family," *Portland Oregonian* (10 Jul. 1892), 11.

75. "Fiction," *Current Literature* 11 (Oct. 1892), 254; "Current Literature" *Inter-Ocean* (3 Sep. 1892), 10.

76. "New Books," *Life* (20 Oct. 1892), 218.

77. "Fiction," *Literary World* (22 Oct. 1892), 375; "Silhouettes of American Life," *Art Amateur* 27 (Nov. 1892), 162.

78. "Profits of Popular Writers," *Roanoke Times* (4 Oct. 1892), 6.

79. "The Man About Town," *Art in Advertising* 6 (Nov. 1892), 88.

80. "Not a Good Day for Gunning," *Richmond Times* (4 Dec. 1892), 1.

81. "Public Ledger Fire," *New York Times* (7 Dec. 1892), 1.

82. "Comment on New Books," *Atlantic Monthly* 70 (Dec. 1892), 853.

83. "Books for Boys," *Christian Union* (3 Dec. 1892), 1066; "Fiction," *Art Amateur* (Dec. 1892), 35; "Stories for Young People," *Independent* (1 Dec. 1892), 20; "Kent Hampden," *Literary World* (3 Dec. 1892), 446.

84. See, for example, *Annual Report and Course of Study of the Public Schools of Baraboo, Wisconsin* (Baraboo: J. S. Briscoe, 1901).

85. See, for example, "Cleveland's Plans," *Pittsburgh Dispatch* (9 Dec. 1892), 1.

86. Letter, Richard Harding Davis to RHD, [c. 1892], UVA.

87. RHD, "A Grumble," *New Peterson's Magazine* 1 (Jan. 1893), 103. Louise Hogan picked up on Davis's comments for an article in the July 1893 issue of *New Peterson's*, "A Plea for Baby."

88. Letter, Richard Harding Davis to Rebecca Harding Davis, Feb. 12, [1893], UVA.

89. Letter, Richard Harding Davis to Charles Belmont Davis, March 1893, UVA.

90. Edmund Robins, "Some Philadelphia Men of Letters," *Pennsylvania Magazine of History and Biography* 50.1 (1926), 334.

91. The notice of her continuing role was syndicated, appearing in newspapers across the country; see, for example, Item, *Sentinel* (13 Feb. 1893), 8.

92. Letter, RHD to William Hayes Ward, Mar. 22, [1893], quoted in Shaeffer, "RHD," 281. Shaeffer dates the letter 1889, but this article with references to Marsden was written in 1893.

93. "The Cleveland Circle," *Boston Daily Advertiser* (13 Mar. 1893), 8.

94. "Honor Mr. Burnham," *Inter-Ocean* (26 Mar. 1893), 1.

95. Letter, RHD to Howard Allen Bridgman, Mar. 10, [1893?], (KAL 261), HL.

96. "Gossip of the Authors," *Kansas City Times* (9 Apr. 1893), 9.

97. "New York Notes," *Literary World* (8 Apr. 1893), 112. There was a Midwestern novelist, Nora Davis, with whom RHD's daughter was probably confused.

98. Letter, Richard Harding Davis to L. Clarke Davis, Apr. 7, [1893], UVA.

99. See, for example, "L. Clarke Davis," *Galveston Daily News* (10 Apr. 1893), 4, or *Roanoke Times* (14 Apr. 1893), 6.

100. "Under Which Name?" *Ladies' Home Journal* 10 (May 1893), 2.

101. Lydia Hoyt Farmer, ed., *The National Exposition Souvenir: What America Owes to Women* (Chicago: Charles Wells Moulton, 1893), 199.

102. "Stage Folks Honor the Bard of Avon," *Philadelphia Inquirer* (26 Apr. 1893), 4.

103. "The Duke to Hear 'La Gioconda,'" and "Item," *Philadelphia Inquirer* (21 June 1893), 2.

104. Letter, Richard Harding Davis to RHD, [c. June 1893], UVA.

105. Letter, Richard Harding Davis to RHD, May 27, [1893], UVA.

106. "July Magazines," *Philadelphia Inquirer* (26 June 1893), 6.

107. Letter, Richard Harding Davis to RHD, June 13, [1893], UVA.

108. "A Philadelphia Honored," *Philadelphia Inquirer* (28 Oct. 1893), 10.

109. "New Books," *Philadelphia Inquirer* (10 Jul. 1893), 5.

110. "Stories of the South," *The Sentinel* (21 Aug. 1893), 4.

111. "The Magazines," *Philadelphia Inquirer* (31 Jul. 1893), 5.

112. "The President's Health," *Charlotte Observer* (2 Sep. 1893), 1.

113. Item, *Topeka Weekly Capital* (7 Sep. 1893), 4.

114. RHD, "What Did Not Happen," *New Peterson's Magazine* 2 (Sep. 1893), 887.

115. Lubow, *The Reporter Who Would Be King*, 76–77.

116. Ibid., 103.

117. Letters, Richard Harding Davis to family, n.d. [winter 1893–94], UVA.

118. Lubow, *The Reporter Who Would Be King*, 113.

119. Ibid., 99–100.

120. *The Tribune Almanac and Political Register* (1893), 123.

121. Item, (New Orleans) *Times-Picayune* (6 Nov. 1893), 6.

122. "Society," *Philadelphia Inquirer* (11 Nov. 1893), 12.

123. RHD, "The Newly Discovered Woman," *Independent* (30 Nov. 1893), 5.

124. A Smith Graduate, "The Girl Graduate and Her Grandmother," *Independent* (14 Dec. 1893), 6.

125. Letter, Richard Harding Davis to Charles Belmont Davis, [1893], UVA.

126. Letter, Richard Harding Davis to Charles Belmont Davis, Nov. 29, [1893], UVA.

127. Letter, Richard Harding Davis to Charles Belmont Davis, Dec. 28, [1893], UVA.

128. "Repudiates Cleveland," (Shenandoah, PA) *Evening Herald* (5 Dec. 1893), 1.

CHAPTER 11. A RETURN TO NOVEL-WRITING (1894–1896)

1. Letters, Richard Harding Davis to Charles Belmont Davis, Jan. 5 and Jan. 16, [1894], UVA.

2. Letter, Richard Harding Davis to Charles Belmont Davis, Jan. 16, [1894], UVA.

3. Letter, Richard Harding Davis to Family, Jan. 24, [1894], UVA.

4. Letter, Richard Harding Davis to RHD, undated [c. early Feb. 1894], UVA.

5. *Public Ledger Almanac* (Philadelphia: George W. Childs Publisher, 1894), 67.

6. "L. Clarke Davis," *Olean Democrat* (16 Feb. 1894), 1.

7. Letter, Richard Harding Davis to Charles Belmont Davis and Nora Davis, undated, [c. Feb. 1894], UVA.

8. "Magazines," *Household News* 2 (Apr. 1894), 418.

9. Charles Belmont Davis, "The Great Sympathetic Strike," *Century Illustrated Magazine* 47 (Mar. 1894), 655.

10. Ibid., 656.

11. The complete version of CBD's report is in *Consular Reports: Commerce, Manufactures, etc.* (Washington, D.C.: General Printing Office, 1894): 7–9.

12. Letter, Richard Harding Davis to "My Dear Old Man" [Charles Belmont Davis], Mar. 1, [1894], UVA.

13. Letter, Richard Harding Davis to "My Dear Old Man" [Charles Belmont Davis], Mar. 1 and Mar. 16, [1894], UVA.

14. Letter, Richard Harding Davis to Charles Belmont Davis, Mar. 16, [1894], UVA.

15. Letter, Richard Harding Davis to Charles Belmont Davis, Mar. 27, [1894], UVA. Mrs. Gebhard was Louise Hollingsworth Morris, whom the wealthy Gebhard married earlier that year after a years-long relationship with Lillie Langtry. Commander Vanderbilt was the millionaire Cornelius Vanderbilt III.

16. "Arts and Letters," *Hartford Courant* (3 May 1894), 6. I have been unable to locate a copy of the May 1894 issue of *Romance* or of other early issues to indicate if RHD published more than once in the magazine.

17. Letter, Richard Harding Davis to Charles Belmont Davis, May 28, [1894], UVA.

18. Letters, "H.S.C." [Henry S. Chandler] to Susan Hayes Ward, June 14 and June 15, 1894, BCL.

19. Letter, Richard Harding Davis to Charles Belmont Davis, Dec. 22, [1894], UVA.

20. Letters, "H.S.C." [Henry S. Chandler] to Susan Hayes Ward, June 14 and June 15, 1894, BCL.

21. William Hayes Ward to RHD, June 16, 1894, BCL.

22. Letters, RHD to William Hayes Ward, June 11 and 18, [1894], BCL.

23. RHD, "Achill," *Independent* (16 Aug. 1894), 1.

24. "The Peasants of Achill," *Independent* (23 Aug. 1894), 12.

25. Moses Purnell Handy, "Three Davises," *Mail and Express*; rpt. *New Haven Register* (7 June 1894), 2.

26. Margaret H. Welch, "Is Newspaper Work Healthy for Women?" *Journal of Social Science* 32 (Nov. 1894), 110. Lucia Runkle's middle name was actually Calhoun.

27. "Gotham by 'Phone," *Philadelphia Inquirer* (7 June 1894), 4.

28. Item, *Philadelphia Inquirer* (4 Aug. 1894), 4.

29. According to Rachel Loden's research, a farewell dinner was given for Emilie's husband, John Gow, Jr. by the county Bar Association on Jan. 8, 1893, RLC.

30. Item, *Boston Globe* (2 Sep. 1894), 21.

31. "Personal and Political," *Boston Daily Advertiser* (27 Sep. 1894), 4.

32. Letter, Richard Harding Davis to Charles Belmont Davis, Nov. 3, [1894], UVA.

33. "When Is a Woman at Her Best?" *Ladies' Home Journal* 11 (Nov. 1894), 3–4.

34. "Dined with Grover" *San Francisco Call* (4 Jan. 1895), 2.

35. *Proceedings of the Assay Commission of 1894* (Washington, DC: US Treasury Document no. 1669, 1894), 3–5.

36. See, for example, the illustrated "Impromptu Bohemian Meals. New York's Swell Set Takes up the Fad of Cooking Their Own Food," *Philadelphia Inquirer* (30 Dec. 1894), 17.

37. Letter, Richard Harding Davis to Charles Belmont Davis, undated [early 1895], UVA.

38. Letter, RHD to Richard Watson Gilder, n.d., ALS 821, LUL.

39. Across the top of her letter, Gilder wrote, "Accept Sketch (pay $100)," and initialed the authorization. It is unknown if RHD knew what Richard was paid compared to her own stated price for a story, though he often sent her detailed accounts of what he was earning. It is unlikely the difference would have mattered to her; she had established what she felt was an equitable rate for her work, and she maintained it with all publishers.

40. John Tasker Howard, *Ethelbert Nevin* (New York: Thomas Y. Crowell, 1935), 253; Vance Thompson, *The Life of Ethelbert Nevin* (Boston: Boston Music Company, 1913), 176.

41. Letter, Richard Harding Davis to Charles Belmont Davis, Apr. 14, [1895], UVA.

42. "Maternal Example," *Boston Daily Advertiser* (14 June 1895), 4.

43. Letter, Richard Harding Davis to Family, Feb. 1, [1895], UVA. The difference between Richard and his mother was evident here, too; as a young writer, RHD had insisted James Fields send her any negative reviews so she could learn from them. Richard, according to his biographer, kept a scrapbook of derogatory newspaper comments at this time with the intention of rebutting them (Lubow, *The Reporter Who Would Be King*, 128–29).

44. Letter, Richard Harding Davis to RHD, [c. June 1895], UVA.

45. Rosbe, *Marion in the Golden Age*, 105–107.

46. Contract between RHD and Harper's, 17 Sept. 1894, Harper Bros. Collection, CUL.

47. "A Line from Frank Leslie's," *The Critic* (2 Nov. 1895), 285.

48. Lillian Guerra, *The Myth of José Marti: Conflicting Nationalisms in Early Twentieth-Century Cuba* (Chapel Hill: U of North Carolina P, 2006), 75; Claude Matthews, *The Cuban Patriots' Cause Is Just* (Philadelphia; C. F. Simmons, 1895), 1–4.

49. Charles Belmont Davis, *Letters and Adventures*, 169; Letter, Richard Harding Davis to RHD, Nov. 1895, UVA.

50. Quoted in Phyllis Robbins, *Maude Adams: An Intimate Portrait* (New York: G. P. Putnam's Sons, 1956), 38; "Gibson-Langhorne Wedding," *Philadelphia*

Inquirer (8 Nov. 1895), 3; Ethel Barrymore, *Memories: An Autobiography* (London: Hulton Press, 1956), 45.

51. Tasker, *Ethelbert Nevin*, 267.

52. Letter, Ellen Terry to Richard Harding Davis, Christmas Day, 1895, UVA. "Sir Henry" is the actor Henry Irving.

53. Letter, Ellen Terry to L. Clarke Davis, Christmas Day, 1895, UVA.

54. Henry S. Chubb, ed., *Full Proceedings of the Conference in Favor of International Arbitration* (Philadelphia: Universal Peace Union, 1896).

55. "Historical Background," Universal Peace Union Records, Swarthmore College Peace Collection, https://www.swarthmore.edu/library/peace, Nov. 17, 2015.

56. "The St. Paul's Passengers," *New-York Tribune* (18 Mar. 1896), 1; Item, *North American* (19 Mar. 1896).

57. Letter, RHD to Richard Watson Gilder, undated, ALS 820, LUL. I have been unable to locate any publication by RHD of this event. This letter is the only extant correspondence from any of RHD's European travels.

58. "Literary," *New York Observer ad Chronicle* (12 Mar. 1896), 371; "Stories," *Congregationalist* (19 Mar. 1896), 483; quoted in *Harper's Bazar* (21 Mar. 1896), 263; "Current Fiction," *Literary World* (16 May 1896), 154; "Dr. Warrick's Daughters," *San Francisco Call* (1 Mar. 1896), "New Novels," *Philadelphia Inquirer* (9 Mar. 1896), 7.

59. "Recent Fiction," *The Dial* (1Jul. 1896), 20.

60. Letter, Publisher to Charles Belmont Davis, May 18, 1923, Harper Bros. Collection, CUL.

61. "Women in Journalism," *San Francisco Call* (24 May 1896), 17.

62. "Americans in Florence," *Kansas City Star* (15 Apr. 1896), 8.

63. Lubow, *The Reporter Who Would Be King*, 132.

64. McKinley, *The People's Choice* (Canton, OH: Repository Press, 1896), 132.

65. "Three Gringoes in Central America," *San Francisco Call* (1 Mar. 1896), 4.

66. Robbins, *Maude Adams*, 35.

67. "Poor, Poor Dick," *Philadelphia Inquirer* (1 June 1896), 6; "Too Much of the Czar," *Philadelphia Inquirer* (3 June 1896), 6; "He's in Moscow," *Philadelphia Inquirer* (4 June 1896), 6.

68. "Gibson Has a Brand New Girl," *Philadelphia Inquirer* (21 Feb. 1897), 33.

69. Letter, Richard Harding Davis to Charles Belmont Davis, Nov. 12, [1896], UVA.

70. "A Dark Mystery in A. W. Cooper's Death," *Philadelphia Inquirer* (11 Nov. 1896), 5.

71. Letter, Richard Harding Davis to RHD, Dec. 19, 1896, UVA: Charles Belmont Davis, *Letters and Adventures*, 198.

CHAPTER 12: WAR YEARS (1897–1899)

1. Letter, RHD to Richard Watson Gilder, June 7, [1896], ALS 822, LUL.
2. Ibid. Gilder's side of the correspondence is not extant.
3. RHD, *Frances Waldeaux* (New York: Harper's Brothers, 1897), 15.
4. Ibid., 19.
5. Ibid., 204.
6. "Sociology," *Western Christian Advocate* (27 Jan. 1897), 105; "Review of New Books," *Portland Oregonian* (27 Dec. 1896), 12; "Novels and Tales," *Outlook* (2 Jan. 1897), 97.
7. "Novels and Tales," *Outlook* (2 Jan. 1897), 97; "Frances Waldeaux," *Literary World* (23 Jan. 1897), 27; "Recent Fiction," *The Dial* (1 Jul. 1896), 20; "Literary Notes," (Lexington) *Morning Herald* (14 Sep. 1896), 6.
8. Contract between Harper's Brothers and RHD, Feb. 17, 1896, Harper Bros. Collection, CUL.
9. See, for example, Letter, Richard Harding Davis to RHD, Jan. 4, 1897, UVA, when he learns about RHD's anxieties from Mrs. Remington.
10. Letter, L. Clarke Davis to Richard Harding Davis, [mid-Jan. 1897], UVA.
11. Letter, Richard Harding Davis to RHD, Jan. 20, [1897], UVA.
12. Richard Harding Davis "Davis and Remington Tell of Spanish Cruelty," *New York Journal* (2 Feb. 1897), 2.
13. Richard Harding Davis, "The Death of Rodriguez," *New York Journal* (2 Feb. 1897).
14. Item, *Philadelphia Inquirer* (1 Feb. 1897), 6. The comments were collected from the *Chicago Times-Herald*, *Atlanta Evening Constitution*, and the *New Orleans Picayune*.
15. Letter, Richard Harding Davis to Charles Belmont Davis, Mar. 5, [1897], UVA.
16. Charles Belmont Davis, *Life and Adventures*, 204; Letter, Richard Harding Davis to RHD, Apr. 15, [1897], UVA.
17. Letters, Richard Harding Davis to Family and to RHD, undated [Feb.-Mar. 1897], UVA.
18. Letter, Richard Harding Davis to RHD, Apr. 7, [1897], UVA.
19. RHD, "Some Hobgoblins in Literature," *Book Buyer* 14 (Apr. 1897), 231.

20. As Lubow notes, "More than any other [of Richard's books] *Soldiers of Fortune* glorified ascendant American power" (*The Reporter Who Would Be King*, 125). Richard's position has been widely debated. See, for example, Amy Kaplan, *The Anarchy of Empire in the Making of US Culture* (Cambridge: Cambridge UP, 2003); John D. Seelye, *War Games: Richard Harding Davis and the New Imperialism* (Amherst: U of Massachusetts P, 2003); and Nirmal Trivedi, "Staging Unincorporated Power: Richard Harding Davis and The Critique of Imperial News," *Journal of Transnational American Studies* 3.2 (2011), http://escholarship.org, April 16, 2015.

21. "Peculiar Things," *Philadelphia Inquirer* (13 May 1897), 11.

22. Bowen, *History of Lehigh University*, 33–34.

23. For a representative sample of the coverage of their movements for many years, see *Social Register*, August 1897 8 (Aug. 1897), 72.

24. Carolyn Wells, "A B C of Literature," *Life* (22 Jul. 1897), 68.

25. "Among the Magazines," *Philadelphia Inquirer* (26 Jul. 1897), 10.

26. "An Evening with Celia Thaxter and Her Poetry" and Untitled Item, *Boston Globe* (25 Jul. 1897), 21, columns 5 and 6.

27. James D. Law, *Here and There in Two Hemispheres* (Lancaster, PA: Home Publishing Co., 1903), 458; Silber, *The Romance of Reunion* 1997.

28. Letter, RHD to Richard Watson Gilder, "Monday" [c. 1897], Letter Collection, Box 7, Folder 279, YUL.

29. RHD, "Two Points of View," *Independent* (9 Sep. 1897), 1.

30. Ibid.

31. Ibid., 2.

32. "Consul Davis Resigns," (Columbia, SC) *State* (29 Sep. 1897), 2. That this was not the case was revealed in family letters; see, for example, Letter, Richard Harding Davis to RHD, [early fall 1897], UVA, in which he remarked to his mother, "I am very sorry about Gus. It is very tough luck indeed."

33. Richard lived at 10 E. 28th Street at this time.

34. RHD, "The Passing of Niagara," *Independent* (5 Nov. 1897), 3–4.

35. "An Exposition May Be Held," *North American* (12 Oct. 1897), 2; "National Export Exposition and International Commercial Congress," *Philadelphia Record Almanac of 1899* (Philadelphia: Philadelphia Record, 1899), 119.

36. Dexter Marshall, "Story Writers' Pay," *Atchison Daily Globe* (4 Jan. 1898), 2.

37. Letter, Richard Harding Davis to his family, undated [late 1897], UVA.

38. Julia R. Tutwiler, "Rebecca Harding Davis," *Women Authors of Our Day in Their Homes*, ed. Francis Whiting Halsey (New York: James Pott and Co., 1898), 271–76.

39. Ibid.
40. Ibid.
41. Ibid.
42. Ibid.
43. RHD, "Two Methods with the Negro," *Independent* (31 Mar. 1898), 1–2.
44. "How Our Readers Will Get War News," *Philadelphia Inquirer* (25 Apr. 1898), 7.
45. "How the Ledger Got Left," *Philadelphia Inquirer* (1 May 1898), 8.
46. Letter, Richard Harding Davis to Charles Belmont Davis, May 17, 1898, UVA.
47. "Business Notes," *Publisher's Weekly* (4 June 1898), 909.
48. RHD, "Women and Patriotism," *Harper's Bazar* (28 May 1898), 455.
49. RHD, "In Old Florence," *St. Nicholas* (25 May 1898), 586.
50. RHD, "One Word More," *Ladies' Home Journal* 15 (June 1898), 4. I have been unable to locate extant letters between RHD and Willard.
51. Tutwiler, "Rebecca Harding Davis," 273.
52. "The Warm Spring," (Richmond) *Dispatch* (4 Aug. 1898), 5.
53. "The Debutante," *North American* (6 Sep. 1898), 5.
54. RHD, "The Surprises of War," *Independent* (25 Aug. 1898), 528.
55. Ibid.
56. "The World of 1898: The Spanish-American War," www.loc.gov/rr/hispanic/1898, Dec. 12, 2016.
57. John D. Seelye, *War Games*, 2003.
58. RHD, "In Proof of To-Morrow," *Harper's Bazar* (17 Sep. 1898), 787.
59. "Olla Podrida," (Lexington, KY) *Morning Herald* (9 Oct. 1898), 6.
60. Letter, Richard Harding Davis to Charles Belmont Davis, Nov. 8 [1898?], UVA.
61. Letter, Richard Harding Davis to RHD, Oct 25, 1898, UVA.
62. RHD, "An Indian Woman's Tale," *Harper's Bazar* (7 Jan. 1899), 18.
63. John Pollack, *Kitchener: The Road to Omdurman and Savior of the Nation* (Boston: Little, Brown, 2013), Chapter 17.
64. RHD, "The Work Before Us," *Independent* (19 Jan. 1899), 177–78; Editorial, 218.
65. Ibid.
66. "The Queer Davis Twins," *Broadway Magazine* 2 (Jan. 1899), 739.
67. Item, *North American* (1 Jan. 1899), 5.
68. Letter, RHD to Richard Harding Davis, undated, UVA.
69. Letter, Richard Harding Davis to RHD, [Mar. 1899], UVA.

70. RHD, "Two 'Servants of the Republic,'" *Independent* (13 Apr. 1899), 1002–1004. There is no record that RHD's husband received a pension; he was one who had paid for a substitute when he was drafted.

71. "Editorial: The Pension Roll," *Independent* (25 May 1899), 1443.

72. "Richard Harding Davis Marries," *San Francisco Call* (5 May 1899), 3; Rosbe, *Marion Art Center*, 59–60, 119.

73. Charles Belmont Davis, *Letters and Adventures*; Letters, Richard Harding Davis to RHD and Cecil Davis to Charles Belmont Davis and others, UVA.

74. RHD, "The Curse of Education," *North American Review* 168 (May 1899), 614.

75. Editorial, *Independent* (8 June 1899), 1578.

76. "Letters and Art," *Literary Digest* (3 June 1899), 634.

77. Mrs. Schuyler Van Renssalaer, "Our Public Schools. A Reply," *North American Review* 169 (Jul. 1899), 78.

78. "L. Clarke Davis, Public Ledger; Rebecca Harding Davis; Richard Harding Davis," (Columbia, SC) *State* (25 May 1899), 4.

79. RHD, "The Mean Face of War," *Independent* (20 Jul. 1899), 1931–33.

80. Editorial, *Independent* (20 Jul. 1899), 1968.

81. Lubow, *The Reporter Who Would Be King*, 203–204.

82. RHD, "A Royal Procession," *Independent* (7 Sep. 1899), 2414.

83. Letter, Richard Harding Davis to Charles Belmont Davis, Sep. 11, 1899, UVA.

84. Lubow, *The Reporter Who Would Be King*, 205.

CHAPTER 13: TRANSITIONS (1900–1904)

1. US Census, 1900. Charley identified himself in the census as "Publisher" and Richard as "War Correspondent." Clarke was noted as an "Editor," but, as was typical for many women, no occupation was listed for RHD.

2. RHD, "Under the Old Code," *Harper's New Monthly Magazine* 100 (Feb. 1900), 400.

3. "A Family of Writers," *Ladies' Home Journal* 17 (Jan. 1900), 37.

4. Willa Cather, "The Passing Show," *Lincoln Courier* (13 Jan. 1900), 2.

5. Charles Belmont Davis, *Letters and Adventures*, 282.

6. Ibid., 261ff; Rosbe, *Marion Art Center*, 89; Lubow, *The Reporter Who Would Be King*, 205ff.

7. Charles Belmont Davis, *Adventures and Letters*, 289; Lubow, *The Reporter Who Would Be King*, 221.

8. See, for example, Item, (Washington, D.C.) *Times* (9 Sep. 1900), 4.

9. Denis Brian, *Pulitzer: A Life* (New York: John Wiley & Sons, 2001).
10. Ibid., 1.
11. RHD, "The Temple of Fame," *Independent* (25 Oct. 1900), 2225–26.
12. Ibid.
13. RHD, "Two American Boys," *Independent* (4 Oct. 1900), 2375.
14. "Improvement among the Colored People in the North," Friends' *Intelligencer* (27 Apr. 1901), ii.
15. RHD, "On the Jersey Shore," *Independent* (15 Nov. 1900), 2731–33.
16. "Magazines," *Cedar Rapids Republican* (4 Nov. 1900), 13.
17. Lubow, *The Reporter Who Would Be King*, 222–223.
18. RHD, "Lord Kitchener's Methods," *Independent* (7 Feb. 1901), 326–27.
19. Ibid., 327–28.
20. Editorial, *Independent* (4 Apr. 1901), 804.
21. Letter, RHD to Charles Wells Moulton, Mar. 15 [c. 1901], BEPL-CWM.
22. Editorial, *Youth's Companion* (18 Apr. 1901), 205.
23. RHD, "A Quiet Half-Hour," *Independent* (30 May 1901), 1232.
24. Quoted in Charles Belmont Davis, *Letters and Adventures*, 293.
25. L. Clarke Davis, "Different Points of View," *Independent* (26 Sep. 1901), 2287–90.
26. RHD, "Is It All for Nothing?" *Independent* (24 Oct. 1901), 2513.
27. Ibid., 2514.
28. Emphasis added.
29. RHD, "The 'Black North,'" *Independent* (6 Feb. 1902), 338–40.
30. Letter, Richard Harding Davis to RHD, undated; from Mt. Kisco, UVA.
31. "Weber & Fields' Music Hall this season," *National Magazine* 16 (May 1902), 208–10.
32. Lubow, *The Reporter Who Would Be King*, 251.
33. "The Return to the Soil," *Duluth News-Tribune* (4 May 1902), 10.
34. My comments on the goals and practices of the *Post* are indebted to Jan Cohn's *Creating America: George Horace Lorimer and The Saturday Evening Post* (Pittsburgh: U of Pittsburgh P, 1989), Chapters 1 and 2.
35. RHD, "Some Modern Buccaneers," *Saturday Evening Post* (24 May 1902), 4–5.
36. RHD, "The Late G. W. Childs," Pinckney (MI) *Dispatch* (24 Jul. 1902), 3; I have been unable to locate the original *Congregationalist and Christian World* article.
37. RHD, "The Disease of Money-Getting," *Independent* (19 June 1902), 1459. The quote was from a statement made two years earlier by Richard Olney, Secretary

of State in the Cleveland administration (see "The Progress of the Presidential Campaign," The Speaker, *The Liberal Review* 2 [29 Sep. 1900], 698).

38. "The Current Magazine," *Houston Daily Post* (4 May 1902), 19.

39. RHD, "Country Girls in Town," *Independent* (17 Jul. 1902), 1691.

40. See, for example, the *Oakland Tribune* (11 Oct. 1902), 15.

41. Item, *Womanhood* 8 (Nov. 1902), 421.

42. RHD, "New Traits of the New American," *Independent* (12 Jul. 1902), 694–98.

43. "Adolph Ochs Buys Philadelphia Ledger," *Scranton Tribune* (22 Jul. 1902), 1; "Philadelphia Papers to Consolidate," *Washington Times* (11 Aug. 1902), 1; "Papers Combined," *Honolulu Evening Bulletin* (21 Aug. 1902), 3.

44. Law, *Here and There in Two Hemispheres*, 457–58.

45. Letter, Richard Harding Davis to RHD, [Sep. 1902], UVA.

46. I am indebted to Jane Atteridge Rose for identifying RHD's unsigned articles in the *Saturday Evening Post*. See "A Bibliography of Fiction and Non-fiction by RHD," *American Literary Realism* 22.3 (Sp 1990), 67–86.

47. Quoted in Lubow, *The Reporter Who Would Be King*, 227.

48. Frank Luther Mott, *A History of American Magazines* (Cambridge, MA: Harvard UP, 1968), 3:74.

49. RHD, "In Remembrance," *Independent* (29 Jan. 1903), 238–39.

50. RHD, "A Peculiar People," *Saturday Evening Post* (19 Jan. 1903), 9, 48.

51. Letter, Grover Cleveland to RHD, Jan. 9, 1903, UVA.

52. RHD, "The Blot on the Great Man's Name," *Saturday Evening Post* (21 Feb. 1903), 12.

53. RHD, "Hard Times for the Old Man," *Saturday Evening Post* (28 Mar. 1903), 14.

54. RHD, "The Man in the Iron Mask," *Saturday Evening Post* (11 Apr. 1903), 18.

55. RHD, "The Rage for Writing," *Saturday Evening Post* (25 Apr. 1903), 12.

56. Nevins, *Letters of Grover Cleveland*, 568.

57. "Roosevelt Congratulates Francis in Address at President's Dinner," *St. Louis Republic* (1 May 1903), 1.

58. RHD, "The Bogey Man Banished," *Saturday Evening Post* (23 May 1903), 14.

59. RHD, "Friend Paul," *Saturday Evening Post* (6 June 1903), 21.

60. RHD, "Red Names for Red Men," *Saturday Evening Post* (20 June 1903), 14.

61. Ada Patterson, *Maude Adams: A Biography* (New York: Meyer Brothers, 1907), 64–65.

62. RHD, Literary Folk—Their Ways and Their Work: Race Books," *Saturday Evening Post* (4 Jul. 1903), 20–21.

63. Ibid., 21–22.
64. Ibid., 22.
65. Item, *New-York Tribune* (9 Aug. 1903), 15.
66. "Town and Country Life," *Town and Country* (11 Jul. 1903), 27.
67. RHD, "The Porch Climbers," *Saturday Evening Post* (8 Aug. 1903), 12.
68. Letters, Theodore Roosevelt to L. Clarke Davis, Aug. 20; Aug. 24; Aug. 27, 1903, UVA.
69. Ibid.
70. Barrymore, *Memories,* 141–42.
71. RHD, "Literary Folk—Human and Inhuman Books," *Saturday Evening Post* (5 Sep. 1903), 13–14.
72. Letters, Theodore Roosevelt to L. Clarke Davis, Oct. 5, 1903, UVA.
73. Letters, Theodore Roosevelt to L. Clarke Davis, Oct. 7, 15, and 30, 1903, UVA.
74. RHD, "A Shelf of Idols," *Saturday Evening Post* (21 Nov. 1903), 20.
75. Charles Belmont Davis, "A Life Sentence," *Smart Set* 11 (Nov. 1903), 113.
76. See, for example, "News of the Book World: Richard Harding Davis Guillotined," *Minneapolis Journal* (2 Jan. 1904), 4.
77. Letter, Richard Harding Davis to RHD, [Feb. 1904], UVA.
78. Letters, RHD to Samuel E. Moffett, June 16–20, [1904], Moffett Collection, Box 1, HL.
79. "Publishers' Meeting To-Day," *St. Louis Republic* (19 May 1904), 1.
80. RHD, "Presidential Campaigns of To-Day and Yesterday: Some of the Signs of an Odd and Significant Change in Public Feeling," *Saturday Evening Post* (17 Sep. 1904), 8–9.
81. RHD, "Literary Folk: Their Ways and Their Work. The Summer Harvest," *Saturday Evening Post* (10 Sep. 1904), 18–19.
82. Decree Admitting Foreign Will to Probate, King County, Washington, Jan. 18, 1907.
83. "Death of Mrs. E. H. Gow," (Maysville, KY) *Evening Bulletin* (14 Nov. 1904); Item, *San Juan Islander* (19 Nov. 1904), 8.
84. Letter, Nora Davis to Amy Gow, June 13, 1952, quoted in Lasseter and Harris, eds. *Rebecca Harding Davis*, 136.
85. For a discussion of RHD's work as a "cultural autobiography," see "Introduction," in Lasseter and Harris, eds. *Rebecca Harding Davis*, 1–22.
86. RHD, "Bits," preface.
87. Ibid., 25.
88. Ibid., 65.

89. Ibid., 76.
90. Ibid., 77.
91. Ibid., 79.
92. Ibid., 80.
93. Ibid., 126–28.
94. Ibid., 130.
95. "Bits of Real Gossip," *Washington Times* (29 Oct. 1904), 6.
96. "Review," *Life* (15 Dec. 1904), 626; "Books and Authors," *Living Age* (10 Dec. 1904), 702.
97. "'Bits of Gossip,'" *New-York Tribune* (6 Nov. 1904), 8.
98. "Some Books of the Week," *Spectator* (4 Feb. 1905), 185–86.
99. Letter, Richard Harding Davis to Charles Belmont Davis, undated, UVA.
100. "Current Events," *Friends' Intelligencer* (24 Dec. 1904), 825.
101. Last Will and Testament, with codicils, of L. Clarke Davis, "Pennsylvania, Wills and Probate Records, 1683–1993," ancestry.com, June 27, 2016.
102. Ibid.

CHAPTER 14: THE WIDOWED WRITER (1905–1910)

1. "Catalogue of the library…of L. Clarke Davis, Esq.," New York: Anderson Auction Co., 1905.
2. Because only Richard's letters to and from RHD were preserved, there is only one extant letter from RHD to Charley. But that letter and references in other letters indicate she wrote as prolifically and lovingly to Charley as to Richard.
3. Letter, RHD to Clara Wilson Baird, Jan. 10, [1905] (quoted in Shaeffer, 333).
4. RHD, "Literary Folk: Their Ways and Their Work. Five Riddles," *Saturday Evening Post* (14 Jan. 1905), 20–22.
5. RHD, "Literary Folk: Their Ways and Their Work," *Saturday Evening Post* (25 Feb 1905), 22–24.
6. RHD, "Literary Folk: Their Ways and Their Work: The Children of Despair," *Saturday Evening Post* (8 Apr. 1905), 17–18.
7. Letter, Richard Harding Davis to RHD, Apr. 30, [1905?], UVA.
8. RHD, "The Story of a Few Plain Women." *Ladies' Home Journal* 22 (May 1905): 4–5.
9. Ibid., 5.
10. *Social Register*, 1905, 109.
11. "Plenty to Do at Point Pleasant," *New York Times* (2 Jul. 1905), X7.

12. RHD, "Literary Folk: Their Ways and Their Work. The Smart Set," *Saturday Evening Post* (17 June 1905), 15–16.

13. Letter, Richard Harding Davis to RHD, undated [Dec. 1905], UVA.

14. "Entertain Mark Twain," *New-York Tribune* (22 Dec. 1905), 7.

15. "American Players Abroad," *Green Book Magazine* 12 (Aug. 1914), 319.

16. RHD, "Undistinguished Americans," *Independent* (26 Apr. 1906), 962–64.

17. RHD, book blurb for James E. McGirt's *For Your Sweet Sake: Poems* (Philadelphia: John C. Winston Co., 1906), 78.

18. Letter, RHD to Richard Harding Davis, Apr. 23, [1906], UVA.

19. Letter, RHD to Richard Harding Davis, [c. late Apr./early May, 1906], UVA.

20. Letter, RHD to Richard Harding Davis, May 1, [1906], UVA.

21. Just as RHD and Nora set sail, another "Davis Family" item appeared in *The Critic*. See "The Lounger" column for May 1906.

22. Letter, RHD to Richard Harding Davis, May 5, [1906], UVA.

23. Ibid.

24. "A Remarkable Short Story," *Minneapolis Journal* (11 Nov. 1906), 10.

25. Decree Admitting Foreign Will to Probate, King County, Washington, Jan. 18, 1907; Will of Hugh Wilson Harding, Jul. 5, 1905, Northampton County, Commonwealth of Pennsylvania.

26. Letter, Richard Harding Davis to RHD, [Dec. 1906], UVA.

27. Letter, RHD to Richard Harding Davis, Feb. 3, [1907], UVA.

28. Lubow, *The Reporter Who Would Be King*, 259–61.

29. Letter, RHD to Richard Harding Davis, Feb. 19, [1907], UVA. In the letter, RHD referred to "the darkies" of Africa, a term she had not used for decades.

30. Letter, RHD to Richard Harding Davis, Feb. 22, [1907], UVA.

31. RHD, "Girls in Business," *Churchman* (2 Mar. 1907), 338–39.

32. Lubow, *The Reporter Who Would Be King*, 259–61.

33. Letter, RHD to Richard Harding Davis, Mar. 1 [1907], UVA.

34. Letter, RHD to Richard Harding Davis, Mar. 3, [1907], UVA.

35. Letter, RHD to Richard Harding Davis, Mar. 11?, [1907], UVA.

36. Letter, RHD to Richard Harding Davis, [Mar. 31, 1907], UVA.

37. Letter, RHD to Richard Harding Davis, Apr. 9, 1907, UVA.

38. Letter, RHD to Richard Harding Davis, [c. Apr. 1907], UVA.

39. RHD, "Some Strange True Stories," *New-York Tribune* (31 Mar. 1907), 7–8.

40. Letter, RHD to Richard Harding Davis, [June 1907], UVA. The quote is a paraphrase from Psalm 33.

41. Letter, RHD to Richard Harding Davis, Apr. 12, 1907, UVA.

42. RHD, "One Woman's Question," *Independent* (18 Jul. 1907), 132–33.

43. Letters, RHD to Richard Harding Davis, [late Jul./early Aug. 1907], UVA.
44. Sinclair Lewis, "Editors Who Write," *Life* 10 (Oct. 1907), 3.
45. Letter, RHD to Richard Harding Davis, [fall 1907], UVA.
46. Letter, Richard Harding Davis to RHD, [Jul.? 23, 1908], UVA.
47. Item, *Washington Times* (25 Jan. 1908), 4.
48. Letter, RHD to Charles Belmont Davis, [Jan. 1908?], UVA.
49. Letter, RHD to Richard Harding Davis, undated [c. 1908], UVA.
50. Letter, Richard Harding Davis to RHD, [c. spring 1908], UVA.
51. Will of RHD, Commonwealth of Pennsylvania, County and City of Philadelphia, Mar. 17, 1908, with appended Executor documents of Oct. 3, 1910.
52. "Fiction," *World To-Day* 15 (Aug. 1908), 877.
53. "Chronicle and Comment," *Bookman* 27 (Jul. 1908), 449; "Books," *Outlook* (4 Jul. 1908), 532.
54. See, for example, letter, Richard Harding Davis to Charles Belmont Davis, Sep. 26 [1908], UVA.
55. RHD, "A Family History by Rebecca Harding Davis" in Lasseter and Harris, eds., *Rebecca Harding Davis*, 135–48; Letter, Nora Davis Farrar to Amy Gow, June 13, 1952 (quoted in Lasseter and Harris, *Rebecca Harding Davis*), 136.
56. Letter, RHD to Richard Harding Davis, undated [c. Aug. 1908], UVA.
57. Numerous diary entries by Cecil Clark Davis in 1908. Cecil's diaries are privately held, and I thank Wendy Bidstrup for allowing me access to the documents and permission to quote from them.
58. See RHD's undated letters from c. fall 1908, UVA.
59. Judith Westlund Rosbe, *Marion* (Charleston, SC: Arcadia Publishing, 2000).
60. Cecil Clark Davis diary, Oct. 8, 1908.
61. Ibid., Oct. 19 and 20, 1908.
62. RHD, "In the Old Days," *Independent* (12 Nov. 1908), 1100.
63. Advertisement, *Christian Advocate* (3 Dec. 1908), 1986.
64. The play based on *Vera the Medium* would not have a New York opening, unlike most of Richard's plays.
65. Letters, Richard Harding Davis to Charles Belmont Davis throughout the first decade of the century, UVA.
66. Cecil Clark Davis diary, Nov. 18–26, 1908.
67. RHD, "An Old-Time Love Story," *Century Illustrated Magazine* 77 (Dec. 1908), 219.
68. Letter, RHD to Richard Harding Davis, [c. 1908], UVA.
69. Cecil Clark Davis diary, Dec. 26, 1908.
70. Letter, RHD to Richard Harding Davis, [Dec. 1908], UVA.

71. RHD, "What We Can," *St. Nicholas* 36 (Jan. 1909), 249.

72. Census, 1910. Originally from Virginia, Lilly apparently lived in the Davis household until RHD's death.

73. Letter, RHD to Richard Harding Davis, [c. spring 1908], UVA.

74. Cecil Clark Davis diary, Mar. 8, 1909.

75. Ibid., Apr. 13, 1909.

76. RHD, "Three Little Stories," *St. Nicholas* 36 (May 1909), 633–34.

77. Cecil Clark Davis diary, June 7, 1909.

78. Letter, RHD to Richard Harding Davis, [summer 1909], UVA.

79. George Jean Nathan, "Drama's Trial Marriage with Art," *Smart Set* 30 (Jan. 1910), 151.

80. Accounts of the luncheon appeared in numerous newspapers; see, for instance, Item, *Kansas City Star* (13 Apr. 1910), 5.

81. Shaeffer, "RHD," 342.

82. Executor Petition, Oct. 3, 1910, appended to RHD's Will; Shaeffer, "RHD", 343.

83. Shaeffer, "RHD," 343.

84. Ibid.

85. Executor documents appended to Will of RHD.

86. "Press Comment," *The State* (Columbus, SC) from the *Springfield Republican* (3 Oct. 1910), 4.

87. "Rebecca Harding Davis," *New-York Tribune* (1 Oct. 1910), 6. This obituary was reprinted in several newspapers.

88. Item, *Washington Herald* (25 Dec. 1910), 7.

CHAPTER 15: FINAL PAGES

1. Frank Moore Colby, et.al, *The New International Yearbook* (New York: Dodd, Mead, 1911), 204.

2. RHD, "Bits," 86.

3. Item, *Philadelphia Inquirer* (4 June 1911), 10.

4. In *The Reporter Who Would Be King*, Lubow surmises that Cecil was lesbian and the marriage was never consummated, but of course there is no evidence to suggest what their marital relations actually were. Although he never states outright that Richard was gay, the implications for that assumption are evident throughout the biography, a charge that largely rests on how close Richard was to his mother. But RHD was this close to all of her children, as their letters imply; the fact that only Richard's letters have survived distorts the impression.

5. See, for example, "R.H. Davis, Novelist, Is to Wed Bessie McCoy," *New York Sun* (2 Jul. 1912), 4.

6. "Wedding Receptions," *Washington Times* (10 Jul. 1912), 6.

7. Ibid.

8. "R. H. Davis, Noted Writer, Falls Dead," *Public Ledger* (12 Apr. 1916), 1; "Richard Harding Davis On His Last Journey," *Evening Public Ledger* (14 Apr. 1916), p. 1, 4.

9. Charles Belmont Davis, *Letters and Adventures*, 312.

10. This previously unpublished letter is privately held by the author.

11. "String to Fortune Left the 'Yama Girl,'" *Day Book* (14 Apr. 1916); "Curious Kink in 'Dickie' Davis' Character," *Philadelphia Inquirer* (14 May 1916), 8.

12. Diary of Cecil Clark Davis, May 11, 1916. There was an attempt to romanticize Richard and Bessie's relationship after his death. Gouverneur Morris edited and published "The Love Letters of Richard Harding Davis to Bessie McCoy Davis" in *Metropolitan Magazine* in Oct. and Nov. 1916, and Bessie made headlines by insisting she communicated regularly with Richard's spirit. She did not, however, allow her daughter to know her aunt and uncle well, although during World War II, Hope wrote Nora a long letter in order to reconnect. [Privately held by the author, with appreciation to Wendy Bistrup for the donation.]

13. "R. H. Davis Left $50,375," *New-York Tribune* (2 Mar. 1918), 2; this is as recorded in the White Plains Surrogate Court by the executors.

14. Bessie McCoy Davis, "Appreciation of the Late Richard Harding Davis," *New-York Tribune* (23 Nov. 1919), 8; "Richard Harding Davis and Bessie McCoy," *New York World*; rpt. *Fort Wayne Journal Gazette* (7 Apr. 1922), 5.

15. What Cecil's role was in this event is unknown.

16. Letter, Nora Davis to Cecil Clark Davis, Apr. 15, 1916. This previously unpublished letter, and the only extant letter written by Nora, is owned by the author.

17. Charles Belmont Davis, "A Coronation Sideshow," *Collier's* (22 Jul. 1911); "The New World," *Collier's* (16 Sep. 1911).

18. Charles Belmont Davis, "Palm Beach and the Pilgrim Fathers," *Collier's* (25 Apr. 1913), 16–17, 35–38.

19. "Gayety at Palm Beach," *New York Sun* (25 Feb. 1912), sec. 3, 2.

20. George Jean Nathan, "On the Trail of a Thousand Girls," *Smart Set* 41 (Oct. 1913), 147; ellipses are in the original.

21. "Charles Belmont Davis and Dai," newspaperarchive.com, Nov. 12, 2014.

22. "Charles Belmont Davis Marries Illinois Girl," *Janesville Daily Gazette* (17 Jan. 1914), 1. Turgeon had lived in Illinois for a year before coming to New York.

23. "Miss Dai Turgeon Wed Abroad," *Chicago Tribune* (18 Jan. 1914), A1; *Washington Herald* (18 Jan. 1914), 7.

24. "C. Belmont Davis Weds in London," *Philadelphia Inquirer* (18 Jan. 1914), 2.

25. "Selwyn Will Repeat Big Broadway Dinner," (Columbia) *University Missourian* (20 Dec. 1915), 3.

26. Joyce Kilmer, "Financial Aspects of Story Writing," *New York Times*; rpt. *The Editor* (17 Jul. 1915), 74–76.

27. "The Stage Door," *New-York Tribune* (18 Dec. 1919), 13; "New York Has Become Theatrical Capital of the Whole World," *New York Evening World* (17 Jan. 1920), 9.

28. "In Town and Country," *Town and Country* (15 Apr. 1911), 41.

29. "Bright Bits about Folk in Society," *Philadelphia Inquirer* (14 May 1911), 10.

30. "Chaplain Farrar Is Dismissed by King George," *Washington Herald* (23 Nov. 1911), 2; "Davis-Farrar," *Lexington Herald* (9 Apr. 1911), society section, 1.

31. "Chaplain Farrar is Dismissed by King George," *Washington Herald* (23 Nov. 1911), 2.

32. "Twenty-First Street House Sold," *Philadelphia Inquirer* (23 May 1911), 5.

33. "Chaplain Farrar Is Dismissed by King George," *Washington Herald* (23 Nov. 1911), 2; "King Dismisses Chaplain, "*New-York Tribune* (23 Nov. 1911), 2; "Disgraced Rector French War Hero," *Philadelphia Inquirer* (10 Nov. 1916), 2; "King Fires His Chaplain," *Kansas City Star* (23 Nov. 1916), 9; "Not King's Chaplain," *Charlotte Observer* (23 Nov. 1911), 13.

34. Letter, Richard Harding Davis to Charles Belmont Davis, undated, UVA.

35. "Farrar Dismissed," *London Gazette* (21 Nov. 1911), 1; "Royal Chaplain Has Disappeared," *New York Times* (23 Nov. 1911), 2.

36. "Now Seek Farrar," *Washington Herald* (24 Nov. 1911), 1.

37. "Disgraced Chaplain Coming to America," *Washington Times* (4 Dec. 1911), 4; "King Fires His Chaplain," *Kansas City Star* (23 Nov. 1911), 9; "Wife Clings to Disgraced Pastor," *San Francisco Call* (29 Nov. 1911), 1.

38. Item, *San Jose Mercury News* (29 Nov. 1911), 1.

39. "Chaplain Farrar is Dismissed by King George," *Washington Herald* (23 Nov. 1911), 1.

40. "Farrars Are Seen in Paris Streets," *Washington Herald* (31 Dec. 1911), 3.

41. Ibid.

42. "Wife Clings to Disgraced Pastor," *San Francisco Call* (29 Nov. 1911), 1.

43. "Mrs. Percival Farrar Here," *New York Sun* (27 May 1912), 9.

44. "Wife of Unfrocked Chaplain in America," *Washington Times* (27 May 1912), 2.

45. "Rector, Known Here, Wipes Out Disgrace By Bravery in War," *Public Ledger* (10 Nov. 1916), 2; "Disgraced Rector French War Hero," *Philadelphia Inquirer* (10 Nov. 1916), 2; "Rector Farrar Found Fighting in France," *New York Sun* (11 Nov. 1916), 2.

46. "Obituaries," (Wilmington, DE) *News Journal* (12 Mar. 1946), 19. Whether they were visiting Peru or were living there is unknown.

47. "Mrs. Percival Farrar," *New York Times* (20 Jul. 1958), 65.

Bibliography

For a complete bibliography of Rebecca Harding Davis's writings, please see the website of *Rebecca Harding Davis: The Complete Works*: http://rebeccahardingdaviscompleteworks.com/

Index

Abolitionists, 21, 22, 40, 55, 65–66, 71, 76, 78, 133, 153, 306
  See also under Davis, Rebecca Harding, themes in the writing of
Adams, Maude, 244, 266, 298, 305, 306, 361, 383
Addison, Rev. Thomas G., 37, 70
African Americans, 59, 61, 100–101, 102, 141, 149, 186, 243, 320
  In Wheeling, 15, 21, 22, 27, 416n90
  In Philadelphia, 76, 122, 147, 160–61
  See also under Davis, Rebecca Harding, themes in the writing of
After Prison—What? (Booth, M.B.), 377
Agassiz, Louis, 66
Ainslee's Magazine, 362
Albion, Eliza, 55
Albion, John, 55
Alcott, Abby May, 57, 137
Alcott, Bronson, 57, 58, 343
Alcott, Louisa May, 55–56, 57, 58, 62, 80–82, 136–37, 148, 158, 161, 173, 194, 281, 343, 346
Aldrich, Thomas Bailey, 213, 233
All-Story Magazine, 377
All the Year Round, 64–65
American Apiculturist, 230
American Homes, 171–72
American Literary Gazette, 132
American Magazine, 239
Anthony, Susan B., 135, 200
Appleton's Journal, 170, 193, 206–7
  RHD's publications in, 190, 192, 193
Archie Lovell (Edwards), 115, 118
Argosy, 289
Armstrong, William, 18
Art in Advertising, 275, 279

Arthur, Chester, 71, 212
Atherton, Gertrude, 280
Atlantic Monthly, 43, 44, 45, 47, 50, 55, 58, 60, 62, 63–64, 81, 89, 92, 98, 104, 108, 111, 117, 126, 129–30, 142, 143, 146, 162, 164, 193–94, 202–3, 230, 258, 265, 281, 320
  Competition with other magazines, 41, 42, 63, 103, 178, 206
  RHD's publications in, 29, 31, 32, 34, 45–46, 52, 61, 68–69, 78, 83–84, 87, 88, 90, 94, 96, 100, 101–2, 107, 110, 122, 158, 230, 235
Atlantic Tales, The, 108

Bailey, Thomas Aldrich, 230
Baird, Andrew Todd, 84, 104, 215
Baird, Clara Wilson. See Wilson (Baird), Clara
Baker, William M., 225
Bangs, John Kendrick, 366
Banner of Light, 107
Barlow, Harriet Preble, 20
Barr, Amelia, 285, 302
Barrington, Jonah, 361
Barrymore, Ethel, 171, 182, 215, 244, 266, 305, 306, 330, 334, 363, 379–80
Barrymore, Georgiana Drew. See Drew, Georgiana
Barrymore, John, 171
Barrymore, Lionel, 171
Barrymore, Maurice, 171
Bartol, Elizabeth, 55
Bartol, Cyrus, 42, 55, 216
Bartol, Lizzie, 55
Battle with the Slum, The (Riis), 377

Beard, George M., 239
Beecher, Henry Ward, 76, 126, 172
Bell, Alexander Graham, 256
Bellamy, Edward, 200
Benedict, Elias C., 256, 261, 359–60
Benedict, Frank Lee, 280, 288
Benedict, Helen, 256, 261, 281, 306
Bénézet, Antoine, 346
Bernhardt, Sarah, 237
Beulah (Evans), 354
Bishop, William Henry, 224
"Black Bess, The" (Spofford), 109
Blaine, James (RHD's uncle), 11, 14, 15, 22, 23
Blaine, James G. (RHD's "cousin"), 11, 14, 15, 20, 29, 180, 196–97, 200, 205, 206, 212, 226, 246, 258, 274–75, 372
Blaine, Rebecca Leet Wilson (RHD's aunt), 11, 23, 24, 101
Blavatsky, Madame, 181–82
Boer War, 338, 340–41, 343, 345–46, 347, 367
Boker, George Henry, 205, 217, 233
Booth, Edwin, 99, 183, 256
Booth, John Wilkes, 99
Booth, Maud Ballington, 377
Boston Daily Advertiser, 112, 159, 194, 302, 304
Boston Evening Transcript, 219
Boston Globe, 255, 301
Boston Sunday Journal, 334
Boston Traveller, 223
Bowden, Clara Wilder. *See* Wilder (Bowden), Clara
Bowen, Henry Chandler, 172, 173, 299–300, 320
Brace, Charles Loring, 188–89
Brackett, Anna Callender, 168
Bradford, John, 366
Bradwell v. Illinois, 190, 191
Bridgman, Howard Allen, 284
"Brier-wood Pipe, The" (Shanly), 73
"Bright Eyes." *See* La Flesche, Suzette
Brisbane, Arthur, 252, 266
Broadway Magazine, 332
Brodhead, Jefferson Davis, 216, 389
Brontë, Charlotte, 378, 379
Brooklyn Magazine, 234
Brooks, Noah, 155, 158

Brown, Dr. John, 44
Brown, John, 28, 35
Browning, Robert, 83–84
Bryan, William Jennings, 310, 311–12, 316
Bryant, William Cullen, 161
Buccaneers, The (Wharton), 368
Bunner, H. C., 224
Burleigh, Margaret, 76, 141
Burlingame, Edward, 247
Burnett, Frances Hodgson, 182, 213, 215, 233, 247, 285, 324
Butler, Benjamin, 74, 83

Cable, George Washington, 233, 243, 440n11
Campbell, Alexander, 13, 25
Campbell, Archibald, 25, 26, 27, 28–29, 33, 37, 50, 67–68, 212
Campbell, Helen, 217, 234
Carroll, Ellen, 28, 94–95, 101
"Case of George Dedlow, The" (Mitchell, S.W.), 104
Cassell and Company Publishers, 234
Cather, Willa, 340
Catherwood, Mary Hartwell, 269
Catholics, 18, 232, 322
  See also Davis, Rebecca Harding, themes in the writing of: Religion/religious sects
Cecil Dreeme (Winthrop), 44
Centennial Exposition, 177, 179–80, 181–82, 184–85, 190, 251
  See also Davis, Rebecca Harding, themes in the writing of: Centennial celebration
Century Illustrated Magazine, 206, 229, 244–45, 247, 262, 263, 268, 278, 296, 307–8, 313
  RHD's publications in, 217, 219, 225, 233–34, 303, 320, 345, 392–93
Century of Dishonor, A (Jackson, H.H.), 211
Century's End Magazine, 265
Champney, Elizabeth W., 298
Chandler, Henry S., 299–300, 303
Channing, Mrs., 62
Channing, William Ellery, 62
Charles Auchester (Sheppard), 60

Charles Scribner Publishing, 270, 277, 279, 351, 390
Chase sisters, 112–13
Chicago *Times-Herald*, 309
Chicago World's Fair. *See* Columbian Exposition
Children of the Tenements (Riis), 377
Children's Hour, The, 161
Childs, Emma Peterson, 352
Childs, George W., 240–41, 256, 266, 272, 274, 288–89, 292, 295, 352–53, 408
"Chimney Corner" (Stowe), 97
Christian Advocate, 27
Christian Examiner, 51
Christian World. See *Congregationalist*
Christmas Traveller, 223
Church, Frank P., 103, 107, 108–10, 111–20, 121, 127
Church, William Conant, 103, 107, 108–10, 111–20, 121, 123, 126, 127, 141, 160, 162
Churchill, Winston, 341, 382
Churchman, The, 309
  RHD's publications in, 367, 384
Civil War, 33, 34–35, 36–37, 38–39, 40, 41, 50, 53, 57, 59, 65–66, 69, 80, 84, 90, 98, 99, 157, 306
  See also under Davis, Rebecca Harding, themes in the writing of
Clark, Bruce (Cecil's brother), 401
Clark, Cecil. *See* Davis, Cecil Clark
Clark, Louise, 244, 330
Clark, Nancy Reagan (Cecil's sister-in-law), 401–2
Clarke, Edward, 168
Clarke, James Freeman, 42
Clarke, William Fayal, 379
Clay, Henry, 20, 202, 372, 414n62
Cleary, Kate, 303
Clemens, Sherrard, 21
Clemens, Samuel. *See* Twain, Mark
Cleveland, Frances Folsom, 240–41, 243, 245, 251, 261, 265–66, 268, 270, 281, 288, 344, 365, 384
Cleveland, Francesca, 270
Cleveland, Grover, 200, 226, 227, 240–41, 243, 245, 246, 251, 261, 263, 265–66, 268, 270, 274, 275–76, 281, 283, 286, 287, 288–89, 290–91, 292, 296, 306, 310, 344, 356, 358, 359–60, 365
Clough, Arthur, 42
Clubb, Henry, 307
Collier's Weekly, 3, 349, 350, 367, 376–77, 383, 395, 400, 404, 405, 406
Columbian Exposition, 273, 283, 285–86, 288, 289, 290, 291
Comfort, Anna Manning, 168
Commonwealth, 80
"Complaint of Friends, A," (Dodge, M.A.), 62
Cone, Helen Gray, 263
Congdon, Charles Taber, 301
Congregationalist, 227, 232, 243, 267, 275, 284, 308, 352
  RHD's publications in, 215, 222, 226–27, 230, 232, 241, 242, 243, 244, 245–46, 250, 255, 258, 260, 264, 273, 274, 289, 301, 329, 342, 349, 353
Congregationalists, 172, 195
  See also *Congregationalist*; *Independent*; *Sunday Afternoon*
Continental Monthly, 41–42
Cooke, Rose Terry, 173, 195, 200, 221, 232, 361
Cooper, Almyr (Clarke's nephew), 311–12
Cooper, Carrie Davis (Clarke's sister), 71, 73, 75, 79, 85, 86, 88, 102
Cosmopolitan, 265, 404
Coward, Eddie, 298
Crane, Stephen, 26, 316
Critic, The, 234, 238, 264, 305, 318, 332
Crute, F. Jennings, 255–56
Cuban War of Independence, 306, 307, 312, 323
  See also Spanish-American War
Cult of celebrity, 237, 238, 279–80, 378
  See also Davis, Rebecca Harding: Cult of celebrity, opposition to; Davis, Richard Harding: Cult of celebrity advocate
Cult of personality, 237, 265, 270, 324
Current Literature, 245, 247, 250, 278
Curtis, Cyrus H., 351–52
Curtis, George William, 209, 233, 264
Cuyler, Theodore L., 209

Dahlgren, Madeleine Vinton, 234
Dall, Caroline, 125, 200
D'Almeida, Joseph-Charles, 65–66
Daly, Augustin, 184, 222–23, 283, 286
Dana, Richard Henry, 56
Daudet, Alphonse, 298
Davis, Bessie McCoy (RHD's daughter-in-law), 390–91, 392, 395, 396, 400–401
Davis, Cecil Clark (RHD's daughter-in-law), 244, 305, 338, 344, 349, 361, 373, 403–4
   Career as an artist, 334, 350
   Divorce, 393–94, 395, 396, 400
   Marriage, 333, 334–36, 391–92, 393, 401–2
   Relationship with RHD, 334, 379, 391, 394, 395
   Travels, 338, 341, 351, 367, 370, 376, 383, 392–93, 394
Davis, Charles Belmont (RHD's son), 3, 373, 374, 389, 391, 400–402
   American Consul to Florence, Italy, 9, 284, 290–91, 294, 296, 298, 304, 307, 311, 312, 319, 321, 322
   Early life, 99–100, 102, 105, 106, 109, 110, 117, 120, 131, 139–40, 148, 171, 182, 183
   Education, 139, 187, 204, 216, 222, 229, 230, 238
   Financial manager, 252, 326–27, 350, 376, 383, 389, 392
   Health, 102, 105, 131, 332, 379
   High society member, 328, 389, 405
   Journalism career, 266–67, 277, 287–88, 295, 382
   Literature career: Author, 255, 272, 278, 279–80, 283, 284, 288, 291–92, 293, 296, 330, 332, 350, 362, 365, 366, 369, 376, 382, 384, 386, 388–89, 390, 394, 404, 406; Editor, 349, 350, 376–77, 388, 404–5, 406, 407 (*see also* Davis, Charles Belmont, theater career: Editor of plays); Inheritor of mother's talents, 272, 330, 366, 404
   Literary style, 238, 272, 291–92, 294, 303, 351, 390
   Marriage to Dai Turgeon, 405–6
   Motion pictures career, 270, 399–400, 406
   Relationship with his siblings, 99, 157, 187, 197, 198, 204, 222, 267, 276, 282, 283, 290, 291, 294, 298, 305, 326–27, 328, 332, 334, 338, 350, 376, 379, 383, 389, 392, 394, 396, 400, 402–3, 404, 408–9
   Relationship with the Clevelands, 266, 268, 274, 281, 283, 287–88, 290–91, 301
   Residences, 266, 322
   Theater career, 252, 379–80, 392, 405, 407; Editor of plays, 317, 321–22, 340, 377; Manager of Weber and Fields, 338, 341, 350–51, 363; Shaped by parents, 139–40, 150, 183, 198, 283, 322, 384; Theatrical reviewer for *New-York Tribune*, 322, 407
Davis, Charles Belmont, works of
Adventures and Letters of Richard Harding Davis, 407
"American Pantomime Season, The," 350
Borderland of Society, The, 330, 332, 340
"Charmichael's Christmas Spirit," 388–89
"City of Homes," 298
"Coccaro the Clown," 382
"Conquerers, The," 395
"Cost of Transporting Big Shows, The," 392
"Countess Veschi's Jewels," 406
"Few Stray Thoughts on Ocean Travel, A," 361
"Freak's Midsummer Night's Dream, A," 283
"Friend of the Family, A," 278, 279
"Great Sympathetic Strike, The," 296
Her Own Sort, and Others, 405
In Another Moment, 405
"La Gommeuse," 316, 318
"Last Chance, The," 272
Lodger Overhead and Other Stories, The, 394
"Miss Marr's Lovers," 365
"Mother O' Mine," 406
Nothing a Year, 407
Octopus, The, 404, 406
"Out of Her Class," 291, 294
"Rise of the Dancing Girl, The," 288
Stage Door, The, 390
Tales of the Town, 405

"Vaudeville Club, The," 283
Woman's Business, A, 407
Davis, Charles (Clarke's brother), 99
Davis, Dai Turgeon (RHD's daughter-in-law), 334, 401–2, 405–6
Davis, David (Clarke's father), 71
Davis, Edward, 75
Davis Family fame, 3, 236, 239, 255, 262, 265, 278, 279, 280, 284, 293, 300–301, 302, 318, 330, 332, 336, 340, 362–63, 381–82, 386, 390, 401, 407
Davis, Hope (RHD's granddaughter), 400–401, 402, 407
Davis, Jefferson, 37
Davis, L. Clarke (RHD's husband), 2, 3, 32–33, 40, 59, 66–67, 68, 70, 74, 80, 83, 86–87, 88, 105, 131–32, 139, 144–45, 153, 219, 225, 227, 228, 229, 236, 237, 238, 239, 262, 264, 267, 273, 275, 305–6, 311–12, 316, 334, 336, 343, 373–74
  Aids RHD's career, 78, 107, 109, 113, 114, 116, 126, 212
  Career aided by RHD, 117–18, 120–21, 126, 136, 192, 212, 260, 347, 369
  Club activities, 160, 177, 180, 220–21, 256, 322, 349
  Collaborative projects with RHD, 89, 133, 142–43, 224
  Early years, 70–72
  Health, 85, 96, 102, 108–9, 114, 280, 301, 312, 317, 322, 328, 346, 358, 359, 367, 368, 373; Depression, 152, 201, 275–76, 295, 328
  Influence on sons' interest in theater, 139–40, 150, 183, 198, 247, 283
  Journalism career, 42–43, 71–72, 89, 133–34, 136, 138, 139, 141, 177, 180, 240–41, 250, 272, 295, 326, 349, 355, 357; Reputation as editor, 9, 136, 204, 237, 241, 275, 281, 286, 288–89, 292, 295, 373–74
  Lawyer, 71–72, 89, 100, 116–17, 136
  Literary career, 42–43, 123, 126, 136, 160, 206–7, 222, 260
  Politics, 40, 184, 206, 214, 224, 226, 246, 310: On war, 81, 88, 94, 273, 306, 307, 323; Relationship with Benjamin Harris, 258, 281; Relationship with Grover Cleveland, 200, 226, 227, 240–41, 245, 263, 265–66, 270, 280, 281, 283, 286, 288–89, 292, 302, 357, 359–60, 365; Relationship with James G. Blaine, 180–81, 196–97, 200, 206, 226, 258, 274–75; Relationship with Theodore Roosevelt, 357, 359–60, 363–64, 365–66; Relationship with William McKinley, 310, 311, 323
  Theater critic/supporter, 99, 110, 117, 160, 192, 198, 200, 220, 222–23, 250, 255, 268, 283, 286, 322, 375
Davis, L. Clarke, works of
  "Among the Comedians," 117
  "At and After the Play," 200
  "Dick Lyle's Fees," 136, 206–7
  "Different Points of View," 347–48
  "Gossip About Actors," 160
  "Joe Jefferson in London," 192
  "Modern Lettre de Cache, A," 129–30, 142
  "Play and an Actor, A," 268
  "Queen of Burlesque, The," 206–7
  Stranded Ship, The, 136–37, 206–7
  "With Stick and Thread," 260
  "Wreck on the Shore, The," 127
Davis (Farrar), Nora (RHD's daughter), 3, 244, 284, 306, 313, 345, 374, 383, 385, 386, 389, 390, 391, 403–4
  Early life, 157, 158, 183
  Education, 204, 223, 407–8
  Health, 166, 179, 204, 317, 338, 380
  Marriage to F. Percival Farrar, 275, 407–10
  Relationship with her siblings, 157, 281, 282, 295–96, 304, 305, 328, 330, 389, 394, 402–3, 408–9
  Relationship with the Clevelands, 266, 281, 301, 365
  Socialite, 9, 255, 266, 268, 277, 286, 291, 293, 312, 318–19, 328, 330, 353, 379, 389, 408
  Strength in crises, 374, 383, 394, 395, 407, 408–10
Davis, Maria, 75
Davis, Rebecca Harding
  Adulthood in Wheeling, 22–72

Davis, Rebecca Harding (*continued*)
  Aid to family members' careers, 89, 116, 117–18, 212, 237, 258, 267: Access to periodicals, 117, 120–21, 126, 136, 192, 236, 237, 261–62, 264–65, 272, 278, 280, 332, 347–48, 365; Critique/editing of manuscripts, 236, 252, 261, 267, 282, 286, 291–92, 294, 302, 316, 377, 384, 390–91
  Authorial pseudonyms: "Author of 'Life in the Iron-Mills,'" 107; "Author of *Margret Howth*," 63, 107–8, 138; "Author of 'The Second Life,'" 68, 107, 138, 206, 223, 224, 236, 264; "New Contributor," 46; "R.H.D.," 229
  Career aided by L. Clarke Davis, 78, 107, 109, 113, 114, 116, 126, 212
  Cult of celebrity, opposition to, 3, 242, 245, 248, 253, 280, 288, 317, 342, 346, 348
  Early years, 14–18, 340
  Editorial work in magazines: *Century Illustrated Magazine*, 320, 359; *Independent*, 172, 248–49, 255, 293, 381; *Lippincott's*, 197, 205, 209–10; *Saturday Evening Post*, 352, 356–57, 359, 360, 363, 366, 367; *Scribner's Monthly*, 192–93; *Youth's Companion*, 253–54, 283, 289, 293. See also Davis, Rebecca Harding: Journalism career
  Education, 17, 18–22, 24
  English publication, 41, 61, 64–65, 92, 127, 178, 189–90, 277, 313, 338, 382
  Financial management, 83, 92, 304, 305, 315, 317, 374, 397
  Health, 82–83, 85–86, 104, 117, 120, 204, 238, 283–84, 387, 388, 393, 394, 396–97: Eye problems, 378–79, 381, 386–87, 389, 394–95; Love of walking, 19, 82–83, 86, 320, 387, 388, 394
  High society, member of, 1, 75, 104, 136, 286, 291, 319, 328, 362–63
  Interviews, 232, 245, 323–25, 328
  Journalism career, 139, 142, 205, 211–12, 230, 239, 309: *New-York Tribune*, 1, 133–134, 139, 145–46, 155, 158, 204, 210–11, 212, 219, 225–26, 239, 248, 300–301, 444n55; *New York World* 341–42, 344, 349, 366–67, 375, 378; Philadelphia *Press*, 1, 211, 233, 239; *Wheeling Intelligencer*, 25–28, 29
  Literary genres/styles: Book reviews for *Atlantic Monthly*, 64, 70, 83–84, 370; Book reviews (general), 89, 128, 331; Book reviews for *Saturday Evening Post*, 352, 361–62, 364, 367, 368, 370, 373, 375–76, 377, 378; Children's/Young Adult literature, 140–41, 147–48, 196, 230, 262–63, 281, 346 (see also *St. Nicholas*, *Youth's Companion*); Genre-blending, 90, 96, 109, 173, 207–8, 223, 239; Gothic/Ghost stories, 43, 151–52, 171–72, 235; Historical narratives, 141, 142, 148, 157, 158, 179, 181–82, 199–200, 202, 222, 232, 258, 273, 281, 317, 327, 343, 369, 370, 382, 390, 392–93 (*see also* Davis, Rebecca Harding, themes in the writing of: John Page stories); Mysteries, 43, 47–48, 91–92, 129, 138, 166, 386 (*see also* Davis, Rebecca Harding, themes in the writing of: John Page stories); Realism, 1, 97, 105, 109, 126, 142, 145, 156, 159, 173, 192, 206, 273–74, 313–15; Romance, 109, 132, 138, 145, 156, 177, 214, 222, 242, 297–98, 318, 387–88; Silhouettes, 222, 278–79, 358; Sketches, 94, 96, 101–2, 179, 215
  Marriage, 64, 66–67, 70–71, 72, 73–75, 78, 81, 82, 90, 131–32, 141, 203, 239, 242, 271, 374
  Motherhood, 84–85, 90, 99, 100, 104, 109, 113, 114–15, 131–32, 135, 155, 162, 166, 183, 256–57, 297, 383: Relationship with Charles, 131, 280, 282, 294, 308, 322, 364, 384, 387, 388, 389, 395; Relationship with Nora, 216–17, 238, 252, 295–96, 297, 313, 353, 380–82, 385, 394–95, 407–8; Relationship with Richard, 86–87, 131, 204, 216, 225, 235, 236–37, 259–60, 270, 277, 279, 282, 286, 287, 304, 306, 311, 312, 332–33, 346–47, 356, 377, 383–84, 386, 388, 395
  Nursing family members, 77–78, 102, 108–9, 247, 251, 275, 290, 292, 295–96, 297, 317, 328

On being a writer, 105, 107, 128, 141, 143
Pay for writings, 30, 45, 50, 63, 70, 78, 83, 97–98, 107–8, 111, 113–114, 115, 169, 178, 214, 217, 223, 224, 228, 252, 253, 267, 268–69, 274, 277, 298–300, 303, 305, 309, 315, 320, 323, 359, 452n39
Philanthropy/charitable work, 98, 141, 152–53, 155, 221, 227, 256
Photographs of, 44–45, 60–61, 245, 248, 298, 334, 414n55
Political alliances, 27, 102, 105, 147, 226, 328, 341–42
Relationships with editors/publishers, 43, 108, 298–99: Negotiations with, 39–40, 44–46, 47, 63, 78, 83, 92, 94–95, 101–2, 103, 108–10, 111–120, 121, 122–23, 248, 267–69, 274, 283, 299–300; Friendships, 50, 58, 78, 86, 88, 90, 92, 108, 114, 120, 126, 270
Religious affiliations/views, 18, 20, 32, 74–75, 123, 195, 212, 275, 373, 375, 385, 393, 413n49
Residences, 73, 88, 96, 106, 120, 136, 137, 139–40, 145, 215–16, 245, 270–71, 339
Salon for artists, 140, 184, 311, 322, 362–63
Servants, 22, 204–5, 296–97, 339, 394
Theater attendance/support of, 99, 110, 192, 198, 222–23, 250, 255, 307, 310, 322
Travels, 89, 169–70, 389, 506: Through the South, 199, 207, 225, 229, 239; To Bethlehem, PA, 197, 200; To Chicago World's Fair, 285–86; To Europe, 9, 192, 267, 268, 270, 272, 307–10, 380–82; To Marion, Massachusetts, 244–45, 252, 261–63, 270–71, 277–78, 287–89, 301–2, 305, 310, 319–20, 328, 347, 355, 361; To New England, 54–58; To New York City, 54–55, 58, 78, 200, 222–23, 255, 300–301; To North Carolina, 168–69, 201, 207–9; To Ocala, Florida, 312, 315, 332, 346, 349, 358; To Point Pleasant, New Jersey, 87–88, 94–96, 104–5, 120–21, 131–32, 137–38, 144–45, 150–51, 154, 168, 172, 181–82, 183, 192, 197, 201–2, 213, 215–16, 225, 239–40, 252, 260–61, 378, 386–87, 391, 396–97; To England/United Kingdom, 270, 307–8, 380–81; To Warm Springs, Virginia, 319–21, 328–29, 347, 355–56, 361, 363, 368, 378–79, 387, 390–91, 395; To Washington, D.C., 211, 212, 243, 283, 387; To Wheeling/Washington, PA, 78–79, 82, 84–85, 88, 89, 105–7, 158, 163–64
War opposition, 50–51, 57, 62–63, 327, 329, 331–32, 336–37. *See also* Davis, Rebecca Harding, themes in the writing of: War
Xenophobia, 251, 321, 322, 335, 380
Davis, Rebecca Harding, themes in the writing of, 87–88
Abolitionists, 28, 29, 47, 53, 66, 76, 185–86, 358, 372
African Americans, 88–89, 111, 260–61, 386: Mixed-race characters/people, 46, 49, 111, 122, 171, 212, 222, 257, 329–30; Progressive depictions, 112–13, 114, 160–61, 186–87, 194–95, 199, 207–8, 230–32, 240, 248–49, 257, 277, 320–21, 324–25, 342–43, 346, 349–50, 380; Racialized depictions, 96, 148–49, 214, 230–32, 277–78, 321, 324–25, 349–50; Slavery, 32, 62–63, 89, 186–87, 210, 246, 273, 321
Aging, 256–57, 314, 346, 368, 393
Anti-imperialism, 274, 310, 329, 331–32, 339
Asylums. *See* Davis, Rebecca Harding, themes in the writing of: Insanity/asylums
Autobiography, 49, 185–86, 205, 232, 259, 322, 340, 343, 352, 358, 359, 367. *See also* Davis, Rebecca Harding, works of: *Bits of Gossip*
"Blood" traditions in America, 49, 149, 156, 166, 277, 340
Capitalism, 31, 100, 126, 145, 156, 164–66, 259
Centennial celebration, 161, 179–80, 181–83, 184–85, 186
Charity, 187–88, 191, 196, 212, 219–20, 223, 226, 250–51, 289, 353
Chinese, 185, 214

Davis, Rebecca Harding, themes (*continued*)
Civil War, 32, 40, 53, 172, 185–86, 197, 199, 333–34, 336, 367, 371–72. *See also* Davis, Rebecca Harding, themes in the writing of: John Page stories
Class, 163, 167, 223: High society, 88, 149, 150, 196, 221, 241, 278, 298, 353, 358, 368; Middle class, 150–51, 273; Servant class, 149, 214; Working class, 29–30, 31–32, 33, 35–36, 149, 150, 186, 196, 199, 218–19, 224, 278, 346, 368
Con artists, 126, 127, 190–91, 213, 220, 352, 399
Convict labor. *See* Davis, Rebecca Harding, themes in the writing of: Prison reform/prisoners
Copyright laws, 151, 233–34, 243, 265, 268, 305–6
Crime. *See* Davis, Rebecca Harding, themes in the writing of: Prison reform/prisoners
Depression, 152, 243–44
Disabilities, 31, 46, 121, 156, 159, 217
Domestic woman, 134, 159–60, 168
Education, 182–83, 186–87, 199, 231–32, 235, 243–44, 257, 258, 277–78, 284, 309, 335–36
Ethnic representations, 140, 148, 163–64, 206, 214, 218–19, 232, 251, 269, 370, 378
Immigrants, 158, 209, 251, 260–61, 274, 300, 327, 380. *See also* Davis, Rebecca Harding, themes in the writing of: Xenophobia
Imperialism, opposition to, 274, 336–37
Insanity/asylums, 28, 129–31, 133, 142–43, 166, 176, 224, 353
John Page stories, 47–49, 83, 105, 126, 129, 157, 194–95, 199, 209
Journalism, 142, 145, 156, 163, 210–11, 217, 255, 356, 375
Labor. *See* Davis, Rebecca Harding, themes in the writing of: Class
Law, 31–32, 43, 189–92, 206, 337. *See also* Davis, Rebecca Harding, themes in the writing of: John Page stories
Marriage, 91, 126, 160, 163, 166, 170–71, 201, 206, 212, 234, 264, 368, 392–93
Mesmerism, 107, 213, 214
Motherhood, 170–71, 173, 251–52, 256–57, 289
Native Americans, 260: Progressive depictions, 151–52, 171–72, 173–76, 209–11, 214, 253, 258–59, 331, 342–43, 360, 362, 376; Racialized depictions, 96–97, 166, 170, 181, 259, 360
New England arrogance, 81, 88, 91–92, 200, 260, 370
New Jersey shore stories, 87, 92, 125–26, 145, 148, 173, 177–78, 184, 343
New Woman, the, 159–60, 191, 251–52, 291, 327, 349
North, the, 173, 222, 239–40, 248–49, 253, 257, 308–9, 320–21, 349–50, 372. *See also* Davis, Rebecca Harding, themes in the writing of: New England arrogance; Philadelphia stories
North Carolina stories, 169, 172, 173–76, 193, 198, 206, 207–9, 218, 247
Philadelphia stories, 179–80, 181–83, 184–85, 196, 228, 249, 255, 300, 314, 333–34
Physicians, 48, 82, 111, 148, 151–52, 159, 160–61, 168, 190, 197, 207–8, 221–22, 228, 308–9
Politics, 100–101, 164–66, 246, 369, 392: Support of Radical Republicans 100–101, 246
Prison reform/prisoners, 125, 146, 154, 155, 193, 196, 208, 223, 245–46, 360, 377, 440n11
Prostitution, 69, 353
Religion/religious sects, 32, 122, 134, 136, 139, 142, 143, 148, 150, 169–70, 176, 178, 181, 195–96, 209, 215, 225, 232, 243, 248, 249, 250–51, 275, 301, 322, 347–48, 353, 367, 377, 380, 399, 432n55
Science, 160, 364, 370
South, the, 43, 47, 60, 157, 167, 169, 194–95, 199–200, 207–8, 212, 221, 222, 230–32, 239–40, 249, 257, 288, 308–9, 372. *See also* Davis, Rebecca Harding, themes in the writing of: John Page stories; North Carolina stories; Virginia/West Virginia stories

Spiritualism, 107–8, 128, 129, 154, 190–91, 235–36
Tarrytown stories, 177–78, 222
Temperance, 95, 134–35, 138, 154, 170, 195, 273, 368
Thought transference, 107, 205
True womanhood. *See* Davis, Rebecca Harding, themes in the writing of: Domestic woman
Virginia/West Virginia stories, 125–26, 177, 185–86, 190, 195, 196, 199, 202, 207–9, 218–19, 262–63, 281, 318, 370. *See also* Davis, Rebecca Harding, themes in the writing of: John Page stories; Davis, Rebecca Harding, works of: "Life in the Iron-Mills;" *Margret Howth*
War: In fiction, 95, 100; In letters, 62–63, 80, 90–91, 94, 383–84; In nonfiction, 95, 307, 327, 329, 331–32, 333–34, 336–37, 343, 371–72
Wasted lives, 107, 163, 219, 257, 303
Woman artist, 162–63, 170–71
Women's rights/suffrage, 126, 135–36, 160, 168, 191
Work for women, 27, 126, 138–39, 141–42, 159–60, 163, 167–68, 193, 199, 212, 215, 217, 230, 246, 291, 314–15, 318, 327, 357, 384
Davis, Rebecca Harding, works of
"About the Painter of Little Penelope," 179
"Achill," 299–300, 301
"Across the Gulf," 213
"Aglae," 218
"Alien Brothers, The," 277
"Alsatian Hound, The," 88–89
"American Convents," 176
"American Family, An," 380
"Annie's Mother," 157
"As I Remember," 356
"As We Grow Old," 256–57
"Asylums for the Insane," 133
"At Bay," 121
"At Kittery," 221
"At Noon," 241
"At Our Gates," 250
"At the Foot of the Class," 309
"At the Races," 169
"At the Station," 247
"Balacchi Brothers," 156, 168, 224
"Barred Acres," 151–52
"Berrytown." *See* Davis, Rebecca Harding, works of: *Kitty's Choice*
"Best Fellow in the World," 166
"Best of Company, The," 356
"Between Man and Wife," 166
Bits of Gossip, 340, 343, 352, 359, 367, 368, 370–73
"Black North, The" 349–50
"Blind Tom," 61, 64–65, 92, 97
"Blot on The Great Man's Name, The," 358
"Bogey Man Banished, The," 360
"Boy Who Was Himself, The," 152
"Boy's Flight, A," 353
"Brand Left to Burn, A," 219
"Brave" ("Brave Dick"), 196
"Break in the Sand, The," 173
"By-Paths in the Mountains," 207–9
"Captain Jean," 138
"Captain's Story, The," 107–8, 109, 205
"Cave-Man, The," 363
"Charities of St. Matthew's, The," 196
"Charity's Secret," 138
"Cheating the Children," 358
"Chip," 169
"Christina," 214
"Clergyman's Wife, The," 91, 166
"Colonel's Venture, The," 199, 200
"Comedy in a Garden, A," 212
"Coming of the Night, The," 393
"Common Fault, A," 260
"Compensation," 149
"Conards, The," 199
"Conductor's Story, A," 151
"Country Girls in Town," 353–54
"Cured by Active Work," 244
"Curse of Education, The," 335–36
Dallas Galbraith, 124, 125–26, 127, 132, 192, 324
"David Conn and His Wife," 212
"David Evans' Christmas," 223
"David Gaunt," 52–53, 54, 61, 63, 92
"Daughter-in-Law, The," 126
"Day with Doctor Sarah, A," 198
"Deacon's Surprise, The," 148

Davis, Rebecca Harding, works (*continued*)
"Deaf and The Dumb, The." *See* Davis, Rebecca Harding, works of: *Margret Howth*
"Death of John Payne, The," 328–29
"Defeated," 241
"Despondency Cured," 243–44
"Disease of Money-Getting, The," 353
"Doctor Pajot," 190
Doctor Warrick's Daughters, 264, 273, 294, 304, 305, 308–9, 313, 346–47
"Doctor's Story, The," 160–61
"Doctor's Wife, The," 166–67
"Dolly," 169
"Dominque," 232
"Earthen Pitchers," 162–63
"Education of Bob, The," 318
"Effie," 177
"Elise," 158
"Elizabeth's Romance," 387–88
"Elizabeth's Thanksgiving," 306
"Elk Heights Tragedy, The," 224
"Ellen," 94–95, 96, 101
"Enchanted Prince," 162
"English Passion Play, An," 345
"Faded Leaf of History, A," 158
"Fire Opal, The," 209
"For Sale?" 264
"Forgotten Worthies," 232
"Fox and A Raven, A," 170
Frances Waldeaux, 312, 313–15, 324
"Friend Paul," 360
"From Door to Door," 241
"George Bedillion's Knight," 110
"George Frost's Madness," 169
"Gertrude," 154, 155
"Gilbert Stuart," 179
"Girls in Business," 384
"Glimpse of Philadelphia in July, 1776, A," 181
"Gossip on the Jersey Beach," 173
"Great Air-Engine, The," 78
"Great Kean Estate, The," 214
"Grumble, A," 281
"Gurneys, The." *See* Davis, Rebecca Harding, works of: "Paul Blecker"
"Hand to Hand," 141–42, 243
"Hard Tack," 148

"Hard Times for an Old Man," 358–59
"Harmonists, The," 94, 101–2
"He Did His Best," 186
"Here and There in the South," 239–40, 245, 320
"Herod," 178
"Heroine, A," 145
"Hetty Fanning," 169
"Hetty's Christmas Gift," 264
"High Tide of December, The," 100
"His Great Deed," 198
"Home Industries for Women," 217–18
"Homely Hints for Everyday," 395
"Homely Hints on Homely Occupations," 215
"Homely Story of Home, A," 139
"Homely Story of A Home, A," 206, 277
"House on the Beach, The," 177–78
"How Jack Went Tiger-Hunting," 149
"How the Widow Crossed the Line," 185–86
"How We Spent the Summer," 150–51, 166
"Human and Inhuman Books," 364
"Hundred Years Ago, A," 143
"Ignoble Martyr, An," 257
"In a Way She Knew Not," 273–74
"In an Inn," 223
"In Old Florence," 327
"In Proof of To-morrow," 329–30
"In Re Silas Rhawn," 200
"In St. Paul's Place," 228
"In the Chronicle Office," 156
"In the Dark," 107
"In the Debatable Lands," 367
"In the Gray Cabins of New England," 303
"'In the Market,'" 126
"In the Old Days," 392
"In the Ore," 259
"Indiscriminate Charity," 188, 191
"Ingenuity in Earning a Living," 357
"Inside Story of It, The," 369
"Is It All for Nothing?" 348
"Jack Graham," 154
"Jenny's Hero," 154, 155
John Andross, 100, 158, 162, 164–66, 190, 247

"John Copley," 215
"John Lamar," 46–47, 51, 56, 88, 92
"John Sorby," 222
"Kennairds, The," 242
Kent Hampden, 262–63, 264, 279, 281, 332, 414n62
Kitty's Choice, 159–60, 168, 170, 198, 273
"Knight and The Castle, The," 171
"La Barrone," 209
"Landry's Strange Story," 199
Law Unto Herself, A, 189–92, 419n53
"Ledoux Crevasse, The," 169
"Leonard Heath's Fortunes," 142, 168
"Leroy Gold Mine, The," 274
"Lesson from France, A," 363
"Life in the Iron-Mills," 1, 24, 29–30, 31–32, 33, 42, 43, 59, 61, 108, 112, 113, 121, 124, 142, 156, 250, 252, 263, 347, 377
"Life-Saving Station," 177–78
"Little Gossip, A," 343
"Little Street-Sweeper, The," 97
"Lois Platner," 136
"Longest Journey, The," 110
"Lord Kitchener's Methods," 345–46
"Losing Her Hold," 246
"Lost," 360
"Lost and Found," 148
"Lost Colony, A," 197–98
"Lost Estate, The," 85
"Love Story of Charlotte Bronte, The," 379
"Low Wages for Women," 246
"Luck of Abel Steadman, The," 94, 96–97, 101
"Madam Bourne," 163
"Mademoiselle Joan," 235, 236, 277
"Man in the Cage, The," 193
"Man in the Iron Mask, The," 359
"Man Who Came Back, The," 366
"Marcia," 178
Margret Howth, 33–34, 35–36, 39–40, 41, 42, 45–46, 50, 51–52, 55, 56, 61, 78, 92, 107, 121, 124, 128, 142, 159, 324, 418n28, 419n59
"Market for Art Work, A," 192–93
"Marty's Cabbage Crop," 212
"Mean Face of War, The," 336–37
"Men's Rights," 135, 163

"Mesmerism vs. Common Sense," 213, 214
"Messenger, The," 157
"Middle-Aged Woman, A," 368
"Missing Diamond, The," 91–92
"Modern Irishman, The," 274
"Modern Phyllis, The," 251–52
"Modest Naturalized Citizen, The," 260–61
"Mother and Baby," 173
"Mountain Shanty, The," 149, 156
"Mrs. Loper's Ambition," 273
"Murder in the Glen Ross, The," 46, 47
"My First Case," 49
"Natasqua," 145, 234–35
"Ned Moxon's Grievances," 250
"Needs of the Reservations," 258–59
"Negro's Ring, The," 170
"New National Trait, A," 253
"New Religious 'What Is It?'" 248
"New Traits for New Americans," 354
"New Year's Story, A," 91
"Newly Discovered Woman, The," 291
"Next Door," 214
"Nicholas Cleever's Money," 264
"Nicholas Harbour's Work," 195
"Night in the Mountains, A," 193
"November Afternoon, A," 141–42, 277
"November Night, The," 194–95
"Odd Corners of the Centennial," 184–85
"Old Black Teapot, The," 359, 360
"Old Lamps for New," 275
"Old Landmarks in Philadelphia," 181
"Old Legend, An," 258
"Old Philadelphia," 179
"Old-Time Hospitality," 374
"Old-Time Love Story, An," 392–93
"Old Time Political Campaigns," 392
"Olden Type of Woman and The New, The," 349
"On Sunday Afternoon," 215
"On the Jersey Shore," 343, 344
"On the Trapeze," 397
"On the Uplands," 353
"One or Two Plain Questions," 391
"One Woman's Question," 387
"One Week an Editor," 163
"Only Father," 209

Davis, Rebecca Harding, works (*continued*)
"Open Doors," 138–39, 142, 215
"Other Side, The," 152
"Our Creditors," 248
"Our National Vanities," 253
"Out of Sight," 277
"Out of the Sea," 92
"Outlook for the Boys, The," 298
"Passing of Niagara, The," 322
"Paul," 224
"Paul Blecker," 70, 74, 83, 121
"Pawned Watch, The," 235
"Peculiar People, A," 358
"Pepper-Pot Woman, The," 149, 166–67
"Phonz," 169
"Poem That Never Was Written, The," 219
"Polly's Venture," 257
"Porch Climbers, The," 363
"Pot of Gold," 152
"Pragues' Ambition, The," 245
"President-Making in Old Times," 317
"Presidential Campaigns of To-Day and Yesterday," 369
"Prisoners' Sunday," 245–46
"Promise of Dawn, The," 68–69, 70
"Put Out of the Way," 142–43
"Qualla," 173–76
"Quiet Half-Hour, A," 346
"Races at Shark Bay, The," 184
"Rage for Writing, The," 359
"Rainy Day, A," 215
"Rainy Day at the Exposition, A," 184–85
"Red Names for Red Men," 360–61
"Religion in the Days of Our Fathers," 380
"Reporter's Work, A," 255
"Return to the Soil, The," 351
"Rope of Sand, A," 358
"Rose of Carolina," 169
"Royal Procession, A," 337
"Saar Secret, The," 166
"School-Boy's Story, The," 186–87
"Second Life, The," 68, 419n54
"Secretary Schurz's Apology," 210–11
"Senor," 148
"Seventy-Seven," 196
"Shan Van Voght, The," 141
"Shelf of Idols, A," 366
"Silhouette, A," 222, 278
Silhouettes of American Life, 273, 277, 278–79, 281
"Slave in Algeria, The," 273
"Some Hobgoblins in Literature," 317, 318
"Some Modern Buccaneers," 352
"Some Old-Time Christmases," 374
"Some Significant Facts," 251
"Some Strange True Stories," 386
"Some Testimony in the Case," 230–32
"South Branch Farm, The," 206
"St. Matthew's and St. Mark's," 196
"Stolen Bond, The," 97–98, 100
"Stephen Yarrow," 83
"Stones of Power," 395
"Story of a Few Plain Women, The," 377–78
"Story of a Newspaper, The," 217, 230
"Story of a Shadow, A," 154
"Story of a Song, The," 87–88
"Story of Ann, The," 170
"Story of Christine, The," 105
"Story of Christmas Eve, The," 122
"Story of Hetty, The," 236
"Story of Life-Insurance, A," 318
"Story of the Plague, A," 199–200
"Story of To-Day, A." *See* Davis, Rebecca Harding, works of: "Life in the Iron-Mills"; *Margret Howth*
"A Strange True Story," 386
"Strawberry Girl, The," 179
"Success," 83
"Such Stuff As Dreams Are Made Of," 205
"Sunday in Limeburgh, A," 195
"Surprises of War, The," 329
"Swift's Comet," 160
"Taneo," 170
"Tembroke Legacy, The," 134, 154
"Temple of Fame, The," 342
"Text for a Sermon, A," 367
"Thanksgiving, A," 156
"Thanksgiving Story, A," 151
"That Akers Girl," 264
"Three Little Stories," 394
"Through Rough Ways," 157
"Tirar y Soult," 241, 288
"To Americans Seeking New Homes," 219

"Tom Gillette's Fortune," 156, 158
"Tom Hardy," 202
"Tragedy of Fauquier, The," 129
"True Story of Wolfenden, The," 171–72
"Two American Boys," 342–43
"Two Brave Boys," 396
"Two Hunted Men," 241
"Two Methods," 283
"Two Methods with the Negro," 324–25
"Two Points of View," 320–21
"Two Servants of the Republic," 333–34
"Two Women," 143, 150, 173
"Uncle Abel," 222
"Under the Old Code," 340
"Unfinished Page of History, An," 209–10
"Unhappy International Marriages," 368
"Unlighted Lamp, An," 347, 413n49
"Unpublished Tragedies," 386
"Unwritten History, An," 344
"University Extension in Canterbury," 284
"Unto the Least of These," 301
"Vacation Sketches Among the Alleghenies," 215
Waiting for the Verdict, 102, 103, 105, 107, 108, 109, 111–20, 121–22, 124–25, 127, 128, 161, 164, 174, 190, 192, 246, 263, 324, 430n1
"Wayside Episode, A," 221
"Weed in the Wheat, The," 226
"What About the Northern Negro?" 248
"What Did Not Happen," 289
"What Does It Mean?" 356
"What John Found," 230
"What We Can," 393
"When Is a Woman at Her Best?" 302
"White Peddler, The," 232
"Wife, Yet Not a Wife, A," 156
"Wife's Story, The," 85, 87, 91, 425n43
"Without Foundations," 289
"Woman's Message, A," 215
"Women and Patriotism," 327
"Women and Politics," 26–27, 31
"Women as Beekeepers," 230
"Women in Literature," 269–70
"Work Before Us, The," 331–32
"Yares of The Black Mountains, The," 172, 278

Davis, Richard Harding (RHD's son), 3, 256, 302, 306–7, 311, 346–47, 349, 357, 373, 374, 380, 383, 388, 389 391, 407
Cult of celebrity advocate, 3, 237, 247, 255
Divorce, 391–92, 393–94, 395, 396, 400. *See also* Davis, Richard Harding: Marriages
Early life, 85–87, 88, 94, 96, 100, 105, 106, 110, 120, 131, 139–40, 148, 150, 171, 182, 183–184
Editorial work, 220, 247, 264–65, 281–82, 290
Education, 139, 171, 187, 197, 198–99, 200, 202, 204, 209, 213, 215–16, 228, 229, 230, 235
Financial management, 252–53, 270, 282, 304, 317, 337
Health, 88, 96, 102, 247, 251, 294, 295–96, 328, 400: Depression, 217, 290, 292
Imperialism, 310, 316, 318, 329, 340–41, 455n20
Journalism career, 228–29, 230, 235, 236, 252, 257, 337: War correspondent, 282, 286, 311, 312, 315–16, 326, 338, 340–41, 347, 367, 400
Literary style, 261, 272, 279, 291–92, 294, 303, 351
Literary career, 213, 220, 225, 236–37, 247, 252, 255, 258, 267, 282, 287, 288, 298, 323, 337, 340, 349, 350, 356, 382, 389–90, 394, 400
Marriages, 306: To Bessie McCoy, 400, 401, 402; To Cecil Clark, 244, 333, 334–36. *See also* Davis, Hope; Davis, Richard Harding: Divorce
Model for Gibson Girl illustrations, 290
Motion pictures career, 270, 399–400
Political ambitions, 274, 284–85, 294
Relationship with his siblings, 157, 198, 204, 222, 272, 276, 282, 283, 284–85, 290, 294, 298, 302, 305, 326–27, 330, 338, 376, 389, 394, 396, 400, 408–9
Relationship with the Clevelands, 266, 268, 274, 281, 286, 294, 301
Residences, 252, 266, 337, 338, 344, 350, 361, 379
Satirized in magazines/newspapers, 279–80, 304, 311, 316, 319, 343, 366–67

Davis, Richard Harding, (*continued*)
 Theatrical productions/playwriting career, 256, 284, 341, 344, 350, 361, 367, 379: Influence of parents, 139–40, 183, 198
Davis, Richard Harding, works of
 Adventures of My Freshman Year, The, 225
 "American in Africa," 283
 "Boys in the Adariondacks," 213
 Captain Macklin, 356
 "Dictator, The," 367
 "Disreputable Mr. Raegen, The," 399–400
 Englishman in Paris, The, 286
 Gallagher and Other Stories, 261, 270, 319
 "Galloper, The," 379
 "Goddess in Mid-Air," 259–60
 "Hat and Its Inmate, The," 213
 "Her First Appearance," 326–27
 "His Bad Angel," 288
 "How Hefty Burke Got Even," 267
 "Inside Stories of Recent History," 350
 "Miss Civilization," 379
 "My Brother's Keeper," 386
 "Other Woman, The," 267, 284
 Ransom's Folly, 351
 Real Soldiers of Fortune, The, 382, 384
 "Romance of Hefty Burke, The," 399
 Rulers of the Mediterranean, 287
 Scarlet Car, The, 385, 386
 Soldiers of Fortune, 318, 344, 350, 455n20
 Three Gringos in Venezuela and Central America, 303, 310
 Van Bibber and Other Stories, 279, 319, 341
 Vera the Medium, 389–90, 392
 "Walk Up the Avenue, A," 261–62
 White Mice, 390, 394, 395
 With Both Armies in Africa, 341
Dean, Mary, 269
"Debby's Debut" (Alcott, L.M.), 81–82
DeForest, John, 108, 170
Deland, Margaret, 267, 324, 332, 378, 385
DeStaël, Germaine, 53
Dial, The, 309, 315
Dicey, Edward, 60, 79
Dickens, Charles, 64–65, 92, 128–29, 144, 422n131
Dickinson, Anna, 78, 126
Dickson, Cyrus, 23, 25, 32, 59, 60–61, 214
Dickson, Mrs. Cyrus, 60–61, 150
Doctor Johns (Mitchell, D.G.), 102
Dodge, Grace, 269
Dodge, Mary Abigail ("Gail Hamilton"), 56, 62, 82, 143, 194, 302
Dodge, Mary Mapes, 161, 169, 179, 233, 236, 243, 260, 276, 302, 327, 379
 Friendship with RHD, 162, 276
Dole, Sanford B., 323
"Done For" (Cooke), 232
Doran, John, 99
Dorr, Julia C. R., 234
Douglass, Frederick, 233, 321
Doyle, Arthur Conan, 305, 323
Dressler, Marie, 341
Drew, Georgiana, 171, 182, 215
Drew, John, 182, 184, 244, 283, 296–97, 306
Drew, Louisa Lane, 171, 182
Drexell, Anthony, 266, 295
Drexell, George W. Childs, 295, 355, 391
DuBois, W.E.B., 278, 320–21, 325, 349–50
du Chaillu, Paul Belloni, 149, 360
Duffey, Elizabeth Bisbee, 168
Dumas, Alexandre, 359
Dunbar, Paul Laurence, 350, 356
Dwight, Theodore, 155, 233
Dwight's Journal of Music, 65

Eakins, Thomas, 365
Eastman, Charles, 376
Edwards, Annie, 115, 429n90
Education of American Girls (Brackett), 168
Eggleston, Edward, 233, 247
Eight Cousins (Alcott, L.M.), 281
Elam, Charles, 134, 138, 159
Emerson, Edith, 57
Emerson, Lydia, 56–57, 79
Emerson, Ralph Waldo, 52, 57, 58, 66, 79, 82, 140, 343
Emily Chester (Seemuller), 89
Episcopalians, 18, 37, 33, 334
 See also Davis, Rebecca Harding, themes in the writing of: Religion/religious sects
Evans, Augusta, 354
Every Saturday, 163
Everybody's Magazine, 376
Evesson, Isabelle, 312

Farmer, Lydia Hoyt, 286
Farrar, Frederic William, 275, 376, 408
Farrar, F. Percival (Nora Davis's husband), 266, 275, 374, 376, 408–10
Faulkner, William, 48
Faust, Lotta, 362
Field, Kate, 56, 60, 61, 79, 102, 158, 189–90, 217
Fields and Osgood, 138, 140
Fields, Annie Adams, 39, 54, 64, 66–67, 70, 73, 85, 99, 117, 120, 181
    Discussions of friends/authors with RHD, 60, 61–62, 79, 80–82, 96, 104, 111, 128–129, 137–38, 144
    Discussions of war, 62–63, 80, 81, 88, 90–91
    Friendship with RHD, 50, 51, 55–56, 58, 59, 69, 77–78, 80, 86, 92–93, 97, 103, 105, 111, 123, 126, 143, 146, 153–54, 155–56, 162, 201–2
    Work for the *Atlantic Monthly*, 34, 74, 79, 80, 83–84, 102–3, 105
Fields, James T., 41, 44–45, 63, 66, 89, 92, 110, 128–29, 138, 140, 144, 146
    Friendship with RHD, 39, 50, 53, 55–56, 58, 62, 77–78, 79–80, 111, 123, 143, 153–54, 155–56, 162
    Negative responses to RHD's work, 33–34, 36, 69, 94–95, 101–2, 104, 122–23
    Positive responses to RHD's work, 29–30, 42, 61, 64–65, 85, 108
    Revision discussions, 39–40, 43, 54, 83–84
Fireside Teacher, 243–44
Flipper, Henry Ossian, 186–87
Flower-de-Luce (Longfellow), 111
Fool's Errand, A (Tourgee), 212, 239–40
Foote, Mary Hallock, 269
Ford, Daniel S., 147–48, 169, 173, 221, 372
Forrest, Edwin, 183–84, 286
Foster, Sarah Hanna, 18–19, 20, 167–68
Frank Leslie's Pleasant Hours, 305
Fraser, Margaret, 386
Frederic, Harold, 303, 316, 330, 356
Freeman, Mary E. Wilkins. *See* Wilkins (Freeman), Mary E.
Frémont, Jessie Benton, 53, 54–55, 56, 58–59, 62, 64, 65, 69, 70, 78, 100, 357, 372
Frémont, John C., 40, 53, 54, 58–59, 62, 78, 100, 357

Frémont, Lily, 54, 58
Friend's Intelligencer, 231, 250
Fuller, Margaret, 92, 309, 317
Furness, Horace Howard, 182, 205, 215, 235–36, 319, 396
Furness, William H., 318–19

Gage, Frances, 75–76
Galaxy, The, 102–3, 109, 110, 121, 123, 126, 133, 160, 163, 164, 229
    RHD's publications in, 105, 107, 110, 111–20, 141–42, 143, 154, 163
Gallitzin, Dimitri, 232
Gardner, Isabella Stewart, 267
Garfield, James A., 11, 200, 206, 212
Garland, Hamlin, 164, 280, 298, 356
Garrick, David, 160
Garsed v. Beall, 116–17
Gibson, Charles Dana, 244, 261, 266, 290, 301–2, 304, 305, 306, 332, 334, 379, 395
Gibson, Irene Langhorne, 302, 306, 379, 395
Gilder, Helena de Kay, 243
Gilder, Jeannette, 264, 305, 332
Gilder, Joseph, 305, 332
Gilder, Richard Watson, 166–67, 192, 206, 270, 288, 307–8, 313, 320
    Friendship with RHD, 166, 244–45, 270
Gladden, Washington, 195, 377
Glasgow, Ellen, 395
Godey's Lady's Magazine, 43, 51, 124, 132, 242–43
Golden Argosy, 230
Gompers, Samuel, 365
Good Company, 206
    RHD's publications in, 202, 206, 212
    See also *Sunday Afternoon*
Good Housekeeping, 248
Good Literature, 213–14
Gosse, Edmund, 233, 245, 305
Gow, Amy, 370
Gow, Emilie Mary Harding. *See* Harding (Gow), Emilie Mary
Gow, John L., Jr., 150, 200, 451n29
Grant, Ulysses S., 173, 180
Great South, The (King), 207–8, 239–40
Greeley, Horace, 27, 65, 133, 155, 158
Greenwood, Grace, 148, 158

Grew, Mary, 76, 141
Griffith Gaunt (Reade), 102

Hadden, Jane, 22
Haden, Francis Seymour, 219
Hale, Edward Everett, 82, 140, 148, 195, 200, 213, 247, 358
Hale, Lucretia, 178
Halstead, Murat, 253
Hamilton, Gail. *See* Dodge, Mary Abigail
Hammond, William A., 82
Handy, Moses Purnell, 1, 133, 211–12, 239, 300–301
Harding (Gow), Emilie Mary (RHD's sister), 16, 24, 82, 83, 88, 150, 200, 217, 275, 301, 319, 370, 373
Harding, Emily (RHD's aunt), 12, 16
Harding, Henry Grattan (RHD's brother), 16, 25, 26, 28, 89, 101, 144, 227, 424n39
Harding, Hugh ("Wilse") Wilson (RHD's brother), 14, 23, 24, 54, 77, 79, 94, 101, 105, 144, 197, 198–99, 204, 215, 216, 235, 281, 315, 370, 382–83
    Career in education, 24, 26, 101, 156–57, 169, 200–201, 319
Harding, Isabel Harris (RHD's grandmother), 12, 16
Harding, Rachel Leet (RHD's mother), 10, 11, 12–18, 25, 34, 38, 52, 85–86, 88, 89, 104, 158, 198, 204, 209, 217, 223, 227
Harding, Richard Harris (RHD's brother), 16, 25, 28, 38, 105, 202, 281, 315, 424n39
    Treason and imprisonment, 38–39, 40, 41, 49, 84
Harding, Richard William (RHD's father), 12–18, 22–23, 32, 38, 39, 52, 54, 84, 85, 89, 227, 251, 390
Harding, Thomas (RHD's grandfather), 12, 232
Harding, William (RHD's brother), 14
Harland, Marion, 243, 269, 324
Harper, Frances E. Watkins, 76
Harper and Brothers Publishing, 178, 262, 265, 290, 313, 382
Harper's Bazar, 241–42, 305
    RHD's publications in, 241, 305, 313–14, 327, 329, 331

Harper's New Monthly Magazine, 103, 121, 163, 178, 181, 247, 261, 283, 285, 287, 288, 298, 316, 318, 340
    RHD's publications in, 178, 179, 192, 193, 198, 199–200, 207–9, 222, 239–40, 250, 255, 257, 278, 284, 318, 340
Harper's Weekly, 3, 37, 193, 262, 265, 266, 276–77, 281–82, 283, 290
    RHD's publications in, 184–85
Harrington (O'Connor), 29
Harris, Joel Chandler, 217, 246, 288, 356
Harrison, Benjamin, 11, 200, 246, 258
Harrison, George Leib, 85, 193
Harrison, Lucretia Mitchell, 85, 193
Harrison, William Henry, 202
Harte, Bret, 161, 247, 356
Hartford Courant, 151, 297–98
Hassard, John R. G., 155, 301
Hawthorne, Julian, 170, 217, 233, 280, 335
Hawthorne, Nathaniel, 29, 32–33, 35, 44, 50, 55, 56–58, 62, 67, 81, 86, 137, 225, 343
Hawthorne, Rose, 55
Hawthorne, Sophia, 55, 56–57, 60, 62, 420n83
Hay, John, 155, 243, 301, 349
Hayes, Rutherford B., 181, 200, 206, 210
Hayne, Paul Hamilton, 127–28, 142
Hearst, William Randolph, 298, 404
Hearth and Home, 134, 141, 161, 229
    RHD's publications in, 134, 138–39, 149, 151, 157, 215
Hennessey, William John, 107, 115
Henry, O., 369
Higginson, Ella, 280
Higginson, Thomas Wentworth, 233, 243, 280, 305
"Highest Type of Girl, The" (Howe, J.W.), 349
Hilliard, Robert, 326–27
Holland, Josiah Gilbert, 145, 158, 162, 166, 167, 219–20, 236, 247
    Friendship with RHD, 158–59, 372
Holloway, Laura C., 247–48
Holmes, Amelia, 55
Holmes, Oliver Wendell, 29, 44, 50, 55, 56, 57, 58, 60, 138, 203, 216, 243, 248, 257, 267, 343
Holt, Hamilton, 337

Hope, Anthony, 323
Hopkins, Pauline, 149
Hopper, DeWolf, 252, 341
"Hospital Sketches" (Alcott, L.M.), 80–81
Hours at Home, 145, 158
House and Home Papers (Stowe), 97
House of Mirth, The (Wharton), 273
How the Other Half Lives (Riis), 257
Howe, Julia Ward, 168, 203, 267, 269, 302, 349, 398
Howe, Mark De Wolfe, 216
Howells, William Dean, 135, 146, 158, 192, 193, 202–3, 230, 232, 233, 243, 247, 265, 267
H. S. Stone Publishing, 330
Hugh Wynne (Mitchell, S.W.), 281
Humphrey Ward, Mrs., 361
Huntingdon Journal, 164
Hutchinson, Nellie, 225

Ibsen, Henrik, 322
Independent, 132, 172, 195, 209, 217, 224, 246, 267, 268–69, 272, 274, 283, 299–300, 312, 320, 335, 347, 354
  Editorial responses to RHD's publications, 250, 331–32, 334, 337, 346
  RHD's publications in, 150, 186, 199, 209, 214, 217, 218, 222, 224, 230, 243, 246, 248, 250, 251, 255, 260–61, 269–70, 275, 291, 298, 300, 322, 324–25, 328–29, 331–32, 333–34, 336–37, 342–43, 344, 345, 346, 347, 348, 349, 353–54, 356, 357, 359, 360, 364, 368–69, 370, 378, 379, 380, 381, 387, 388, 392
Indian Boyhood (Eastman), 376
Inter-Ocean, 278, 310
Interior, RHD's publications in, 368

Jackson, Carlisle, 34
Jackson, Helen Hunt, 209, 210, 211, 440n20
Jackson, Stonewall, 53
James, Alice, 3
James, Henry, 3, 108, 121–22, 126, 164, 192, 232, 243, 244, 273, 330
James, William, 3, 107, 205
Jefferson, Charles, 244, 280
Jefferson, Joseph, 117, 182, 183, 184, 192, 200, 229, 244, 252
Jewett, Sarah Orne, 195, 200, 269, 378
Joaquin et.al. (Miller), 137–38
Johnson, Andrew, 102, 105
Johnston, Mary, 355, 395
Jones, Henry Arthur, 268
Journal of Medicine and Science, 353
Jungle, The (Sinclair), 164

Kean, Edmund, 160, 184, 283
Kilmer, Joyce, 406
King, Edward, 207–8, 239
Kipling, Rudyard, 323, 341, 393
Kirk, John Foster, 129
Kirkbride, Thomas Story, 130, 133
Kitchener, Lord, 331–32, 341, 345–46

La Flesche, Francis, 342–43, 362
La Flesche, Suzette (Inshata Theumba), 209–10, 211, 331, 362
Ladies' Home Journal, 245, 329, 340, 351, 392
  RHD's publications in, 285, 302, 327–28, 377–78, 392
Lambdin, A.C., 355
Lambdin, George, 181
Lancaster Intelligencer, 125
Larcom, Lucy, 140, 161, 346
Law Reports, 42, 71–72
Lee, Robert E., 40, 77, 82, 90
Legal Intelligencer, 42, 71–72, 89, 117
Lehigh Burr, 220, 222, 225, 229
Leet, Isaac, 10
Leet, Margaret (RHD's aunt), 11
Leet, Rebecca Vahan, 10
Leland, Charles Godfrey, 41–42, 52, 309
Leland, Emily Hewitt, 221
LeMoyne, F. Julius, 18, 20–22, 29, 111, 215, 358
LeMoyne (Reed), Madelaine, 215
Lewis, Sinclair, 388
Life of Dean Farrar, 376
Life Magazine, 234–35, 279–80, 319
Life Stories of Undistinguished Americans, The (Holt), 380
Lili'uokalani, Queen, 323

Lilly, Alice Selby, 394
Lincoln, Abraham, 29, 35, 37, 40, 88, 91, 99, 365, 367
Lippincott, J.B., 233
Lippincott's New Monthly Magazine, 121, 127, 129, 136, 163, 178, 392
  RHD's publications in, 125–26, 142, 156, 159–60, 172, 173–74, 177–78, 181, 185–86, 189–92, 197–98, 199, 200, 205, 213, 221
Literary criticism/trends, 126, 206–7, 265, 290, 298–99
  Canonizing of American literature, 221, 245, 247, 250, 263, 265, 318, 345–46, 376
  Cheap book series, 234–35, 288, 351
  Civil War/Reconstruction themes, 170, 172, 179, 328
  Honoring male authors, 193–94, 202–3
  Increased publisher control over authors' works, 305–6
  Modernism, 278–79
  Women authors' collective articles, 234, 285, 302, 364
Literary Digest, 335
Literary World, 158, 231–32, 233, 279, 284, 308, 315
"Little Money of Her Own, A" (Leland, E.H.), 221
Littlest Girl, The (Hilliard), 327
Livermore, Mary, 269
London, Jack, 368
London *Mail*, 241
London Times, 323
Long, John D., 210
Longfellow, Henry Wadsworth, 44, 52, 58, 66, 111
Lorimar, George Horace, 351–52, 356
Loring, Alonzo, 28
Love, Albert, 307
Lovejoy, Elijah, 65
Lowell, James Russell, 76, 233
Lowell, Josephine Shaw, 188–89, 191

Macmillan's Magazine, 41
Mail and Express, 300–301, 310
"Man Without a Country, The" (Hale), 82
Manchester Times, 178

Mann, William d'Alton, 369
Marden, Orison Swett, 349
Marlowe, Julia, 250
Martineau, Harriet, 1, 301, 309
Massachusetts Ploughman, RHD's publications in, 151, 158
Matthers, Brander, 224
May, Sophie (Rebecca Sophia Clarke), 158
McCarthy, Justin, 298, 303
McClellan, George B., 35
McClure, Alexander K., 228, 229
McClure's, 298
McDermot, John F., 25
McGirt, James E., 380
McKean, William, 272
McKinley, William, 292, 310, 312, 316, 321, 323, 348
McMichael, Morton, 242
McMichael, Morton, Jr., 242–43, 247
McVeigh, Wayne, 298
Medical and Surgical Reporter, 112
Merrill, William Bradford, 368
Methodists, 18, 259, 413n49
Metropolitan Magazine, 365, 405
  RHD's publication in, 365
Middle Five, The (La Flesche, F.), 342–43, 362
Middleman, The (Jones), 268
Miles, Nelson A., 363–64
Miller, Joaquin, 137–38
Mitchell, Donald G., 102, 161, 217
Mitchell, S. Weir, 82, 85, 104, 105–6, 205, 235–36, 281, 298
Modjeska, Helena, 237
Moffett, Samuel E., 367–68
More Letters of Jayne Welsh Carlyle, 364
Mormons, 136
Moravians, 169–70, 212, 232
Morton, Levi P., 212
Mott, Lucretia, 75–76, 112, 205
Mott, Marianna Pelham, 75, 102
Mott, Thomas, 75, 102, 205
Moulton, Charles Wells, 346
Moulton, Louise Chandler, 148, 170
Munsey, Frank, 289
Munsey's, 377
Murfree, Mary, 269

Nathan, George Jean, 405
Nation, The, 121, 122, 192, 354
National Exhibition Souvenir, The, 285–86
National Magazine, 350
Native Americans, 10, 209–11, 331
  See also Davis, Rebecca Harding, themes in the writing of
Negro Problem, The (DuBois), 278
Neilson, Adelaide, 160, 183
Nesbitt, Evelyn, 244
Nevin, Anne, 304
Nevin, Ethelbert, 304
New-Hampshire Patriot, 151
New International Yearbook, 399
New Peterson's Magazine, 280, 283, 284, 288
  RHD's publications in, 281, 289
New York Evening Sun, 252, 257, 261, 265, 266, 267, 272
New York Freeman, 232
New York Herald, 323, 326, 340–41
New York Journal, 312, 316
New York Times, 378, 379, 406
New-York Tribune, 1, 27, 71, 141, 158, 164, 166, 189, 200, 211, 219, 239, 254, 347, 373, 382, 388, 397–98, 400, 405
  RHD's publications in, 133, 139, 142, 155, 167–68, 182–83, 187–89, 196, 206, 210–11, 214, 225–26, 386
  See also Davis, Rebecca Harding: Journalism career
New York World, 1, 264, 266–67, 277, 279, 287–88, 295, 341–42
  RHD's publications in, 341–42, 344, 349, 367–68, 375, 378, 379
Nightingale, Florence, 398
No Sex in Education (Duffey), 168
Norris, Frank, 356, 358
North American, 241, 242
North American Review, 42, 51, 83, 249, 253, 335–36
Norton, Charles Eliot, 42, 83,
Norwood (Beecher, H.W.), 126
Noyes, George, 151

Ochs, Adolph, 355
O'Connor, William Douglas, 29, 372
Olcott, Henry Steel, 105, 182

Old Chester Tales (Deland), 332
Omaha Indians, 25
Oo-mah-hah Ta-wah-thah, 362
O'Shea, John J., 300
Osler, William, 82, 227, 408
Ouida (Maria Louise Ramé), 138, 233
Our Continent, 212, 217
  RHD's publication in, 217
Our Young Folks, 140, 152, 161
  RHD's publications in, 140–41, 152
Outing, 361, 362, 377
Outlook, 315, 354
  RHD's publication in, 354
"Outside Glimpses of English Poverty" (Hawthorne, N.), 81

Page Act of 1875, 185
Page, Thomas Nelson, 288, 316
Paine, Albert Bigelow, 332
Pan-Republic Congress, 273
Pattison, Robert E., 266, 273
Payne, William Morton, 315
Peabody, Elizabeth Palmer, 57, 60, 61–62, 67
People of the Abyss, The (London), 368
Pepper, William, 221, 227, 235–36
Perkins, E. T., 37
Peterson, Charles J., 43, 47, 89, 136, 238
  Friendship with RHD, 75, 78, 79, 126, 195, 372
Peterson, Elizabeth, 75, 78, 79, 86, 88, 89
Peterson, Sarah, 242, 280
Peterson's Magazine, 42–43, 52, 63–64, 97–98, 107, 110, 140, 142, 242–43, 280
  RHD's publications in, 43–44, 46, 47–48, 83, 85, 87, 88–89, 91–92, 94–95, 97, 100, 104, 105, 121, 129, 136, 139, 142–43, 145, 148, 149, 150, 152, 156, 158, 163, 166, 169, 177, 192, 194–95, 199, 200, 202, 209, 212, 213, 215, 217, 219, 221, 223, 224, 228, 230, 241, 242, 243, 255
  See also New Peterson's Magazine
Pfaelzer, Jean, 1
Phelps, Austin, 105
Phelps (Ward), Elizabeth Stuart, 105, 121, 140, 156, 194, 200, 213, 233, 267–68, 269, 285, 346

Philadelphia *Evening Bulletin*, 111–12, 132, 135
Philadelphia *Evening Telegraph*, 139, 272
Philadelphia *Inquirer*, 2, 133, 138, 139, 164, 184, 197, 200, 217, 228, 241, 255, 256, 272, 285, 286, 288, 309, 311, 316, 319, 326, 328, 408
Philadelphia Medical Times, 221
Philadelphia Negro, The (DuBois), 278
Philadelphia *Press*, 1, 211–12, 230, 237, 239, 310
Philadelphia *Record*, 235, 236
Philadelphia *Times*, 211, 228, 355
Phillips, David Graham, 265
Phillips, Wendell, 76
Physician's Problems, A (Elam), 134, 138
Pierce, Charles Caleb, 367
Pinero, Arthur W., 322
Pit, The (Norris), 358
Poe, Edgar Allan, 317, 372
Portland Oregonian, 278, 314–15
Portrait of an Artist, The (James, H.), 273
Powell, John S., 104–5
Prescott, Harriet. *See* Spofford, Harriet Prescott
Prince and The Pauper, The (Twain), 281
Public Ledger, 2, 240–41, 246, 250, 256, 272, 273, 275, 280, 288–89, 292, 295, 312, 326, 341, 355, 365, 396, 408, 410
Pugh, Thomas Burnett, 153
Pulitzer, Joseph, 264, 298, 341
Putnam's Magazine, 135, 136, 141, 145, 206–7, 390
  RHD's publication in, 135

Quakers, 32, 75–76, 139, 141, 158, 161, 181, 232, 249–50, 367, 394

Rab and His Friends (Brown, Dr.), 44
Ramsay, Milne, 181
Reade, Charles, 102
Reader, The, 95, 377
Rebecca of Sunnybrook Farm (Wiggins), 378
Red Book, 362
Reed, Alexander, 18

Rehan, Ada, 184, 222–23, 283, 286
Reid, Whitelaw, 158, 219, 248, 391, 408
Religio-Philosophical Journal, 107
Remington, Frederick, 312
Reno Evening Gazette, 246
Repplier, Agnes, 298, 324
Reynolds, Paul, 338
R. H. Russell Publishing, 317, 321–22, 327
Rhys, Grace, 361
Richmond *Dispatch*, 328
Riis, Jacob, 257, 377
Ripley, George, 56, 158
Ripley, Sophia, 56
Rivals, The (Sheridan), 53
Riverside Magazine for Young People, 141
  RHD's publications in, 141, 143
Robert Elsmere (Ward, M.A.), 249
Robertson, Harrison, 288
Rockefeller, John D., 189
Romance, 297–98, 451n16
"Romeo and Juliet" (Shakespeare), 25, 250
Roosevelt, Theodore, 348, 357, 363–64, 365–66, 369, 370
Rose, Jane Atteridge, 1
Rosecrans, William S., 37, 40, 53
Rossell, David, 111
Rostand, Edmond, 322
Round Table, The, 124, 125, 130
Ruff, Margaret, 182
Runkle, Lucia Calhoun, 155, 225, 301, 309
Russell, Lillian, 341, 364
Russo-Japanese War, 367

Sackville-West, Lionel, 214
Saint-Gaudens, Augustus, 244
Salvini, Tommaso, 220
San Francisco Call, 308–9, 400
Sanborn, Kate, 158
Sangster, Margaret, 305
Saturday Evening Post, 342, 351–52, 356, 365, 390, 400
  RHD's publications in, 135, 356–57, 358, 360–62, 364, 366, 367, 368, 369, 372, 374, 375, 377, 378, 379, 380, 381
Scribner, Charles, 224, 247
  See also Charles Scribner Publishing

Scribner's Magazine, 247, 316, 330, 340, 341, 400, 405
  RHD's publications in, 247, 343, 393
Scribner's Monthly Magazine, 145, 158, 162, 163, 164, 178, 192, 206, 229, 247, 261, 267, 299
  RHD's publications in, 145, 149, 162–63, 166, 168–69, 181, 192, 195, 206, 241
Scudder, Horace Elisha, 141, 195, 258
Schurz, Carl, 210–11
Seemuller, Anne M., 89
Seger, Louise Godey, 242
Seward, William H., 33
Sex and Education (Howe), 168
Sex in Education (Clarke, E.), 168
Seybert, Henry, 235
Shaeffer, Helen Woodward, 1
Shanly, Charles Dawson, 73
Shaw, Francis George, 59
Shaw, Robert Gould, 59, 244
Shaw, Sarah Blake Sturgis, 59
Sheldon & Company, 119, 120, 121, 124, 141
Sheppard, Elizabeth Sara, 60
Sheridan, Richard Brinsley, 53
Siddons, Sarah, 160
Simms, William Gilmore, 125
Sinclair, Upton, 164
Smart Set, 362, 366, 369, 405
  RHD's publication in, 369
Smith, Lloyd P., 125, 129
Smyth, Albert Henry, 250
Social Salvation (Gladden), 377
Sordello (Browning), 83–84
"Southern Sketches" (Warner), 239
Spanish-American War, 306, 323, 326, 329, 336–37, 339, 357
Spectator, The, 373
Spencer, Herbert, 189
Spiritualism. *See* Davis, Rebecca Harding, themes in the writing of
Spofford, Harriet Prescott, 56, 102, 109, 173, 194, 213, 246, 285, 305, 324
Spoil of Office, A (Garland), 164
Sport of the Gods, The (Dunbar), 350
St. Nicholas, 140, 152, 161, 236, 252, 260, 276, 332, 379
  RHD's publications in, 162, 163, 169, 170, 171, 178, 179, 327, 329, 379, 381, 382, 388, 392, 393, 394, 395, 396
Stage, The, 247
Standing Bear, 210–11
Stanton, Elizabeth Cady, 135, 200
Starr, Louis, 179, 268, 290
Stedman, Edmund Clarence, 135, 158
Stevens, Thaddeus, 100
Stevenson, Robert Louis, 243, 370
Still, William, 76
Stockton, Frank R., 71, 215
Stoddard, Elizabeth, 135
Stone, Lucy, 234, 269
Stories of the South, 288
"Story of a Masterpiece" (James, H.), 243
Story of the Guard, The (Frémont, J.B.), 70
Stowe, Harriet Beecher, 97, 122, 134, 148, 194, 217, 239–40, 281, 346
Success Magazine, 349
  RHD's publications in 349, 351, 353, 368, 377
Sullivan, Margaret, 301
Sunday Afternoon, 195, 200
  RHD's publications in, 195, 196, 199, 200
  See also *Good Company*
Sunday School Teacher, 112
Sumner, Charles, 65
Sweeney, Sarah, 19
Swell Set, 303, 405

Tanner, Benjamin, 321
Tarbell, Ida, 1, 239
Taylor, Bayard, 224
Terry, Ellen, 306–7
Thanet, Octave, 200, 302
Thaxter, Celia, 56, 60, 161, 319
"*Their Majesties' Servants*" (Doran), 99
Thomas, Augustus, 322, 344
Thomas, Edith, 309
Thoreau, Henry David, 79
Thurston, William W., 216, 235
Ticknor and Fields, 32, 36, 44, 54, 64, 79, 107
Ticknor, George, 58, 63
Ticknor, William, 86
Tilton, Theodore, 172

Tolstoy, Leo, 398
Tourgee, Albion, 212, 217, 239–40
Town and Country, 362–63
Towne, Charles Hanson, 369
Traubel, Horace, 237
"Treasure of Franchard, The" (Stevenson), 243
Trollope, Anthony, 233
Trowbridge, John Townsend, 140
Twain, Mark, 243, 244, 281, 288, 379, 398
Turgeon, Dai. *See* Davis, Dai Turgeon
Turner, Elizabeth (Eliza) Randolph, 76, 394
Tutwiler, Julia R., 324–25, 328
Tyndal, John, 160

Uncle Tom's Cabin (Stowe), 25, 97, 112, 239–40, 281
Unitarians, 59, 249–50, 319
United States Gazette, 20
Uzanne, Octave, 370

Van Rensselaer, Marianna Schuyler, 244, 335–36
Vaughan, Father, 18

Wallace, Benjamin J., 79
Wallace, Sarah, 79–80
Ward, Mary A., 249
Ward, Susan Hayes, 299
Ward, William Hayes, 172, 214, 218, 248, 267–69, 274, 275, 299–300, 320
Warner, Charles Dudley, 161, 178, 239
Washington, Booker T., 321, 325, 342–43, 349–50
Washington Female Seminary, 18–22, 24, 167–68
See also Davis, Rebecca Harding: Education
Washington Herald, 398
Washington Times, 373, 400
Wasson, David Atwood, 42, 65, 79, 96
Watchman and Southron, 243
Webster, Daniel, 358
Welch, Margaret, 301

Wells, Carolyn, 319
Western Christian Advocate, 314
Wharton, Edith, 273, 324, 368, 373, 378
What Answer? (Dickinson), 126
Wheeler, "Fighting Joe," 355
Wheeling Intelligencer, 24, 25, 33, 34, 39, 44, 69, 72, 86, 133, 212
RHD's publications in, 26–27, 28, 196
See also Davis, Rebecca Harding: Journalism career
Wheeling Union, 33
Whipple, Edwin P., 55
White, Helen, 330
White, Stanford, 244, 256, 330, 383
Whitney, Adeline, 285
Whitman, Walt, 237, 317, 372
Whittier, John Greenleaf, 29, 52, 76, 178, 193, 194, 203, 246
Wiggins, Kate Douglas, 378
Wiggins, Thomas, 61, 65, 97
Wilcox, Ella Wheeler, 285
Wilde, Oscar, 217
Wilder (Bowden), Clara, 298
Wilkins (Freeman), Mary E., 269, 287, 302, 303, 323, 324
Willard, Frances, 194, 250, 269, 327–28, 372, 378
Willard, Mary, 378
Willetts, Gilson, 297
Wills, Charlotte LeMoyne, 19–20
Wilson (Baird), Clara (RHD's cousin), 20, 84, 97, 104, 108, 215, 375
Wilson, Edward Preble (RHD's cousin), 20
Wilson, Francis, 252
Wilson, Hugh W. (RHD's uncle), 10–11, 18, 20, 28, 33, 34, 38
Wilson, James Blaine (RHD's cousin), 20, 38
Wilson, James, Sr., (RHD's grandfather), 10, 12, 15
Wilson, Johnny, 346
Wilson, Margaret (RHD's grandmother), 10, 11
Wilson, Margaret Fleming, 11
Wilson, Rachel (RHD's aunt), 10–11
Wilson, Rachel Leet. *See* Harding, Rachel Leet (RHD's mother)

Wilson, Rebecca Leet (RHD's aunt), 11, 23, 24, 101
Wines, Enoch, 155
Winthrop, Theodore, 44, 137
Wister, Owen, 298
"Woman in American Literature" (Cone), 263
Woman's Story, The (Holloway), 247–48
Womanhood, 354
"Women in Journalism" (Tarbell), 239
Women Authors of Our Day (Tutwiler), 324–25
Women's Education and Women's Health (Comfort), 168
Women's Home Companion, RHD's publication in, 392
Wooing of Sheila, The (Rhys), 361

Woolman, John, 232, 346
Woolson, Constance Fenimore, 269, 298

Youth's Companion, 147–48, 173, 221, 253–54, 283, 289, 302, 346
  RHD's publications in, 148, 151, 152, 154, 156, 157, 160, 161, 163, 169, 170, 177–78, 186, 192, 196, 199, 209, 215, 217, 221, 225, 230, 232, 235, 238, 241, 243, 246, 250, 255, 262–63, 264, 309, 317, 347

Zagonyi, Charles, 53
Zeisberger, David, 232
Zola, Émile, 361

www.ingramcontent.com/pod-product-compliance
Lightning Source LLC
Chambersburg PA
CBHW072231240426
43670CB00040B/2385